6. Can a local account be used in a trust relationship? Explain.
7. In a complete trust domain model that uses 4 different domains, what is the total number of trust relationships required to use a complete trust domain model?

## Exam Questions

The following questions are similar to those you will face on the Microsoft exam. Answers to these questions can be found in section Answers and Explanations, later in the chapter. At the end of each of those answers, you will be informed of where (that is, in what section of the chapter) to find more information..

1. ABC Corporation has locations in Toronto, New York, and San Francisco. It wants to install Windows NT Server 4 to encompass all its locations in a single WAN environment. The head office is located in New York. What is the best domain model for ABCís directory services implementation?

   A. Single-domain model

   B. Single-master domain model

   C. Multiple-master domain model

   D. Complete-trust domain model

2. JPS Printing has a single location with 1,000 users spread across the LAN. It has special printers and applications installed on the servers in its environment. It needs to be able to centrally manage the user accounts and the resources. Which domain model would best fit its needs?

   A. Single-domain model

   B. Single-master domain model

   C. Multiple-master domain model

   D. Complete-trust domain model

5. What must be created to allow a user account from one domain to access resources in a different domain?

   A. Complete Trust Domain Model

   B. One Way Trust Relationship

   C. Two Way Trust Relationship

   D. Master-Domain Model

## Answers to Review Questions

1. Single domain, master domain, multiple-master domain, complete-trust domain. See section, Windows NT Server 4 Domain Models, in this chapter for more information. (This question deals with objective Planning 1.)
2. One user, one account, centralized administration, universal resource access, synchronization. See section, Windows NT Server 4 Directory Services, in this chapter for more information. (This question deals with objective Planning 1.)
6. Local accounts cannot be given permissions across trusts. See section, Accounts in Trust Relationships, in this chapter for more information. (This question deals with Planning 1.)

**Answers and Explanations:** For each of the Review and Exam questions, you will find thorough explanations located at the end of the section. They are easily identifiable because they are in blue type.

**Exam Questions:** These questions reflect the kinds of multiple-choice questions that appear on the Microsoft exams. Use them to become familiar with the exam question formats and to help you determine what you know and what you need to review or study more.

**Suggested Readings and Resources**

The following are some recommended readings on the subject of installing and configuring NT Workstation:

1. Microsoft Official Curriculum course 770: *Installing and Configuring Microsoft Windows NT Workstation 4.0*
   - Module 1: Overview of Windows NT Workstation 4.0
   - Module 2: Installing Windows NT Workstation 4.0
2. Microsoft Official Curriculum course 922: *Supporting Microsoft Windows NT 4.0 Core Technologies*
   - Module 2: Installing Windows NT
   - Module 3: Configuring the Windows NT Environment
3. *Microsoft Windows NT Workstation Resource Kit Version 4.0* (Microsoft Press)
   - Chapter 2: Customizing Setup
   - Chapter 4: Planning for a Mixed Environment
4. Microsoft TechNet CD-ROM
   - *MS Windows NT Workstation Technical Notes*
     - MS Windows NT Workstation Deployment Guide – Automating Windows NT Setup
     - An Unattended Windows NT Workstation Deployment
5. Web Sites
   - `www.microsoft.com/train_cert`

**Suggested Readings and Resources:** The very last element in each chapter is a list of additional resources you can use if you wish to go above and beyond certification-level material or if you need to spend more time on a particular subject that you are having trouble understanding.

| OBJECTIVE | PAGE REFERENCE |
|---|---|
| Install, configure, and remove hardware components for a given situation. Hardware components include: | Installing, Configuring, and Removing Hardware Components, pg. 87–93 |
| • Network adapter drivers | Working with Network Adapter Drivers, pg. 88–89 |
| • SCSI device drivers | Working with SCSI Device Drivers, pg. 89 |
| • Tape device drivers | Working with Tape Device Drivers, pg. 89 |
| • UPS | Working with Uninterruptible Power Supplies, pg. 90 |
| • Multimedia devices | Working with Multimedia Devices, pg. 90–91 |
| • Display drivers | Working with Display Drivers, pg. 91–92 |
| • Keyboard drivers | Working with Keyboard Drivers, pg. 92 |
| • Mouse drivers | Working with Mouse Drivers, pg. 93 |
| Use Control Panel applications to configure a Windows NT Workstation computer in a given situation. | Using Control Panel Applications to Configure Windows NT Workstation, pg. 94–95 |
| Upgrade to Windows NT Workstation 4.0 in a given situation. | Upgrading to Windows NT Workstation 4.0, pg. 85–86 |
| Configure server-based installation for wide-scale deployment in a given situation. | Configuring Server-Based Installation, pg. 86–87 |

## Managing Resources

| OBJECTIVE | PAGE REFERENCE |
|---|---|
| Create and manage local user accounts and local group accounts to meet given requirements. | Implementing Local User and Group Accounts, pg. 123–139 |
| Set up and modify user profiles. | Setting Up and Modifying User Profiles, pg. 139–146 |
| Set up shared folders and permissions. | Setting Up Shared Folders and Permissions, pg. 146–157 |
| Set permissions on NTFS partitions, folders, and files. | Setting Permissions on NTFS Partitions, Folders, and Files, pg. 157–171 |
| Install and configure printers in a given environment. | Installing and Configuring Printers in a Given Environment, pg. 171–187 |

TRAINING GUIDE

# MCSE

Second Edition

# Windows NT® Workstation 4

Exam: 70-073

DENNIS MAIONE

**MCSE Training Guide: Windows NT Workstation 4, Second Edition**

Copyright © 1998 by New Riders Publishing

All rights reserved. No part of this book shall be reproduced, stored in a retrieval system, or transmitted by any means, electronic, mechanical, photocopying, recording, or otherwise, without written permission from the publisher. No patent liability is assumed with respect to the use of the information contained herein. Although every precaution has been taken in the preparation of this book, the publisher and author assume no responsibility for errors or omissions. Neither is any liability assumed for damages resulting from the use of the information contained herein.

International Standard Book Number: 1-56205-918-1

Library of Congress Catalog Card Number: 98-85733

Printed in the United States of America

First Printing: September, 1998

00 99 98 4 3

## Trademarks

All terms mentioned in this book that are known to be trademarks or service marks have been appropriately capitalized. New Riders Publishing cannot attest to the accuracy of this information. Use of a term in this book should not be regarded as affecting the validity of any trademark or service mark. Windows NT Workstation 4 is a registered trademark of Microsoft Corporation.

## Warning and Disclaimer

Every effort has been made to make this book as complete and as accurate as possible, but no warranty or fitness is implied. The information provided is on an "as is" basis. The author and the publisher shall have neither liability or responsibility to any person or entity with respect to any loss or damages arising from the information contained in this book or from the use of the CD or programs accompanying it.

**EXECUTIVE EDITOR**
Mary Foote

**ACQUISITIONS EDITOR**
Nancy Maragioglio

**DEVELOPMENT EDITOR**
Scott Warner

**MANAGING EDITOR**
Sarah Kearns

**PROJECT EDITOR**
Christopher Morris

**COPY EDITOR**
Audra McFarland

**INDEXER**
Cheryl Jackson

**TECHNICAL EDITOR**
Marc Savage

**SOFTWARE DEVELOPMENT SPECIALIST**
Jack Belbot

**PRODUCTION**
Jeanne Clark
Heather Stephenson

New Riders is an independent entity from Microsoft Corporation, and not affiliated with Microsoft Corporation in any manner. This publication may be used in assisting students to prepare for a Microsoft Certified Professional Exam. Neither Microsoft Corporation, its designated review company, nor New Riders warrants that use of this publication will ensure passing the relevant Exam. Microsoft is either a registered trademark or trademark of Microsoft Corporation in the United States and/or other countries.

# Contents at a Glance

# Table of Contents

# About the Author

**Dennis Maione** lives in Winnipeg, Canada, where he is a full-time trainer for PBSC Computer Training Centres—the largest Canadian ATEC. He is an MCSE and has been in the computer training business for three years. He has a Computer Science degree and more than 15 years of experience programming and administering networks in a variety of environments (who'da thought that a TRS-80 would take me so far?).

Dennis is also the author of *MCSE Training Guide: Windows NT Server 4, Second Edition* and is co-author of *CLP Training Guide: Lotus Notes*. You should buy them, they're both really good!

Dennis is married to a wonderfully supportive wife (Debra) and has three stunningly intelligent children (Emma, Alexander, and Noah). He never sees them anymore, though, because he spends all his free time at his hobbies (this is the product of one of them).

Dennis would like to be a rock star when he grows up and if you hear that Third Eye Blind or Jars of Clay are looking for a new lead singer, email him at `Dennis_Maione@PBSC.COM`. You can email him at that address if you just have comments or questions about the book (or if any other famous bands are looking for lead singers).

# Dedication

*This book is dedicated to my family:*

*Debra: I'm still thankful you said "Yes" and keep saying "Yes" every time you sacrifice something of your life to allow me to pursue my dreams and "hobbies."*

*Emma, Alexander, and Noah: For all the little things that only you can do to encourage me when I am down ... "my butterflies."*

*My parents (biological and adoptive): For giving to me when I could never give back and teaching me the way to walk.*

*God: How can I thank you for being Father and supporter to me...so this is what grace is like.*

# Acknowledgment

I have to acknowledge all the people who made this project possible:

Nancy: Thanks for the "gentle" prodding to get this all done and thanks for a chance to write again. (OK, I'll take the pins out now!)

Scott, Marc, and Luther: How could I have done it without your expert advice? (Scott, you're far too laid back, though...get the tough-as-nails-DE course from Ami!)

Brian, Tami, Rob, and Jason: You have and continue to encourage me to be the best at what I do...thanks for the chance to do that.

All the people who supported me and my family during long hours of writing, without whose prayers and encouragement we would have fallen apart long ago.

# Tell Us What You Think!

As the reader of this book, *you* are our most important critic and commentator. We value your opinion and want to know what we're doing right, what we could do better, what areas you'd like to see us publish in, and any other words of wisdom you're willing to pass our way.

As the Executive Editor for the Certification team at Macmillan Computer Publishing, I welcome your comments. You can fax, email, or write me directly to let me know what you did or didn't like about this book—as well as what we can do to make our books stronger.

*Please note that I cannot help you with technical problems related to the topic of this book, and that due to the high volume of mail I receive, I might not be able to reply to every message.*

When you write, please be sure to include this book's title and author, as well as your name and phone or fax number. I will carefully review your comments and share them with the author and editors who worked on the book.


Fax: 317-581-4663

Email: `certification@mcp.com`

Mail: Executive Editor<br>
Certification<br>
Macmillan Computer Publishing<br>
201 West 103rd Street<br>
Indianapolis, IN 46290 USA

# How to Use This Book

**New Riders Publishing has made an effort in the second editions of its Training Guide series to make the information as accessible as possible for the purposes of learning the certification material. Here, you have an opportunity to view the many instructional features that have been incorporated into the books to achieve that goal.**

## Chapter Opener

Each chapter begins with a set of features designed to allow you to maximize study time for that material.

**List of Objectives:** Each chapter begins with a list of the objectives as stated by Microsoft.

**Objective Explanations:** Immediately following each objective is an explanation of it, providing context that defines it more meaningfully in relation to the exam. Because Microsoft can sometimes be vague in its objectives list, the objective explanations are designed to clarify any vagueness by relying on the authors' test-taking experience.

**Objectives**

Microsoft provides the following objectives for "Connectivity":

**Add and configure the network components of Windows NT Workstation.**

- This objective is necessary because someone certified in the use of Windows NT Workstation technology must understand how it fits into a networked environment and how to configure the components that enable it to do so.

**Use various methods to access network resources.**

- This objective is necessary because someone certified in the use of Windows NT Workstation technology must understand how resources available on a network can be accessed from NT Workstation.

**Implement Windows NT Workstation as a client in a NetWare environment.**

- This objective is necessary because someone certified in the use of Windows NT Workstation technology must understand how NT Workstation can be used as a client in a NetWare environment and how to configure the services and protocols that make this possible.

**Use various configurations to install Windows NT Workstation as a TCP/IP client.**

- This objective is necessary because someone certified in the use of Windows NT Workstation technology must understand how TCP/IP is important in a network environment and how Workstation can be configured to use it.

CHAPTER 4

**Connectivity**

## OUTLINE



**Chapter Outline:** Learning always gets a boost when you can see both the forest and the trees. To give you a visual image of how the topics in a chapter fit together, you will find a chapter outline at the beginning of each chapter. You will also be able to use this for easy reference when looking for a particular topic.

## STUDY STRATEGIES

- Disk configurations are a part of both the planning and the configuration of NT Server computers. To study for Planning Objective 1, you will need to look at both the following section and the material in Chapter 2, "Installation Part 1." As with many concepts, you should have a good handle on the terminology and know the best applications for different disk configurations. For the objectives of the NT Server exam, you will need to know only general disk configuration concepts—at a high level, not the nitty gritty. Make sure you memorize the concepts relating to partitioning and know the difference between the system and the boot partitions in an NT system (and the fact that the definitions of these are counter-intuitive). You should know that NT supports both FAT and NTFS partitions, as well as some of the advantages and disadvantages of each. You will also need to know about the fault-tolerance methods available in NT—stripe sets with parity and disk mirroring—including their definitions, hardware requirements, and advantages and disadvantages.

  Of course, nothing substitutes for working with the concepts explained in this objective. If possible, get an NT system with some free disk space and play around with the Disk Administrator just to see how partitions are created and what they look like.

  You might also want to look at some of the supplementary readings and scan TechNet for white papers on disk configuration.

- The best way to study for Planning Objective 2 is to read, memorize, and understand the use of each protocol. You should know what the protocols are, what they are used for, and what systems they are compatible with.

  As with disk configuration, installing protocols on your NT Server is something that you plan for, not something you do just because it feels good to you at the time. Although it is much easier to add or remove a protocol than it is to reconfigure your hard drives, choosing a protocol is still an essential part of the planning process because specific protocols, like spoken languages, are designed to be used in certain circumstances. There is no point in learning to speak Mandarin Chinese if you are never around anyone who can understand you. Similarly, the NWLink protocol is used to interact with NetWare systems; therefore, if you do not have Novell servers on your network, you might want to rethink your plan to install it on your servers. We will discuss the uses of the major protocols in Chapter 7, "Connectivity." However, it is important that you have a good understanding of their uses here in the planning stage.

**Study Strategies:** Each topic presents its own learning challenge. To support you through this, New Riders has included strategies for how to best approach studying in order to retain the material in the chapter, particularly as it is addressed on the exam.

# INSTRUCTIONAL FEATURES WITHIN THE CHAPTER

These books include a large amount and different kinds of information. The many different elements are designed to help you identify information by its purpose and importance to the exam and also to provide you with varied ways to learn the material. You will be able to determine how much attention to devote to certain elements, depending on what your goals are. By becoming familiar with the different presentations of information, you will know what information will be important to you as a test-taker and which information will be important to you as a practitioner.

EXAM TIP

**Only One NTVDM Supports Multiple 16-bit Applications**
Expect at least one question about running Win16 applications in separate memory spaces. The key concept is that you can load multiple Win16 applications into the same memory space only if it is the initial Win16 NTVDM. It is not possible, for example, to run Word for Windows 6.0 and Excel for Windows 5.0 in one shared memory space and also run PowerPoint 4.0 and Access 2.0 in another shared memory space.

**Exam Tip:** Exam Tips appear in the margins to provide specific exam-related advice. Such tips may address what material is covered (or not covered) on the exam, how it is covered, mnemonic devices, or particular quirks of that exam.

**Note:** Notes appear in the margins and contain various kinds of useful information, such as tips on the technology or administrative practices, historical background on terms and technologies, or side commentary on industry issues.

8 Chapter 1 PLANNING

## INTRODUCTION

Microsoft grew up around the personal computer industry and established itself as the preeminent maker of software products for personal computers. Microsoft has a vast portfolio of software products, but it is best known for its operating systems.

Microsoft's current operating system products, listed here, are undoubtedly well-known to anyone studying for the MCSE exams:

- Windows 95
- Windows NT Workstation
- Windows NT Server

NOTE

**Strange But True** Although it sounds backward, it is true: Windows NT boots from the system partition and then loads the system from the boot partition.

Some older operating system products—namely MS-DOS, Windows 3.1, and Windows for Workgroups—are still important to the operability of Windows NT Server, so don't be surprised if you hear them mentioned from time to time in this book.

Windows NT is the most powerful, the most secure, and perhaps the most elegant operating system Microsoft has yet produced. It languished for a while after it first appeared (in part because no one was sure why they needed it or what to do with it), but Microsoft has persisted with improving interoperability and performance. With the release of Windows NT 4 which offers a new Windows 95-like user interface, Windows NT has assumed a prominent place in today's world of network-based computing.

## WINDOWS NT SERVER AMONG MICROSOFT OPERATING SYSTEMS

WARNING

**Don't Overextend Your Partitions and Wraps** It is not necessary to create an extended partition on a disk; primary partitions might be all that you need. However, if you do create one, remember that you can never have more than one extended partition on a physical disk.

As we already mentioned, Microsoft has three operating system products now competing in the marketplace: Windows 95, Windows NT Workstation, and Windows NT Server. Each of these operating systems has its advantages and disadvantages.

Looking at the presentation of the desktop, the three look very much alike—so much so that you might have to click the Start button and read the banner on the left side of the menu to determine which operating system you are looking at. Each offers the familiar Windows 95 user interface featuring the Start button, the Recycling

**Objective Coverage Text:** In the text before an exam objective is specifically addressed, you will notice the objective is listed and printed in color to help call your attention to that particular material.

**Warning:** In using sophisticated information technology, there is always potential for mistakes or even catastrophes that can occur through improper application of the technology. Warnings appear in the margins to alert you to such potential problems.

STEP BY STEP

**5.1 Configuring an Extension to Trigger an Application to Always Run in a Separate Memory Space**

1. Start the Windows NT Explorer.
2. From the View menu, choose Options.
3. Click the File Types tab.
4. In the Registered File Types list box, select the desired file type.
5. Click the Edit button to display the Edit File Type dialog box. Then select Open from the Actions list and click the Edit button below it.
6. In the Editing Action for Type dialog box, adjust the application name by typing **cmd.exe /c start /separate** in front of the existing contents of the field (see Figure 5.15).

**FIGURE 5.15**
Configuring a shortcut to run a Win16 application in a separate memory space.

**Step by Step:** Step by Steps are hands-on tutorial instructions that walk you through a particular task or function relevant to the exam objectives.

**Figure:** To improve readability, the figures have been placed in the margins so they do not interrupt the main flow of text.

14 Chapter 1 PLANNING

You must use NTFS if you want to preserve existing permissions when you migrate files and directories from a NetWare server to a Windows NT Server system.

Windows 95 is Microsoft's everyday workhorse operating system. It provides a 32-bit platform and is designed to operate with a variety of peripherals. See Table 1.1 for the minimum hardware requirements for the installation and operation of Windows 95. Also, if you want to allow Macintosh computers to access files on the partition through Windows NT's Services for Macintosh, you must format the partition for NTFS.

**MAKING REGISTRY CHANGES**

To make Registry changes, run the REGEDT32.EXE program. The Registry in Windows NT is a complex database of configuration settings for your computer. If you want to configure the Workstation service, open the HKEY_LOCAL_MACHINE hive, as shown in Figure 3.22.

The exact location for configuring your Workstation service is

```
HKEY_LOCAL_MACHINE\System\CurrentControlSet\Services\
LanmanWorkstation\Parameters
```

To find additional information regarding this Registry item and others, refer to the Windows NT Server resource kit.

This summary table offers an overview of the differences between the FAT and NTFS file systems.

REVIEW BREAK

## Choosing a File System

But if the system is designed to store data, mirroring might produce disk bottlenecks. You might only know whether these changes are significant by setting up two identical computers, implementing mirroring on one but not on the other, and then running Performance Monitor on both under a simulated load to see the performance differences.

This summary table offers an overview of the differences between the FAT and NTFS file systems.

**In-Depth Sidebar:** These more extensive discussions cover material that perhaps is not as directly relevant to the exam, but which is useful as reference material or in everyday practice. In-Depths may also provide useful background or contextual information necessary for understanding the larger topic under consideration.

**Review Break:** Crucial information is summarized at various points in the book in lists or tables. At the end of a particularly long section, you might come across a Review Break that is there just to wrap up one long objective and reinforce the key points before you shift your focus to the next section.

## CASE STUDIES

Case Studies are presented throughout the book to provide you with another, more conceptual opportunity to apply the knowledge you are developing. They also reflect the "real-world" experiences of the authors in ways that prepare you not only for the exam but for actual network administration as well. In each Case Study, you will find similar elements: a description of a Scenario, the Essence of the Case, and an extended Analysis section.

**CASE STUDY: REALLY GOOD GUITARS**

**ESSENCE OF THE CASE**

Here are the essential elements in this case:

- need for centralized administration
- the need for WAN connectivity nation-wide
- a requirement for Internet access and e-mail
- the need for Security on network shares and local files
- an implementation of Fault-tolerant systems

**SCENARIO**

Really Good Guitars is a national company specializing in the design and manufacturer of custom acoustic guitars. Having grown up out of an informal network of artisans across Canada, the company has many locations but very few employees (300 at this time) and a Head Office in Churchill, Manitoba. Although they follow the best traditions of hand-making guitars, they are not without technological savvy and all the 25 locations have computers on-site which are used to do accounting, run MS Office applications, and run their custom made guitar design software. The leadership team has recently begun to realize that a networked solution is essential to maintain consistency and to provide security on what are becoming some very innovative designs and to provide their employees with e-mail and Internet access.

RGG desires a centralized administration of its

*continues*

**Essence of the Case:** A bulleted list of the key problems or issues that need to be addressed in the Scenario.

**Scenario:** A few paragraphs describing a situation that professional practitioners in the field might face. A Scenario will deal with an issue relating to the objectives covered in the chapter, and it includes the kinds of details that make a difference.

**CASE STUDY: PRINT IT DRAFTING INC.**

*continued*

too, which is unacceptable. You are to find a solution to this problem if one exists.

**ANALYSIS**

The fixes for both of these problems are relatively straightforward. In the first case, it is likely that all the programs on the draftspeople's workstations are being started at normal priority. This means that they have a priority of 8. But the default says that anything running in the foreground is getting a 2-point boost from the base priority, bringing it to 10. As a result, when sent to the background, AutoCAD is not getting as much attention from the processor as it did when it was the foreground application. Because multiple applications need to be run at once without significant degradation of the performance of AutoCAD, you implement the following solution:

1. On the Performance tab of the System Properties dialog box for each workstation, set the Application Performance slider to None to prevent a boost for foreground applications.
2. Recommend that users keep the additional programs running alongside AutoCAD at a minimum (because all programs will now get equal processor time).

The fix to the second problem is to run each 16-bit application in its own NTVDM. This ensures that the crashing of one application will not adversely affect the others, but it still enables interoperability between the applications because they use OLE (and not shared memory) to transfer data. To make the fix as transparent as possible to the users, you suggested that two things be done:

1. Make sure that for each shortcut a user has created to the office applications, the Run in Separate Memory Space option is selected on the Shortcut tab.
2. Change the properties for the extensions associated with the applications (for example, .XLS and .DOC) so that they start using the `/separate` switch. Then any file that is double-clicked invokes the associated program to run in its own NTVDM.

**Analysis:** This is a lengthy description of the best way to handle the problems listed in the Essence of the Case. In this section, you might find a table summarizing the solutions, a worded example, or both.

**CHAPTER SUMMARY**

**KEY TERMS**

Before you take the exam, make sure you are comfortable with the definitions and concepts for each of the following key terms:

- FAT
- NTFS
- workgroup
- domain

This chapter discussed the main planning topics you will encounter on the Windows NT Server exam. Distilled down, these topics revolve around two main goals: understanding the planning of disk configuration and understanding the planning of network protocols.

- Windows NT Server supports an unlimited number of inbound sessions; Windows NT Workstation supports no more than 10 active sessions at the same time.
- Windows NT Server accommodates an unlimited number of remote access connections (although Microsoft only supports up to 256); Windows NT Workstation supports only a single remote access connection.

**Key Terms:** A list of key terms appears at the end of each chapter. These are terms that you should be sure you know and are comfortable defining and understanding when you go in to take the exam.

**Chapter Summary:** Before the Apply Your Learning section, you will find a chapter summary that wraps up the chapter and reviews what you should have learned.

# EXTENSIVE REVIEW AND SELF-TEST OPTIONS

At the end of each chapter, along with some summary elements, you will find a section called "Apply Your Learning" that gives you several different methods with which to test your understanding of the material and review what you have learned.

Chapter 1 PLANNING 23

**APPLY YOUR LEARNING**

This section allows you to assess how well you understood the material in the chapter. Review and Exam questions test your knowledge of the tasks and concepts specified in the objectives. The Exercises provide you with opportunities to engage in the sorts of tasks that comprise the skill sets the objectives reflect.

## Exercises

**1.1 Synchronizing the Domain Controllers**

The following steps show you how to manually synchronize a backup domain controller within your domain. (This objective deals with Objective Planning 1.)

**Time Estimate:** Less than 10 minutes.

1. Click Start, Programs, Administrative Tools, and select the Server Manager icon.
2. Highlight the BDC (Backup Domain Controller) in your computer list.
3. Select the Computer menu, then select Synchronize with Primary Domain Controller.

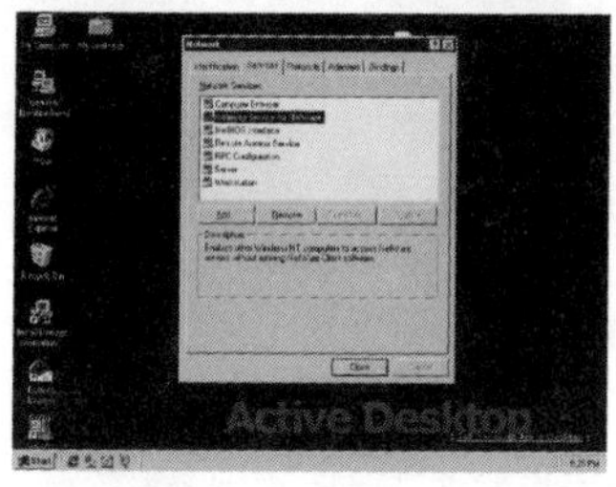


FIGURE 1.2
The login process on a local machine.

**12.2 Establishing a Trust Relationship between Domains**

The following steps show you how to establish a trust relationship between multiple domains. To complete this exercise, you must have two Windows NT Server computers, each installed in their own domain. (This objective deals with objective Planning 1.)

**Time Estimate:** 10 minutes

1. From the trusted domain select Start, Programs, Administrative Tools, and click User Manager for Domains. The User Manager.
2. Select the Policies menu and click Trust Relationships. The Trust Relationships dialog box appears.
4. When the trusting domain information has been entered, click OK and close the Trust Relationships dialog box.

## Review Questions

1. List the four domain models that can be used for directory services in Windows NT Server 4.
2. List the goals of a directory services architecture.
3. What is the maximum size of the SAM database in Windows NT Server 4.0?
4. What are the two different types of domains in a trust relationship?
5. In a trust relationship which domain would contain the user accounts?

**Exercises:** These activities provide an opportunity for you to master specific hands-on tasks. Our goal is to increase your proficiency with the product or technology. You must be able to conduct these tasks in order to pass the exam.

**Review Questions:** These open-ended, short-answer questions allow you to quickly assess your comprehension of what you just read in the chapter. Instead of asking you to choose from a list of options, these questions require you to state the correct answers in your own words. Although you will not experience these kinds of questions on the exam, these questions will indeed test your level of comprehension of key concepts.

6. Can a local account be used in a trust relationship? Explain.
7. In a complete trust domain model that uses 4 different domains, what is the total number of trust relationships required to use a complete trust domain model?

## Exam Questions

The following questions are similar to those you will face on the Microsoft exam. Answers to these questions can be found in section Answers and Explanations, later in the chapter. At the end of each of those answers, you will be informed of where (that is, in what section of the chapter) to find more information..

1. ABC Corporation has locations in Toronto, New York, and San Francisco. It wants to install Windows NT Server 4 to encompass all its locations in a single WAN environment. The head office is located in New York. What is the best domain model for ABC's directory services implementation?
   A. Single-domain model
   B. Single-master domain model
   C. Multiple-master domain model
   D. Complete-trust domain model
2. JPS Printing has a single location with 1,000 users spread across the LAN. It has special printers and applications installed on the servers in its environment. It needs to be able to centrally manage the user accounts and the resources. Which domain model would best fit its needs?
   A. Single-domain model
   B. Single-master domain model
   C. Multiple-master domain model
   D. Complete-trust domain model
5. What must be created to allow a user account from one domain to access resources in a different domain?
   A. Complete Trust Domain Model
   B. One Way Trust Relationship
   C. Two Way Trust Relationship
   D. Master-Domain Model

## Answers to Review Questions

1. Single domain, master domain, multiple-master domain, complete-trust domain. See section, Windows NT Server 4 Domain Models, in this chapter for more information. (This question deals with objective Planning 1.)
2. One user, one account, centralized administration, universal resource access, synchronization. See section, Windows NT Server 4 Directory Services, in this chapter for more information. (This question deals with objective Planning 1.)
6. Local accounts cannot be given permissions across trusts. See section, Accounts in Trust Relationships, in this chapter for more information. (This question deals with Planning 1.)

**Exam Questions:** These questions reflect the kinds of multiple-choice questions that appear on the Microsoft exams. Use them to become familiar with the exam question formats and to help you determine what you know and what you need to review or study more.

**Answers and Explanations:** For each of the Review and Exam questions, you will find thorough explanations located at the end of the section. They are easily identifiable because they are in blue type.

**Suggested Readings and Resources**

The following are some recommended readings on the subject of installing and configuring NT Workstation:

1. Microsoft Official Curriculum course 770: *Installing and Configuring Microsoft Windows NT Workstation 4.0*
   - Module 1: Overview of Windows NT Workstation 4.0
   - Module 2: Installing Windows NT Workstation 4.0
2. Microsoft Official Curriculum course 922: *Supporting Microsoft Windows NT 4.0 Core Technologies*
   - Module 2: Installing Windows NT
   - Module 3: Configuring the Windows NT Environment
3. *Microsoft Windows NT Workstation Resource Kit Version 4.0* (Microsoft Press)
   - Chapter 2: Customizing Setup
   - Chapter 4: Planning for a Mixed Environment
4. Microsoft TechNet CD-ROM
   - *MS Windows NT Workstation Technical Notes*
     - MS Windows NT Workstation Deployment Guide – Automating Windows NT Setup
     - An Unattended Windows NT Workstation Deployment
5. Web Sites
   - `www.microsoft.com/train_cert`
   - `www.prometric.com/testingcandidates/assessment/chosetest.html` (take online

**Suggested Readings and Resources:** The very last element in every chapter is a list of additional resources you can use if you want to go above and beyond certification-level material or if you need to spend more time on a particular subject that you are having trouble understanding.

# Introduction

*MCSE Training Guide: Windows NT Workstation 4, Second Edition* is designed for advanced end-users, service technicians, and network administrators with the goal of certification as a Microsoft Certified Systems Engineer (MCSE). The "Implementing and Supporting Microsoft Windows NT Workstation 4.0" exam (#70-073) measures your ability to implement, administer, and troubleshoot information systems that incorporate Windows NT Workstation.

## Who Should Read This Book

This book is designed to help you meet the goal of certification by preparing you for the "Implementing and Supporting Microsoft Windows NT Workstation 4.0" exam.

This book is your one-stop shop. Everything you need to know to pass the exam is in here, and Microsoft has approved it as study material. You do not *need* to take a class in addition to buying this book to pass the exam. However, depending on your personal study habits or learning style, you may benefit from taking a class in addition to the book.

This book also can help advanced users and administrators who are not studying for the exam but are looking for a single-volume reference on Windows NT Workstation 4.

## How This Book Helps You

This book leads you on a guided tour of all the areas covered by the "Implementing and Supporting Microsoft Windows NT Workstation 4.0" exam and teaches you the specific skills you need to achieve your MCSE certification. You'll also find helpful hints, tips, real-world examples, exercises, and references to additional study materials. Specifically, this book is designed around four general concepts to help you learn.

**Organization.** This book is organized first by major exam topics and then by individual exam objectives. Every objective you need to know for the "Implementing and Supporting Microsoft Windows NT Workstation 4.0" exam is covered in this book. We attempt to make the information accessible in several different ways:

- The full list of exam topics and objectives is included in this introduction.
- Each chapter begins with a list of the objectives covered in that particular chapter.
- Each chapter also includes an outline that provides an overview of the material in the chapter and the page numbers on which particular topics can be found.
- To help you quickly locate where the objectives are addressed in the chapter, each objective is restated at the beginning of its corresponding section, and it appears in blue print.
- Information about where the objectives are covered is also conveniently condensed on the tearcard at the front of this book.

**Instructional Features.** This book has been designed to provide you with multiple ways to access and reinforce the exam material. The book's instructional features include the following:

- *Objective Explanations.* As mentioned earlier, each chapter begins with a list of the objectives covered in the chapter. In addition, immediately following each objective is an explanation of it, in a context that defines it more meaningfully.
- *Study Strategies.* The chapter also includes strategies for how to approach studying and retaining the material in the chapter, particularly as it is addressed on the exam.
- *Exam Tips.* Exam Tips appear in the margin to provide specific exam-related advice. Such tips may address what material is covered (or not covered) on the exam, how it is covered, mnemonic devices, or particular quirks of that exam.
- *Reviews and Summaries.* Crucial information is summarized at various points in the book in lists or tables. Each chapter ends with a summary as well.
- *Key Terms.* A list of key terms appears at the end of each chapter.
- *Notes.* These appear in the margin and contain various kinds of useful information, such as tips on the technology or administrative practices, historical background on terms and technologies, or side commentary on industry issues.
- *Warnings.* When you use sophisticated information technology, there is always potential that mistakes or even catastrophes can occur as a result of improper application of the technology. Warnings appear in the margin to alert you to such potential problems.
- *In-Depth Sidebars.* These more extensive discussions cover material that is, perhaps, not directly relevant to the exam, but which is useful as reference material or in everyday practice. In-Depth Sidebars may also provide useful background or contextual information necessary for understanding the larger topic under consideration.
- *Step by Steps.* These are hands-on tutorial instructions that walk you through particular tasks or functions relevant to the exam objectives.
- *Exercises.* Found at the end of the chapters in the "Apply Your Learning" section, Exercises may include additional tutorial material as well as other types of problems and questions.
- *Case Studies.* Case Studies are presented throughout the book. They provide you with another, more conceptual opportunity to apply the knowledge you are gaining. They include a description of a Scenario, the Essence of the Case, and an extended Analysis section. They also reflect the "real-world" experiences of the authors in ways that prepare you not only for the exam but for actual network administration as well.

**Extensive practice test options.** The book provides numerous opportunities for you to assess your knowledge and practice for the exam. The practice options include the following:

- *Review Questions.* These open-ended questions appear in the "Apply Your Learning" section at the end of each chapter. They allow you to quickly assess your comprehension of what you just read in the chapter. Answers to the questions are provided later in the chapter.
- *Exam Questions.* These questions also appear in the "Apply Your Learning" section. They reflect the kind of multiple-choice questions that appear on the Microsoft exams. Use them to practice for

the exam and to help you determine what you know and what you need to review or study further. Answers and explanations for them are provided.

- *Practice Exam.* A Practice Exam is included in the Final Review section. The Final Review section and the Practice Exam are discussed below.
- *Top Score.* The Top Score software included on the CD-ROM provides further practice questions.

> NOTE
> **Top Score** For a complete description of New Riders' Top Score test engine, see Appendix D, "Using the Top Score Software."

**Final Review.** This part of the book provides you with three valuable tools for preparing for the exam.

- *Fast Facts.* This condensed version of the information contained in the book will prove extremely useful for last-minute review.
- *Study and Exam Prep Tips.* Read this section early on to help develop your study strategies. It provides you with valuable exam-day tips and information on new exam question formats, such as adaptive tests and simulation-based questions.
- *Practice Exam.* A full Practice Exam is included. Questions are written in the styles used on the actual exam. Use it to assess your readiness for the real thing.

The book includes other features, such as a section titled "Suggested Readings and Resources" at the end of each chapter that directs you toward further information that could aid you in your exam preparation or your actual work. There are several valuable appendices as well, including a glossary (Appendix A), an overview of the Microsoft certification program (Appendix B), and a description of what is on the CD-ROM (Appendix C). These and all the other book features mentioned previously will prepare you thoroughly for the exam.

For more information about the exam or the certification process, contact Microsoft:

Microsoft Education: (800) 636-7544

Internet: `ftp://ftp.microsoft.com/Services/MSEdCert`

World Wide Web:
`http://www.microsoft.com/train_cert`

CompuServe Forum: GO MSEDCERT

## What the Implementing and Supporting Microsoft Windows NT Workstation 4.0 Exam (#70-073) Covers

The "Implementing and Supporting Microsoft Windows NT Workstation 4.0" exam (#70-073) covers the seven main topic areas represented by the test objectives. Each chapter represents one or more of these main topic areas. The exam objectives are listed by topic area in the following sections.

## Planning

Create unattended installation files.

Plan strategies for sharing and securing resources.

Choose the appropriate file system to use in a given situation. File systems and situations include:

- NTFS
- FAT
- HPFS
- Security
- Dual-boot systems

## Installation and Configuration

Install Windows NT Workstation on an Intel-based platform in a given situation.

Set up a dual-boot system in a given situation.

Remove Windows NT Workstation in a given situation.

Install, configure, and remove hardware components for a given situation. Hardware components include:

- Network adapter drivers
- SCSI device drivers
- Tape device drivers
- UPSs
- Multimedia devices
- Display drivers
- Keyboard drivers
- Mouse drivers

Use Control Panel applications to configure a Windows NT Workstation computer in a given situation.

Upgrade to Windows NT Workstation 4 in a given situation.

Configure server-based installation for wide-scale deployment in a given situation.

## Managing Resources

Create and manage local user accounts and local group accounts to meet given requirements.

Set up and modify user profiles.

Set up shared folders and permissions.

Set permissions on NTFS partitions, folders, and files.

Install and configure printers in a given environment.

## Connectivity

Add and configure the network components of Windows NT Workstation.

Use various methods to access network resources.

Implement Windows NT Workstation as a client in a NetWare environment.

Use various configurations to install Windows NT Workstation as a TCP/IP client.

Configure and install Dial-Up Networking in a given situation.

Configure Microsoft Peer Web Services in a given situation.

## Running Applications

Start applications on Intel and RISC platforms in various operating system environments.

Start applications at various priorities.

## Monitoring and Optimization

Monitor system performance by using various tools.

Identify and resolve a given performance problem.

Optimize system performance in various areas.

## Troubleshooting

Choose the appropriate course of action to take when the boot process fails.

Choose the appropriate course of action to take when a print job fails.

Choose the appropriate course of action to take when the installation process fails.

Choose the appropriate course of action to take when an application fails.

Choose the appropriate course of action to take when a user cannot access a resource.

Modify the Registry using the appropriate tool in a given situation.

Implement advanced techniques to resolve various problems.

# Hardware and Software Needed

Intended as a self-paced study guide, this book was designed with the expectation that you will use Windows NT 4.0 as you follow along through the exercises while you learn. The theory covered in *MCSE Training Guide: Windows NT Workstation 4, Second Edition* is applicable to a wide range of actual situations, and the exercises in this book encompass that range.

Your computer should meet the following criteria:

- All devices should be listed on the Microsoft Hardware Compatibility List
- 486DX2 66Mhz (or better) processor for Windows NT Server
- 340MB (or larger) hard disk for Windows NT Server, with 100MB of free space formatted NTFS
- 3.5-inch 1.44MB floppy drive
- VGA (or Super VGA) video adapter
- VGA (or Super VGA) monitor
- Mouse or equivalent pointing device
- Double-speed (or faster) CD-ROM drive (optional)
- Network Interface Card (NIC)
- Presence on an existing network, or use of a 2-port (or more) mini-port hub to create a test network is optional but very helpful
- Microsoft Windows NT Workstation version 4 (CD-ROM version)

It is somewhat easier to obtain access to the necessary computer hardware and software in a corporate business environment. It can be difficult, however, to allocate enough time within the busy workday to complete a self-study program. Most of your study time will occur after normal working hours, away from the everyday interruptions and pressures of your regular job.

## ADVICE ON TAKING THE EXAM

More extensive tips are found in the Final Review section in the chapter titled "Study and Exam Prep Tips." But keep the following suggestions in mind as you study:

- **Read all the material.** Microsoft has been known to include material on its exams that's not expressly specified in the objectives. This book has included additional information not reflected in the objectives in an effort to give you the best possible preparation for the examination and for the real-world network experiences to come.
- **Do the Step by Steps and complete the Exercises in each chapter.** They will help you gain experience using the Microsoft product. All Microsoft exams are task- and experienced-based and require you to have used the Microsoft product in a real networking environment.
- **Use the questions to assess your knowledge.** Don't just read the chapter content; use the questions to find out what you know and what you don't. Then study some more, review, and assess your knowledge again.
- **Review the exam objectives.** Develop your own questions and examples for each topic listed. If you can make and answer several questions for each topic, you should not find it difficult to pass the exam.

> NOTE
>
> **Preparation Includes Practice**
> Although this book is designed to prepare you to take and pass the Implementing and Supporting Microsoft Windows NT Workstation 4.0 certification exam, there are no guarantees. Read this book and work through the questions and exercises, and when you feel confident, take the Practice Exam and additional exams using the Top Score test engine. This should tell you whether you are ready for the real thing.
>
> When taking the actual certification exam, make sure you answer all the questions before your time limit expires. Do not spend too much time on any one question. If you are unsure about an answer, answer the question as best you can and mark it for later review; you can go back to it when you have finished the rest of the questions.

Remember, the primary objective is not to pass the exam—it is to understand the material. If you understand the material, passing the exam should be simple. Knowledge is a pyramid: To build upward, you need a solid foundation. This book and the Microsoft Certified Professional programs are designed to ensure that you have that solid foundation.

Good luck!

## NEW RIDERS PUBLISHING

The staff of New Riders Publishing is committed to bringing you the very best in computer reference material. Each New Riders book is the result of months of work by authors and staff who research and refine the information contained within its covers.

As part of this commitment to you, the NRP reader, New Riders invites your input. Please let us know if you enjoy this book, if you have trouble with the information or examples presented, or if you have a suggestion for the next edition.

Please note, however, that New Riders staff cannot serve as a technical resource during your preparation for the Microsoft certification exams or for questions about software- or hardware-related problems. Please refer instead to the documentation that accompanies the Microsoft products or to the applications' Help systems.

If you have a question or comment about any New Riders book, you can contact New Riders Publishing in several ways. We will respond to as many readers as we can. Your name, address, or phone number will never become part of a mailing list or be used for any purpose other than to help us continue to bring you the best books possible. You can write to us at the following address:

New Riders Publishing
Attn: Publisher
201 W. 103rd Street
Indianapolis, IN 46290

If you prefer, you can fax New Riders Publishing at (317) 581-4663.

You also can send email to New Riders at the following Internet address:

`certification@mcp.com`

Thank you for selecting *MCSE Training Guide: Windows NT Workstation 4, Second Edition*!

PART I

# EXAM PREPARATION

## OBJECTIVES

Microsoft provides the following objectives for "Planning":

**Create unattended installation files.**

- This objective is necessary because an individual certified in the use of Windows NT Workstation technology must be able to plan and execute strategies for effective installation of NT Workstation in a large-deployment situation. This includes creating unattended answer files and uniqueness databases to provide full hands-off installation of a number of workstations. In addition, it also extends to the use of tools such as SYSDIFF to automate the installation of applications in addition to the operating system.

**Plan strategies for sharing and securing resources.**

- In order to satisfy this objective, you must be able plan strategies that will allow for security to be put in place when workstations are configured. This includes the creation of groups, the use of system groups, and the sharing of public and private folders.

**Choose the appropriate file system to use in a given situation. File systems and situations include NTFS, FAT, HPFS, security, and dual-boot systems.**

- This objective is necessary because an individual certified in the use of Windows NT Workstation technology must be able to choose which disk file system to implement given the projected use of the Workstation and its security needs. This includes knowing about the different file systems NT supports, the security for each, and the implications of multi-booting on the file system of choice.

This chapter will help you prepare for the "Planning" section of Microsoft's Exam 70-73 by giving you information necessary to make intelligent choices regarding automating installation, securing resources, and selecting a disk file system.

CHAPTER 1

# Planning

## OUTLINE

## Study Strategies

- You must know how to perform an unattended installation, including the purpose of the answer file and the uniqueness database file. You should also memorize all the appropriate commands, especially the switches.

  Although SYSDIFF and WINDIFF are not covered in any depth in the Microsoft curriculum (SYSDIFF is mentioned in the Core Technologies class and WINDIFF is not mentioned at all), the exam is bound to include one or two questions on each. You should get a copy of the NT Resource Kit and read through the help information on both of these utilities.

  Work out strategies to implement an automated installation of Workstation, with and without the installation of applications. This will fix in your mind the way that all these utilities fit together in the overall installation strategy; it will be well worth your time to use it as a study technique.

- Be sure that you understand how the different sharing strategies outlined in this chapter are implemented. There are bound to be some questions on the exam relating to accessing Workstation both locally and over the network and how share-level permissions interact with local NTFS permissions. In addition, be sure you understand the groups that are described in this chapter and how they can be used to implement security.

- Finally, be sure you understand the file systems that are supported by NT. You must know the advantages and disadvantages for each and when it is appropriate to use each one. The exam will include scenario questions in which you will be expected to analyze situations based on your knowledge of the features of each system.

## INTRODUCTION

Effective planning prior to implementation of Windows NT Workstation 4.0 is critical. This chapter focuses on planning the unattended installation of Windows NT Workstation 4.0, planning how to most effectively share and secure resources, and deciding on the appropriate file system to use on your Windows NT Workstation.

This chapter discusses the following Planning topics:

- Creating and using unattended answer files and uniqueness database files.
- Using SYSDIFF to create snapshot files, difference files, and .INF files.
- Planning the use of built-in Windows NT groups.
- Sharing folders for use as users' home directories, shared application folders, and common access folders.
- Choosing the right file system (FAT, NTFS, HPFS) for use in various situations and taking dual-boot systems and file security into consideration.

In terms of the number of questions on the exam, Planning tends to be one of the major topic areas. Understanding how planning applies to an effective implementation of Windows NT Workstation should help you significantly in passing the exam.

## CREATING UNATTENDED INSTALLATION FILES

Create unattended installation files.

One reason it is important to plan before you start rolling out Windows NT Workstation is that you can create and implement an unattended installation of the Windows NT Workstation operating system. This keeps the team doing the rollout from having to visit every computer to install the operating system manually either from a CD or from a shared network installation point.

## Files Used for Unattended Installation

In a relatively small environment—one with fewer than 10 machines—manually installing Windows NT Workstation might be an option. In any larger environment, however, the time is better spent developing an unattended installation plan for rolling out Windows NT. Based on the size of the environment (the number of workstations to install), using an unattended installation could save significant time in the total installation process.

Although doing an unattended installation takes more time up-front, it is time well spent if it decreases the total time of the migration process. Some of the files and tools related to this unattended installation process include the following:

- Unattended answer file (UNATTEND.TXT)
- Uniqueness database file (UDF)
- SYSDIFF.EXE
- WINDIFF.EXE

An unattended installation gives a network administrator the ability to both *customize* and *automate* the installation of Windows NT as explained here:

*Customization.* User-specific or organization-specific information can be tailored to a particular installation through a combination of unattended answer files and uniqueness database files.

*Automation.* Using an unattended answer file and a uniqueness database file enables the administrator to perform a hands-free installation of Windows NT.

Windows NT 4.0 uses a combination of an unattended answer file and uniqueness database files to both customize and automate the installation of Windows NT Workstation. A third utility used in the installation process, SYSDIFF, enables the administrator to automate the installation of other applications in addition to the operating system itself. Using these three tools, an administrator can perform an entire installation of the operating system and all necessary applications. A final utility called WINDIFF allows quick analysis of changes in the contents of files or folders to determine which files need to be copied from one installation to another (in cases where manual intervention is required).

## Answer Files

Using an answer file frees the administrator from having to sit at a particular computer and manually reply to the prompts of the setup program. The manual approach is fine if you are installing only a few machines, but it can become quite time-consuming if you are rolling out Windows NT Workstation in a large-scale environment.

The administrator implements an unattended answer file (a text file) as part of the Windows NT setup process by using the `/u` switch after the `WINNT` (or `WINNT32`) command. The syntax of this command is as follows:

`Winnt /u:`*`answer file`* `/s:`*`source path`* when NT is being installed on a non-NT machine

`Winnt32 /u:`*`answer file`* `/s:`*`source path`* when NT is being installed on an existing NT machine

Take a look at this breakdown of the command syntax:

`/u` is the switch that specifies this is an unattended installation.

*`answer file`* represents the name of the answer file that you have created. (The default name of the sample answer file is UNATTEND.TXT.)

`/s` is the switch that points to the location of the Windows NT installation files.

*`source path`* represents the location of the Windows NT installation files (the I386 directory for an Intel installation); this is probably on the CD or on a network share.

The main function of the unattended answer file is to reply automatically to the prompts that the end user, or the person doing the installation, usually must respond to manually as part of the setup process. You can use the same unattended answer file across a number of installations. If you are using an unattended answer file only, however, it is difficult to completely automate the setup process because of the unique information that is required to install Windows NT Workstation. For example, the NetBIOS computer name of each NT Workstation must be unique.

NOTE

**Speed Up Installation by Specifying Multiple File Sources** In Windows NT 4.0, you can list more than one source path location for a particular installation. If, for example, the Windows NT installation files are stored in two network locations, you can point to both of them. That way, Setup can draw from both locations, which speeds up the installation.

One possible solution to this problem of supplying unique information is to include the computer name as part of the unattended answer file. After the installation finishes, you must then go to all the installed machines and change the computer names so that each is unique on the network or in the domain. This solution is not ideal, however, because it requires the administrator to "touch" every machine that has been installed after the installation process is complete.

## STEP BY STEP

### 1.1 Changing the Computer Name

1. Log on to the computer using the default administrator account created during installation.
2. Open the Start menu, select Settings, click Control Panel, and open the Network applet.
3. Click on the Change button next to the computer name, and then enter a unique name in the Identification Changes dialog box (shown in Figure 1.1).
4. If this machine will belong to a domain, you must change the domain name (by default, it shows the name of the workgroup into which the machine was originally installed).

In addition to changing the computer name after the installation, you must also change the domain membership after the installation. Because all the installed computer names must be identical, none of the machines could have joined the domain during the installation process. Thus you must add them to the domain after changing the computer names. In a medium- to large-sized environment, this requires a significant amount of post-installation work from the administrator.

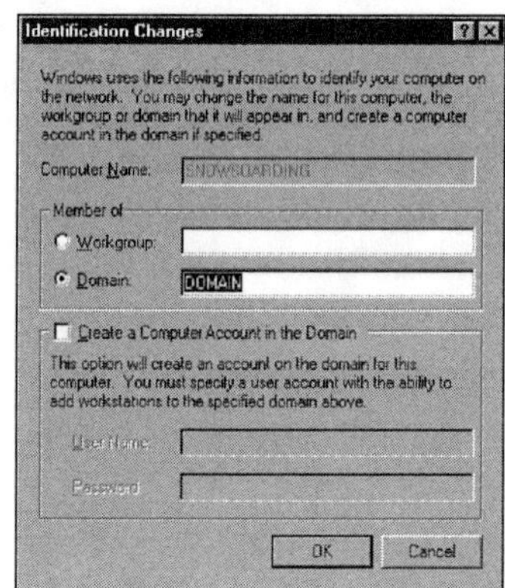


**FIGURE 1.1**
The Control Panel's Network applet is used to change the computer name and domain name on a Windows NT workstation.

WARNING

**Manually Changing Computer Names** Although changing each workstation's computer name after the installation works in a smaller LAN environment, it is not the most efficient solution for most larger network environments. Imagine what it would be like to have to manually modify the names of 100 or 1,000 workstations after the installation is complete. Then, consider what it would be like if the workstations were scattered all over a large city, region, or country.

An alternative to changing computer names after the installation is to have the installation process stop and prompt the user during the network portion of the setup so that the unique information can be added at that time. If your goal is to fully automate the installation process, however, you do not want the installation to stop in the middle and wait for user input.

## Uniqueness Database Files (UDF)

One method of providing unique information in the unattended answer file is to create what is called a *uniqueness database file* or UDF. A UDF is a text file that supplies the information that must be unique to each computer or each user. A Uniqueness database file can be used in conjunction with an unattended answer file to provide a complete installation of Windows NT Workstation that requires no user intervention during the setup process. The uniqueness database file provides the capability to specify computer-specific parameters for the installation, such as the computer name or username.

The UDF is used to merge or to replace sections of the unattended answer file during the GUI portion of the Windows NT setup process. For the installation of Windows NT Workstation 4.0, you can use one unattended answer file for the information that applies to all installations, and one or more UDF files to specify the settings intended for a single computer or for a group of computers. It is possible to have one UDF that contains settings for multiple computers or users within it.

## SYSDIFF

In addition to installing Windows NT Workstation, you may need to install various applications as well. If those applications do not support a scripted installation, you can use the SYSDIFF utility to install the applications on the destination computers. By using SYSDIFF, you can automate the installation of all desired applications. This enables you to automate and customize not only the installation of the operating system, but also the installation of all applications required for your environment. The SYSDIFF function is made up these three tasks:

1. Creating a snapshot file

2. Creating a difference file
3. Applying the difference file

Alternatively, SYSDIFF can be used to create an .INF file and dump the contents of a difference file.

## Creating an Unattended Answer File

As you have learned already, an unattended answer file is a text file that answers the prompts of the setup program during installation so that no one has to manually answer the setup prompts on every machine. A sample unattended answer file, called UNATTEND.TXT, is included with the Windows NT Workstation CD. You can use it as a template for creating or customizing an unattended installation file. You can also use the Windows NT Setup Manager, a graphical application included with the Windows NT Workstation Resource Kit CD, to create an unattended answer file.

### Modifying the UNATTEND.TXT Sample File

On the Windows NT Workstation 4.0 CD, open the UNATTEND.TXT file with any text editor (such as Notepad). In general, the information in UNATTEND.TXT can be categorized as section headings, parameters, and values associated with the parameters. Most of the actual section headings are predefined and do not need to be changed. If necessary, however, you can add sections. The UNATTEND.TXT file follows this format:

```
[section]
;comments
;comments
parameter=value
```

Information in the UNATTEND.TXT file is divided into the following main sections. You may or may not choose to modify all the sections, depending on your particular environment.

`[Unattended]`. This section is used during text mode setup and can be modified only in the answer file. This section tells the setup program that this is an unattended setup. It also specifies settings such as whether this is an upgrade installation, what file system to use, and the path for the installation.

`[OEMBootFiles]`. This section specifies OEM boot files and can be specified only in the answer file, not in the UDF.

`[MassStorageDrivers]`. This section is used during the text mode portion of Setup to specify which SCSI drivers to install. If this section is missing, Setup tries to detect SCSI devices on the computer. This section can be specified only in the answer file, not in the UDF.

`[DisplayDrivers]`. This section contains a list of display drivers to be loaded by the text mode setup process. If this section is missing, setup tries to detect the display devices on the computer.

`[KeyboardDrivers]`. This section includes a list of keyboard drivers to be loaded by Setup. This setting can be specified only in the answer file, not in the UDF.

`[PointingDeviceDrivers]`. This section is run during the text mode portion of Setup and contains a list of pointing device drivers to be used during Setup. This section must be specified in the answer file, not in the UDF.

`[OEM_Ads]`. This section can be used to modify the default user interface of the setup program. It enables you to modify the banner, background bitmap, and logo used during the GUI portion of Setup.

`[GuiUnattended]`. This section specifies settings for the GUI portion of Setup. It can indicate the time zone and hide the administrator password page.

`[UserData]`. This section is used to provides user-specific data such as the username, organization name, computer name, and product ID.

`[LicenseFilePrintData]`. This section is valid only during installation of Windows NT Server. It enables you to specify the licensing option you want to use for your Windows NT server.

`[Network]`. This section specifies network settings such as network adapters, services, and protocols. If this section is missing, networking components won't be installed. If the `[Network]` section is specified but is empty, the user is presented with a number of error messages during the installation. This section is also used to specify the domain or workgroup and to create a computer account in the domain.

[Modem]. This section indicates whether a modem should be installed. This section must be specified if you want to install modems by using RAS in unattended mode.

[Display]. This section indicates specific display settings for the display adapter that is being installed. These settings must be correct and supported by the adapter.

[DetectedMassStorage]. This section specifies which mass storage devices Setup should recognize, even if they are not connected to the system during installation. This setting must be specified in the answer file, not in the UDF.

Those items that can be specified only in the answer file and not in the UDF must be the same for all installations performed using that answer file. If, for example, you have a need to install different keyboard drivers or SCSI drivers on certain machines, this requires you to create a different answer file for each of those instances.

> **WARNING**
>
> **Be Sure to Specify Network Specifications in Your Answer File**
> If a [Network] section is not specified in your unattended answer file, no networking components for Windows NT Workstation will be installed. If the computer you are installing does not have a CD-ROM and you are trying to install across the network, the system will have no way of connecting to the installation files to add the networking components.

> **NOTE**
>
> **Commonly Used UDF Sections** The sections of the unattended answer file that pertain to individual user settings are the most likely candidates for inclusion in a UDF. They are [GuiUnattended], [UserData], and [Network].

## Using Setup Manager to Create an Unattended Answer File

Setup Manager is a graphical application that comes on the Windows NT Workstation Resource Kit CD. You can use it to graphically create an unattended answer file instead of editing the UNATTEND.TXT template file directly. You can specify the following three areas in the Setup Manager:

- General Setup
- Networking
- Advanced

### General Setup Options

The General Setup Options dialog box enables you to specify the installation directory, display settings, time zone, license mode, user information, computer role, and general information for hardware detection and upgrade information (see Figure 1.2).

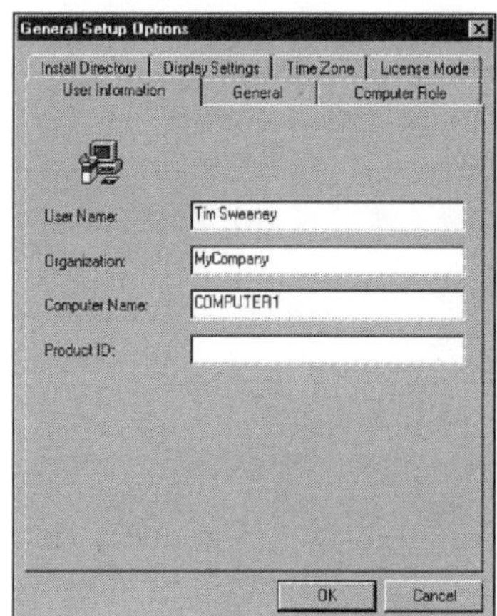


**FIGURE 1.2**
The General Setup Options dialog box contains parameters for user settings and general information.

The General Setup Options dialog box contains the following tabs of options:

- *User Information.* This tab contains fields for the user's name, organization name, computer name, and product ID.
- *General.* The General tab contains settings for whether or not to confirm hardware as part of the installation and for the capability to run a program with Setup. It also includes specifications if this is an upgrade installation. The following upgrade options are available:

  *Prompt User for Windows NT Installation to Upgrade.* This is used if there is more than one installation of Windows NT on the machine.

  *Upgrade the Current Single Windows NT Installation.* This is used to upgrade a single Windows NT installation.

  *Upgrade the First Windows NT Installation Found.* This is used if there is more than one installation of Windows NT on the machine and you do not want the user to choose which one to use.

  *Upgrade Windows 3.1 or Windows for Workgroups.* This is used to upgrade Windows 3.x.

- *Computer Role.* This tab contains options for the role the computer will play. The following are the valid options for NT Workstation computers:

  *Workstation in Workgroup.* This option is used for installing Windows NT Workstation into a workgroup. You use this option in either a small environment with no domains or an environment in which you will later add the computer to the domain.

  *Workstation in Domain.* If this option is selected, an additional prompt appears, asking you to create a computer account in the domain.

- *Install Directory.* The options on this tab enable you to specify the install directory. You can use the default directory, have Setup prompt the user for the directory, or use a particular directory that you specify.

- *Display Settings.* This tab contains the display settings. You can have Setup configure them automatically, or you can specify that they will be set during logon.
- *Time Zone.* On this tab, you can select the time zone for the user location from a list.
- *License Mode.* This tab is used only in the installation of Windows NT Server. It is used to specify the license settings for the Windows NT Server.

## Networking Options

The Networking Options dialog box enables you to specify adapters, protocols, services, and modem settings, and whether this portion of the GUI setup should be manual or automatic (see Figure 1.3).

The settings that you can configure through the Networking Options dialog box are grouped on these six tabs:

- *General.* This tab enables you to specify whether the networking components will be configured manually or unattended. For an unattended installation, you can tell Setup to automatically configure the first detected adapter or to search for a particular adapter.
- *Adapters.* The Adapters tab contains options with which you can specify which adapters will be detected.
- *Protocols.* The Protocols tab enables you to specify which protocols are installed and which configuration parameters are used.
- *Services.* On the Services tab, you can specify which services are installed and what their configuration parameters are. Services include RAS, CSNW, and SNMP.
- *Internet.* The Internet tab is used only during the installation of Windows NT Server.
- *Modem.* The Modem tab is used only if the RAS service is selected for installation on the Services tab.

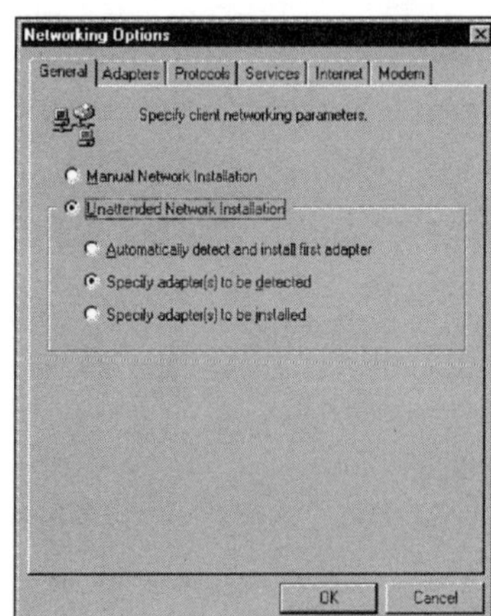


**FIGURE 1.3**
The Networking Options dialog box allows you to set specifications to completely configure networking in an automated installation.

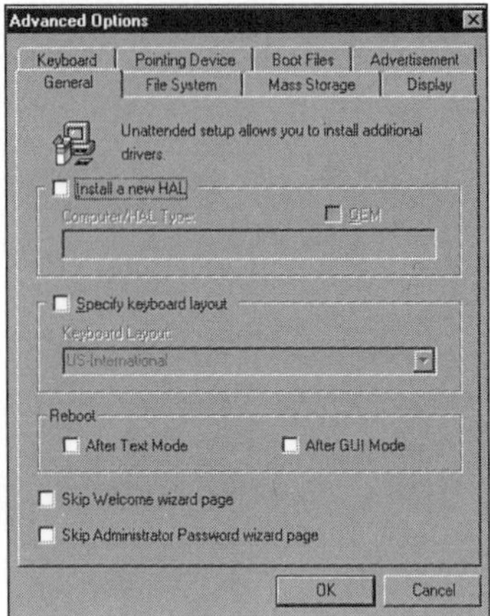


**FIGURE 1.4**
In the Advanced Options dialog box, you can specify additional device drivers and advertisement information for use during the GUI portion of Setup.

## Advanced Options

The Advanced Options dialog box enables you to specify which device drivers to install, the file system to use, and the banner and background information to use during the GUI portion of Setup. As Figure 1.4 shows, this section also lets you control the reboots during the setup process and whether to skip the display of the administrator password page.

The Advanced Options dialog box offers eight tabs of options:

- *General.* This tab enables you to skip the welcome page, set the administrator password, specify the automatic reboot after text and GUI modes of Setup, and indicate keyboard layout and HAL type.
- *File System.* On this tab, you can indicate whether to keep the current file system or convert to NTFS as part of the installation.
- *Mass Storage.* This tab enables you to specify a list of driver descriptions.
- *Display.* This tab enables you to specify a list of display driver descriptions.
- *Keyboard.* This tab enables you to specify a list of keyboard driver descriptions.
- *Pointing Device.* This tab enables you to specify a list of pointing device driver descriptions.
- *Boot Files.* This tab enables you to specify a list of boot files.
- *Advertisement.* This tab enables you to specify banner text, a logo graphics file, and a background graphics file for use during the GUI portion of installation.

> NOTE
>
> **Combine Methods for Creating an Unattended Answer File** You can combine methods, such as using Setup Manager to configure most of the settings for the unattended answer file, and then using a text editor to make changes to that file directly.

# Creating Uniqueness Database Files

Uniqueness database files extend the functionality of the unattended answer file, enabling the specification of computer-specific settings. The function of a UDF is to merge with sections of the answer file to provide the computer-specific settings. The UDF is a text file that should be located with the other Windows NT installation files on the distribution server.

The UDF contains two sections: one for unique IDs and one for unique ID parameters. The first section identifies which areas of the answer file will be replaced or modified. In it, you specify the particular users or computers for which unique information will be specified. The unique ID parameters section contains the actual data that will be merged into the answer file, such as a computer name or time zone information.

You use one of these syntax examples to specify a UDF:

```
Winnt /u:answerfile /s:x:\ /udf:userid,x:\udf.txt
```

or

```
Winnt32 /u:answerfile /s:x:\ /udf:userid,x:\udf.txt
```

Here is a breakdown of the elements that make up the syntax:

`answerfile` represents the name of the unattended answer file.

`/s` points to the source path of the Windows NT installation files.

`/udf` indicates the unique ID and the path to the UDF file.

The first section of the UDF lists the uniqueness IDs. Following the uniqueness IDs are the sections that they refer to. For example, a UDF might look like this:

```
[UniqueIDs]
User1 = UserData, GuiUnattended, Network
User2 = UserData, GuiUnattended, Network
[User1:UserData]
FullName = "User 1"
OrgName = "MyCompany"
ComputerName = "Computer1"
[User1:GuiUnattended]
TimeZone = "(GMT-08:00) Pacific Time (US & Canada);
➥Tijuana"
[User1:Network]
JoinDomain = "DomainName"
[User2:UserData]
FullName = "User 2"
OrgName = "MyCompany"
ComputerName = "Computer2"
[User2:GuiUnattended]
TimeZone = "(GMT-08:00) Pacific Time (US & Canada);
➥Tijuana"
[User2:Network]
JoinDomain = "OtherDomain"
```

So how do you use a combination of the unattended answer file and the UDF? For each environment (similar hardware, certain department, certain geography), create a single unattended answer file. In addition, create at least one UDF file that specifies the unique IDs of all machines that will be installed. For each unique ID, indicate those parameters that should be defined on a computer-specific basis or user-specific basis.

## The $OEM$ Directory

In some instances, your customized installation might include drivers that do not ship with NT and need to be installed by hand, or it might include the installation of application software. You can have files copied to the destination machine during the text setup phase, and you can then configure your unattended installation to use those files. In order for this to work, however, two things must be done:

- You must create a $OEM$ directory in the network share from which you are installing NT Workstation.
- You must enable the preinstallation copy of these OEM files by specifying the command `OEMInstall=Yes` in the `[Unattended]` section of your unattended installation file.

When the unattended installation begins the copying phase of installation, the contents of the $OEM$ directory will be copied to the destination computer. Customized files can then be accessed by the automated installation. In addition, .INF files created by the SYSDIFF utility (discussed in the next section) can also be copied and invoked after the installation of NT Workstation is complete.

## Using SYSDIFF

SYSDIFF, unlike the unattended answer file and the uniqueness database file, is not used during the actual installation of the Windows NT operating system. Instead, it is used to install applications after the operating system is in place. However, you can use it in conjunction with the unattended answer file and the uniqueness database file to create a fully automated installation of both the operating system and the necessary applications.

This tool gives you the ability to track the changes between a standard installation of Windows NT Workstation and an installation that has been modified to your particular environment. It does this by creating a *snapshot* of your system before the changes. The snapshot documents the freshly installed Windows NT Workstation as it was configured by the automated installation. After you make the desired changes to your system (adding applications), SYSDIFF records a *difference file*, which documents the changes that were made.

After the difference file has been created, you can use it to generate either an .INF file or an expandable package. The .INF file is a set of instructions that tell NT how to apply a set of files to create an installation. It does not contain the installation files, though; they are kept in a separate place. An expandable package, on the other hand, is like a .ZIP file in that it contains all the files and Registry settings required to apply the differences detected between the original configuration and the one after the difference file was made.

> **WARNING**
>
> **The SYSDIFF Utility Is Version-Specific** The SYSDIFF utility is for Windows NT 4 only. Do not try to use it to install Windows 95 or Windows NT 3.51.

## Creating a Snapshot File

The first step in running SYSDIFF is to install Windows NT Workstation on a sample system. After the operating system is installed, you then use SYSDIFF to take a snapshot of that reference machine. The command syntax for taking a snapshot of the system is

```
Sysdiff /snap [/log:log file] snapshot file
```

where `log file` is the name of an optional log file that can be created by SYSDIFF and `snapshot file` is the name of the file that will contain the snapshot of the system.

This command creates the snapshot file, which is then used as the original configuration. SYSDIFF uses this original configuration as the baseline for comparison with the changed system.

The reference machine (the one you are taking a snapshot of) must be of the same platform type (x86, Alpha, and so on) as the destination computers (those on which you will run the unattended installation). Similarly, the Windows NT root directory (d:\winnt, for example) must be the same on both the reference machine and the target machines (those on which the difference file will be applied).

> **NOTE**
>
> **Copying Empty Directories** When propagating the directory structure, SYSDIFF does not copy empty directories. As a workaround, you can either copy a temporary file into those directories so SYSDIFF will copy them, or you can copy them as part of the Windows NT installation.

## Creating a Difference File

After the snapshot has been taken, install all applications that will be needed on the machine. Then perform the second step of SYSDIFF—creating the difference file. Use the following command to create the difference file:

```
Sysdiff /diff [/c:title] [/log:log file] snapshot file
➥difference file
```

Within that command, replace the following variables:

`title` is the title for the difference file.

`log file` is the name of an optional log file that can be created by SYSDIFF.

`snapshot file` is the name of the file that contains the snapshot of the system. This file must specify the same snapshot file you created with the `/snap` command. If you use a file created on another system, SYSDIFF will not run.

`difference file` is the name of the file that contains the changes between the original configuration and the current configuration of the system.

> **WARNING**
>
> **Don't Change Computer Name on Reference Machine** Make certain that you do not change the computer name of the reference machine after you start the SYSDIFF process. If you do, you'll have to re-create the snapshot and the difference file.

This mode uses the snapshot file (the original configuration) created in the first step to find the changes that were made in the directory structure and the Registry entries during the application installations. These changes will be added to the difference file.

## Using the Difference File

Now that the difference file has been created, you have two options for using that file to install software along with the installation of NT Workstation. You can use SYSDIFF with either `/apply` or `/inf`.

When you use `/apply`, you create a single, potentially large file that contains all the files and Registry settings indicated by the difference file. When you use `/inf`, you create an .INF file that defines the process by which the installation is to be carried out. During the first phase of Workstation installation, both the operating system files *and* the configuration for application installation are copied. With `/apply`, one large file is copied; with `/inf`, a configuration file and a number of smaller files (which comprise the changed files identified by the difference file) are copied.

When the installation of NT is complete, the files copied during installation setup are used to complete the application setup.

Microsoft suggests you use `/inf` whenever possible for the following reasons:

- Although both options require a large quantity of data to be moved to the workstation during installation, the `/inf` option moves the information in smaller pieces and, therefore, is potentially more efficient, especially on a busy network.
- Both options require that the installation process be configured to include both the files to be copied with the NT installation files and the instructions as to how to apply those files. However, the `/inf` option performs the configuration automatically, and the `/apply` option does not.

## Creating an .INF File

An .INF file created from the difference file contains only the Registry and initialization file directives. It is, therefore, significantly smaller than the difference file itself. You use the following command to initiate the .INF portion of the installation:

```
Sysdiff /inf /m [/u] sysdiff_file oem_root
```

Here's a breakdown of the command's elements:

`/m` indicates that the changes made to the menu structure should map to the default user profile structure instead of to the profile of the user who is currently logged on. Otherwise, these menu changes would be made to only one user account instead of being made globally on the whole system. (And that one user account might not even exist on the destination workstation.)

`/u` indicates that the .INF should be generated as a Unicode text file. The default is to generate the file using the system ANSI codepage.

*`Sysdiff_file`* is the path to the file created by the `/diff` command.

*`Oem_root`* is the path to the directory where the $OEM$ structure required for the .INF will be created, and where the .INF will be placed.

> **WARNING**
>
> **$OEM$ Directory Path Name Limitation** The initial phase of Windows NT installation is DOS based and cannot copy directories whose path names are longer than 64 characters. Make sure the $OEM$ directory does not exceed that length.

This command creates the .INF file as well as a $OEM$ directory structure, which contains all the files from the difference file package. You should create this directory under the I386 directory (if you're installing x86 machines) on the distribution server. If the directory is not under the I386 directory, you can move it.

## Using the .INF File

To use this .INF file after it has been created, you must add a line to the file CMDLINES.TXT located in the $OEM$ directory. Fortunately, this line is automatically added when you use the `/inf` option with SYSDIFF.

To invoke the .INF you created, add this line to the CMDLINES.TXT file

```
"RUNDLL32 syssetup,SetupInfObjectInstallAction section 128
➥inf"
```

where *`section`* specifies the name of the section in the .INF file, and *`inf`* specifies the name of the .INF file. This needs to be specified as a relative path.

The CMDLINES.TXT file is placed in the root of the $OEM$ directory on the network share containing the NT installation files. This file, along with the rest of the $OEM$ directory, will be copied to the destination machine. Then, when the installation of NT is complete, the command lines in the CMDLINES.TXT file will be executed. If an .INF file is included, this can be used to install the applications of your choice.

Using an .INF file instead of the entire difference file package can save time during your unattended installation.

## Applying the Difference File

The final step in the SYSDIFF process is to apply the difference file to a new installation as part of the unattended setup. To do so, use this command

```
Sysdiff /apply /m [/log:log file] difference file
```

Take a look at a few of those elements more closely:

`/m` indicates that the changes made to the menu structure should map to the default user profile structure instead of to the profile of the user who is currently logged on. Otherwise, these menu changes would be made to only one user account instead of being made globally on the system. (And that one user account may not even exist on the destination workstation.)

`log file` is the name of an optional log file that SYSDIFF uses to write information regarding the process. This is good to use for troubleshooting if SYSDIFF fails during the apply process.

`difference file` is the file created by the `/diff` command. The Windows NT root must be the same (d:\winnt, for example) as it is on the system that created the difference file. This means that for all the unattended installations you will perform using this difference file, the location of the system root must be the same.

You do not have to run this command as part of the unattended installation. You can run it at any time after Windows NT Workstation is installed. To make the installation of Windows NT and your applications fully automated, you might want to have it run as part of the installation.

Because this difference file contains all the files and Registry settings for the applications you installed, it can be quite large (depending on how many applications you install). Applying such a potentially large package as part of the installation can add a significant amount of time to your setup process.

## Dumping the Difference File

If you are uncertain about the configuration of the installation you are applying to your NT installation and you want to confirm the files being applied or check for errors if applications do not function properly, you may want a list of the files being applied. You can use the `/dump` option to dump the difference file into a file that you can review. This command enables you to read the contents of the difference file. The syntax of this command is

```
Sysdiff /dump difference file dump file
```

where `difference file` specifies the name of the difference file you want to review, and `dump file` specifies the name you want to give to the dump file.

After creating the dump file, you can view it with any text editor, such as Notepad.

## The WINDIFF Utility

The utility called WINDIFF analyzes files and/or directories for differences. (Like SYSDIFF, it is distributed with the NT Resource Kit.) If you are concerned about ensuring that files changed during the installation of software are all identified properly, or if you just want to compare two directories for differences in filename and content, you can use the WINDIFF utility.

After installing the Resource Kit, you can invoke this utility from a command line by typing **WINDIFF**. Once it is running, the utility allows you to run file-level or directory-level comparisons from the File menu. These comparisons are then presented in a combination of graphical and text-based styles, depending on your preference.

Although it is not used frequently, the WINDIFF utility can be very valuable for file comparison and is a prime candidate for questions on the NT Workstation exam.

# PLANNING STRATEGIES FOR SHARING AND SECURING RESOURCES

Plan strategies for sharing and securing resources.

Another thing to consider when you're installing Windows NT Workstation 4.0 is how you will make resources available to users without sacrificing security. Giving users access to resources does not require you to "give away the shop." To effectively share and secure resources for Windows NT Workstation, you must understand the built-in groups and what rights those groups give the users within them, as well as how sharing one folder affects the other folders in the hierarchy below it.

## Built-In NTW Groups

Windows NT Workstation has six built-in groups that are added during the installation process. You can use the following built-in groups to give users certain rights and abilities on the Windows NT system:

- Users
- Power Users
- Administrators
- Guests
- Backup Operators
- Replicator

When you're administering user accounts and assigning user rights, it is typically easier to assign rights to a group than to assign them to an individual. Table 1.1 identifies and explains the default rights initially assigned to users or groups on a Windows NT workstation.

**TABLE 1.1**

**DEFINITION OF DEFAULT USER RIGHTS**

| *User Right* | *Description* | *Granted To* |
|---|---|---|
| Access This Computer from the Network | Enables a user to connect to the computer over the network. | Administrators, Everyone, Power Users |
| Back Up Files and Directories | Enables a user to back up files and directories. This right supersedes file and directory permissions when used with the NT Backup utility. | Administrators, Backup Operators |
| Change the System Time | Enables a user to set the internal clock of the computer. | Administrators, Power Users |
| Force Shutdown from a Remote System | Enables a user to shut down a remote computer. | Administrators, Power Users |
| Load and Unload Device Drivers | Enables a user to install and remove device drivers. | Administrators |
| Log On Locally | Enables a user to log on at the computer from the computer keyboard. | Administrators, Backup Operators, Guests, Everyone, Power Users, Users |
| Manage Auditing and Security Log | Enables a user to specify what types of resource access (such as file access) are to be audited and to view and clear the security log. This right does not enable a user to set system auditing policy using the Policies, Audit command in the User Manager. Members of the Administrators group can always view and clear the security log. | Administrators |

*continues*

**TABLE 1.1** *continued*

**DEFINITION OF DEFAULT USER RIGHTS**

| *User Right* | *Description* | *Granted To* |
|---|---|---|
| Restore Files and Directories | Enables a user to restore backed up files and directories. This right supersedes file and directory permissions when used with the NT Backup utility. | Administrators, Backup Operators |
| Shut Down the System | Enables a user to shut down Windows NT. | Administrators, Backup Operators, Power Users, Users, Everyone |
| Take Ownership of Files or Other Objects | Enables a user to take ownership of files, directories, printers, and other objects on the computer. This right supersedes permissions protecting objects. | Administrators |

Table 1.1 describes what each default user right enables a user to do. You can add a user to one of the existing groups on Windows NT Workstation to give that user the ability to perform any of these tasks, or you can add that user's account to the list of accounts with permissions via the User Rights Policy dialog box (see Figure 1.5).

If you're trying to determine whether to add a particular user account to the list of default user rights or to just add the user to an existing Windows NT Workstation group that has that right, it is helpful to know which groups are assigned certain rights by default. Table 1.2 shows this.

In addition to these default user rights, Windows NT also has built-in user capabilities. You cannot modify the built-in capabilities. The only way to give a user one of these abilities is to put that user in a group that has been granted the capability. If you want to give a user the right to create and manage user accounts on a Windows NT workstation, for example, you must make that user a member of either the Power Users or the Administrators group. Table 1.3 lists Windows NT Workstation's built-in capabilities.

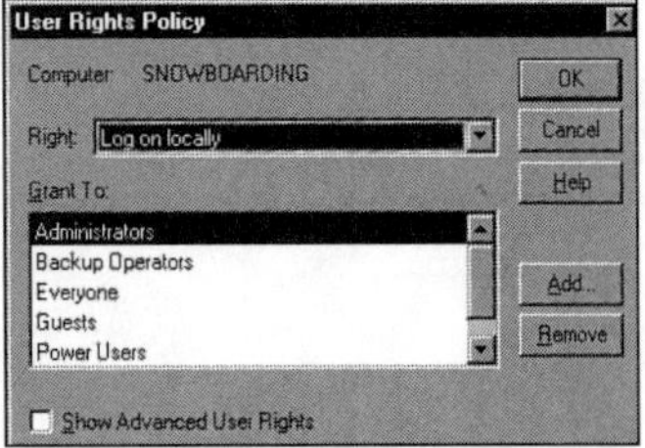


**FIGURE 1.5**
In User Manager, you can select the Policies, User Rights command to modify the default user rights assigned in Windows NT.

TABLE 1.2

## ASSIGNMENT OF DEFAULT USER RIGHTS

| *Right* | *Administrators* | *Power Users* | *Users* | *Guests* | *Everyone* | *Backup Operators* |
|---|---|---|---|---|---|---|
| Access This Computer from the Network | X | X | | | | X |
| Back Up Files and Directories | X | | | | | X |
| Change the System Time | X | X | | | | |
| Force Shutdown from a Remote System | X | X | | | | |
| Load and Unload Device Drivers | X | | | | | |
| Log On Locally | X | X | X | X | X | X |
| Manage Auditing and Security Log | X | | | | | |
| Restore Files and Directories | X | | | | | X |
| Shut Down the System | X | X | X | | X | X |
| Take Ownership of Files or Other Objects | X | | | | | |

TABLE 1.3

## BUILT-IN USER CAPABILITIES

| *Built-In Capability* | *Administrators* | *Power Users* | *Users* | *Guests* | *Everyone* | *Backup Operators* |
|---|---|---|---|---|---|---|
| Create and Manage User Accounts | X | X | | | | |
| Create and Manage Local Groups | X | X | | | | |
| Lock the Workstation | X | X | X | X | X | X |
| Override the Lock of the Workstation | X | | | | | |
| Format the Hard Disk | X | | | | | |
| Create Common Groups | X | X | | | | |
| Share and Stop Sharing Directories | X | X | | | | |
| Share and Stop Sharing Printers | X | X | | | | |

NOTE

**Placement of Power Users Members**
Users created by a member of the Power Users group can only be placed into the Power Users group or groups with lesser permissions. Members of the Power Users group cannot create users that can be placed in the Administrators group.

Knowing about these built-in user rights on Windows NT Workstation is an important step toward understanding how to give users the right to perform certain tasks on the system.

## Users

The Users group provides the user with the necessary rights to use the computer as an end user. By default, all accounts created on Windows NT Workstation are put into the Users group, except for the built-in Administrator and Guest accounts.

## Power Users

The Power Users group gives members the ability to perform certain system tasks without giving the user complete administrative control over the machine. One of the tasks a Power User can perform is the sharing of directories. An ordinary user on Windows NT Workstation cannot share directories (refer to Table 1.2).

## Administrators

The Administrators group has full control over the Windows NT workstation. This account has the most control on the computer. However, members of the Administrators group do not automatically have control over all files on the system. File permissions on an NTFS partition can be set to restrict even an administrator's access. If the administrator needs to access the file, he or she can take ownership of the file and then access it.

## Guests

The Guests group gives its users limited access to the resources on the Windows NT workstation. The Guest account is automatically added to this group.

The Guest account is disabled by default on Windows NT Workstation 4.0. This is a change from Windows NT 3.51, which enabled the Guest account by default for the workstation.

## Backup Operators

Members of the Backup Operators group can back up and restore files on the Windows NT system. If a user is not part of this group, she has the right to back up only those files or directories that she has access to. When a user is part of the Backup Operators group, she has the ability to back up and restore files that she normally would not have access to; but she has access to those files only when she's using the NT Backup utility to back up files.

> WARNING
>
> **Use Trusted Backup Operators**
> A backup operator has the ability to back up files and then restore them without the permissions that they originally had. Consequently, the people with the ability to back up and restore information need to be trusted members of your organization. Some organizations give the backup right to a group but do not give the restore right, thereby ensuring that the ability to back up is disconnected from the ability to restore.

## Replicator

The Replicator group is used for only one task: to enable directory replication. This is the process by which an export server (which must be an NT Server) provides files that are imported by another computer (which could be NT Workstation or NT Server). In order to start the Replicator service, you must create an account for replication and place it in this Replicator group. The Replicator group has no rights other than the ability to replicate. For more information on replication, see the *MCSE Training Guide: Windows NT Server 4, Second Edition.*

## Special Groups

In addition to the default groups created by Windows NT Workstation, Windows NT Workstation uses four other special groups. You cannot assign users to these groups. That assignment happens as part of the Windows NT functionality. These are the four special groups:

- Network
- Interactive
- Everyone
- Creator Owner

The Network group contains any user who is accessing this computer from across the network (instead of sitting down at the computer locally). For example, if Kelley is connecting to a shared printer on your Windows NT Workstation, she is part of your Network group.

The Interactive group contains all users who are logged on locally to the Windows NT workstation. Consider again the preceding example in which Kelley is accessing your shared printer. On her own machine, Kelley is part of the Interactive group; but on your machine, she is part of the Network group.

The Everyone group contains all users who access the Windows NT workstation. This includes all users defined on the computer or domain, as well as guests, interactive users, network users, and users from other domains. This also includes users from other network operating systems—such as NetWare—who have access to your LAN.

Creator Owner refers to the user account that created a resource, such as a file or printer. The Creator Owner automatically has full control over the resource that he or she created.

## Sharing Home Directories

NOTE

**Administrators Can Take Ownership** An administrator always has the ability to "Take Ownership" of a user's home directory. This could be useful if, for instance, a user leaves the company and his files need to be retrieved (see Chapter 3, "Managing Resources").

One of the issues that you have to decide on during the planning process is whether to give your users their own home directories or personal directories for storing information either on the server or on their local workstations. A *home directory* provides a location in which an individual user can store his or her own data or files and to which only that particular user has access.

If you decide to give every user his own home directory, you must decide whether that directory should be on the user's local machine or on the server. Each option has its own advantages, as described in Table 1.4.

EXAM TIP

**Using Comparisons to Prepare for the Test** Comparison tables offer excellent summaries of the information in a section. Although you should know all the detail in a section for the exam, you really need to memorize the information in the tables because they give "boiled-down" versions of section information.

### Structure

Typically when you are creating home directories on the server or a user's workstation, it is best to centralize those directories in one larger directory (for example, called Users). If your company has five users—named Tina, Mark, Carla, Corey, and Fritz—your directory structure would look like that shown in Figure 1.6.

TABLE 1.4

**HOME DIRECTORIES ON THE SERVER VERSUS HOME DIRECTORIES ON THE LOCAL COMPUTER**

| *Server-Based Home Directories* | *Local Home Directories* |
|---|---|
| Centrally located so that users can access them from any location on the network. | Available only on the local machine. For *roaming users* (who log in from more than one computer on the network), the directory is not accessible from other systems. |
| During a regular backup of the server, information in users' home directories is also backed up. | Often users' local workstations are not backed up regularly as part of a scheduled backup process. If the user's machine fails, lost data cannot be recovered. |
| Windows NT does not provide a way to limit the size of a user's directory. Thus, if a lot of information is being stored in home directories the directories use up a lot of server disk space. | If a user stores a lot of information in his home directory, the space is taken up on his local hard drive instead of on the server. |
| If the server is down, the user won't have access to their files. | The user has access to his files even when the network is down because the files are stored locally. |
| Some network bandwidth is consumed due to the over-the-network access of data or files. | No network traffic is generated by a user accessing his or her files. |

If you were to share these directories at the "users" level, you would have a problem because all the directories would be accessible to all users. Given that setup, if Tina wanted to access Mark's directory, you could not prevent her from doing so. If you use share-only permissions, you must share each user's directory individually at the folder level. Therefore, you would share Tina's directory only to Tina, Mark's only to Mark, and so on.

## Permissions

Sharing each individual user's home directory separately at the folder level can be tedious, especially if you have a large environment with many users. One way around this is to create the "Users" directory on an NTFS partition instead of a FAT partition. On an NTFS partition, you can use NTFS permissions for each specific directory (such as the directory called Tina), and then use share permissions to share the top-level "Users" directory to the Users group. By combining NTFS and share permissions in this manner, you can solve the problem of giving individual access without creating a lot of extra work for the administrator. (For a more thorough discussion of NTFS versus share permissions, see Chapter 3.) Table 1.5 lists the directory permissions.

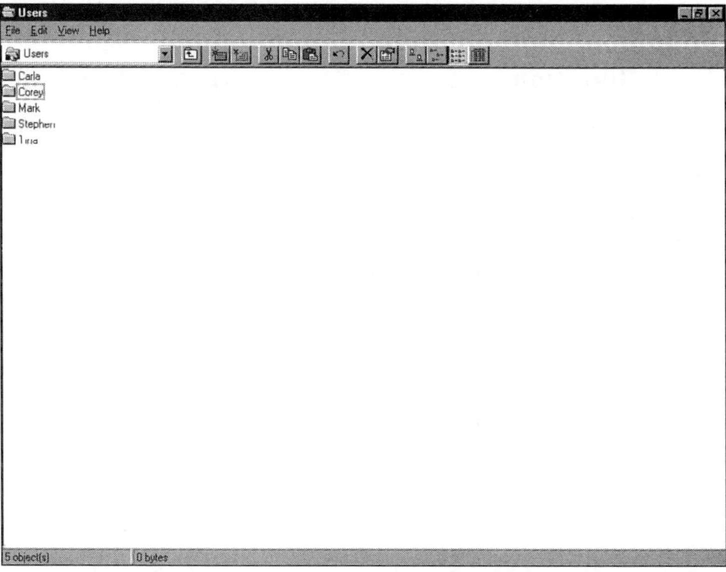


**FIGURE 1.6**
In some way, users' home directories should identify which directory belongs to which user.

**TABLE 1.5**

**DIRECTORY STRUCTURE PERMISSIONS FOR USERS' HOME DIRECTORIES USING NTFS AND SHARE PERMISSIONS**

| *Directory* | *User/Group* | *Permission* |
|---|---|---|
| \Users | Users | Full Control |
| \Tina | Tina | Full Control |
| \Mark | Mark | Full Control |
| \Carla | Carla | Full Control |
| \Corey | Corey | Full Control |
| \Fritz | Fritz | Full Control |

In this sample situation, all users can access the top-level Users folder, but only each particular user can access his or her own home directory. In other words, only Fritz has full control to his own home directory. Because Fritz is not listed in the directory permissions for Carla's home directory, he does not have access to it or anything in it.

## Sharing Application Folders

Another issue you may have to plan for is whether to give your users access to shared network applications. Shared application folders typically give users access to applications that they will run from a network share point. Another option, however, is to have users run applications locally from their own computers. Table 1.6 compares the two alternatives.

As you can see, there are advantages and disadvantages to both shared network and locally installed implementations.

### Structure

If you choose to use shared network applications, you must plan your server directory structure so that these folders can be shared in the most efficient and secure method. If, for example, you use a shared copy of Word, Excel, and PowerPoint, your directory structure might look something like that shown in Figure 1.7.

In this example, you want all your users to be able to access these folders for running applications, but you do not want them to be able to change the permissions or delete any files from within the directories. A group called the "Applications group" is in charge of updates to these applications. Therefore, users in that group need the ability to modify the application directories, but not to modify the permissions on the directory structure.

**TABLE 1.6**

**SHARED NETWORK APPLICATIONS VERSUS LOCALLY INSTALLED APPLICATIONS**

| *Shared Network Applications* | *Locally Installed Applications* |
|---|---|
| Take up less disk space on the local workstation. | Use more local disk space. |
| Easier to upgrade/control. | Upgrades must "touch" every machine locally. |
| Use network bandwidth. | Use no network bandwidth for running applications. |
| Slower response time because applications are accessed from the server. | Faster, more responsive. |
| If the server is down, users can't run applications. | Users can run applications regardless of server status. |

**FIGURE 1.7**
Creating a directory to contain the folders for all shared applications makes it easier to control access to those files.

## Permissions

The permissions on this shared network applications directory structure need to allow the Applications group to make updates to files within any of the three directories as needed, and they need to allow the users to access the directories to execute the applications. To fulfill both requirements, set up the directory structure like that shown in Table 1.7.

Because you are sharing the top-level folder SharedApps, you do not need to share the lower-level folders Word, Excel, and PowerPoint unless you want them to be individually available to users. By giving the Administrators group Full Control, you give them the ability not only to add files but also to change the permissions on the directory structure. By giving the Applications group the Change permission, you allow them to upgrade the applications in these directories as needed.

TABLE 1.7

**DIRECTORY STRUCTURE PERMISSIONS FOR SHARED NETWORK APPLICATIONS**

| *Directory* | *Group* | *Permission* |
|---|---|---|
| \SharedApps | Administrators, Applications group, Users | Full Control, Change, Read |
| \Word | Inherited from SharedApps | Inherited from SharedApps |
| \Excel | Inherited from SharedApps | Inherited from SharedApps |
| \PowerPoint | Inherited from SharedApps | Inherited from SharedApps |

## Sharing Common-Access Folders

Another situation that you may face when planning how to appropriately share and secure resources is the need to have a directory structure that allows for certain groups to work together on files and to access certain directories based on this group membership. You might have a top-level directory called Departments, for example, with subdirectories of Sales, Accounting, Human Resources, and Finance.

### Structure

To create a directory structure to support the need for certain groups to share access over certain directories, you may want to create a directory structure like that shown in Figure 1.8.

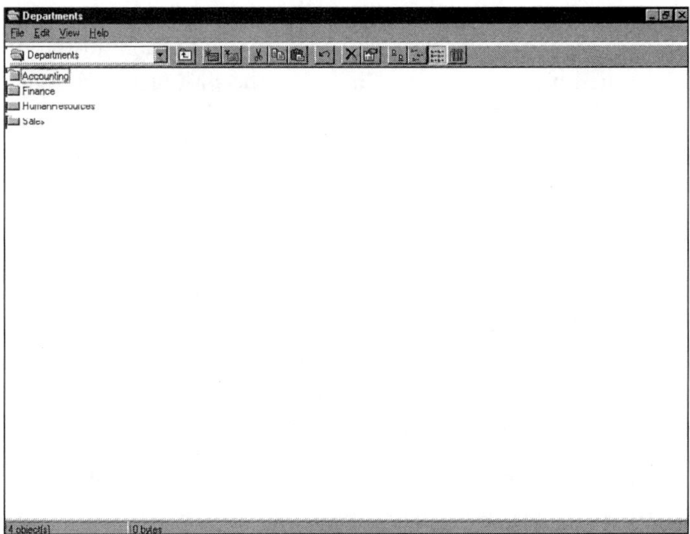


**FIGURE 1.8**
A directory structure for common-access folders can be based on departments, regions, or a combination of the two.

By creating the departmental folders under one main folder, you centralize the administration of the folder hierarchy. This structure offers a common location in which the sales personnel can store their files and access information. Because you may not want the sales personnel to access the accounting data, however, you need to plan your shared directories accordingly.

## Permissions

To set share permissions on this folder hierarchy, you need to assign permissions separately to each directory, as outlined in Table 1.8.

**TABLE 1.8**

**DIRECTORY STRUCTURE PERMISSIONS FOR COMMON-ACCESS FOLDERS**

| *Directory* | *Group* | *Permission* |
|---|---|---|
| \Departments | Administrators | Full Control |
| \Sales | Sales | Change |
| \Accounting | Accountants | Change |
| \HumanResources | HR | Change |
| \Finance | Finance | Change |

On a volume that is FAT formatted, giving the Administrators group Full Control over the Departments share makes the administration of the shared hierarchy possible and gives the administrators access to all the shared folders below the top-level folder (Departments). No specific department can be given access at the top level because you do not want any department to have access to any other department's data. Therefore, you need to share each departmental folder at the folder level and only to that particular department. The Sales folder, for example, is shared to the Sales group with Change permission. The Sales group will probably need to add or modify data in this directory, but they should not need to modify the directory itself or the directory's permissions. Because of this, the Sales group is given the Change permission instead of Full Control.

If, on the other hand, this structure exists on an NTFS volume, you can give shared permissions to allow everyone to access the

Departments directory, and then you can apply NTFS permissions to the individual subdirectories. As a result, everyone would be able to see that the directories for the other groups existed, but they would be able to access only the directory that gave them access. All other directories would be restricted. (For a more thorough discussion of NTFS versus share permissions, see Chapter 3.)

## Choosing the Appropriate File System to Use in a Given Situation

Choose the appropriate file system to use in a given situation. File systems and situations include NTFS, FAT, HPFS, security, and dual-boot systems.

Windows NT Workstation 4.0 supports two file systems: FAT16 (not FAT32) and NTFS. Windows NT 3.51 contained support for HPFS (the High Performance File System used with OS/2), but that support has been eliminated in NT 4.0.

Windows NT 4.0 supports the use of either or both the NTFS and FAT file systems. An important decision to make when planning your Windows NT Workstation environment is which file system to use. Which file system you use on each workstation or each partition within a workstation depends on the needs of your particular environment. When choosing a file system, you must consider the following issues:

- Performance
- Size of partition
- Recoverability
- Dual-boot capabilities
- Security
- File compression

# NT Partitions

A *partition* is an area of a physical disk that functions as though it were a separate unit. Each physical disk can be divided into as many as four partitions, and each partition can be as large as 4GB if formatted FAT or—theoretically—as large as 16 exabytes (that's 18 billion GB) if formatted NTFS. Actually, given current hardware limitations, the upper limit is 2 terabytes (that's 2200GB).

Being familiar with the types of partitions that can be created under NT Workstation is essential to planning for implementation properly.

## Primary Partitions

A *primary partition* is a partition on which you can load the files needed to boot a particular operating system. A primary partition cannot be further partitioned. Thus if you want multiple partitions on your system, be careful not to use all the available free space for the primary partition. Each physical disk can be divided into as many as four primary partitions. One primary partition is needed for the Windows NT system partition.

- *System partition.* The volume that contains the files needed to load Windows NT Workstation (including NTLDR, NTDETECT.COM, and so on). Only a primary partition can be used as the system partition, and that primary partition must be marked active.
- *Boot partition.* The volume that contains the Windows NT operating system files (\winnt directory and subdirectories). This can be, but does not have to be, the same volume as the system partition.

## Extended Partitions

An *extended partition* is created from free space on the physical disk and can be further partitioned into multiple logical drives. An extended partition is not assigned a drive letter or formatted with a file system. Only the logical drives within the extended partition can be assigned drive letters or formatted with a particular file system. Creating an extended partition enables you to exceed the four-partition limitation.

By creating multiple logical drives within the extended partition, you can format each drive with a particular file system as needed. If you create a single logical drive within the extended partition, you cannot change the partition information in Windows NT without deleting the logical drive and then re-creating logical drives.

If you have multiple physical disks, it is possible to have a disk that has only an extended partition on it and no primary partitions. To do this, you must have at least one physical disk that has a primary partition for the Windows NT system partition.

WARNING

**Don't Waste Space** You are limited to one extended partition per physical disk, so plan your partitions accordingly. If you have three primary partitions and you create an extended partition that does not include all the free space available on the drive, you end up wasting the remaining free space.

## The High Performance File System (HPFS)

High Performance File System (HPFS) is the file system used with OS/2. Windows NT 3.51 supported partitions already formatted with the HPFS file system, but it did not allow you to format new drives as HPFS. In Windows NT 4.0, the support for HPFS has been eliminated entirely. Therefore, if your system currently has an HPFS partition, you need to reformat that drive as either FAT or NTFS before installing Windows NT Workstation 4.0 or upgrading to Windows NT 4.0. Essentially, you must remove the HPFS partition before setting up Windows NT 4.0 in order to perform the installation. You can eliminate the HPFS partition in one of two ways:

- Reformat the HPFS partition as either FAT or NTFS
- Convert the HPFS partition to NTFS prior to the installation

Which option you should choose depends on whether you want to preserve the data on the partition. If you do *not* want to preserve the data, you can simply reformat the partition; if you *do* want to preserve the data, convert the partition.

NOTE

**Change Existing Partitions with Third-Party Partition Managers** Some third-party partition managers, such as Partition Magic, enable you to change the size of an existing partition without deleting the partition or losing data. Keep in mind, however, that it is always a good idea to back up important data before resizing partitions.

### Reformatting an HPFS Partition

If you choose to format the existing HPFS drive as either FAT or NTFS, you must back up the existing data from the drive that you want to keep.

If the HPFS drive is your system partition (the one that you boot from) or your boot partition (the one that contains the Windows

WARNING

**Reformatting Deletes All Existing Data** Reformatting the drive erases all existing data on the drive. Do not choose that option unless you have made a backup of the data or you know for sure that you do not need to keep the existing data.

NT operating system files), you cannot reformat that partition from within Windows NT. The following procedures explain how you can reformat the system and boot partitions (respectively).

## STEP BY STEP

### 1.2 Formatting the System Partition

1. Create a DOS bootable floppy.
2. Boot the computer from the floppy.
3. Use the DOS `format` command with the `/s` option to format the drive as FAT and make it bootable to DOS.
4. From DOS, launch the Windows NT installation.

   If the \winnt directory is not on the system partition (the one that you just formatted), you didn't blow away Windows NT by formatting the system partition. If you can boot off a Windows NT bootable floppy, you can run the upgrade from within Windows NT instead of DOS.

## STEP BY STEP

### 1.3 Formatting the Boot Partition

1. If the system partition is FAT formatted, boot to DOS.
2. After booting under DOS, format the boot partition with the DOS `format` command.
3. From DOS, launch the Windows NT installation.

> **WARNING**
>
> **Make Sure You Have a Bootable Disk** If you are reformatting your system partition, make certain that you have either a DOS bootable or Windows NT bootable floppy available so that you can restart your computer after you have reformatted.

If the HPFS partition that you are trying to delete is not your system or boot partition, you can reformat the partition by using the Windows NT Disk Administrator program (see Figure 1.9).

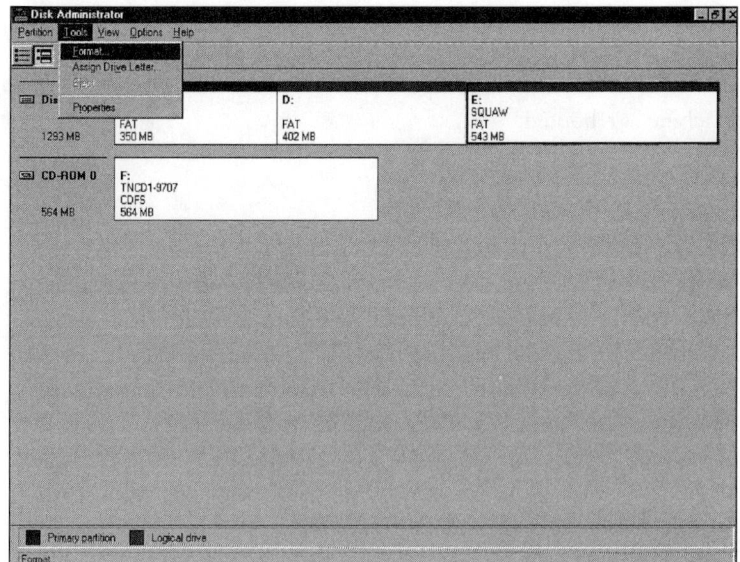


**FIGURE 1.9**
You can use the Windows NT Disk Administrator program (in Windows NT 3.51) to reformat an HPFS drive as either FAT or NTFS in preparation for the upgrade to NT 4.0.

If there are any files in use on the HPFS partition that is being reformatted, the `format` command prompts you to close those files. After you have reformatted the drive, you are ready to upgrade the system to Windows NT Workstation 4.

## Converting an HPFS Partition

If you do not want to lose the data on your HPFS partition, you can use the `convert` command (from within Windows NT 3.51) to convert the HPFS partition to NTFS before you upgrade to Windows NT 4.0. The `convert` command is run from the command line with the syntax

```
Convert drive: /FS:NTFS /v
```

where

*`drive`* is the drive letter of the HPFS partition you want to convert.

`/FS:NTFS` specifies the file system to which you want to convert (NTFS is the only option).

`/v` runs the command in verbose mode.

NOTE

**Be Patient** Converting a drive to NTFS can take a long time, especially if the drive is large or fragmented. Because the `convert` command does not display any status information, it might appear to be hung up when it is actually still converting the file system.

You cannot convert the Windows NT boot partition while you are running Windows NT. If you do attempt to convert the boot partition, you will receive a prompt to convert it the next time the machine is rebooted.

# FAT

Windows NT Workstation 4.0 supports the FAT file system. This file system is named for its method of organization: the File Allocation Table. The File Allocation Table resides at the top, or beginning, of the volume. Each volume contains two copies of the FAT in case one becomes damaged. FAT supports the following four attributes:

- Read Only
- Archive
- System
- Hidden

## Understanding the Benefits

The FAT file system is typically a good choice for a small partition. Because FAT is required for DOS, it is also a good option for a dual-boot system with Windows 95 or Windows 3.x. Using the FAT file system on Windows NT has a number of benefits over using FAT on a DOS-based system. Under Windows NT, the FAT file system supports the following features:

- Long filenames (up to 255 characters)
- Multiple spaces in filenames
- Multiple periods in filenames
- Filenames that are not case sensitive but that do preserve case

The FAT file system has a fairly low file-system overhead, which makes it good for smaller partitions.

## Knowing the Limitations

Although the FAT file system is necessary for dual-boot configurations, it has some significant limitations when used with Windows NT:

- *Inefficiency on larger partitions.* There are two reasons that FAT is inefficient on larger partitions (greater than 400MB). First, FAT uses a linked list for its directory structure. If a file grows in size it might become fragmented on the disk, which results in slower access time for retrieving the file. Second is the default cluster size used on a FAT partition. For partitions up to 255MB, FAT uses a 4KB cluster size. For partitions greater than 512MB, however, FAT uses 16KB clusters and greater, up to 256KB clusters for drives above 8192MB on Windows NT 4. Thus, if you are using Windows NT and have an 800MB FAT formatted partition that contains a lot of smaller files (under 32KB), you end up wasting a lot of space on the drive due to the cluster size.
- *Lack of local security.* Because the FAT file system does not support local security, there is no way to prevent a user from accessing a file if that user can log on locally to the workstation.
- *No support for compression under Windows NT.* Although the FAT file system supports compression by DriveSpace or DoubleSpace, neither of those utilities is supported under Windows NT. Therefore, there is no way to use compression on FAT under Windows NT.

Whether you choose to use the FAT file system depends on the needs of your particular workstation.

# NTFS

NTFS tends to be the preferred file system for use under Windows NT in environments that can support it (those that don't need to dual-boot, for instance). Only Windows NT supports NTFS.

## Understanding the Benefits

Using NTFS has many benefits, including the following:

- *Support for long filenames.* NTFS supports long filenames of up to 255 characters.
- *Preservation of case.* NTFS is not case sensitive, but it does have the capability to preserve case for POSIX compliance.
- *Recoverability.* NTFS is a recoverable file system. It uses transaction logging to automatically log all file and directory updates so that if a power outage or system failure occurs, the information can be used to redo failed operations.
- *Security.* NTFS provides the user with local security for protecting files and directories.
- *Compression.* NTFS supports compression of files and directories to optimize storage space on your hard disk.
- *Size.* NTFS partitions can support much larger partition sizes than FAT can. NTFS can support partitions up to 16 exabytes in size. (An exabyte is a little larger than one billion gigabytes.)

Using NTFS gives you security and enhanced functionality when compared with the FAT file system.

## Knowing the Limitations

The main limitations with NTFS are its lack of compatibility with other operating systems and its high overhead. If you need to dual-boot with another operating system, at least one of the partitions must be formatted FAT in order for the second operating system to function. As well, if your NT system becomes unbootable, you cannot boot from a floppy disk and recover the information. However, an emergency repair process will allow most broken NT systems to be repaired. For more information on the emergency repair process, see Chapter 7, "Troubleshooting."

The amount of overhead required to maintain the NTFS file structure is also a factor. It takes between 7.5MB and 15MB to maintain an NTFS partition. Therefore, Microsoft recommends that for partitions smaller than 400MB you consider formatting the partition as FAT unless other circumstances make that unadvisable.

## Comparison of FAT and NTFS

As you have learned, there are benefits to using both FAT and NTFS partitions on Windows NT Workstation. Many of these are dependent on your particular configuration and needs. Table 1.9 provides a comparison of the two file systems.

**TABLE 1.9**

**COMPARISON OF NTFS AND FAT FILE SYSTEMS USING WINDOWS NT WORKSTATION**

| *Feature* | *FAT* | *NTFS* |
|---|---|---|
| Support for long filenames (up to 255 characters) | Yes | Yes |
| Compression | No | Yes |
| Security | No | Yes |
| Dual-boot capabilities with non–Windows NT systems | Yes | No |
| Maximum file/partition size | 4GB | 16EB |
| Recommended partition size | 0–400MB | 400MB–16EB |
| Capability to format a floppy | Yes | No |
| Recoverability (transaction logging) | No | Yes |

## Using Compression

NTFS compression enables you to make more efficient use of limited hard disk space. If you need more space on your hard disk but do not want to (or are unable to) purchase an additional drive, you can use NTFS compression to fit more information on your existing disk.

The compression state of a folder does not necessarily reflect the compression state of the files in that folder. It is possible to have a folder that is compressed even if none of the files within that folder are compressed. To use NTFS compression under Windows NT Workstation 4.0, you can initiate it either through the file or folder properties or through the command line using the COMPACT utility.

WARNING

**Compact Instead of Compress** A utility called compress enables you to compress folders and files. However, it is not recommended that you use this utility for compression because you cannot open a file that has been compressed in this way.

## Implementing Security

In a discussion of how security relates to file systems, it is necessary to define security. The NTFS file system gives you the ability to implement local security. *Local security* is defined as a means of restricting access to a file or directory from someone who is sitting at the keyboard of that particular machine. Even if someone logs on to your Windows NT workstation locally (or interactively), for example, you can still prevent him from accessing your files and directories if you use NTFS security.

NTFS is the only file system supported by Windows NT 4 that has the ability to provide local security. The FAT file system can secure a directory only with share-level permissions, not local permissions. Share-level permissions apply only to users accessing the directory across the network. Therefore, share-level permissions cannot prevent someone logged on locally from accessing your files or directories.

## Choosing Dual-Boot Scenarios

If you want to dual boot between Windows NT 4.0 and any other non–Windows NT operating system, you must use the FAT file system for universal access across operating systems. The NTFS file system is accessible only by Windows NT. Thus if you are dual booting with Windows 95, the NTFS partition will not be visible in Windows 95.

If want to dual boot a machine between Windows NT Workstation 4.0 and Windows 95, you *can* use an NTFS partition if you want, even though it is inaccessible from Windows 95. If you do, however, you must be careful not to format your active partition (your C: drive) or the partition that has the Windows directory on it. Otherwise, you won't be able to boot into Windows 95.

WARNING

**Windows NT Can't Access FAT32 File Systems** If you are using the FAT32 file system with Windows 95, you must remove it before installing Windows NT for a dual-boot system. The FAT32 file system for Windows 95 is inaccessible from within Windows NT.

If you choose to dual boot between Windows 95 and Windows NT Workstation 4.0, you must install all applications under each operating system individually.

## CASE STUDY: RIVER WIDE TRAINING

### ESSENCE OF THE CASE

Here are the essential elements in this case:

- Automated installation
- NT Workstation installation
- Application software installation
- Fast processor speed
- Reliable results
- Consistent configuration for all machines used in a given course
- Security is not an issue
- Performance in classroom is of paramount importance

### SCENARIO

River Wide Training is a Microsoft Authorized Technical Education Center (ATEC). As a prerequisite to technical training courses, River Wide offers introductory courses on Windows NT for end-users. Because a single classroom may be used for many different classes from day to day, and because the instructors have found that students tend to make dramatic changes to workstation configurations during training, River Wide reformats its hard drives at the end of each class and then reinstalls Windows NT Workstation at the end of each day.

Although the end result of this is desirable, the amount of work has been found to be excessive. On busy days, as many as 30 machines may have to be installed with NT Workstation. To make matters more complex, many companies are now requesting that their employees receive training in application packages, such as Word 97 and Excel 97, on a Windows NT Workstation platform. This could increase the number of daily Workstation installations to as many as 100.

As a consultant to River Wide Training, you are made aware that security is not an issue in this environment because no information on any of the systems is private. In addition, you are told that speed of response to students' software requests is of paramount importance in classes. Therefore, a longer setup time is preferred over having sluggish performance in the classroom.

*continues*

## CASE STUDY: RIVER WIDE TRAINING

### ANALYSIS

Drawing from the beginning of this chapter, the conclusions are to automate the setup of workstations using WINNT.EXE, answer files, and uniqueness database files. One answer file could be constructed for each machine configuration (assuming that not all of River Wide's computers are identical). If three or four machine types exist, that many answer files would be constructed. In addition, a single uniqueness database file could be constructed with the unique information for each workstation to be installed; at minimum, this would consist of the workstation name.

Installation is made simpler by the lack of security requirements. This means that a simple workgroup can be configured, and FAT partitions can remain on the systems. FAT formatted partitions make for easier clean-up at the end of the day because machines can be booted to DOS and hard drives can be reformatted without the need for special utilities that read from or remove NTFS partitions.

When the need for application training comes to fruition, it will be simple to create some difference files using SYSDIFF and to have it build and configure .INF files that can be executed at the end of the installation. This use of .INF files ensures that the downloads will be fast, especially at peak load times when the network is being used to install NT and applications on 100 machines at once. Using .INF files also ensures consistency in the installation and, therefore, consistent configuration of student stations. With these .INF files, performance would remain high in the classroom because the software would be available on each workstation instead of having to be accessed from an applications server (thus preventing the network from bearing the load of applications during class times).

## CHAPTER SUMMARY

Looking back at this chapter, you can see that the information fell into three main topics: unattended installation, sharing and securing resources, and file systems. In the unattended installation section you learned about the elements needed to perform a successful unattended installation—the answer file and the UDF. In addition, you learned about using the SYSDIFF and WINDIFF as aids to completing an installation by installing applications.

In the section on sharing and securing resources, you learned about groups and how to use them to provide security. You also examined how groups play into sharing home directories, application folders, and common access folders.

Finally, you studied file systems on NT Workstation. Beginning with partitions, you learned about FAT and NTFS, the two file systems supported by Windows NT Workstation 4.0. In addition, you were introduced to the HPFS file system, which was supported in NT 3.51 but is not supported in NT 4.0.

### KEY TERMS

Before you take the exam, make sure you are comfortable with the definitions and concepts for each of the following key terms:

- unattended answer file
- uniqueness database file (UDF)
- SYSDIFF
- WINDIFF
- difference file
- built-in Windows NT groups
- primary partition
- extended partition
- HPFS
- FAT
- NTFS

## APPLY YOUR LEARNING

The following section allows you to assess how well you understood the material in the chapter. The exercises enable you to engage in the sorts of tasks that comprise the skill sets the objectives reflect. Review and exam questions test your knowledge of the tasks and concepts specified in the objectives. Answers to the review and exam questions follow in the answers sections.

For additional review- and exam-type questions, use the Top Score test engine on the CD-ROM that came with this book.

## Exercises

### 1.1 Using the Setup Manager to Create an Unattended Answer File

This exercise helps you work with the Setup Manager to create an unattended answer file that could be used to automate an installation of Windows NT Workstation.

**Estimated Time:** 30 minutes

1. Log on to Windows NT Workstation as an administrator.
2. Insert the Windows NT Workstation CD into the CD-ROM drive. From the CD, click on the Support/deptools/i386 directory. Launch Setup Manager by double-clicking on it.
3. Click on the General button. Click on the User Information tab and fill in the following fields:

   *User Name.* Enter your name.

   *Organization Name.* Enter the name of your company.

   *Computer Name.* Enter the name assigned to your computer.

   *Product ID.* Leave this field blank.

   Click on the Computer Role tab and fill in the following information:

   *Role.* Choose the role of Workstation in Workgroup.

   *Workgroup Name.* Enter a workgroup name, such as Sierras.

   Click on the Time Zone tab and select your time zone from the list. Then click the OK button.
4. Click on the Networking Setup button. Click on the General tab, select Automatically Detect, and then install the first adapter. When you finish, click OK.
5. Click on the Advanced Setup button. On the Advertisement tab, enable banner text and type **This is a customized NT Setup**. On the General tab, put a check mark in the following check boxes:
   - Reboot After Text Mode
   - Reboot After GUI Mode
   - Skip Welcome Wizard Page
   - Skip Administrator Password Page

   Then click on OK.
6. Click on the Save button and save this file as c:\custom.txt. Then exit out of Setup Manager.
7. Launch Notepad by clicking the Start button and selecting Programs, Accessories, Notepad. In Notepad, open the File menu and choose Open. In the File Name field, type **c:\custom.txt**. Review the contents of the file.
8. Exit Notepad and log off Windows NT Workstation.

## APPLY YOUR LEARNING

### 1.2 Assigning User Rights to a User Account

This exercise helps you understand the rights of built-in Windows NT Workstation groups by examining the user rights within User Manager and testing to see what happens when they are changed.

**Estimated Time:** 40 minutes

1. Log on to Windows NT Workstation with the built-in Administrator account.
2. Launch User Manager by choosing Start, Programs, Administrative Tools, User Manager.
3. Within User Manager, click on the Policies menu and choose User Rights.
4. What groups can log on locally to the Windows NT workstation by default?
5. What groups can change the system time?
6. Close out of the User Rights dialog box.
7. Within User Manager, create a new user account by clicking on the User menu and choosing New User. Respond to the following controls:

    *Username.* Enter your username, such as MarinaS.

    *Full Name.* Enter your full name, such as Marina Sugar.

    *Password.* Leave this field blank.

    *Description.* Choose User.

    *User Must Change Password at Next Logon.* Uncheck this box.

    Click on the Add button to create the user account for MarinaS.

8. Open the Policies menu and choose User Rights. From the list of user rights, select Change the System Time. Click on the Add button to add the new account MarinaS to the list of accounts with the right to change the system time.
9. Log off of Windows NT Workstation.
10. Log on as MarinaS with a blank password.
11. On the taskbar, double-click on the clock.
12. Change the time to 12:00 AM. Were you successful?
13. Log off of Windows NT.
14. Log on as the default administrator.
15. Launch User Manager by choosing Start, Programs, Administrative Tools, User Manager.
16. Within User Manager, click on the Policies menu and choose User Rights.
17. From the list, select Change the System Time. Then remove the account for MarinaS from the list of accounts with the right to change the system time.
18. Close out of the User Rights dialog box. Exit out of User Manager.
19. Log off of Windows NT Workstation.
20. Log on as MarinaS with a blank password.
21. Double-click on the clock on the taskbar. Change the system time to 2:30 PM. Were you successful?
22. Log off of Windows NT Workstation.

## APPLY YOUR LEARNING

### 1.3 Creating a Partition Using Disk Administrator and Converting an Existing FAT Partition to NTFS

In this exercise, you work with partitions and Disk Administrator to create an NTFS partition and to convert a FAT partition to NTFS. (This lab exercise requires that you have either unpartitioned space on your hard disk or a FAT partition that you can convert to NTFS.)

**Estimated Time:** 30 minutes

**Creating an NTFS Partition from Free Space**

1. Log on to Windows NT Workstation as an administrator.
2. Launch Disk Administrator by choosing Start, Programs, Administrative Tools, Disk Administrator.
3. If this is the first time that you have run Disk Administrator, it prompts you to write a signature on the disk. Accept the defaults when prompted.
4. Within Disk Administrator, how many partitions do you have? How many primary? How many secondary? How can you tell the difference within Disk Administrator?
5. Select an area of free space, signified by diagonal lines, by clicking on it. From the Partition menu, choose Create. In the Create dialog box, select the size you want to use for your new partition (make it at least 10MB).
6. Click on the new partition. Then open the Partition menu and choose Commit Changes Now. When you're prompted to save the changes, click on Yes. A dialog box appears indicating that disks were updated successfully. Click on OK.
7. With the new partition selected, go to the Tools menu and choose Format. Under File System, select NTFS. In the Format dialog box, click on Start. Then click OK to clear the warning message.
8. Click on OK in the Format Complete message dialog box. Then click on Close to exit the Format dialog box.

**Converting a FAT Partition**

1. Log on to Windows NT Workstation as an administrator.
2. Launch Disk Administrator by choosing Start, Programs, Administrative Tools, Disk Administrator.
3. View the partitions on your system to determine which is a FAT partition. You will convert that partition to NTFS. (If you do not want to convert an existing partition, create a new FAT partition with Disk Administrator.) Close Disk Administrator.
4. Go to a command prompt and type **convert *drive letter:* /fs:ntfs**. Then press Enter. Windows NT begins the conversion process. If files are in use on this partition, you receive the following message:

   ```
   Convert cannot gain exclusive access to
   your drive. Would you like to schedule it
   to be converted the next time the system
   restarts?
   ```

   Type **Y** to answer Yes and press Enter.
5. Exit the command prompt by typing **Exit** and pressing Enter. Then restart Windows NT Workstation by clicking on the Start button and

choosing Restart the Computer. When the computer reboots, it will convert the drive to NTFS. When the conversion is complete, the system restarts and boots into Windows NT Workstation.

## Review Questions

1. As a network administrator of a 500-user network, you need to roll out Windows NT Workstation 4.0 to all the machines in your network. You have standardized hardware across departments, and you want to perform an unattended installation of NT Workstation. You also need to install Office 97 as part of this rollout. What should you do?
2. You need to create home directories for the 250 users in your network so they have a place to store personal files. Where should you create these directories? How will you make them available to users?
3. Leslie needs to work on some confidential files on her Windows NT Workstation. She shares a machine with Scott, who should not have access to these files. How can Leslie secure her files so that Scott cannot access them while he is sitting at the machine?
4. Roger wants to dual boot his Windows 95 system with Windows NT Workstation 4.0. His drive is divided into three partitions: C:, D:, and E:. How should Roger format these partitions for use with both Windows NT and Windows 95?
5. Jack wants to fully automate the installation of 50 Windows NT Workstation 4.0 computers. What files does he need to use for these installations to make them automated and capable of setting computer-specific parameters?
6. What are three major disadvantages of using the FAT file system as compared with NTFS?

## Exam Questions

1. You are in charge of your company's rollout of Windows NT Workstation 4.0. You need to install 500 machines, all of which will be part of the same domain. Each has identical hardware, and you want Windows NT installed identically on all machines.

   **Required Result:**

   To install Windows NT Workstation on all machines, configured correctly to work on the network.

   **Optional Results:**

   Install in the shortest possible amount of time.

   Install with no user intervention.

   **Solution:**

   You decide to create one unattended answer file to use for the installation, but you will not use UDFs. You will manually install the network settings during the installation.

   **Analysis:**

   Which of the following statements best describes the proposed solution?

   A. This solution fulfills the required result as well as both optional results.

   B. This solution fulfills the required result and one of the optional results.

## APPLY YOUR LEARNING

C. This solution fulfills the required result but does not fulfill either of the optional results.

D. This solution does not fulfill the required result.

2. You are in charge of your company's rollout of Windows NT Workstation 4.0. You need to install 500 machines, all of which will be part of the same domain. Each has identical hardware, and you want Windows NT installed identically on all machines.

**Required Result:**

To install Windows NT Workstation on all machines, configured correctly to work on the network.

**Optional Results:**

Install in the shortest possible amount of time.

Install with no user intervention.

**Solution:**

Create one unattended answer file and one UDF file that specifies the computer names, and then use those for the installation.

**Analysis:**

Which of the following statements best describes the proposed solution?

A. This solution fulfills the required result as well as both optional results.

B. This solution fulfills the required result and one of the optional results.

C. This solution fulfills the required result but does not fulfill either of the optional results.

D. This solution does not fulfill the required result.

3. You are in charge of your company's rollout of Windows NT Workstation 4.0. You need to install 500 machines, all of which will be part of the same domain. Each has identical hardware, and you want Windows NT installed identically on all machines.

**Required Result:**

To install Windows NT Workstation on all machines, configured correctly to work on the network.

**Optional Results:**

Install in the shortest possible amount of time.

Install with no user intervention.

**Solution:** Install Windows NT Workstation directly from the CD.

**Analysis:**

Which of the following statements best describes the proposed solution?

A. This solution fulfills the required result as well as both optional results.

B. This solution fulfills the required result and one of the optional results.

C. This solution fulfills the required result but does not fulfill either of the optional results.

D. This solution does not fulfill the required result.

4. Margie wants to upgrade her OS/2 system to Windows NT Workstation 4.0. She has a 486 with 32MB RAM, a 6x CD-ROM drive, and 1.2GB hard disk with 500MB free. Her system is configured as one drive formatted with the HPFS file system. What steps should she take to upgrade this machine?

## APPLY YOUR LEARNING

A. Run `winnt /b` from the Windows NT Workstation CD.

B. Run Setup from the Windows NT Workstation CD.

C. Run `winnt32 /b` from the Windows NT Workstation CD.

D. Format the drive as FAT, and then install Windows NT Workstation.

5. Pat wants to prevent other people who use his workstation from accessing files he has been working on. He has converted his FAT partitions to NTFS. What else does he have to do to restrict access to those who will be sitting at his system?

A. Store the files in the briefcase. The briefcase has a security option that enables him to password-protect his files.

B. Compress his files to ensure that only he can read them.

C. Share out his files in a folder and only grant himself access to them.

D. Assign NTFS permissions to his files to restrict everyone but him from accessing them.

6. Joyce has a dual-boot system with Windows 95 and Windows NT Workstation 4. She needs to run both operating systems to test out an application she is writing. However, she is running out of space on her C: drive and would like to take advantage of the extra space she could gain through compression. What should Joyce do?

A. Get the Windows 95 Plus Pack, which comes with a compression agent.

B. Use DOS DoubleSpace to compress the drive.

C. Format the drive as NTFS and use the `compress` command to compress the drive.

D. You cannot support this configuration.

7. Which of the following are valid methods for creating an unattended answer file? (Choose all that apply.)

A. Use the Setup Manager on the Windows NT Resource Kit.

B. Use the System Policy Editor installed with Windows NT Workstation.

C. Create the file with a text editor such as Notepad.

D. Use the sample UNATTEND.TXT file as a template, and then customize it to your environment.

8. Which of the following is a valid method for creating a uniqueness database file?

A. Use the Setup Manager on the Windows NT Resource Kit.

B. Use the System Policy Editor installed with Windows NT Workstation.

C. Create the file with a text editor such as Notepad.

D. Use the sample UNATTEND.TXT file as a template, and then customize it to your environment.

## Apply Your Learning

9. Winnie needs to be able to share files on her Windows NT workstation with other users on the network. To do this, yet grant her the fewest other rights that she doesn't need, the administrator should make her a member of which built-in group in Windows NT Workstation?

   A. Users

   B. Power Users

   C. Guests

   D. Domain Administrators

10. Harry is an administrator of a 200-person network. He needs to set up home directories for all the users on the network. The data that users will be storing in their home directories is sensitive and should not be viewed by other users. This data is vital to the company's business. Users will need to access this data from anywhere on the network. How should Harry set up the home directories?

    A. Create a directory called Users on a FAT partition on the server and put each user's home directory underneath it. Share the Users directory to all users.

    B. Create a common directory on the server in which all users can store their files.

    C. Create a directory called Users on an NTFS partition on the server and put each user's home directory underneath it. Share the Users directory to all users. The NTFS permissions prevent each specific user from accessing any directory other than his or her home directory.

    D. Create a home directory on each user's workstation.

11. Fred needs to upgrade a Windows NT 3.51 workstation to Windows NT 4.0. He has a Pentium 100 with 32MB RAM, a 1.2GB hard disk, and an 8x CD-ROM drive. His hard drive is currently partitioned in this way:

    - C drive: FAT format and contains the system partition
    - D drive: HPFS format and contains the boot partition
    - E drive: NTFS format and contains data files

    What should he do to upgrade this system?

    A. Connect to the network share with the Windows NT Workstation 4.0 files and run `winnt32 /b` to install Windows NT.

    B. Use Disk Administrator to format drive D: as FAT, and then connect to the network share with the Windows NT Workstation 4.0 files and run `winnt32 /b` to install Windows NT.

    C. Use Disk Administrator to convert drive D: to FAT, and then connect to the network share with the Windows NT Workstation 4.0 files and run `winnt32 /b` to install Windows NT.

    D. From a command prompt, use the `convert` command to convert drive D: to NTFS. After the system reboots, connect to the network share with the Windows NT Workstation 4.0 files and run `winnt32 /b` to install Windows NT.

12. What is the name of the partition in which the Windows NT operating system files are located?

    A. The system partition

    B. The boot partition

## APPLY YOUR LEARNING

C. The NT partition

D. The OS partition

13. What is the name of the partition in which the files needed to boot Windows NT are located?

    A. The system partition

    B. The boot partition

    C. The NT partition

    D. The OS partition

14. Which of the following is a benefit of using FAT over NTFS?

    A. FAT supports local security and file compression; NTFS does not.

    B. FAT supports long filenames and local security; NTFS does not.

    C. FAT supports additional local operating system's efficient storage for hard drives smaller than 400MB; NTFS does not.

    D. FAT supports formatting floppy disks and efficient storage for hard drives smaller than 400MB; NTFS does not.

15. What are three benefits of using NTFS over FAT? (Select the best answer.)

    A. NTFS supports local security, file compression, and floppy disk formatting; FAT does not.

    B. NTFS supports partitions larger than 4GB, long filenames, and file compression; FAT does not.

    C. NTFS supports conversion to HPFS, file compression, and partitions larger than 4GB; FAT does not.

    D. NTFS supports local security, file compression under NT, and partitions larger than 4GB; FAT does not.

16. Under Windows NT 4.0, FAT supports long filenames up to:

    A. 175 characters.

    B. 8.3 characters.

    C. 255 characters.

    D. It depends on the size of the partition.

17. Kirk has a dual-boot system with Windows 95 and Windows NT Workstation 4.0. It is configured with the following drive partitions:

    - C drive: FAT format and contains the system partition
    - D drive: FAT format and contains the Windows 95 operating system files
    - E drive: FAT format and contains the Windows NT Workstation operating system files
    - F drive: used for storing data

    Attempting to take advantage of all the functionality of NTFS, Kirk converts drive E: to NTFS. What will happen the next time he tries to boot into Windows 95?

    A. Nothing. The system will boot into Windows 95 as before.

## APPLY YOUR LEARNING

B. The system will boot into Windows 95 Safe mode.

C. The system cannot boot into Windows 95 because of the conversion.

D. The system will no longer give the option to boot into Windows 95. He would have to modify the BOOT.INI file to re-enable the dual boot option.

18. Tempest has a dual-boot system with Windows 95 and Windows NT Workstation 4.0. It is configured with the following drive partitions:

    - C drive: FAT format and contains both the system partition and the Windows 95 files
    - D drive: FAT format
    - E drive: FAT format and contains the Windows NT Workstation operating system files
    - F drive: used for storing data

    Attempting to take advantage of all the functionality of NTFS, Tempest converts drive C: to NTFS. What will happen the next time she tries to boot into Windows 95?

    A. Nothing. The system will boot into Windows 95 as before.

    B. The system will boot into Windows 95 Safe mode.

    C. The system cannot boot into Windows 95 because of the conversion.

    D. The system will no longer give the option to boot into Windows 95. She would have to modify the BOOT.INI file to re-enable the dual boot option.

19. Eric moves a file from his D: drive to his C: drive. His D: drive is formatted NTFS and is compressed. His C: drive is FAT formatted. What will happen to the file when it is copied to the C: drive?

    A. It will remain compressed.

    B. It will no longer be compressed.

    C. It will be converted to FAT compression.

    D. It will be compressed using the DOS DriveSpace utility.

20. Mitch has a system configured with Windows 95 and Office 97. He would like to dual boot with Windows NT Workstation 4.0 but still be able to use his Office applications. His machine is a Pentium 100 that has 32MB RAM and a 1GB hard disk formatted with FAT32. What should he do to upgrade his machine?

    A. Install Windows NT 4.0 using the `winnt32` command, and then reinstall Office 97 under Windows NT.

    B. Upgrade Windows 95 to Windows NT Workstation by deleting his Windows directory after he installs Windows NT Workstation.

    C. Install Windows NT 4.0 using the `winnt` command, and then reinstall Office 97 under Windows NT.

    D. Mitch cannot install Windows NT Workstation on this machine with its current configuration.

APPLY YOUR LEARNING

## Answers to Review Questions

1. Use an unattended answer file with a single UDF file that specifies the computer-specific settings. To install Office 97, use SYSDIFF to take a snapshot of the original (post-installation) configuration and then create a difference file after Office 97 is installed. For more information, refer to the section "Creating Unattended Installation Files."

2. Most likely you will want to create the users' home directories on the server so that they will be backed up and can be accessed from any location in the network. You should make them available to users through a combination of NTFS and share-level permissions so that you do not have to share each individual folder to each user. For more information, refer to the section "Sharing Home Directories for Users' Private Use."

3. Leslie should store the files on an NTFS partition. NTFS provides local security, which enables Leslie to restrict access to the files—even from someone who is sitting locally at the machine. For more information, refer to the section "Choosing the Appropriate File System to Use in a Given Situation."

4. Roger will need to format all partitions with the FAT file system because that is the only file system that can be read by both Windows NT Workstation and Windows 95. He should not format partitions with NTFS or FAT32 because each will be inaccessible to one of the operating systems. For more information, refer to the section "Choosing the Appropriate File System to Use in a Given Situation."

5. Minimally Jack will need to use an unattended answer file and a UDF, which specifies the computer-specific settings for each of the 50 machines. If Jack's environment is not standardized in terms of hardware or the installation directory, he may need to use multiple unattended answer files. For more information, refer to the section "Creating Unattended Installation Files."

6. The following are three disadvantages to formatting with FAT: It is inefficient for large partitions (greater than 400MB); it does not support file compression under NT; and it does not support local security. Conversely, these are all supported by NTFS on NT. For more information, refer to the section "FAT."

## Answers to Exam Questions

1. **C** is correct. Although creating one unattended answer file and manually responding to the network prompts fulfills the required result of having Windows NT installed properly, it does not fulfill either of the optional results because it is not the quickest option and it does prompt for user intervention. For more information, refer to the section "Creating an Unattended Answer File."

2. **A** is correct. By using one unattended answer file and a UDF file, you can automate the installation with no user intervention and have it ready to function on the network after the installation is complete. For more information, refer to the section "Creating an Unattended Answer File."

3. **C** is correct. Although this method will get Windows NT Workstation installed, and it does

## APPLY YOUR LEARNING

meet the required result, it does not meet either of the optional results for shortest time taken or for no user intervention. For more information, refer to the section "Creating Unattended Installation Files."

4. **D** is correct. This is the only option because the drive is formatted HPFS. For more information, refer to the section "The High Performance File System."

5. **D** is correct. The briefcase does not provide security, nor does file compression. A share provides security, but only over the network and not to local users. NTFS permissions are the only way Pat can restrict access to everyone but himself. For more information, refer to the section "Choosing the Appropriate File System to Use in a Given Situation."

6. **D** is correct. While dual booting Windows 95 and Windows NT Workstation, you cannot implement compression through either operating system without sacrificing access by the other operating system. For more information, refer to the section "Choosing the Appropriate File System to Use in a Given Situation."

7. **A, C, and D** are correct. You can create an unattended answer file through the Setup Manager, by using the UNATTEND.TXT template file, or by creating it with Notepad. For more information, refer to the section "Creating Unattended Installation Files."

8. **C** is correct. To create a UDF, use any text editor, such as Notepad. For more information, refer to the section "Creating Unattended Installation Files."

9. **B** is correct. To be able to share resources, Winnie needs to be a member of the Power Users group. Members of the Users group on Windows NT Workstation do not have the right to share directories. And although domain administrators do have that ability, that group is not a Windows NT Workstation group. For more information, refer to the section "Planning Strategies for Sharing and Securing Resources."

10. **C** is correct. To most easily set up the users' home directories so that only each particular user can access his or her home directory, Harry should put the Users directory on an NTFS partition. This will implement the appropriate rights after the Users directory is shared and the users' home directories are created. For more information, refer to the section "Sharing Home Directories for Users' Private Use."

11. **D** is correct. The D: drive must be converted before the upgrade. This must be done as a convert because the D: drive contains the boot partition. For more information, refer to the section "Choosing the Appropriate File System to Use in a Given Situation."

12. **B** is correct. The boot partition contains the NT operating system files (those required to boot NT after the computer starts). For more information, refer to the section "Choosing the Appropriate File System to Use in a Given Situation."

13. **A** is correct. The system partition contains the files necessary to initiate the boot process and direct that process to the boot partition for the actual starting of NT. For more information, refer to the section "Choosing the Appropriate File System to Use in a Given Situation."

14. **C** is correct. FAT supports other local operating systems, while NTFS is a proprietary file system that is accessible only by NT. In addition, FAT

## APPLY YOUR LEARNING

provides an efficient file system for small partitions (smaller than 400MB) because of its low overhead. Choice A is incorrect because FAT does not support either local security or file compression. Choice B is incorrect because although FAT does support long filenames, it does not support local security and, in fact, NTFS supports both. Choice D is incorrect because although FAT supports the formatting of floppy disks (which NTFS does not), it is not an efficient system to use for large partitions (larger than 400MB). For more information, refer to the section "Choosing the Appropriate File System to Use in a Given Situation."

15. **D** is correct. NTFS supports local security, file compression under NT, and partitions larger than 4GB, but FAT does not. Choice A is incorrect because NTFS does not support floppy disk formatting. Choice B is incorrect because although the statements are true about NTFS, it is incorrect to say that they are not true about FAT because FAT does support long filenames and file compression (just not under NT). Choice C is incorrect because there is no way to convert from NTFS to HPFS. For more information, refer to the section "Choosing the Appropriate File System to Use in a Given Situation."

16. **C** is correct. There is support for filenames up to 255 characters under Windows NT. For more information, refer to the section "Choosing the Appropriate File System to Use in a Given Situation."

17. **A** is correct. Because Kirk formatted drive E:, which has Windows NT installed on it, that conversion will not affect Windows 95. The only result Kirk will see from this is that he will not be able to access drive E: from within Windows 95. For more information, refer to the section "Choosing the Appropriate File System to Use in a Given Situation."

18. **C** is correct. Because Tempest converted the C: drive, which had Windows 95 installed on it, she will no longer be able to boot into Windows 95. For more information, refer to the section "Choosing the Appropriate File System to Use in a Given Situation."

19. **B** is correct. Because Eric moved the file from NTFS to FAT, the file lost the compression attribute. For more information, refer to the section "Choosing the Appropriate File System to Use in a Given Situation."

20. **D** is correct. Because Mitch's system is formatted with FAT32, he cannot install Windows NT Workstation on it. For more information, refer to the section "Choosing the Appropriate File System to Use in a Given Situation."

## Suggested Readings and Resources

The following are some recommended readings related to Planning:

1. Microsoft Official Curriculum course 922: *Supporting Microsoft Windows NT 4.0 Core Technologies*
   - Module 1: The Windows NT 4.0 Environment
   - Module 5: Managing File Systems
   - Module 6: Managing Partitions
   - Module 7: Managing Fault Tolerance
   - Module 10: Configuring Windows NT Protocols
   - Module 15: Implementing Network Clients
2. *Microsoft Windows NT Server 4.0 Networking Guide* (Microsoft Press; also available in the Windows NT Server 4.0 Resource Kit)
   - Chapter 1: Windows NT 4 Networking Architecture
   - Chapter 6: TCP/IP Implementation Details
   - Chapter 13: Using NetBEUI with Windows NT
3. Microsoft TechNet CD-ROM
   - *Concepts and Planning: MS Windows NT Server 4.0*
     - Chapter 1: Managing NT Server Domains
     - Chapter 7: Protecting Data
     - Chapter 11: Managing Client Administration
4. Web sites
   - `www.microsoft.com/ntserver`
   - `www.microsoft.com/train_cert`
   - `www.prometric.com/testingcandidates/assessment/chosetest.html` (take online assessment tests)

## Objectives

Microsoft provides the following objectives for "Installation and Configuration":

**Install Windows NT Workstation on an Intel platform in a given situation.**

- This objective is necessary because an individual certified in the use of Windows NT Workstation technology must be able to install Windows NT Workstation on an Intel platform. This includes not only knowing the mechanics of installation but also understanding the options and why one would choose certain options under certain conditions.

**Set up a dual-boot system in a given situation.**

- This objective is necessary because an individual certified in the use of Windows NT Workstation technology must understand the concept of dual booting and know when it is appropriate to dual boot a computer. In addition, you must understand the limitations you place on NT by having another operating system reside locally on your hard drive.

**Remove Windows NT Workstation in a given situation.**

- This objective is necessary because an individual certified in the use of Windows NT Workstation technology must be able to remove an installation of Windows NT Workstation. This includes understanding what makes NT boot as NT, which files to remove, and how to restore another operating system to boot on your machine.

**Upgrade to Windows NT Workstation 4.0 in a given situation.**

- This objective is necessary because an individual certified in the use of Windows NT Workstation technology must understand the upgrade paths from various operating systems, as well as how to execute the upgrade processes.

CHAPTER 2

# Installation and Configuration

## Objectives

**Configure a server-based installation for wide-scale deployment in a given situation.**

- To satisfy this objective, you must be able to set up a server for the installation of Windows NT Workstation over the network. In addition, you should be able to execute an installation from such a platform.

**Install, configure, and remove hardware components for a given situation. Hardware components include network adapter drivers, SCSI device drivers, tape device drivers, UPSs, multimedia devices, display drivers, keyboard drivers, and mouse drivers.**

- To satisfy this objective, you must understand and be able to configure the various hardware devices that NT Workstation supports, and you should know how to remove these devices when they are no longer needed or are being upgraded. In addition to installing and removing devices, you must be able to make reasonable decisions regarding the use of these devices and the situations in which they are appropriate.

**Use Control Panel applications to configure a Microsoft Windows NT Workstation computer in a given situation.**

- This objective is necessary because an individual certified in the use of Windows NT Workstation technology must be able to configure the software components related to the hardware installed. In addition, this person should be able to configure all the software components of NT Workstation itself, which are configurable from the Control Panel.

## Outline

## Outline



## Study Strategies

- Because installation and configuration are so fundamental to understanding and working with NT Workstation, you can expect to see a number of questions related to these topics. The best way for you to study the subjects of installation, dual booting, removal, and network installation objectives is by working through the material presented here and then performing installations. You should try installations in as many different contexts as possible, such as installing using the setup disks from DOS; installing with Windows 95 already present; installing with another version of NT already present; and installing over the network from a share point on a server. Such practice will reinforce the installation concepts you've read about and give you a good feel for the kinds of options that are available. Finally, after you have installed NT Workstation, try removing it. This will enable you to see what must be removed in order to provide a clean break from the operating system.

- With regard to the hardware and Control Panel objectives, you do not have to worry too much about the fine details. That is, if you have never worked with a SCSI drive, it's probably not necessary that you seek one out to study for the exam. Of course, having as broad an experience as possible is always more helpful than not. But the questions on the exam have more to do with general concepts of using the various components and where you would go to configure them than they do with the nitty-gritty of IRQ settings and DMA channels. You need to have a solid theoretical understanding of the concepts presented in this chapter. Beyond that, however, being familiar with the icons in the Control Panel and what hardware or software components to which they are connected should be sufficient for this component of the exam.

# INTRODUCTION

Before people can use Windows NT Workstation, it must be installed and configured. In fact, arguably the most important factor in an NT implementation is that it is installed and configured correctly. An improperly installed or configured NT system can lead to nothing but headaches and grief for you and the users you support, who need to use NT.

Installation of operating systems and application software on client desktops is one of the most time-consuming activities performed by network administrators. Being able to efficiently carry out these functions can result in significant time savings (just consider the time you could gain by saving one hour at each of 200 client desktops).

Configuration of NT is not just a matter of making sure that the right adapter cards are installed; it involves working with all the drivers for all the hardware. It also means ensuring that the operating system is adequate to meet all the users' needs, and if it is not, adding the necessary components to make it so.

# INSTALLING NT WORKSTATION

Install Microsoft Windows NT Workstation 4.0 on an Intel platform in a given situation.

Before you try to install Microsoft Windows NT Workstation 4.0, you must be able to answer the following questions:

1. Is your hardware on the Microsoft Windows NT 4.0 Hardware Compatibility List (HCL)?

2. Does your hardware meet the minimum requirements for processor, RAM, and hard disk space?

3. Are you attempting to install Microsoft Windows NT Workstation 4.0 on a "clean" system, or are you planning to upgrade a computer with an existing operating system?

4. If you are upgrading a computer with an existing operating system, will the Microsoft Windows NT 4.0 operating system

be replacing the other operating system? Or do you want to be able to use both operating systems and switch between them by dual booting?

5. Which file system(s) do you want to use: FAT or NTFS?
6. Will your Windows NT Workstation 4.0 be a member of a workgroup or a domain?
7. Which type of installation do you want to perform: typical, portable, compact, or custom?
8. Where are the installation files that you will use to install Microsoft Windows NT Workstation 4.0 located: on a local hard disk or CD-ROM, or on a network distribution server?

Write down the answers to these questions. Your answers will help you choose the proper options during the setup process.

## Using the Windows NT Hardware Qualifier Tool (NTHQ.EXE)

One way to make sure all your hardware is on the official Hardware Compatibility List (HCL) is to execute the Windows NT Hardware Qualifier Tool (NTHQ.EXE), which is available only for Intel x86-based computers or compatibles. A batch file (MAKEDISK.BAT) that actually creates a special MS-DOS bootable disk containing NTHQ.EXE can be found in the \Support\HQTool folder on the Windows NT Workstation 4.0 installation CD. Exercise 2.1 (later in this chapter) provides complete instructions on how to create the special bootable disk and then use NTHQ.

WARNING

**Avoid Unnecessary System Failures** The Hardware Compatibility List (HCL) specifies all the computer systems and peripheral devices that have been tested for operation with Microsoft Windows NT 4.0. Devices not listed on the HCL can cause intermittent failures or, in extreme cases, system crashes.

Qualification lists are only as good as they are current. Unfortunately, the HCL and, therefore, the NTHQ.EXE that comes on the CD-ROM is already outdated. A lot of time has passed, and a number of drivers have been produced since the NT 4.0 CD-ROMs were created. This means that, although NTHQ.EXE is a good tool, it might not give you correct information.

If the NTHQ tells you that all your hardware is supported by NT, you can be sure that it is. However, if it tells you that some of your hardware is not supported, that may not necessarily be the case. Many devices work perfectly well under NT 4.0 even though they hang the NTHQ. The bottom line is that you should check all your hardware against the most current HCL, which you can get from Microsoft TechNet or the Microsoft Web site (`http://www.microsoft.com/ntworkstation/info/hcl.htm`).

NTHQ presents detected hardware devices in four categories:

- System
- Motherboard
- Video
- Others

The Others category is used for device types that the tool cannot positively identify. If a system has an old PCI adapter that does not support PCI version 2.0 or later, for example, the tool might not be able to identify its device type. Click on the appropriate tabs to view detection results for each category, or save the results to a text file named NTHQ.TXT.

You should then check the list of detected devices with the Windows NT 4.0 HCL to avoid unpleasant surprises during installation. The information in NTHQ.TXT is also very useful for avoiding IRQ conflicts when adding new hardware because, unlike Windows 95, Windows NT does not support Plug and Play.

The following is part of the data generated by the Windows NT Hardware Qualifier tool (NTHQ.EXE), which includes IRQ, DMA, and I/O addresses for detected devices:

```
Hardware Detection Tool For Windows NT 4.0

Master Boot Sector Virus Protection Check
Hard Disk Boot Sector Protection: Off.
No problem to write to MBR

ISA Plug and Play Add-in cards detection Summary Report

No ISA Plug and Play cards found in the system
ISA PnP Detection:  Complete

Legacy Detection Summary Report

System Information
Device: System board
Computer Name: Toshiba
Machine Type: IBM PC/AT
Machine Model: fc
```

```
Microprocessor: Pentium
Conventional memory: 655360
Available memory: >=48
Can't locate BIOSName
BIOS Version: 430CDS  V6.30   TOSHIBA
BIOS Date: 01/09/97
Bus Type: ISA

Device: Standard 101/102-Key or Microsoft Natural Keyboard
Hardware ID (for Legacy Devices): *PNP0303
I/O: 60 - 60
I/O: 64 - 64
IRQ: 1

Device: Standard PS/2 Port Mouse
Hardware ID (for Legacy Devices): *PNP0F0E
IRQ: 12

Device: Chips & Tech. Super VGA
Hardware ID (for Legacy Devices): *PNP0930
I/O: 3b0 - 3bb
I/O: 3c0 - 3df
Memory: a0000 - affff
Memory: b8000 - bffff
Memory: e4000 - effff

Device: Standard Floppy Disk Controller
Hardware ID (for Legacy Devices): *PNP0700
I/O: 3f2 - 3f5
IRQ: 6
DMA: 2

Enumerate all IDE devices

IDE Devices Detection Summary Report
Primary Channel: master drive detected
Model Number: TOSHIBA MK1301MAV
Type of Drive: Fixed Drive
Disk Transfer Rate: >10Mbs
Number of Cylinders: 2633
Number of Heads: 16
Number of Sectors Per Track: 63
Number of unformatted bytes per sector Per Track: 639
LBA Support: Yes
DMA Support: Yes
Drive Supports PIO Transfer Cycle Time Mode:   1
Drive Supports Fast PIO Mode: 3
Drive Supports Fast PIO Mode: 4

Secondary Channel: ATAPI device as a master drive detected
Model Number: TOSHIBA CD-ROM XM-1502B
Firmware Revision: 2996
Protocol Type: ATAPI
Device Type: CD-ROM drive
```

```
LBA Support: Yes
DMA Support: Yes
Drive Supports PIO Transfer Cycle Time Mode:   1
Drive Supports Fast PIO Mode: 3

IDE/ATAPI: Complete
PCI Detection: Complete

===============End of Detection Report==================
Adapter Description: Chips & Technologies Super VGA
Listed in Hardware Compatibility List: Yes

Adapter Description: Joystick/game port
Listed in Hardware Compatibility List: Yes
```

## Minimum Requirements for Installation

Make sure that your computer hardware meets the minimum requirements for the installation of Windows NT Workstation 4.0 (see Table 2.1). If your hardware does not meet the minimum requirements, you need to make whatever upgrades are necessary before you attempt to install Windows NT Workstation 4.0. If any of your hardware devices are not listed in the HCL, you should check with the devices' manufacturers to see whether device drivers that support Windows NT 4.0 are available. Unlike with Windows 95, you cannot use older 16-bit device drivers with Windows NT. If you cannot obtain the proper device drivers, you cannot use unsupported devices after you install Windows NT.

NOTE

**Take Advantage of Hardware Emulation** If you have unsupported devices, see if they emulate another device that has drivers for Windows NT 4.0. Then try to use the drivers for the emulated device (for example, try using standard VGA for video, Sound Blaster for audio, and Novell NE2000-compatible for generic network adapter cards).

**TABLE 2.1**

**WINDOWS NT WORKSTATION 4.0 MINIMUM INSTALLATION REQUIREMENTS**

| *Component* | *Minimum Requirement* |
|---|---|
| CPU | 32-bit Intel x86-based (80486/33 or higher) microprocessor or compatible (the 80386 microprocessor is no longer supported) |
| | Intel Pentium, Pentium Pro, or Pentium II microprocessor |
| | Digital Alpha AXP-based RISC microprocessor |
| | MIPS Rx400-based RISC microprocessor |
| | PowerPC-based RISC microprocessor |

| *Component* | *Minimum Requirement* |
|---|---|
| Memory | Intel x86-based computers: 12MB RAM |
| | RISC-based computers: 16MB RAM |
| Hard disk | Intel x86-based computers: 110MB |
| | RISC-based computers: 148MB |
| Display | VGA or better resolution |
| Other drives | Intel x86-based computers require a high-density 3 1/2" floppy drive and a CD-ROM drive (unless you are planning to install Windows NT over a network) |
| Optional | Network adapter card |
| | Mouse or other pointing device, such as a trackball |

Microsoft Windows NT 4.0 actually requires slightly more hard disk space during the installation process (to hold some temporary files) than it requires after installation. If you don't have at least 119MB of free space in your partition, the Setup routine displays an error message and halts. The Setup routine also displays an error message and halts if you attempt to install Windows NT Workstation 4.0 to a Windows NT software-based volume set or stripe set (RAID 0). If you have a hardware-based volume set or stripe set, you might be able to install Windows NT Workstation 4.0 on it; ask your manufacturer.

WARNING

**Avoid FAT32 Formatting When Upgrading** If you are replacing Windows 95 with Windows NT Workstation 4.0, make sure that you do not have any compressed drives and that you are not using FAT32. FAT32 is the new, optional partitioning format that is supported by Windows 95 OEM Service Release 2 (which is also called Windows 95b). Windows 95 compressed drives and FAT32 partitions cannot be accessed by Windows NT.

Keep in mind that Table 2.1 lists the *minimum* requirements for installation of Windows NT Workstation 4.0. After you install your application software and data, you will probably find out that your actual hardware requirements are higher than the minimum values given.

## Installation Options

During installation, you can make use of your knowledge from Chapter 1, "Planning," to decide whether you want to change the partitioning of your hard disk or convert hard disk partitions from FAT to NTFS.

Regardless of whether you install Microsoft Windows NT Workstation 4.0 locally via the three floppies and the CD or by means of a network connection to a network distribution server, you have four setup options:

- Typical
- Portable
- Compact
- Custom

These four setup options install varying components from several categories (see Table 2.2).

Compact setup is designed to conserve hard disk space; therefore, it installs no optional components. The only way to install Windows Messaging or games during installation is to choose Custom setup. You can change installation options after installation via the Add/Remove Programs application in Control Panel.

## Beginning the Installation

You actually have several choices of how to install Microsoft Windows NT Workstation 4.0:

- Locally via the three Setup floppies and a CD
- Locally by using the CD and creating and using the three Setup floppies
- Locally by using the CD without the Setup floppies and booting to an operating system that recognizes the CD-ROM

**TABLE 2.2**

**VARYING COMPONENTS IN FOUR SETUP OPTIONS**

| *Component* | *Typical* | *Portable* | *Compact* | *Custom* |
|---|---|---|---|---|
| Accessibility options | X | X | None | All options |
| Accessories | X | X | None | All options |
| Communications programs | X | X | None | All options |
| Games | | | None | All options |
| Windows Messaging | | | None | All options |
| Multimedia | X | X | None | All options |

- Locally by booting to the CD-ROM, where the computer recognizes the CD-ROM as a boot device
- Over the network by creating and using the three Setup floppies
- Over the network but without the Setup floppies

Exercises 2.2, 2.3, and 2.4 offer step-by-step instructions for the actual installation procedures. After you install Microsoft Windows NT Workstation 4.0, you need to install all your applications.

## Installing Windows NT Workstation 4.0 on an Intel Computer with an Existing Operating System

If your computer has an existing operating system with support for CD-ROM, you can install Windows NT Workstation 4.0 directly from the installation CD. All you have to do is execute WINNT.EXE, which is a 16-bit program compatible with MS-DOS, Windows 3.x, and Windows 95. WINNT.EXE is located in the \I386 folder on the Microsoft Windows NT Workstation 4.0 CD. It performs the following tasks:

1. Creates the three Setup boot disks (requires three blank high-density formatted disks)
2. Creates the $WIN_NT$.~LS temporary folder and copies the contents of the \I386 folder to it
3. Prompts the user to restart the computer from the first Setup boot disk

You can also modify the installation process by using the switches outlined in Table 2.3.

TABLE 2.3

**MODIFYING THE WINNT.EXE INSTALLATION PROCESS**

| *Switch* | *Effect* |
|---|---|
| `/b` | Prevents creation of the three Setup boot disks. Creates a temporary folder named $WIN_NT$.~BT and copies to it the boot files that would normally be copied to the three floppies. The contents of the temporary folder are used instead of the Setup boot disks to boot the machine when the user is prompted to restart. |
| `/c` | Skips the step of checking for available free space. |
| `/I:`*`inf_file`* | Specifies the name of the Setup information file. The default filename is DOSNET.INF. |
| `/f` | Prevents verification of files as they are copied. |
| `/l` | Creates a log file called $WINNT.LOG, which lists all errors that occur as files are being copied to the temporary directory. |
| `/ox` | Creates the three Setup boot disks and then stops. |
| `/s:`*`server_path`* | Specifies the location of the installation source files. |
| `/u` | Allows all or part of an installation to proceed unattended (as detailed in Chapter 1). The `/b` option for floppyless installation is automatically invoked, and the `/s` option for location of the source files must be used. The `/u` option can be followed with the name of an answer file to fully automate installation. |
| `/udf` | During an unattended installation, specifies settings unique to a specific computer, which are contained in a uniqueness database file (see Chapter 1). |
| `/w` | This *undocumented* flag enables the WINNT.EXE program to execute in Windows (normally, it must be executed from an MS-DOS command prompt). |
| `/x` | Prevents creation of the three Setup boot disks. You must already have the three boot disks. |

There is also a 32-bit version of the installation program called WINNT32.EXE, which is used to upgrade earlier versions of Windows NT and cannot be used to upgrade Windows 95. WINNT32.EXE does not support the `/f`, `/c`, or `/l` options. See the later section "Upgrading to Windows NT Workstation 4.0" for more information.

## SETTING UP A DUAL-BOOT SYSTEM

Set up a dual-boot system in a given situation.

If you are in the process of migrating your users to Windows NT Workstation, they might feel better if they could continue to use their previous operating system for a limited period of time. Additionally, they might need to be able to execute applications that are not compatible with Windows NT. Another possibility is that you might need to support users running different operating systems, but you need to be able to do so using only one computer. If you need to solve any of these problems, you may want to set up a dual-boot system.

*Dual booting* is a term for having more than one operating system on a single computer. A dual-boot system also has, typically, a boot menu that appears whenever the computer is started. The boot menu enables users to choose which of the available operating systems they would like to start.

You can install Windows NT Workstation 4.0 to operate as a dual-boot system that works side by side with any version of MS-DOS, Microsoft Windows, Windows NT, or even OS/2.

Although it is possible to set up a dual-boot system with Windows 95 and Windows NT, Microsoft recommends that you do not, for a number of reasons:

- One of the security features of Windows NT prevents a user from accessing the computer locally without logging in with a valid user account. Creating a dual-boot scenario would allow a local user to boot using the less-secure operating system (Windows 95) and gain access to files in that way.
- A second security feature of Windows NT enables you to format drives with NTFS, which provides local security on specific files and folders. In a dual-boot scenario, you must format any common drives as FAT in order to allow both operating systems to access them. If you share data between your operating systems, you are forced to format these drives as FAT and sacrifice any local security you may have had.
- Because Windows 95 and Windows NT maintain their own Registries, you must install each application that needs to be

NOTE

**Know Which Install Program Is Right for a Given Environment** Remember that WINNT32.EXE is used to install Windows NT only when you already have NT installed (you're performing an upgrade or configuring a dual-boot NT machine). WINNT.EXE is used in all other situations. The exam might ask questions about installing NT in different situations; know which program to use.

EXAM TIP

**Dual Booting** You are likely to see questions on the exam dealing with dual booting or issues involving dual-boot scenarios. Be sure to remember that dual booting allows for bypassing NT security; dual booting requires a FAT partition; and dual booting requires dual-installation of files.

used by both operating systems twice: once for each operating system. This forces you to use twice as much disk space for your application installations.

On the other hand, there are still some benefits to dual booting. The primary one is related to software that is not compatible with NT. If any user needs to use software that cannot be run on NT, you must provide some way to run it. Dual booting may be the only way to ensure that this capability is maintained.

## Removing Windows NT Workstation

Remove Windows NT Workstation 4.0 in a given situation.

To remove Windows NT Workstation from a computer, you must first determine whether there are any NTFS partitions on the computer. If any partitions on the computer are formatted NTFS, you must remove them because Windows 95 and MS-DOS cannot use them. If the NTFS partitions contain only data and no Windows NT system files, you can use the Windows NT Disk Administrator program to remove them. If the NTFS partitions contain Windows NT system files, or if they are logical drive(s) in an extended partition, the MS-DOS FDISK utility cannot be used to remove them; instead, you should use the procedure outlined in Exercise 2.5.

After you remove all the NTFS partitions, you must start the computer with a Windows 95 or MS-DOS system disk that contains the SYS.COM file. Then type the command **sys c:** to transfer the Windows 95 or MS-DOS system files to the boot track on drive C:. When that process is complete, you must manually remove the following Windows NT Workstation files:

- All paging files (C:\PAGEFILE.SYS)
- C:\BOOT.INI, C:\BOOTSECT.DOS, C:\NTLDR, C:\NTDETECT.COM (these are hidden, system, read-only files)
- *.PAL on Alpha computers

- NTBOOTDD.SYS on computers with SCSI drives with the BIOS disabled
- The *winnt_root* folder
- The C:\Program files\Windows Windows NT folder

You can now install your choice of operating systems on your computer.

> **WARNING**
>
> **Problems Will Occur If the Windows NT Boot Track Is Not Removed** If you fail to remove the Windows NT boot track from your computer, the following error message appears when you restart your computer:
>
> ```
> BOOT: Couldn't find NTLDR.
> Please insert another disk.
> ```

# Upgrading to Windows NT Workstation 4.0

Upgrade to Windows NT Workstation 4.0 in a given situation.

You can upgrade to Windows NT Workstation only from a previous version of NT Workstation (Workstation 3.51, for example). In such upgrades, you must use WINNT32.EXE, the 32-bit version of the installation program. WINNT32.EXE was previously mentioned in the section "Installing Windows NT Workstation 4.0 on an Intel Computer with an Existing Operating System." Installations of any version of Windows NT Server cannot be upgraded to Windows NT Workstation 4.0; to make that change, you must install Workstation into a new folder and reinstall all your Windows applications.

> **WARNING**
>
> **Windows 95 Settings Are Lost** Because of differences in hardware device support and in the internal structure of the Registry, there is no upgrade path from Microsoft Windows 95 to Microsoft Windows NT 4.0. You must perform a new installation of Windows NT to a new folder and then reinstall all your Windows applications. No system or application settings are shared or migrated. After you install Microsoft Windows NT Workstation 4.0 and necessary applications, you should delete the Windows 95 directory.

When Windows NT Workstation 3.x is upgraded to Windows NT Workstation 4.0, all the existing Registry entries are preserved, including those for the following settings:

- User and group settings
- Preferences for applications
- Network settings
- Desktop environment

To upgrade Windows NT Workstation 3.x to Windows NT Workstation 4.0, install to the same folder that contains the existing installation and answer yes to the upgrade question that you are asked during the installation process. Then follow the instructions.

For a significant performance increase during the file transfer portion of a network-based upgrade from a previous version of Windows NT Workstation to Windows NT Workstation 4.0, use multiple /s switches with WINNT32.EXE to specify multiple servers that contain the source files (see the next section).

## CONFIGURING SERVER-BASED INSTALLATION

Configure server-based installation for wide-scale deployment in a given situation.

The quickest way to install Windows NT Workstation 4.0 on a large number of computers is to use a network distribution server as the source of the installation files (especially when you need to install Windows NT Workstation 4.0 on computers that have network connectivity but don't have CD-ROM drives).

To set up a network distribution server, use one of the following methods:

- Copy the distribution files from the CD-ROM to a network file server and share it, making sure that the permissions allow authorized users to access the files. The distribution files for Intel-based machines are found in the I386 folder. (This method is faster than the next one; however, you need approximately 100MB of free space on your file server to copy all the distribution files.)
- Share the I386 folder on the Workstation CD-ROM from a network file server. This method slows installation as compared to the previous method because the speed of data transfer from the CD-ROM is a significant bottleneck. However, it is useful if sufficient disk space is not available to copy the distribution files to a hard drive.

Keep in mind that if you use Windows NT Explorer or Windows 95 Explorer to copy the files, the default options must be changed to allow for hidden files and system files with extensions such as .DLL, .SYS, and .VXD to be displayed and copied. To display such files, select View, Options to open the Options dialog box and select the Show All Files option button (see Figure 2.1).

If you are using WINNT32.EXE to upgrade an existing copy of Windows NT, you can use more than one network server to significantly speed up the rate at which the installation files are downloaded to your client computers. If you set up two network servers called SERVER1 and SERVER2 with installation shares called NTW, for example, the proper command line option to use both servers during the installation process is

```
WINNT32 /B /S:\\SERVER1\NTW /S:\\SERVER2\NTW
```

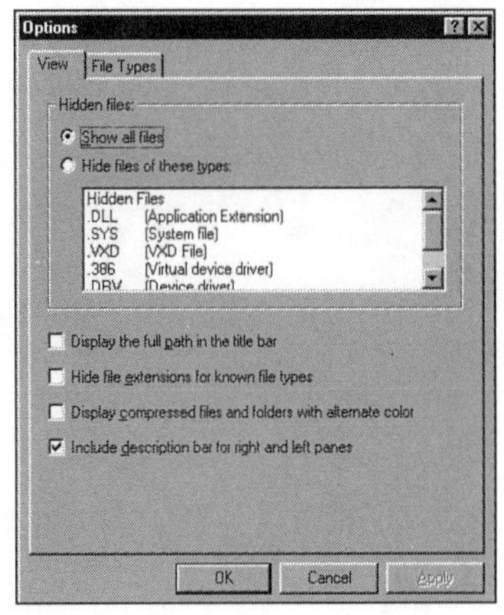


**FIGURE 2.1**
Displaying hidden and system files in Windows NT Explorer.

## Installing, Configuring, and Removing Hardware Components

Install, configure, and remove hardware components for a given situation. Hardware components include the following: network adapter drivers, SCSI device drivers, tape device drivers, UPSs, multimedia devices, display drivers, keyboard drivers, and mouse drivers.

Some configurable hardware components in Windows NT Workstation include the following:

- Network adapter drivers
- SCSI device drivers
- Tape device drivers
- UPSs
- Multimedia devices
- Display drivers
- Keyboard drivers
- Mouse drivers

This section covers each of the preceding items, which are accessible via programs in Control Panel (see Figure 2.2). The section explains how you can configure these types of devices in Windows NT.

EXAM TIP

**Control Panel Nuances Are Not Covered in Detail on the Exam**
Subtle characteristics of working with Control Panel applications are not tested on the exam. Instead, it includes general questions about what applications are useful in particular situations. You should know what applications are available and what each one is used for.

**FIGURE 2.2**
The default options in Control Panel.

## Working with Network Adapter Drivers

You can configure network adapters by double-clicking on the Network icon in the Control Panel and then selecting the Adapters tab (see Figure 2.3).

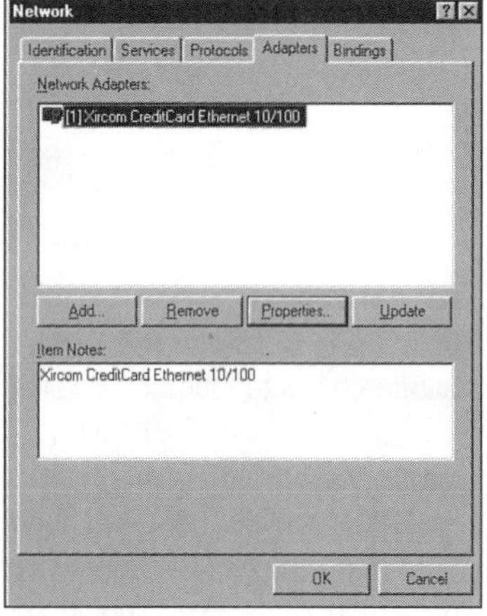


**FIGURE 2.3**
Viewing the current network adapters.

Windows NT 4.0 allows for an unlimited number of network adapters, as you'll learn in Chapter 4, "Connectivity." You can also configure each network adapter separately. To configure a specific network adapter, go to the Adapters tab of the Network dialog box, and then click on the Properties button.

Figure 2.4 shows a sample network adapter properties dialog box. The actual dialog boxes for network adapter properties are manufacturer-specific, so what your system shows might look different from this example. In addition, some network adapters (such as Intel's Token Ring 16/4 adapters) have only limited configuration options from within NT; in such cases, the I/O port, memory address, and IRQ settings may have to be set from DOS using a manufacturer-supplied setup disk.

**WARNING**

**Older Drivers Are Incompatible with NT** Windows NT cannot use any 16-bit legacy device drivers or device drivers from Windows 95, which uses NDIS 3.1 drivers. It may not be able to use Windows NT 3.x drivers, either. So make sure you don't get caught when you upgrade.

You also need to make sure that you have the proper device drivers for your network adapter. Windows NT 4.0 is compatible with any device drivers that are compliant with Network Driver Interface Specification (NDIS) version 4.0 or version 3.0.

When you modify the settings in the network adapter properties dialog box, be careful to select the proper settings. Microsoft Windows NT does not support Plug and Play and has no way of determining whether the values you select are correct. Incorrect values in this dialog box can lead to loss of network connectivity and, in extreme cases, can cause system crashes.

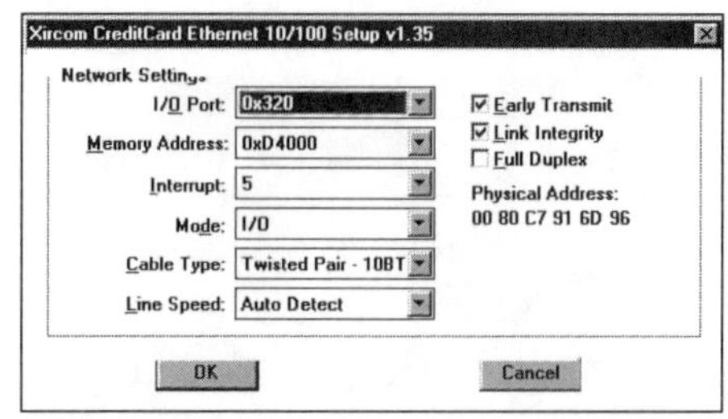


**FIGURE 2.4**
Specifying the hardware settings for a network adapter.

## Working with SCSI Device Drivers

In Windows NT 4.0, you can access the user interface for viewing configuration information on SCSI host adapters by clicking the SCSI icon in the Control Panel.

To view device properties, open the SCSI Adapters dialog box (see Figure 2.5). Select the Devices tab, select the device, and then click on the Properties button. You can then view information on the device's properties and the revision data on its device drivers (as shown in Figure 2.6).

Although the dialog box is titled SCSI Adapters, you can also view and modify information regarding your IDE adapters and devices. You must restart Windows NT 4.0 if you add or delete any SCSI or IDE adapters.

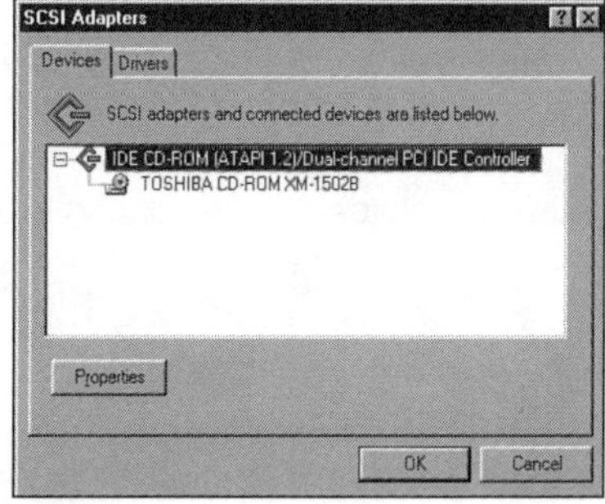


**FIGURE 2.5**
This dialog box lists SCSI and IDE adapters and devices.

## Working with Tape Device Drivers

In Windows NT 4.0, you can access the user interface for viewing configuration information on tape devices in Windows NT 4.0 by selecting the Tape Devices icon in the Control Panel (see Figure 2.7).

If you want Windows NT 4.0 to automatically detect tape devices, click on the Devices tab and click on Detect. If you would rather view device properties, click on Properties. You can also add and remove device drivers by using the Add and Remove buttons available on the Drivers tab. You do not have to restart Windows NT if you add or delete tape devices.

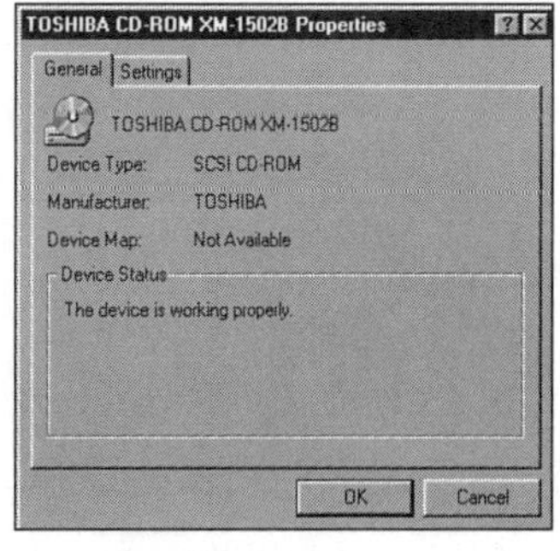


**FIGURE 2.6**
Viewing the settings for a SCSI or IDE device.

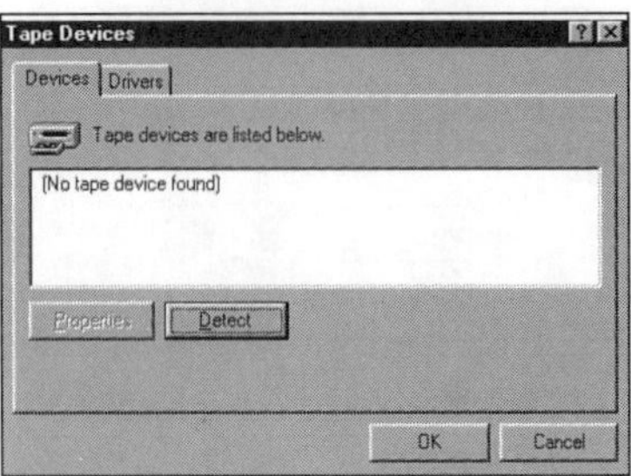


**FIGURE 2.7**
Viewing configured tape devices.

> **WARNING**
>
> **Serial Mouse Test Can Cause Shutdown** You must be sure to test the UPS unit after you configure it. During startup of Intel-based computers, NTDETECT.COM sends test messages to all serial ports to determine whether a serial mouse is attached. Some UPS units misinterpret these test messages and shut down. To prevent your UPS unit from shutting down like this, add the `/NoSerialMice` switch to the BOOT.INI file.

## Working with Uninterruptible Power Supplies

An Uninterruptible Power Supply (UPS) provides backup power in case your local power source fails. Power for UPS units is typically provided by batteries that are continuously recharged and are rated to provide power for a specific (usually highly limited) period of time. Figure 2.8 shows the UPS option dialog box available through Control Panel.

During a power failure, the UPS service of Windows NT communicates with the UPS unit until one of the following events occur:

- Local power is restored.
- The system is shut down by the UPS service or by an administrator.
- The UPS signals to Windows NT that its batteries are low.

When a power failure occurs, the Windows NT Server service is paused (which prevents any new users from establishing sessions with the server). Any current users are warned to save their data and to close their open sessions. All users are notified when normal power is restored.

The UPS and the Windows NT system communicate via a standard RS-232 port. The cable is not, however, a standard cable. A special UPS cable must be used for proper communications between the UPS system and your computer.

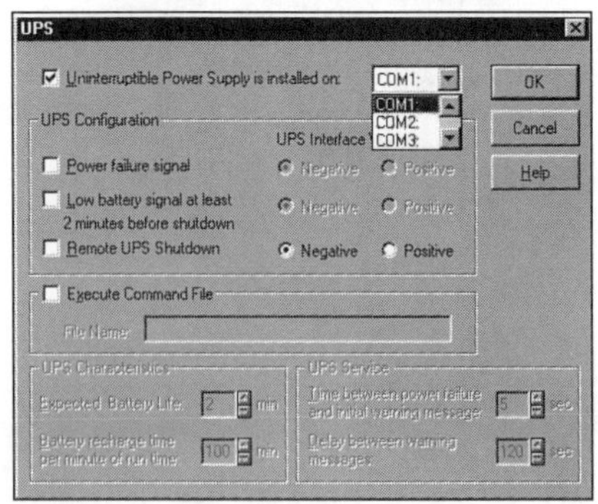


**FIGURE 2.8**
Configuring your UPS.

## Working with Multimedia Devices

Use the Multimedia icon in Control Panel to access a dialog box from which you can install, configure, and remove multimedia devices. Categories of multimedia devices that can be modified include audio, video, MIDI, and CD music (see Figure 2.9). There is also a Devices tab that enables you to view information about all the multimedia devices and drivers installed on your system (see Figure 2.10).

You must install drivers for sound cards after you have successfully installed Windows NT. Those drivers cannot be configured during an unattended installation. For step-by-step instructions on how to install a sound driver, see Exercise 2.9.

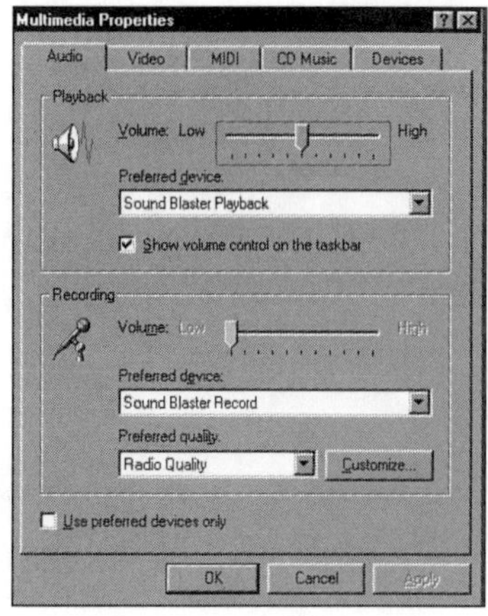


**FIGURE 2.9**
Viewing the properties of multimedia devices.

## Working with Display Drivers

Use the Settings tab of the Display dialog box (accessible through Control Panel) to choose display options. You can control such settings as refresh frequency, font sizes, video resolution, and the number of colors (see Figure 2.11).

Table 2.4 describes the various display options.

**TABLE 2.4**

**OPTIONS FOR CONFIGURING DISPLAY SETTINGS**

| *Option* | *Description* |
|---|---|
| Color Palette | Lists color options for the display adapter. |
| Desktop Area | Configures screen area used by the display. |
| Display Type | Displays options about the display device driver and allows installation of new drivers. |
| Font Size | Allows selection of large or small display font sizes. |
| List All Modes | Gives the option to configure color, desktop area, and refresh frequency simultaneously. |
| Refresh Frequency | Configures the frequency of the screen refresh rate for high-resolution drivers only. |
| Test | Tests screen choices. If you make changes and do not test them, you are prompted to test your choices when you try to apply them. |

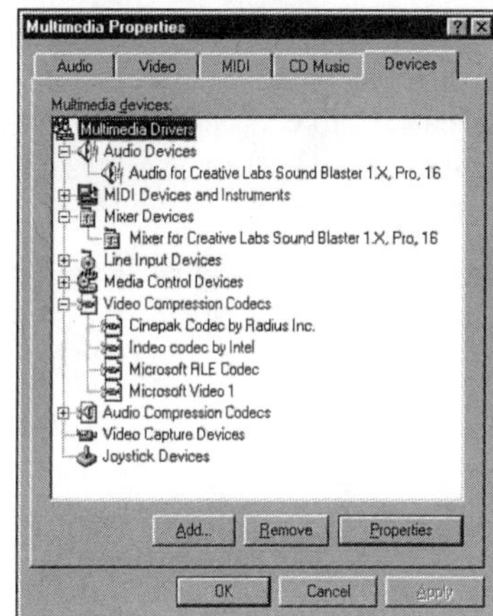


**FIGURE 2.10**
Viewing the current multimedia devices.

Whenever you make changes to your display driver settings, you are prompted to test them before they are saved. If you ignore the test option and save incompatible values, your screen may become unreadable. You can restore normal operations by restarting your computer and selecting the VGA option from the Boot menu. The VGA option forces your video card into 16-color standard VGA. You can then try selecting different values in the Display Properties dialog box.

> **WARNING**
>
> **Incorrect Settings Can Cause Damage** Be careful when changing the settings for your display driver. In extreme cases, it is possible to damage your display card or monitor with incorrect settings.

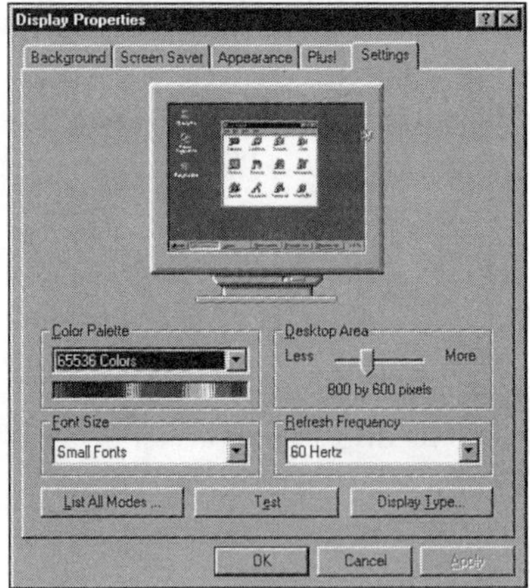


**FIGURE 2.11**
Viewing the display properties.

## Working with Keyboard Drivers

> NOTE
> **Keyboards Can Take Advantage of Special Accessibility Options** The Control Panel's Accessibility Options application contains keyboard options you can set to configure a system to match the capabilities of a physically challenged user.

Figure 2.12 shows the Keyboard Properties dialog box accessible through the Control Panel. It contains the following three tabs of options:

- *Speed.* Controls repeat character delay, character repeat rate, and cursor blink speed.
- *Input Locales.* Specifies the international keyboard layout.
- *General.* Enables you to view and change the keyboard driver. You might want to change your keyboard driver if you need to support an international keyboard or if your prefer a Dvorak-style keyboard over the standard QWERTY keyboard.

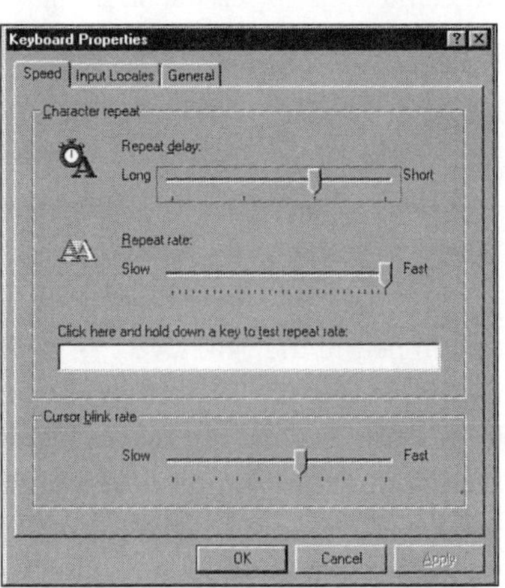


**FIGURE 2.12**
Viewing the properties of your keyboard.

## Working with Mouse Drivers

Use the Mouse program in Control Panel to change mouse options. Those options are grouped onto these four tabs: Buttons, Pointers, Motion, and General (see Figure 2.13).

Table 2.5 describes the various options you can configure with the Mouse program.

**TABLE 2.5**

**CONFIGURING MOUSE OPTIONS**

| *Tab* | *Options Enable You to...* |
|---|---|
| Buttons | Configure mouse for right-hand or left-hand operation and set double-click speed |
| Pointers | Choose which pointer shapes are associated with various system events |
| Motion | Control pointer speed and select whether you want the mouse pointer to snap to the default button in dialog boxes |
| General | View current mouse driver and change mouse driver, if desired |

With the exception of the mouse driver controls, all the mouse options described in Table 2.4 can be configured individually for each user account and are saved in the user's profile.

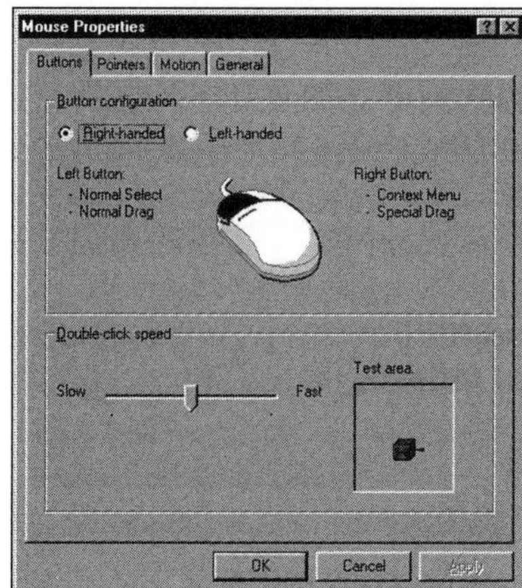


**FIGURE 2.13**
Viewing your mouse settings.

# Using Control Panel Applications to Configure Windows NT Workstation

Use the Control Panel applications to configure a Microsoft Windows NT Workstation 4.0 computer in a given situation.

In addition to working with the Control Panel applications for configuring hardware (which were described in the section "Installing, Configuring, and Removing Hardware Components"), you can use several other options to configure Windows NT Workstation.

## Adding and Removing Programs

You can modify the components that were installed automatically based on the installation option (Typical, Portable, Compact, or Custom) that you chose when you installed Windows NT Workstation 4.0. You do so by choosing the Add/Remove Programs icon in Control Panel and then selecting the Windows NT Setup tab (see Figure 2.14).

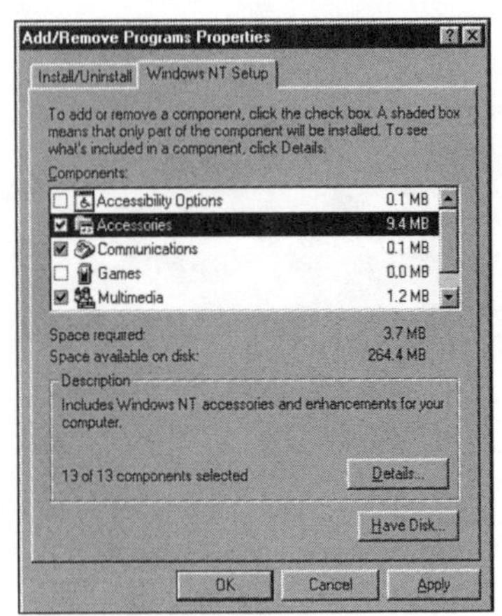


**FIGURE 2.14**
Adding and removing optional components.

The Windows NT Setup tab enables you to add and delete optional components and applications in the following categories:

- Accessibility Options
- Accessories
- Communications
- Games
- Multimedia
- Windows Messaging

Note that the check boxes shown in Figure 2.14 actually can have the following three states:

- *Clear boxes.* Indicate that *none* of the selected components or applications in that category is installed.
- *Clear checked boxes.* Indicate that *all* the selected components or applications in that category are installed.
- *Gray checked boxes.* Indicate that *some* of the selected components or applications in that category are installed. For details on which of the components or applications are actually installed, click on the Details button.

WARNING

**Deleting a Program Folder Doesn't Completely Remove the Program** Deleting the folder that contains a program does not remove any files installed in other folders that are associated with the program, nor does it remove any Registry entries made by that program.

You can also add and remove applications from your system by choosing the Add/Remove Programs icon in Control Panel and then selecting the Install/Uninstall tab.

## Modifying the Date, Time, or Time Zone

You can also use the Control Panel to modify your computer's date and time or to change which time zone is selected (see Figure 2.15). To access this dialog box, you must be a member of either the Administrators or Power Users group or have been granted the user right to Change the System Time.

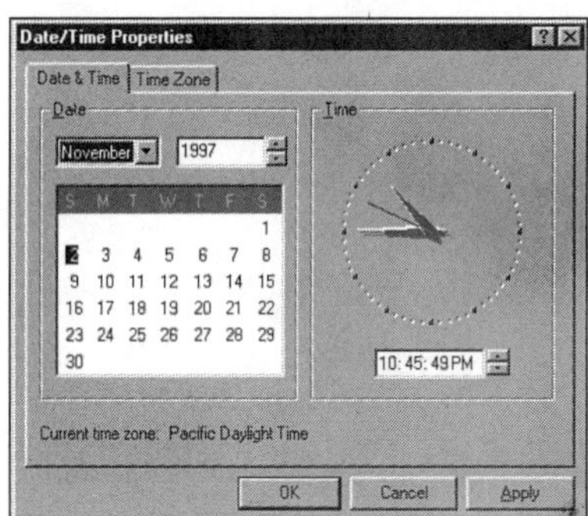


**FIGURE 2.15**
Setting your time, date, and time zone.

## CASE STUDY: LARSON, WATTERSON, AND ADAMS

### ESSENCE OF THE CASE

Here are the essential elements in this case:

- High security in general
- Local file security
- Support for Office 97
- Support for WordPerfect 7.0
- Ability to operate in a workgroup configuration

### SCENARIO

The accounting firm Larson, Watterson, and Adams is currently using WordPerfect 5.0 for DOS on their Windows 95 machines. Their support people report that they need more functionality in their desktop applications as well as greater security. For personal and political reasons, they have decided to use the Microsoft Office 97 suite with the addition of WordPerfect 7.0.

The partners recently saw a presentation on Windows NT Workstation 4.0 and have decided that Workstation is the way to go to maintain the best security, especially on their spreadsheets, which they are concerned about giving people access to. They operate in a small workgroup, and each person has an account locally on each machine to ensure that they can access resources from the other machines. Unfortunately, although Microsoft Office 97 will work on an NT platform, the version of WordPerfect that has been agreed upon will not. And despite your best efforts, you cannot get the partners to change their minds. Therefore, you must implement a desktop solution that provides the best possible security but also supports the needed applications.

You think the release of WordPerfect 8.0 (which is supposed to be NT compatible) is right around the corner, but you need a solution that works in the meantime.

## CASE STUDY: LARSON, WATTERSON, AND ADAMS

### ANALYSIS

The demands of this case put you, the system architect, in an awkward situation. You must provide the users of these systems with the highest-level services possible, yet stay within the bounds of the requirements set by the partners.

Of the five essential points previously listed, Windows NT Workstation provides the ideal solution to four. Workstation can be configured in a workgroup, it provides high security, and with NTFS partitions, it provides local file security. In addition, Workstation supports all the Microsoft Office 97 applications. The only problem is that you cannot run WordPerfect 7.0 on that platform.

The solution to the WordPerfect problem is to configure the client systems to dual boot Workstation and Windows 95. This poses a problem with local file security, however, because Windows 95 will not read NTFS partitions. So you will store your WordPerfect files on the Windows 95 boot partition so that you will be able to access the WordPerfect files from your Windows 95 system.

Finally, you submit a proposal to remove Windows 95 from all the machines as soon as a version of WordPerfect that will run under NT becomes available.

## CHAPTER SUMMARY

### KEY TERMS

- Hardware Compatibility List (HCL)
- NTHQ.EXE
- WINNT.EXE
- WINNT32.EXE
- dual boot
- `/NoSerialMice`

This chapter presented information on two major topics: installation and upgrade of Windows NT, and configuration of hardware and software using the Control Panel. Beginning with installation, you read about the complete process for getting an NT Workstation up and running. This included installing from an MS-DOS base, installing from a Windows 95 base, and upgrading from an existing version of Windows NT. This discussion also included two different methods of installing: from the CD-ROM and over the network from a share point on a server. In addition, you saw how to remove NT from a computer and how to ensure that the computer booted to whatever operating system was desired after NT was completely removed.

You also learned about the process for creating a dual-boot system and learned of some cautions about dual booting. And you discovered why you should create a dual-boot system only when it is absolutely necessary.

The last sections of the chapter dealt with configuration of NT Workstation, particularly as it applies to hardware and the Control Panel. First, you examined some common hardware components and their configurations within NT. Then you learned about common configurations of software, which are established in the Control Panel. You got to see a number of the programs available through the Control Panel, and you learned of their various uses.

## Apply Your Learning

The following section allows you to assess how well you understood the material in the chapter. The exercises enable you to engage in the sorts of tasks that comprise the skill sets the objectives reflect. Review and exam questions test your knowledge of the tasks and concepts specified in the objectives. Answers to the review and exam questions follow in the answers sections.

For additional review- and exam-type questions, use the Top Score test engine on the CD-ROM that came with this book.

## Exercises

The following exercises provide step-by-step procedures of various ways to install and configure Windows NT Workstation 4.0 on your computer. Other lab exercises show you how to use options in Control Panel to configure a current installation of Windows NT Workstation 4.0.

### 2.1 Creating and Using an NTHQ Boot Floppy

This exercise shows you how to create a Windows NT Hardware Qualifier (NTHQ) boot floppy. You can then use the NTHQ boot floppy to examine the hardware configuration of your computer.

**Estimated Time:** 20 minutes

1. Insert the Windows NT Workstation 4.0 CD into your CD-ROM drive.
2. Type **D:** at the command prompt to switch the default drive to the CD-ROM drive (or whatever the correct drive letter is for your computer).
3. Type **CD \Support\HQTool** to switch to the HQTool directory.
4. Insert a formatted $3^1/_2$-inch floppy into floppy drive A:.
5. Type **Makedisk** at the command prompt. The Makedisk utility begins transferring all necessary files to the floppy disk.
6. When the Makedisk utility finishes, reboot your computer, leaving the floppy that you just made in drive A.
7. When the NTHQ dialog box appears, click on Yes to approve device detection.
8. Click on Yes to approve comprehensive detection.
9. When system detection is complete, click on the various buttons at the bottom of the screen and observe the details that were detected for the various devices in your computer.
10. Click on the Save button at the bottom of the screen.
11. Click on OK to save the detection results to A:\NTHQ.TXT.
12. Click on the Exit button.
13. Remove the floppy from drive A:.
14. Reboot your computer.
15. Reinsert the NTHQ floppy into your floppy drive.
16. View the contents of A:\NTHQ.TXT.

## APPLY YOUR LEARNING

### 2.2 Installing Windows NT Workstation 4.0 from CD on a Computer That Has No Existing Operating System

This exercise shows you how to perform a CD-based installation of Windows NT on a computer that doesn't have an existing operating system.

**Estimated Time:** 70 minutes

1. Before you start the installation, verify that your hardware (especially your CD-ROM drive) is listed on the Windows NT HCL.
2. Locate your Windows NT Workstation 4.0 CD and the three floppies that came with it.
3. Insert the Windows NT Workstation CD into the CD-ROM drive.
4. Insert the Windows NT Workstation Setup Boot Disk into your floppy drive, and then restart your computer.
5. When prompted, insert Windows NT Workstation Setup Disk #2.
6. At the Windows NT Workstation Setup – Welcome to Setup screen, press Enter to start the installation process.
7. Press Enter to detect mass storage devices.
8. When prompted, insert Windows NT Workstation Setup Disk #3.
9. Press Enter to approve the list of detected mass storage devices. (Don't worry if your IDE hard disk controller isn't detected; the installation process should proceed just fine anyway.)
10. Press Page Down repeatedly, until you reach the last page of the Windows NT Licensing Agreement.
11. Press F8 to approve the Windows NT Licensing Agreement.
12. Press Enter to approve the list of detected hardware components.
13. Select the desired installation partition, and then press Enter.
14. Press Enter to indicate that you do *not* want to convert the installation partition to NTFS.
15. Press Enter to install to the default directory named \WINNT.
16. Press Enter to examine the hard disk for errors.
17. Wait for hard disk examination.
18. Wait while files are copied.
19. When prompted, remove the floppy disk from the drive and press Enter to restart the computer and begin the graphical portion of the setup process.
20. When the computer restarts, click on Next.
21. Select the Typical option for installation, and then click on Next.
22. Enter your name and organization, and then click on Next.
23. Enter your CD-ROM key, and then click on Next.
24. Enter your computer name (specify a computer named **Test**), and then click on Next. The maximum length for a computer name is 15 characters.

**APPLY YOUR LEARNING**

25. Enter and confirm the password for the administrator account, and then click on Next. Make sure that you write down your selected password and keep it in a secure location. If you forget your administrator password, you will find yourself locked out of your own system and you will have to reinstall Windows NT to restore access.
26. Click on Yes to create an Emergency Repair Disk (ERD).
27. Click on Next to install the most common components.
28. Click on Next to install Windows NT Networking.
29. Specify whether your computer will be participating in a network, and then click on Next. If your computer will not be participating in a network, skip ahead to step 36.
30. Click on either Start Search for Your Adapter or Select from List.
31. If you chose Select from List in step 30, select your adapter from the list and click on Next.
32. Make sure that NetBEUI is the only specified protocol, and then click on Next.
33. Click on Continue to approve the network card settings. (Remember that Windows NT 4.0 doesn't support Plug and Play, and your network card settings *must* be correct.)
34. Click on Next to start the network.
35. Click on Next to install the computer named Test into a workgroup named Workgroup.
36. Click on Next to finish setup.
37. Select the proper time zone, and then click on Close.
38. Click OK to approve the detected video adapter.
39. Click on Test to test the video adapter.
40. Click OK to start the video test, and then wait five seconds.
41. Click on Yes (if you saw the bitmap properly).
42. Click OK to save the video settings.
43. Click OK in the Display Properties dialog box.
44. Wait while files are copied.
45. Wait while the configuration is saved.
46. Insert a floppy that will become your ERD, and then click OK.
47. Wait while the ERD is formatted and files are copied.
48. Wait while the temporary configuration files are removed.
49. When prompted to do so, press the button to restart your computer. The installation process is now complete.

### 2.3 Upgrading an Existing System to Windows NT Workstation 4.0 from CD-ROM Without the Setup Disks

This exercise shows you how to re-create the Setup disks and then upgrade an existing system to Windows NT Workstation 4.0 from CD-ROM.

**Estimated Time:** 80 minutes

1. Format three high-density floppies and label them the following:

## APPLY YOUR LEARNING

Windows NT Workstation Setup Boot Disk

Windows NT Workstation Setup Disk #2

Windows NT Workstation Setup Disk #3

2. Place the Windows NT Workstation 4.0 CD in the CD-ROM drive. (This exercise assumes that your CD-ROM drive is drive D:.)
3. From a command prompt, type **D:\I386\WINNT** to upgrade a 16-bit system, or type **D:\I386\WINNT32** to upgrade a previous version of Windows NT.
4. Insert Windows NT Workstation Setup Disk #3, into the floppy drive.
5. When prompted by the Windows NT 4.0 Upgrade/Installation screen, click on Continue.
6. Wait while files are copied.
7. When prompted, insert Windows NT Workstation Setup Disk #2.
8. When prompted, insert Windows NT Workstation Setup Boot Disk.
9. Leave the Windows NT Workstation Setup Boot Disk in the drive and restart your computer when prompted.
10. Wait while the computer restarts and files are copied.
11. When prompted, insert Windows NT Workstation Setup Disk #2.
12. At the Windows NT Workstation Setup – Welcome to Setup screen, press Enter to start the installation process.
13. Press Enter to detect mass storage devices.
14. When prompted, insert Windows NT Workstation Setup Disk #3.
15. Press Enter to approve the list of detected mass storage devices. (Don't worry if your IDE hard disk controller isn't detected. The installation process should proceed just fine anyway.)
16. Press Page Down repeatedly, until you reach the last page of the Windows NT Licensing Agreement.
17. Press F8 to approve the Windows NT Licensing Agreement.
18. Press Enter to approve the list of detected hardware components.
19. Select the desired installation partition, and then press Enter.
20. Press Enter to indicate that you do *not* want to convert the installation partition to NTFS.
21. Press Enter to install to the default directory named \WINNT.
22. Press Enter to examine the hard disk for errors.
23. Wait for hard disk examination.
24. Wait while files are copied.
25. When prompted, remove the floppy disk from the drive and press Enter to restart the computer and begin the graphical portion of the setup process.
26. When the computer restarts, click on Next.
27. Select the Typical option for installation, and then click on Next.
28. Enter your name and organization, and then click on Next.
29. Enter your CD-ROM key, and click on Next.
30. Enter your computer name (specify a computer named **Test**), and then click on Next.

## APPLY YOUR LEARNING

31. Enter and confirm the password for the administrator account, and then click on Next.
32. Click on Yes to create an Emergency Repair Disk (ERD).
33. Click on Next to install the most common components.
34. Click on Next to install Windows NT Networking.
35. Specify whether your computer will be participating in a network, and then click on Next. If your computer will not be participating in a network, skip ahead to step 42.
36. Click on either Start Search for Your Adapter or Select from List.
37. If you chose Select from List in the previous step, select your adapter from the list, and then click on Next.
38. Make sure that NetBEUI is the only specified protocol, and then click on Next.
39. Click on Continue to approve the network card settings. (Remember that Windows NT 4.0 doesn't support Plug and Play, and your network card settings *must* be correct.)
40. Click on Next to start the network.
41. Click on Next to install the computer named Test into a workgroup named Workgroup.
42. Click on Next to finish setup.
43. Select the proper time zone, and then click on Close.
44. Click OK to approve the detected video adapter.
45. Click on Test to test the video adapter.
46. Click OK to start the video test, and then wait five seconds.
47. Click on Yes (if you saw the bitmap properly).
48. Click OK to save the video settings.
49. Click OK in the Display Properties dialog box.
50. Wait while files are copied.
51. Wait while the configuration is saved.
52. Insert a floppy that will become your ERD, and then click OK.
53. Wait while the ERD is formatted and files are copied.
54. Wait while the temporary configuration files are removed.
55. Press the button to restart your computer, and the installation process is complete.

### 2.4 Installing Windows NT Workstation 4.0 from a Network Server

This exercise describes how to upgrade an existing MS-DOS system to Microsoft Windows NT Workstation 4.0 when the installation files are located on a network server.

**Estimated Time:** 60 minutes

1. Format three high-density floppies and label them the following:

   Windows NT Workstation Setup Boot Disk

   Windows NT Workstation Setup Disk #2

   Windows NT Workstation Setup Disk #3

## APPLY YOUR LEARNING

2. From a command prompt, enter the appropriate command to connect a network drive to drive letter X. The appropriate command for a Microsoft based network would be:

   ```
   NET USE X: \\server\sharename
   ```

3. Change to drive X.
4. Start the Windows NT installation process by typing **WINNT** and pressing Enter.
5. Insert Windows NT Workstation Setup Disk #3 into the floppy drive.
6. When prompted by the Windows NT 4.0 Upgrade/Installation screen, click on Continue.
7. Wait while files are copied.
8. When prompted, insert Windows NT Workstation Setup Disk #2.
9. When prompted, insert Windows NT Workstation Setup Boot Disk.
10. Leave the Windows NT Workstation Setup Boot Disk in the drive and restart your computer when prompted.
11. Wait while the computer restarts and files are copied.
12. When prompted, insert Windows NT Workstation Setup Disk #2.
13. At the Windows NT Workstation Setup – Welcome to Setup screen, press Enter to start the installation process.
14. Press Enter to detect mass storage devices.
15. When prompted, insert Windows NT Workstation Setup Disk #3.
16. Press Enter to approve the list of detected mass storage devices. (Don't worry if your IDE hard disk controller isn't detected. The installation process should proceed just fine anyway.)
17. Press Page Down repeatedly, until you reach the last page of the Windows NT Licensing Agreement.
18. Press F8 to approve the Windows NT Licensing Agreement.
19. Press Enter to approve the list of detected hardware components.
20. Select the desired installation partition, and then press Enter.
21. Press Enter to indicate that you do *not* want to convert the installation partition to NTFS.
22. Press Enter to install to the default directory named \WINNT.
23. Press Enter to examine the hard disk for errors.
24. Wait for hard disk examination.
25. Wait while files are copied.
26. When prompted, remove the floppy disk from the drive and press Enter to restart the computer and begin the graphical portion of the setup process.
27. When the computer restarts, click on Next.
28. Select the Typical option for installation, and then click on Next.
29. Enter your name and organization, and then click on Next.
30. Enter your CD-ROM key, and then click on Next.

## APPLY YOUR LEARNING

31. Enter your computer name (specify a computer named **Test**), and then click on Next.
32. Enter and confirm the password for the administrator account, and then click on Next.
33. Click on Yes to create an Emergency Repair Disk (ERD).
34. Click on Next to install the most common components.
35. Click on Next to install Windows NT Networking.
36. Specify whether your computer will be participating in a network, and then click on Next. If your computer will not be participating in a network, skip ahead to step 43.
37. Click on either Start Search for Your Adapter or Select from List.
38. Select your adapter from the list, and then click on Next.
39. Make sure that NetBEUI is the only specified protocol, and then click on Next.
40. Click on Continue to approve the network card settings. (Remember that Windows NT 4.0 doesn't support Plug and Play, and your network card settings *must* be correct.)
41. Click on Next to start the network.
42. Click on Next to install the computer named Test into a workgroup named Workgroup.
43. Click on Next to finish setup.
44. Select the proper time zone, and then click on Close.
45. Click OK to approve the detected video adapter.
46. Click on Test to test the video adapter.
47. Click OK to start the video test, and then wait five seconds.
48. Click on Yes (if you saw the bitmap properly).
49. Click OK to save the video settings.
50. Click OK in the Display Properties dialog box.
51. Wait while files are copied.
52. Wait while the configuration is saved.
53. Insert a floppy that will become your ERD, and then click on OK.
54. Wait while the ERD is formatted and files are copied.
55. Wait while the temporary configuration files are removed.
56. Press the button to restart your computer. The installation process is complete.

### 2.5 Removing NTFS Partitions

This exercise gives instructions on how to remove Windows NT from a computer configured with NTFS partitions that are logical drives in extended partitions. Logical NTFS partitions cannot be removed using FDISK.

**Estimated Time:** 30 minutes

1. Insert the Windows NT Workstation Setup Boot Disk into your floppy drive and restart your computer. (If you don't have the three Setup Boot Disks, you can create them with the command `WINNT /OX`.)

## APPLY YOUR LEARNING

2. When prompted, insert Windows NT Workstation Setup Disk #2.
3. At the Windows NT Workstation Setup – Welcome to Setup screen, press Enter to start the installation process.
4. Press Enter to detect mass storage devices.
5. When prompted, insert Windows NT Workstation Setup Disk #3.
6. Press Enter to approve the list of detected mass storage devices. (Don't worry if your IDE hard disk controller isn't detected; the installation process should proceed just fine anyway.)
7. Press Page Down repeatedly, until you reach the last page of the Windows NT Licensing Agreement.
8. Press F8 to approve the Windows NT Licensing Agreement.
9. Press Enter to approve the list of detected hardware components.
10. Select the desired installation partition, and then press Enter.
11. Specify that you want to convert the desired partition from NTFS to FAT.
12. When the conversion to FAT is complete, press F3 to exit from the Setup program.
13. Restart your computer with an MS-DOS system disk that contains the Sys.com program.
14. From a command prompt, type **SYS C:**, which transfers the MS-DOS boot sector to the hard disk.

### 2.6 Changing Hardware Settings for a Network Adapter

This exercise shows the necessary steps for changing the hardware settings for a network adapter.

**Estimated Time:** 10 minutes

1. Double-click on the Network icon in Control Panel.
2. Click on the Adapters tab.
3. Select the desired network adapter in the Network Adapters section.
4. Click on Properties.
5. Modify the network card properties to the desired settings, and then click on OK.
6. Click on Close in the Network dialog box.
7. Wait while your bindings are recalculated.
8. Click on Yes to restart your computer.

### 2.7 Adding Additional SCSI Adapters

This exercise shows you how to add additional SCSI adapters to a computer already running Windows NT 4.0.

**Estimated Time:** 10 minutes

1. Double-click on the SCSI Adapters icon in Control Panel.
2. Click on the Drivers tab.
3. Click on Add.
4. Wait while the driver list is being created.

## APPLY YOUR LEARNING

5. Select the appropriate SCSI adapter from the list, or click on Have Disk.
6. Insert the installation CD or the device manufacturer's installation disk when prompted, and then click OK.
7. Click on Close to close the SCSI Adapters dialog box.

### 2.8 Adding Tape Devices

This exercise shows you how to add tape devices to a computer already running Windows NT Workstation 4.0.

**Estimated Time:** 10 minutes

1. Double-click on the Tape Devices icon in Control Panel.
2. Click on Detect to see whether your tape drive can be automatically detected.
3. If your tape drive is not automatically detected, click on the Drivers tab.
4. Click on Add.
5. Select the appropriate SCSI adapter from the list, or click on Have Disk.
6. Click OK.
7. Insert the installation CD or the device manufacturer's installation disk when prompted, and then click OK.
8. Click on Close to close the Tape Devices dialog box.

### 2.9 Installing a Sound Card

This exercise leads you through the steps for installing a driver for a sound card.

**Estimated Time:** 10 minutes

1. Double-click on the Multimedia icon in Control Panel.
2. Click on the Devices tab.
3. Click on Add.
4. Select the appropriate device from the list (or choose Unlisted or Updated Driver if you have a manufacturer's installation disk).
5. Click OK.
6. Place the installation CD (or manufacturer's installation disk) in your drive and click OK.
7. Configure the appropriate hardware settings for your sound card in all the dialog boxes that appear.
8. Restart your computer when prompted.

### 2.10 Configuring Display Settings

This exercise leads you through the steps for changing your display settings.

**Estimated Time:** 10 minutes

1. Double-click on the Display icon in Control Panel.
2. Click on the Settings tab in the Display Properties dialog box.
3. Click on Display Type.

## APPLY YOUR LEARNING

4. In the Display Type dialog box, click on Change.
5. Select the appropriate device from the list (or click Have Disk if you have a manufacturer's installation disk).
6. Click OK.
7. Place the installation CD (or manufacturer's installation disk) in your drive and click OK.
8. In the Display Type dialog box, click on Close.
9. Click on Test to test the new video settings.
10. Click OK, and then wait five seconds to perform the video test.
11. Click on Yes (if you saw the test bitmap correctly).
12. In the Display Properties dialog box, click OK.
13. If you're prompted to do so, restart the computer.

### 2.11 Adjusting Keyboard Drivers

This exercise shows you how to adjust the repeat delay and the repeat speed for your keyboard.

**Estimated Time:** 5 minutes

1. Double-click on the Keyboard icon in Control Panel.
2. Adjust the Repeat Delay to the desired setting.
3. Adjust the Repeat Rate to the desired setting.
4. Click OK to save your settings.

### 2.12 Configuring Your Mouse

This exercise leads you though the steps for configuring your mouse.

**Estimated Time:** 5 minutes

1. Double-click on the Mouse icon in Control Panel.
2. Click on the Buttons tab to specify right-handed or left-handed operation, and then set the double-click speed.
3. Click on the Pointers tab to specify the desired style for the mouse pointer.
4. Click on the Motion tab to specify the desired pointer speed and snap to default setting.
5. Click on the General tab to view the current mouse driver.
6. Click OK to save your mouse settings.

### 2.13 Adding Optional Components

This exercise shows you how to add additional optional components that you didn't select when you installed Windows NT Workstation 4.0.

**Estimated Time:** 10 minutes

1. Double-click on the Add/Remove icon in Control Panel.
2. Click on the Windows NT Setup tab.
3. Click on the appropriate category in the displayed list.

## APPLY YOUR LEARNING

4. Click on Details.
5. Select the optional component(s) that you want to add.
6. Click OK.
7. Click OK in the Add/Remove Properties dialog box.
8. If you're prompted to do so, insert the installation CD in your CD-ROM drive, and then click OK.

### 2.14 Modifying Your System Time

This exercise shows you how to change your system time, date, and time zone.

**Estimated Time:** 5 minutes

1. Double-click on the Date/Time icon in Control Panel.
2. Change the month, date, and time, as desired.
3. Click on the Time Zone tab to select the proper time zone and the settings for daylight savings time.
4. Click OK to save the new date/time settings.

## Review Questions

1. You have an MS-DOS system with a CD-ROM drive configured as drive D:. What command should you use to install Windows NT Workstation 4.0?
2. You have a Windows 95-based computer that uses compressed drives. What do you have to do before you upgrade it to Windows NT Workstation 4.0?
3. You want to set up a computer to dual boot Microsoft Windows NT Workstation 4.0 and Microsoft Windows NT Server 4.0. What do you need to do to use the same 32-bit application program with both versions of the operating system?
4. You want to remove Windows NT Workstation 4.0 from your computer that was set up to dual boot with Windows 95. You delete all the Windows NT operating systems files and the hidden files in the system partition. However, you receive the following error message when you boot your computer:

   ```
   BOOT: Couldn't find NTLDR.
   Please insert another disk.
   ```

   How do you fix this problem?
5. Which program should you use to install a new network adapter card: Windows Setup or Control Panel?
6. What program should you use to install a new SCSI host adapter card: Windows Setup or Control Panel?
7. Your UPS unit is being deactivated when Windows NT Workstation 4.0 boots. Which file needs to be modified to prevent your UPS unit from being turned off?

## APPLY YOUR LEARNING

8. What available tool enables you to check a computer to see if its components are on the NT Hardware Compatibility List?

9. If you want to dual boot Windows NT and Windows 95, which file system must be used on the partition that stores common data? Which file system must be used on the primary partition from which both systems boot?

10. In order to install NT Workstation over the network, what must you do to prepare the server from which the installation will be performed?

11. Microsoft does not recommend that you dual boot Windows NT with Windows 95. List the three reasons for that recommendation that were given in this chapter.

## Exam Questions

1. Mitch has a system configured with Windows 95 and Office 97. He would like to dual boot with Windows NT Workstation 4.0 but still be able to use his Office applications. His machine is a Pentium 100 that has 12MB RAM and a 1GB hard disk formatted with FAT. What should he do to upgrade his machine?

   A. Install Windows NT 4.0 using the `WINNT` command, and then reinstall Office 97 under NT.

   B. Upgrade Windows 95 to Windows NT Workstation by deleting his Windows directory after he installs Windows NT Workstation.

   C. Install Windows NT 4.0 using the `WINNT32` command, and then reinstall Office 97 under NT.

   D. Mitch cannot install Windows NT Workstation on this machine in its current configuration.

2. You want to install Microsoft Windows NT Workstation 4.0 on 10 Microsoft Windows for Workgroups computers that are connected to your Microsoft Windows NT Server 4.0. What is the fastest way to perform the installation?

   A. Using floppies

   B. Using the Setup Boot floppies and CD

   C. Over the network

   D. Over the network, specifying the `/b` option for `WINNT`

3. You want to upgrade a Windows 95 computer to Windows NT Workstation 4.0. You have the installation CD and a CD-ROM drive. What program should you use to perform the upgrade?

   A. SETUP

   B. WINNT

   C. WINNT32

   D. UPGRADE

4. You want to upgrade a Windows NT Workstation 3.51 computer to Windows NT Workstation 4.0. You have the installation CD and a CD-ROM drive. What program should you use to perform the upgrade?

   A. SETUP

   B. WINNT

## APPLY YOUR LEARNING

C. WINNT32

D. UPGRADE

5. You are setting up a network-based distribution server so that you can perform over-the-network installations of Microsoft Windows NT Workstation 4.0. What program or command should you use to place the necessary files on your server? Choose two.

   A. The `SETUP /A` command

   B. The `XCOPY` command

   C. Server Manager

   D. Explorer

6. What version of network adapter drivers does Microsoft Windows NT Workstation 4.0 support? Choose two.

   A. ODI

   B. NDIS 3.0

   C. NDIS 3.1

   D. NDIS 4

7. You need to re-create the three Setup Boot Disks that originally came with your installation CD. What command switch enables you to re-create the disks without installing Windows NT Workstation 4.0?

   A. `/b`

   B. `/a`

   C. `/ox`

   D. `/x`

8. How do you configure network hardware and software?

   A. Use Windows Setup.

   B. In Control Panel, click on the Network program.

   C. In Control Panel, click on the Devices program.

   D. In Control Panel, click on the Services program.

9. What command will use a script file to install Windows NT?

   A. `Netsetup`

   B. `Setup setup.txt`

   C. `WINNT /U:setup.txt /s:\\server1\ntwWINNT32 /b`

   D. `Install setup.txt`

10. You need to upgrade a computer from Windows 95 to Windows NT Workstation 4.0. The computer is Pentium based and has 32MB of RAM and 750MB of free hard disk. Which of the following methods should you use?

    A. Run `WINNT` and install Windows NT Workstation 4.0 in the same directory as Windows 95.

    B. Run `WINNT` and install Windows NT Workstation 4.0 in a different directory from Windows 95; then delete the Windows 95 directory.

## APPLY YOUR LEARNING

C. Run WINNT32 and install Windows NT Workstation 4.0 in the same directory as Windows 95.

D. Run WINNT32 and install Windows NT Workstation 4.0 in a different directory from Windows 95; then delete the Windows 95 directory.

11. When you upgrade a computer from a previous version of Windows NT Workstation, which Registry settings are preserved? Choose all that apply.

    A. User and group accounts.

    B. All desktop settings.

    C. Network adapter settings and protocols.

    D. You cannot perform this upgrade.

12. You need to upgrade a computer from Windows 95 to Windows NT Workstation 4.0. The computer is Intel 386-based and has 32MB of RAM and 750MB of free hard disk. Which of the following methods should you use?

    A. Run WINNT and install Windows NT Workstation 4.0 in the same directory as Windows 95.

    B. Run WINNT and install Windows NT Workstation 4.0 in a different directory from Windows 95; then delete the Windows 95 directory.

    C. Run SETUP and install Windows NT Workstation 4.0 in a different directory from Windows 95; then delete the Windows 95 directory.

    D. You cannot perform this upgrade.

13. What is the maximum length for a computer name?

    A. 15 characters

    B. 12 characters

    C. 32 characters

    D. 256 characters

14. What is the minimum amount of RAM required to install Windows NT Workstation 4.0 on an Intel processor?

    A. 4MB

    B. 12MB

    C. 16MB

    D. 32MB

15. You need to install the Windows Messaging system when you install Windows NT Workstation 4.0. Which Setup option should you choose?

    A. Compact

    B. Portable

    C. Typical

    D. Custom

16. Your computer has Windows 95 installed. You want to install Windows NT Workstation 4.0 and configure it to dual boot both operating systems. Which of the following statements are true? Choose two.

    A. You must reinstall all your 32-bit Windows applications before they will run under Windows NT Workstation 4.0.

## APPLY YOUR LEARNING

B. Do nothing after you install Windows NT Workstation 4.0. All your 32-bit Windows applications will continue to execute as they did before.

C. All your user profile settings will be migrated from Windows 95 to Windows NT 4.0 Workstation.

D. None of your user profile settings will be migrated from Windows 95 to Windows NT Workstation 4.0.

17. You need to upgrade 50 Pentium-based computers with network cards to Windows NT Workstation 4.0. To prepare for over-the-network installations, which folder on the installation CD must you share?

    A. \I386

    B. \NETSETUP

    C. OEMSETUP

    D. \WINNT

18. In an over-the-network installation of Windows NT Workstation 4.0, what is the name of the temporary folder that contains the installation files?

    A. WIN_NT.TMP

    B. $WINNT.LS

    C. $WIN_NT$.~LS

    D. $WIN_NT$.TMP

19. You need to upgrade a computer from Windows NT 3.51 Workstation to Windows NT Workstation 4.0. The computer is Pentium based and has 32MB of RAM and 750MB of free hard disk. Which of the following methods should you use?

    A. Run `WINNT` and install Windows NT Workstation 4.0 in the same directory as Windows NT 3.51.

    B. Run `WINNT` and install Windows NT Workstation 4.0 in a different directory from Windows NT 3.51.

    C. Run `WINNT32` and install Windows NT Workstation 4.0 in the same directory as Windows NT 3.51.

    D. Run `WINNT32` and install Windows NT Workstation 4.0 in a different directory from Windows NT 3.51.

20. Which of the following switches needs to specified along with the `/s` switch to enable an unattended installation of Windows NT Workstation 4.0?

    A. `/b`

    B. `/u`

    C. `/oem`

    D. `/ox`

**APPLY YOUR LEARNING**

## Answers to Review Questions

1. `d:\I386\WINNT /b` is the command you should use to install Windows NT Workstation 4.0. For more information, refer to the section "Installing Windows NT Workstation 4.0 on an Intel Computer with an Existing Operating System."

2. Windows NT Workstation 4.0 cannot access Windows 95 compressed partitions. You have to uncompress the compressed drives. For more information, refer to the section "Minimum Requirements for Installation."

3. To execute 32-bit applications in a dual-boot configuration, you must install them twice. Boot the computer with Windows NT Workstation 4.0, and then install the application. Then boot the computer with Windows NT Server 4.0 and reinstall the application. For more information, refer to the section "Setting Up a Dual-Boot System."

4. You can restore the Windows 95 boot track by booting the computer with a Windows 95 boot disk and executing the SYS command. For more information, refer to the section "Removing Windows NT Workstation."

5. Control Panel contains the options for installing new network adapters. (In Windows NT 3.51, you would have used Windows Setup.) For more information, refer to the section "Working with Network Adapter Drivers."

6. Control Panel contains the options for installing new SCSI host adapters. (In Windows NT 3.51, you would have used Windows Setup.) For more information, refer to the section "Working with SCSI Device Drivers."

7. BOOT.INI is the file that needs to be modified to prevent your UPS from being deactivated (add the NoSerialMice option). For more information, refer to the section "Working with Uninterruptible Power Supplies."

8. The tool is NTHQ (the NT Hardware Qualifier); it is a floppy-based tool to which you boot your computer to have it analyze your hardware for compatibility. Its limitation is that it uses the HCL located on the NT CD-ROM from which it was built. Consequently, it may be a few years outdated. For more information, refer to the section "Using the Windows NT Hardware Qualifier Tool (NTHQ.EXE)."

9. To share information on a dual-boot system, you must have a partition formatted FAT. To perform the boot itself, your primary partition must also be formatted FAT. For more information, refer to the section "Setting Up a Dual-Boot System."

10. In order for you to install NT Workstation over the network, your server must have the hardware-specific files shared. For example, if you wanted to install NT Workstation on an Intel-based computer, you would share the I386 folder from the CD-ROM on the server. You can either share this folder from the CD itself (slow) or copy it onto the server and share it from there (faster). For more information, refer to the section "Configuring Server-Based Installation."

11. This chapter identifies three serious drawbacks to dual booting Windows NT with Windows 95:

    - Booting to Windows 95 allows you to bypass NT logon requirements and access the hard drive.

## APPLY YOUR LEARNING

- Dual booting requires that at least one partition be formatted FAT, and on that partition, you will not be able to implement local security via NTFS.
- Because Windows NT and Windows 95 maintain their own Registries, you will have to install application software twice if it is to be used by both operating systems.

For more information, refer to the section "Setting Up a Dual-Boot System."

## Answers to Exam Questions

1. **A** is correct. Mitch will be able to install Windows NT Workstation, but he must reinstall his Office 97 applications in order to use them. For more information, refer to the section "Setting Up a Dual-Boot System."
2. **D** is correct. Performing an over-the-network installation with the `/b` option does not waste time creating the three Setup Boot Disks and reading them back. For more information, refer to the section "Installing Windows NT Workstation 4.0 on an Intel Computer with an Existing Operating System."
3. **B** is correct. You cannot use `WINNT32` with Windows 95. For more information, refer to the section "Installing Windows NT Workstation 4.0 on an Intel Computer with an Existing Operating System."
4. **C** is correct. You cannot use `WINNT` to upgrade Windows NT. For more information, refer to the section "Installing Windows NT Workstation 4.0 on an Intel Computer with an Existing Operating System."
5. **B and D** are both correct. There is no `SETUP /A` command for Windows NT, and Server Manager is used for other functions. For more information, refer to the section "Installing Windows NT Workstation 4.0 on an Intel Computer with an Existing Operating System."
6. **B and D** are both correct. ODI and NDIS 3.1 are types of network device drivers that are supported by Windows 95. For more information, refer to the section "Working with Network Adapter Drivers."
7. **C** is correct. The switch `/ox` will start what looks like an installation setup, but it will only create the three setup disks and then stop. For more information, refer to the section "Installing Windows NT Workstation 4.0 on an Intel Computer with an Existing Operating System."
8. **B** is correct. To configure network hardware and software, you must run the network application in the Control Panel. For more information, refer to the section "Working with Network Adapter Drivers."
9. **C** is correct. The command `WINNT /U:setup.txt /s:\\server1\ntwWINNT32 /b` will install NT Workstation using the configuration described in the file SETUP.TXT and will use the path \\server1\ntwWINNT32 to obtain the installation files, but it will not create the three setup disks. For more information, refer to the section "Installing Windows NT Workstation 4.0 on an Intel Computer with an Existing Operating System."

## APPLY YOUR LEARNING

10. **B** is correct. There is no upgrade path from Windows 95, and you can use WINNT32 only when you are upgrading previous versions of Windows NT. For more information, refer to the section "Upgrading to Windows NT Workstation 4.0."

11. **A, B, and C** are all correct. When you upgrade a previous version of Windows NT, all Registry settings are preserved. For more information, refer to the section "Upgrading to Windows NT Workstation 4.0."

12. **D** is correct. Windows NT Workstation 4.0 is not supported on Intel 386 microprocessors. For more information, refer to the section "Upgrading to Windows NT Workstation 4.0."

13. **A** is correct. Due to limitations in NetBIOS naming, the maximum length for an NT computer name is 15 characters. For more information, refer to Exercise 2.2.

14. **B** is correct. The minimum RAM required to install NT Workstation on an Intel-based computer is 12MB. If you have less memory, the installation will stop to tell you so. For more information, refer to the section "Minimum Requirements for Installation."

15. **D** is correct. You can install the messaging components only if you choose a Custom installation. For more information, refer to the section "Installation Options."

16. **A and D** are both correct. Because of incompatibilities between Windows NT and Windows 95, you must install all 32-bit applications, and none of the profiles will be migrated. For more information, refer to the section "Setting Up a Dual-Boot System."

17. **A** is correct. There is no upgrade path from Windows 95 to Windows NT. For more information, refer to the section "Configuring Server-Based Installation."

18. **C** is correct. The temporary directory used to store the installation files during an over-the-network installation is called $WIN_NT$~LS. For more information, refer to the section "Installing Windows NT Workstation 4.0 on an Intel Computer with an Existing Operating System."

19. **C** is correct. The 16-bit version of the installation program does not work under Windows NT. For more information, refer to the section "Upgrading to Windows NT Workstation 4.0."

20. **B** is correct. To perform an unattended installation, you must specify both the source files (/s) and the unattended answer file (/u). For more information, refer to the section "Installing Windows NT Workstation 4.0 on an Intel Computer with an Existing Operating System."

## Suggested Readings and Resources

The following are some recommended readings on the subject of installing and configuring NT Workstation:

1. Microsoft Official Curriculum course 770: *Installing and Configuring Microsoft Windows NT Workstation 4.0*
   - Module 1: Overview of Windows NT Workstation 4.0
   - Module 2: Installing Windows NT Workstation 4.0
2. Microsoft Official Curriculum course 922: *Supporting Microsoft Windows NT 4.0 Core Technologies*
   - Module 2: Installing Windows NT
   - Module 3: Configuring the Windows NT Environment
3. *Microsoft Windows NT Workstation Resource Kit Version 4.0* (Microsoft Press)
   - Chapter 2: Customizing Setup
   - Chapter 4: Planning for a Mixed Environment
4. Microsoft TechNet CD-ROM
   - *MS Windows NT Workstation Technical Notes*
     - MS Windows NT Workstation Deployment Guide – Automating Windows NT Setup
     - An Unattended Windows NT Workstation Deployment
5. Web sites
   - `www.microsoft.com/train_cert`
   - `www.prometric.com/testingcandidates/assessment/chosetest.html` (take online assessment tests)

## Objectives

Microsoft provides the following objectives for "Managing Resources":

**Create and manage local user accounts and local group accounts to meet given requirements.**

- This objective is necessary because someone certified in the use of Windows NT Workstation technology must be able to manage users and groups on an NT Workstation. This would include creating new users, creating new groups for maintaining permissions, and configuring user accounts.

**Set up and modify user profiles.**

- This objective is necessary because someone certified in the use of Windows NT Workstation technology must understand the use of profiles and how to create and modify those profiles.

**Set up shared folders and permissions.**

- This objective is necessary because someone certified in the use of Windows NT Workstation technology must understand how to control access to resources by sharing those resources and then configuring share-level permissions.

**Set permissions on NTFS partitions, folders, and files.**

- To satisfy this objective, you must understand how to control access to local resources by assigning NTFS permissions. You also must understand how to decide between FAT and NTFS partitions and what factors affect that decision. It is also important to understand how share-level permissions interact with NTFS partitions.

CHAPTER 3

# Managing Resources

## Objectives

**Install and configure printers in a given environment.**

- This objective is necessary because someone certified in the use of Windows NT Workstation technology must be able to install both local and network printers. In addition, this person should be able to configure printers and share them to the network.

This chapter will help you prepare for the "Managing Resources" section of Microsoft's Exam 70-73 by covering the stated objectives. This includes the management and creation of user and group accounts and user profiles. In addition, it covers creating shared folders and configuring permissions on those folders and on NTFS partitions, folders, and files. Finally, this chapter covers the installation and configuration of printers on an NT Workstation.

## Outline

## OUTLINE

## STUDY STRATEGIES

- For the NT Workstation exam, you have to know all the ins and outs of user accounts. Begin by walking through the material presented here. That will give you a good feel for the scope of the exam coverage. From there, look into User Manager, create a user, and look at all the options for configuration of that user. You should know all the buttons on the User Properties dialog boxes and what options each button gives you access to. You might be asked a multiple choice question like, "Where do you configure a user's profile path?," and being comfortable with the User Properties dialog boxes will help you answer such questions.

  In addition, you'll want to look at the contents of the Policies menu, especially the Account command (what can you configure from there?) and the User Rights command (what are the default rights and whom are they given to?). Finally, you need to understand the function of groups, which groups are present by default, what they can do, and how to build your own groups.

- The profile objective follows on the accounts section. First, read through the profiles section in this chapter, and then look back at the User Manager. Experiment with creating new profiles—both personal and mandatory profiles. Then log on as a new user and see what those profiles do. If you have another machine available, create a roaming profile so you can see the effect of moving from one machine to another.

- You can study shared folders and NTFS permissions together. Of course, you want to read through the material, but then you should get as much hands-on exposure to the options as possible. Because sharing is the same whether you're sharing from NTFS or from FAT, you can kill two birds with one stone by sharing from an NTFS partition: Doing so enables you to learn about sharing procedures and permissions, NTFS local security, and how the two interact. You might even want to begin playing and testing these concepts while you read so you can see firsthand how the concepts work. When you study NTFS permissions, be sure to look at the special permissions as well as the standard ones, just to see how you can make granular modifications to the standard permissions.

- Finally, you need to understand how printing works. Of course, you can't really test the architecture, but you must understand the related terminology. This is strictly memorization: You have to know what the terms mean in order to understand the exam questions. You will not be told the difference between a printer and a print device on the exam, but you will be expected to know what each one is.

  Because there are so many printing options, you won't be able to test all of them unless you have numerous printers. The more you can try out, though, the better off you will be when taking the exam. For those options you can't try out, you just have to take the configuration process as far as you can and then rely on your memory. For example, you might not have enough print devices to actually test printer pools, but Windows NT doesn't know that. So when you configure your system, you can tell Windows NT that you have a number of print devices of the same type, which will enable you to configure a printer pool.

# INTRODUCTION

Managing resources is important in the administration of Windows NT Workstation. Managing resources refers to the computer accounts on the workstation—both for users and groups—as well as the resources on the workstation.

Being able to set appropriate permissions to either allow or restrict access to resources based on a user or group account is the key to an effective implementation of Windows NT Workstation. And remember that "resources" refers not only to files and directories on the Windows NT Workstation, but to printers as well.

# IMPLEMENTING LOCAL USER AND GROUP ACCOUNTS

Create and manage local user accounts and local group accounts to meet given requirements.

Windows NT has a mandatory logon. That means that every user who wants to use a Windows NT Workstation must have a logon name and password before he or she can use Windows NT Workstation. Whether you are in a small workgroup or a large domain, it is a good idea to plan the implementation of user accounts as well as local group accounts.

> NOTE
> **Use Local Group Accounts to Give Multiple Users Access** Local group accounts are used to give multiple users access to resources. For a particular resource such as a printer, it is easier to give access to a group than to each user individually.

In relation to user and group accounts, you need a working knowledge of how to perform the following tasks:

1. Planning user and group accounts
2. Creating user and group accounts
3. Managing user and group accounts

Each of these tasks is important for an effective implementation of Windows NT Workstation.

## Planning User Accounts

Before you create any user accounts, it is a good idea to plan how you will implement user accounts under Windows NT Workstation. Planning user accounts includes deciding on the password requirements you want to implement, your naming conventions, the location of a user's home directory, and whether you want to grant users dial-in access.

### Modifying Account Policy

While planning your user accounts, you must answer certain questions such as the following about how each account will be handled:

- How often do you want users to have to change their passwords?
- What do you want to have happen to an account if there are multiple bad logon attempts?
- How many passwords do you want NT to "remember"?

All these items are manipulated with the NT Policy. You configure the Account Policy within User Manager by choosing Account from the Policies menu (see Figure 3.1).

The following list outlines the available password restrictions:

*Maximum Password Age.* This option enables you to specify how long a user's password will be valid. The default is that passwords expire in 42 days.

*Minimum Password Age.* This specifies how long a user must keep a particular password before she can change it again. If you force a user to change her password and you leave this set to Allow Changes Immediately, after the user changes her password, she can change it right back to the old one. If you are trying to implement password changes for security reasons, this breaks down your security. For that reason, you might want to set a minimum password age.

*Minimum Password Length.* The default on Windows NT is to allow blank passwords. Once again, for security reasons, you might not want to allow this. You can set a minimum password length of up to 14 characters, which is the maximum password length allowed under Windows NT.

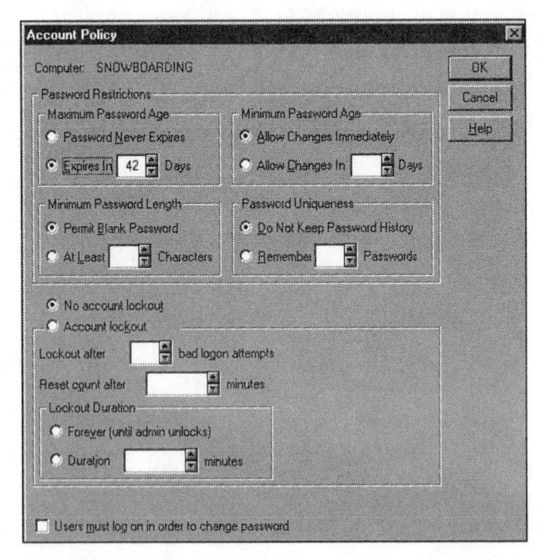


**FIGURE 3.1**
You can modify password options within the Account Policy screen of User Manager.

*Password Uniqueness.* If you want to force users to use different passwords each time they change their passwords, you can set a value for password uniqueness. If you set the password uniqueness value to remember two passwords, when a user is prompted to change her password, she cannot use the old password again until she changes her password for the third time. The maximum password uniqueness value is 24.

WARNING

**User Settings Override Account Policy** If the Account Policy is configured so that the password expires but the user's account is configured so that the password never expires, the user setting overrides the Account Policy setting.

The following list outlines the Account Lockout options:

*Lockout After Bad Logon Attempts.* Setting a value for this option prevents the account from being used after this number is reached, even if the right password is finally entered. For example, if you set this value to five (which is the default setting for Account Lockout), on the sixth attempt—even if the user (or hacker) types in the correct username and password—he cannot log on to Windows NT.

*Reset Counter After.* This value specifies when to refresh the counter for bad logon attempts. The default value is 30 minutes. This means that if Account Lockout is set to five, a user who tries to log on unsuccessfully four times can try again in 45 minutes; because the counter will have been reset, the account will not be locked out, and the user can try up to four more times.

*Lockout Duration.* This value specifies how long the account should remain locked out if the lockout counter is exceeded. It is generally more secure to set Lockout Duration to forever so that the administrator must unlock the account. That way the administrator is warned of the activity on that account.

*Users Must Log On to Change Password.* This setting requires a user to log on successfully before changing his password. If a user's password expires, the user cannot log on until the administrator changes the password for her.

EXAM TIP

**Know the Account Policy Screen** For the exam, you should be familiar with the Account Policy screen and how to configure each option on it.

When you're planning an account policy, it is important that you give your environment the required security but also make the password requirements manageable. If you forced users to change their passwords every day and you set the password history to remember 24 passwords (the maximum), you might create a situation in which users start writing down their passwords and sticking them on the monitor or under the keyboard or in the desk drawer. That would compromise your security more than it would enhance it.

## Using a Naming Convention

Planning your naming convention is another important part of creating user accounts. If you are going to be implementing Windows NT Workstation in a domain environment, the usernames must be unique in the domain. If you are implementing Windows NT Workstation as a standalone machine, usernames must be unique on that machine.

You must implement a naming convention to allow for this uniqueness of names. You might choose to use employee identification numbers as logon names. In a very large company where each employee is given a unique employee number, that may be a good way to ensure uniqueness. In a smaller company, you may choose to use a naming convention of first name followed by last initial. If you had an employee named Kendra McCormick, for example, her logon name would be KendraM. If, later on, your company hired someone named Kendra McClarty, you would have to determine what to do about her username. You cannot use the name KendraM because that is already used. One option is to add a number to the username, making it KendraM1. Another option is to add the second letter of the last name, which would make it KendraMc. In a larger environment, this type of naming convention can become unwieldy due to the possibility of having so many duplicate names.

It is highly likely that you would have more than one StephenR, for instance, in a 10,000-user company. In a larger environment, it might make more sense to use a naming convention of first initial followed by last name. In this environment, if you had a user named David Kayano, his username would be DKayano. An even better way to implement a naming convention for a large company is to use a few letters of the first name, followed by the middle initial, followed by the last name. Even with this naming convention, you may have duplicates, however. So you would need to account for that possibility. In a large environment, it is likely that you may have more than one user named Mike Smith, for instance.

Once you have decided on a naming convention for the users in your environment, you can consider whether you want to implement home directories. A home directory provides each user with a place to store personal files, either locally on his own PC or on a server.

## Designing a Home Directory Location

Whether you will grant users home directories for storing personal information is another issue you must consider when planning user accounts. A home directory is a storage location available only to one particular user for storing his or her own files.

You can create a home directory either on the local Windows NT Workstation or on a remote location such as a Windows NT Server. When deciding whether to create a user's home directory locally or remotely, you must take into account the needs of your environment. Do users "roam" from machine to machine in your network? If so, you need to store users' home directories centrally so they can access them from anywhere in the network. If you are in a workgroup of just Windows NT Workstations, however, you would probably create users' home directories on each Windows NT Workstation locally because there is no central server on which to create them.

If you choose to create the home directories on a Windows NT Server, you must give the users access to the Shared Users directory on the server. For more information on that task, see Chapter 1, "Planning."

## Granting Dial-In Permission

If you have users who will be working from home or who travel and need to access your network remotely from the road, you need to grant those users dial-in access. By default, Windows NT does not grant the right to dial in to the network remotely. You must specifically grant that right to all users who need it.

To give a user the permission to dial in to the network and to configure the options available after dial-in has been established, you use the User Manager (see Figure 3.2).

Having opened the properties dialog box for a particular user in User Manager, click the Dialin button in the lower-right corner to bring up the Dialin Information dialog box shown in Figure 3.3.

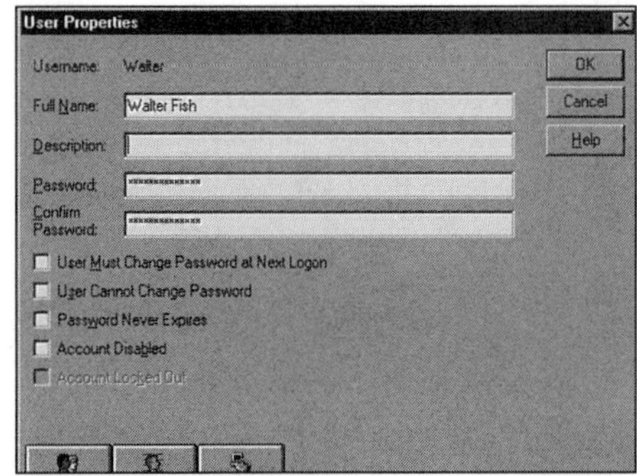


**FIGURE 3.2**
Click the Dialin button in the User Properties dialog box.

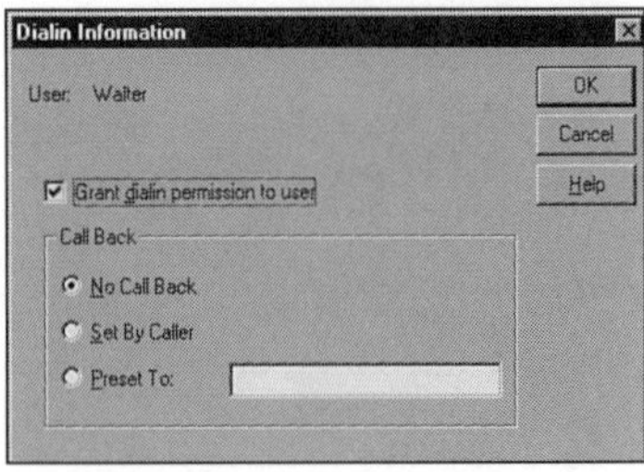


**FIGURE 3.3**
Configure dialin permissions from the Dialin Information dialog box.

You need to configure the following call back options for dial-in access:

- *No Call Back.* This setting disables call back for a particular user account. If this is set, the user must initiate the phone call with the RAS server, and the user is responsible for the phone charges.
- *Set By Caller.* This enables the remote user to specify a number at which the server can call the user back. When this option is enabled, the server is responsible for the phone charges instead of the user.
- *Preset To.* When set, this option specifies a number at which the server can call the user back when the user initiates a dial-in session. This tends to be used for security so that a user is called back only at the predefined number.

WARNING

**Dial-In Permissions Are Different for Workstations and Domains** If you are creating user accounts for a Windows NT Workstation rather than a domain, granting the dial-in permission applies only to that one Windows NT Workstation.

WARNING

**Don't Use the Preset To Option for Traveling Users** Don't set the Preset To option in the dial-in permissions if a user will be traveling and calling from a hotel or other location that has a switchboard instead of from a direct line.

## Built-In User Accounts

Windows NT Workstation creates two built-in user accounts when it's installed:

- *Administrator.* The default Administrator account has full power over the Windows NT Workstation. It has the right to create and delete user accounts, share and stop sharing resources, create and format partitions, set password policies, and use the administrative tools of Windows NT. Because this default Administrator account is always created on Windows NT, you should rename the account after installation if you have concerns about security.
- *Guest.* This built-in Windows NT account enables people who do not have accounts on the Windows NT Workstation (or on the domain that the workstation is a part of, if it's in a domain environment) to access the Workstation. This account has the fewest privileges of all accounts on the Windows NT Workstation and is not allowed to share resources, create users, or manage user policies. This account exists primarily to allow the user to log on to the Windows NT Workstation, but it may also be used to allow the user to access resources on that system or on the network. You might want to rename this built-in account after installation for security purposes.

Because unidentified guests are generally allowed to access the system only in low-security environments, this account is disabled by default.

You can use these two built-in accounts for administration of Windows NT Workstation and to allow guest access to the Windows NT Workstation. Although you can rename both of the built-in accounts on Windows NT Workstation, you cannot delete them. If you try to delete either of them, an error message appears, stating that you cannot delete the account.

> EXAM TIP
>
> **Initial User Account Is No Longer Installed** During installation, Windows NT Workstation 3.51 created an additional user account called the Initial User account. Windows NT Workstation 4.0 does not create that account during installation. On the exam, be careful of questions referring to this Initial User account; they may try to trick you.

### Accounts You Create

Along with the accounts created on Windows NT Workstation during installation, you must create additional user accounts on each workstation for those who need to log on to that Windows NT Workstation. You must create an account for every user who will log on to the Windows NT Workstation, unless the user will be using the Guest account or the default Administrator account.

Under Windows NT, logging on the workstation is mandatory for gaining access to any resources on it; this is unlike Windows 95, in which the user has the opportunity to cancel out of the logon screen. In Windows NT Workstation, a user must have a valid username and password in order to log on to the machine.

## Creating User Accounts

After you have planned your account policy, naming convention, and user account settings, you are ready to actually start creating user accounts. To create user accounts, you must be logged on with an account that has that right. On a Windows NT Workstation, the only two groups that can create user accounts are the Administrators group and the Power Users group. To create a user account, you use User Manager (see Figure 3.4).

You must configure many items when creating a new user account. The following sections discuss those items.

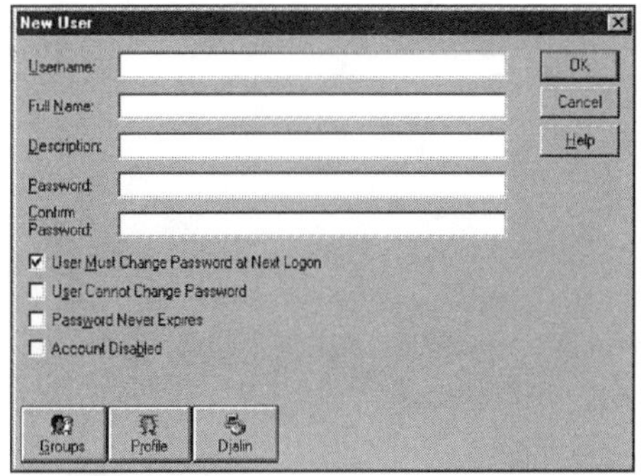


**FIGURE 3.4**
User Manager enables you to create user accounts.

## Setting User Information

Within the User Information section (the main screen), only the Username field is required. The username can contain a maximum of 20 characters but cannot contain the following special characters:

“ / \ [ ] : ; | = , + * ? < >

The Full Name and Description fields are for informational purposes. If you choose to preassign a password to users when creating their accounts, you specify that password in both the Password field and the Confirm Password field. A password in Windows NT can be up to 14 characters long. If you have specified an account policy that requires a minimum password length, you must enter a password at least that long when creating the user account.

## Establishing Password Options

The password options are not required fields when creating a new user account. You may choose to implement some of the following options, however, when creating user accounts.

- *User Must Change Password at Next Logon.* When this is selected (which is the default when creating new users), the user is prompted to change his password when he logs on to Windows NT. This setting is not compatible with the account policy that forces a user to log on to change his password. If both are selected, the user must contact the administrator to change the password.
- *User Cannot Change Password.* Setting this option prevents a user from changing her password. If both this setting and User Must Change Password are selected when you attempt to add the account, you get an error message stating that you cannot check both options for the same user.
- *Password Never Expires.* You can use this option to override the setting for password expiration in the Account Policy. This option tends to be used for accounts that will be assigned to services, but it can also be applied to user accounts. If you have both this option and User Must Change Password at Next Logon selected, a warning tells you that the user will not be required to change her password.

- *Account Disabled.* Instead of deleting a user's account when he or she leaves the company, it is a good idea to disable the account instead. If the employee will be replaced, it is likely that the new individual hired will need the same rights and permissions the previous user had. By disabling the account, you prevent the previous employee from being able to access your Windows NT Workstation or domain. When the new individual is hired, you can rename the old account with the new name and have the new user change the password.
- *Account Locked Out.* This option is visible only if you have Account Lockout enabled in the Account Policy. You, as an administrator, can never check this box—it will be grayed out. The only time this box is available is when a user's account has been locked out because someone has exceeded the set number of bad logon attempts. If the Lockout Duration is set to forever, the administrator must go into that user's account and uncheck the Account Locked Out check box.

## Configuring a User Environment Profile

You can configure the User Environment Profile settings to manage the user's working environment. To access these options, click the Profile button in the dialog box for the user's account. Figure 3.5 shows the settings that you can modify.

When deciding how to create and configure your user accounts for Windows NT Workstation, it is important that you understand the settings you can define for the user's environment. You can control the following settings:

- *User Profile Path.* This setting is used to specify a path for a user profile that is available centrally on a server or to assign a mandatory user profile for this user. To use a roaming or mandatory user profile, you must create a share on a server and then specify the path to that share in the user's profile, where the path follows this syntax:

  *\\servername\sharename\profilename*

  For more information on mandatory user profiles, see the section "Mandatory User Profiles," later in this chapter.

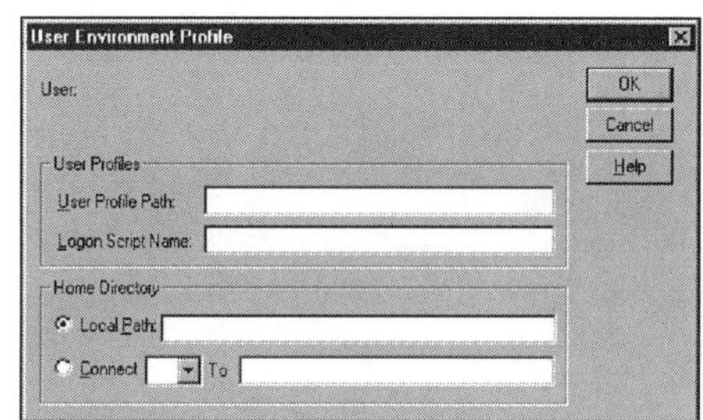


**FIGURE 3.5**
You use the Profile button to configure the user's working environment.

- *Logon Script Name.* This setting enables you to specify the logon script you want used. If a logon script is specified, it will be launched when the user logs on to the Windows NT Workstation. If the logon script is in a subdirectory of the machine's logon script path (typically c:\winnt\system32\repl\import\scripts), you must specify that subdirectory within the logon script name (for example, users\LailaL.bat). Logon scripts can have the extension .CMD, .BAT, or .EXE.
- *Home Directory.* To specify a home directory for a user's personal use, use the controls in this section. Indicate whether the home directory is to be local or remote by choosing the appropriate radio button.

  If it is to be local, enter the full path in the Local Path field (for example, enter C:\users\JillB).

  If you want to use a remote home directory, you must select a drive letter and specify the path to that remote share like this:

  *servername*\users\JillB

  For a discussion of the pros of cons of local versus remote home directories, see Chapter 1, "Planning.")

The settings within the User Environment Profile dialog box enable you to manage the location of both the user's profile and the user's home directory. For each item, you just need to decide whether you want to store it centrally or allow it to be stored on each individual user's workstation.

## Using a Template Account

You should use a template account if certain information will be the same for multiple user accounts you will create. For instance, if you will be creating Windows NT accounts for a group of salespeople, you may want the Description field for all of them to read Sales Representative. You could manually add that to each user account that you create, but that would require unnecessary effort if you were creating a lot of accounts. Instead, you could create a user account called Template that had the Description field filled in. In addition, you could put this Template account in the Sales group and specify the home directory and logon script settings that you want to apply to all users (see Figure 3.6).

When a user account is created from a template, the following properties of the template also become properties of the new user account:

- Account description
- User Must Change Password at Next Login property
- User Cannot Change Password property
- Password Never Expires property
- Group memberships
- All User Environment profile properties
- All dial-in properties

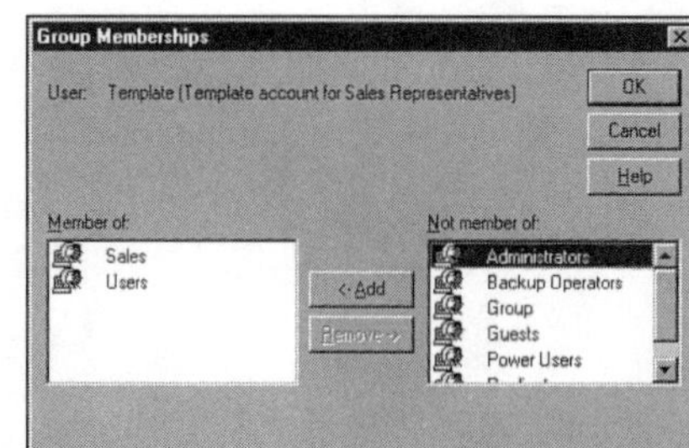


**FIGURE 3.6**
You can create a template user account to make creating user accounts more efficient.

Microsoft recommends that when you name your template account, you call it by the name of the group it best represents and precede that name with an underscore character. For example, if you were making a template for creating accounts for users in Sales, you might call the template _Sales. This does two things. First, it ensures that the name stands out from the rest in its form; no other accounts will begin this way. Second, it ensures that the templates stand out in their position in the user list. Because the list of users is alphabetical, the accounts beginning with an underscore will be sorted first and displayed at the beginning of the list. This second point also ensures that when you go to create a new user from a template, the template you want to use will be easily accessible.

---

### %USERNAME% VARIABLE

Because a template represents a generic setup that will be copied for many users, it is helpful to make the settings as nonspecific as possible. One way to do this is to use environment variables in place of actual directories and usernames. When you specify the path of the home directory in a template, it does you no good to use a path like C:\Users\JillB.

If you did, all your users would get the same path, and you would end up having to modify the properties for each user. Instead, you can use the environment variable %username% to represent the name of the person currently logged in (which NT tracks when

*continues*

*continued*

during login). So instead of including a specific username in the home directory path, you would enter the following:

```
C:\Users\%Username%
```

That way, when JillB logs in, her path will be C:\Users\JillB. But when EmmaM logs in, her path will be C:\Users\EmmaM.

After the Template account is created, you can use that account to create the user accounts for the sales representatives.

## STEP BY STEP

### 3.1 Creating User Accounts from a Template Account

1. Highlight the Template account in User Manager.
2. From the User menu, choose Copy.
3. Fill in the Username and Full Name fields for this new account.

You can create more than one template account. Then use each template to create a group of user accounts that share certain information regarding description, group memberships, home directories, logon scripts, user profile paths, or dial-in access.

## Managing User Accounts

After you create user accounts, you might need to manage them. This management can include renaming user accounts or deleting user accounts. It is important to understand that renaming a user account is usually preferred over deleting an account; however, you will need to be able to weigh individual situations and decide which is the appropriate course of action.

## Renaming User Accounts

When a user account is created in Windows NT, it is given a unique identification called a security identifier (SID). This SID is designed to be unique in all of space and time. It is not based on the user's name, so renaming the user account does not make a difference to NT.

If your company's Chief Information Officer (CIO) has left the company and you hire a new CIO, you can rename the old account with the name of the new CIO, and it retains all the rights and permissions the original account had. It is likely that the new CIO would need the same rights and permissions as the former one, so this would save you the work of reassigning them.

## Deleting User Accounts

In Windows NT, it is not usually a good idea to delete a user account. If CindyF has permissions to a particular directory and you accidentally delete her user account, you cannot just create another account called CindyF. When the original CindyF account was created, it was given a SID, which was unique in all of space and time. When you deleted her account, you deleted the SID. If you re-create her account, even though it carries the same username, the SID is different.

It is actually the SID that is given resource access. So CindyF no longer will have access to that directory until you add her new account to the list of directory permissions. Because of this issue with the SID, it is generally better to disable an account using the User Manager than to delete the account.

In the case of the CIO who left the company, for example, you would probably want to disable that account so that the former CIO would not be able to access your network. When the new CIO is hired, you enable the account and rename it with the name of the new CIO. If you had deleted the account, you would have had to re-create all the rights and permissions the former CIO had.

NOTE

**Paths Don't Change with Rename** If you used the %Username% variable to configure the names to server paths (for example, the path to a user's home directory), you will have to make sure you rename the paths in the user's account. NT will not adjust the path for the new user, nor will the name of the folder it refers to be changed. For example, if the account name of the previous CIO was HerbertH, the home directory path may have been called C:\Home\HerbertH. When you change the name of that account to WalterF, you will have to manually change the path to C:\Home\WalterF, and then you will have to change the folder's name on your NT machine.

## Planning Local Group Accounts

Local group accounts are used to organize users to give them rights on the workstation, as well as to give them access to resources. Built-in local groups are used to give users the rights to perform certain actions on the workstation. Local groups that you create are used to logically organize users to give them the ability to access a particular resource, such as a folder or a printer.

### Built-In Local Groups

NOTE **That's All You Get** Local groups are the only type of group created on Windows NT Workstation. When Windows NT Server is installed as a domain controller, it contains both local groups and global groups.

If you want to give a user the ability to create additional user accounts, create disk partitions, format those partitions, and share directories, you can put that user in the Administrators built-in group. The following list describes the six built-in groups on Windows NT Workstation. Assigning users to these built-in groups can help you manage Windows NT Workstation.

- *Administrators.* The Administrators group has full control over the Windows NT Workstation. This account has the most control on the computer. As a member of the Administrators group, however, the user does not automatically have control over all files on the system. On an NTFS partition, a file's permissions could be set to restrict access from the administrator. If the administrator needs to access the file, she can take ownership of the file and then access it. Administrative privilege is one of three different levels of privilege that you can assign to a user in Windows NT. It is the highest level of privilege that can be assigned within Windows NT.
- *Guests.* The Guests group gives a user limited access to the resources on the Windows NT Workstation. The Guest account is automatically added to this group. The Guests group is one of the three levels of privilege you can assign to a Windows NT user account.
- *Users.* The Users group provides the user with the necessary rights to use the computer as an end user. By default, all accounts created on Windows NT Workstation are put into the Users group, except for the built-in Administrator and Guest accounts. User privilege is one of the three levels of privilege you can assign in Windows NT.

- *Power Users.* The Power Users group gives members the ability to perform certain system tasks without giving the user complete administrative control over the machine. One of the tasks a power user can perform is the sharing of directories. An ordinary user on Windows NT Workstation cannot share directories.
- *Backup Operators.* The Backup Operators group gives its members the ability to bypass the security placed on any files when using the NTBackup utility. This allows for complete resource access, but only for the specialized job of backing up files, not for general access.
- *Replicator.* The Replicator group is used only to enable directory replication. This process allows file transfer to take place between an export server (which must be an NT Server) and an import computer (which can be NT Workstation or NT Server). You will not be tested on this group and its service in the NT Workstation exam, but if you want more information, you can consult the NT Server book in this MCSE series.

For more information on the default rights and abilities of these built-in groups, see the section "Built-In Groups" in Chapter 1.

## Local Groups You Create

If you have to assign permissions to a shared resource or if you implement NTFS permissions on directories or printers, it is recommended that you create a group. The built-in groups can be used to give users certain rights on the workstation or in the domain, but you may need to allocate access to resources based on department or geographical location. In such situations, you may choose to create a group for each department, each city, or each logical grouping of users to which you need to assign rights. If you need to share a printer to the Education Department, for example, it might make more sense to put all those users in the Education Department into a group and then assign that group access to the printer.

## Creating Local Group Accounts

To create a local group account, you must be logged on to Windows NT with an account that has administrative permissions. The tool for creating user accounts on Windows NT Workstation is User Manager; the tool for creating user accounts on a Windows NT domain is User Manager for Domains. To create a local group account on Windows NT Workstation, you must fill in the fields as shown in Figure 3.7. Whereas you need special system rights to create a user account, any user can create a local group.

> NOTE
> **Account Names Must Be Unique**
> Any account name you create must be unique within the database in which it resides. That means that on a local machine, no local group account can have the same name as any user on that machine, nor can it have the same name as any group that has been created or any system group that NT has created.

**STEP BY STEP**

**3.2 Creating a Local Group**

1. Highlight those accounts that you would like to make part of this group by holding down Ctrl and selecting them.
2. Within User Manager, go to the User menu and choose New Local Group.
3. Type in a Group name for this group and, optionally, a description.
4. Add any additional user accounts to this group by clicking the Add button and working through the resulting dialog box.
5. Click the OK button to create the local group.

   You can now use this local group to assign permissions to resources such as a directory or a printer.

> NOTE
> **Automatically Add Users When Creating a New Local Group** If a user account is highlighted when you begin to create a new local group, the new user account is automatically put in that group. This can be used as a shortcut when creating local groups. If you would like to automatically add more than one user account to the group, you can highlight multiple user accounts by holding down the Ctrl key.

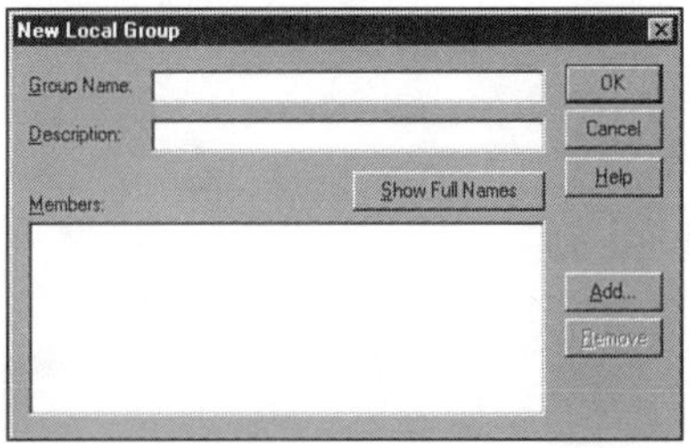

**FIGURE 3.7**
To create a local group account on Windows NT Workstation, use User Manager.

## Managing Local Group Accounts

It may be necessary to manage your local group accounts after they are created. Management tasks might include adding user accounts to the group or deleting the group. If you need to add additional users to a local group, you can do that when you create each user account by selecting the Groups button within the user account dialog box. Or you can add a user account after you have created it by double-clicking on the local group account within User Manager. To add a user account to the local group, click the Add button and select the desired user account.

### Renaming Local Group Accounts

You cannot rename a local group account. If you decide that you want to change the name of a group, you must create a new group with the new name. You can then give that group the appropriate rights to resources and reassign the members of the original group to the new one.

### Deleting Local Group Accounts

If you delete a group account, that group will be gone forever. Just as an individual user account is given a SID when it is created, so is a group account. If you delete the group accidentally, you must re-create the group and reassign all the permissions for the group. Deleting a group does not delete the individual user accounts within the group, just the group itself.

NOTE

**Built-In Accounts Cannot Be Deleted**
You cannot delete any of the built-in system groups on NT. This includes Administrators, Power Users, Users, Guests, Backup Operators, and the Replicator.

## SETTING UP AND MODIFYING USER PROFILES

Set up and modify user profiles.

User profiles are automatically created when a user logs on to Windows NT. A user profile establishes the settings that contribute to a user's working environment. This includes such things as wallpaper, desktop shortcuts, and network connections. The user's profile contains all user-definable settings for the user's environment.

EXAM TIP

**You Must Know How Windows NT Workstation Handles User Profiles**
On Windows NT Workstation, a user profile is automatically created for every user who logs on to the workstation. In Windows 95, on the other hand, you can choose whether to use user profiles. This is the type of issue you might see in a test question.

### Understanding User Profiles

User profiles enable each user on Windows NT to store his own individual settings for his own work environment. User profiles are primarily used for convenience, but they can be used by an administrator to establish control over a user's environment. For more information, see the section "Mandatory User Profiles."

WARNING

**User Profiles Are Not Interchangeable** User profiles for Windows NT Workstation 4.0 are not interchangeable with user profiles for Windows NT Workstation 3.51 or Windows 95. If a user deploys all three operating systems, that user must have three different user profiles, one for each operating system.

A user profile can be stored either locally on the user's Windows NT Workstation or centrally on a server so they are accessible from any location in the network. If user profiles are stored on the server and set as roaming user profiles, they can be accessed from any machine on the network running Windows NT 4.0.

## User Profile Settings

Items that are specific to each user's own working environment are stored in a user profile. Table 3.1 identifies these items in regard to the areas in which they are located.

TABLE 3.1

**ITEMS INCLUDED IN A USER PROFILE**

| *Area* | *Specific Items* |
|---|---|
| Accessories | Any user-specific settings that affect the user's environment, such as settings for Calculator, Clock, Notepad, and Paint. |
| Control Panel | Any user-defined settings defined within the Control Panel, such as mouse pointers, modem dialing properties, and mail and fax properties. |
| Printers | Any printer connections made within Windows NT Workstation to network printers. |
| Start menu | Any personal program groups and their properties, such as the working directory. |
| Taskbar | Any taskbar settings, such as Always on Top or Auto Hide. |
| Windows NT Explorer | Any user-specific settings for Windows NT Explorer, such as whether to view the toolbar, whether to show large icons, and how to arrange icons. |

Items managed on a per-user basis that define the user's working environment are part of the user's profile settings.

## User Profile Directory Structure

By default in Windows NT Workstation, when a user logs on to the workstation, a user profile is stored locally on that machine for that user. This profile is created under the user's name in the Profiles folder within the Windows NT root directory. The first time a user logs on to the computer, this directory is created for that user. The user's profile inherits the settings of the Default User directory structure that is located in the Winnt root user Profiles\Default User. You'll learn more about this default user profile later, in the section "Default User."

Also combined into the user profile are the groups common to all users, which are found in the All Users directory structure (under WinntRoot\Profiles\All Users). After a user logs off the Windows NT Workstation, any changes the user made to her environment while she was logged on are saved to her user profile.

Below the user's directory within the Profiles directory is a structure of settings relating to the user's profile. Table 3.2 outlines that structure.

**TABLE 3.2**

**FOLDERS WITHIN A USER'S PROFILE DIRECTORY**

| *Folder* | *Description of Contents* |
|---|---|
| Application Data | Application-specific data. Application vendors determine the contents of this folder. |
| Desktop | Desktop items, such as shortcuts, folders, documents, or files. |
| Favorites | A list of favorite locations, such as Internet URLs for different Web sites. |
| NetHood | Shortcuts to Network Neighborhood items. |
| Personal | Shortcuts to program items. |
| PrintHood | Shortcuts to printers. |
| Recent | Shortcuts to recently used items. |
| SendTo | Shortcuts to items in the SendTo context menu. You can add items such as Notepad or printers to this folder. |
| Start menu | Shortcuts to the program items found in the Start menu. |
| Templates | Shortcuts to any template items. |

The NetHood, PrintHood, Recent, and Templates folders are not visible by default. If you would like to display these folders, you must open Windows NT Explorer's View menu and choose Options, select the View tab, and then click the Show All Files radio button. This displays the hidden folders.

### All Users

The All Users public folder is used for Start menu shortcuts that apply to all users of the Windows NT Workstation. These settings are not added to a user profile, but they are used in conjunction with the profile to define a user's working environment.

The common program groups (common to all users who log on to the Windows NT Workstation) are stored under the All Users directory. If you want to add a menu shortcut to a Windows NT Workstation, you can do so by adding it to the All Users folder. Only members of the Administrators group can add items to the All Users folder for common access.

### Default User

The Default User folder contains settings that each new user who logs on to the workstation inherits the first time he or she logs on. If no preconfigured profile exists for a user when he logs on, he inherits the settings from the Default User folder; those settings are copied into that user's new user profile directory. Any changes the user makes while logged on are saved into his own new user profile, so the Default Users folder remains unchanged.

## Setting Various User Profiles

Setting user profiles can help you configure the environment for your users. User profiles can be used either to restrict users or as a convenience for users so they can retain their own settings when they move from one machine to another throughout your network. Setting user profiles requires the configuration of three main categories: mandatory user profiles, local user profiles, and roaming user profiles.

## Mandatory User Profiles

You might decide you do not want users to have the convenience of storing their own desktop settings in personal or individual profiles, but instead that you want to impose a more consistent working environment. You can use mandatory user profiles when a higher level of control is required than that of the standard user profile environment. Users cannot change mandatory user profiles. An administrator can create a mandatory user profile and can assign it to one or more users. You configure user profiles through the Control Panel's System application (see Figure 3.8).

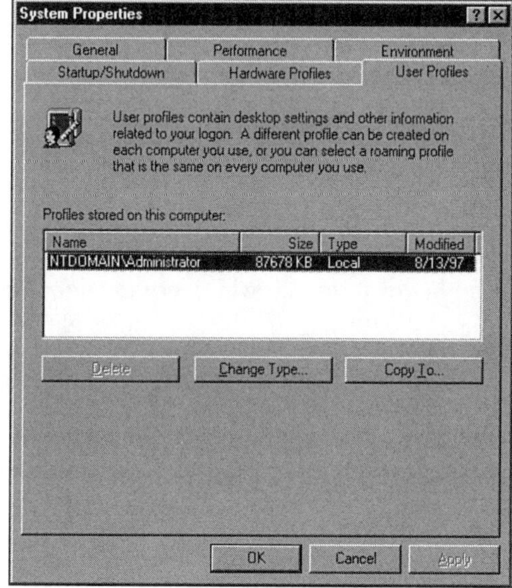


**FIGURE 3.8**
User profiles are managed through the System Properties dialog box.

Because a mandatory user profile cannot be changed, it remains consistent from one logon to the next. A user can change her settings once she is logged on, but those changes are never written back to the mandatory profile. As a result, a user would have to make the same changes to the environment every time she logs on. In addition, because a mandatory user profile cannot be changed, it can be used for multiple users in your network. You can use mandatory user profiles to present a consistent working environment for users within certain departments or for all users in your company.

## Local User Profiles

A local user profile is a user's profile that is created on the Windows NT Workstation that she is logging on to. Local user profiles are created by default in Windows NT Workstation the first time that a user logs on to a Windows NT Workstation.

Local user profiles are stored locally on the Windows NT Workstation, under the Profiles directory. If a user uses only one machine and will never need to use his settings while sitting at another Windows NT Workstation, a local user profile might be the best choice for that user.

## Roaming User Profiles

Local user profiles are allowed in Windows NT. However, if users must "roam" from one Windows NT Workstation computer to another in your environment, you might not want to use local user profiles.

A roaming user profile is configured by the administrator to allow the user to retain her own settings wherever she might land on the network, as long as she is using another Windows NT 4.0 machine. When the user makes a change to her roaming user profile, that change is saved on the server where the profile is stored. If the user is logged on to two machines simultaneously, the settings from the last session to be logged off will be retained for the user's profile.

An administrator can create a roaming mandatory profile, which users cannot change. A roaming mandatory profile can be used for multiple users. If the administrator needs to make a change to the profile, she makes the change only once, and it will affects all users who have been assigned that mandatory profile.

A roaming profile is configured as a UNC path in the Profile field of the User dialog box in User Manager.

WARNING

**References to Local Resources Will Not Function on Different Machines** Some configuration changes that are stored in a roaming profile will not produce the functionality a user may want. For example, although the desktop settings that a user configures are stored as part of the user profile, objects like shortcuts may point to files that are locally resident on a specific machine. If that is the case, the shortcut will persist from computer to computer; however, it will work only on a computer in which the application is stored in the same path as the one on which it was created. Other settings, such as password protection on a screen saver, are also stored locally on a machine and, therefore, will not persist from one machine to another even though a user is using a roaming profile.

# Creating a User Profile

Now that you are aware of the different reasons to use mandatory or roaming user profiles with NT Workstation, you must actually implement user profiles.

## STEP BY STEP

### 3.3 Creating a User Profile

1. Log on to Windows NT Workstation with an account that has administrative permissions.
2. Create a test user account.
3. Log off and log on as the test user account. This creates a folder under the Profiles directory for that test user.
4. Configure the desktop environment as you would like it to be for the new mandatory profile.
5. Log off and log back on with the administrative account.
6. Create a centralized location for storing user profiles on a server (for example, enter ***servername*\Profiles*username***), and then share that directory.
7. Go into the Control Panel, double-click the System icon, and select the User Profiles tab.
8. Select the profile for the test user and click on Copy To. Under Copy Profile To, enter the path to the shared profiles directory: ***servername*\Profiles*username*.**
9. Under Permitted to Use, make sure the right user name is selected.
10. Launch User Manager and double-click on the test user's account.
11. Click the Profile button and enter the path to the mandatory profile: ***servername*\Profiles*username*.**

    To make a profile mandatory, rename the file NTUSER.DAT to NTUSER.MAN. The user's profile directory contains this file.

Regardless of whether they are used for convenience for the user or to restrict user actions, user profiles can be helpful in managing the NT Workstation environment.

## Testing a User Profile

To test the creation of a user profile, log on to the Windows NT Workstation as a user who has been assigned a user profile. If you receive the proper settings while logged on as that user, your test is successful. If you do not receive those settings, go back to the Control Panel, choose the System icon, and select the User Profiles tab to determine whether you have set up the user's profile properly. Also, check the properties of that user account within User Manager to make sure you entered the path to the user account properly. Finally, check the actual directory structure on the machine storing the profile to verify that the share point has been set up correctly and that the profile has been copied to the correct folder.

# SETTING UP SHARED FOLDERS AND PERMISSIONS

Set up shared folders and permissions.

To allow remote access of your resources, you must make them available on the network to other users on other computers. Just because you make some resources available on the network does not mean that you have to make all resources available on the network, nor does it mean that you have to make a resource available to everyone. Windows NT enables you to selectively choose which folders you want to allow access to and which you want to remain private to that workstation.

To share a folder in Windows NT means to make that folder available to other users on the network. If you have a resource that you want others to access, you must choose to share that resource. Sharing can only be established at the folder or directory level; it cannot be established at the individual file level. Therefore, if you want to share only one file, you must create a folder and put just that one file into the folder. After you put the file in the folder, you need to share that folder. When a folder is shared, users with rights to that shared folder have access to all the files and subfolders within it.

## Planning Shared Folders

When you're planning to share folders, it is important that you structure your directories appropriately and that you plan for the naming convention that you will use for the share names.

### Location of Resources

When you share a directory, all files and folders below that directory are shared with the same access permissions as the parent directory. Because of this, you need to plan where to locate resources so you can limit access to only the resources you choose to share.

As an example, take a look at Figure 3.9. It shows three application folders (Excel, PowerPoint, and Word) within a SharedApps folder. If you were the administrator of this network, you would have to decide how you wanted to implement sharing of these application folders.

If you want users to have the same access to all three application folders, you can create the share at the SharedApps level. If, however, you want users to have access to certain applications but not others, you have to create the share at the level of each application folder, such as Word or Excel.

The effective permissions can be changed if the files exist on an NTFS partition because you can apply local permissions in addition to the shared permissions. That is discussed in detail in the section "File and Folder Permission Interaction."

### Naming Convention for Shared Folders

When deciding on a naming convention for shared resources, you must consider the type of clients in the environment. If all clients are Windows 95 or Windows NT, using long share names is an option. If your environment contains Windows 3.x clients or DOS clients, however, you must take that into account when determining your naming convention for shared resources. Because Windows 3.x clients and DOS clients cannot view long share names, you must keep the share names to 8.3 characters or fewer.

Also, when creating shared folders, it is a good idea to use share names that are indicative of what is found within that shared

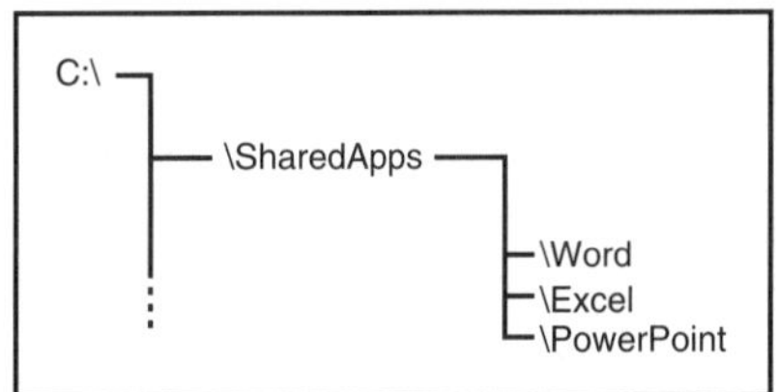


**FIGURE 3.9**
Planning the location of shared resources.

resource. The share name Share01, for example, does not really describe what the resource is.

## Establishing Shared Folder Permissions

Establishing permissions on shared folders gives you some measure of control over what specific users or groups of users can do with the information in the folders. Windows NT provides four levels of permission that you can give to users who will access your shared folder over the network. You can apply these permissions at either the user level or the group level, depending on the needs of your environment. Remember, however, that these permissions apply only to access gained to these resources over the network; they do not apply to users who access the resources by logging in locally to the machine on which the resource is resident.

You can assign the following four levels of permission to a shared folder:

- *No Access.* If a user or group is given the No Access permission to a shared folder, that user or group cannot even open the shared folder even though he can see the shared folder on the network. The No Access permission overrides all other permissions that a user or group might have to the folder.
- *Read.* The Read permission allows the user or group to display files and subfolders within the shared folder. It also allows the user or group to execute programs that might be located within the shared folder.
- *Change.* The Change permission allows the user or group to add files or subfolders to the shared folder and to append or delete information from existing files and subfolders. The Change permission also gives a user or group all rights included within the Read permission.
- *Full Control.* If a user or group is given the Full Control permission, that user or group has the ability to change file permissions, take ownership of files (on an NTFS partition), and perform all tasks allowed by the Change permission.

EXAM TIP

**Use Groups to Assign Access to Resources** Microsoft recommends that you use groups instead of users to assign permissions to resources. Therefore, you should be prepared for exam questions about that. If you're asked about it or presented with related options, always choose the answer that favors groups over users for assignment of resource permissions.

## Enabling Folder Sharing

To share a folder so others can access it on the network, you must have the right to share folders. This right is not given to ordinary users (members of the Users group) in Windows NT Workstation. To share a network resource under Windows NT, you must be a member of one of the following groups:

- Power Users (on Windows NT Workstation)
- Administrators (on Windows NT Workstation or Server)
- Server Operators (on the Windows NT Domain Controller)

If you are not a member of one of those groups, you must be added to one of the groups before you can share resources.

### Sharing a Folder Locally

To share a folder locally—meaning that you are sitting at the workstation that holds the folder you would like to share—right-click on the folder and choose the Sharing option. This brings up the folder's properties dialog box, with the Sharing tab at the front (see Figure 3.10). Step by Step 3.4 contains specific instructions for setting up the share.

## STEP BY STEP

### 3.4 Sharing a Folder Locally

1. On the Sharing tab of the folder's properties dialog box, click on the Shared As radio button.
2. Enter the Share Name you would like to use. (Remember that DOS and Windows 3.x clients cannot access share names longer than 8 characters.)
3. (Optional) Enter a comment to describe this shared resource.

*continues*

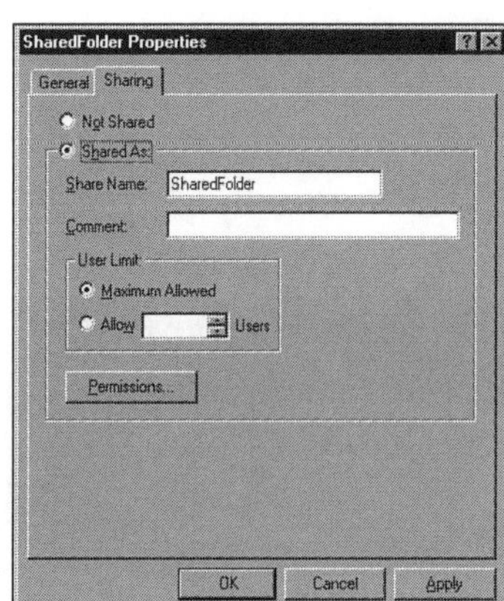


**FIGURE 3.10**
The Sharing tab of a folder within My Computer.

*continued*

4. (Optional) Set a user limit for the number of simultaneous connections. The maximum number of connections NT Workstation will allow is 10, regardless of what you place in this field.

5. Assign permissions to the shared folder by clicking the Permissions button and working through the resulting dialog boxes.

## Sharing a Folder Remotely

To share a folder remotely—meaning that you would like to attach to a remote server or workstation and share its resources with other users on the network—you must use Server Manager, which comes with the Client-Based Network Tools for Windows NT Workstation. Server Manager is a tool you can use to create remote shared directories (see Figure 3.11).

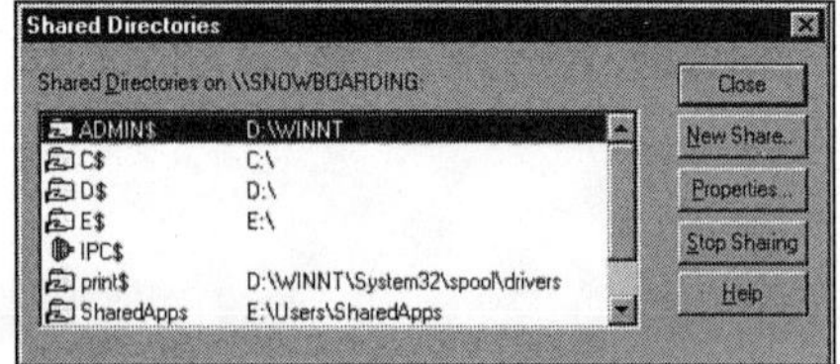


**FIGURE 3.11**
You can create shared directories on a remote machine by using Server Manager.

## STEP BY STEP

### 3.5 Sharing a Folder Using Server Manager

1. Highlight the computer on which you would like to create the shared folder.

2. From the Computer menu, choose Shared Directories.

3. In the Shared Directories dialog box, click the New Share button.

4. Enter the share name that you want to use for this new share.

5. Enter the path to the share as it would be specified according to the remote machine. For example, if you wanted to share the directory C:\Info, that is what you would type. Because there is no Browse button available, you must know the path for the folder you want to share.

6. (Optional) Enter a comment to describe the shared resource.
7. (Optional) Set a user limit for the shared resource. If the resource is on a Windows NT Workstation, the maximum number of inbound connections is 10. If the resource is on a Windows NT Server, the number of inbound connections is unlimited.
8. Click the Permissions button and work through the resulting dialog boxes to set permissions for the shared resource.
9. Click OK to create the shared resource.

## Setting Permissions on a Shared Folder

To set permissions on a shared folder, highlight the folder and right-click on it. From the context menu, choose Sharing. In the folder's properties dialog box, select the Sharing tab and click on the Permissions button. This button is available only if the folder is being shared. By default in Windows NT, the share permissions are set to give the Everyone group Full Control (see Figure 3.12).

These default share permissions should be changed if there is a need for security because the group Everyone includes everyone who has network access to your computer, whether they are from your workgroup, domain, or even from another network operating system. To change the default permissions, click Add. By default just groups are shown. To grant access to a specific user account, click the Show Users button. After you have selected the appropriate user or group, open the Type of Access field and select the access you want to assign to that user or group. After you have granted permissions to the necessary users or groups to make the share more secure, you should remove the Full Control permission from the Everyone group.

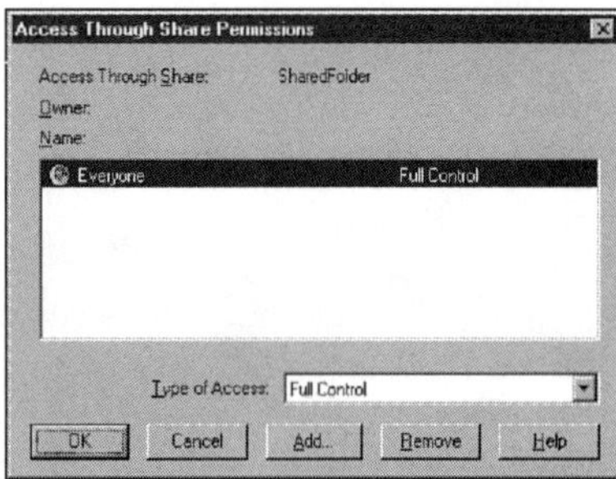


**FIGURE 3.12**
The default permissions on a shared folder give Everyone Full Control.

WARNING

**Be Sure to Share with Someone** Before you remove the permission for Everyone Full Control, be sure to give another user or group access to the shared directory. Otherwise, you might have a shared directory to which no one has been granted access.

# Managing Shared Folders

After you have created your shared folders, you probably will need to manage them at a later point. Managing folders includes creating a new share from an existing share, stopping sharing on a folder, modifying permissions on a shared folder, and modifying the share name after a folder has been shared.

## Creating a New Share

As part of managing shared folders, you might need to create an additional new share name for a directory that has already been shared. The steps for creating an additional share are slightly different than those for creating the shared directory in the beginning; it's important that you understand those differences both for their real-life value for implementation and for the exam. When you configure a new share for an existing shared directory, a New Share button appears in the folder's properties dialog box (see Figure 3.13).

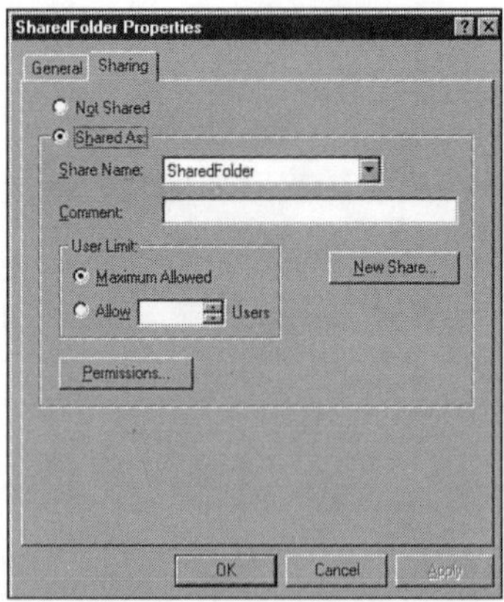


**FIGURE 3.13**
Creating a new share from an existing shared directory.

**STEP BY STEP**

**3.6 Creating an Additional Share on a Shared Directory**

1. Right-click on the existing shared folder and choose the Sharing option.
2. Click the New Share button. (Notice that you cannot change the existing share name in this dialog box.)
3. In the dialog box that appears, enter the new share name and any comments regarding the share, and then set the permissions for the new shared directory.
4. Click OK to close the New Share dialog box. Click OK again to close the folder's properties dialog box and create the new share.

Many factors may prompt you to reshare an existing shared directory. Perhaps you want to assign the permissions differently to the two directories, or maybe you need to add another reference to the share for the use of other departments.

## Stopping Sharing

After a directory has been shared, it may be necessary to stop sharing that directory. Maybe the information in the directory is not up-to-date or is no longer needed by users in your company. Or maybe you've decided that there is no longer a need to share that information. Whatever the reason, it is possible to stop sharing a directory after it has already been shared.

**STEP BY STEP**

### 3.7 Discontinuing Sharing

1. Right-click on the directory that you would like to stop sharing and choose Sharing from the context menu.
2. Click the Not Shared radio button.
3. Click OK to stop sharing the directory.

## Modifying Permissions on a Shared Directory

After you have set up your shared directories, you may need to change the directory permissions at a later time. Maybe you have created another local group that needs permissions to the resource, or maybe the resource needs in your environment have changed, or maybe you want to be more selective now as to who has access to this resource.

NOTE

**Stop the Server Service to Prevent All Access** One way to prevent any access to your Windows NT Workstation is to stop the Server service through the Control Panel's Services application. Although this also stops the Computer Browser service, it still is the most effective way of preventing access to your workstation.

## STEP BY STEP

### 3.8 Modifying Shared Directory Permissions

1. Log on with an account that has the right to change shared directory permissions (reserved for members of the Administrators or Power Users group).
2. Right-click on the shared directory and choose Sharing from the context menu.
3. On the Sharing tab, click the Permissions button.
4. Add or remove groups as needed from the list of users and groups with permissions.

## Shared Folders and Resource Maintenance

Sharing is not a transferable property. Certain file and folder maintenance tasks automatically remove sharing from a resource. For example, if you move a folder from one location to another or if you change its name, sharing is removed. You are warned of this when you perform either of these tasks, and you are given a chance to change your mind if that result is not desired. If you do move or rename a folder, however, you can simply share that folder again from its new location or by using its new name. In fact, there is no reason in either case why you could not simply share the folder by using the same share name it previously had.

Copying a folder does not transfer the sharing, either. Although the original folder will not have its sharing removed, the new copy will not be shared, and you will have to share it once the copy procedure is complete. Of course, the share name still has to be unique on the computer. So if you copy the folder to another place on the same computer, when you set up sharing, you'll have to give this folder a share name different from that of the original shared folder.

## How Shared Folder Permissions Apply

When you're setting up permissions on shared folders, it is important that you understand how those permissions will apply or be implemented in your environment. Before you set up shared folder permissions, you need to know how user and group permissions will interact, as well as how the No Access permission can override any other permission set for that user or group.

### User and Group Permission Interaction

You can grant shared folder permissions to both users and groups. Because of this, once in a while a user might be given access to a shared resource both as an individual user and as a member of a group. Similarly, a user might be a member of more than one group that has been given access to the resource. In those cases, you need to understand how user and group permissions for shared folders interact.

To see how permissions interact, consider the access permissions outlined in the following table:

| *Account* | *Permission* |
|---|---|
| JohnM | Read |
| Conservatives | Change |
| Politicians | Full Control |

For this example, suppose the user named JohnM is a member of both the Conservatives and the Politicians groups. JohnM is given Read permission, Conservatives are given Change permission, and Politicians are given Full Control. Because JohnM is a member of both groups, his effective permission is Full Control—the cumulative permission of all the groups to which he belongs. Whenever user and group permissions for a shared folder are combined, the effective permission is always the cumulative, or least restrictive, permission except in the case of No Access.

## Using the No Access Permission on a Shared Folder

The No Access permission is unique in that it overrides all other permissions granted for a user or group. If No Access is listed in a user's permissions, it overrides all other permissions. For example, consider the permissions outlined here:

| *Account* | *Permission* |
|---|---|
| JohnM | Full Control |
| Conservatives | Change |
| Politicians | No Access |

In this example, suppose JohnM is a member of both the Conservatives and the Politicians groups. Even though JohnM's account has been given Full Control, the Politicians group has been assigned the No Access permission. Because JohnM is a Politician, his effective permission is No Access. If JohnM needs to access the folder, either he must be removed from the Politicians group, or the permission for the Politicians group must be changed. Alternatively, one other way to give JohnM access yet still restrict access for the Politicians group is to set the permissions as listed here:

| *Account* | *Permission* |
|---|---|
| JohnM | Full Control |
| Conservatives | Change |
| Politicians | |

Here, the effective permissions for JohnM are Full Control. Although Politicians have not been granted the No Access permission, they have not been specified in the list of permissions. Therefore, users who are members of the Politicians group still do not have access to the shared folder, but JohnM's effective permissions are Full Control.

NOTE

**Access Is Assigned at User Login**
During the user login process, a user is given an access token that defines his group membership and access rights. As a result, any changes you make to a user's or group's permissions will take effect only after a user logs off and logs back in.

## Shared Folders Within Shared Folders

It is possible to share a folder that is located within another shared folder. If you do this, however, you must be very careful because it might allow users to gain access to a resource through an unintended "back door."

Like a house with only a single door, you can prevent an undesired person from entering the kitchen by simply restricting access through the front door. Obviously, if that person cannot get into the house, he cannot get to the kitchen. However, if a back door also exists on the house, locking and barring the front door to a person does no good if the back door is left wide open. This theory works the same for shared folders that are located in other shared folders.

When you assign access to a resource by sharing a folder, you also are sharing all the folders within the tree structure that the share point represents. In other words, when you grant a permission to a shared folder, you also grant the same permission to everything else in the tree. Thus, Read access to a share means Read access to everything inside the share's tree. However, if you also share a folder in the shared tree, you are providing another access point to the resource.

Because you get access to the resources inside a tree at the level of access from which you entered, if you enter a tree at a point of low access, you get low access. However, if you enter at a point of high access, you get high access. Users see each share point on the network as a unique access point to resources; they do not see the tree structure in which the shares are located. Therefore, you should be very careful when sharing a folder located inside a folder that is already shared.

## Setting Permissions on NTFS Partitions, Folders, and Files

Set permissions on NTFS partitions, folders, and files.

One of the benefits of using the NTFS file system on a Windows NT Workstation is the added security that NTFS provides. NTFS permissions enable you to get beyond the security limitations of shared folder permissions (that are effective only when a user accesses the directory from across the network) and implement local security on both the folder and the file level.

Shared folder permissions can be assigned only at the folder level and even then, only over the network. NTFS permissions can be applied to individual files as well as shares, and they apply to any access method, whether it is local or over the network. NTFS permissions are applicable only on NTFS partitions; they are not applicable on FAT partitions.

## Planning NTFS Folder and File Permissions

Before you implement NTFS permissions, you must have a good understanding of what NTFS permissions are and how they will affect the resource permissions you assign. When a partition is formatted with NTFS, all files and folders on that partition automatically have their permissions set to allow Everyone Full Control. It is important to understand these default NTFS permissions, especially if you are concerned about implementing security in your Windows NT environment. You might want to remove this Everyone Full Control permission. Be careful how you do that, however. If you remove the Everyone Full Control permission but don't add any other groups and give them NTFS permissions, no one will be able to access that data except Administators who must take ownership of the file to change the access permissions.

When you're assigning NTFS permissions, it is usually a good idea to assign Full Control to the Administrators group. If you choose to remove the Everyone Full Control permission, but you still want validated users to be able to access the files and folders on an NTFS partition, replace Everyone Full Control with Users Full Control. The permissions you choose to assign depend on what resource you are trying to protect. For application folders, for example, you may not want users to have Full Control to add or delete anything to or from that folder.

### NTFS Permissions

You can assign NTFS permissions to files or folders. Table 3.3 lists the NTFS permissions and describes what each one allows a user to do.

TABLE 3.3

**STANDARD NTFS PERMISSIONS**

| *Permission* | *Folder* | *File* |
|---|---|---|
| Read (R) | Enables the user to display the folder and subfolders, attributes, and permissions | Enables the user to display the file, its attributes, and its permissions |
| Write (W) | Enables the user to add files or folders, change attributes for the folder, and display permissions | Enables the user to change file attributes and add or append data to the file |
| Execute (X) | Enables the user to make changes to subfolders, display permissions, and display attributes | Enables the user to run a file if it is an executable and display attributes and permissions |
| Delete (D) | Enables the user to remove the folder | Enables the user to remove the file |
| Change Permission (P) | Enables the user to modify folder permissions | Enables the user to modify file permissions |
| Take Ownership (O) | Enables the user to take ownership of the folder | Enables the user to take ownership of a file |

These NTFS permissions are combined into standard groupings of NTFS permissions at both the file and the folder level.

## NTFS File Permissions

NTFS file permissions are a combination of the various NTFS permissions. You can set NTFS file permissions on a per-file basis, and they override NTFS folder permissions if there is a conflict. Table 3.4 shows the standard NTFS file permissions.

TABLE 3.4

**STANDARD NTFS FILE PERMISSIONS**

| *Standard File Permission* | *Individual NTFS Permissions* |
|---|---|
| No Access | (None) |
| Read | (RX) |
| Change | (RWXD) |
| Full Control | (All Permissions) |

These standard NTFS file permissions are combinations of the individual NTFS permissions.

## NTFS Folder Permissions

NTFS folder permissions are also combined into a standard set of permissions. Table 3.5 shows the NTFS folder permissions. In a list of NTFS folder permissions, the permissions are typically followed by two sets of parentheses. The first set represents the standard permissions on the folder itself. The second set represents the permissions inherited by any file created within that folder.

**TABLE 3.5**

**STANDARD NTFS FOLDER PERMISSIONS**

| *Standard Folder Permissions* | *Individual NTFS Folder Permissions* | *Individual NTFS File Permissions* |
|---|---|---|
| No Access | (None) | (None) |
| Read | (RX) | (RX) |
| Change | (RWXD) | (RWXD) |
| Add | (WX) | (Not Applicable) |
| Add & Read | (RWX) | (RX) |
| List | (RX) | (Not Applicable) |
| Full Control | (All) | (All) |

When "Not Applicable" appears under the file permissions, that particular permission does not apply at a file level, only at a folder level. The List permission, for example, allows you to display a folder's contents—all the files within the folder. Obviously, that permission would not make sense at a file level.

# Setting NTFS Permissions

The default NTFS permission assigned when a partition is created is Everyone Full Control. Thus to be able to use NTFS permissions, you must choose to set them on either a file or a folder level. NTFS permissions can enhance shared folder permissions that you may have already implemented on your Windows NT Workstation. You set NTFS permissions by clicking the Permissions button on the

Security tab of a file's or a folder's Properties dialog box. Figure 3.14 shows the screen in which you set NTFS permissions for a directory.

Keep in mind that to set NTFS permissions you must have the right to do so.

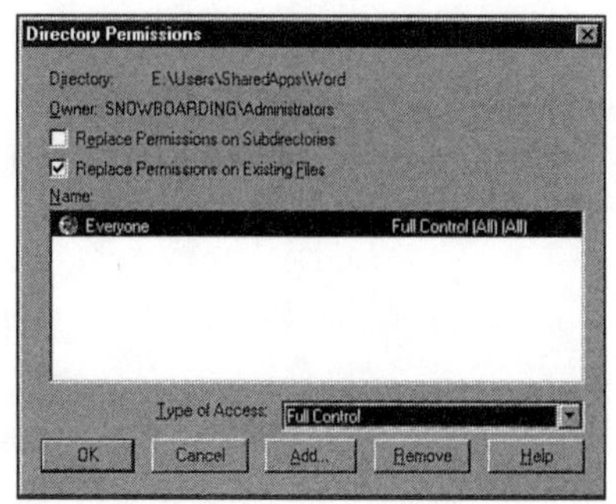


**FIGURE 3.14**
Setting NTFS permissions.

## Requirements for Assigning NTFS Permissions

Not just any user on Windows NT can assign NTFS permissions. To assign NTFS permissions, either you must be a part of a group that has been given that right, or your user account must be given that right. By default, the group Everyone is assigned Full Control when an NTFS partition is created. If that default permission is left, part of the Full Control permission includes the right to Change Permissions (P):

Suppose, however, that the default permission of Everyone Full Control is changed. To assign NTFS permissions, you must meet one of the following criteria:

- *You must be the owner of the file or folder.* You must be the user who created it.
- *You must have been granted Full Control.* This includes the ability to Change Permissions (P).
- *You must have been given special access to Change Permissions (P).* A user can be given just this one permission to a file or folder.
- *You must have been given special access to Take Ownership (O).* With the ability to Take Ownership, a user can give himself the right to Change Permissions (P). (For a description of Taking Ownership, see the section "Taking Ownership of Files or Folders," later in this chapter.)

In order for NTFS permissions to be used effectively, users must be educated about the various NTFS permissions. In addition, they must know how NTFS permissions apply—at both the file and folder levels—and how they enhance shared folder permissions.

## How NTFS Permissions Apply

Because NTFS permissions can be implemented at both a file level and a folder level, you must have an understanding of how these two levels interact. In addition to the standard NTFS permissions, you can also use other combinations of NTFS permissions in certain scenarios.

### File and Folder Permission Interaction

If a file is created within a folder for which NTFS permissions have been set, by default the file inherits the permissions of the folder in which it is created. It is possible, though, to assign permissions to a file that contradict the permissions of the folder in which it is created. Assume, for example, that you're creating an environment like the one outlined here:

| *Resource* | *User or Group Account* | *Permission* |
|---|---|---|
| Folder: Test | Everyone | Full Control |
| File: Top Secret | MyAccount | Full Control |

You create a folder called Test on an NTFS partition. The default permissions for the Test folder are Everyone Full Control. You decide to leave those default permissions. After creating the folder, you decide to create within it a Word document called Top Secret. That file contains information you do not want anyone else to see, so you decide to remove Everyone Full Control from the file permissions and add Full Control for only your own user account. Because no other user account is specified, no one else has access to that file—or do they?

The folder permission is Everyone Full Control. What do you think the effective file permissions are? If another user wants to read what is in Top Secret, will she be able to?

Remember that file permissions always override folder permissions. So in this case, only the account MyAccount has Full Control to that file and can access it. All other users are denied access. Even though Everyone has Full Control at the folder level, because there is only one account specified at the file level, that effectively excludes all other accounts.

## User and Group Permission Interaction

With NTFS permissions, as with shared folder permissions, user and group permissions interact so that the cumulative permission is the effective permission. NTFS permissions can be granted to both users and groups. Because of this, a user might be given access to a resource through individual NTFS permissions and group NTFS permissions that differ. Similarly, a user might be a member of multiple groups that have been given different NTFS permissions to a resource. In such cases, you need to understand how user and group permissions interact in NTFS permissions. To see how this works, study the following example, which uses the same user account and groups from the discussion on shared folder permissions.

| *Account* | *File Permission* |
|---|---|
| JohnM | Read |
| Conservatives | Change |
| Politicians | Full Control |

In this example, JohnM is a member of both the Conservatives and Politicians groups. For this particular file, the NTFS permissions are set so that JohnM is given Read permission, Conservatives are given Change permission, and Politicians are given Full Control to the file. Because JohnM is a member of both groups, his effective NTFS permission is Full Control—the cumulative permission of all the groups to which he belongs.

Whenever user and group NTFS permissions are combined, the effective permission is always the cumulative, or least restrictive, permission except in the case of the No Access permission.

## Using Special Access Permissions

The Special Access permission combines the individual NTFS permissions but is not one of the standard NTFS permissions. Typically, you will assign the standard permissions to files or folders. But in certain situations, you may want to implement a customized version of the individual NTFS permissions. If you need to assign individual permissions, you can assign Special Access permissions. The Special Access permissions are the same for both files and folders. To customize permissions, you choose the permissions you want from a list of the individual NTFS permissions (see Figure 3.15).

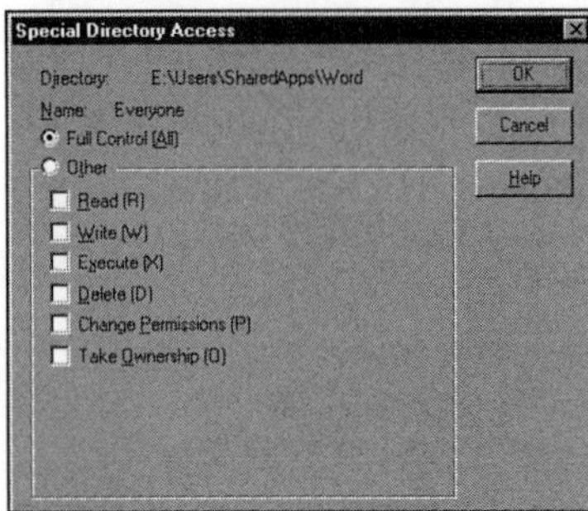


**FIGURE 3.15**
Assigning Special Access permissions.

## STEP BY STEP

### 3.9 Assigning Special Access Permissions to a File or a Folder

1. Right-click on the file or folder and select Properties from the context menu.
2. Click the Security tab and then the Permissions button.
3. From the Type of Access drop-down list, select Special File or Folder Access.
4. In the Special Directory Access dialog box, select the Other radio button and then check each individual NTFS permission that you would like to use.

Special directory access can be used in any situation that requires customization of the NTFS permissions assigned to a resource.

## Taking Ownership of Files or Folders

The ability to take ownership of files or folders is an NTFS permission that can be assigned through special directory or file permissions. Whoever creates a file or a folder is the owner of that file or folder. As the owner, that individual has Full Control to that file or folder. This includes the ability to assign permissions to it, to access it, and to allow others to access it through sharing.

Suppose the user who owns a file or a number of files leaves the company. You or the user's replacement may need to access those files. If the user restricted access to those files so that only he had permissions to them, you must take ownership of the user's files. In order for you to take ownership, however, you must have been given that right through the NTFS permissions. If the user removed everyone but himself from the list of permissions on the resource, only an administrator can take ownership of the files. Administrators can always take ownership, even if they have been given No Access to the file or folder.

There is no way to give ownership to another user or group; even the owner can only give the permission to take ownership. Because of this, if an administrator takes ownership of a user's files, that administrator will remain the owner. The administrator cannot give ownership back to the user to try to "cover up" the fact that he took ownership of the files. This prevents any user or administrator from altering or creating files or folders and then making it look like those files or folders belong to another user.

To give someone the right to take ownership, the owner or administrator must grant that person either Full Control, Take Ownership special permission or Change Permission special permission. Then the owner or administrator must change the resource permissions so that the other person can take ownership.

## Using the No Access Permission for NTFS Permissions

When the No Access permission is set, it overrides all other permissions. Even if the user himself is given Full Control but a group to which he belongs is given No Access, his effective permission is No Access.

As in shared folder permissions, in NTFS permissions, the No Access permission is unique in that it can override all other permissions granted for a user or group if it exists in the list of permissions for that user or group. If No Access is listed in the NTFS permissions, it overrides all other permissions. To see this firsthand, consider how the permissions assigned in the following example would interact.

| *Account* | *File Permission* |
|---|---|
| JohnM | Full Control |
| Conservatives | Change |
| Politicians | No Access |

In this example, JohnM is a member of the Conservatives and the Politicians groups. Even though JohnM's account has been given Full Control to the file, the Politicians group has been assigned the No Access NTFS permission. Because JohnM is a Politician, his effective NTFS permission is No Access. If JohnM needs to access the file, either he must be removed from the Politicians group or the NTFS permission for the Politicians group must be changed. Alternatively, one other way to give JohnM access yet still restrict access for the Politicians group is to set the NTFS file permissions as shown here:

| *Account* | *File Permission* |
|---|---|
| JohnM | Full Control |
| Conservatives | Change |
| Politicians | |

Here, the effective NTFS permissions for JohnM are Full Control. Although Politicians have not been granted the No Access permission, they have not been specified in the list of NTFS permissions. Therefore, users who are members of the Politicians group still do not have access to the file, but JohnM's effective NTFS permissions are Full Control.

## File Delete Child

File Delete Child refers to a specific scenario relating to NTFS permissions under Windows NT. If a user has been given the NTFS No Access permission to a particular file but has been given Full Control to the directory that contains the file, the user can actually delete the file even though he doesn't even have the ability to read it. This is true only if the user actually tries to delete the file, not if he attempts to move it to the Recycle Bin. This situation is called File Delete Child, and it is a part of Windows NT because of requirements for POSIX compliance.

Because the File Delete Child feature can allow a user to breach security, Windows NT offers a way to prevent the possibility of such an act.

## STEP BY STEP

### 3.10 Removing File Delete Child Loophole

1. Access the properties for the directory that contains the file.
2. Instead of selecting Full Control as the directory permission, select Custom.

3. In the list of custom options, put a check in each check box. This is the same as granting Full Control, except that it bypasses the File Delete Child problem.

4. Make sure the file permissions are still set to No Access for that user.

## NTFS Permissions and Resource Maintenance

NTFS permissions are transferable properties, at least under certain circumstances. In the ongoing maintenance of files and folders, you might need to perform any of these three tasks on a file or a folder:

- Rename the file or folder
- Copy the file or folder
- Move the file or folder

Let's look at the effect of each task separately.

The renaming of a resource has no effect on its NTFS permissions. The resource (file or folder) has the same permissions after it has been renamed that it had before.

When you copy a file or folder from one location to another, the file or folder always inherits the properties of the object into which the file or folder is copied. For example, if a file that has permissions giving Joe Full Control is copied into a folder where Everyone has Full Control, the result is that for the new copy of the file, Everyone has Full Control (the permissions on the original file, however, remain unchanged).

When you move a file or folder from one location to another, the result depends on the location of the destination. If the destination location is on the same partition that the file or folder was originally, the file or folder retains its original permissions. This means that if Joe has Full Control of a file that is moved to a folder on the same partition that Joe has Change access to, Joe continues to have Full Control of his file. If, however, the destination for the moved file or folder is another partition, the file or folder inherits the permissions of the destination location, just like in a copy. That is because when a file or folder is moved from one partition to another, what really happens is that the file or folder is copied to the new location, and then it is deleted from its original location.

## Combining Shared Folder and NTFS Permissions

When combining shared folder permissions with NTFS permissions, you must understand when each of these permissions is effective. Shared folder permissions apply only to those users accessing the directory from across the network. Shared folder permissions do not apply to the user sitting interactively on the machine. NTFS permissions, on the other hand, apply to both the user sitting locally at the machine and the user accessing the computer from across the network.

When shared folder permissions and NTFS permissions are combined, the most restrictive permission is the effective permission. To see how this works firsthand, examine the permissions described in the following example:

| *Account* | *Shared Folder Permission* | *NTFS Permission* |
|---|---|---|
| JohnM | Full Control | Read |
| Conservatives | Read | Change |
| Politicians | Change | Read |

In this example, JohnM is a member of two groups: Conservatives and Politicians. Two sets of permissions have been assigned to each of those groups. To determine a user's effective permissions, you must first determine the effective shared folder permissions, and then determine the effective NTFS permissions, and then compare the two.

In this example, JohnM's effective shared folder permissions would be Full Control because the cumulative permission is the effective permission. In the case of the NTFS permissions, JohnM's effective permission would be Change because it is the cumulative of the NTFS permissions. Knowing that, consider these questions:

- *What would JohnM's effective permissions be if he were sitting locally at the Windows NT Workstation?* (Hint: Do shared folder permissions apply if the user is sitting locally at the workstation?)

  JohnM's effective permissions if he were sitting locally at the workstation would be Change because only NTFS permissions apply locally.

- *What would JohnM's effective permissions be if he were accessing this resource from across the network?*

  JohnM's effective permissions if he were accessing this resource from across the network would be Change. To determine this, you must combine the shared folder permissions and the NTFS permissions and take the *most restrictive* permission.

The following scenario provides another example of combining shared folder permissions and NTFS permissions.

| ***Account*** | ***Shared Folder Permission*** | ***NTFS Permission*** |
|---|---|---|
| JohnM | Full Control | Full Control |
| Conservatives | No Access | Change |
| Politicians | Change | Read |

Again, JohnM is a member of both the Conservatives and the Politicians groups and is given Full Control at the share level. This time, however, the Conservatives group has been given No Access at the share level. Given those facts, consider the following questions:

- *What would JohnM's effective permissions be if he were accessing this resource from across the network?*

  For shared folder permissions, the effective permission is the cumulative permission, except in the case of No Access. Thus, even though JohnM has Full Control, he effectively has No Access because No Access is in the list of permissions for the resource.

- *What would JohnM's local permissions be if he were sitting at the workstation instead of accessing it from across the network?*

  For the NTFS permissions, JohnM's cumulative permission is Full Control. Share permissions do not apply when a user is

WARNING

**Shared Folders Are the Only Security for FAT** Shared folder permissions are the only security that you can implement on a FAT partition.

sitting locally at the workstation. Thus, if JohnM were sitting locally at the machine, he would have Full Control of the resource. If he were accessing it from across the network, however, he would have No Access.

Understanding the interaction between shared folder permissions and NTFS permissions is critical to understanding how to manage the security of resources in your Windows NT environment. First, you must understand how user and group permissions apply in terms of shared folder permissions. Second, you must understand how user and group permissions apply for NTFS permissions, as well as how NTFS file and folder permissions interact. Finally, you must understand how shared folder and NTFS permissions interact, which depends on how the user is accessing the resource.

Keep the following rules in mind to help you understand permissions:

- When user and group permissions for shared folders are combined, the effective permission is the cumulative permission.
- When user and group permissions for NTFS security are combined, the effective permission is the cumulative permission.
- When shared folder permissions and NTFS permissions are combined, the most restrictive permission is always the effective permission.
- With NTFS permissions, file permissions override folder permissions.
- Using NTFS permissions is the only way to provide local security.
- Shared folder permissions are the only way to provide security on a FAT partition and are effective only when the folder is accessed from across the network.

---

### MANAGING INTERACTION BETWEEN NTFS AND SHARED PERMISSIONS

Using a combination of NTFS and shared permissions is a very effective way of providing access to resources over the network as well as providing security against unwanted access. In order for someone to access a resource over the network, that resource must first be shared. The main issues to consider are how to manage the interaction between NTFS and shared permissions, and how to ensure that access remains the same locally as it does over the network.

The easiest method of doing this entails three steps. First, make sure that all shared resources (or as many as is practical) are located on NTFS partitions. Second, share the resources you want to allow access to and leave the share permission at Everyone, Full Control. Third, assign access to all resources using NTFS permissions.

How does this method ensure ease of management as well as security of resources? First of all, it eliminates the possibility of conflict between shared permissions and NTFS permissions: Because the shared permission allows everyone to have access to everything, the only permissions that have any weight are the NTFS permissions. Second, NTFS permissions apply the same whether a user is sitting locally at a machine or accessing it over the network. Therefore, if you assign NTFS permissions of Read to Bob, you do not have to worry about whether Bob logs in locally at the computer or accesses it from over the network; in either case, Bob has only Read access.

# INSTALLING AND CONFIGURING PRINTERS IN A GIVEN ENVIRONMENT

Install and configure printers in a given environment.

"Why can't I print to that printer?" "Why is the print job garbled?" "What do I need to do to print?" How do I set print permissions?" "How do I configure printing in my environment?"

Printing questions tend to be among the more frequent troubleshooting questions asked regarding a network environment. To effectively manage and install printers in your Windows NT environment, you must know the answers to these questions and understand the related concepts.

## Printing Vocabulary

Before you can discuss printing under Windows NT, you must know the "language" of printing. You must understand the definitions of at least a few terms for a discussion of printing to be meaningful:

- *Printer.* A printer is the software component for printing. Also referred to as a *logical printer*, it is the software interface between the application and the print device.
- *Print device.* This term refers to the actual hardware that the paper comes out of. This is what most people traditionally think of as a printer. In Windows NT terminology, however, it is called a print device.
- *Print job.* The print job refers to the information that is sent to the print device. It contains both the data and the commands for print processing.
- *Print spooler.* The print spooler is a collection of DLLs (Dynamic Link Libraries) that accept, process, schedule, and distribute print jobs.
- *Creating a printer.* Creating a printer refers to the act of defining a printer from your Windows NT Workstation. When you create a printer, you are actually specifying that the machine on which you are creating it will be the print server for that print device. Creating a printer is necessary when no other Windows NT system has created the printer, or when the print device is on a non–Windows NT operating system (such as Windows 95).
- *Connecting to a printer.* Connecting to a printer is necessary when the print device has already been defined by another Windows NT system and a printer has been created on that Windows NT system. If that is the case, to use the created printer from your Windows NT Workstation, you need to connect to the printer.
- *Print server.* The print server is the computer that has created the printer on which the printer is defined. Typically, this is a Windows NT Server; however, a Windows NT Workstation or even a Windows 95 system can act as a print server.

- *Print queue.* The print queue refers to the list of print jobs waiting to print on the print server.
- *Printer driver.* The printer driver is the software that enables applications to communicate properly with the print device.
- *Spooling.* The process of storing documents on the hard disk and then sending them to the printer. After the document is stored on the hard disk, the user regains control of the application.

These terms are all essential to the understanding of how to install and configure printing in a Windows NT environment so that it works effectively.

EXAM TIP

**Know the Printer Terminology**
The terminology listed here frequently comes up on the Workstation exam, especially in scenarios that use the term "printer." It is very important that you remember that a printer is a piece of software and not a physical device. You do not put paper into a printer; you put paper into a print device. You must be prepared for the proper use of these terms. Simply knowing the concept is not enough if you do not have the terminology to describe it correctly.

## Installing a Printer

The first step toward implementing effective printing in your Windows NT environment is to install a printer. Before you install a printer, you should check the Windows NT Hardware Compatibility List (HCL) to make sure that your print device is on it. If Windows NT does not have a printer driver for the print device, you must get a Windows NT 4.0–compatible printer driver for that device. To install a printer, you must also be logged on with an account that has the right to install or create a printer. In Windows NT Workstation, the Administrators and Power Users groups have that right.

To install a printer in Windows NT 4.0, you use the Add Printer Wizard. The Add Printer Wizard gives you the option of installing the printer to either My Computer or a network print server.

EXAM TIP

**Don't Be Fooled by Questions About Print Manager** Print Manager is no longer used in Windows NT 4.0; the Add Printer Wizard took its place. Be on the lookout for exam questions that refer to configuring or adding printers by using Print Manager.

### My Computer (Creating a Printer)

If you want to install a printer locally (when the print device is connected to LPT1, for instance), you use the My Computer option. You also use this option to install a network printer (one that your computer accesses indirectly across the network) if that network printer is to be managed by your computer. Choosing My Computer designates the machine that the printer is being installed on as the print server.

> **WARNING**
>
> **NT Workstation Limits Inbound Network Connections** If you are using Windows NT Workstation as a print server, remember that Windows NT Workstation accepts only 10 simultaneous inbound network connections. If you must support more users than that, you will have to designate a Windows NT Server as the print server.

To install a printer, choose the My Computer option in the Add Printer Wizard screen shown in Figure 3.16.

## STEP BY STEP

### 3.11 Installing a Printer Using My Computer

1. Log on to Windows NT with an account that has the right to install a printer.
2. Open the Start menu, choose Settings, and select Printers.
3. Double-click the Add Printer icon, and the Add Printer Wizard starts.
4. Select the My Computer radio button to install the printer.
5. You must specify which port should be used to access the print device. If the print device is local to the machine, select the local LPT port. If the print device is a network print device, select the appropriate port for connecting to the print device. (For more information on printer ports, see the section "Configuring Printer Ports," later in this chapter.)
6. Select the appropriate printer driver. If the right driver for your print device is not on the list, click the Have Disk button and install the correct driver from a floppy or other location.
7. In the next dialog box, you can enter a name for the printer. This is called a friendly name, and it is for your own use. This name combined with the print server name cannot be more than 31 characters.
8. Indicate whether you want this to be the default printer for Windows-based applications.
9. If you would like to share this printer on the network, select the Shared radio button and select additional operating systems to which you want to make the printer available. (For more information on sharing a printer, see the section "Sharing a Printer," later in this chapter.)

**FIGURE 3.16**
Installing a printer using the My Computer option.

10. The final question of the Add Printer Wizard is whether you would like to print a test page. You should do so because printing a test page enables you to determine whether the printer has been installed properly and the print device is functioning.

If you have a print device locally attached to your Windows NT Workstation or you are setting up the initial definition of a network print device, you will use the My Computer (Creating a Computer) option in the Add Printer Wizard.

## Network Printer Server (Connecting to a Printer)

If a printer has already been defined and you just need to send a print job to it from your Windows NT Workstation, you can use the Network Printer Server option to install that network printer. You would use that option when the print device is being managed by another Windows NT 4.0 system. Figure 3.17 shows the Add Printer Wizard with the Network Printer Server option selected.

If a print device is being managed by a non–Windows NT 4.0 computer (server or workstation), you must create the printer on your own system by using the My Computer option.

## STEP BY STEP

### 3.12 Connecting to an Installed Printer

1. Log on to Windows NT with an account that has the right to install a printer.
2. Open the Start menu, choose Settings, and select Printers.
3. Double-click the Add Printer icon, and the Add Printer Wizard starts.
4. Select the Network Printer Server radio button to install the printer.

*continues*

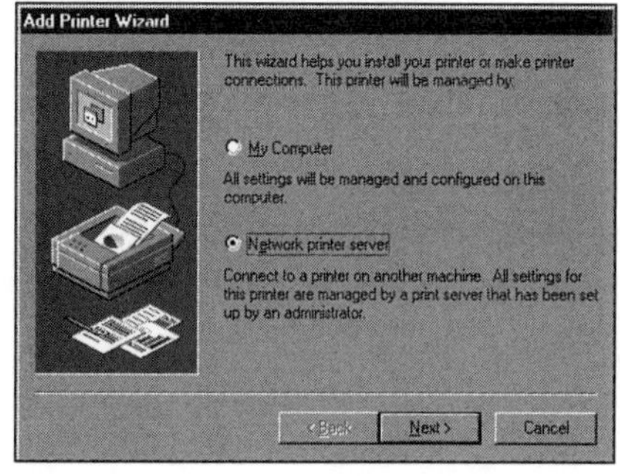


**FIGURE 3.17**
Using the Network Printer Server option to install a printer.

*continued*

5. From the list of available print servers, select the one that has the printer you would like to install. You can do so either by double-clicking on that print server or by typing the full path (as in **\\printserver\printer**) in the Printer field.
6. Indicate whether you want this to be the default printer for all Windows-based applications.
7. Click Finish to set up the printer.

To install a printer that has already been defined and is being managed by another print server, you choose the Network Printer Server option in the Add Printer Wizard to have the driver downloaded to your local machine.

## Configuring a Printer

Configuring a printer refers to the management of the printer after it has been installed. Configuring a printer includes performing the following tasks:

- Configuring printer ports
- Sharing a printer
- Setting printer permissions
- Scheduling when a printer is available
- Modifying the spool settings
- Setting the print priority

Configuring a printer is essential to being able to administer printing effectively.

### Configuring Printer Ports

When you install a printer using the My Computer option on your Windows NT Workstation, you have the option to set a printer port. This might be a local LPT port (if the print device is local to your machine) or an additional port (if it is a network print device that you will manage from your machine).

If you are creating a printer for a network print device, you must use a port that is compatible with that particular device. If you will be creating a printer for an HP Jet Direct print device using DLC, for example, you first need to install the DLC protocol on the machine acting as the print server. Then you go to the Ports tab of the printer's properties dialog box to configure a port for the HP Jet Direct print device.

## Configuring a Printer Pool

If the throughput that a single print device provides to a group of users is not sufficient for their needs, you might choose to set up a *printer pool*: a port that controls many print devices instead of just one. You configure a printer pool from the Ports tab of the printer's properties dialog box (see Figure 3.18).

When using a printer pool, each user prints to a single printer, which then prints to whichever print device is currently unused or has the fewest print jobs pending. In order to take advantage of such a configuration, you must ensure the following:

- *The print devices are all the same or, at the very least, can all be configured to use the same driver.* If the print devices do not use the same driver, some of the printouts will come out garbled because the driver is assigned to the printer, not to the print device.
- *The print devices are in close proximity to one another.* Because the users do not know which print device their printout is being sent to, they need to be able to go to a single place to find it.

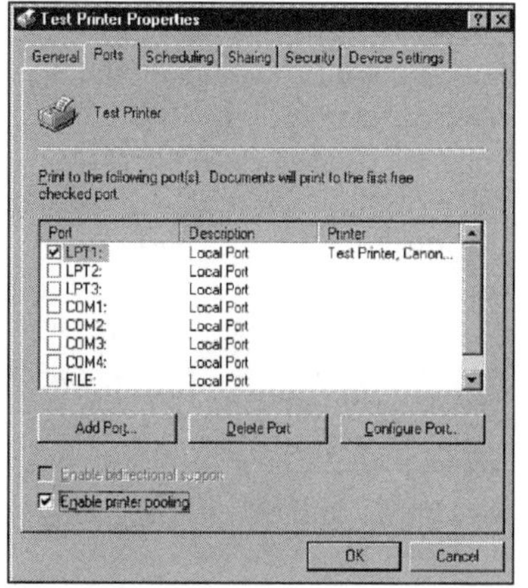


**FIGURE 3.18**
Setting up a printer pool.

## Sharing a Printer

It is likely that in your Windows NT environment, you will need to share printers for use by multiple users. Sharing a printer can be done during the installation or creation of the printer, or it can be done after the printer has already been installed. To share a printer that's already installed, you use the options on the Sharing tab of the printer's properties dialog box (see Figure 3.19).

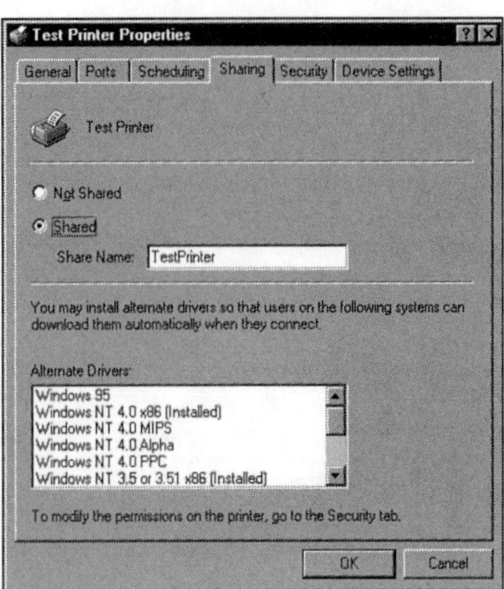


**FIGURE 3.19**
Sharing a printer.

**You Can Only Share Local Printers** You can only share a printer that has been defined by your computer. You cannot share a printer that you connect to using the Network Printer Server option.

NOTE

**Keep Printer Drivers Updated from a Single Location** Each time a Windows NT Workstation prints to your printer, there will be a verification that the client's printer driver is the current printer driver. If you need to update the printer driver, update it on the print server, and it will be downloaded automatically to the client workstations. (The exception to this occurs with Windows 95. If a Windows 95 client prints to your shared printer, it downloads the driver only the first time that it prints to it.)

## STEP BY STEP

### 3.13 Sharing a Local Printer

1. Log on to Windows NT with an account that has administrative permissions.
2. Open the Start menu, choose Settings, and select Printers.
3. Right-click on the printer you want to share and choose the Sharing option from the context menu.
4. Click the Shared radio button and enter a share name for the printer.
5. If only Intel platforms use Windows NT 4.0 in your environment, click OK to share the printer. When another Windows NT 4.0 Workstation tries to print to your shared printer, the printer driver is downloaded to that machine automatically.
6. If other clients (such as Windows 95 or Windows NT 3.51 or other platforms of Windows NT 4.0) exist in your environment, select those operating systems from the list of alternate drivers.
7. After you have selected those alternate operating systems from the list, you receive a prompt for the location of the drivers for each operating system. This is so the drivers for each operating system you have selected can be downloaded when the client tries to print to your printer. Specify those driver locations and click OK.

You must share a printer in order for your users to be able to print to it. Setting up a shared printer for other operating systems assists your users in printing to your shared printer.

## Setting Printer Permissions

Windows NT Workstation provides the following four printer permissions:

- Full Control
- Manage Documents
- Print
- No Access

> **WARNING**
>
> **Windows 3.x Does Not Automatically Load Printer Drivers**
> Windows 3.x clients must install their own drivers locally. Printer drivers for Windows 3.x are not installed when a printer is shared.

By default, all users are given the Print permission, the creator owner is given Manage Documents permission, and administrators are given Full Control. As you will see in this chapter, you might want to change these default printer permissions after installing the printer. Table 3.6 lists the capabilities you can grant to users and specifies which printer permissions enable each capability.

**TABLE 3.6**

**CAPABILITIES GRANTED WITH PRINTER PERMISSIONS**

| *Capability* | *Full Control* | *Manage Documents* | *Print* | *No Access* |
|---|---|---|---|---|
| Print documents | X | X | X | |
| Pause, resume, restart, and cancel the user's own documents | X | X | X | |
| Connect to a printer | X | X | X | |
| Control job settings for all documents | X | X | | |
| Pause, restart, and delete all documents | X | X | | |
| Share a printer | X | | | |
| Change printer properties | X | | | |
| Delete a printer | X | | | |
| Change printer permissions | X | | | |

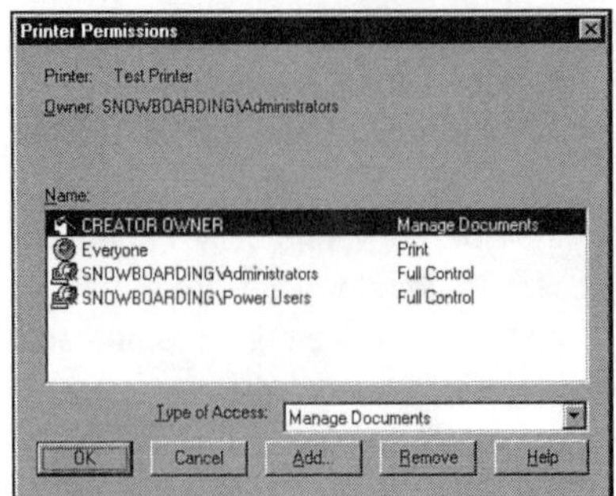


**FIGURE 3.20**
Setting printer permissions.

You can assign permissions or change permissions assigned to a printer via the Printer Permissions dialog box (see Figure 3.20).

## STEP BY STEP

### 3.14 Assigning or Changing Printer Permissions

1. Log on with an account that has Full Control to the printer.
2. Go to the Printers folder by choosing Start, Settings, Printer. To view the properties for the printer, select the printer, right-click on it, and choose Properties.
3. Select the Security tab, and then click the Permissions button.
4. Add or remove users or groups from the list of permissions assigned to the printer.

Understanding how to set printer permissions is crucial to implementing printing security in your Windows NT environment.

## Scheduling Printing

Scheduling printing means you specify the available printing times on a per-printer basis. If, for instance, your Accounting Department needs to print large printer-intensive documents every day but you do not want the printer to be bogged down during the day, you can create a printer for the Accounting group that is available only from 7 p.m. until 7 a.m. so that those documents do not dominate the printer during the day. Figure 3.21 shows the Scheduling tab of a printer's properties dialog box.

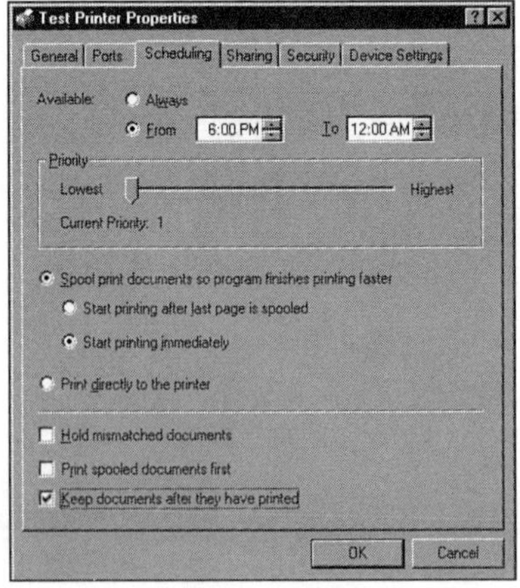


**FIGURE 3.21**
Setting the scheduling options for a printer.

Setting the scheduling options helps you control the traffic on your shared printer and enables you to distribute that traffic most efficiently.

## Modifying Spool Settings

You can also set spool settings on a per-printer basis. You can configure the following spool settings to make the printing process more efficient:

- *Spool Print Documents so Program Finishes Printing Faster.* If you choose this option, the documents will spool. You then need to choose one of two options that control when the job prints:
    - *Start Printing After Last Page Is Spooled.* Documents will not print until they are completely spooled, and the application that is printing is not available during the spooling. This requires that you have adequate space on the partition of the spool directory to hold the entire print job.
    - *Start Printing Immediately.* Documents will print before they have spooled completely, which speeds up printing.
- *Print Directly to the Printer.* This prevents the document from spooling. Although this option speeds up printing, it is not an option for a shared printer, which must support multiple incoming documents simultaneously.
- *Hold Mismatched Documents.* This prevents incorrect documents from printing. Incorrect documents are those that do not match the configuration of the printer.
- *Print Spooled Documents First.* Spooled documents will print ahead of partially spooled documents, even if they have a lower priority. This speeds up printing.
- *Keep Documents After They Have Printed.* Documents remain in the spooler after they have been printed.

Setting the spool settings to fit your environment can greatly increase printing efficiency.

## Controlling Printer Availability

Although most printers need to be available all the time, it is sometimes useful to configure a printer to be available only at certain times. For example, if large print jobs are printed frequently, those jobs could tie up a print device and leave other, perhaps more critical, documents in a long print queue. One solution is to configure a printer that is available only at certain times and simply holds documents that are sent to it outside of those times.

## STEP BY STEP

### 3.15 Implementing Printer Priorities

1. Define two or more printers pointing to the same print device from the same print server.
2. Connect both printers to the same port to the print device.
3. Set a different priority for each of the printers.
4. Assign permissions to the printers based on the priorities set.

If you wanted to set up the previously described scenario so that management would have a higher printing priority than other users, for example, you could set up one printer called Management Printer as shown in Figure 3.22. To make sure that management's print jobs have the highest priority, set the Management Printer's priority to 99 (the highest priority). Then set up another printer called Users Printer and give it the default priority of 1 (the lowest).

What is to keep ordinary users from printing to the management printer after they find out that it has a higher priority? You can set permissions on the Security tab to prevent it. In the permissions list for the management printer, remove the permission Everyone Print and replace it with Management Print. That way if a user is not in the group called Management, she cannot print to the high-priority printer. Assigning priorities to different printers enables you to manage the printing environment within Windows NT.

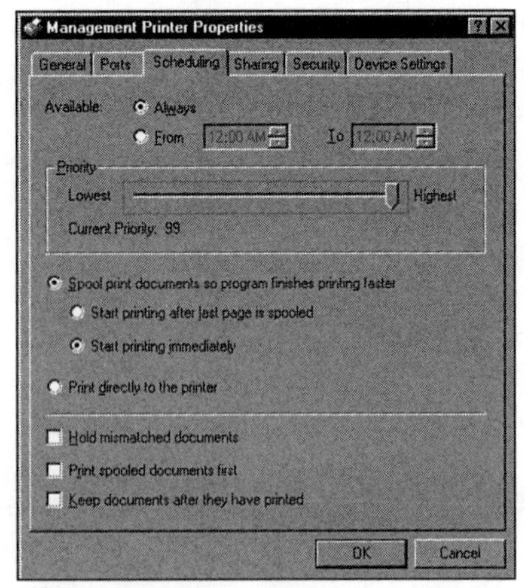


**FIGURE 3.22**
Setting priorities on a shared printer.

## Managing Printing

Managing printing entails performing certain tasks after the printer is installed and configured for your environment. Those tasks include day-to-day things that might need to be done in a Windows NT printing environment, such as pausing a printer or deleting a print job.

## Pausing and Resuming a Printer

Pausing and resuming a printer might be necessary for troubleshooting printing problems. You may want to pause a printer to prevent garbled output from spanning multiple pages (which happens when a user has the wrong printer driver configured).

### STEP BY STEP

#### 3.16 Pausing a Printer

1. Open the Printers folder by choosing Start, Settings, Printers.
2. Double-click on the printer.
3. From the Printer menu, choose Pause Printing.

After you pause a printer and solve whatever problem had occurred, you must resume the printer.

### STEP BY STEP

#### 3.17 Resuming a Paused Printer

1. Open the Printers folder by choosing Start, Settings, Printers.
2. Double-click on the printer.
3. From the Printer menu, choose Pause Printing. This removes the check mark next to the command and resumes the printer.

Pausing and resuming a printer is not a common task, but it might be necessary in troubleshooting situations.

## Redirecting Printing

Redirecting printing is the process of changing which print device a printer prints to. You can redirect a printer to either a local or a remote print device. You may need to redirect a printer, for example, if there is a problem with the print device that requires it to be taken offline for maintenance. Redirecting a printer redirects all documents sent to that printer. There is no way to redirect printing on a document-by-document basis.

## STEP BY STEP

### 3.18 Redirecting Documents to a Remote Print Device

1. Open the Printers folder by choosing Start, Settings, Printers.
2. Right-click on the printer you want to redirect and select Properties.
3. Click the Ports tab.
4. Click the Add Port button.
5. Click Local Port, and then click New Port.
6. In the Port Name field, enter the UNC path to the other printer (**\\printserver\printer2**, for example).
7. Click OK, and documents will be redirected to the new printer.

WARNING

**Redirected Documents Must Still Use the Same Printer Driver** For redirection to work properly, both the original and the new printer must use the same printer driver. Also, change the original port so that the printer does not attempt to print to the old port.

Redirecting documents is typically done only in troubleshooting situations. Why wouldn't you just tell all your users to print to the new printer while the original is being serviced? You could, but that would mean redefining the printer settings on all client machines in your environment. By redirecting printing, you make the change once on the print server, and it is invisible to the clients.

## Deleting Print Jobs

Sometimes the ongoing maintenance of a printer involves removing a print job from the print queue. Maybe you need to clear a document error that "jams" the print queue, or maybe a user has sent a large document to the wrong printer. The owner of a document and anyone with Full Control or Manage Documents permissions can delete a print job from the queue.

---

**STEP BY STEP**

**3.19 Deleting a Document from a Print Queue**

1. Open the Printers folder by choosing Start, Settings, Printers.
2. Double-click the printer whose queue you want to manage.
3. Select the document you want to delete and press the Delete key on your keyboard.

---

# Troubleshooting Printing

In addition to performing the preceding tasks as a means of troubleshooting printing problems, you must understand a few more issues that relate to troubleshooting. You need this information both for providing support within your network environment and for the exam.

## Spooler Service

The Spooler service controls the print spooling process in Windows NT. If your users cannot print to a printer, and there are documents in the print queue that will not print and cannot be deleted (even by the administrator), you may need to stop and restart the Spooler service. You do so through the Services dialog box (shown in Figure 3.23).

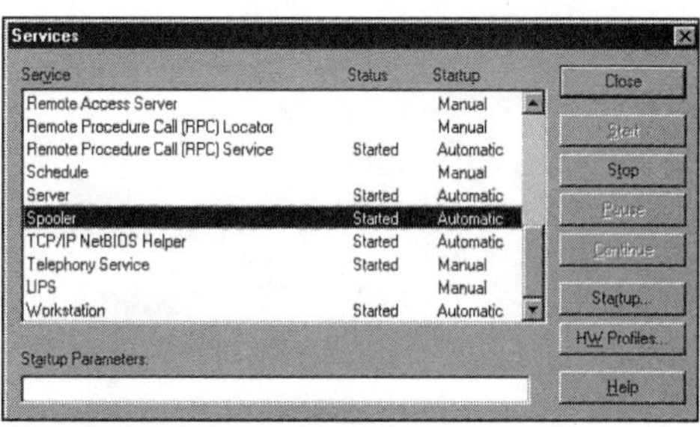


**FIGURE 3.23**
Stopping and restarting the Spooler service can clear a jammed print queue.

## STEP BY STEP

### 3.20 Stopping and Restarting the Spooler Service

1. Open the Control Panel by choosing Start, Settings, Control Panel.
2. Double-click the Services icon.
3. Click the Spooler service in the list of services.
4. Click Stop. When you're prompted to verify that you want to stop the service, click Yes.
5. After the service has been stopped, you can click the Start button in the Services dialog box to restart the Spooler service.

Stopping and restarting the Spooler service clears only the jammed print job from the queue. The other print jobs continue printing.

**WARNING**

**The Shared Printer Is Unavailable While Spooler Service Is Stopped** While the Spooler service is stopped, no one can print to the shared printer.

## Spool Directory

Another seldom-seen player in the spooling process in Windows NT is the *spool directory*, which is the location on the hard disk where print jobs are stored while spooling. By default, this directory is the Windows NT Root\system32\spool\printers directory. This one directory is used for spooling all printers defined on the print server.

If you notice the hard disk thrashing or see that documents are not printing or not reaching the print server, check to make sure that available space exists on the partition where the spool directory is located. If there is not sufficient disk space available (minimally about 5MB, more for complex print jobs), you must free up some disk space. If that is not possible, you must move the spool directory to another location. You can do this from the Print Server Properties dialog box (see Figure 3.24).

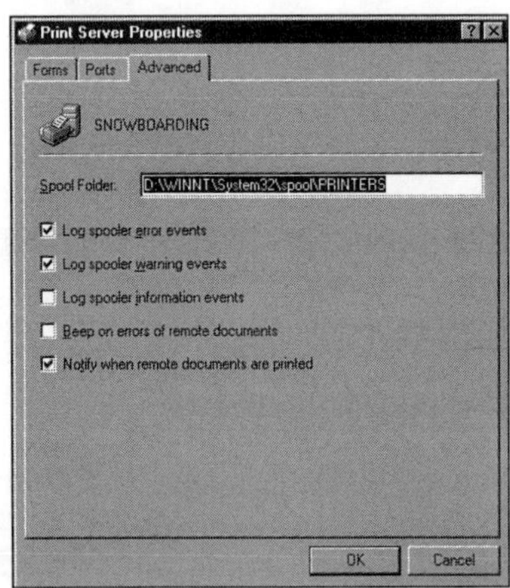


**FIGURE 3.24**
You can change the location of the spool directory.

## STEP BY STEP

### 3.21 Changing the Spool Directory

1. Open the Printers folder by choosing Start, Settings, Printers.
2. From the File menu, choose Server Properties.
3. On the Advanced tab, type the new location for the spool directory in the Spool Folder field.

EXAM TIP

**The Process Changed in NT Workstation 4** In Windows NT 3.51, there was no graphical interface for changing the spool directory. It could be changed only in the Registry. Because this is something different in Windows NT 4.0, watch for it on the exam.

## CASE STUDY: LARSON, WATTERSON, AND ADAMS

### ESSENCE OF THE CASE

Here are the essential elements in this case:

- Not enough machines to be dedicated to specific workstations
- Large jobs cannot interfere with the general printer availability
- The print jobs of the partners should take precedence over other print jobs
- Printers that are not being used should be used before more jobs are queued to busy printers
- Access to the color printer needs to be restricted to authorized personnel

### SCENARIO

You are analyzing the network configuration for the Larson, Watterson, and Adams accounting firm. They have completed their upgrade to Windows NT Workstation, and everyone has an Office suite that runs on an NT platform. In addition, at your suggestion, they have completely removed Windows 95 from their systems. Now, however, they are having printing problems.

Currently, there are printers all over the company, but all of them are dedicated to single machines, and none are available over the network. In total, they have 10 HP4 printers, all of which were purchased at the same time along with a number of other hardware upgrades. In addition to the standard black-and-white printers, they have one HP LaserJet 5M color printer, which was purchased to print brochures and customer reports.

The partners are hearing complaints about printing, and they also have some of their own. First, a number of people are complaining that they need to be able to print but don't have a printer. So there are requests for 10 more printers (an

*continues*

## CASE STUDY: LARSON, WATTERSON, AND ADAMS

*continued*

expense the partners are not excited about approving). Second, although they know about print sharing, they are concerned about implementing it because of large jobs (especially at month- and year-end) that might swamp any shared printers. They are also concerned about jobs from one group interfering with the reports that they (the partners) need to print immediately for meetings. They are also concerned about some printers remaining idle while others are being heavily utilized. Finally, they have found that the color printer is being overused—especially by people who simply want to spruce up common reports—and they want to restrict access to it so that only personnel who need it can use it.

Your job is to propose a printer configuration strategy that will allow for the most efficient use of their resources while also providing the best possible print performance.

### ANALYSIS

A number of techniques can be implemented to address the essential needs. First, the problem of not having enough machines for the number of workstations can be handled by sharing some or all of the printers by use of network connections to the printers. Second, by setting printer availability so that some printers are available only at certain times, you restrict large jobs to printing to only those printers. Third, the printers the partners user can be set to have a higher priority than those for the rest of the employees so that the partners' jobs will move to the front of any print queue and be printed quickly. Fourth, implementing a printer pool with some of the printers allows NT to decide which printer should be used (instead of letting the users decide). The users' printers can then be configured to print to a certain printer that is actually a printer pool in a central location. Finally, the computer that the color printer is connected to would need to be configured with a group account that contains only the names of those people who are allowed to use it and that group would then be assigned print permissions to the printer. You will also want to assign someone the Manage Printer permission and give someone administrator access to that printer.

Of course, it may not be prudent to configure any person's workstation as a print server, especially the one that controls the printer pool. To avoid that, you recommend the configuration of one or more dedicated workstations or NT Servers (standalone machines) as print servers to ensure that no user's ability to work is compromised because her system resources are consumed by print jobs.

## CHAPTER SUMMARY

The material in this chapter was divided into three major sections: user management, folder and file management, and printer management. Beginning with user management, you looked at the creation and configuration of user accounts as well as the creation of group accounts to ease the management of users. In addition, you learned how user profiles can be used to ensure standard configuration of users' desktops and to retain users' desktop modifications.

This chapter also covered resource access as it pertains to local and network access to files and folders. You learned how to share folders and configure access to those shares. In addition, you discovered how you can secure local files and folders through the use of NTFS permissions, and you got a detailed look at the interaction between shared and NTFS permissions.

Finally, you studied printer configuration. This included printer installation, sharing, and general setup for most efficient usage.

### KEY TERMS

Before you take the exam, make sure you are comfortable with the definitions and concepts for each of the following key terms:

- Account Policy
- built-in user accounts
- SID
- local group accounts
- user profiles
- shared folder
- NTFS permissions
- No Access permission
- File Delete Child
- printer
- print device
- spooling
- print server
- printer pool
- scheduling printing
- printer priorities
- Spooler service

## APPLY YOUR LEARNING

The following section allows you to assess how well you understood the material in the chapter. The exercises provide you with opportunities to engage in the sorts of tasks that comprise the skill sets the objectives reflect. Review and exam questions test your knowledge of the tasks and concepts specified in the objectives. Answers to the review and exam questions follow in the answers sections.

For additional review- and exam-type questions, use the Top Score test engine on the CD-ROM that came with this book.

## Exercises

### 3.1 Creating User Accounts Using a Template Account

This exercise teaches you how to create a template account to use for creating user accounts with similar configuration settings. It also teaches you how to create a location for users' home directories, as well as a new local group.

**Estimated Time:** 40 minutes

To create a local group, follow these steps:

1. Log on to Windows NT with an account that has administrative permissions.
2. Launch User Manager by choosing Start, Programs, Administrative Tools, User Manager.
3. Open the User menu and choose New Local Group to create a new local group.
4. In the Group Name field, type **Sales**.
5. In the Group Description field, type **Sales Representatives**.
6. Make sure there are no user accounts included in the group. (You add the user accounts later in the exercise.)
7. Click OK to create the local group.

To create a Users directory to store users' home directories in, follow these steps:

1. Log on to Windows NT with an account that has administrative permissions.
2. Launch Windows NT Explorer by choosing Start, Programs, Windows NT Explorer.
3. Create a new subfolder under the C: drive and name it **Users**.
4. Right-click on the Users folder and choose the Sharing option. Leave the default settings and click OK to share the Users folder.

To create the template account, follow these steps:

1. Log on to Windows NT with an account that has administrative permissions.
2. Launch User Manager by choosing Start, Programs, Administrative Tools, User Manager.
3. Choose the User, New User command to create a new user account.
4. In the Username field, type **_Sales_Template**.
5. In the Description field, type **Sales Representative**.
6. Click the Profile button. For the Home Directory, select Connect To and enter the path for the home directory: ***server*\users\%username%**, where *server* is the name of your Windows NT Workstation. Then click OK.

## APPLY YOUR LEARNING

7. Click the Dialin button. Click the check box to grant dial-in permission to the user. Click OK, and then click OK again to create the user account.

To create additional accounts using the template, follow these steps:

1. Log on to Windows NT with an account that has administrative permissions.
2. Launch User Manager by choosing Start, Programs, Administrative Tools, User Manager.
3. Click on the _Sales_Template account to highlight it.
4. With the _Sales_Template account highlighted, click on the User menu and choose Copy.
5. Enter **Sales1** for the Username. Notice that the description is already filled in for this user.
6. Click the Profile button. Notice that the Home Directory is already filled in for this user. Click OK.
7. Click the Dialin button. Notice that the dial-in permissions are already granted for this user. Click OK.
8. Click OK to create this user account.
9. Exit User Manager.

### 3.2 Implementing User Profiles

This exercise shows you how to create a profile for a user.

**Estimated Time:** 35 minutes

To create a test user profile, follow these steps:

1. Log on to Windows NT with an account that has administrative permissions.
2. Launch User Manager by choosing Start, Programs, Administrative Tools, User Manager.
3. Create a new user called User Profile. Accept the default settings except for the User Must Change Password check box. Remove the check from that box so the user will not have to change the password.
4. Log off and log on as User Profile.
5. Make a change to the wallpaper on the system by using the options on the Background tab of the Control Panel's Display application.
6. Log off and log back on as the account with administrative permissions.
7. Select Start, Settings, Control Panel. Then double-click the System icon and select the User Profiles tab.
8. What profiles are stored on your machine?
9. Exit the System application.

To create a shared profiles directory, follow these steps:

1. Log on to Windows NT with an account that has administrative permissions.
2. Create a directory on the C: drive called Profiles.
3. Share the Profiles directory, leaving the default settings.
4. Within the Profiles directory, create a folder called TestProfile.

## APPLY YOUR LEARNING

To test your configuration using the User Profile account, follow these steps:

1. Log on to Windows NT with an account that has administrative permissions.
2. Launch User Manager by choosing Start, Programs, Administrative Tools, User Manager.
3. Create a new user called TestProfile. Accept the defaults except for the User Must Change Password check box. Remove the check from that box so the user will not have to change the password.
4. Click the Profile button. In the User Profile Path field, enter the path that you created to the Profiles directory: ***server*\profiles\testprofile**, where *server* is your computer's name.
5. Click OK to create the user account and exit User Manager.
6. Select Start, Settings, Control Panel. Then double-click the System icon and select the User Profiles tab.
7. Under Profiles Stored on This Computer, click on the profile for Profile User and click Copy To.
8. In the Copy To field, type the network path to the folder you created: ***server*\profiles\profile**, where *server* is your computer name.
9. For Permitted to Use, click the Change button and select the account for Test Profile.
10. Log off Windows NT and log on as Test Profile.
11. What settings do you get?

### 3.3 Creating and Managing Shared Directories

This exercise shows you how to create a shared directory, set the permissions for it, and manage the shared directory after it is created.

**Estimated Time:** 25 minutes

1. Log on to Windows NT Workstation as an account with administrative permissions on that workstation.
2. On an NTFS partition (or FAT if you do not have NTFS), create a directory called **Antigua**.
3. Right-click on the directory and choose Sharing from the context menu.
4. Click the Shared As button and leave the share name as Antigua.
5. In the Comment field, type **This is a Shared Directory**.
6. Click on the Permissions button.
7. Remove the group Everyone from the list of shared permissions. Add Administrators with Full Control and Users with Read access.
8. Click OK to create the shared directory.
9. Double-click on the Network Neighborhood icon on your desktop, and then double-click on your computer. Does Antigua show up?
10. Close Network Neighborhood.
11. Launch Windows NT Explorer. Right-click on the Antigua directory and choose Sharing from the context menu.

## APPLY YOUR LEARNING

12. Click the New Share button to create a new share.
13. Type **Guatemala** for the new share name. In the Comment field, type **Second Share**.
14. Click the Permissions button and remove the Everyone Full Control permission. Do not add any other permissions.
15. Click OK. You receive a prompt with a warning that your shared directory will be inaccessible because you have removed all the permissions. Click the Yes button to continue.
16. Double-click the Network Neighborhood icon on your desktop. Double-click on your computer. Does Antigua show up? Does Guatemala show up?
17. Double-click on Guatemala. What happens?
18. Close Network Neighborhood.

### 3.4 Implementing NTFS Permissions and Using No Access

This exercise helps you set up NTFS permissions on folders and files and see how the No Access permission works. (This exercise requires you to have an NTFS partition on your Windows NT Workstation.)

**Estimated Time:** 35 minutes

1. Log on to Windows NT Workstation as an account with administrative permissions on that workstation.
2. Launch Windows NT Explorer. Right-click on the Antigua directory created in the preceding lab and choose Properties from the context menu.
3. Click the Security tab, and then click the Permissions button.
4. What are the default NTFS permissions for the Antigua directory?
5. Remove the group Everyone Full Control.
6. Click Add and add Administrators Full Control.
7. Click Add and add Users Read access.
8. Log off Windows NT.
9. Log on with an account that has user permissions.
10. Launch Windows NT Explorer, and then double-click on the Antigua directory. Can you open it?
11. Choose File, New, Folder to create a new folder within the Antigua directory. Were you successful? Why or why not?
12. Log off Windows NT.
13. Log on to Windows NT Workstation as an account with administrative permissions on that workstation.
14. Launch Windows NT Explorer. Right-click on the Antigua directory you created in the preceding lab and choose Properties from the context menu.
15. Click the Security tab, and then click the Permissions button.
16. Highlight the Users group and change the permission from Read to No Access.
17. Log off Windows NT.
18. Log on with an account that has user permissions.

## APPLY YOUR LEARNING

19. Launch Windows NT Explorer and double-click on the Antigua directory. Can you open it? Why or why not?
20. Log off Windows NT.

### 3.5 Installing and Configuring a Printer

This exercise walks you through installation and configuration of a printer in Windows NT Workstation.

**Estimated Time:** 35 minutes

To install and share a printer, follow these steps:

1. Log on to Windows NT Workstation as an account with administrative permissions on that workstation.
2. Open the Printers folder by choosing Start, Settings, Printers.
3. Double-click the Add Printer icon.
4. In the first Add Printer Wizard screen, leave the default of My Computer selected and click Next.
5. Click on Enable Printer Pooling, and then click LPT2 and LPT3.
6. From the list of printers, select HP on the left and then HP LaserJet 4 on the right. Click Next.
7. For the printer name, type **My Printer**.
8. When prompted to share the printer, click the Shared radio button. Do not share the printer to other operating systems.
9. When you're asked if you want to print a test page, select No.
10. Click Finish. When you're prompted to do so, enter the path to the Windows NT Workstation installation files.

To set printer permissions, follow these steps:

1. Log on to Windows NT Workstation as an account with administrative permissions on that workstation.
2. Open the Printers folder by choosing Start, Settings, Printers.
3. Right-click on My Printer and choose Properties from the context menu.
4. Click the Security tab and then the Permissions button.
5. What are the default permissions for your newly created printer?
6. Click the Add button and select an existing Windows NT Workstation group to add to the list of permissions. Under Type of Access, select Manage Documents.
7. Click OK to exit the printer properties for My Printer.

To set the schedule for a printer, follow these steps:

1. Log on to Windows NT Workstation as an account with administrative permissions on that workstation.
2. Open the Printers folder by choosing Start, Settings, Printers.
3. Right-click on My Printer and choose Properties from the context menu.
4. Click the Scheduling tab and set the printer to be available from 6 p.m. to 5 a.m.
5. Set the priority to 50.
6. For the spool settings, select the option to print spooled documents first.
7. Close the properties for My Printer.

## APPLY YOUR LEARNING

To view the spool directory location, follow these steps:

1. Log on to Windows NT Workstation as an account with administrative permissions on that workstation.
2. Open the Printers folder by choosing Start, Settings, Printers.
3. From the File menu, choose Server Properties.
4. Click on the Advanced tab.
5. What is the location of the spool directory?
6. Close the Printers folder.

To stop and restart the Spooler service, follow these steps:

1. Log on to Windows NT Workstation as an account with administrative permissions on that workstation.
2. Launch the Control Panel by choosing Start, Settings, Control Panel.
3. Double-click on the Services icon.
4. Highlight the Spooler service in the list.
5. Click the Stop button, and then continue when prompted.
6. After the Spooler service has been stopped, go to the properties dialog box for My Printer and click the General tab.
7. Click the Print Test Page button. What message did you get?
8. Restart the Spooler service.
9. Log off of Windows NT.

## Review Questions

1. You've set up a shared directory called Information and assigned the following permissions to the shared directory:

| *Account* | *Permission* |
|---|---|
| CherriL | Change |
| Users | Read |
| Operations | Full Control |

   If CherriL is a member of the Users group and a member of the Operations group, what are CherriL's effective permissions for the shared directory if she is sitting locally at the workstation?

2. You've set up a shared directory called Information and assigned the following permissions to the shared directory:

| *Account* | *Permission* |
|---|---|
| CherriL | Change |
| Users | Read |
| Operations | Full Control |

   If CherriL is a member of the Users group and of the Operations group, what are CherriL's effective permissions for the shared directory if she is accessing it from across the network?

3. You've set up NTFS permissions on a directory called Sales Data and assigned the following NTFS permissions to the directory:

| *Account* | *Permission* |
|---|---|
| JasonM | Read |
| Users | Read |
| Sales | Full Control |

## APPLY YOUR LEARNING

If JasonM is a member of the Users group and of the Sales group, what are JasonM's effective permissions for this directory if he is sitting locally at the workstation?

4. You've set up a directory called Market Research and assigned the following NTFS and share permissions to the directory:

| *Account* | *NTFS Permissions* | *Share Permissions* |
|---|---|---|
| CarlaH | Change | Change |
| Users | Read | Read |
| Marketing | Full Control | Full Control |

If CarlaH is a member of the Users group and of the Marketing group, what are CarlaH's effective permissions for this directory if she is sitting locally at the workstation?

5. You've set up a directory called Market Research and assigned the following NTFS and share permissions to the directory:

| *Account* | *NTFS Permissions* | *Share Permissions* |
|---|---|---|
| CarlaH | Change | Change |
| Users | Read | Read |
| Marketing | Full Control | No Access |

If CarlaH is a member of the Users group and of the Marketing group, what are CarlaH's effective permissions for this directory if she is accessing the Market Research directory from across the network?

6. Your boss tells you to delete the account for SpenceB because SpenceB is leaving the company. You delete the account. Two hours later, your boss calls you to tell you he was wrong: SpenceB was gone on vacation. He's not leaving the company, and he needs his account back. You re-create his account, giving it the same name as before. In the afternoon, SpenceB calls you to tell you he cannot access his files in his home directory or other files in shared directories that he used to be able to access. What is the problem?

7. You receive a call from your boss who is quite angry because the report he needs will not print. He tells you that all that is coming out of the printer is "garbage text" on multiple pages. What do you think the problem is?

8. You receive a call from your boss who is quite angry because the report she needs will not print. She tells you that nothing is coming out of the printer. You look at the print queue for the printer and see five other documents behind her job, waiting to print. What should you do to troubleshoot this problem?

9. You want to add a shortcut to the Start menu and want the shortcut to be available to all users who log on to that workstation. How should you do that?

10. You want to have the same desktop settings no matter where you log on within your Windows NT domain. All the client machines are Windows NT Workstation 4.0. How can you set this up?

## APPLY YOUR LEARNING

## Exam Questions

1. If you are concerned about security in your network, what can you do to make the default Administrator and the default Guest accounts more secure? (Choose all that apply.)

   A. Delete them and create new ones.

   B. Delete the built-in Guest account, and change the password for the built-in Administrator account.

   C. Create difficult passwords for both accounts.

   D. Rename both accounts.

2. What directories are created in the profile folder when a user logs on to a Windows NT Workstation for the first time?

   A. Default User

   B. All Users

   C. A directory called Users

   D. A directory named after that user

3. What is the difference between a *roaming user profile* and a *local user profile*?

   A. A roaming user profile is available from anywhere on the network; a local user profile is available only from the machine on which it resides.

   B. A roaming user profile is available only on the machine on which it was created; a local user profile is available from anywhere on the network.

   C. A roaming user profile is available from anywhere on the network; a local user profile is available only on an NT workstation.

   D. A roaming user profile requires an NT Server to administrate it; a local user profile does not.

4. What is the difference between a *personal user profile* and a *mandatory user profile*?

   A. A personal user profile can be used only from your workstation; a mandatory user profile can be used from anywhere on the network.

   B. A personal user profile can be modified by the user to whom it belongs; a mandatory user profile cannot be modified.

   C. Applying a personal profile is optional, whereas applying a mandatory user profile is not.

   D. A mandatory profile has an extension of .MAN; a personal user profile has an extension of .CAN.

5. What does it mean if the Account Locked Out check box is checked for a user's account?

   A. That user chose to have his account locked out by indicating it in his user profile.

   B. Someone has exceeded the number of bad logon attempts allowed by the Account Policy.

   C. Another administrator checked that option for the user's account because the user is going to be on leave for three months.

   D. It is the default setting when you create a user account.

## APPLY YOUR LEARNING

6. What are the built-in group accounts on Windows NT Workstation?

   A. Administrators

   B. Users

   C. Power Users

   D. Account Operators

   E. Print Operators

7. A user in your network will be on a leave of absence for the next six months. What should you do with his user account?

   A. Delete it and re-create it when he returns.

   B. Rename the account so that no one else can use it.

   C. Disable the account while the user is gone.

   D. Leave the account alone.

8. Of which of the following groups do you have to be a member to be able to share resources on a Windows NT Workstation? (Choose all that apply.)

   A. Administrators

   B. Power Users

   C. Users

   D. Server Operators

9. You want to set up both shared folder permissions and NTFS permissions on your Windows NT Workstation computer. You have two FAT partitions, and you would like to create the shares on the C: drive. What should you do?

   A. First set the share permissions, and then set the NTFS permissions.

   B. First set the NTFS permissions, and then set the shared folder permissions.

   C. You cannot share folders on a FAT partition.

   D. You cannot implement NTFS permissions on a FAT partition.

10. You create a shared folder with the following permissions:

| *Account* | *Permissions* |
|---|---|
| KelleyD | Full Control |
| Sales | Change |
| Users | Read |

    If KelleyD is a member of the Sales and of the Users group, what are KelleyD's effective permissions?

    A. Full Control.

    B. Change.

    C. Read.

    D. The result cannot be determined.

11. You have assigned the following NTFS permissions on a folder:

| *Account* | *Permissions* |
|---|---|
| KelleyD | Full Control |
| Sales | Change |
| Users | Read |

    If KelleyD is a member of the Sales group and the Users group, what are KelleyD's effective permissions?

    A. Full Control.

## APPLY YOUR LEARNING

B. Change.

C. Read.

D. The result cannot be determined.

12. You have shared a folder with the following permissions:

| *Account* | *Shared Folder Permissions* | *NTFS Permissions* |
|---|---|---|
| KelleyD | Full Control | |
| Sales | Read | Change |
| Users | No Access | Read |

If KelleyD is a member of the Sales group and the Users group, what are KelleyD's effective permissions when accessing this resource locally?

A. Full Control.

B. Change.

C. No Access.

D. The result cannot be determined.

13. You have shared a folder with the following permissions:

| *Account* | *Shared Folder Permissions* | *NTFS Permissions* |
|---|---|---|
| KelleyD | | |
| Sales | Read | Change |
| Users | | Read |

If KelleyD is a member of the Sales group and the Users group, what are KelleyD's effective permissions when accessing this resource from across the network?

A. No Access.

B. Change.

C. Read.

D. The result cannot be determined.

14. What is a print device?

A. A document that you print

B. The software interface between the client and the printer

C. The physical device that prints (such as an HP LaserJet)

D. The computer that receives documents from clients

15. What is a printer?

A. The physical device that prints (such as an HP LaserJet)

B. The file that stores print jobs waiting to be printed

C. The software interface between the client and the printer

D. Another word for the Spooler service

16. What is a printer pool?

A. A single printer that controls many print devices

B. A single print device that controls many printers

C. A hardware device that allows you to manually switch printing between multiple printers

D. A place where printers go to cool off in summer

## Apply Your Learning

17. You want to print to a printer managed by a Windows NT Server 4.0. What should you do?

    A. Use Print Manager to connect to the printer.

    B. Use Print Manager to create a printer.

    C. Use the Add Printer Wizard to connect to the printer.

    D. Use the Add Printer Wizard to create a printer.

18. What is File Delete Child?

    A. The phenomena of files being deleted when you delete the parent folder

    B. The ability to delete a file when you have only Read access to it

    C. The ability to delete a file to which you have no access

    D. The ability to delete the files in a folder to which you have no access

19. What groups on a Windows NT Workstation have the right to take ownership?

    A. Users

    B. Administrators

    C. Account Operators

    D. Print Operators

20. Which of the following is the appropriate method for clearing a jammed print job from the queue?

    A. Delete the printer and re-create it.

    B. Stop the Printer service.

    C. Delete the spool directory.

    D. Stop and restart the Spooler service.

## Answers to Review Questions

1. CherriL's permissions are Full Control. The share permissions that you assign do not apply to her because she is sitting locally at the machine. Share permissions only apply when a user is accessing the resource from across the network. For more information, see the section "Setting Up Shared Folders and Permissions."

2. CherriL will have Full Control to the resource because her effective permissions are the cumulative permissions. Because the Operations group has Full Control, and she is a member of that group, and she is accessing the resource from across the network, CherriL will have Full Control. For more information, see the section "Setting Up Shared Folders and Permissions."

3. JasonM's effective permissions to the directory are Full Control. With NTFS permissions, the effective permissions are cumulative for user and group permissions. Because he is sitting locally at the machine, the NTFS permissions apply to him. For more information, see the section "Setting Up Shared Folders and Permissions."

4. CarlaH's effective permissions are Full Control because that is her cumulative NTFS permissions. Shared folder permissions do not apply because CarlaH is sitting locally at the machine. For more information, see the section "Setting Up Shared Folders and Permissions."

## APPLY YOUR LEARNING

5. CarlaH's effective permissions are No Access. Because she is accessing the resource from across the network, both shared folder permissions and NTFS permissions apply. And because there is a No Access permission granted to the Marketing group CarlaH is a part of, CarlaH has No Access. Anytime there is a No Access in a user's permissions, it overrides all other permissions. For more information, see the section "Setting Up Shared Folders and Permissions."

6. When you deleted the account for SpenceB, the SID was also deleted. A SID is uniquely tied to a particular user account and is unique in history. So when you re-create the account for SpenceB, even though the account has the same name, there is a new SID. Because there is a new SID and the old SID is no longer valid, the user's resource rights must be redefined. For more information, see the section "Setting Up Shared Folders and Permissions."

7. Typically when "garbage text" comes out of the print device, the wrong printer driver is being used or a printer driver is corrupt. Reinstall the printer driver to fix the problem. For more information, see the section "Installing and Configuring Printers in a Given Environment."

8. The problem is probably that a print job is stuck in the queue. To remove a jammed print job from the queue, access Control Panel's Services application and stop and restart the Spooler service. That is the appropriate method for troubleshooting a jammed print job. For more information, see the section "Installing and Configuring Printers in a Given Environment."

9. Add the shortcut to the All Users folder under the Profiles directory. This adds the shortcut to the Start menu for all current and new users who log on to the Windows NT Workstation. For more information, see the section "Setting Up and Modifying User Profiles."

10. Set up your User account to have a roaming user profile, and then place that profile in a central location such as a server. (Note: This assumes that you are using Windows NT Workstation in a domain environment.) For more information, see the section "Setting Up and Modifying User Profiles."

### Answers to Exam Questions

1. **C and D** are correct. The default Administrator and Guest accounts cannot be deleted, so they should be renamed and given difficult passwords to prevent unauthorized access. For more information, see the section "Implementing Local User and Group Accounts."

2. **D** is correct. When a user logs on to a Windows NT Workstation for the first time, a profile directory is created for that user and is named after that user's logon name. For more information, see the section "Setting Up and Modifying User Profiles."

3. **A** is correct. A roaming user profile is available to the user from any Windows NT 4.0 Workstation on the network. A local user profile is available only on the user's local workstation. For more information, see the section "Setting Up and Modifying User Profiles."

## APPLY YOUR LEARNING

4. **B** is correct. A personal user profile stores the user's personal settings. It is mainly used for the convenience of the user, enabling her to store her own settings. A mandatory user profile does not allow the user to save any changes made to the profile. For more information, see the section "Setting Up and Modifying User Profiles."

5. **B** is correct. The Account Locked Out box can be checked only if the number set for bad logon attempts has been exceeded. For more information, see the section "Implementing Local User and Group Accounts."

6. **A, B, and C** are correct. Account Operators and Print Operators are default groups on Windows NT Server installed as a domain controller but not on Windows NT Workstation. For more information, see the section "Implementing Local User and Group Accounts."

7. **C** is correct. Because the user will be coming back to the company, you should disable the account so that it will not be used while he is gone. Do not delete the user account, however, because that will delete the SID as well. For more information, see the section "Implementing Local User and Group Accounts."

8. **A and B** are correct. Only Administrators and Power Users can share directories on Windows NT Workstation. For more information, see the section "Setting Up Shared Folders and Permissions."

9. **D** is correct. You cannot use NTFS permissions on a FAT partition. For more information, see the section "Setting Permissions on NTFS Partitions, Folders, and Files."

10. **A** is correct. When user and group permissions are combined, the effective permissions are the cumulative permissions. For more information, see the section "Setting Up Shared Folders and Permissions."

11. **A** is correct. When user and group permissions are combined, the effective permissions are the cumulative permissions. For more information, see the section "Setting Permissions on NTFS Partitions, Folders, and Files."

12. **B** is correct. When user and group permissions are combined, the effective permissions are the cumulative permissions. The shared folder permissions do not apply because KelleyD is sitting locally at the computer. For more information, see the section "Setting Permissions on NTFS Partitions, Folders, and Files."

13. **C** is correct. When user and group permissions are combined, the effective permissions are the cumulative permissions. For more information, see the section "Setting Permissions on NTFS Partitions, Folders, and Files."

14. **C** is correct. A print device is an actual hardware that the paper comes out of, such as an HP LaserJet. For more information, see the section "Installing and Configuring Printers in a Given Environment."

15. **C** is correct. A printer is a software component that interfaces between the application and the print device. For more information, see the section "Installing and Configuring Printers in a Given Environment."

16. **A** is correct. A printer pool is defined as one printer pointing to multiple print devices, which

## APPLY YOUR LEARNING

must be of the same type. For more information, see the section "Installing and Configuring Printers in a Given Environment."

17. **C** is correct. Because the printer is already managed by the Windows NT Server, all the user must do is use the Add Printer Wizard to connect to the printer. For more information, see the section entitled "Installing and Configuring Printers in a Given Environment."

18. **C** is correct. File Delete Child refers to a specific scenario relating to NTFS permissions under Windows NT. If a user has been given both the NTFS No Access permission to a particular file and Full Control access to the directory that contains the file, the user is actually able to delete the file even though he does not even have the ability to read the file. For more information, see the section "Setting Permissions on NTFS Partitions, Folders, and Files."

19. **B** is correct. By default, only the Administrators group has the right to take ownership of files or folders. For more information, see the section "Setting Permissions on NTFS Partitions, Folders, and Files."

20. **D** is correct. The appropriate course of action for troubleshooting jammed print jobs is to stop and restart the Spooler service. For more information, see the section "Installing and Configuring Printers in a Given Environment."

## Suggested Readings and Resources

The following are some recommended readings in the area of "managing resources" for Windows NT Workstation:

1. Microsoft Official Curriculum course 770: *Installing and Configuring Microsoft Windows NT Workstation 4.0*
   - Module 3: Working with Windows NT Workstation 4.0
   - Module 4: Configuring Windows NT Workstation 4.0
2. Microsoft Official Curriculum course 803: *Administering Microsoft Windows NT 4.0*
   - Module 2: Setting Up User Accounts
   - Module 3: Setting Up Group Accounts
   - Module 4: Administering User and Group Accounts
   - Module 5: Securing Network Resources with Shared Folder Permissions
   - Module 6: Securing Network Resources with NTFS Permissions
   - Module 7: Setting Up a Network Printer
   - Module 8: Administering Network Printers
3. *Microsoft Windows NT Workstation Resource Kit Version 4.0* (Microsoft Press)
   - Chapter 6: Windows NT Security
   - Chapter 7: Printing
   - Chapter 34: Managing User Work Environments
4. Microsoft TechNet CD-ROM
   - *Concepts and Planning: MS Windows NT Server 4.0*
     - Chapter 2: Working with User and Group Accounts
     - Chapter 3: Managing User Work Environments
     - Chapter 4: Managing Shared Resources and Resource Security
     - Chapter 5: Setting Up Print Servers
5. Web sites
   - `www.microsoft.com/train.cert`
   - `www.prometric.com/testingcandidates/assessment/ chosetest.html` (take online assessment tests)

## OBJECTIVES

Microsoft provides the following objectives for "Connectivity":

**Add and configure the network components of Windows NT Workstation.**

- This objective is necessary because someone certified in the use of Windows NT Workstation technology must understand how it fits into a networked environment and how to configure the components that enable it to do so.

**Use various methods to access network resources.**

- This objective is necessary because someone certified in the use of Windows NT Workstation technology must understand how resources available on a network can be accessed from NT Workstation.

**Implement Windows NT Workstation as a client in a NetWare environment.**

- This objective is necessary because someone certified in the use of Windows NT Workstation technology must understand how NT Workstation can be used as a client in a NetWare environment and how to configure the services and protocols that make this possible.

**Use various configurations to install Windows NT Workstation as a TCP/IP client.**

- This objective is necessary because someone certified in the use of Windows NT Workstation technology must understand how TCP/IP is important in a network environment and how Workstation can be configured to use it.

CHAPTER 4

# Connectivity

## Objectives

**Configure and install Dial-Up Networking in a given situation.**

- This objective is necessary because someone certified in the use of Windows NT Workstation technology must understand how NT Workstation can participate as a Dial-Up Networking client and what configuration is necessary for this to happen.

**Configure Microsoft Peer Web Services in a given situation.**

- This objective is necessary because someone certified in the use of Windows NT Workstation technology must understand how Peer Web Services can enable NT Workstation to act as an Internet or intranet server. As well, you must know how to configure such a server after the software is installed.

This chapter will help you prepare for the "Connectivity" section of Microsoft's Exam 70-73 by introducing you to a variety of connectivity situations involving Windows NT Workstation. These involve network connectivity, the configuration of networking components in a LAN environment, and connectivity with Novell NetWare environments. This chapter also covers NT Workstation as a dial-up client and server using the Remote Access Service. And finally, you learn about connectivity in an Internet or intranet context as it relates to Peer Web Server.

## Outline

## Outline



## Study Strategies

- The connectivity section of this book is very important because it is a weighted topic on the Workstation exam. Most specifically, the topics of NetWare connectivity and RAS are the subject of an inordinate number of questions on the Workstation exam, so you should make sure you are familiar with those concepts.

  You should try to get hands-on experience using both NetWare and RAS. If you can't get production access, set up a test lab where you can install the services and practice the configuration. Begin with the theory here, but then practice repeatedly. If you are not comfortable with these two topics, you may miss too many questions to pass the exam.

- RAS is a particularly sticky topic, and you need to be prepared for a variety of configuration questions. Be familiar with the dialog boxes that come up throughout the installation and configuration of RAS. Also, make sure you understand the authentication methods, as you are sure of getting a question on those. You should understand how PPTP works, but there is not a lot of focus on it on the exam.

- The Personal Web Services section is not a major portion of the test. Still, make sure you know what services come in the PWS bundle and what they are used for. In addition, you should know how they are generally configured. Knowing the information in this book is sufficient for answering PWS questions on the exam.

# INTRODUCTION

A *local area network* (LAN) is a collection of computers in a specific area that are connected by a communications network. LANs can range in size from just two computers to hundreds or even thousands of computers in a single location. Networks can also consist of LANs in multiple locations that are connected into a *wide area network* (WAN).

Because this is an NT certification book, it primarily discusses purely Microsoft topics. However, it is common for Microsoft-based computer networks to include non-Microsoft-based computers, such as Novell NetWare, Apple Macintosh, or UNIX-based computers. Conversely, it is also common for non-Microsoft networks to include Microsoft-based computers. In addition, connectivity with the Internet is also increasingly important. Therefore, for a Windows NT Workstation 4.0 to participate in various LAN and WAN configurations, you must be able to properly configure its network components.

# THE WINDOWS NT NETWORKING MODEL

Before reviewing how to configure the network components of Windows NT, you should examine the underlying components that make up the networking architecture. The networking architecture is made of several different interlocking layers in which lower levels affect higher levels. Knowledge of how all the different levels work together is important in understanding how the Windows NT networking architecture enables the various computers in a network to communicate.

NOTE

**Distributed Applications Can Execute on Multiple Machines** A *distributed application,* also referred to as a client/server application, has its component pieces executing on more than one computer. A *front-end* process running on a client computer communicates with a *back-end* process that runs on a server.

All the networking components of Windows NT Workstation 4.0 are built into the operating system (although some of them are not installed automatically and must be manually configured). A Windows NT Workstation 4.0–based computer can participate in a network in any of the following roles:

- A client or a server in a *distributed application* environment
- A client or a server in a *peer-to-peer networking* environment

The built-in networking components enable Windows NT Workstation 4.0 to share files, printers, and applications with other networked computers (including other computers that aren't based on Windows NT).

NOTE

**Peer-to-Peer Networks Allow Resources to Be Shared** A *peer-to-peer network* enables any computer to connect to files and printers on any other computer in the network, not just to specialized servers.

## Windows NT Networking Versus the OSI Reference Model

The *Open Systems Interconnection* (OSI) model is a format designed to help people understand the networking architecture of Windows NT. The OSI model was developed by the International Standards Organization (ISO). The OSI model describes a layered architecture that standardizes how various computers in a network should exchange information.

The components of the Windows NT networking architecture can be organized into three categories: network adapter card drivers, transport drivers, and file system drivers. The advantages of this modular design are increased flexibility and reliability because it is much easier to test and change a small module than to test and change the entire block of network software. Also, each layer must be written to be compatible with only the layers immediately above and below it in the overall architecture, which makes adding new capabilities much easier. Figure 4.1 compares the Windows NT network architecture model with the OSI model.

EXAM TIP

**Know the Relationship Between NT Networking and the OSI Model** The OSI model is only a theoretical model. There is not a one-to-one match between the layers of the OSI model and the layers of the Windows NT network architecture. As a result, knowing just the OSI model is not sufficient for the exam. You will want to know what features of NT Networking correspond to what OSI layers.

### NDIS-Compatible Network Adapter Card Drivers

The bottom layer of the Windows NT network architecture, as shown in Figure 4.1, is the network adapter card driver. These drivers must be 32-bit and compliant with the Network Device Interface Specification (NDIS) 3.0 or 4.0. NDIS is the specification that controls how network adapter card drivers need to be written.

Because the adapter card drivers and any protocols being used are completely independent of one another, you can substitute protocols without changing adapter card drivers.

WARNING

**Windows NT Requires Specific Device Drivers** Windows NT cannot use older 16-bit device drivers or the 32-bit NDIS 3.1–compliant drivers that were developed for Windows 95.

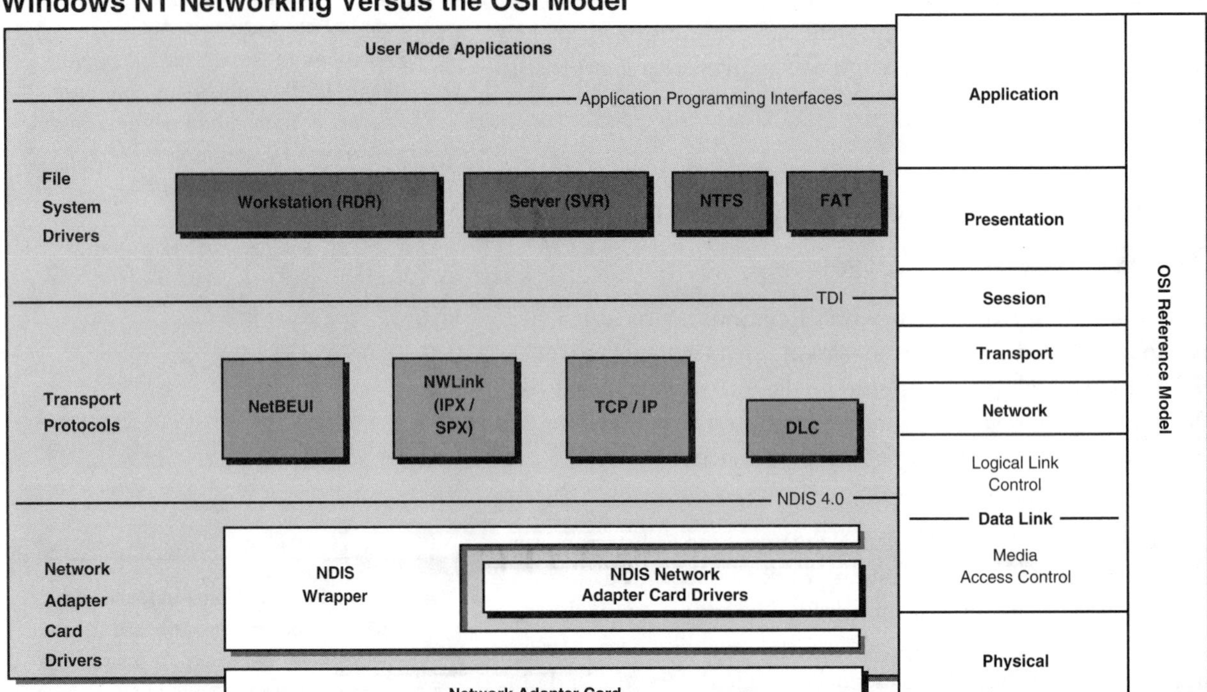


**FIGURE 4.1**
Windows NT network architecture viewed alongside the OSI model.

## NDIS 4.0

NDIS 4.0 is an updated version, for Microsoft Windows NT 4.0, of the boundary layer that defines the interaction of network protocols and network adapter card drivers. Any network protocol compliant with NDIS 4.0 can communicate with any network card driver compliant with NDIS 4.0.

The initial connection made between each protocol being used and the network card driver is referred to as network *binding*. The actual set of networking components used is called the *protocol stack*. If you have more than one network adapter in your computer, each adapter card's protocol stack can be configured individually.

In Windows NT 4.0, NDIS 4.0 enables the following:

- An unlimited number of network adapter cards
- An unlimited number of network protocols bound to a single network adapter card

- Independence between protocols and adapter card drivers
- Communication links between adapter cards and their drivers

## Network Protocols

The network protocols, as shown in Figure 4.1, control the communications between computers on a network. Different network protocols provide varying communications services and capabilities.

> WARNING
>
> **NT Workstation Doesn't Support AppleTalk** Windows NT Workstation 4.0 doesn't support AppleTalk connectivity. Only Windows NT Server 4.0 can be configured with Services for Macintosh.

### TCP/IP

*Transmission Control Protocol/Internet Protocol* (TCP/IP) is the default protocol for Windows NT 4.0 and is an industry standard suite of protocols used for wide area networks (WANs) and the Internet. TCP/IP is commonly used in wide area networks that consist of a variety of computer types.

Microsoft's implementation of TCP/IP provides a number of advantages, including the following:

- Routing support
- Connectivity with the Internet
- Interoperability with most operating systems and computer types
- Support as a client for Dynamic Host Configuration Protocol (DHCP)
- Support as a client for Windows Internet Name Service (WINS)
- Support as a client for Domain Name System (DNS)
- Support for Simple Network Management Protocol (SNMP)

### NWLink IPX/SPX Compatible Transport

NWLink IPX/SPX Compatible Transport is Microsoft's NDIS-compliant version of Novell's Internetwork Packet Exchange (IPX/SPX). The primary function of NWLink in a Microsoft-based network is to provide connectivity with NetWare resources. However, it can also be used for communication on pure Microsoft networks if that is desired.

The advantages of NWLink include the following:

- Connectivity with NetWare resources
- Routing support
- Support from a wide variety of other operating systems
- Large installation base

NWLink is only a transport protocol, and by itself it doesn't enable a Windows NT Workstation 4.0–based computer to access files and printers on a Novell NetWare server or to act as a file and print server to NetWare clients. To access files and printers on a NetWare server, you must also use a NetWare-compatible redirector, such as Microsoft Client Services for NetWare (see the section "File System Drivers" for details).

EXAM TIP

**Don't Confuse NetBIOS and NetBEUI** Although the names seem similar, don't make the common mistake of confusing the NetBEUI transport protocol with the NetBIOS API. NetBIOS and NetBEUI serve very different functions in the networking components of Windows NT (as discussed in the section "Network Application Program Interfaces").

### NetBEUI

*NetBIOS Extended User Interface* (NetBEUI) was originally developed to support small departmental LANs of up to 150 users. Because it was assumed that gateway devices would connect these small departmental LANs, no support for routing was included. Therefore, if you want to connect two or more NetBEUI-based LANs, you must use a bridge instead of a router. Although it is possible to configure some routers to function with NetBEUI, that configuration is usually not a good choice. Only Microsoft-based computers typically use NetBEUI.

The main characteristics of NetBEUI include the following:

- No routing support
- Transmissions are broadcast-based and, therefore, generate a lot of traffic
- Fast performance on small LANs
- Small memory overhead
- No tuning options

### DLC

*Data Link Control* (DLC) is not used for general networking by Windows NT Workstation 4.0. The main use for DLC by Windows NT is for connectivity to printers directly attached to the network, such as Hewlett-Packard JetDirect devices. Additional software is required for connectivity to Systems Network Architecture (SNA) mainframes.

> **WARNING**
>
> **Other Protocols Might Require DLC for Certain Situations** Even if you are planning to use another protocol such as TCP/IP or NWLink to communicate with printers directly attached to your network, you must install the DLC protocol. Some of the networking components needed to establish network sessions with network attached printers are installed only when and if the DLC protocol is installed.

## Transport Driver Interface

The *Transport Driver Interface* (TDI) boundary layer provides the connection between the file system drivers and the individual transport protocols (refer to Figure 4.1). The TDI standard enables transport protocols to be added or removed from a system independently of any file systems that might be in use. TDI is a Microsoft standard.

### File System Drivers

File system drivers are used to access files. Whenever an application attempts to access a file, the I/O Manager determines if the I/O request is for a local disk or for a network resource. If the request is for a network resource, a redirector then passes it to the appropriate network components. The default redirector included with Windows NT Workstation 4.0 is called the Workstation service. It is possible for a Windows NT Workstation 4.0 computer to have more than one redirector to enable network communications with non-Microsoft-based servers, such as UNIX or Novell NetWare.

In addition to the Workstation service, Windows NT Workstation 4.0 also includes a component called the Server service. The Server service is responsible for responding to I/O requests from other computers on the network that have been passed up to it by the lower network components.

> **WARNING**
>
> **Don't Confuse Services with Product Names** Don't confuse the Workstation service and the Server service with the products Windows NT Workstation 4.0 and Windows NT Server 4.0. Both products have both services and can function as either a client or a server during network sessions.

### Network Application Program Interfaces

An *application program interface* (API) is the set of routines that an application program uses to request and carry out lower-level services performed by the operating system. Two network APIs are used by Windows NT to establish communications sessions and to transfer data to other computers in a network:

- *NetBIOS (Network Basic Input/Output System).* The original network API supported by Microsoft. IBM originally developed NetBIOS.
- *Windows Sockets (also called WinSock).* A newer network API originally developed by the UNIX community. Now Microsoft also supports it.

The NetBIOS interface is used by most of the networking services found on NT. This includes the Workstation, Server, and Browser services. Windows Sockets are used by many applications including the TCP/IP utilities DHCP, FTP, and Telnet.

## File and Print Sharing Process

Figure 4.2 details the interaction between the Workstation service on a client computer and the Server service on a server computer as the client attempts to open a file at the server. Note that to simplify this example, the user at the client computer is assumed to have the necessary security authorization to access the file on the server.

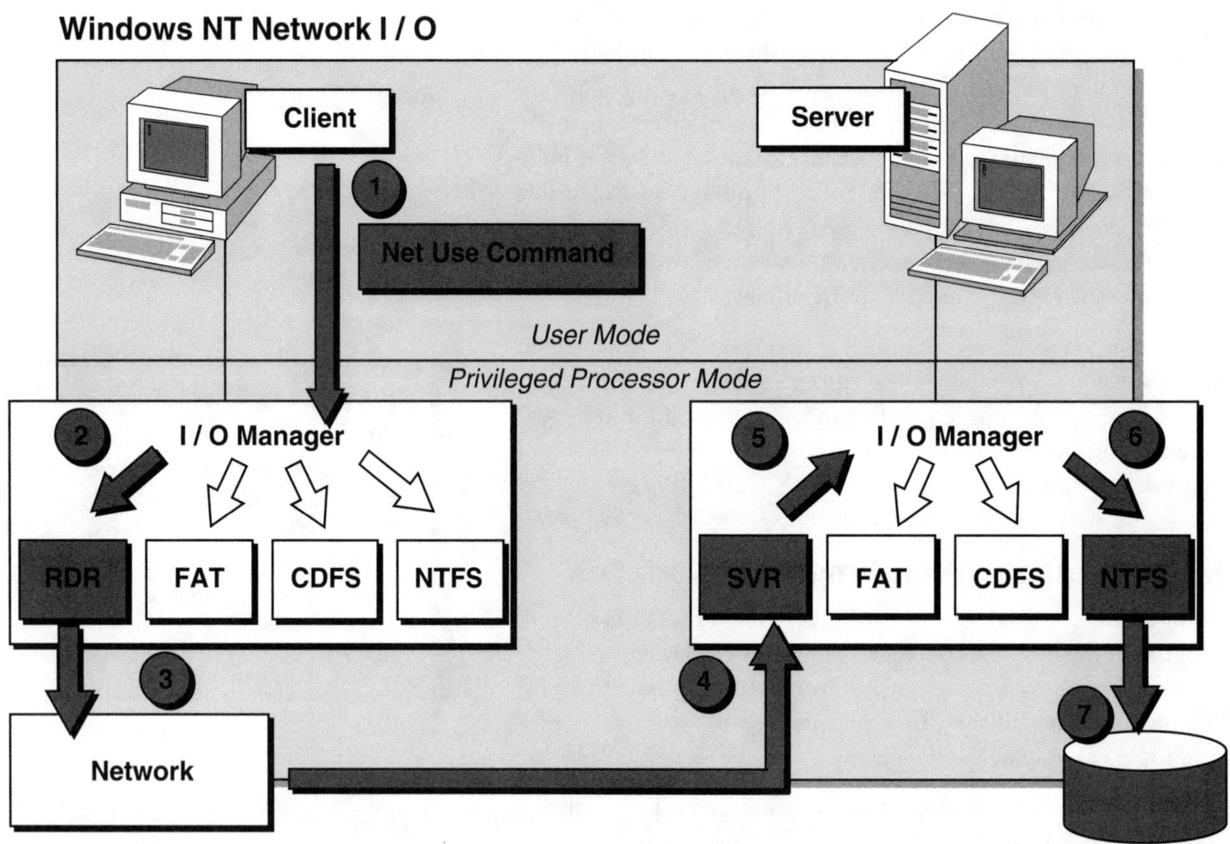


**FIGURE 4.2**
The input/output process in Windows NT.

The following steps outline the sequence of operation illustrated in Figure 4.2:

1. A client initiates a file open command (via a program option or at a command prompt).
2. The I/O Manager at the client determines that the file is located on a remote computer.
3. The Workstation service at the client passes the I/O request to the lower-level networking layers, which send the request to the remote server.
4. The Server service at the server receives the I/O request asking to open a file that resides at the server.
5. The Server service at the server passes the I/O request to the I/O Manager at the server.
6. The I/O Manager at the server passes the I/O request to the local file system driver.
7. The local file system driver at the server performs the desired action. An acknowledgment is then sent back to the requesting client.

In this process, either computer could be Windows NT Workstation 4.0 or Windows NT Server 4.0.

WARNING

**End User License Agreement Limits Concurrent Inbound Sessions** Although Windows NT Workstation 4.0 can function as a network server, the Microsoft End User License Agreement (EULA) limits usage to 10 concurrent inbound sessions. There are no limitations on outbound sessions from Windows NT Workstation 4.0.

You should deploy Windows NT Server 4.0 if you need more than 10 concurrent inbound sessions.

## Distributed Processing

In distributed processing applications (sometimes called *client/server* applications), computing requirements are divided into pieces that run on more than one computer. The minimal *front-end* processes run on a client, and the resource-intensive (CPU and/or hard disk) *back-end* processes are executed on a server. The server shares its processing power by executing applications at the request of clients. Microsoft SQL Server and Microsoft Exchange Server are examples of distributed applications.

## Interprocess Communications Mechanisms

In a distributed processing application, a network connection that enables data to flow back and forth between the client and the server must be established. Table 4.1 lists the various types of network connections you can establish to perform that function.

**TABLE 4.1**

**TYPES OF INTERPROCESS COMMUNICATIONS**

| *IPC Mechanism* | *Typical Uses* |
|---|---|
| Named pipes | Named pipes establish a guaranteed bidirectional communications channel between two computers. After the pipe is established, either computer can read data from or write data to the pipe. |
| Mailslots | Mailslots establish a unidirectional communications channel between two computers. Receipt of the message is not guaranteed, and no acknowledgment is sent if the data is received. |
| Windows Sockets (WinSock) | WinSock is an API that enables applications to access transport protocols such as TCP/IP and NWLink. |
| RPCs | RPCs enable the various components of distributed applications to communicate with one another via the network. |
| Network Dynamic Data Exchange (NetDDE) | NetDDE is an older version of an RPC that is based on NetBIOS. |
| Distributed ActiveX Component Object Model (DCOM) | DCOM is an RPC based on Microsoft technology; it enables the components of a distributed application to be located on multiple computers across a network simultaneously. |

Figure 4.3 shows where the various interprocess communications mechanisms fit into the overall Windows NT 4.0 network architecture.

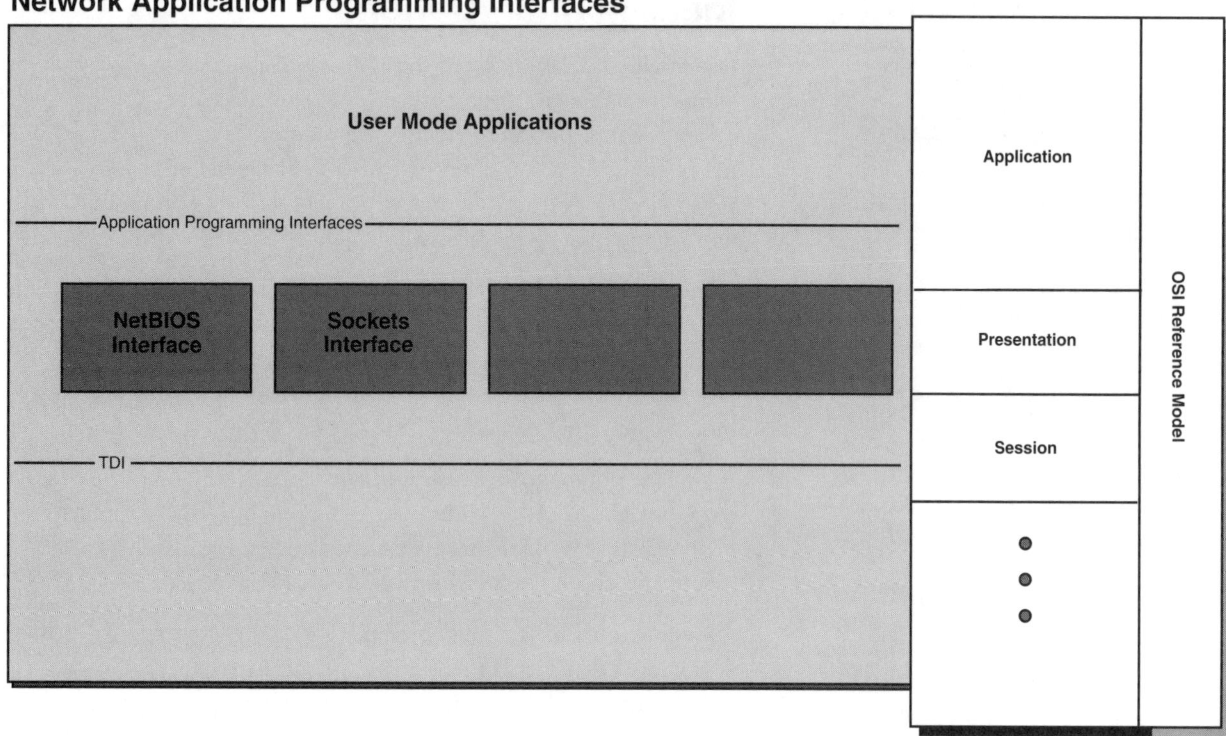


**FIGURE 4.3**
Network application programming interfaces.

## Adding and Configuring the Network Components of Windows NT Workstation

Add and configure the network components of Windows NT Workstation.

You can configure all your network components when you first install Windows NT Workstation 4.0. If you want to examine how your network components are configured, or if you want to make changes to your network configuration, double-click on the Network icon in Control Panel to view the Network dialog box (see Figure 4.4).

> NOTE
> **Administrators Only** You must be an administrator to make changes to the network settings on your computer.

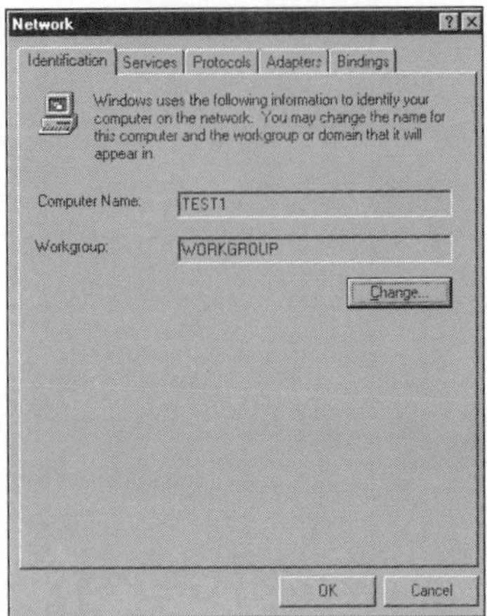


**FIGURE 4.4**
The Network program in Control Panel.

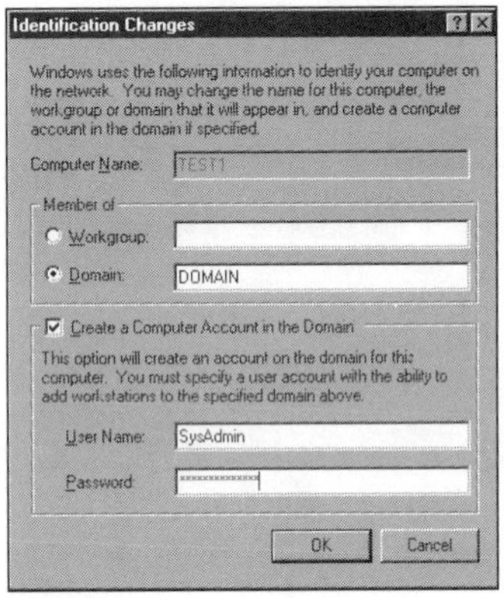

**FIGURE 4.5**
Joining a domain.

## Identification Options

Use the Identification tab of the Network dialog box to view your computer name and your workgroup or domain name. You can click on the Change button to change your computer name (the maximum length for a computer name is 15 characters) or to join a workgroup or domain (the maximum length for a workgroup or domain name is 15 characters) (see Figure 4.5).

Windows NT security requires that every Windows NT computer in a domain has an account. Only domain administrators and other users who have been granted the user right of "Add Workstations to Domain" by a domain administrator can create computer accounts in a Windows NT domain.

If you are a domain administrator, you can give any user or group the user right of "Add Workstations to Domain." To do so, open User Manager for Domains, select the Policies, User Rights command, and check the Show Advanced User Rights box.

To join a domain, you must have network connectivity to the primary domain controller (PDC) in the domain that you want to join. Also, make sure that you do not have a network session open with that PDC. If you must have open network sessions with that PDC, close all open files. Then join that domain, restart your computer, and reopen the files.

You can use either of the following two methods to change your domain name:

- If a domain administrator has already created a computer account for your computer, type the domain name into the Domain box and click on OK.
- You can create your computer account in the domain by using the options in the Identification Changes dialog box as shown in Figure 4.5. To create computer accounts, the username specified must be that of a domain administrator or must have been granted the user right of "Add Workstations to Domain" by a domain administrator.

Regardless of which method you use to join a domain, you should see a status message welcoming you to your new domain. You then must restart your computer to complete the process of joining the new domain.

## Services Options

Use the Services tab in the Network dialog box to view and modify the network services for your computer (see Figure 4.6).

You might want to add some of the following network services to a Windows NT Workstation 4.0:

- *Client Services for NetWare (CSNW).* Enables you to access files and printers on a NetWare server.
- *Microsoft Peer Web Services.* Installs an intranet Web server on your computer.
- *Microsoft TCP/IP Printing.* Configures your computer to act as a print server to which TCP/IP-based clients, such as UNIX systems, can submit print jobs.
- *Remote Access Server.* Enables your computer to connect via telephone lines or the Internet to remote networks.
- *SNMP Service.* Enables your computer to transmit status information via TCP/IP to network management stations.

WARNING

**Computer Account Only Good as Long as a Computer Stays a Member** A computer account is good only as long as the computer remains a member of a domain. If the computer leaves the domain, joins another domain, and then returns to the original domain, for example, the computer account must be re-created in the original domain.

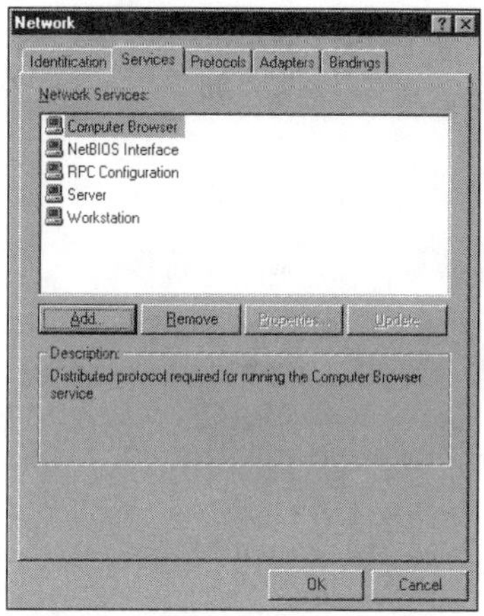


**FIGURE 4.6**
Network services in Windows NT 4.0.

## Protocols Options

Use the Protocols tab in the Network dialog box to view and modify the transport protocols for your computer (see Figure 4.7).

Windows NT Workstation 4.0 allows an unlimited number of network transport protocols. You might want to add some of the following network transport protocols to a Windows NT Workstation 4.0:

- *TCP/IP.* The default protocol for Windows NT Workstation 4.0. It is required for Internet connectivity.
- *NWLink IPX/SPX Compatible Transport.* Required for connectivity to NetWare servers.
- *NetBEUI.* Typically allows connectivity only to other Microsoft-based computers.

You can also add *third-party* transport protocols compatible with TDI and NDIS, which have not been developed by Microsoft.

NOTE

**Eliminate Unused Protocols** For maximum performance, remove any unnecessary protocols and always make sure that your most frequently used protocol is configured to be your default protocol.

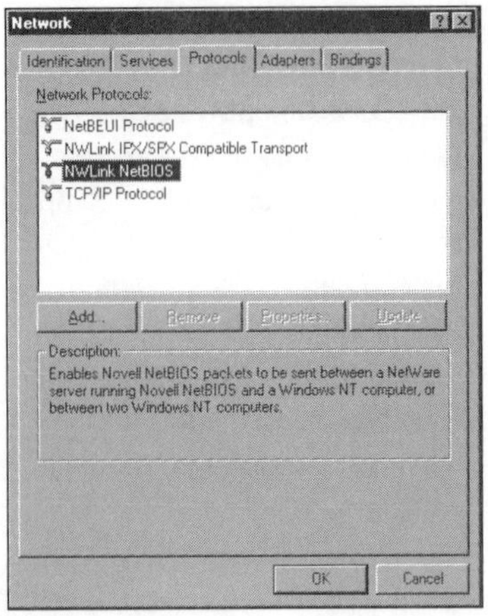

FIGURE 4.7
Transport protocols in NT Workstation.

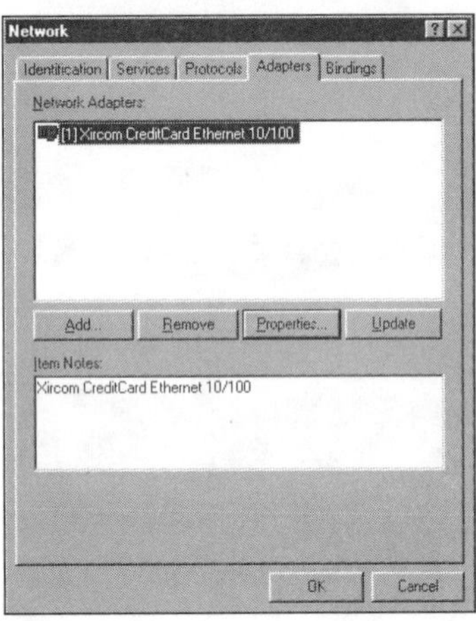


FIGURE 4.8
Viewing current network adapters.

> **NOTE**
>
> **Practice Without a Network Adapter**
> Even if you don't have a network adapter, you can still practice installing some of the network services that will not install without a network adapter. Just select the MS Loopback Adapter from the Network Adapter list.

## Adapters Options

You can use the Adapters tab in the Network dialog box to add, remove, view properties of, or update your network adapter drivers (see Figure 4.8). Windows NT Workstation 4.0 allows an unlimited number of network adapters. It must be noted, however, that certain network options require separate configuration for every card. In particular, if you have TCP/IP installed as a protocol, each adapter must be configured with a unique TCP/IP address in order to function properly.

## Bindings Options

Network bindings are the connections between network services, transport protocols, and adapter card drivers. You can use the Bindings tab in the Network dialog box to view, enable, disable, and change the order of the bindings on your computer (see Figure 4.9). The current default protocol for each network service appears at the top of each section in the display. The default protocol for the Server service in Figure 4.9, for example, is TCP/IP.

Notice in Figure 4.9 that the binding from the Server service to the NetBEUI protocol has been disabled. Given this configuration, client computers that are configured only with the NetBEUI protocol cannot establish network sessions with this computer. However, this computer can still establish network sessions with servers configured with the NetBEUI protocol only, because the Workstation service is still bound to the NetBEUI protocol.

# Accessing Network Resources

Use various methods to access network resources.

Windows NT Workstation 4.0 offers several methods of working with network resources. This gives you multiple ways to determine what network resources are available to you and enables you to make multiple types of connections to those network resources.

## Universal Naming Convention

The *Universal Naming Convention* (UNC) is a standardized way of specifying a share name on a particular computer. The share names can refer to a folder or a printer. The UNC path takes the form of *computer_name**share_name*. For example, the UNC path to a share called Accounting on a server called ACCTSERVER is \\ACCTSERVER\Accounting. Connections made via UNC paths take place immediately and do not require the use of a drive letter.

You can also use UNC connections to connect to network printers. For example, \\ACCTSERVER\ACCTPRINT is the UNC path to a printer named ACCTPRINT on a server named ACCTSERVER.

WARNING

**Some Applications Require a Mapped Drive** Many 16-bit applications do not work with UNC paths. If you need to work with a 16-bit application that doesn't work with UNC paths, you must map a drive letter to the shared folder or connect a port to the network printer.

## Network Neighborhood

If your Windows NT Workstation 4.0 computer has a network card installed, the Network Neighborhood icon appears on your desktop. When you double-click on the Network Neighborhood icon, the list of all computers in your workgroup or domain appears. By double-clicking on the Entire Network icon, you can also view all computers connected to your network that are not members of your workgroup or domain.

When you view lists of computers in Network Neighborhood, you are actually viewing a graphical representation of what is called a *browse list*. The browse list is actually maintained by a computer that has been designated as the Browse Master. All computers in the network that have an active Server service periodically announce their presence to the Browse Master to keep the browse list current.

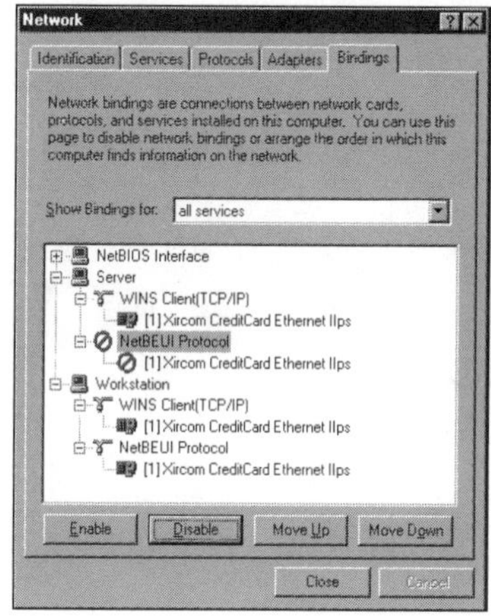


**FIGURE 4.9**
Viewing the network bindings on your computer.

The browse list is very useful in a network environment because it enables a single computer to be the source of information about what resources are available on the network. This is much better than each machine having to maintain its own list or, worse, having to send out a query on the network each time a resource is required.

When a computer wants to display a list of resources in Network Neighborhood, it requests that list from the Browse Master on its LAN. The Browse Master is a computer that is chosen in a browser election. The winner of an election is the machine with the highest credentials to become such a master. These credentials include the following:

- The operating system it uses (NT takes precedence over Windows 95)
- How long the computer has been up and running (the longer the better)
- The role of the computer on the network (in a domain, a domain controller will take precedence over all other computers)

Once elected, the Master Browser then chooses one or more machines to be backup browsers (the number of backup browsers is based on the number of clients on the network at the time). Backup browsers are chosen from a list of machines designated as potential browsers. By default, any machine with its Server service enabled is a potential browser (this includes all NT machines and all Windows 95 and Windows for Workgroups machines enabled for File and Print Sharing).

It may not always be prudent for all machines to be potential browsers, though, especially on a workgroup where the potential exists for any machine to win an election. If a low-powered machine is elected as the Browse Master, network response could slow down considerably. Consequently, many machines are configured to not become browsers under any circumstances. On an NT machine, you can configure a machine that way by changing the following Registry key:

HKEY_Local_Machine\System\CurrentControlSet\Services\Browser\Parameters\MaintainServerList

If the above key is set to "Yes," the NT computer will always attempt to become a browser; if the key is set to "No," the computer will never attempt to become a browser and can never become a backup browser; if the key is set to "Auto," the computer participates in elections, and if it does not win, it is listed as a potential browser, which means it can be enlisted as a backup browser if required.

## `Net View` Command

You can also access the current browse list from the command prompt by typing `Net View`. The current browse list will be displayed on your screen. A sample browse list looks like this:

```
C:\>net view
Server Name              Remark

-------------------------------------------------
\\TEST1
\\TEST2
\\TESTPDC
The command completed successfully.
```

### Net Use Command

You can associate network resources with drive letters from the command prompt by using the `Net Use` command and the UNC path of the resource. For example, to connect drive letter X: to a share called GoodStuff on a server named SERVER1, you would type the following command at a command prompt:

```
Net Use X: \\SERVER1\GoodStuff
```

You can also use the `Net Use` command to connect clients to network printers. If you want to connect port LPT1 to a network printer named HP5 on a server named SERVER1, you can use the following command:

```
Net Use LPT1: \\SERVER1\HP5
```

To disconnect the network resources for the two preceding commands, you would use the following two commands:

```
Net Use X: /d

Net Use LPT1: /d
```

## WINDOWS NT WORKSTATION IN A NETWARE ENVIRONMENT

Implement Windows NT Workstation as a client in a NetWare environment.

In order to access shared resources on a NetWare server, an NT Workstation must first share a common protocol with that server. The protocol of choice on a Novell network is IPX/SPX, and Microsoft's implementation of that protocol is NWLink.

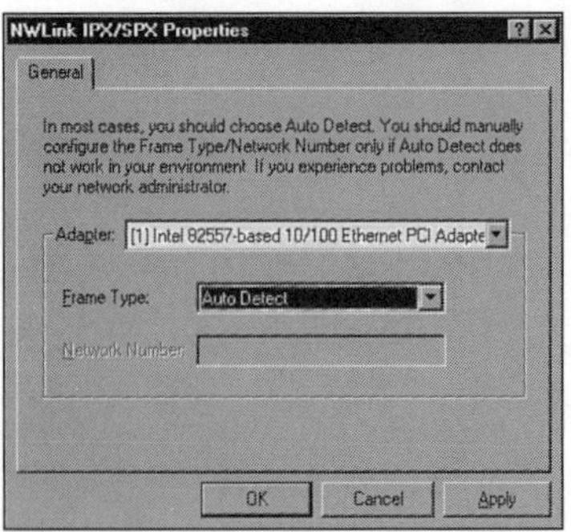


**FIGURE 4.10**
The NWLink IPX/SPX Properties dialog box with Auto Detect selected.

# Installing and Configuring NWLink

As you learned in the section "Protocols Options," you install NWLink through the Protocols tab of the Network dialog box (refer to Figure 4.7). After installing the protocol, you might have to configure it. To do so, you select NWLink IPX/SPX Compatible Transport in the installed protocol list, and then click the Properties button. The NWLink IPX/SPX Properties dialog box appears (see Figure 4.10).

In this dialog box, you can specify the frame type and network number that are associated with a particular network adapter. The frame type and network number must conform to the same configuration as the resource you are trying to access, or you have no hope of connecting to it. Of course, if you have a router on your network, you may be able to get away with having a different network number, provided that the resource is indeed on a different network.

The frame type indicates which kind of IPX/SPX packet is being transmitted by the NetWare resource you are trying to connect to. This frame type will differ with different versions of NetWare and with different types of networks (ethernet versus token-ring, for example). If only one frame type is being used on your network, you can leave the frame type at Auto Detect to ensure that the first frame type detected will be configured for the adapter. If more than one frame type is being used on your network (which is typical when more than one version of NetWare is running), only one frame type will be configured. The default frame type is 802.2; if any 802.2 frames are detected, that will become the only frame type NT will respond to. To allow interoperability with multiple frame types, you have to configure NWLink manually. Manual configuration consists of simply selecting a frame type from the list of available types (see Figure 4.11), which include the following:

- Ethernet II
- Ethernet 802.3
- Ethernet 802.2
- Ethernet SNAP
- ARCnet

You need to make sure that you select a frame type that is being used by the NetWare resource on your network, which you can find out from the NetWare resource itself. In a NetWare 3.x environment, the default frame is 802.3. In a NetWare 4.x environment, the default frame type is 802.2.

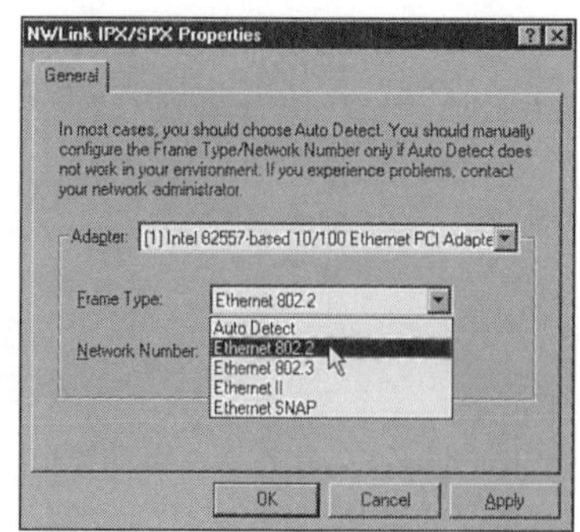


**FIGURE 4.11**

Select the frame type manually if necessary.

If you need to configure multiple frame types, you begin by selecting one of the frame types manually. Whereas NT Server has a GUI configuration for multiple frame types, NT Workstation does not. After selecting the frame type, you will need to edit the Registry and add more frame types to the list. You need to modify the Registry key

> HKEY_LOCAL_MACHINE\System\CurrentControlSet\Services \NwlinkIpx\NetConfig*network adapter card1*

where *network adapter card1* represents the network adapter card you are configuring.

This Registry key can contain multiple values. You enter multiple values separated by <Enter> to configure properly (see Figure 4.12). The entries are hex numbers corresponding to the frame types. The correspondence is as follows: Ethernet II (0); 802.3 (1); 802.2 (2); SNAP (3); and ARCnet (4).

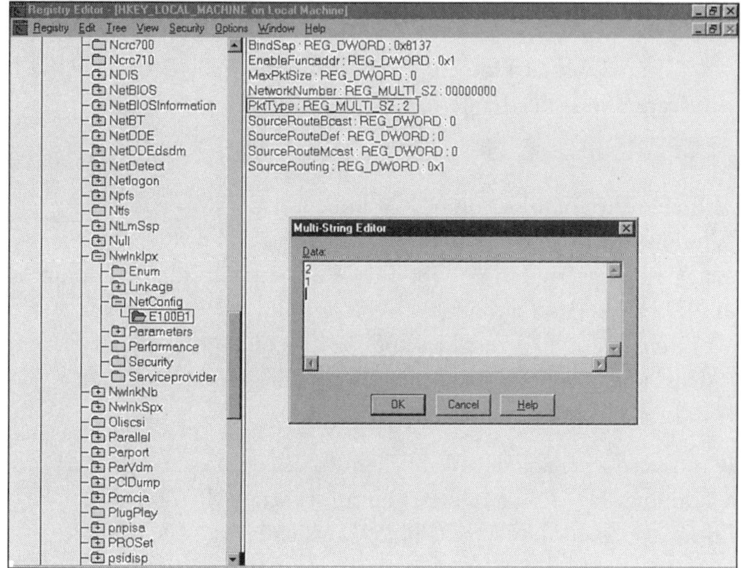


**FIGURE 4.12**

Editing the Registry to configure multiple frame types (802.2 and 802.3).

## Client Services for NetWare

To enable a Windows NT Workstation 4.0 computer to access and share resources on a NetWare server, you might have to install additional software besides the NWLink protocol on the Windows NT Workstation 4.0 computers. What type of access you are trying to establish determines whether additional software must be installed. NWLink can establish client/server connections, but it does not provide access to files and printers on NetWare servers.

If you want to be able to access files or printers on a NetWare server, you must install the Microsoft Client Services for NetWare (CSNW), which is included with Windows NT Workstation 4.0. CSNW enables Windows NT Workstation 4.0 to access files and printers at NetWare servers running NetWare 2.x or later (including NetWare 4.x servers running NDS). CSNW installs an additional network redirector.

Windows NT Workstation 4.0 computers that have NWLink and CSNW installed gain the following:

- A new network redirector compatible with NetWare Core Protocol (NCP). NCP is the standard Novell protocol for file and print sharing.
- Support for long filenames, when the NetWare server is configured to support long filenames.
- Large Internet Protocol (LIP) to automatically determine the largest possible frame size to communicate with NetWare servers.

NOTE

**Connect to NetWare Without Installing Client Services for NetWare** Windows NT Workstation 4.0 can access files and printers on a NetWare server without adding CSNW if Workstation is connecting through a Windows NT Server configured with Gateway Services for NetWare (GSNW). GSNW can be installed only on Windows NT Server.

Although the combination of NWLink and CSNW enables a Windows NT Workstation 4.0 to access files and printers on a NetWare server running NDS, it does not support administration of NDS trees. Also, although CSNW enables a Windows NT Workstation 4.0 to access files and printers on a NetWare server, it doesn't enable NetWare clients to access files and printers on a Windows NT Workstation 4.0.

If you need to enable NetWare clients to access files and printers on a Windows NT 4.0 computer, you must install Microsoft File and Print Services for NetWare (FPNW), which is available separately from Microsoft on a Windows NT Server 4.0.

## Installing Client Services for NetWare

CSNW is installed the same way as any other network service, through the Network program in the Control Panel. After you install CSNW, you will notice a new CSNW program listed in the Control Panel. Exercise 4.4 (later in the chapter) provides full instructions on how to install CSNW.

If after you install NWLink and CSNW you cannot establish connectivity to your NetWare servers, you should check to see what IPX frame type they are configured for. There are actually two different, incompatible versions, 802.2 and 802.3. Windows NT Workstation 4.0 attempts to automatically determine the correct frame type, but you might have to manually specify the frame type to make the connection work (see Exercise 4.5 in the "Exercises" section).

WARNING

**Passwords Are Not Synchronized** Even though Windows NT Workstation 4.0 attempts to automatically connect you to your NetWare system, there is no direct link between the two account databases. If you change either network password, the other password does not automatically change to match your new network password.

## Configuring Client Services for NetWare

After you have installed CSNW on your computer, each user that logs on receives a prompt to enter the details of his or her NetWare account. Each user can enter either a preferred server for NetWare 2.x or 3.x or his or her default tree and context for NDS. Or the user can specify <None> if he doesn't have a NetWare account. Each time the same user logs on to that computer, he automatically connects to his NetWare account in addition to his Windows NT account.

Each user is asked to enter his NetWare account information only once. The only way to change a user's recorded NetWare account information is to double-click on the CSNW program in Control Panel (see Figure 4.13). You can also use the CSNW program in Control Panel to modify your print options for NetWare printers—to add form feeds or print banners, for example.

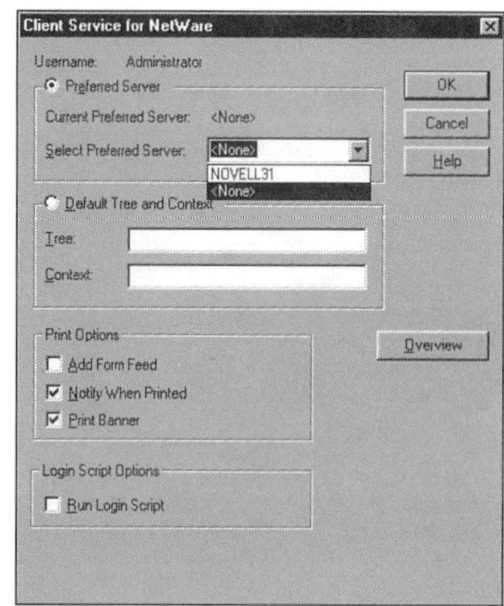


**FIGURE 4.13**
Modifying NetWare account information.

## Connecting to NetWare Resources

After you install NWLink and CSNW, you access the NetWare servers in your network using the same methods you would to connect to any other Windows NT Server. You can connect to files and printers on the NetWare servers without any special procedures.

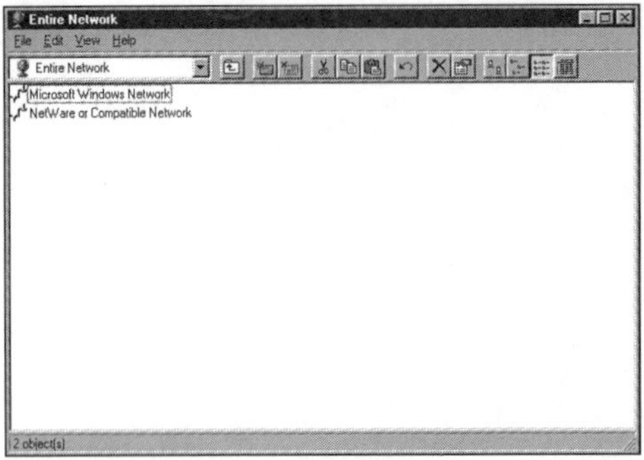


**FIGURE 4.14**
Browsing NetWare servers.

## Browsing

After you install NWLink and CSNW, when you double-click on Network Neighborhood and then double-click on Entire Network, you can choose to browse either the Microsoft Windows Network or the NetWare or Compatible Network (see Figure 4.14).

## Map Command

After you install NWLink and CSNW, right-click on Network Neighborhood and choose Map Network Drive from the menu. You can then assign any drive letter to any shared directory on a NetWare server (see Figure 4.15).

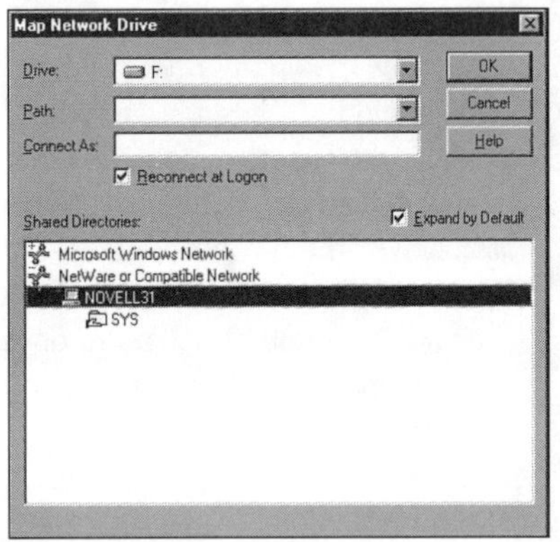


**FIGURE 4.15**
Mapping network drives to NetWare servers.

## Connecting to NetWare Printers

Suppose the resources you want to connect to are not file resources but are printer resources. Actually, the configuration is the same for printer access as for file access. Installation of NWLink and CSNW enables you to connect to NetWare print queues (see Figure 4.16 and Exercise 4.9).

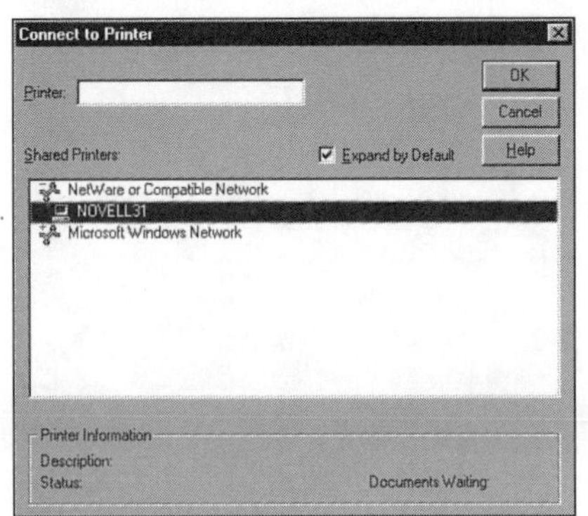


**FIGURE 4.16**
Connecting to a NetWare print queue.

# NT Workstation as a TCP/IP Client

Use various configurations to install Windows NT Workstation as a TCP/IP client.

TCP/IP, the default protocol for Windows NT Workstation 4.0, is a suite of protocols designed for both LANs and WANs. TCP/IP is supported by most common operating systems and is required for connectivity to the Internet. When you manually configure a computer as a TCP/IP host, you must at least configure a TCP/IP address and a subnet mask that are compatible with other hosts on your LAN. The most common network settings and their definitions are outlined here:

- *IP address.* A logical 32-bit address used to identify a TCP/IP host. Each network adapter configured for TCP/IP must have a unique IP address, such as 10.100.5.43.

- *Subnet mask.* A subnet is a division of a larger network environment that's typically connected with routers. Whenever one TCP/IP host tries to communicate with another TCP/IP host, the subnet mask is used to determine whether the other TCP/IP host is on the same network or a different network. If the other TCP/IP host is on a different network, the message must be sent via a router that connects to the other network. A typical subnet mask is 255.255.255.0; this is the default subnet mask for a class C license. All computers on a subnet must have identical subnet masks.
- *Default gateway (router).* This optional setting is the address of the router for this subnet that controls communications with all other subnets. If this address is not specified, this TCP/IP host can communicate only with other TCP/IP hosts on its subnet.
- *Windows Internet Name Service (WINS).* Computers use IP addresses to identify one another, but users generally find it easier to use other means, such as computer names. Therefore, some method must be used to provide *name resolution,* the process in which references to computer names are converted into the appropriate IP addresses. WINS provides name resolution for the NetBIOS computer names typically used on Microsoft networks. If your network uses WINS for name resolution, your computer needs to be configured with the IP address of a WINS server (the IP address of a secondary WINS server can also be specified).
- *Domain Name Service (DNS) Server Address.* DNS is an industry standard distributed database that provides name resolution and a hierarchical naming system for identifying TCP/IP hosts on the Internet and on private networks. That means that instead of specifying a TCP/IP address for a computer, you can use its fully distinguished name (such as microsoft.com). A DNS address must be specified to enable connectivity with the Internet or with UNIX TCP/IP hosts. You can specify more than one DNS address, and you can specify the order in which the addresses should be used. Whereas WINS is used to resolve NetBIOS names, DNS is used to resolve names when NetBIOS names are not available, typically with UNIX hosts on the Internet.

NOTE

**Name Resolution** Name resolution is the process of translating user-friendly computer names to IP addresses.

WARNING

**Incorrect TCP/IP Protocol Settings Cause Problems** If the settings for the TCP/IP protocol are incorrectly specified, you will experience problems that keep your computer from establishing communications with other TCP/IP hosts in your network. In extreme cases, communications on your entire subnet can be disrupted.

If two computers on your network have the same TCP/IP address, the message shown in Figure 4.17 will be displayed on one or both of the conflicting machines.

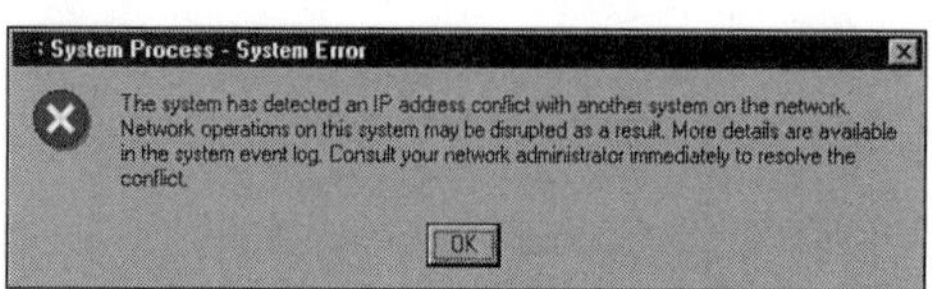


**FIGURE 4.17**
This message appears when two computers on the same LAN have the same TCP/IP address.

You can specify all the settings for the TCP/IP protocol manually, or you can have them configured automatically through a network service called *Dynamic Host Configuration Protocol* (DHCP).

## Dynamic Host Configuration Protocol

One way to avoid the possible problems of administrative overhead and incorrect settings for the TCP/IP protocol—which are caused by incorrect manual configurations—is to set up your network so that all your clients receive their TCP/IP configuration information automatically through Dynamic Host Configuration Protocol (DHCP).

DHCP automatically centralizes and manages the allocation of the TCP/IP settings required for proper network functionality for computers that have been configured as *DHCP clients*. One major advantage of using DHCP is that most of your network settings have to be configured only once—at the DHCP server. Also, the TCP/IP settings that the DHCP client receives from the DHCP server are only *leased* to it and must be periodically renewed. This lease and renewal sequence enables a network administrator to change client TCP/IP settings if necessary.

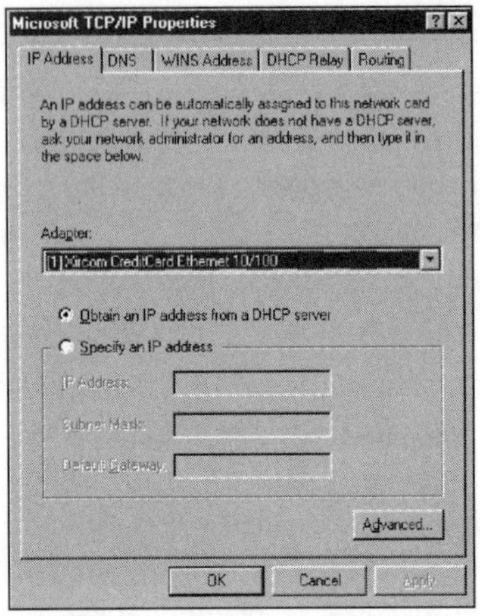

**FIGURE 4.18**
Specifying a TCP/IP host to be a DHCP client.

To configure a computer as a DHCP client, you choose Obtain an IP Address from a DHCP Server in the TCP/IP Properties box (see Figure 4.18). Exercise 4.2 contains complete instructions.

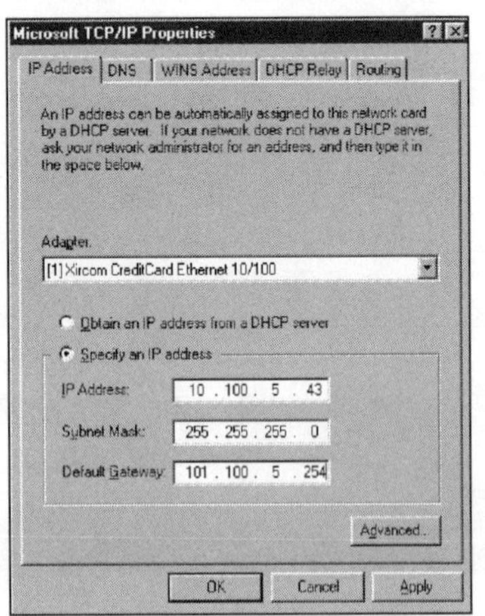


**FIGURE 4.19**
Manual configuration of a TCP/IP host.

## Manually Configuring TCP/IP

To manually configure your TCP/IP settings, you must enter all the required values into the TCP/IP Properties dialog box (see Figure 4.19). For complete details, see Exercise 4.1 (later in this chapter).

## Name Resolution with TCP/IP

DNS and WINS are not the only name resolution methods available for Windows NT Workstation 4.0 TCP/IP hosts. Microsoft also provides two different lookup files, LMHOSTS and HOSTS, for this purpose. These files both provide static name resolution for a local workstation for situations when no network name resolution system exists. The files consist primarily of mappings between common names (NetBIOS or Host) and TCP/IP addresses. As a rule of thumb, WINS replaces LMHOSTS, and DNS replaces HOSTS.

You can find samples of both LMHOSTS and HOSTS in the *winnt_root*\SYSTEM32\DRIVERS\ETC folder under the names LMHOSTS.SAM and HOSTS.SAM. In order to use either of these, configure it with the resolution you need for your network, and then rename it to eliminate the .SAM extension but leave it in the path in which you found it. If you do not eliminate the .SAM extension, or if you move one of these files from the \winnt_root\SYSTEM32\DRIVERS\ETC folder, NT will not be able to use it for resolution. The .SAM files contain instructions on how they are to be used.

## TCP/IP Tools

The TCP/IP protocol suite comes with a number of tools, some for data communication and others for diagnostics and configuration. Two important tools for determining the correctness of configuration and the ability to communicate properly are PING and IPCONFIG.

### Using IPCONFIG

To determine the current configuration of TCP/IP on your computer, you can use the command line tool IPCONFIG (short for TCP/IP configuration). The syntax of the command is as follows:

```
IPCONFIG
```

This command will return basic TCP/IP information for your computer:

```
Windows NT IP Configuration

Token Ring Adapter TXP162:

IP Address:. . . . . . . . . . : 131.107.2.200
Subnet Mask: . . . . . . . . . : 255.255.255.0
Default Gateway: . . . . . . . : 131.107.2.1
```

If you want a complete listing of all TCP/IP configuration information, you can append the `/all` switch to the command as follows:

```
IPCONFIG /all
```

The following is a sample output from the IPCONFIG command with the /all switch:

```
Windows NT IP Configuration

Host Name . . . . . . . . . . : bazyl.ikthuse.com
DNS Servers . . . . . . . . . : 131.107.2.2
Node Type . . . . . . . . . . : Hybrid
NetBIOS Scope ID. . . . . . :
IP Routing Enabled. . . . . : No
WINS Proxy Enabled. . . . . : No
NetBIOS Resolution Uses DNS : No

Token Ring Adapter txp162:

Description . . . . . . . . . : ISA Token-Ring Network 16/4
Adapter
Physical Address. . . . . . : 00-55-00-81-5A-96
DHCP Enabled. . . . . . . . : Yes
IP Address. . . . . . . . . : 131.107.2.200
Subnet Mask . . . . . . . . . : 255.255.255.0
Default Gateway . . . . . . : 131.107.2.1
DHCP Server . . . . . . . . . : 131.107.2.2
Primary WINS Server . . . . : 131.107.2.2
Lease Obtained. . . . . . . : Saturday, June 06, 1998
➥12:31:29 PM
Lease Expires . . . . . . . : Tuesday, June 09, 1999
➥6:31:29 PM
```

Note that, if you are a DHCP client, IPCONFIG also gives you full details on the duration of your current DHCP lease. You can verify whether a DHCP client has connectivity to a DHCP server by releasing the client's IP address and then attempting to lease an IP address. You can conduct this test by typing the following sequence of commands from the DHCP client at a command prompt:

```
IPCONFIG /release

IPCONFIG /renew
```

## Using PING

The command-line utility called PING is used to verify that TCP/IP hosts are reachable from your computer, which thereby confirms the accuracy of both your TCP/IP configuration and your connectivity to other hosts. The PING command uses a series of TCP/IP echoes to determine if an Internet host can be located. If you are having trouble communicating using TCP/IP, the first thing you should do is use IPCONFIG to confirm that your computer is configured properly. Then you should use a series of pings to determine how much of the LAN or WAN you can communicate with.

The command syntax for `PING` is as follows:

```
PING hostaddress
```

When you ping successfully, a series of four responses are generated, indicating that communication with the host you pinged was successful. The successful communication response looks like this:

```
D:\PING 131.107.2.1

Pinging 131.107.2.1 with 32 bytes of data

Reply from 131.107.2.1: bytes = 32 time<10ms TTL=128
Reply from 131.107.2.1: bytes = 32 time<10ms TTL=128
Reply from 131.107.2.1: bytes = 32 time<10ms TTL=128
Reply from 131.107.2.1: bytes = 32 time<10ms TTL=128
```

If the `PING` command is unsuccessful, you will receive a message like this:

```
D:\PING 131.107.2.1

Pinging 131.107.2.1 with 32 bytes of data

Request timed out.
Request timed out.
Request timed out.
Request timed out.
```

A methodology for troubleshooting using PING is discussed in Chapter 7, "Troubleshooting."

# Dial-Up Networking

Configure and install Dial-Up Networking in a given situation.

*Remote Access Service* (RAS) and *Dial-Up Networking* (DUN) enable you to extend your network to unlimited locations. RAS servers and DUN clients enable remote clients to make connections to your LAN either via ordinary telephone lines or through higher-speed techniques, such as ISDN or X.25. The incoming connections can also be established via industry standard *Point-to-Point Protocol* (PPP) or the newer *Point-to-Point Tunneling Protocol* (PPTP) that makes use of the Internet. DUN also supports the use of Serial Line Internet Protocol (SLIP) to initiate dial-up connections with SLIP servers.

> NOTE
>
> **PPTP Provides Added Security**
>
> The *Point-to-Point Tunneling Protocol* (PPTP) is an extension to PPP that enables clients to connect to remote servers over the Internet with security not normally present in that environment.

After clients establish a connection to a RAS server, they are registered into the local network and can take advantage of the same network services and data that they could if they were actually physically connected to the local network. The only difference clients might notice is that WAN connections are much slower than a direct physical connection to their LAN is.

## Line Protocols

The network transport protocols (NetBEUI, NWLink, and TCP/IP) were designed for the characteristics of LANs and are not suitable for use in phone-based connections. To make the network transport protocols function properly in phone-based connections, it is necessary to encapsulate them in a line protocol. Windows NT Workstation 4.0 supports two line protocols: SLIP and PPP. In addition, NT Workstation also supports PPTP, an extension of PPP that allows for increased security through the establishment of an encrypted "tunnel" between the RAS client and a RAS server.

### Serial Line Internet Protocol (SLIP)

SLIP is an industry standard that support TCP/IP connections made over serial lines. Unfortunately, SLIP has several limitations:

- Supports only TCP/IP; does not support IPX or NetBEUI
- Requires static IP addresses; does not support DHCP
- Transmits authentication passwords as clear text; does not support encryption
- Usually requires a scripting system for the logon process

Windows NT Workstation 4.0 supports SLIP client functionality only; operation as a SLIP server is not supported.

NOTE

**Pool Modems to Increase Access Speed** New to NT Workstation 4.0 is support for PPP Multilink, which enables you to combine multiple physical links into one logical connection. A client with two ordinary phone lines and two 28.8Kbps modems, for example, could establish a PPP Multilink session with a RAS server to produce an effective throughput of up to 57.6Kbps. The two modems do not have to be the same type or speed. Both the RAS server and the DUN client must have PPP Multilink enabled.

### Point-to-Point Protocol (PPP)

The limitations of SLIP prompted the development of a newer industry standard protocol, Point-to-Point Protocol (PPP). Some of the advantages of PPP include the following:

- Supports TCP/IP, IPX, NetBEUI, and others
- Supports DHCP or static addresses
- Supports encryption for authentication
- Doesn't require a scripting system for the logon process

## Point-to-Point Tunneling Protocol

New to Windows NT Workstation 4.0 is an extension to PPP called Point-to-Point Tunneling Protocol (PPTP). PPTP enables a DUN client to establish a communications session with a RAS server over the Internet. PPTP enables multiprotocol virtual private networks (VPNs), so remote users can gain secure encrypted access to their corporate networks over the Internet. Because PPTP encapsulates TCP/IP, NWLink, and NetBEUI, it enables the Internet to be used as a backbone for NWLink and NetBEUI.

To use PPTP, you must first establish a connection from the DUN client to the Internet using PPP and then establish a connection to the RAS server over the Internet using a VPN.

# Installing and Configuring the Dial-Up Networking Client

You can install DUN either when you install Windows NT Workstation 4.0 or later. If you select remote access to the network during setup, both RAS and DUN will be installed. However, either or both services can be installed separately after installation of Windows NT Workstation 4.0.

**STEP BY STEP**

### 4.1 Installing Dial-Up Networking Client

1. Install and configure a modem. (This step is required only if the RAS connection is to be established using a phone connection.)
2. Install and configure PPTP. (This step is required only if you are using PPTP for additional security.) This step may be performed in conjunction with step 1 or as an alternative to step 1.
3. Install the RAS service.
4. The first time you access Dial-Up Networking, you must configure a location document and set up one or more Phonebook entries.

WARNING

**NT Workstation Supports Only One RAS Session at a Time** Windows NT Workstation 4.0 is limited to one RAS session at a time, either dial-out or receive. If you need to support more than one simultaneous RAS session, you should purchase Windows NT Server 4.0.

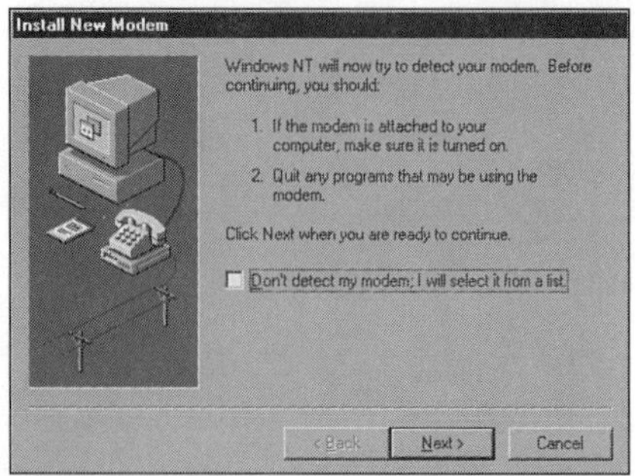


**FIGURE 4.20**
The Install New Modem Wizard begins the process of modem installation.

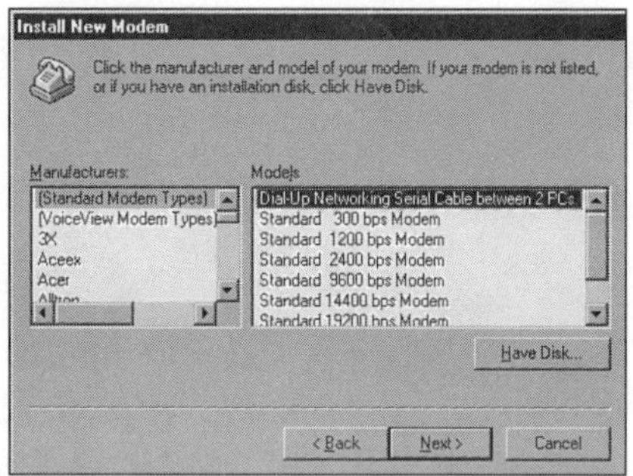


**FIGURE 4.21**
When specifying the modem to install, you must indicate both manufacturer and model.

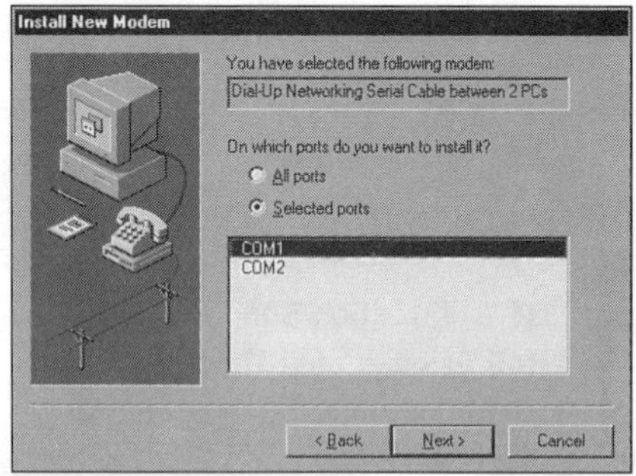


**FIGURE 4.22**
Manual installation involves indicating which COM port the modem will communicate over.

## Installing and Configuring a Modem

If you are going to be using phone lines to connect to a RAS server, either directly or through an Internet service provider (ISP), you will have to install a modem and then configure it through the Control Panel. This can be done during or after the installation process.

---

## STEP BY STEP

### 4.2 Installing a Modem

1. Open the Control Panel and double-click the Modems icon.
2. Allow NT to try to detect your modem by clicking the Next button in the Install New Modem dialog box (see Figure 4.20). If NT will not detect your modem, select the Don't Detect My Modem option, as shown in the figure.
3. If you chose to tell NT what modem you have, select the modem manufacturer and model from the lists in the Install New Modem dialog box (see Figure 4.21), and then click Next.
4. If you chose to install the modem manually, choose the port (or ports) through which your modem will be communicating from the list presented in the next dialog box (see Figure 4.22). Then click Next.
5. If this is the first modem or RAS device you have installed, you will be asked to configure a location (see Figure 4.23). Choose your country from the pull-down list and enter your area code. If you have to dial a number to get an outside line—like 9, for example—enter that and choose the type of phone system you are using (most North American cities use tone dialing). Click Next to continue.
6. When you're told that your modem has successfully been installed, click the Finish button.
7. A dialog box appears, telling you which modems are installed. Click the Close button.

---

## Installing the RAS Service

The RAS service allows your NT Workstation to act as either a RAS client or a RAS server. Usually, NT Workstation is configured as a RAS client; however, it has limited capability as a server. Because it is limited to a single inbound connection, a Workstation could provide a single user with access to a workgroup LAN, or each Workstation could allow the owner to dial in from home or a travel location.

In order to complete the configuration of the RAS service, you must have a RAS-capable device installed on your system. This could take the form of a modem or a PPTP Virtual Private Network (the configuration of which is discussed in an upcoming section).

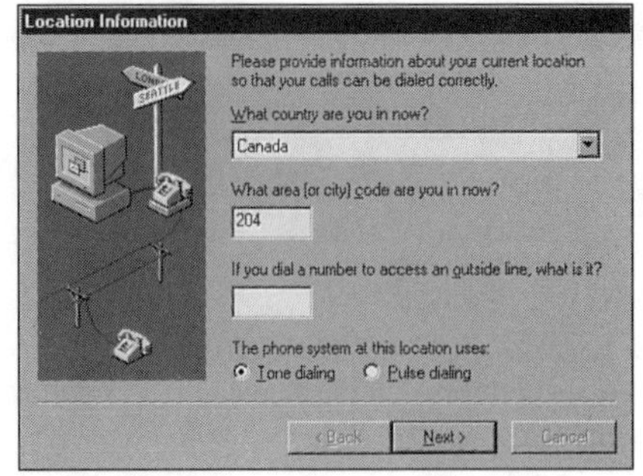


**FIGURE 4.23**
The Location Information dialog box allows you to specify location-specific information.

## STEP BY STEP

### 4.3 Installing and Configuring the RAS Service

1. Open the Network dialog box and click the Services tab.
2. Click the Add button, and select Remote Access Service from the list of services to install.
3. When prompted, enter the path to the NT files used for installing RAS.
4. When the Add RAS Device dialog box appears, select a RAS-capable device from the pull-down list (see Figure 4.24). If you have not already installed a modem, you can install one at this point by clicking the Install Modem button and following the wizard's instructions.
5. When the Remote Access Setup dialog box appears, click the Configure button to configure whether the selected RAS device will dial out, receive, or both (see Figure 4.25). Normally, you will leave Dial Out Only selected; however, if your Workstation is to be a RAS server, select either Receive Calls Only or Dial Out and Receive Calls. Then click OK to continue.
6. Assuming that you are only dialing out, click the Network button in the Remote Access Setup dialog box to specify

*continues*

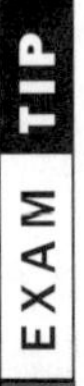

**The Exam Focuses on RAS Client Functionality** The exam does not expect that you know how to configure a RAS server, even on an NT Workstation. All you will be required to know is the client side of RAS. Server configuration is covered in the Server exam.

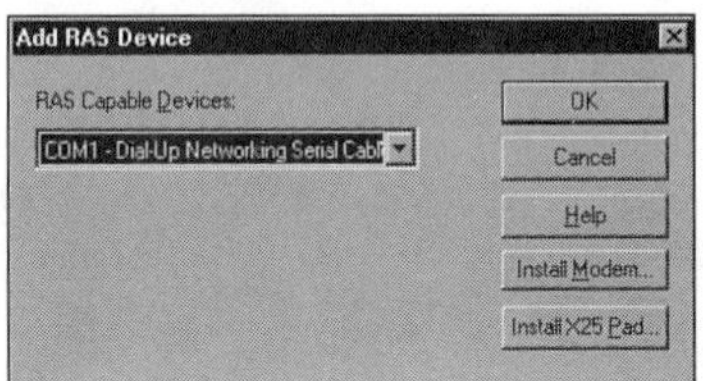


**FIGURE 4.24**
From this dialog box, you configure RAS to work with a specific device.

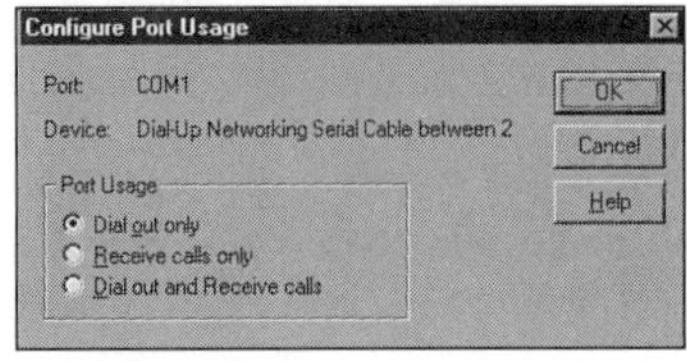


**FIGURE 4.25**
The Configure Port Usage dialog box allows you to indicate whether this device should be used to dial out, receive calls, or both.

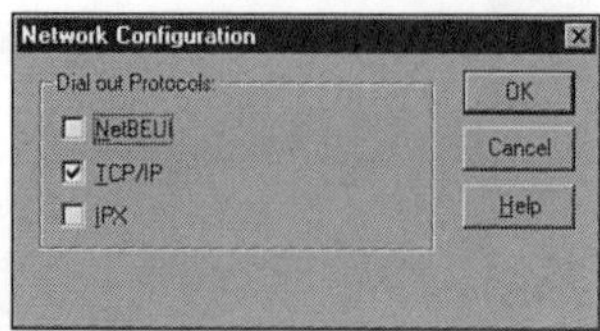


**FIGURE 4.26**
The Network Configuration dialog box allows you to indicate which protocols will be used to communicate on the remote network.

*continued*

the protocol you want to use to communicate on the Remote network (see Figure 4.26).

7. Click the Continue button in the Remote Access Setup dialog box to continue the installation of RAS.
8. After RAS has been installed, click Close to close the Network dialog box.
9. When prompted, click the Yes button to restart NT Workstation.

## Configuring a Phonebook Entry

The phonebook is a central place for configuration of phone numbers to RAS servers. When you connect to a remote LAN using RAS, you must use a phonebook entry to dial. This entry specifies not only the phone number, but also the type of server you are connecting to (PPP or SLIP).

## STEP BY STEP

### 4.4 Adding a Phonebook Entry

1. Open the My Computer window and double-click the Dial-Up Networking icon. If this is the first phonebook entry you have entered, you are told that the phonebook is empty. Click OK to enter a new entry.
2. In the New Phonebook Entry Wizard, type a name describing the server you are connecting to in the Name the New Phonebook Entry field and then select the I Know All About Phonebook Entries… check box to exit the wizard (see Figure 4.27). Then click the Finish button.
3. In the New Phonebook Entry dialog box, type the phone number of the dial-up server in the Phone Number field (see Figure 4.28). Type the number as you would dial it from your location if you were phoning by hand (for example, 1-204-555-1212).

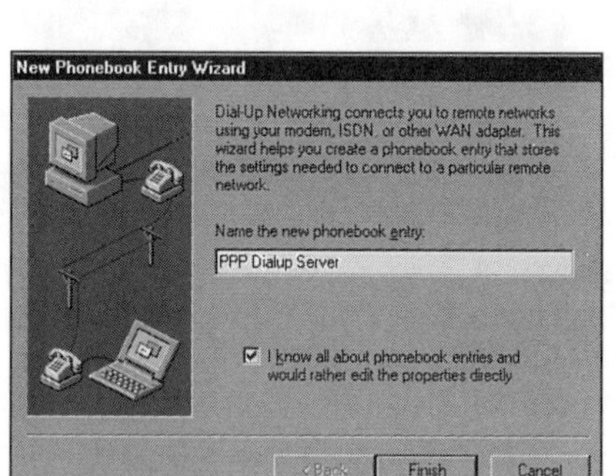


**FIGURE 4.27**
The New Phonebook Entry Wizard begins the process of creating the first phonebook entry.

4. Choose the device to connect with from the Dial Using pull-down list.
5. Click the Server tab to configure the expectations of the server that this entry calls (see Figure 4.29).
6. In the Dial-Up Server Type field, choose the type of server you are dialing. If the server is an NT 4.0 server, you will choose PPP; if the server is a SLIP server, choose SLIP; if the server is NT 3.1, select Windows NT 3.1.
7. Select the protocols you want to use to communicate on the remote network, and then click the configuration button to the right of the protocol name to configure it. For this example, click the configuration button for TCP/IP to see the dialog box shown in Figure 4.30.
8. If the server you are dialing will provide you with a TCP/IP address, leave the default setting of Server Assigned IP Address selected. Otherwise, select Specify an IP Address, and then enter your IP address.
9. If DNS and WINS servers will be provided by the server you are dialing, leave the default setting of Server Assigned Name Server Addresses selected. Otherwise, select Specify Name Server Addresses, and then enter TCP/IP addresses for your name servers.
10. The Use IP Header Compression check box enables you to configure special compression that's only available on new versions of PPP. Some servers do not recognize this compression (called *Van Jacobson compression*) and may not respond well if it is enabled. If you have problems transmitting data after a RAS connection has been established, you may want to deselect this check box. However, you should leave it selected unless problems occur.
11. If RAS is your only network connection mechanism, leave the Use Default Gateway on Remote Network option selected. However, if you are connected to a LAN and a remote LAN, you may want to ensure that the gateway on the remote LAN is never used when you cannot resolve an address on your LAN. If you deselect this check box, you can be sure that the remote gateway is never used.

*continues*

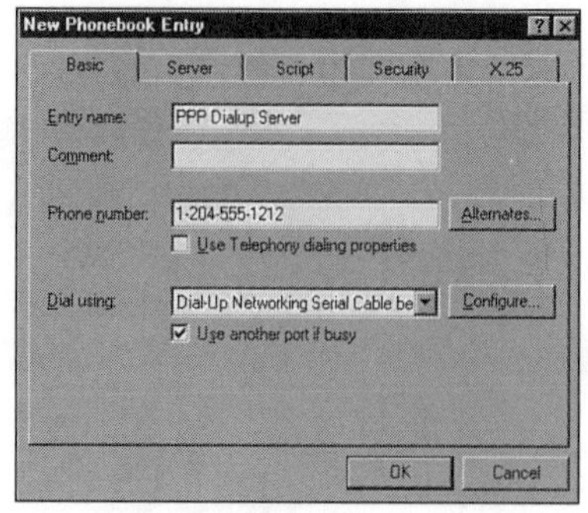


**FIGURE 4.28**
The Basic tab of the New Phonebook Entry dialog box allows you to name the entry, specify the phone number to dial, and indicate which device will be used to dial.

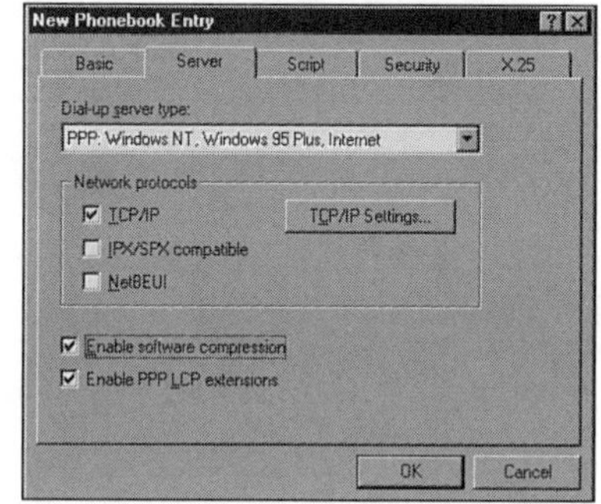


**FIGURE 4.29**
The Server tab allows you to define the expected configuration of the server you are dialing in to.

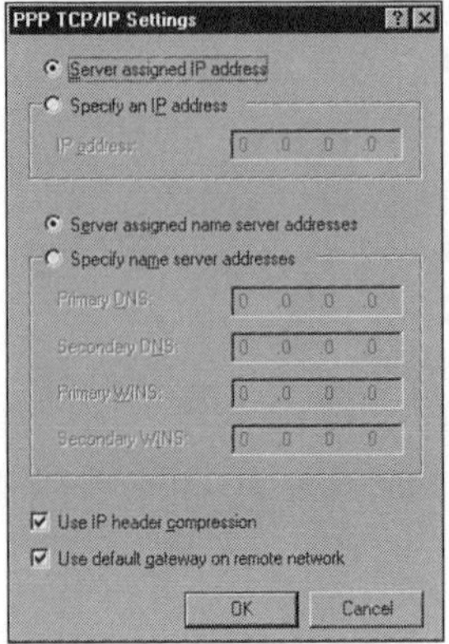


**FIGURE 4.30**
Use the PPP TCP/IP Settings dialog box to specify configuration settings for TCP/IP on the dial-up connection.

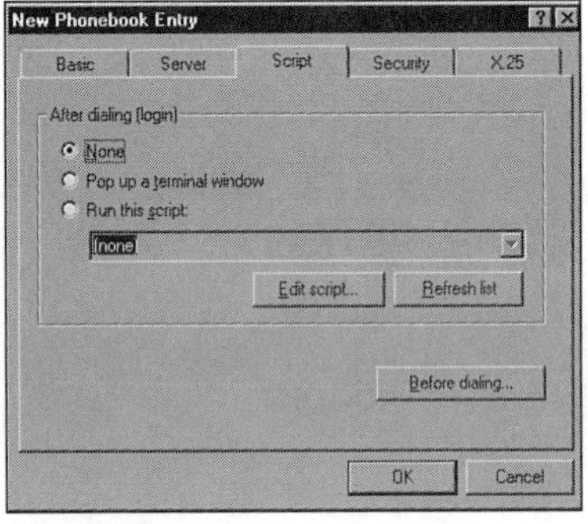


**FIGURE 4.31**
The Script tab allows you to configure scripts to run before and after dialing.

*continued*

**12.** Click OK to save the configuration and return to the New Phonebook Entry dialog box.

**13.** Click the Script tab to configure scripts to run before or after dialing (see Figure 4.31). Generally, scripts are used only with SLIP connections and are not required with PPP connections. However, the administrator of the server you are connecting to will be able to give you more information on that. The default is not to run scripts before or after dialing, but you can choose to have a script run or just to have a terminal window appear after dialing. In addition, if you want to run a script or have a terminal window appear before you dial, click the Before Dialing button and configure those settings.

**14.** Click the Security tab to configure dial-up security (see Figure 4.32).

The security settings you set up here are dependent on what the server you are dialing to will accept. You cannot ask for more security than the server you are dialing is willing to provide. Unless you know otherwise, you want to configure as much security as you can. When you connect, if you are told that the server does not support the level of security you are asking for, just back down the list. The highest level of security is Microsoft encrypted authentication, which requires data encryption and uses the current username and password. This kind of security is supported only by Microsoft servers. If you are dialing a non-Microsoft server, you will have to back down the authentication at least one more level. If you use the Accept Only Encrypted Authentication selection, you can use external encryption methods such as RSA, DES, and Shiva. The first choice, Accept Any Authentication Including Clear Text, will allow your workstation to send all information without any security at all (which may not be a suitable method to ensure security of data transmission).

**15.** To configure an X.25 connection, click the X.25 tab (see Figure 4.33). Select the network type, the X.25 network address, and if required, the User Data and Facilities information required by the X.25 network you are dialing into.

16. Click the Close button to complete the phonebook entry, and then click the Close button in the Dial-Up Networking dialog box to exit the phonebook setup.

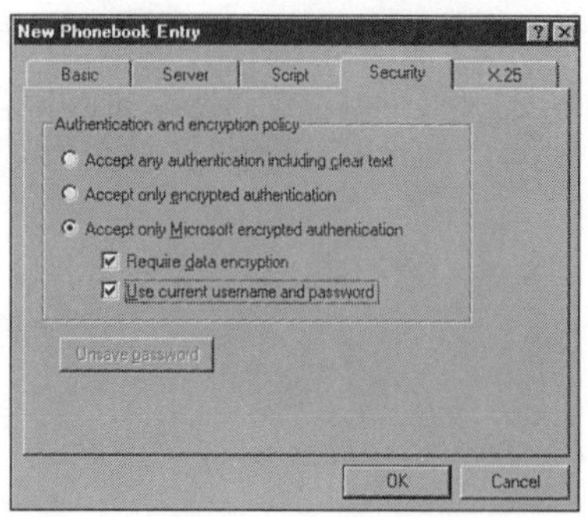


**FIGURE 4.32**
The Security tab allows you to configure the minimum security settings the workstation is willing to use when communicating with a RAS server.

After you have created the first phonebook entry, you can create a new entry or modify any entry that has already been created.

## STEP BY STEP

### 4.5 Adding Phonebook Entries

1. Open the My Computer window and double-click the Dial-Up Networking icon to access the Dial-Up Networking dialog box (see Figure 4.34).
2. Click the New button to bring up the New Phonebook Entry dialog box. Then create and configure the new entry using steps 3 through 16 of Step by Step 4.4.

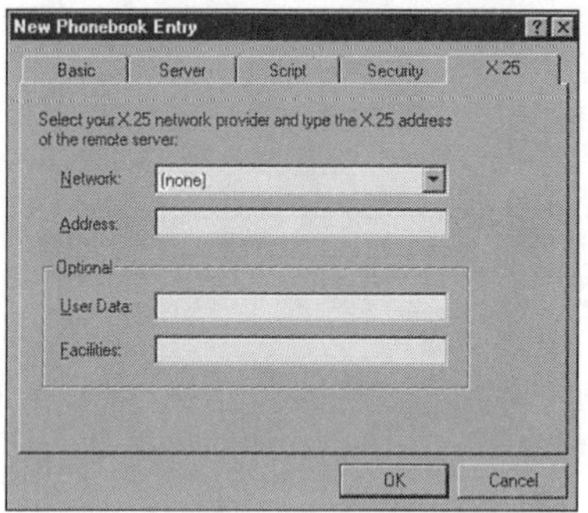


**FIGURE 4.33**
The X.25 tab allows you to configure X.25 settings for the dial-up connection.

Modifying a phonebook entry also begins by opening the Dial-Up Networking dialog box.

## STEP BY STEP

### 4.6 Modifying a Phonebook Entry

1. Open the My Computer window and double-click the Dial-Up Networking icon to access the Dial-Up Networking dialog box (see Figure 4.34).
2. From the Phonebook Entry to Dial drop-down list, select the phonebook entry you want to modify.
3. Click the More button, and then select the Edit, Modem Properties command to open the Edit Phonebook Entry dialog box (which is exactly the same as the New Phonebook Entry dialog box).
4. Modify the settings required, and then click the Close button to exit the dialog box.

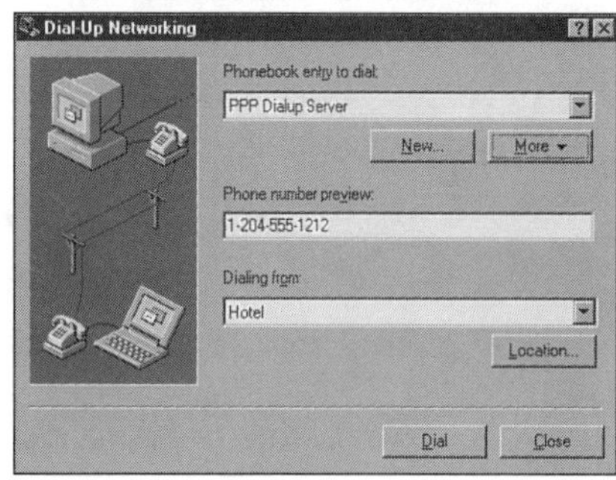


**FIGURE 4.34**
You begin most Dial-Up Networking configurations from the Dial-Up Networking dialog box.

## Adding and Modifying Locations

Locations are used to specify particular dialing locations and their properties. In the simplest of cases, this includes configuration of dialing prefixes and suffixes. In situations that are more complex, it includes configuration for calling cards and for disabling call waiting. The dialog boxes you use to configure simple versus complex configurations are different and are controlled by a check box that appears in any phonebook entry configuration. If, on the Basic tab of any phonebook entry the check box labeled Use Telephony Dialing Properties is selected (refer to Figure 4.28), the complex configuration dialog boxes will appear; otherwise, the simple configuration dialog boxes will appear.

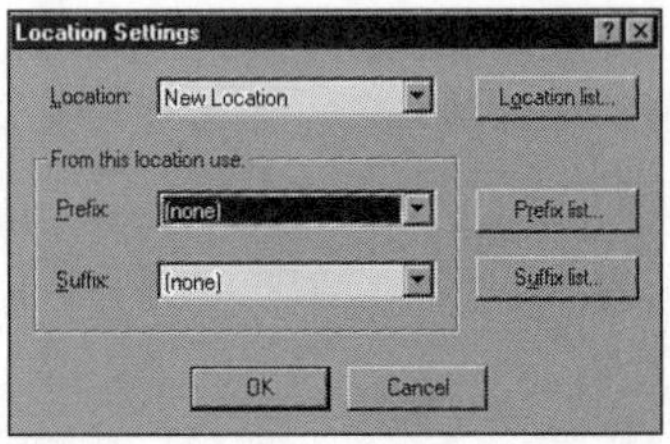

**FIGURE 4.35**
The Location Settings dialog box looks like this when Telephony Dialing Settings are not used.

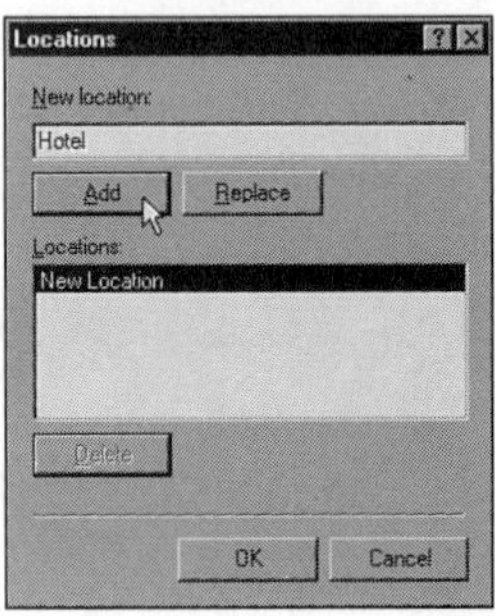


**FIGURE 4.36**
You add new locations from the Locations dialog box.

## STEP BY STEP

### 4.7 Adding a New Location with Telephony Dialing Properties Disabled

1. Open the My Computer window and double-click the Dial-Up Networking icon to access the Dial-Up Networking dialog box (refer to Figure 4.34).
2. Click the Location button at the bottom of the dialog box, and the Location Settings dialog box appears (see Figure 4.35).
3. Click the Location List button. Then, in the Locations dialog box (see Figure 4.36), type the name of the new location and click the Add button. Click OK to exit.
4. In the Location Settings dialog box, choose the location you just created from the Location field, and then choose a prefix and a suffix from the pull-down lists. If an appropriate choice is not available, you can click the Prefix List or Suffix List button and add a new entry in the resulting dialog box. Figure 4.37 shows the dialog box for prefixes.
5. Click OK to complete the addition of the location.

If the location you want has already been created and you simply want to modify its options, you can do so using Step by Step 4.7. Simply select the location to modify and skip step 3.

If Telephony Dialing Properties are enabled, you have a wider selection of available configuration options.

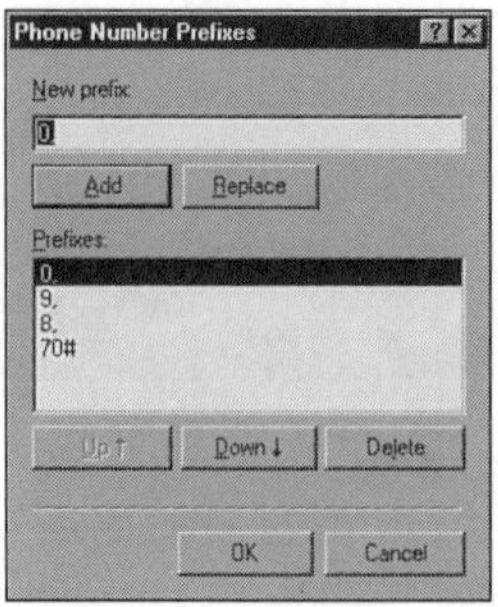


**FIGURE 4.37**
You add phone number prefixes in the Phone Number Prefixes dialog box.

## STEP BY STEP

### 4.8 Adding a New Location with Telephony Dialing Properties Enabled

1. Open the My Computer window and double-click the Dial-Up Networking icon to access the Dial-Up Networking dialog box (refer to Figure 4.34).
2. Click the Location button at the bottom of the dialog box, and the Dialing Properties dialog box appears (see Figure 4.38).
3. Click the New button. The current location will be cloned, and a message will appear telling you that a new location has been created.
4. Type the name of the location into the I Am Dialing From field.
5. Configure the appropriate area code and location. Then add prefix codes for dialing local and long distance calls, if necessary.
6. If a calling card will be used to dial from this location, select the Dial Using Calling Card check box. Then click the Change button to open the Change Calling Card dialog box (see Figure 4.39).
7. Select an appropriate calling card from the Calling Card to Use field, or if the correct one is not available, add a calling card name by clicking the New button and typing in the calling card name.
8. If you create a new Calling Card definition, you will be told that you must configure rules in order for the card to work properly. Clear that message by clicking OK, and the Dialing Rules dialog box appears (see Figure 4.40). The rules define what number will be called and what additional pauses or numbers are required. For a full list of the

*continues*

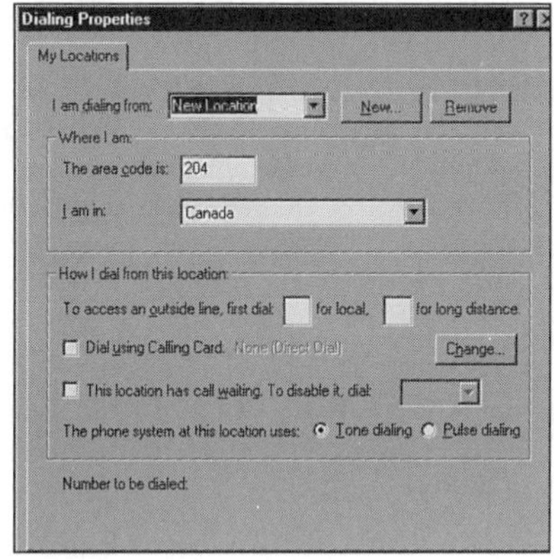


**FIGURE 4.38**
The Dialing Properties dialog box is more extensive when Telephony Dialing Properties are enabled.

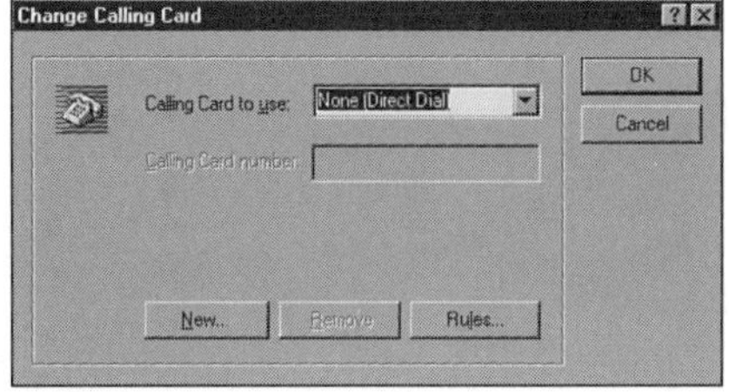


**FIGURE 4.39**
The Change Calling Card dialog box allows you to specify a calling card type and number for long distance dialing.

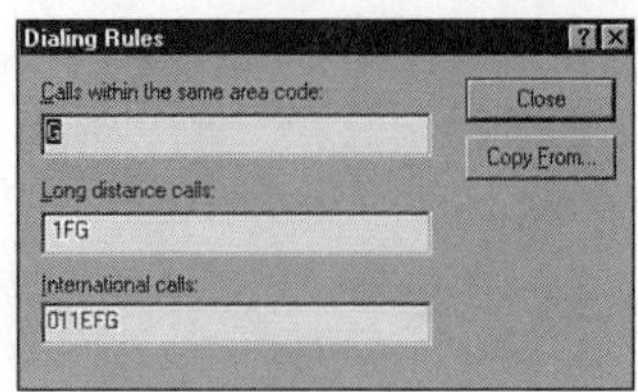


**FIGURE 4.40**
The Dialing Rules dialog box allows you to specify dialing settings for a new calling card entry.

*continued*

codes, click the "?" at the top of the box, and then click in any of the three fields.

9. If any of the codes in the Rules include an "H," a calling card number will automatically be dialed. In this case, you will be able to type your calling card number into the Calling Card Number field. Then click OK to exit back to the location you are creating.

10. If you have call waiting on the line you are dialing from, you will need to disable it to ensure that tones on the line do not cause disruptions to your RAS connection. Select the check box labeled This Location Has Call Waiting, and then choose the code appropriate for your location to disable call waiting.

11. Finally, choose the dialing type your location uses and click OK to exit the Dialing Properties dialog box.

If the location you want is already created and you simply want to modify its options, you can do so using Step by Step 4.8. Just select the location you want to modify and skip steps 3 and 4.

## Installing and Configuring PPTP

If you require more security on your RAS connection than the standard PPP configuration can provide, you may want to install and use Point-to-Point Tunneling Protocol (PPTP). Using a connection that has already been established (through a dial-up PPP connection or on a LAN), a PPTP connection then creates a secure tunnel through which PPTP packets can travel. This secure tunnel is established by means of a Virtual Private network (VPN).

PPTP is a protocol and must be installed like any other protocol. Although PPTP does not require a modem to function, it does require that Dial-Up Networking be present through the installation of RAS. If RAS is not already installed when PPTP is installed, it will be installed at that time. Step by Step 4.9 outlines the process of installing PPTP assuming that RAS is already installed.

## STEP BY STEP

### 4.9 Installing PPTP with RAS Installed

1. Open the Network dialog box (through Control Panel or by right-clicking Network Neighborhood) and click the Protocols tab.
2. Click the Add button and select Point to Point Tunneling Protocol from the list.
3. When prompted, supply the path to the NT files for PPTP installation.
4. When asked, enter the number of Virtual Private networks you want to configure (see Figure 4.41). If you have multiple dial-up connections, you may want to configure multiple VPNs; however, you usually need only one.
5. A dialog box appears, informing you that you will have to configure RAS to use PPTP. Click OK to accept that.
6. In the Remote Access Setup dialog box, click the Add button. Then in the Add RAS Device dialog box, choose the VPN that you want to use with RAS (see Figure 4.42). Click OK to return to the RAS Setup dialog box.
7. Click the Configure button to configure your VPN to dial out or receive (or both) for the selected RAS device (refer to Figure 4.25). Normally, you will leave Dial Out Only selected. However, if your Workstation is to be a RAS server, select either Receive Calls Only or Dial Out and Receive Calls. Then click OK to continue.
8. Assuming that you are only dialing out, click the Network button in the Remote Access Setup dialog box to specify the protocol you want to use to communicate on the remote network (refer to Figure 4.26).
9. Click the Continue button in the Remote Access Setup dialog box to return to the Network dialog box. Then click Close to complete PPTP installation. When you're prompted to do so, restart NT.

**FIGURE 4.41**
After installing the PPTP protocol, you will have to specify how many VPNs you want to install.

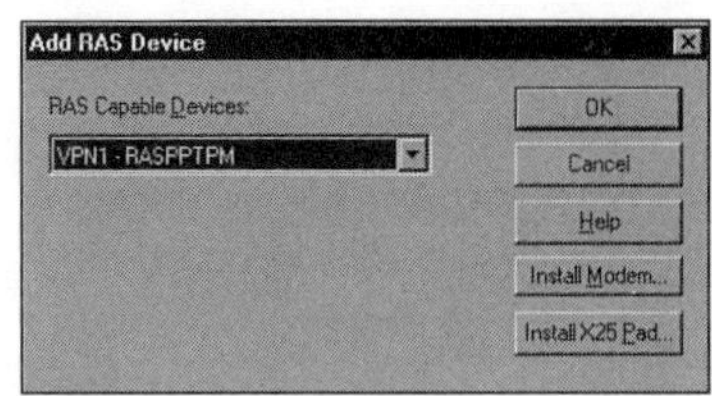


**FIGURE 4.42**
The Add RAS Device dialog box allows you to configure a VPN for RAS connection.

## Configuring the Phonebook for PPTP

To use PPTP, you must begin with a PPP or LAN connection to the RAS server. If you are connecting via LAN, you do not have to have a modem or a dial-up connection to the RAS server. If you are using a PPP connection, you must configure RAS and phonebook entries as indicated in the Step by Steps that preceded the discussion of PPTP. In addition to the connection to the RAS server, you must also configure a connection using PPTP; this enables the secure tunnel through the current connection.

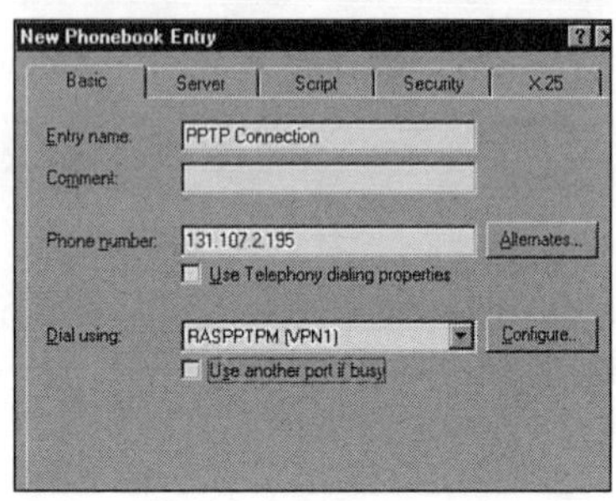


**FIGURE 4.43**
The phonebook entry for a PPTP connection has a TCP/IP address instead of a phone number to dial.

## STEP BY STEP

### 4.10 Configuring a PPTP Phonebook Entry

1. Open the My Computer window and double-click the Dial-Up Networking icon to access the Dial-Up Networking dialog box.
2. Click the New button to bring up the New Phonebook Entry dialog box, and then enter a distinguishing name in the Entry Name field (see Figure 4.43).
3. In the Phone Number field, enter the TCP/IP address of the server you are connecting to (if you use a resolution method, you can also enter the host name).
4. In the Dial Using field, choose a VPN entry.
5. Configure the rest of the phonebook entry as you would a regular PPP connection.
6. Click OK to return to the Dial-Up Networking dialog box, and then click Close to exit.

Using an established phonebook entry is very easy. After you have established a connection to the RAS server using PPP, use the PPTP connection to dial using PPTP.

## Configuring the Client on the Dial-Up Server

Although the configuration of RAS on the dial-up server is not a Workstation topic, the user account configuration needed to allow dial-up is. In order for a user to be able to log on to a machine that is configured as a RAS server, that user account must be configured to allow dial-up access.

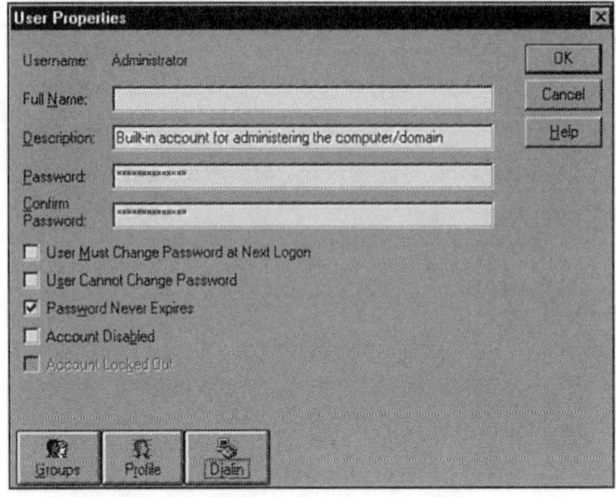


**FIGURE 4.44**
Select the Dialin button to access the Dialin Information dialog box.

### STEP BY STEP

#### 4.11 Configuring Dial-Up Server Account Information

1. Open User Manager and double-click the name of the user to whom you want to give dial-up permission. (You can also select multiple users and choose the User, Properties command to configure them all at once.)
2. In the User Properties dialog box, click the Dialin button in the lower-right corner (see Figure 4.44).
3. In the Dialin Information dialog box, indicate that the user has dialin permissions by selecting the Grant Dialin Permission to User check box (see Figure 4.45).
4. If required, configure the Call Back options.
5. Exit User Manager, approving the changes to the accounts as you go.

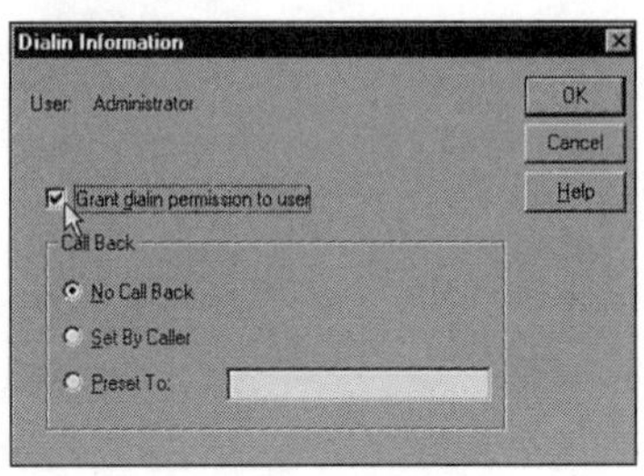


**FIGURE 4.45**
Select the Grant Dialin Permission check box to allow this user to dial in to the RAS server.

# PEER WEB SERVER

Configure Microsoft Peer Web Services in a given situation.

Peer Web Server (PWS) enables users to publish information on private intranets or the public Internet. PWS includes capabilities for hypertext documents, interactive Web applications, and client/server applications and is optimized for use as a small-scale Web server. PWS supports the following industry standard Internet services:

WARNING

**IIS Is Better for Large Jobs**
Internet Information Server (IIS), which is included with Windows NT Server 4.0, should be deployed for larger-scale requirements, whether those are on an intranet or the Internet.

- *HyperText Transfer Protocol (HTTP).* Used for the creation and navigation of hypertext documents.
- *File Transfer Protocol (FTP).* Used to transfer files between TCP/IP hosts.
- *Gopher.* A hierarchical indexing system that identifies files in directories to make searching for data easier.

PWS also supports Microsoft's Internet Server Application Programming Interface (ISAPI). You can use ISAPI to create interactive Web-based applications that enable users to access and enter data into Web pages.

## Installing Peer Web Server

Before you start installing Peer Web Server (PWS), you need to remove all other Internet services (Gopher, FTP, and so on) that are already installed. Also, make sure you have properly configured your computer to function as a TCP/IP host. Then you can proceed with the installation.

### STEP BY STEP

#### 4.12 Installing Peer Web Server

1. Open the Network dialog box and click the Services tab.
2. Click Add, select Microsoft Peer Web Services, and click OK to begin the installation.
3. When you're prompted to do so, enter the path to the NT Workstation CD-ROM or installation share.
4. Click OK in the Microsoft Peer Web Services Setup dialog box to continue the installation (see Figure 4.46).
5. When the Options dialog box appears, you can choose what components of PWS you want to install (see Figure 4.47) and the path into which they should be installed. By default, all components are installed except Web access to the management software.

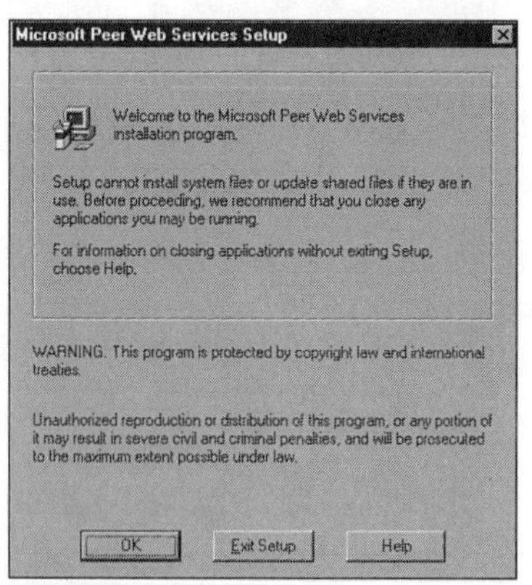


**FIGURE 4.46**
The Microsoft Peer Web Services Setup dialog box begins the installation process.

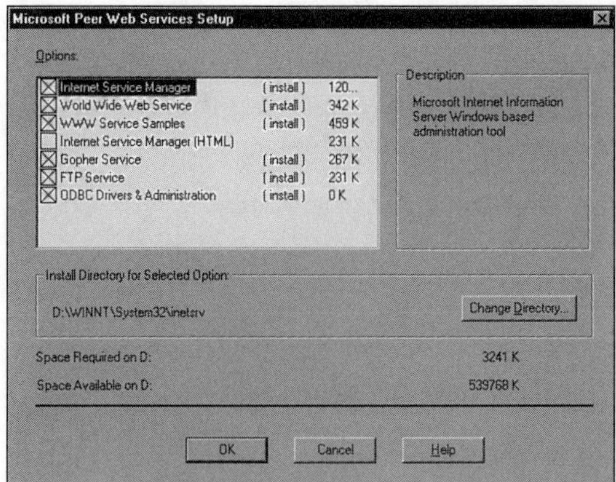


**FIGURE 4.47**
The Options dialog box allows you to indicate which components to install and where to install them.

6. A dialog box appears, asking if the installation process can create the inetsrv folders. Click Yes to continue.

7. When the publishing directories dialog box appears, click OK to allow the creation of directories for published information (see Figure 4.48). If desired, you can specify alternate locations by typing new paths or by browsing for existing paths. If the directories do not exist, you will be asked for permission to create them.

   The installation program will install and start the specified services.

8. If you selected the ODBC drivers for installation, you will be prompted for which drivers you want (see Figure 4.49). Select from the list of drivers available on your system, and then click OK to continue.

9. Click OK to complete the installation of PWS, and then click Close to close the Network dialog box.

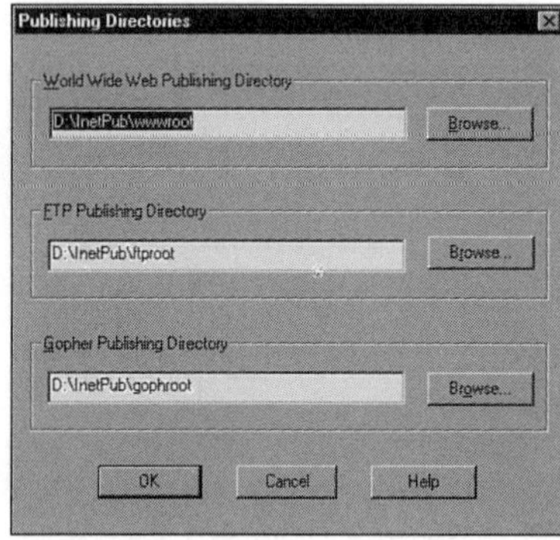


**FIGURE 4.48**
In the Publishing Directories dialog box, you specify the location for published information for each of the publishing components of PWS.

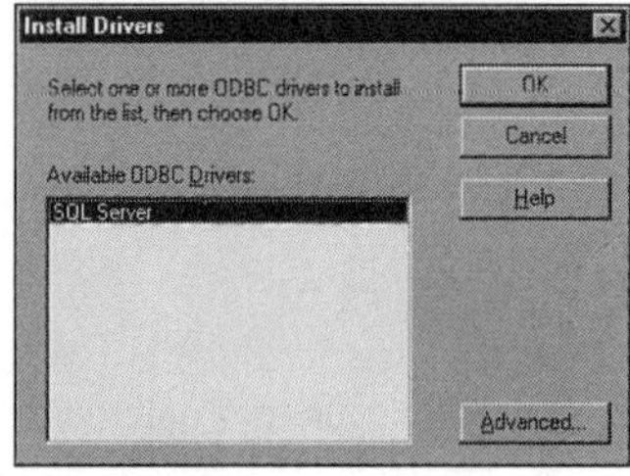


**FIGURE 4.49**
Choose which ODBC drivers you want to install from the list presented in the Install Drivers dialog box.

When the installation is complete, the following changes will have been made to your NT Workstation:

- An INETPUB directory has been created on the root of your boot partition, and it contains four subfolders: ftproot, gophroot, wwwroot, and scripts.

- An Internet guest account has been created locally in the Workstations directory database. This account is called IUSR_WORKSTATION, and it is the account used when anonymous users access published data.
- A program group called Microsoft Peer Web Services (Common) is created.

## Configuring Peer Web Server

After you install PWS, a new program group containing the PWS utilities is added to your desktop (see Figure 4.50). The following PWS utilities are available from this program group:

- Internet Service Manager
- Internet Service Manager (HTML)
- Key Manager
- Peer Web Services Setup
- Product Documentation

The most important of these utilities is the Internet Service Manager. The Internet Service Manager (shown in Figure 4.51) allows you to manage the publishing services available on your NT Workstation and on any others to which you have administrative rights.

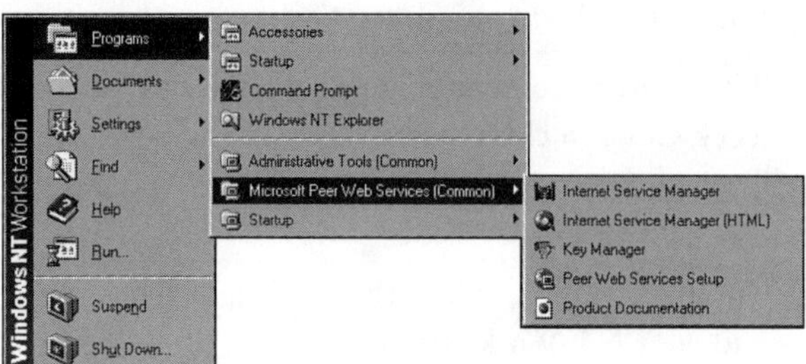


**FIGURE 4.50**
Peer Web Server configuration utilities.

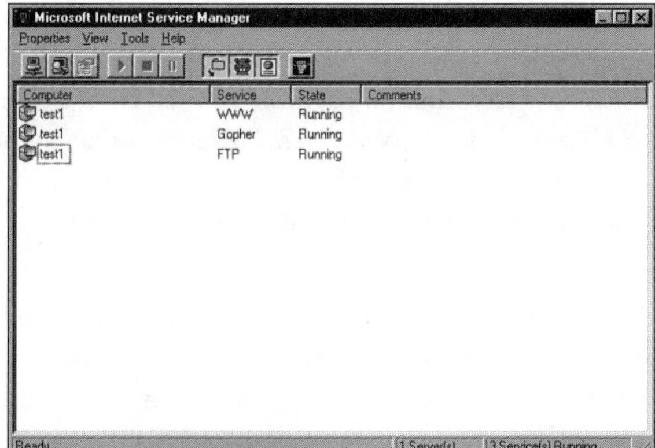


**FIGURE 4.51**
Peer Web Server Internet Service Manager.

The Internet Service Manager enables you to perform the following tasks:

- Find and list all PWS and IIS servers on your network
- Connect to servers and view their installed services
- Start, stop, or pause any service
- Configure service properties

You can also choose to install a version of the Internet Service Manager accessible via HTML, which enables you to manage your PWS server with any standard Web browser.

## Securing Your PWS

By default, the security of PWS is very loose. Anonymous access is given to all the publishing folders, which means that anyone who has the TCP/IP address of your NT Workstation will be able to access the wwwroot, ftproot, and gophroot folders and see anything inside them.

You can tighten security in a number of ways:

- *Disable all services that are not required (see Step by Step 4.13).* This ensures that you have not left a door open that you have forgotten about. (It's easier to keep tabs on a service that is used often than on one that is enabled but is never used.)

- *Make sure that the FTP service uses only anonymous connections (see Step by Step 4.14) and that only Read permission is given.* There is no encryption on passwords passed from a client to the FTP service on a PWS server. This means that anyone who has a packet analyzer or some other way of capturing network packets will be able to get your users' passwords in a clear text format.
- *Make sure that the WWW service does not allow anonymous access and that NT Challenge/Response authentication is required (see Step by Step 4.15).* The WWW service is able to use Microsoft Encryption to secure password authentication for client access. By forcing access using NT user accounts, you can be sure that only certain people get access to information. As well, if you then secure files and folders locally using NTFS permissions, you can limit access to that information to only those people who need it.

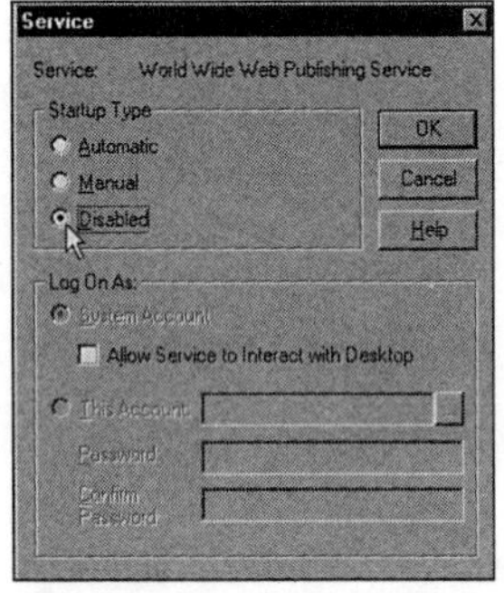


**FIGURE 4.52**
From the Service dialog box, you can permanently disable a service.

## STEP BY STEP

### 4.13 Disabling Unused PWS Services

1. Open the Control Panel and double-click the Services icon.
2. Scroll down to the service you want to disable and double-click it to open the Service dialog box for that service (see Figure 4.52). The services are listed as FTP Publishing Service, Gopher Publishing Service, and World Wide Web Publishing Service.
3. Click the Disabled option and click OK. If the service is running, it will be stopped, and you will not be able to start it again until you change this option back to Manual or Automatic.
4. Click OK to exit the main Service dialog box.

You can secure the FTP service by ensuring that anonymous access is always used and that only Read permission is given.

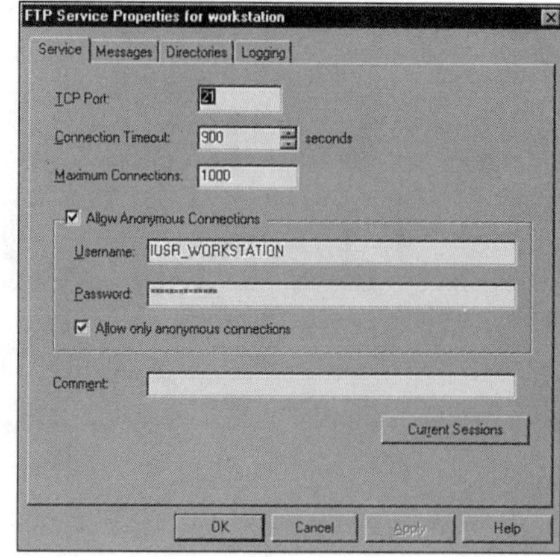


**FIGURE 4.53**
Use the FTP Service Properties dialog box to adjust configuration and security settings for the FTP service.

## STEP BY STEP

### 4.14 Securing FTP Access

1. Start the Microsoft Internet Service Manager by choosing Start, Programs, Microsoft Peer Web Services (Common), Internet Service Manager.
2. Double-click the entry for FTP to access the FTP Service Properties dialog box (see Figure 4.53).
3. On the Service tab, select the Allow Anonymous Connections check box and the Allow Only Anonymous Connections check box. This means that you will allow anonymous connections, but all others will be rejected.
4. Click the Directories tab to display a list of the directories being published (see Figure 4.54).
5. Double-click the \InetPub\ftproot entry, and then make sure that the Read check box is selected and the Write check box is not selected (see Figure 4.55). This means that only people who access from the local computer—and not those who access through FTP—are allowed to modify the contents of the FTP folders.
6. Close the dialog boxes and exit the Internet Service Manager.

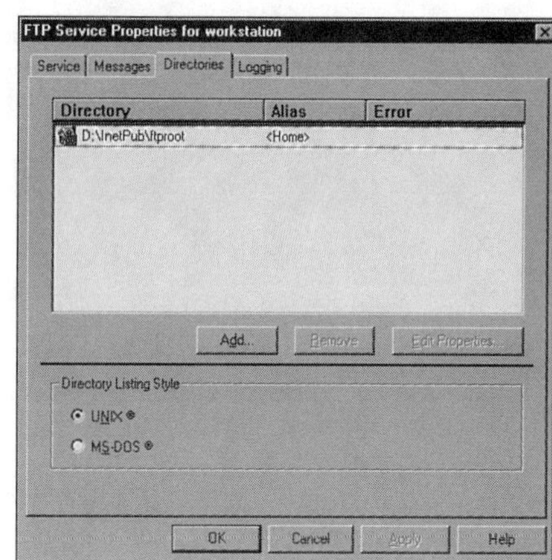


**FIGURE 4.54**
The Directories tab allows you to configure access to the directories being published.

You can enhance security on the WWW service by preventing anonymous access and forcing NT Challenge/Response authentication. In addition, you should configure all published directories to be Read Only.

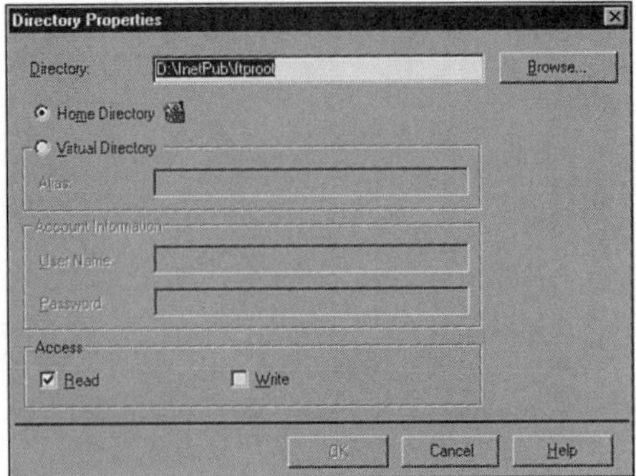


**FIGURE 4.55**
You can set the Read and Write properties for each published directory individually.

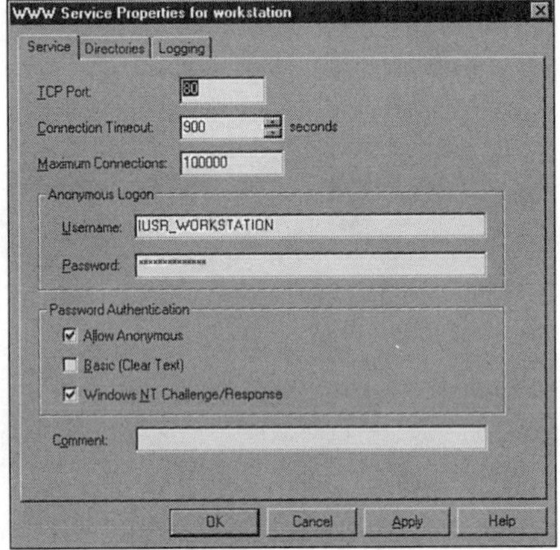


**FIGURE 4.56**
Use the WWW Service Properties dialog box to adjust configuration and security settings for the WWW service.

## STEP BY STEP

### 4.15 Securing WWW Access

1. Start the Microsoft Internet Service Manager by choosing Start, Programs, Microsoft Peer Web Services (Common), Internet Service Manager.
2. Double-click the entry for WWW to access the WWW Service Properties dialog box (see Figure 4.56).
3. Deselect the Allow Anonymous check box and the Basic (Clear Text) check box, and select the Windows NT Challenge/Response check box. This ensures that only valid NT users can access the Web site and that the authentication is encrypted.
4. Click the Directories tab to display the directories being published (see Figure 4.57).
5. Double-click the \InetPub\wwwroot entry. Then make sure that the Read check box is selected and the Execute check box is not selected (see Figure 4.58). This means that only people who access from the local computer—and not those who access through FTP—are allowed to modify the contents of the WWW folders.
6. Close the dialog boxes and exit the Internet Service Manager.

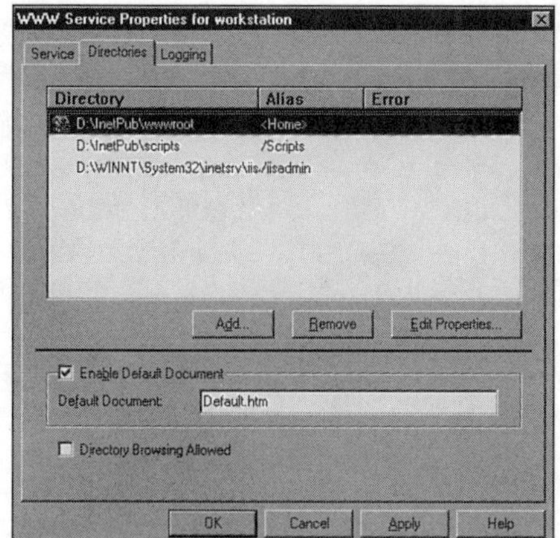


**FIGURE 4.57**
The Directories tab allows you to configure access to the directories being published.

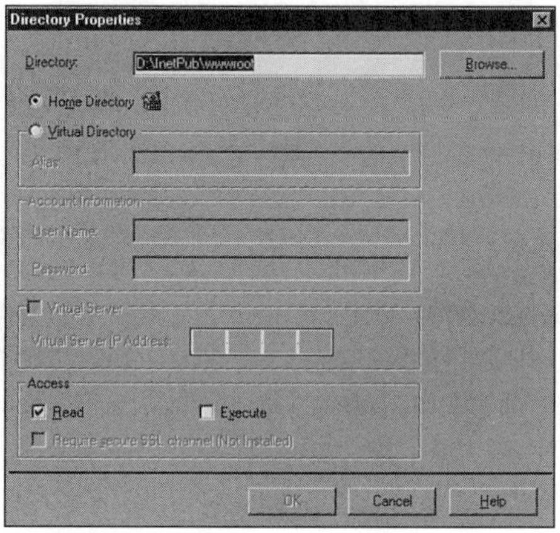

**FIGURE 4.58**
You can set the Read and Execute properties for each published directory individually.

## CASE STUDY: RED IS BEST

### ESSENCE OF THE CASE

Here are the essential elements in this case:

- Connectivity between NT Workstation and NetWare servers
- Ability to administer NetWare servers from NT Workstations
- Dial-up access to the network

### SCENARIO

Red Is Best, a clothing manufacturer specializing in '60s attire, is expanding their computer network. They have seen rapid growth in the last few years because of the interest in retro fashion. Currently, Red Is Best has a NetWare network, but looking to the future, they have decided on a slow migration to NT.

*continues*

## CASE STUDY: RED IS BEST

*continued*

In order to become familiar with NT networking, they have decided to install a few NT Workstation machines for their system administrators to use as desktop PCs. Of course, these people will have to retain access to the NetWare resources, and they will need to be able to administer the NetWare servers from their NT Workstations. In addition, the administrators would like to be able to configure their NT Workstation machines to allow them to access the network from their homes via modem.

### ANALYSIS

Access to NetWare resources from NT revolves around two things: a compatible protocol and the Client Services for NetWare. By installing both NWLink and CSNW on the NT Workstations, you can ensure connectivity between the NT machines and NetWare servers. Of course, you will need to configure the NT machines to log in using recognized NetWare accounts in order to ensure that the administrators will be able to access resources at the level they are used to. Fortunately, no further configuration is required to allow these users to administrate the NetWare network; all they have to do is log in to the NetWare network from the NT Workstations as administrators, and they'll be able to perform administrative duties on their servers.

Adding the dial-up capability introduces a little more complexity to the scenario. Because NT Workstation allows for only a single RAS connection, you will have to configure RAS separately on each NT Workstation machine. The NT machines will have to be physically configured for dial-up access, which means that you must install an NT-compatible modem on each one. Then you will have to install the RAS service, configuring RAS to use the modems installed in the machines. Assuming that the only protocol currently installed is NWLink, you can configure RAS to use only NWLink. In addition, you will probably want to configure the workstations for dial-up only, and not to dial out.

## CHAPTER SUMMARY

Connectivity incorporates a number of different issues. This chapter began with an overview of the NT Networking model and then moved into the configuration of networking in NT Workstation through the Network dialog box. Following that, it covered general access to network resources through UNCs and Network Neighborhood. Finally, you learned about four major connectivity topics: NT Workstation and NetWare resources, NT Workstation and TCP/IP, NT Workstation as a dial-up client, and NT Workstation as a Web server.

### KEY TERMS

- NDIS
- TCP/IP
- NWLink
- NetBEUI
- DLC
- distributed processing
- IPC mechanism
- bindings
- UNC
- NWLink frame type
- CSNW
- subnet mask
- WINS
- DNS
- DHCP
- RAS
- PPTP
- PPP

## APPLY YOUR LEARNING

The following section allows you to assess how well you understood the material in the chapter. The exercises provide you with opportunities to engage in the sorts of tasks that comprise the skill sets the objectives reflect. Review and exam questions test your knowledge of the tasks and concepts specified in the objectives. And answers to the review and exam questions follow in the answers sections. For additional review- and exam-type questions, see the Top Score test engine on the CD-ROM that came with this book.

## Exercises

The following exercises detail step-by-step procedures on various ways to install and configure the networking components of Windows NT Workstation 4.0. Other lab exercises show you how to interoperate with Novell NetWare servers and to install a Peer Web Server on your computer.

### 4.1 Add the TCP/IP Protocol

This exercise shows you the steps for adding and configuring the TCP/IP protocol.

**Estimated Time:** 10 minutes

1. Double-click on the Network icon in Control Panel.
2. Click on the Protocols tab in the Network dialog box.
3. Click on Add.
4. Select the TCP/IP Protocol and click OK.
5. In the TCP/IP Setup box, choose No in answer to the question about DHCP.
6. When you're prompted to do so, insert your installation CD and click on Continue.
7. When the Network dialog box reappears, click on Close.
8. In the Microsoft TCP/IP Properties box, specify the IP address: **10.100.5.27**.
9. Specify the subnet mask of **255.255.255.0**, and then click OK.
10. Restart your computer when prompted.

### 4.2 Change TCP/IP Properties to Use DHCP

This exercise shows you how to change the properties of the TCP/IP protocol so that it becomes a DHCP client and no longer maintains a static IP address.

**Estimated Time:** 10 minutes

1. Double-click on the Network icon in Control Panel.
2. Click on the Protocols tab in the Network dialog box.
3. Select the TCP/IP protocol.
4. Click on Properties.
5. Select Obtain an IP Address from a DHCP Server.
6. Click on Yes to enable DHCP.
7. In the TCP/IP Properties box, click on OK.
8. In the Network dialog box, click on Close.
9. If you're prompted to do so, restart your computer.

## APPLY YOUR LEARNING

10. To verify whether DHCP is functional, go to a command prompt and type **IPCONFIG /ALL**.
11. If you don't see a valid IP address and lease information and you didn't already restart your computer, restart it now.

### 4.3 Add a New Network Adapter Driver

This exercise walks you through the steps required to add a new network adapter driver.

**Estimated Time:** 10 minutes

1. Right-click on Network Neighborhood and select Properties.
2. Click on the Adapters tab.
3. Click on Add.
4. Select MS Loopback Adapter from the Network Adapter list.
5. Click OK.
6. In the MS Loopback Adapter Card Setup box, click OK.
7. Insert your Windows NT Workstation 4.0 installation CD when requested, and then click on Continue.
8. Click on Close in the Network dialog box.
9. Answer any questions having to do with protocols you might have installed.
10. Click on Yes to restart your computer.

### 4.4 Install Client Service for NetWare (CSNW)

In this exercise, you learn how to enable your computer to access files and printers on a NetWare server.

**Estimated Time:** 20 minutes

1. Double-click on the Network icon in Control Panel.
2. Click on the Services tab.
3. Click on Add.
4. Select Client Service for NetWare in the Network Service list, and then click OK.
5. Insert your Windows NT Workstation 4.0 installation CD when prompted, and then click on Continue.
6. Click on Close, and then wait while the bindings are being reset.
7. Click on Yes to restart your computer.
8. Press Ctrl+Alt+Delete and log on to your computer.
9. When the Select NetWare Logon dialog box appears, select your NetWare 3.x preferred server or your NetWare 4.x default tree and context. Then click OK.
10. When your desktop appears, right-click on Network Neighborhood.
11. In the Network Neighborhood menu, choose Who Am I, and your NetWare user information appears.

### 4.5 Change the Frame Type of the NWLink Protocol

This exercise shows you how to adjust the properties of the NWLink protocol to change the frame type from Auto Detect to 802.2.

**Estimated Time:** 10 minutes

## Apply Your Learning

1. Double-click on the Network icon in Control Panel.
2. Click on the Protocols tab in the Network dialog box.
3. Select the NWLink IPX/SPX Compatible Transport protocol.
4. Click on Properties.
5. In the Frame Type drop-down box, select Ethernet 802.2.
6. Click OK.
7. In the Network dialog box, click on Close.
8. Restart your computer when prompted.

### 4.6 Install DUN and Configure a Modem

This exercise walks you through the steps for setting up your computer to access remote networks via a modem.

**Estimated Time:** 15 minutes

1. Double-click on the Dial-Up Networking icon in My Computer.
2. Click on the Install button to start the installation wizard.
3. Insert your installation CD when prompted.
4. Click on Yes to start the modem installer.
5. Select the check box labeled Don't Detect My Modem, I Will Select It from a List, and then click on Next.
6. Select your modem from the list or click on Have Disk.
7. Direct the installation wizard to your modem's installation files.
8. Click on Next to install the modem.
9. Select the port to which the modem is connected, and then click on Next.
10. Wait while the modem is installed.
11. Click on Finish.
12. In the Add RAS Device screen, click OK.
13. In the Remote Access Setup box, click on Configure. (Notice that the default setting for Microsoft NT Workstation 4.0 is Dial Out Only.)
14. Click OK to return to the Remote Access Setup dialog box.
15. Click on Network. In the Network Configuration dialog box, notice that you can choose which of the protocols you want to use after you connect to the remote network.
16. Click OK to return to the Remote Access Setup dialog box.
17. Click on Continue.
18. Wait while the remainder of the RAS software is installed and the bindings are reset.
19. Restart your computer to finish the installation of DUN.

### 4.7 Add a New Dial-Up Networking (DUN) Phonebook Entry

This exercise leads you through the steps of adding a new DUN phonebook entry.

**Estimated Time:** 5 minutes

1. Double-click on the Dial-Up Networking icon in My Computer.

## APPLY YOUR LEARNING

2. Click on New.
3. Enter **New Server** for the name of the new phonebook entry, and then click on Next.
4. For the Server settings, click on Next.
5. Enter the phone number **555-5555**, and then click on Next.
6. Click on Finish.
7. Click on the Phonebook Entry to Dial drop-down box to see how you can choose which phone number to use.
8. Click on Close.

### 4.8 Add a New Dial-Up Networking (DUN) Dialing Location

In this exercise, you learn how to add a new dialing location so that you can use your DUN client from a new location.

**Estimated Time:** 5 minutes

1. Double-click on the Dial-Up Telephony icon in My Computer.
2. Click on New.
3. A dialog box appears, telling you a new location was created. Click OK.
4. Change the area code to your new area code.
5. Indicate whether you need to Dial 9 for an outside line and Dial 8 for long distance.
6. Check the Dial Using Calling Card check box, and then click on Change.
7. Select your Calling Card from the list, and then click OK.
8. Click OK to close the Dialing Properties dialog box.

### 4.9 Connect to a NetWare Print Server

This exercise shows you how to connect your computer to a NetWare print server.

**Estimated Time:** 10 minutes

1. Double-click on the Printers icon in My Computer.
2. Double-click on Add Printer.
3. In the Add Printer Wizard, select Network Printer Server, and then click on Next.
4. In the Connect to Printer screen, select the desired network printer and click OK. (You can double-click on the desired print server to see a list of the printers available on that print server.)
5. Select the proper printer from the list, and then click OK.
6. Insert your installation CD when prompted, and then click OK.
7. Specify whether you want this new printer to be your default Windows printer, and then click on Next.
8. Click on Finish.

### 4.10 Install Peer Web Server (PWS)

This exercise details the step-by-step process required to install a Peer Web Server on a Windows NT Workstation 4.0.

**Estimated Time:** 20 minutes

1. Before starting the installation of Peer Web Server, make sure that the TCP/IP protocol is installed and configured properly.
2. Double-click on the Network icon in Control Panel.

## APPLY YOUR LEARNING

3. Click on the Services tab.
4. Click on Add.
5. Select Microsoft Peer Web Server from the Network Service list, and then click OK.
6. Insert your NT Workstation 4.0 installation CD when prompted, and then click OK.
7. Click OK to start Peer Web Services Setup.
8. Click OK to select which PWS services to set up.
9. Click on Yes to create the Inetsrv directory.
10. Click OK to confirm the names for the publishing directories.
11. Click on Yes to create the publishing directories.
12. Wait while the PWS files are installed, and then click OK in the Install Drivers box.
13. Click OK to finish the installation of PWS.
14. Click on Close in the Network dialog box. You do not have to restart your computer. PWS is now active.

## Review Questions

1. You have an older network adapter card that has drivers only for Windows for Workgroups. Can you use it with Windows NT Workstation 4.0?
2. You have two networks that use the NetBEUI protocol. You connect the two networks with a router, but the computers on the two networks can't connect. What is wrong?
3. You have installed the NWLink IPX/SPX Compatible Transport protocol on your computer, but you cannot establish a session with a NetWare file server. What other component do you need to install?
4. What are network bindings?
5. How many network adapter cards can you put into a single Windows NT Workstation 4.0 computer?
6. What is a Browse Master?
7. What command should you type at a command prompt to redirect port LPT1: to a network printer named HP5 located on a print server named PRINTSERVE?
8. When do you need to specify a default gateway on a computer configured for TCP/IP?
9. You have a computer configured for IPX, but you cannot make a connection to a UNIX SLIP server. What is your problem?
10. You need to set up a Web server for your department. Which component of Windows NT Workstation 4.0 is well-suited for your purposes?

## Exam Questions

1. You have a laptop computer configured with Dial-Up Networking, and you want to configure your system to use a calling card. Which of the following describes the correct procedure for doing so?

## APPLY YOUR LEARNING

A. You can't program calling card numbers.

B. Enter the calling card number after the phone number you want to dial.

C. Edit the dialing location, click on Dial Using Call Card, click on Change, and enter the number.

D. Go to the Control Panel's Network program, select the Services tab, and edit the properties for the Remote Access Service.

2. What three components enable a Windows NT Workstation 4.0 computer to access files and printers on a NetWare server?

   A. Client Services for NetWare

   B. Gateway Services for NetWare

   C. NWLink IPX/SPX Compatible Transport

   D. File and Print Services for NetWare

3. What do you need to do before you install Peer Web Services?

   A. Install NetBEUI

   B. Download the files from the Microsoft Web site

   C. Remove all other Internet services from the computer

   D. Create a dedicated FAT partition

4. You have a TCP/IP network connected to the Internet. What name resolution service enables you to connect to Web sites?

   A. WINS

   B. DHCP

   C. DNS

   D. Browser service

5. Which of the following components must be installed on Windows NT Workstation 4.0 to enable it to access a print queue on a NetWare server?

   A. Client Services for NetWare

   B. Gateway Services for NetWare

   C. NWLink IPX/SPX Compatible Transport

   D. File and Print Services for NetWare

6. What tool should you use to configure Peer Web Server (PWS) after it is installed on your Windows NT Workstation 4.0?

   A. Internet Service Manager.

   B. The Network program in Control Panel.

   C. Windows Setup.

   D. You can configure PWS only during installation.

7. Which of the following are characteristics of the NetBEUI protocol? Choose all that apply.

   A. Fast performance on small LANs

   B. Small memory overhead

   C. No tuning options

   D. Support for routing

8. Which of the following are limitations of SLIP for Dial-Up Networking (DUN) clients?

   A. DUN doesn't support use as a SLIP client.

   B. SLIP doesn't support NWLink or NetBEUI.

   C. SLIP doesn't support DHCP.

   D. SLIP doesn't support encrypted authentication.

## APPLY YOUR LEARNING

9. Which of the following are methods supported by Dial-Up Networking for establishing sessions with remote networks?

   A. ISDN

   B. X.25

   C. Dial-up with modems and ordinary phone lines

   D. XNS

10. Which network environments are supported by Windows NT Workstation 4.0? Choose all that apply.

   A. Microsoft networks

   B. TCP/IP networks

   C. Novell NetWare 3.x and 4.x (including NDS)

   D. AppleTalk

11. What service enables a Windows NT Workstation 4.0 to establish connections to other computers on a network?

   A. Session service

   B. Server service

   C. Workstation service

   D. Routing service

12. In distributed processing, the front-end process does what?

   A. Runs on a server and requires extensive resources

   B. Runs on a client and requires extensive resources

   C. Runs on a server and requires minimal resources

   D. Runs on a client and requires minimal resources

13. Each time you print to a printer on a NetWare server, an extra page is printed that contains your username. How can you prevent this extra page from being printed?

   A. At a command prompt, type **NO BANNER**.

   B. In the CSNW program in Control Panel, clear the Print Banner check box.

   C. In the CSNW program in Control Panel, clear the Form Feed check box.

   D. Clear the Print Banner check box in the printer's properties box.

14. Installing Client Services for NetWare (CSNW) on your Windows NT Workstation 4.0 accomplishes which of the following? Choose all that apply.

   A. It allows NetWare clients to access files on your computer.

   B. It allows you to access files on NetWare servers.

   C. It allows NetWare clients to access printers on your computer.

   D. It allows you to access printers on NetWare servers.

15. You have a Windows NT Workstation 4.0 computer with two modems and two ordinary phone lines. You want to establish the fastest possible connection to a remote network. Which protocol should you use?

   A. Serial Line Internet Protocol (SLIP)

   B. Point-to-Point Tunneling Protocol (PPTP)

   C. Point-to-Point Multilink Protocol

   D. Remote Access Service (RAS)

## APPLY YOUR LEARNING

16. What service enables other computers on a network to establish connections with a Windows NT Workstation 4.0?

    A. Session service

    B. Server service

    C. Workstation service

    D. Routing service

17. You need to purchase a new network adapter for your Windows NT Workstation 4.0. Which types of device drivers are supported? Choose all that are correct.

    A. ODI 3.0

    B. NDIS 3.0

    C. NDIS 3.1

    D. NDIS 4.0

18. Which Windows NT service provides support for remote users that make connections via ordinary phone lines?

    A. Dial-Up service

    B. PPP service

    C. SLIP service

    D. Remote Access Service

19. Which of the following network settings are needed to manually configure a Windows NT Workstation 4.0 to communicate in a routed WAN configuration? Choose all that apply.

    A. IP address

    B. Subnet mask

    C. DHCP server address

    D. Address of the default gateway

20. Which transport protocol provides connectivity with the Internet?

    A. DLC

    B. NetBEUI

    C. NWLink IPX/SPX Compatible Transport

    D. TCP/IP

## Answers to Review Questions

1. Windows NT does not support the use of any 16-bit device drivers. You must use a device driver written to support Windows NT. For more information, see the section "NDIS-Compatible Network Adapter Card Drivers."

2. NetBEUI is not normally supported by routers. You must either configure your router to support NetBEUI or switch your network protocol to IPX or TCP/IP. For more information, see the section "NetBEUI."

3. NWLink is not sufficient to support file and print connectivity to a NetWare server. You must also install CSNW. For more information, see the section "NWLink IPX/SPX Compatible Transport."

4. A network binding is the initial connection made between a protocol being used and the network card driver. For more information, see the section "NDIS 4.0."

5. Windows NT supports an unlimited number of network adapters. (Your hardware, however, limits how many cards you can actually use.) For more information, see the section "NDIS 4.0."

## APPLY YOUR LEARNING

6. A Browse Master is responsible for maintaining a list of all the servers available on the network. For more information, see the section "Network Neighborhood."

7. The command would be `Net Use LPT1: \\PRINTSERVE\HP5`. For more information, see the section "Universal Naming Convention."

8. You must specify a default gateway when your TCP/IP computer needs to communicate with a computer located on a different physical network. For more information, see the section "NT Workstation as a TCP/IP Client."

9. SLIP supports only TCP/IP. For more information, see the section "Serial Line Internet Protocol (SLIP)."

10. Peer Web Server is intended for use as a small-scale Web server. For more information, see the section "Configuring Peer Web Server."

## Answers to Exam Questions

1. **C** is correct. You enter your calling card information when you edit your dialing location. For more information, see the section "Adding and Modifying Locations."

2. **A, B, and C** are correct. FPNW enables NetWare clients to access files and printers on a Windows NT Server. For more information, see the section "Windows NT Workstation in a NetWare Environment."

3. **C** is correct. PWS requires TCP/IP. For more information, see the section "Installing Peer Web Server."

4. **C** is correct. UNIX TCP/IP hosts do not support WINS. For more information, see the section "NT Workstation as a TCP/IP Client."

5. **A and C** are correct. GSNW is supported only for Windows NT Server. For more information, see the section "Windows NT Workstation in a NetWare Environment."

6. **A** is correct. The Microsoft Internet Service Manager is used to configure PWS after installation. For more information, see the section "Configuring Peer Web Server."

7. **A, B, and C** are correct. NetBEUI does not support routing. For more information, see the section "NetBEUI."

8. **B, C, and D** are correct. Windows NT Workstation 4.0 supports usage as a SLIP client, but not usage as a SLIP server. For more information, see the section "Serial Line Internet Protocol (SLIP)."

9. **A, B, and C** are correct. DUN doesn't support XNS. For more information, see the section "Installing and Configuring the Dial-Up Networking Client."

10. **A, B, and C** are correct. Services for Macintosh are supported only by Windows NT Server. For more information, see the section "Network Protocols."

11. **C** is correct. The Workstation service initiates I/O requests to network servers. For more information, see the section "File System Drivers."

12. **D** is correct. A front-end process runs on a client. For more information, see the section "Distributed Processing."

## APPLY YOUR LEARNING

13. **B** is correct. You need to stop printing print banners. For more information, see the section "Configuring Client Services for NetWare."

14. **B and D** are correct. CSNW enables you to access files and printers on a NetWare server, but it does not allow NetWare clients to access files and printers on a Windows NT computer. For more information, see the section "Windows NT Workstation in a NetWare Environment."

15. **C** is correct. The Point-to-Point Multilink Protocol enables you to combine multiple physical links into one logical connection. For more information, see the section "Point-to-Point Protocol (PPP)."

16. **B** is correct. The Server service receives I/O requests from network clients. For more information, see the section "File System Drivers."

17. **B and D** are correct. Although NDIS 4.0 is the newest version, Windows NT 4.0 is also backward compatible with NDIS 3.0. For more information, see the section "NDIS-Compatible Network Adapter Card Drivers."

18. **D** is correct. The Remote Access Service enables Windows NT computers to accept connections from remote clients. For more information, see the section "Installing and Configuring the Dial-Up Networking Client."

19. **A, B, and D** are correct. You need to configure the default gateway to enable TCP/IP connectivity in a WAN. For more information, see the section entitled "NT Workstation as a TCP/IP Client."

20. **D** is correct. The TCP/IP protocol provides connectivity with the Internet. For more information, see the section "TCP/IP."

## Suggested Readings and Resources

The following are some recommended readings on the subject of Connectivity for NT Workstation:

1. Microsoft Official Curriculum course 770: *Installing and Configuring Microsoft Windows NT Workstation 4.0*
   - Module 4: Configuring Windows NT Workstation 4.0
   - Module 5: Working with the Internet and Intranets
2. Microsoft Official Curriculum course 803: *Administering Microsoft Windows NT 4.0*
   - Module 2: Setting Up User Accounts
3. Microsoft Official Curriculum course 922: *Supporting Microsoft Windows NT 4.0 Core Technologies*
   - Module 9: The Windows NT Networking Environment
   - Module 10: Configuring Windows NT Protocols
   - Module 12: Remote Access Service
   - Module 13: Internetworking and Intranetworking
   - Module 14: Interoperating with Novell NetWare
4. *Microsoft Windows NT Workstation Resource Kit Version 4.0*
   - Chapter 30: Microsoft TCP/IP and Related Services for Windows NT
   - Chapter 31: Microsoft TCP/IP Architecture
   - Chapter 32: Networking Name Resolution and Registration
   - Chapter 33: Using LMHOSTS files
   - Chapter 35: Using Windows NT Workstation on the Internet
5. *Microsoft Windows NT Server 4.0 Resource Kit*
   - Chapter 6: Internet Connectivity Using the Remote Access Service
6. *Microsoft Windows NT Server Networking Guide*
   - Chapter 1: Windows NT Networking Architecture
   - Chapter 5: Network Services: Enterprise Level
   - Chapter 6: TCP/IP Implementation Details
   - Chapter 13: Using NetBEUI with Windows NT
   - Chapter 14: Using DLC with Windows NT
7. Web sites
   - `www.microsoft.com/train.cert`
   - `www.prometric.com/testingcandidates/assessment/chosetest.html` (take online assessment tests)

## Objectives

Microsoft provides the following objectives for "Running Applications":

**Start applications on Intel and RISC platforms in various operating system environments.**

- This objective is necessary because someone certified in the use of Windows NT Workstation technology must understand how applications run on NT and how to execute them. This includes applications run not only in the native 32-bit environment but also in the various subsystems.

**Start applications at various priorities.**

- This objective is necessary because someone certified in the use of Windows NT Server technology must understand how priorities on NT applications can be adjusted at runtime and the implications of those changes.

CHAPTER 5

# Running Applications

## OUTLINE

This chapter will help you prepare for the "Running Applications" section of Microsoft's Exam 70-73 by introducing you to a variety of application support issues. This includes issues related to native 32-bit applications, DOS applications, and 16-bit Windows applications. In addition, the chapter touches on two additional application support subsystems: OS/2 and POSIX. Finally, the discussion turns to application execution priority, how priorities can be adjusted, and why.

## STUDY STRATEGIES

- The key to this objective is understanding the fundamentals of application execution in NT. This means knowing what kinds of applications NT supports and what subsystems allow that support. So you need to know about the 32-bit subsystem, NTVDMs, and WOW.EXE. In addition, you must understand execution priority, what the base priorities are for each priority name, and how to change the base priority of an application. Changing base priorities means that you'll have to know both how to specify a priority from a command prompt and how to configure foreground boost to optimize foreground or background processing.

In addition, you must know about the OS/2 and POSIX subsystems and the applications associated with them.

Hands-on experience is useful for these objectives but not required—especially for the OS/2 and POSIX subsystems—because knowledge about the theory of their operation will be sufficient for the exam. In addition, because you can't really try out much in the area of application execution and priority, you'll just have to trust that the priority switches work the way Microsoft says they do.

## INTRODUCTION

Understanding how the Windows NT architecture handles applications from different operating systems enables an administrator to better work with the Windows NT operating system. Knowing what operating system's applications are supported and on what platforms of Windows NT those applications are supported is an important key to using the Windows NT operating system.

This chapter discusses the following topics related to managing applications:

- Windows NT's architectural design, which enables Windows NT to support applications from other operating systems.
- Specifics on how Windows NT handles DOS, Win16, Win32, OS/2, and POSIX applications on Intel and RISC platforms.
- Starting applications at various priorities and changing the priority of a running application.

## WINDOWS NT ARCHITECTURE

The Windows NT operating system was designed to handle applications written both for its native 32-bit environment and for other environments. In addition to supporting software written for legacy Microsoft operating systems and environments (such as MS-DOS and Windows 3.x), NT also has some environment subsystems that offer limited support for non-Microsoft operating systems. The additional operating systems supported are POSIX and OS/2.

All supported applications believe that they are running in their native environments because the environment subsystems provide application programming interfaces (APIs) that the foreign programs can recognize. The environment subsystems translate calls made by the application into commands that the Windows NT Executive can perform for the application.

These subsystems receive all programmatic calls from the applications they support (see Figure 5.1). They either handle the requests themselves or pass the requests on to the Windows NT Executive Services or to the Win32 subsystem. The Win32 subsystem handles all requests for error handling, application shutdown, and console applications display.

All basic operating systems functions are handled by the Windows NT Executive Services, which resides in the Kernel mode. Because it is located in Kernel mode, Executive Services provides stability by preventing any application from directly accessing the hardware. This prevents a malfunctioning user application from causing a Kernel-mode component to malfunction.

All graphics-related requests are passed to the Win32 Windows Manager and GDI component of Executive Services. Using a common executive service ensures that users of applications are provided a consistent user interface.

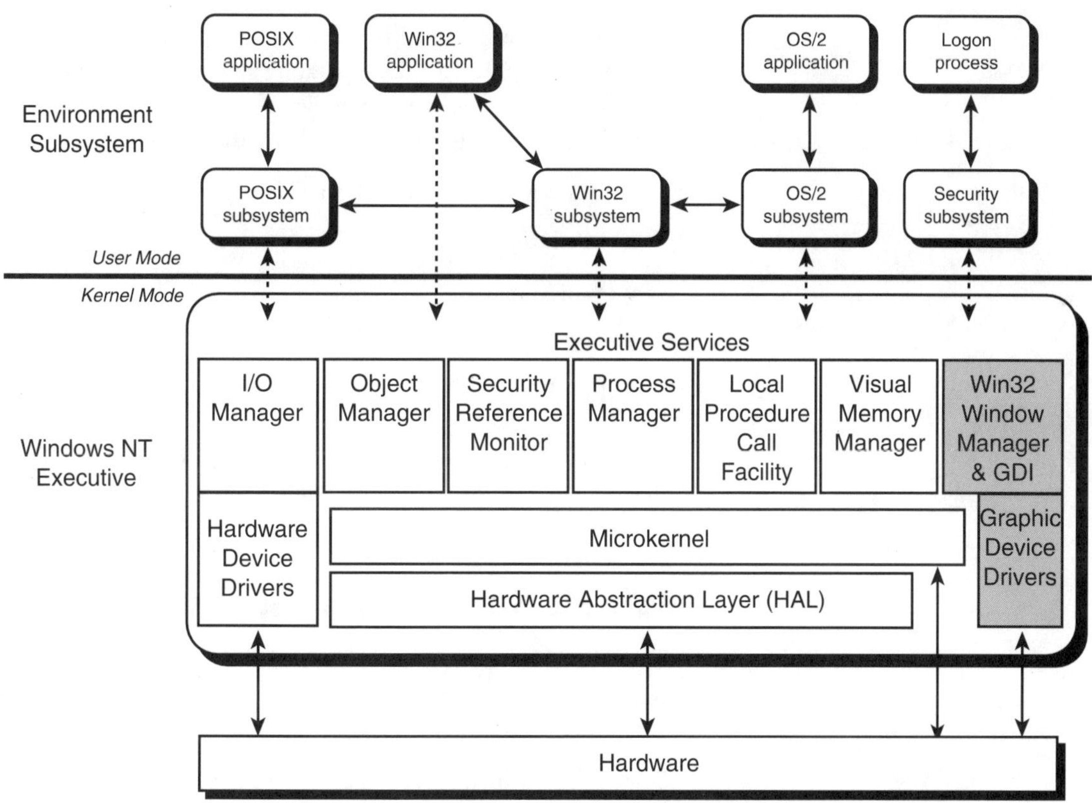


**FIGURE 5.1**
This diagram shows a breakdown of the major components of the Windows NT architecture.

Building each subsystem into the Windows NT architectural model eliminates duplication of services in the environment subsystems. The I/O Manager executive service, for example, handles all disk input/output activity. Because each subsystem relies on the Executive Services, creating future environment subsystems is much easier. It also makes maintenance easier because you have to update only Executive Services instead of every environment subsystem.

## WINDOWS NT SUPPORTED SUBSYSTEMS

Start applications on Intel and RISC platforms in various operating system environments.

Windows NT is designed to run applications that were originally designed to run under other operating systems. Windows NT can support running applications designed for the following operating systems (some to a greater extent than others):

- Windows 95 and Windows NT
- MS-DOS
- Windows 3.x
- OS/2
- POSIX

Windows NT accomplishes this by using the subsystems discussed in the following sections.

### Win32 Subsystem Support

The Win32 subsystem (also known as the Client/Server or CSR subsystem) supports all 32-bit Windows applications and the rest of the environment subsystems.

Some of the primary features of Win32 applications include the following:

- Reliability—because each application has its own 2GB address space
- Support of multithreaded applications
- Capability to take advantage of multiprocessor systems
- Support for preemptive multitasking

Each Windows 32-bit application runs in its own virtual 2GB address space (see Figure 5.2). This space is mapped to true RAM by the virtual memory manager, which controls the paging of memory out to disk (to PAGEFILE.SYS). This design prevents one 32-bit application from overwriting the memory space of another 32-bit application. In other words, a failure of one 32-bit application does not affect other running 32-bit applications.

The major advantage of using 32-bit applications over using 16-bit applications is that 32-bit applications can be multithreaded. Each Windows NT process requires at least one thread. These threads enable execution to be scheduled. 32-bit applications can have more than one thread of execution.

One example of a multithreaded application is a 32-bit setup program. A 32-bit setup program generally has the following three threads of execution:

- A decompression thread that decompresses all files from a centralized archive file

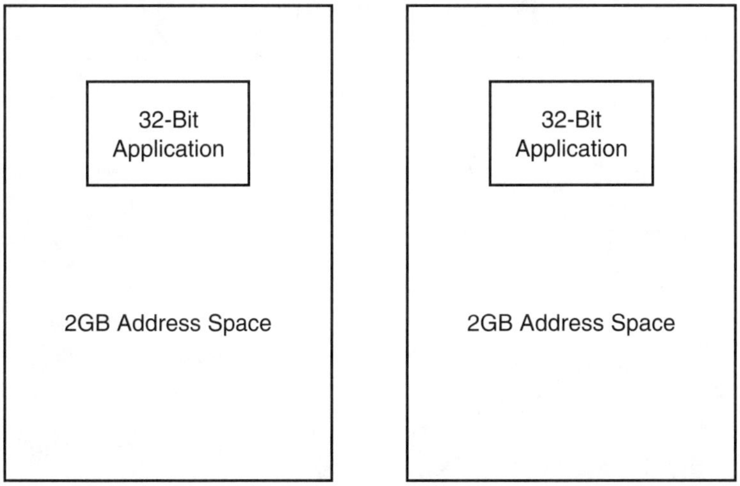

32-Bit Application

2GB Address Space

32-Bit Application

2GB Address Space

**FIGURE 5.2**
Each 32-bit program gets 2GB of virtual memory in which to operate.

- A copying thread that copies the decompressed files to the appropriate installation directory
- A system configuration thread that modifies all necessary configuration files to enable the application to execute correctly

The threads of execution, while independent of one another, must be timed correctly by the developer of the application. The copying thread must wait for the decompression thread to expand the necessary file before the copying thread can place it in the proper directory. Likewise, the system configuration thread must make sure that a file has been copied to the proper directory if it needs to execute the program to enable configuration to take place. Figure 5.3 shows a typical setup progress meter for a 32-bit setup program. Note that a separate setup bar appears for showing the progress of expansion, copying, and configuration.

Having multiple threads also enables 32-bit applications to take full advantage of Windows NT's capability to support Symmetric Multi-Processing (SMP). SMP enables each thread of an application to execute on the first available processor. Figure 5.4 shows how the capability of using Symmetric Multi-Processing can lead to improved execution time by splitting threads between processors. Both threads 1 and 2 display an improvement in execution time because less time

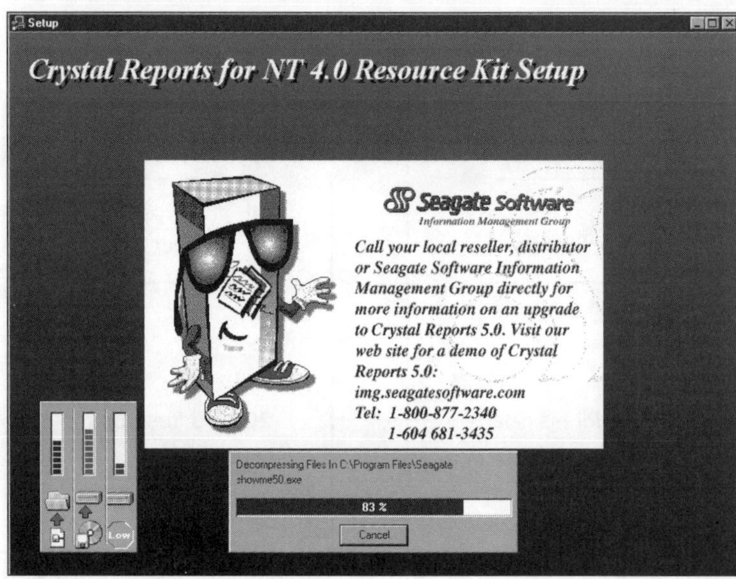


**FIGURE 5.3**
In the lower-left corner of this figure is a 32-bit setup program's progress meter.

is spent in wait states while one thread waits for the other thread to relinquish control of the processor. Windows NT 32-bit multi-threaded applications can take full advantage of a multiprocessor system.

Finally, 32-bit applications can take part in preemptive multitasking. Instead of making the operating system wait for a thread to voluntarily relinquish control of the processor (as Windows 16-bit applications do), the operating system can interrupt a thread when one of the following events occurs:

- A thread runs for a specified length of time.
- A thread with a higher priority is ready to execute.

The scheduling of threads by the operating system makes it less likely that an application will monopolize the processor.

EXAM TIP

**Windows NT Supports Symmetric Multi-Processing** A common exam question relates to multiprocessing. Remember that Windows NT supports *Symmetric Multi-Processing* (SMP). This enables Windows NT to use whichever processor is available instead of scheduling the O/S to only use one processor and applications to only use the other processor(s). Under *Asymmetric Multi-Processing* (ASMP), operating systems set aside one or more processors for exclusive use by the operating system. Windows NT uses SMP because it provides better load balancing between processors. It also provides a degree of fault tolerance. This is because a processor failure in a multiprocessor system results only in a degradation of performance. In an ASMP system, this can cause the entire operating system to crash.

## Supporting MS-DOS Applications

Windows NT supports any MS-DOS applications that do not attempt to directly access hardware. The Windows NT architecture does not allow any user mode processes to directly access the system hardware.

MS-DOS applications run in a special Win32 application known as a Windows NT Virtual DOS Machine (NTVDM). The NTVDM creates a pseudo MS-DOS environment in which the application is capable of running. Each NTVDM has a single thread of execution

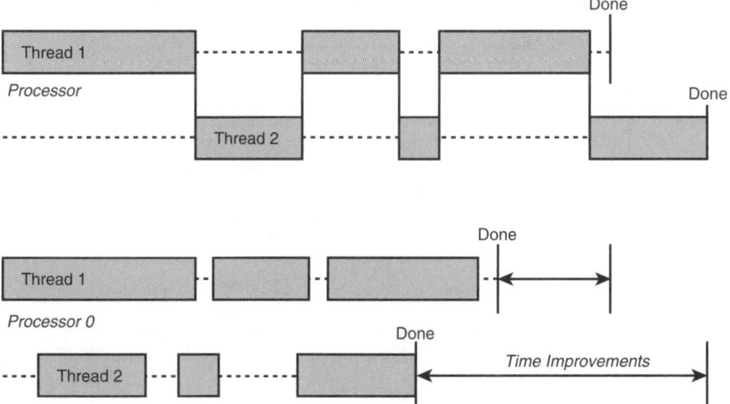


**FIGURE 5.4**
Comparison of a single-processor system and a multiprocessor system.

and its own address space. This enables preemptive multitasking between MS-DOS applications, as well as protection from other MS-DOS application failure. The following components make up the NTVDM:

- *NTVDM.EXE.* Provides the MS-DOS emulation and manages the NTVDM.
- *NTIO.SYS.* The NTVDM's equivalent of IO.SYS in MS-DOS.
- *NTDOS.SYS.* The NTVDM's equivalent of the MS-DOS kernel.
- *Instruction Execution Unit (IEU).* On RISC systems, this emulates an Intel 80486 microprocessor. On x86 computers, the IEU acts as a trap handler. Any instructions that cause hardware traps have their control transferred to the code that handles them in Windows NT.

Figure 5.5 shows the components of the NTVDM and how communication takes place between the various components.

Because applications cannot directly access the hardware in the Windows NT architectural model, the NTVDM's virtual device drivers intercept any attempt by an application to access the hardware. The virtual device drivers translate the calls to 32-bit calls and pass them to the Windows NT 32-bit device drivers. This entire process

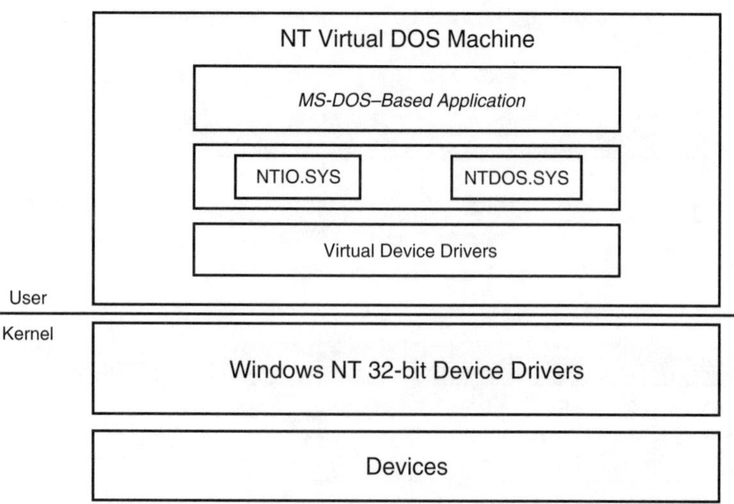


**FIGURE 5.5**
The components of an NTVDM allow MS-DOS applications to execute on an NT Workstation machine.

is hidden from the MS-DOS–based applications. Provided virtual device drivers include drivers for the mouse, keyboard, parallel ports, and COM ports.

You can configure a Windows NT Virtual DOS Machine by customizing the application's Program Information File (PIF). A shortcut created to any MS-DOS application is assigned the extension .PIF. To modify an application's PIF settings, just right-click on the shortcut to the application and choose Properties from the pop-up menu.

> **WARNING**
>
> **You Must Have a Virtual Device Driver for Each Hardware Device**
> If a virtual device driver does not exist for a hardware device, any application that tries to access this hardware directly cannot run in an NTVDM. Many MS-DOS applications do not execute in Windows NT for this reason.

## Configuring the Program Properties of a PIF

The Program tab of of a PIF Properties dialog box enables you to configure default locations for where a program is located on the hard disk and the directory in which the program will execute (see Figure 5.6).

Table 5.1 shows the settings you can configure in the Program tab of the PIF Properties dialog box.

> **NOTE**
>
> **NT Command Prompt Is Not MS-DOS**
> Opening a command prompt window (by choosing Start, Programs, Command Prompt) does not initiate an NTVDM because the NT Command Prompt is not MS-DOS. The Command Prompt is a 32-bit Windows application that provides a command line interface to NT. It is, in fact, a text version of NT, not an MS-DOS window.

**TABLE 5.1**

**PROGRAM SETTINGS**

| *Setting* | *Description* |
|---|---|
| Cmd Line | The full path to the MS-DOS application's executable file. |
| Working | Default directory to which you want to save an application's data files. |
| Batch File | The name of a batch file that runs each time the application is run (only functional in the Windows 95 operating system). |
| Shortcut key | Used to set a shortcut key combination to launch the application. To remove a shortcut key combination, use the Backspace key. |
| Run | Determines what windows state the program starts in. Choices include normal windows, minimized, or maximized. |
| Close on Exit | Forces the closing of the MS-DOS window in which the MS-DOS application runs when the user exits the application. |
| Windows NT | Enables the application to specify tailored AUTOEXEC and CONFIG files that are processed every time the application is run. |
| Change Icon | Enables the user to change the icon displayed for the shortcut. |

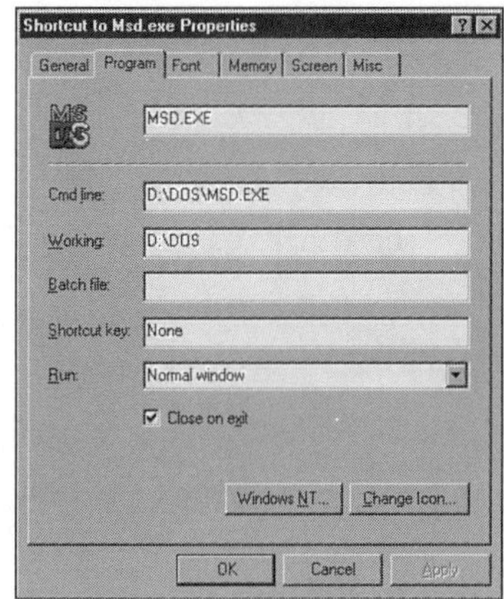


**FIGURE 5.6**
The Program tab of PIF settings.

NOTE

**Use Different AUTOEXEC and CONFIG Files for MS-DOS Applications** Each MS-DOS shortcut can point to a different AUTOEXEC and CONFIG file. By default, these are AUTOEXEC.NT and CONFIG.NT, which are located in the %Systemroot%\System32 directory. These configuration files must follow MS-DOS 5.0 conventions. They can be created using any text editor, and their location is specified in the dialog box that appears when you click the Windows NT button on the Program tab of the PIF properties dialog box (refer to Figure 5.6).

## Configuring the Memory Properties of a PIF

Running MS-DOS applications under Windows NT does ease one area of configuration. MS-DOS applications use one of two methods for providing additional memory beyond conventional memory:

- Expanded memory
- Extended memory

In the MS-DOS applications, to configure these types of additional memory, you had to make configuration changes to the CONFIG.SYS file, modifying the HIMEM.SYS and EMM386.EXE drivers. In addition, you had to reboot the system every time you made a configuration change in order to see the results.

In Windows NT, these configuration settings have been moved from the CONFIG.SYS file to the Memory tab of a PIF Properties dialog box (see Figure 5.7).

From the Memory tab of a PIF Properties dialog box, you can specify the exact amount of expanded memory specification (EMS) or extended memory specification (XMS) to allocate to a program. Then, instead of rebooting the system, you only have to restart the application for the new settings to take effect. You can also use the Memory tab to set the amount of environment space that will be allocated to the Windows NT Virtual DOS Machine. The environment space is used to store all environment variables declared for the application.

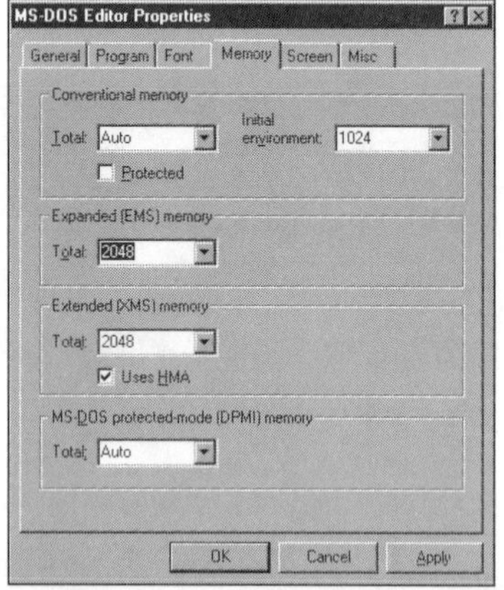


**FIGURE 5.7**
The Memory tab of the PIF Properties dialog box allows you to specify what kind of memory is used and how much of it.

## Configuring a PIF's Miscellaneous Settings

Because Windows NT supports multitasking, one key setting to change for a PIF is to enable an application to run in the background. To do this, clear the Always Suspend check box on the Misc tab of a PIF Properties dialog box (see Figure 5.8).

Another area that must often be configured is the Windows Shortcut Keys section. By clearing any of the key combinations in this section, the user removes that key combination from the set of predefined Windows NT key combinations. Table 5.2 shows the Windows NT definitions for the provided key combinations.

**TABLE 5.2**

**WINDOWS NT SPECIAL KEY COMBINATIONS**

| *Key Combination* | *Windows NT Meaning* |
|---|---|
| Alt+Tab | This key combination is commonly used for switching between running applications. It makes use of a pop-up window that shows the icons of the running applications. |
| Ctrl+Esc | This key combination activates the Start menu. |
| Alt+PrtSc | This key combination is used to capture the active window to the Windows NT clipboard. |
| Alt+Space | This key combination activates the Control menu of the running applications. |
| Alt+Esc | This key combination also enables the user to switch between running applications. It works by pulling each application to the foreground. |
| PrtSc | This key captures the entire screen to the Windows NT clipboard. This is the most commonly disabled Windows NT key. Many MS-DOS programs require the capability to have the Print Screen key print the current window to the printer. This is accomplished by clearing the PrtSc option. |
| Alt+Enter | This key combination switches an MS-DOS application between full screen and windowed modes. |

WARNING

**Be Sure to Configure the Proper Memory for DOS Applications**
One of the most difficult things to configure for a DOS application is the proper memory setting. Most applications support only EMS or XMS memory. Be sure you select the appropriate type of memory. If an application states that it is LIM compatible, you need to provide EMS memory. If the application uses DPMI, you need to provide XMS memory.

## Supporting Win16 Applications

Windows 16-bit applications are supported in Windows NT by a feature called *Win16 on Win32* (WOW). Figure 5.9 shows the Win16 on Win32 architecture.

Note that the WOW environment runs within a Windows NT Virtual DOS Machine. This is just like Windows 3.x, which ran over MS-DOS. Table 5.3 describes the WOW components.

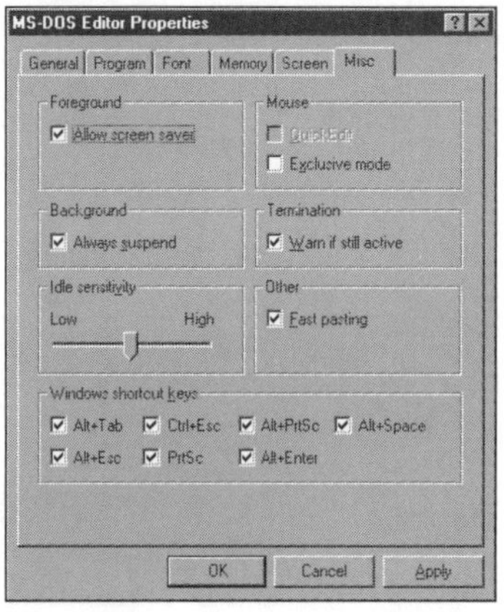


**FIGURE 5.8**
The Misc tab of PIF settings.

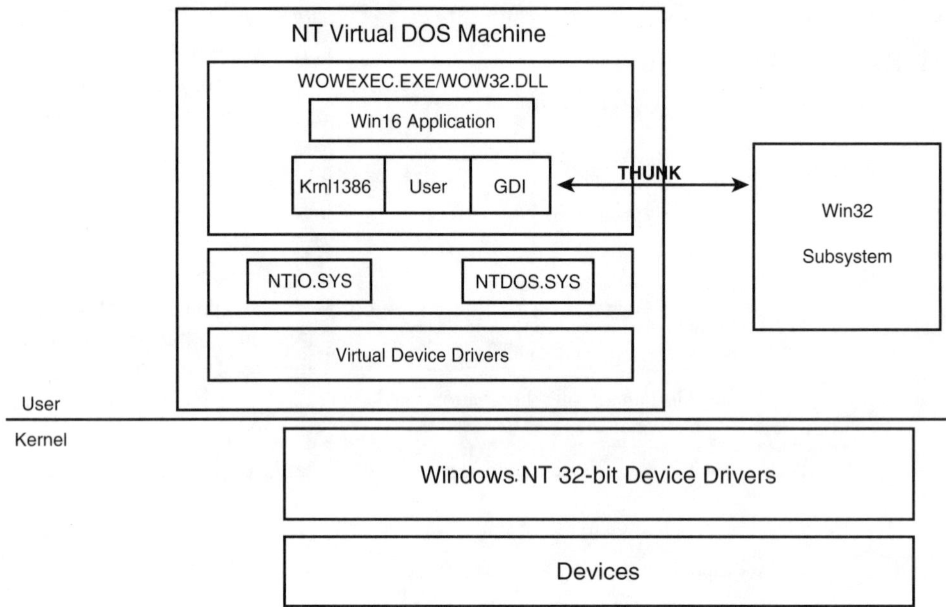


**FIGURE 5.9**
The Win16 on Win32 (WOW) architecture allows 16-bit Windows applications to run on the 32-bit NT platform.

**TABLE 5.3**

**WOW COMPONENTS**

| *Component* | *Description* |
|---|---|
| WOWEXEC.EXE | The WOWEXEC provides the Windows 3.1 emulation for the NTVDM. |
| WOW32.DLL | The supporting dynamic link library for the WOWEXEC. |
| Win16 application | The Windows 16-bit application that is being executed. This application must not use any Windows 16-bit VxDs. Support may not be provided for them in Windows NT. |
| KRNL386.EXE | This is a modified version of the Windows 3.x kernel. It translates calls meant for the Windows 3.x kernel to Win32 calls. Basic operating system functions are handled by KRNL386.EXE. |
| USER.EXE | The USER.EXE is a modified version of the Windows 3.x USER.EXE. It handles all user interface API calls and translates them to Win32 calls. |
| GDI.EXE | The GDI.EXE captures API calls related to graphics and printing. These calls are translated to Win32 calls. |

Based on the API calls that an application makes, the KRNL386.EXE, USER.EXE, or GDI.EXE intercepts the calls and translates them into Win32 calls. This process is known as *thunking*. Also, any responses from the Win32 services must be translated back to 16-bit responses. The time spent translating the calls is offset by the speed increase that results from executing 32-bit instructions.

WARNING

**Certain Applications Are Not Supported** As with MS-DOS applications, certain functions of Win16 applications are not supported. If a Win16 application uses drivers that require direct access to hardware, they will not be allowed to run.

## Running Multiple Win16 Applications

By default, the WOW environment provides nonpreemptive multitasking as provided in Windows 3.x. This means that control of the processor must be voluntarily given up by one application to give another application access to the processor. The implication of this is that one 16-bit application can cause another 16-bit application to fail.

By default, Windows NT starts each 16-bit Windows application in the same Windows NT Virtual DOS Machine. All Win16 applications share a single thread of execution. If one Win16 application hangs, all other Win16 applications will also hang. Figure 5.10 demonstrates how Windows NT handles multitasking with Windows 16-bit and 32-bit applications.

As you can see in the figure, Win16 App1, Win16 App2, and Win16 App3 are all running within a single NTVDM. Within the NTVDM, the three Win16 applications are nonpreemptively

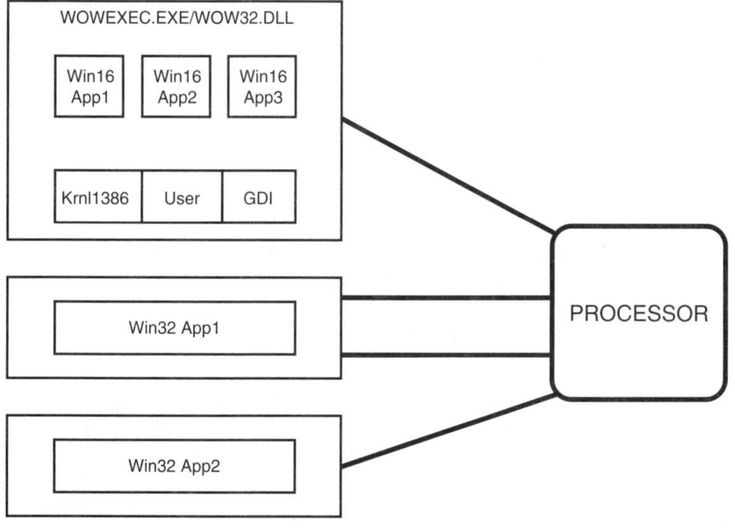


**FIGURE 5.10**
Multitasking with Win16 and Win32 applications.

multitasked. The NTVDM has one thread of execution, and that thread is preemptively multitasked with the two threads of Win32 App1 and the one thread of Win32 App2. If one of the Win16 applications were to fail, it would affect only the other Win16 applications that share its memory space within the NTVDM. It would not affect the two Win32 applications because they are being run in their own memory spaces.

By looking at the running processes in the Task Manager, you can see that, by default, all Win16 applications run in the same NTVDM with the WOWEXEC.EXE program providing them with the 16-bit Windows environment (see Figure 5.11).

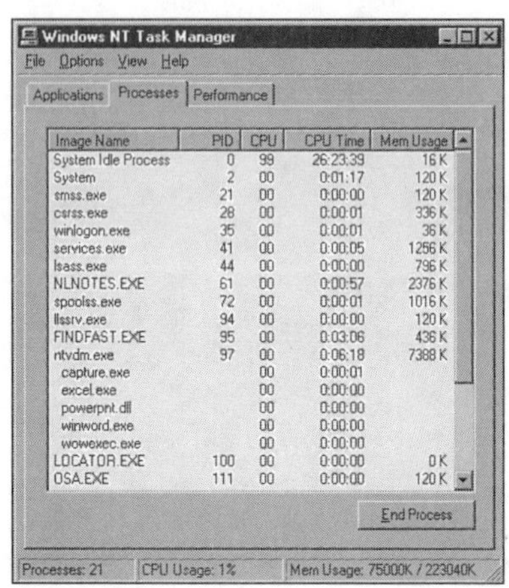


**FIGURE 5.11**
Capture, Word, Excel, and PowerPoint are all running in the same NTVDM.

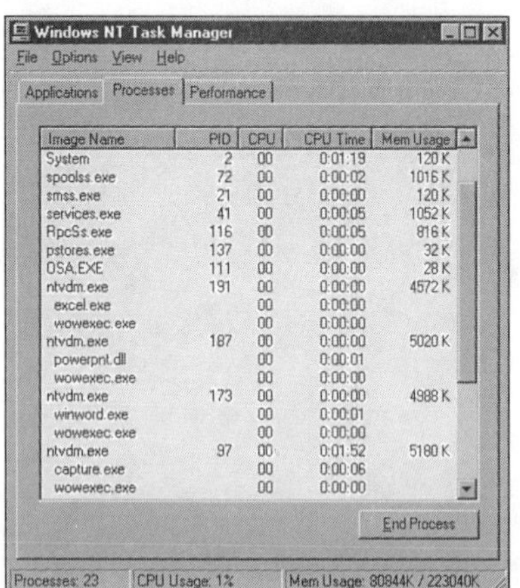


**FIGURE 5.12**
Capture, Word, Excel, and PowerPoint are running in separate NTVDMs.

## Running Win16 Applications in Individual NTVDMs

Win16 applications can be executed in individual NTVDMs under Windows NT. To make that happen, you must configure the Win16 applications to run in separate memory spaces. Architecturally, this generates a separate NTVDM with its own WOW environment for each Win16 application. This enables Win16 applications to preemptively multitask because each Win16 application's NTVDM will have a separate thread of execution. Figure 5.12 shows the same three Win16 applications executing under Windows NT when configured to run in separate NTVDMs.

The reasons for running Win16 applications in their own memory spaces include the following:

- Win16 applications will use preemptive multitasking. An ill-behaved Win16 application will no longer prevent other Win16 applications from executing normally because each Win16 application will have its own memory space and thread of execution.
- Win16 applications will be more reliable because they will not be affected by the problems of other Win16 applications.
- Win16 applications can take advantage of multiprocessor computers. When Win16 applications are run in a common NTVDM, they must share a single thread of execution; starting the applications in individual NTVDMs creates individual threads of execution. Each thread can then potentially be executed on a different processor. So the operating system could

schedule each NTVDM's thread of execution to run on whichever processor is available. In a multiprocessor system, this can lead to multiprocessing. If the Win16 applications were running in a common NTVDM, their single thread of execution would only be able to run on a single processor, no matter how many processors existed on the computer.

- Windows NT will enable Win16 applications running in separate memory spaces to continue to participate in OLE and dynamic data exchange (DDE).

As with any configuration change, there are some tradeoffs for the advantages gained by running Win16 applications in separate memory spaces. These tradeoffs include the following:

- Running separate NTVDMs creates additional overhead. In Figure 5.11, for example, 7388KB was allocated to the shared NTVDM. In Figure 5.12, however, where each Win16 application is run in a separate memory space, a total of 18,744KB of memory is required to support the four separate NTVDMs. This is almost three times as much as for the single NTVDM. If you do not have enough memory installed on the server, this could result in a decrease in system performance.
- Some older Win16 applications did not use the standards of OLE and DDE and would not function properly if they were run in separate memory spaces. Such applications must be run in a common memory space to function correctly. Lotus for Windows 1.0 is an example of this type of application.

EXAM TIP

**Only One NTVDM Supports Multiple 16-bit Applications**
Expect at least one question about running Win16 applications in separate memory spaces. The key concept is that you can load multiple Win16 applications into the same memory space only if it is the initial Win16 NTVDM. It is not possible, for example, to run Word for Windows 6.0 and Excel for Windows 5.0 in one shared memory space and also run PowerPoint 4.0 and Access 2.0 in another shared memory space.

## Configuring Win16 Applications to Run in Separate Memory Spaces

Windows NT provides multiple ways to run Win16 applications in separate memory spaces:

- Anytime you start a Win16 application by using the Start, Run command, you can select the Run in Separate Memory Space option (see Figure 5.13). This technique must be applied every time an application is run from the Run dialog box.

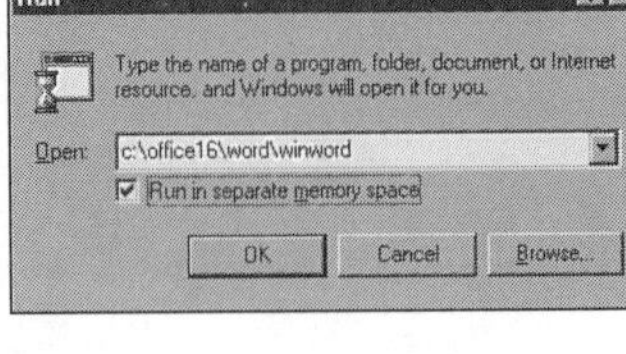


**FIGURE 5.13**
You can run a Win16 application in its own memory space by selecting this option in the Run dialog box.

> **NOTE**
>
> **Run Separate Only Available for Win16 Applications** The Run in Separate Memory Space option is available only when you type in the path to a Win16 application. It is not available for any other type of application because they run in their own memory spaces by default. Only Win16 applications will share the same memory space by default.

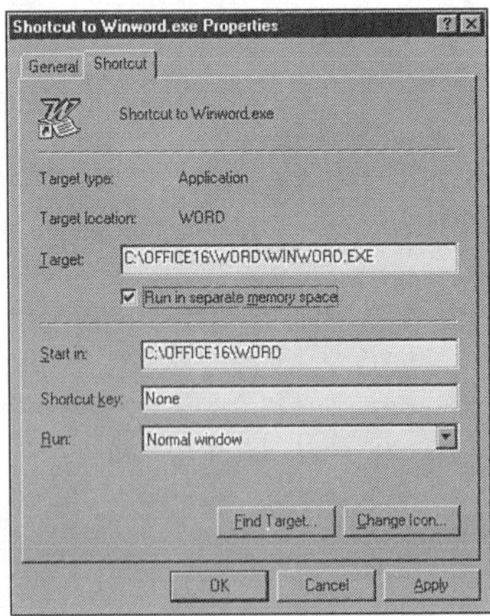


**FIGURE 5.14**
Configuring a shortcut to run a Win16 application in a separate memory space.

- At a command prompt, you can start a Win16 application in its own memory space by typing **start /separate application**. For example, to start Word 6.0 you would type:

```
start /separate c:\office16\word\winword.exe
```

  This technique must be applied every time the application is run from a command prompt.

- Shortcuts that point to Win16 applications can be configured to always run in a separate memory space. This option is available on the Shortcut tab of the properties dialog box for the shortcut (see Figure 5.14). Although this technique will enable an application to run in a separate memory space every time the shortcut is used, it applies only to the particular shortcut modified and not to all shortcuts created to that application.

- You can configure any file with a given extension to always run in a separate memory space when the data document is double-clicked in the Windows NT Explorer. To do so, edit the File Types tab of the Options dialog box as explained in Step by Step 5.1.

## STEP BY STEP

### 5.1 Configuring an Extension to Trigger an Application to Always Run in a Separate Memory Space

1. Start the Windows NT Explorer.
2. From the View menu, choose Options.
3. Click the File Types tab.
4. In the Registered File Types list box, select the desired file type.
5. Click the Edit button to display the Edit File Type dialog box. Then select Open from the Actions list and click the Edit button below it.
6. In the Editing Action for Type dialog box, adjust the application name by typing **cmd.exe /c start /separate** in front of the existing contents of the field (see Figure 5.15).

For example, to ensure that every time you double-click a Word 6.0 document a new NTVDM opens in which to run Word, use the following command:

```
cmd.exe /c start /separate
➥c:\office16\word\winword.exe
```

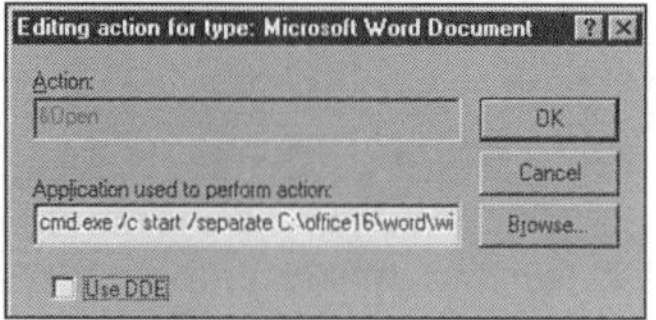


**FIGURE 5.15**
Configuring the Open action for Word 6.0 to always run in a separate memory space.

## Supporting OS/2 Applications Under Windows NT

Windows NT has limited support for OS/2 applications through the OS/2 subsystem. This subsystem creates support for OS/2 1.x character-based applications; however, this subsystem is only present on Intel-based versions of NT. As a result, the only OS/2 applications that will run on a RISC machine are those that are *bound* (that is, they run in either OS/2 or MS-DOS). In order to run bound applications in DOS mode, you must execute them using the `FORCEDOS` command (`FORCEDOS` *<application>*). Any bound OS/2 application can be forced to run in an NTVDM. However, it will run faster in the OS/2 subsystem if that is available. Therefore, it is not recommended that you use `FORCEDOS` in an Intel environment.

> EXAM TIP
>
> **Expect a FORCEDOS Question**
> Expect at least one exam question that deals with the topic of bound applications and the `FORCEDOS` command. Remember also that the only way to execute OS/2 applications on RISC-based systems is to use the `FORCEDOS` command for bound applications.

### Configuring OS/2 Applications

As with all Windows NT configurations, the configuration data for OS/2 applications is stored within the Windows NT Registry. This configuration data is stored in the following two locations:

- Hkey_Local_Machine\System\CurrentControlSet\Control\Session Manager\Subsystems
- Hkey_Local_Machine\Software\Microsoft\OS/2 Subsystem for NT

All of the configuration information for the OS/2 subsystem is stored in the CONFIG.SYS file. However, unless an OS/2 CONFIG.SYS file is copied onto an NT system from a native OS/2 system, that file never actually exists in NT. Instead, it is simulated through a number of Registry settings that NT reads from and writes to.

EXAM TIP

**Edit the CONFIG.SYS File with an OS/2 Editor** A common scenario question on the exam tests your knowledge of configuring the OS/2 subsystem. Typical questions test you on the fact that the CONFIG.SYS file must be edited with an OS/2 text editor.

If an OS/2 editor is started on an NT machine, it invokes the OS/2 subsystem. When the CONFIG.SYS file is edited, NT simulates the presence of that file by building a temporary one. After the file has been saved, the temporary file is deleted, and the changes are written to the Registry. From then on, every time an OS/2 editor is used to edit the CONFIG.SYS file, the simulated file is rebuilt from the Registry and displayed to the user. If, however, a native OS/2 CONFIG.SYS file is present, NT will actually use that file to maintain configuration information.

## Windows NT Add-On Subsystem for Presentation Manager

Windows NT 4 added support for 16-bit OS/2 1.x Presentation Manager applications. Previous versions of Windows NT provided no support for Presentation Manager–dependent applications. This support is provided by the Add-On Subsystem for Presentation Manager. This subsystem replaces the OS/2 subsystem on Intel-based Windows NT systems. It is not available for RISC-based systems.

NOTE

**This Add-On Is Not Free** This add-on subsystem is not provided free of charge. You must purchase it separately in addition to Windows NT.

An executed Presentation Manager application generates a separate Presentation Manager desktop. This desktop is *not* integrated with the Windows NT desktop.

## Removing Support for the OS/2 Subsystem

The Windows NT Resource Kit includes a utility called the C2 Configuration Tool. The National Computer Security Center has created a set of security standards that have been called the *Orange Book*. Windows NT 3.5x was evaluated as being C2 secure according to the specifications of the Orange Book when properly configured. The Windows NT operating system supports security that is not part of the C2 security definition.

The OS/2 Subsystem is not included in the current C2 security definition. To meet the C2 security standards, the OS/2 Subsystem should be disabled. The C2 Configuration Tool accomplishes this by deleting the OS2.EXE and OS2SS.EXE files from the %systemroot%\system32 subdirectory.

## STEP BY STEP

### 5.2 Disabling the OS/2 Subsystem

1. Start the C2 Configuration Tool by choosing Start, Programs, Resource Kit 4.0, Configuration, C2 Configuration (assuming it's in the default location).
2. In the list of Security Features, select the OS/2 Subsystem entry.
3. Double-click the OS/2 Subsystem entry, and a dialog box appears (see Figure 5.16).
4. Click the OK button to disable the OS/2 subsystem. A confirmation dialog box asks you to verify that you do want to remove the OS/2 subsystem from the computer and tells you that this action is not reversible. If this is acceptable, click OK. The icon to the left of the OS/2 subsystem now appears as a red closed lock, indicating full C2 Orange Book compliance.

NOTE

**Remove OS/2 Subsystem to Reduce Overhead** You might want to disable the OS/2 subsystem if you are not using any OS/2 applications. This reduces the amount of overhead the operating system must deal with. If you need to restore the OS/2 subsystem, you simply restore the OS2.EXE and OS2SS.EXE files from the original Windows NT distribution files. To do this, you use the `Expand` command.

## Supporting POSIX Applications

POSIX (Portable Operating System Interfaced based on UNIX) support is provided by Windows NT because of a U.S. government requirement for government computing contracts. Because it includes support for POSIX applications, Windows NT can be considered for government quotes. The implementation of POSIX in Windows NT enables portability of common applications from a UNIX system to Windows NT running the POSIX subsystem.

Table 5.4 describes the components that comprise the POSIX subsystem.

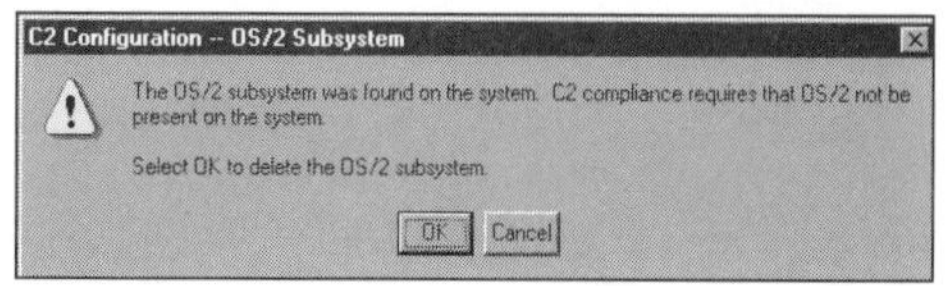


**FIGURE 5.16**
Confirm deletion of the OS/2 subsystem when prompted.

**TABLE 5.4**

**POSIX SUBSYSTEM COMPONENTS**

| *Component* | *Description* |
|---|---|
| PSXSS.EXE | The POSIX server, which is the main component of the POSIX subsystem. It is initialized when the first POSIX application is run. |
| POSIX.EXE | The Console Session Manager is a Windows NT 32-bit application that handles all communication between the POSIX subsystem and the Windows NT Executive Services. |
| PSXDLL.DLL | The dynamic link library support files that handle communications between POSIX applications and the PSXSS.EXE (the POSIX server). |

NOTE

**POSIX Subsystem Is Not Loaded by Default** The POSIX subsystem does not load until a POSIX application is executed; but after that, it remains loaded until the system is restarted. The POSIX subsystem can support up to 32 concurrent POSIX applications.

Windows NT provides POSIX.1 support in its POSIX subsystem. POSIX.1 defines a C language source-code-level application programming interface (API) to an operating system environment. To have full POSIX.1 compliance, the NTFS file system must be implemented on the computer that will be executing POSIX applications. This provides the user with the following POSIX.1 compliance features:

- *Case-sensitive file naming.* NTFS preserves case for both directories and filenames.
- *Hard links.* POSIX applications can store the same data in two differently named files.
- *An additional time stamp on files.* This tracks the last time the file was accessed. The default on FAT volumes is to track when the file was last modified.

## Modifying Support for the POSIX Subsystem

For full POSIX.1 compliance, one of the Windows NT user rights must be modified. By default, the user right Bypass Traverse Checking is granted to the special group Everyone. This right enables a user to change directories through a directory tree even if the user has no permission for those directories. This user right must be disabled for any accounts that will be using POSIX applications.

## STEP BY STEP

### 5.3 Disabling the Bypass Traverse Checking Right

1. Log on as a member of the Administrators local group, and then start the User Manager.
2. Create a global group that contains all users who will *not* be running POSIX applications. It is imperative that no POSIX users be members of this global group.
3. From the Policies menu, choose User Rights.
4. Make sure that the Show Advanced User Rights check box is selected.
5. Select the Bypass Traverse Checking user right.
6. Click Remove to remove the Everyone group.
7. Click Add and select the new global group of non-POSIX users that you created in step 2, and then click OK to add this group.
8. Click OK to complete this user rights change.

## Removing Support for the POSIX Subsystem

Like the OS/2 subsystem, you can also disable the POSIX subsystem by using the C2 Configuration Tool in the Windows NT Resource Kit because it is not included in the current C2 security definition. The C2 Configuration Tool accomplishes this by deleting the PSXSS.EXE file from the %systemroot%\system32 subdirectory.

## STEP BY STEP

### 5.4 Disabling the POSIX Subsystem

1. Start the C2 Configuration Tool by choosing Start, Programs, Resource Kit 4.0, Configuration, C2 Configuration (assuming it's in the default location).

*continues*

EXAM TIP

**Know What POSIX Features the Subsystem Provides** Most exam questions related to the POSIX subsystem focus on what features of NTFS provide support for POSIX.1 requirements. These are case-sensitive file naming, hard links, and access date information. Remember that if a POSIX application does not access file system resources, it can run on the FAT file system.

*continued*

2. In the list of Security Features, double-click the POSIX Subsystem entry.
3. Click OK to disable the POSIX subsystem.
4. Click OK to confirm that you do want to permanently remove support for the POSIX subsystem. The icon to the left of the POSIX subsystem now appears as a red closed lock, indicating full C2 Orange Book compliance.

## Application Support on RISC and Intel Platforms

EXAM TIP

**Know the Terminology** Typically, the exam tests your knowledge of the terms *source-compatible* and *binary-compatible*. Make sure you know the difference and how each type of application is supported on each platform.

Although you can run Windows NT on both the Intel and RISC platforms, you must consider compatibility issues when determining what applications to support. Applications are either *source-compatible* or *binary-compatible.* Source-compatible applications must be recompiled for each hardware platform on which they are going to be executed. Binary-compatible applications can be run on any Windows NT platform without recompiling the application. Table 5.5 outlines application compatibility on the Windows NT platforms.

TABLE 5.5

APPLICATION COMPATIBILITY ACROSS WINDOWS NT PLATFORMS

| *Platform* | *MS-DOS* | *Win16* | *Win32* | *OS/2* | *POSIX* |
|---|---|---|---|---|---|
| Intel | Binary | Binary | Source | Binary | Source |
| Alpha | Binary | Binary | Source* | Binary** | Source |
| Mips | Binary | Binary | Source | Binary** | Source |
| PowerPC | Binary | Binary | Source | Binary** | Source |

* Third-party utilities such as Digital FX!32 enable Win32-based Intel programs to execute on Digital Alpha AXP microprocessors. Although these utilities are interpreting the code on-the-fly, they end up performing faster on the Alpha as a result of the increased processor speed.

** Only bound applications can be run on the three RISC hardware platforms. They will run in a Windows NTVDM because the OS/2 subsystem is not provided in RISC-based versions of Windows NT.

# Starting Applications at Different Priorities

Start applications at various priorities.

Under preemptive multitasking, Windows NT uses priority levels to determine which application should get access to the processor for execution. Each application starts at a base priority level of eight. The system dynamically adjusts the priority level to give all applications access to the processor. The process or thread with the highest priority base at any one time has access to the processor. Some of the factors that cause Windows NT to adjust the priority of a thread or process include the following:

- Windows NT boosts the base priority of whichever process is running in the foreground. This ensures that the response time is maximized for the application currently in use.
- Windows NT randomly boosts the priority for lower-priority threads. This has two major benefits. First, low priority threads that would normally not be able to run can do so after their priority base is raised. Second, if a lower-priority process has access to a resource that is to be shared with a higher-priority process, the lower-priority process could end up monopolizing the resource. The boost in the lower-priority thread's base priority frees up the resource sooner.
- Anytime a thread has been in a voluntary wait state, Windows NT boosts its priority. The size of the boost depends on how long the resource has been in a wait state.

Figure 5.17 shows how Windows NT handles different priority levels.

Priority levels 0 to 15 are used by dynamic applications. Anything running at a dynamic level can be written to the Windows NT pagefile. By default, this includes user applications and operating system functions that are not imperative to the performance of the operating system. Priority levels 16 to 31 are reserved for real-time applications that cannot be written to the Windows NT pagefile. This includes all Executive Services and the Windows NT Kernel.

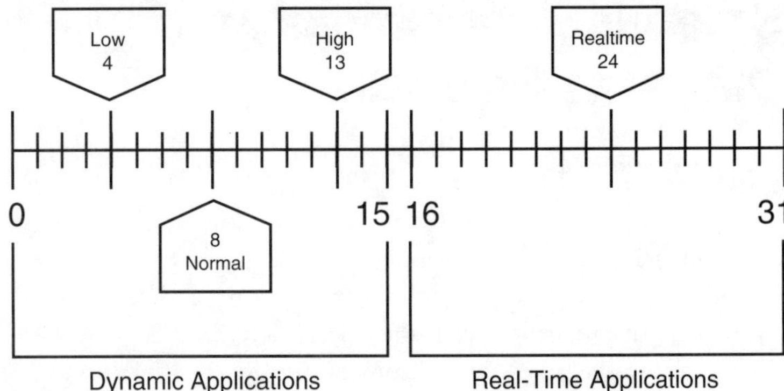


**FIGURE 5.17**
Base priority levels in Windows NT.

## Starting Applications at Different Levels

Windows NT enables the user to change the default priority level from Normal either by using the command prompt to start an application or by using the Task Manager to adjust the priority level after the application has started.

Table 5.6 shows the four priority levels the user can set and the command line switches that can be used with the `start` command to adjust those levels at execution time.

**WARNING**

**Using Realtime Priority Can Be Hazardous to the Operation of Your Workstation** Be very careful about running any application at the Realtime base priority. This could slow down the performance of your system because no other applications will be able to access the processor for I/O. Windows NT protects against the use of Realtime base priority by allowing only members of the Administrators group to run applications at this level.

**TABLE 5.6**

**BASE PRIORITY LEVELS UNDER WINDOWS NT**

| *Priority Level* | *Base Priority* | *Command* |
|---|---|---|
| Low | 4 | `start /low executable.exe` |
| Normal | 8 | `start /normal executable.exe` |
| High | 13 | `start /high executable.exe` |
| Realtime | 24 | `start /realtime executable.exe` |

After an application is running, you can use the Task Manager to change the base priority (see Figure 5.18).

> **EXAM TIP**
>
> **Know the Base Priority Switches** Common questions about base priorities include how to start an application at a different base priority using the `start` command with the `/low`, `/normal`, `/high`, and `/realtime` switches.

## STEP BY STEP

### 5.5 Changing the Priority of a Running Application

1. Right-click on the taskbar to bring up its shortcut menu.
2. Click the Task Manager option.
3. In Task Manager, click the Processes tab to view all running processes.
4. If the Base Priority column is not visible, add it to the view by choosing View, Select Columns and selecting Base Priority in the resulting dialog box.
5. Right-click on the process in the Process list.
6. Click Set Priority, and then click the desired priority at which you want the process to run.

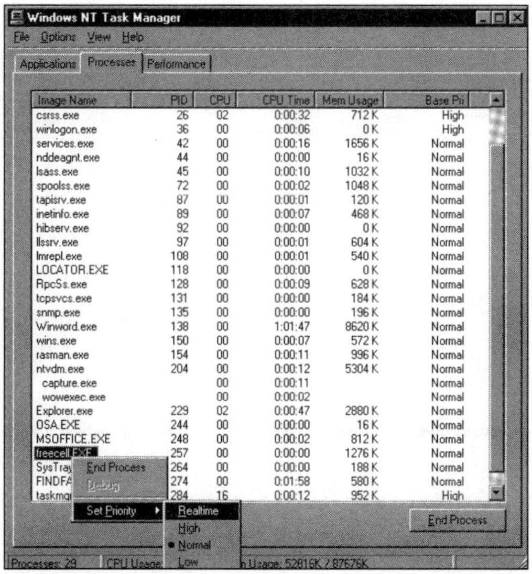

**FIGURE 5.18**
Change the base priorities of running applications by using Task Manager.

## Changing the Default Priority Boost for Foreground Applications

On some Windows NT computers, you might need to improve the responsiveness of background applications. By default, the foreground application is given a priority boost of two levels. This changes the base priority for foreground applications from the default of 8 to 10 in the case of Normal priority applications. However, it may not always be desirable for this boost to be granted to foreground applications, in which case, you may want to change the amount of boost given to foreground applications.

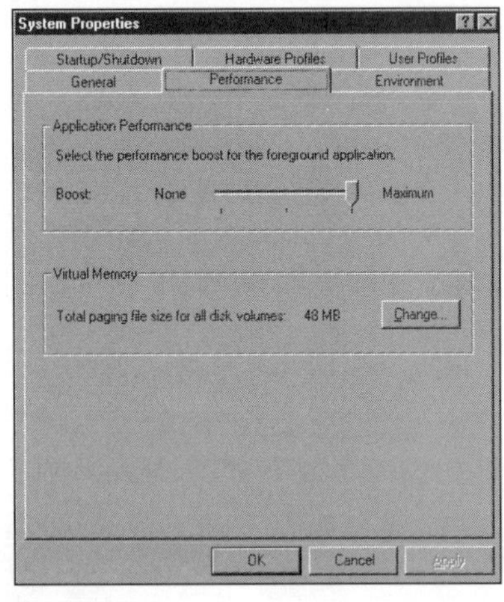


**FIGURE 5.19**
Changing the default priority boost for foreground applications.

### STEP BY STEP

**5.6 Changing the Boost of Foreground Applications**

1. In Control Panel, double-click the System icon.
2. In the System Properties dialog box, click the Performance tab.
3. The Performance tab contains an Application Performance setting that determines whether foreground applications are given a priority boost over background applications (see Figure 5.19). Choose from the three settings.

   If the slider is set to None, no boost is given to foreground applications over background applications. This setting is preferred for file and print servers and application servers so that running a utility on the server will not affect any client connection performance. If the slider is set to the middle setting, the foreground application receives a boost of only one over background applications. The default setting is to have the priority boost set to Maximum. This gives a foreground application a priority increase of two over background applications. This is the preferred setting for Windows NT Workstations acting as client workstations.

## CASE STUDY: PRINT IT DRAFTING INC.

### ESSENCE OF THE CASE

Here are the essential elements in this case:

- AutoCAD's performance is unacceptably slow when running in the background.
- The failure of one 16-bit Windows application causes other 16-bit applications to fail as well.

### SCENARIO

Print It Drafting Inc. is a small drafting and architectural company that employs 100 people. Many facets of the operation are computerized, and they have a small Windows NT domain consisting of 50 NT Workstations and a single NT Server that is functioning as a file and print server as well as the domain controller. Of the 50 Workstations, 25 are running AutoCAD software to produce the many drawings that create the foundation of the business. In addition to AutoCAD, most of the machines have the Microsoft Office Suite 4.3 for Windows 3.1. The company is planning a software upgrade in the future but has no plans for an immediate change in software.

Print It Drafting Inc. has come to you with two problems. First, many of the draftspeople are concerned because it takes such a long time to render their AutoCAD drawings. When they submit the drawings for processing, they usually switch to another application to make the most efficient use of their time; however, this seems to slow the process greatly. On the other hand, it's not acceptable for them to sit around and wait for the documents to process because some drawings take up to an hour to complete. They want you to tune their systems so that running other programs (such as Word or Excel) does not measurably slow their CAD programs.

The second problem is related to the Office Suite products. The administrative and accounting staffs produce many critical documents and spreadsheets, and frequently both Word and Excel are being used at the same time. If one program stops responding to commands for any reason, the other program is always terminated,

*continues*

## CASE STUDY: PRINT IT DRAFTING INC.

*continued*

too, which is unacceptable. You are to find a solution to this problem if one exists.

### ANALYSIS

The fixes for both of these problems are relatively straightforward. In the first case, it is likely that all the programs on the draftspeople's workstations are being started at normal priority. This means that they have a priority of 8. But the default says that anything running in the foreground is getting a 2-point boost from the base priority, bringing it to 10. As a result, when sent to the background, AutoCAD is not getting as much attention from the processor as it did when it was the foreground application. Because multiple applications need to be run at once without significant degradation of the performance of AutoCAD, you implement the following solution:

1. On the Performance tab of the System Properties dialog box for each workstation, set the Application Performance slider to None to prevent a boost for foreground applications.
2. Recommend that users keep the additional programs running alongside AutoCAD at a minimum (because all programs will now get equal processor time).

The fix to the second problem is to run each 16-bit application in its own NTVDM. This ensures that the crashing of one application will not adversely affect the others, but it still enables interoperability between the applications because they use OLE (and not shared memory) to transfer data. To make the fix as transparent as possible to the users, you suggested that two things be done:

1. Make sure that for each shortcut a user has created to the office applications, the Run in Separate Memory Space option is selected on the Shortcut tab.
2. Change the properties for the extensions associated with the applications (for example, .XLS and .DOC) so that they start using the `/separate` switch. Then any file that is double-clicked invokes the associated program to run in its own NTVDM.

## CHAPTER SUMMARY

This chapter presented three major topics: Windows NT architecture, NT subsystems, and management of application execution. In the first section, you looked at the general architecture of NT. This provided background to help you understand the subsystems in place to allow a variety of application types to execute on NT.

Studying the supported subsystems in NT, you first learned about the native subsystem: the Win32 client/server (CSR) subsystem used to execute 32-bit programs. Then you studied the function and configuration of the MS-DOS subsystem and the NTVDMs that are created to run MS-DOS–based programs. As an addition to the NTVDM, you then examined how NT supports Win16 applications through the WOW running in an NTVDM, which gives support for 16-bit Windows programs. Finally, you learned about the architecture and configuration of two subsystems designed to give support to OS/2 and POSIX applications.

The chapter concluded with a discussion of application priorities and how to manipulate those priorities through command lines and system configuration.

### KEY TERMS

Before you take the exam, make sure you are comfortable with the definitions and concepts for each of the following key terms:

- OS/2
- POSIX
- CSR subsystem
- multithreaded
- Symmetric Multi-Processing
- preemptive multitasking
- NT Virtual DOS Machine (NTVDM)
- Program Information File (PIF)
- Windows on Windows (WOW)
- `/separate`
- `FORCEDOS`
- hard links
- source-compatible
- binary-compatible
- base priority
- default performance boost

## APPLY YOUR LEARNING

The following section allows you to assess how well you understood the material in the chapter. The exercises provide you with opportunities to engage in the sorts of tasks that comprise the skill sets the objectives reflect. Review and exam questions test your knowledge of the tasks and concepts specified in the objectives. Answers to the review and exam questions follow in the answers sections. For additional review- and exam-type questions, see the Top Score test engine on the CD-ROM that came with this book.

## Exercises

These lab exercises give you a chance to practice configuring Windows NT to support DOS, Win16, and Win32 applications. They also enable you to investigate changing the priority levels of running applications. You can find the applications used in Exercise 5.2 and Exercise 5.3 on the CD that accompanies this book.

### 5.1 Configuring a Windows NT Virtual DOS Machine

This exercise investigates some of the configuration that can be done to an NTVDM.

**Estimated Time:** 5 minutes

1. Right-click on the desktop and choose New Shortcut.
2. Enter **c:\winnt\system32\edit.com** as the command line. (This assumes that Windows NT is installed in the c:\winnt directory. Substitute the correct directory if yours differs.)
3. Click Next, and the Create Shortcut dialog box should suggest MS-DOS Editor as the shortcut name.
4. Click Finish to finish creating the shortcut.
5. Double-click on the newly created shortcut to start the MS-DOS Editor. Press the Esc key to bypass the display of the survival guide.
6. The MS-DOS Editor runs in a DOS window and, by default, enables you to use the mouse. Press Alt+Enter to switch to full-screen mode. Note that the mouse pointer becomes a box onscreen. You can now modify the NTVDM to automatically run full-screen and you can disable the capability to switch between full-screen and windowed modes.
7. Exit the MS-DOS Editor by choosing File, Exit.
8. Right-click on the shortcut to the MS-DOS Editor and choose Properties from the pop-up menu.
9. On the Program tab, change the command line to read **c:\winnt\system32\edit.com /h** to change the display of the editor to 32 lines.
10. On the Screen tab, set the Usage option to Full Screen. Also increase the initial size to 43 lines.
11. On the Misc tab, deselect the check box next to Alt+Enter. This disables the capability to switch between full-screen and windowed modes.
12. Click OK to apply all your changes to the MS-DOS Editor's NTVDM, and then double-click on its shortcut to start the MS-DOS Editor. Note that the MS-DOS Editor now runs full screen with 43 lines of display. Try switching to windowed mode by using the Alt+Enter key combination. It should not work!

## APPLY YOUR LEARNING

### 5.2 Running Win16 Applications in Separate Memory Spaces

This exercise makes use of the NTSRV16.EXE utility on the accompanying CD to investigate how Windows NT runs Win16 applications in one memory space by default. It then investigates how Windows NT can run Win16 applications in separate memory spaces.

**Estimated Time:** 10 minutes

1. Locate the NTSRV16.EXE file on the accompanying CD and double-click on it.
2. Double-click the NTSRV.EXE file again to open a second instance of the program. Notice that the taskbar now shows instances of the program running.
3. Right-click on a blank area of the taskbar and choose Task Manager from the pop-up menu.
4. On the Processes tab, look for the NTVDM.EXE process. Note that both instances of NTSRV16.EXE are running in the same NTVDM.
5. Close both instances of NTSRV16.EXE by selecting the Option, Exit from This Program command.
6. From the Start menu, choose Run.
7. Click the Browse button, select the NTSRV16.EXE executable from the accompanying CD, and click OK to return to the Run dialog box.
8. Select the Run in Separate Memory Space option and click OK to start NTSRV16.EXE.
9. Repeat steps 6 through 8 to run a second instance of NTSRV16.EXE in a separate memory space.
10. Start the Task Manager. Note that each instance of NTSRV16.EXE is now running in its own NTVDM. In fact, you should also see the default NTVDM running with only WOWEXEC.EXE running in it.
11. Close all instances of NTSRV16.EXE using the Option, Exit from This Program command.

### 5.3 Testing Reliability When Win32 and Win16 Applications Fail

This exercise uses the NTSRV16.EXE, POW_16.EXE, and POW_32.EXE files from the accompanying CD. Using these files, you will investigate the effect an ill-behaved application has on other running applications based on whether the ill-behaved application is 16-bit or 32-bit.

**Estimated Time:** 20 minutes

1. Using the accompanying CD, start the following applications by double-clicking on each one:
   - NTSRV16.EXE
   - POW_16.EXE
   - POW_32.EXE
2. From the Start menu, select Run. Type in **MSPAINT.EXE** as the program name. The Paint program included with Windows NT is 32-bit program, and the NT Server Simulator (NTSVR16.EXE) is a 16-bit program that you will use for testing.
3. First you'll investigate the crash of a Win32 program. Switch to the running version of

## APPLY YOUR LEARNING

POW_32.EXE. Click the POW button to cause a general protection fault.

Note that you can no longer do anything in the POW_32.EXE window, but you can still use NTSVR16.EXE and MSPAINT.EXE. This is because each Win32 application has its own 2GB address space. The crash of one Win32 application does not affect other programs. Click the OK button in the Dr. Watson window to close the POW_32.EXE application.

4. Switch to the POW_16 program. Click the POW button to cause a general protection fault.

   You can still draw in MSPAINT.EXE. However, you cannot operate the NT Server simulator. This is because it is running in the same memory space as Badapp16.

5. For a final test, run both POW_16.EXE and NTSRV16.EXE in separate memory spaces. When you cause a general protection fault in the POW_16.EXE program's execution, it does not affect NTSRV16.EXE. This is because each Win16 application is running in its own memory space.

### 5.4 Changing Priorities of Applications

In this exercise, you investigate starting programs at different base priority levels and then changing the base priority on-the-fly.

**Estimated Time:** 5 minutes

1. Log on as the administrator of your Windows NT Workstation computer.
2. Go to a command prompt by choosing Start, Programs, Command Prompt.
3. Type **start /low sol.exe** to start Solitaire at a low base priority. This sets the base priority to four.
4. Type **start /realtime freecell.exe**.
5. Close the command prompt window.
6. Start the Task Manager.
7. Select the Processes tab. If you do not see the Base Priority Column, add it by choosing View, Select Columns and checking the check box next to Base Priority.
8. Note that the FREECELL.EXE process is currently running at a base priority of Realtime. Right-click on the FREECELL.EXE process in the Process list to change the base priority. In the pop-up menu, choose Set Priority and then select Normal to reset the base priority to its default level.
9. Change the base priority for SOL.EXE to Normal as well.

## Review Questions

1. What type of OS/2 character-based applications can a RISC-based Windows NT Workstation run?
2. Which environment subsystem requires case-sensitive file naming?
3. By default, which handles Symmetric Multi-Processing better: two MS-DOS–based applications or two Win16 applications?
4. How do you run a Windows 16-bit application in its own memory space?

## APPLY YOUR LEARNING

5. What kind of compatibility do Windows 32-bit applications have across hardware platforms?
6. What kind of compatibility do Windows 16-bit applications have across hardware platforms?
7. What other operating systems' applications does Windows NT support with environment subsystems?

## Exam Questions

1. Which of the following are advantages to running Win16 applications in their own separate memory spaces?

   A. OLE runs more efficiently.

   B. Preemptive multitasking.

   C. Nonpreemptive multitasking.

   D. Greater reliability (the crash of one Win16 application does not affect other Win16 applications).

   E. Support for multiple processors.

2. Which of the following are valid switches for the `start` command?

   A. `/base`

   B. `/separate`

   C. `/high`

   D. `/kernel`

3. What standard NT utility is used to stop a nonresponsive program?

   A. Task Manager

   B. Control Panel's System application

   C. KILL.EXE

   D. Server Manager

4. Which groups have the capability to run applications at the Realtime base priority?

   A. Server Operators

   B. Administrators

   C. Account Operators

   D. Replicator

5. An OS/2 application that can also be executed in an NTVDM is known as a ____________ application.

   A. Dynamic

   B. 32-bit

   C. Flexible

   D. Bound

6. Which of the following commands causes an OS/2 application to execute in an NTVDM?

   A. `start /ntvdm os2app.exe`

   B. `start /separate os2app.exe`

   C. `FORCEDOS`

   D. `FORCECMD`

7. POSIX.1 support in Windows NT includes which of the following features?

   A. Additional time stamp

   B. Hard links

   C. Binary compatibility

   D. Case-sensitive naming

## APPLY YOUR LEARNING

8. **Scenario:** Willie is running a Windows NT Workstation with a 200MHz Intel MMX processor. He runs Word 6.0 and PowerPoint 4.0 (two 16-bit Windows applications that both use OLE).

   **Required Result:**

   Ensure that the failure of either application will not force the termination of the other.

   **Optional Desired Results:**

   Use as little memory overhead as possible to accomplish this task.

   Make sure that data can still be exchanged using OLE.

   **Proposed Solution:**

   Configure each of the applications to run in its own NTVDM when a shortcut is used to access the programs or their files.

   **Analysis:**

   Which of the following statements best describes the proposed solution?

   A. The proposed solution produces the required result and both of the optional desired results.

   B. The proposed solution produces the required result and only one of the optional desired results.

   C. The proposed solution produces the required result but does not produce either of the optional desired results.

   D. The proposed solution does not produce the required result.

9. What files are used to configure an NTVDM by default?

   A. AUTOEXEC.BAT

   B. AUTOEXEC.NT

   C. CONFIG.SYS

   D. CONFIG.NT

10. You edit the CONFIG.SYS file to reflect the configuration changes you want for the OS/2 subsystem, but the changes are ignored. What's causing this?

    A. You have a boot-sector virus.

    B. The OS/2 subsystem can be configured only by directly modifying the Registry.

    C. An OS/2 text editor was not used to edit CONFIG.SYS.

    D. OS/2 configuration is saved to the %systemroot%\system32\config.os2 file.

11. You download a new POSIX utility from the Internet to run on your Dec Alpha AXP system running Windows NT. The application does not run. Why?

    A. POSIX applications are binary-compatible.

    B. The POSIX subsystem must be configured to auto start (in the Control Panel) in order to run POSIX applications.

    C. POSIX applications are source-compatible.

    D. The POSIX subsystem must be unloaded.

12. MS-DOS applications are __________ compatible across platforms? Pick any that apply.

    A. Source

## APPLY YOUR LEARNING

B. Processor

C. Thread

D. Binary

13. You have several macros in Excel that you want to run faster in the background while you are working in other applications. How do you accomplish this?

A. Run the foreground processes using the `/separate` switch.

B. Run Excel in its own memory space.

C. Increase the base priority for Excel spreadsheets in the Registry.

D. Use the Control Panel's System application to lower the boost given to foreground applications.

## Answers to Review Questions

1. RISC-based Windows NT Workstations can run only bound OS/2 applications because the OS/2 subsystem is not supported on RISC systems. Bound applications can be run in an NTVDM by using the `FORCEDOS` command. For more information, refer to the section "Supporting OS/2 Applications Under Windows NT."

2. The POSIX subsystem provides support for case-sensitive file naming as long as the NTFS file system is being used. For more information, refer to the section "Supporting POSIX Applications."

3. Two MS-DOS–based applications handle Symmetric Multi-Processing better by default because each MS-DOS application will have a separate thread of execution. By default, Win16 applications share a common memory space with only one thread of execution. For more information, refer to the sections "Supporting MS-DOS Applications" and "Running Multiple Win16 Applications."

4. You can do this by running the Win16 application and typing the command **start /separate app.exe** at the command prompt. Another method is to select the Run in Separate Memory Space check box in the Run dialog box (accessible through the Start menu). For more information, refer to the section "Configuring Win16 Applications to Run in Separate Memory Spaces."

5. Win32 applications are source-compatible across platforms. This means that they must be recompiled for every platform on which they are going to run. You cannot use the same version of the software on Intel, Alpha, Mips, or PowerPC systems. For more information, refer to the section "Application Support on RISC and Intel Platforms."

6. Win16 applications are binary-compatible across platforms. This means that they can be run as is on all versions of Windows NT. For more information, refer to the section "Application Support on RISC and Intel Platforms."

7. The OS/2 subsystem and the POSIX subsystem come with Windows NT to support applications for these operating systems. For more information, see the section "Windows NT Architecture."

**APPLY YOUR LEARNING**

## Answers to Exam Questions

1. **B, D, and E** are correct. Running Win16 applications in their own separate memory spaces enables them to participate in preemptive multitasking because each Win16 application has a separate thread of execution. Running the application in a separate memory space also prevents the crash of one Win16 application from affecting other Win16 applications. Finally, if each Win16 application has a separate thread of execution, they can take advantage of multiple processors in the system because Windows NT can schedule each thread independently. For more information, refer to the section "Running Win16 Applications in Individual NTVDMs."

2. **B and C** are correct. The `/separate` switch is used to start Win16 applications in their own separate memory spaces, and the `/high` switch is used to start an application with a base priority of 13 (instead of the default of 8). For more information, refer to the sections "Configuring Win16 Applications to Run in Separate Memory Spaces" and "Starting Applications at Different Levels."

3. **A** is correct. You can stop most applications by using the Task Manager. Although the Resource Kit's Kill utility enables you to kill any process, it is not a standard NT utility. For more information, refer to the section "Running Win16 Applications in Individual NTVDMs."

4. **B** is correct. Only administrators can start an application using the `/realtime` switch. This level is normally reserved for operating system functions. For more information, refer to the section "Starting Applications at Different Levels."

5. **D** is correct. Bound applications run more efficiently under OS/2 environments, but they can also run in MS-DOS environments. This is the only type of OS/2 application that can be run on a RISC-based Windows NT system. For more information, refer to the section "Supporting OS/2 Applications Under Windows NT."

6. **C** is correct. The `FORCEDOS` command must be used to run bound applications in MS-DOS mode on RISC-based Windows NT systems because RISC systems do not have an OS/2 subsystem. For more information, refer to the section "Supporting OS/2 Applications Under Windows NT."

7. **A, B, and D** are correct. By using the NTFS file system, Windows NT provides hard links, which is the capability to store the same data in two files with different names. Changing the data in one also changes the data of the other. Case-sensitive naming is also supported for POSIX applications, which means that Data.txt and DATA.txt will be two different files. Finally, POSIX support provides not only a last-modified time stamp, but also a last-accessed time stamp. For more information, refer to the section "Supporting POSIX Applications."

8. **B** is correct. Running in separate NTVDMs ensures that if one hangs, the other will not fail as well. In addition, exchange of data using OLE will be maintained. However, this is not the most efficient use of memory because there is overhead associated with each NTVDM—a tradeoff for the added functionality. For more information, see the section "Supporting Win16 Applications."

## APPLY YOUR LEARNING

9. **B and D** are correct. The AUTOEXEC.NT and CONFIG.NT files are stored in the %systemroot%\System32 subdirectory. Remember that each PIF can have its own CONFIG and AUTOEXEC files. These are set via the Advanced button on the Program tab of the PIF Properties dialog box. For more information, refer to the section "Configuring the Program Properties of a PIF."

10. **C** is correct. The CONFIG.SYS file is not simply a text file (as it is under MS-DOS) and must be edited and saved using an OS/2 text editor. This process creates a temporary CONFIG.SYS file from Registry settings and then writes those configuration settings back to the Registry. For more information, refer to the section "Configuring OS/2 Applications."

11. **C** is correct. POSIX applications must be compiled for each platform on which they are going to run. Be careful: By default, most applications for Windows NT that you find on the Internet are compiled for the Intel platform. For more information, refer to the section "Application Support on RISC and Intel Platforms."

12. **D** is correct. MS-DOS applications are binary-compatible across platforms and do not need to be recompiled to run under RISC systems. The Intel Instruction Unit provides the Intel emulation, and the NTVDM provides an environment for the MS-DOS applications to run under. For more information, refer to the section "Application Support on RISC and Intel Platforms."

**D** is correct. Even though the Excel application is running in the background, modifying the priority boost for foreground applications works in this case because you are lessening the boost for the application that you are working on as the macro executes in the background. For more information, refer to the section "Changing the Default Priority Boost for Foreground Applications."

### Suggested Readings and Resources

The following are some recommended readings on the topic of running applications for NT Workstation:

1. Microsoft Official Curriculum course 922: *Supporting Microsoft Windows NT 4.0 Core Technologies*
    - Module 8: Supporting Applications
2. Web sites
    - `www.microsoft.com/train.cert`
    - `www.prometric.com/testingcandidates/assessment/chosetest.html` (take online assessment tests)

## Objectives

Microsoft provides the following objectives for "Monitoring and Optimization":

**Monitor system performance by using various tools.**

- This objective is necessary because someone certified in the use of Windows NT Workstation technology must understand how the Performance Monitor functions and how to configure it to monitor the objects desired.

**Identify and resolve a given performance problem.**

- This objective is necessary because someone certified in the use of Windows NT Workstation technology must understand what the major source of a performance problem us and how to identify bottlenecks in the system when analyzing Performance Monitor output. In addition, a Workstation professional should know what steps to take to resolve performance problems.

**Optimize system performance in various areas.**

- This objective is necessary because someone certified in the use of Windows NT Workstation technology must understand how optimization is to be done under a variety of circumstances. This involves ensuring system recoverability, configuring systems for good performance proactively, and responding to bad performance indicators.

CHAPTER 6

# Monitoring and Optimization

## OUTLINE

This chapter will help you prepare for the "Monitoring and Optimization" section of Microsoft's Exam 70-73 by introducing you to a variety of tools and utilities which can be used to do just that. These utilities will allow you to determine the performance characteristics of your NT Workstation, to analyze these characteristics, and finally to take steps which will improve performance where that is possible.

# Study Strategies

- Microsoft does not usually put much emphasis on performance monitoring in its 70-73 (NT Workstation) exam. It leaves that to the Enterprise exam. However, they do expect you to know the tools that are available to you and how to use them. When reading this chapter, focus on two major areas: the theoretical aspects of performance in general, and the practical use of the tools outlined in the chapter.
- The theoretical aspects of performance are just that, theoretical. You can't touch your processor or actually see it work. All you can do is understand that certain tasks use the processor more intensely than others and that, if your server is doing those tasks, you need a fast processor. The bottom line is that you have to study and memorize the subsystems discussed here and know how each is related to performance.
- Of course, you can't get away with not touching your computer at all for this chapter. Because Microsoft has provided Performance Monitor, Server Manager, Task Manager, and NT Diagnostics as tools you can use to monitor programs, analyze performance, and locate bottlenecks, you need to understand how they are used. You don't need to know all the objects and all the counters associated with Performance Monitor or all the small customizations to Task Manager that are covered in this chapter. However, you do need to know what they are for and under what circumstances you would use them; that is the kind of thing you will be tested on.

# Introduction

Monitoring and optimization of the Windows NT Workstation 4.0 product can be broken down into the following three parts:

- Understanding the tools within Windows NT used to monitor system activity and performance
- Interpreting symptoms and knowing which tool can help diagnose the situation
- Understanding the complete effects of one Windows NT component on others before making changes

Depending on whether the Windows NT Workstation 4.0 product is running as a standalone system or networked in a Windows NT domain, you will have to consider some very different issues. This chapter focuses on Windows NT Workstation 4.0 in a simple Windows NT domain networked environment.

EXAM TIP

**Resource Kit and Third-Party Utilities Mentioned Are Not Test Material** The Windows NT Resource Kit and third-party utilities mentioned in this chapter are covered for information only and will be elaborated on later in this chapter.

Two basic Windows NT Workstation 4.0 tools are discussed in this chapter: Task Manager and Performance Monitor. Additional tools are mentioned for their supporting roles. Each tool is discussed in relation to its merits and purpose. Along with detailed descriptions of the features of these tools, this chapter contains recommended techniques and suggested uses.

To implement changes, you must make use of several Windows NT features. For this reason, a fair understanding of Windows NT is required before you can start to monitor and modify performance.

# Monitoring System Performance

Monitor system performance by using various tools.

This section takes a close look at the activities going on behind the scenes of Windows NT Workstation 4.0. Unfortunately, no absolute correct answer or value can be given to a specific reading. The goal here is to explain the purpose and use of each tool.

The only method for evaluating a given result is to compare it to a *benchmark value*. These benchmarks will be gathered over time and should be kept on record. Microsoft and third-party magazines do publish some guideline values that are mentioned in this chapter. However, these guidelines are examples and suggestions. Remember that each system and situation differs. Thus you may not be able to implement some of the suggestions mentioned in this chapter.

## Using the Task Manager

The Task Manager tool offers a quick overview of key system resources, such as the following:

- Memory and CPU usage
- Status of applications currently running
- Processes in use on the system

You can invoke the Task Manager in several ways, including the following:

- Right-click on the taskbar and select Task Manager.
- Press Ctrl+Alt+Delete, and then select Task Manager.
- Press Ctrl+Shift+Esc.

### Using the Applications Tab

The Applications tab lists all DOS, 16-bit, and 32-bit Windows applications. The application name is listed in the Task column, and the status of `Running` or `Not Responding` appears in the Status column (see Figure 6.1).

Here the terms *task* and *application* are interchangeable. You can use the Applications tab to end a task, start a task, or switch to a task.

The Task Manager's Applications tab identifies a failed application as `Not Responding`. When an application fails, it can tie up critical resources such as memory and the CPU. Therefore, it is in everyone's best interest to end the task as soon as possible.

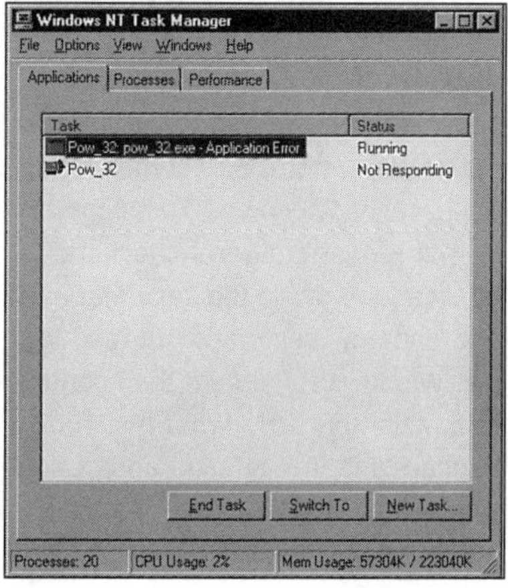


**FIGURE 6.1**
The Applications tab's Status column identifies any failed applications that need to be ended.

## STEP BY STEP

### 6.1 Terminating an Unresponsive Application

1. Right-click the taskbar and choose Task Manager from the menu.
2. Click the Applications tab to see a list of running applications.
3. Select the application to end by clicking it.
4. Click on the End Task button.
5. If a dialog box appears, warning you that you might lose data, click on Wait to allow the application five more seconds to shut down properly.
6. If the application does not terminate and the above dialog box reappears, click on End Task to end it immediately.

DOS, 16-bit, and 32-bit applications are all ended the same way. The big difference is in the resources that may be released. DOS and 32-bit applications run in their own memory address space with very little sharing of resources.

NOTE

**An Unresponsive System Doesn't Necessarily Mean NT Crashed**
Windows NT is designed to prevent application failures from corrupting the entire system. Sometimes it might appear that Windows NT has crashed even if it hasn't. Always check the Applications tab in the Task Manager and end any task that's not responding. Windows NT should then continue to function properly. What may have happened is that a failed application was using a resource needed by the operating system.

However, a 16-bit application is much more intertwined with all other 16-bit applications. All 16-bit applications share the same memory address space and message queue. When one application fails to respond to the user or the operating system, it also blocks all other 16-bit applications from responding because they all share the same message queue.

When you terminate a failed 16-bit application, the system releases the resources that may have been tied up and returns all memory to the common pool. For more information on how applications run under Windows NT Workstation 4.0, see Chapter 5, "Running Applications."

If you do not close down an application properly, you risk losing data. When you use Task Manager to close a currently running application, you receive a prompt to save the current data if desired. You cannot save data when you are ending an application that is not responding. The applications themselves, however, might have an auto-save feature that is able to salvage some data.

## Using the Processes Tab

Each application can run several processes simultaneously. The Windows NT operating system runs several processes at a time. You can consider a process to be a subset of programming code used to run applications.

NT services are also processes. They use system resources such as memory and CPU time. You can monitor each process in the Processes tab of the Task Manager (see Figure 6.2). To free system resources for other applications and processes, you should end services not being used (as detailed in the section "Running Windows NT Services").

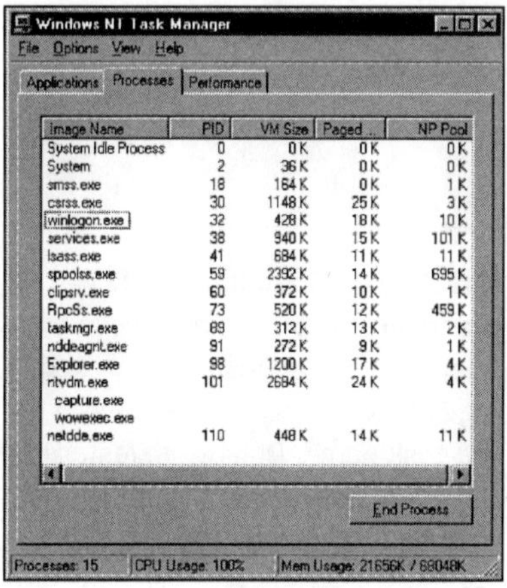

**FIGURE 6.2**
This system currently has only one application running, but several processes still exist and take up system resources.

The processes in the Task Manager can be sorted in ascending or descending order based on any visible column. You can change columns to reflect different information. Fourteen information columns are available. By changing the sort order or the columns listed, you can organize information by importance; thus less time is wasted on idle or low-impact processes. The Processes tab of the Task Manager has five default-selected columns (see Table 6.1).

**TABLE 6.1**

**DEFAULT-SELECTED COLUMNS IN THE PROCESSES TAB OF TASK MANAGER**

| *Column* | *Description* |
|---|---|
| Image Name | The process running. |
| PID | Process identifier. This is a unique number. |
| CPU Usage | Current percentage of CPU's usage allocated to this process. |
| CPU Time | Total time the process has used on the CPU. |
| Memory Usage | The amount of memory allocated to this process. |

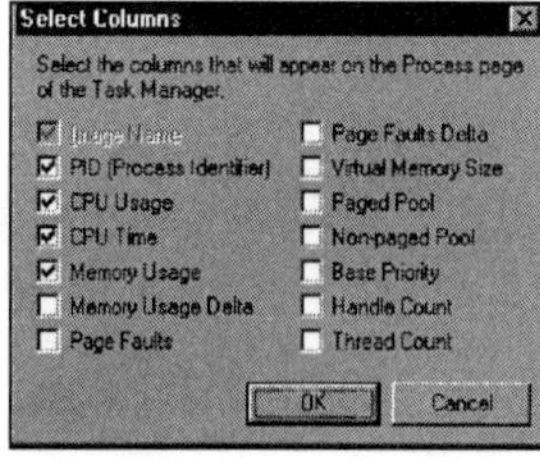

**FIGURE 6.3**
This is the list of all possible columns that can be displayed on the Processes tab of Task Manager.

To add other columns to the list, choose Select Columns from the View menu, and the dialog box shown in Figure. 6.3 appears. The Task Manager screen can display only five columns of information at a time. To view additional columns, use the Scroll button.

NOTE

**Resources for Explanation of Columns** Microsoft does not explain directly in the dialog box what each of the columns does. You can always obtain more information through the Help menu (F1), specifically the Glossary book. Another good source is Microsoft's TechNet CD, discussed in Chapter 7, "Troubleshooting."

To sort the information by a specific column, click on the column heading, and then click on the column a second time to change between ascending and descending order. Listing processes in ascending or descending order of memory usage can help you identify an application's usage—even if it's idle—or a process that's tying up the CPU sort by CPU usage.

Each application or service is a process running on the system and takes up some system resources. An application can be made up of several processes.

Several Windows NT services fall under the SERVICES.EXE process; others have their own processes. The SPOOLSS.EXE process, for example, identifies printing. With this in mind, it becomes important to monitor processes and possibly stop a process that might be using up too many resources.

NOTE

**Restarting a Task from Task Manager** If you end a process by mistake, you can restart it by choosing File, New Task (run) and typing the task name. Otherwise, restarting the computer returns the system to normal.

Not all processes can be ended by using the Task Manager. Using the Services icon in the Control Panel stops only some services. You should end applications by using the Applications tab of the Task Manager (stopping the EXPLORER.EXE process, for example). Then the desktop shuts down, but the operating system does not, which would be necessary if the desktop seems to have stopped responding to user input.

## STEP BY STEP

### 6.2 Ending a Process

1. Right-click the taskbar and choose Task Manager from the menu that appears.
2. Click the Processes tab of Task Manager.
3. Click on the process you want to end.
4. Click on End Process.

## Using the Performance Tab

The Performance tab displays a summary of memory, CPU usage, and general indicators (see Figure 6.4). You can get a more complete analysis of these items by using the Performance Monitor, as described in the section "Using the Performance Monitor."

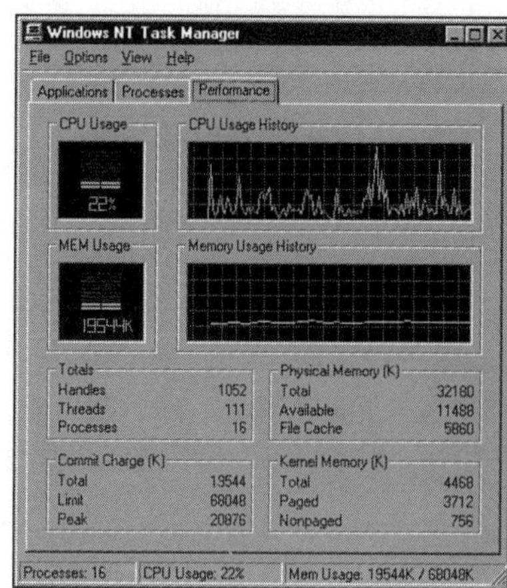


**FIGURE 6.4**
The Performance tab allows you to see a small part of the resources that are currently being used by NT.

The topmost level of the Performance tab displays the CPU usage and CPU history. These indicators show the total usage of the CPU by either the operating system or an application. The CPU Usage indicates the percentage of the CPU in use at the last update count. The CPU Usage History displays the last few updates. The default update time is approximately one second. You can change that value by using the View, Update Speed command. Selecting a low update count allows for a longer time in the history window.

If the computer has several CPUs, you can set up the history portion to show one chart for all CPUs or one chart per CPU. Choose View, CPU History to see the options. You can break down the CPU history to view additional details on the Windows NT kernel (the core of the operating system) by choosing View, Show Kernel Times.

The Totals area of the Performance tab shows the total number of file handles, threads, and processes running. If you compare these counters before and after a new application starts, the difference indicates resource usage for that particular application.

The remaining areas of the screen deal with memory consumption. Table 6.2 lists the counters in the Performance tab, broken down into their four categories.

**TABLE 6.2**

**MAIN CATEGORIES IN THE PERFORMANCE TAB**

| *Category* | *Description* |
|---|---|
| *Totals* | |
| Handles | The number of file handles open on the system. |
| Threads | The total number of application threads in use by all applications. |
| Processes | Total number of processes in use by all applications. |

*continues*

**TABLE 6.2** *continued*

**MAIN CATEGORIES IN THE PERFORMANCE TAB**

| *Category* | *Description* |
|---|---|
| ***Physical Memory*** | |
| Total | Total actual RAM in the computer. |
| Available | Physical RAM available that can be allocated to a process. |
| File Cache | The amount of physical RAM used by the file cache. |
| ***Commit Charge*** | |
| Total | The total amount of memory allocated. This includes physical and virtual memory. |
| Limit | Total amount of memory the system can use before the pagefile needs to be increased. This is using the current size of the pagefile, not necessarily the maximum or minimum. |
| Peak | The largest amount of memory that has been used this session. |
| ***Kernel Memory*** | |
| Total | The amount of memory being used by the operating system itself. |
| Paged | The amount of memory being accessed by other programs. |
| Nonpaged | The amount of memory reserved exclusively for the operating system; cannot be accessed by other programs. |

The Performance Monitor tool shows all these counters in much more detail. The Task Manager is used to obtain a quick overview of the system. Information cannot be logged or printed from the Task Manager.

## Using the Performance Monitor

Whereas Task Manager allows you to get an overview of the applications and processes running on your Workstation (and a small view of the resources used), the Performance Monitor takes you to a completely different level of detail. The entire system's operations as well as the application's performance can be monitored, charted, logged, or displayed in a report. The Performance Monitor also enables you to remotely monitor other Windows NT 4.0 systems, assuming that you have administrative rights for the remote system.

You would use the Task Manager to begin an investigation of a slow system or to terminate a faulty application. You would use Performance Monitor to analyze for and correct systemic weaknesses in your Workstation's configuration.

Information is presented under the following three components:

- *Objects.* Items are categorized as objects.
- *Counters.* Each object has counters that can be monitored.
- *Instances.* There may be multiple instances of each counter.

An object is broken down into several counters, and counters are broken down into instances. There are three types of counters:

- Instantaneous
- Averaging
- Difference

Windows NT 4.0 now includes a "total" instance for most counters, as well as "individual" instances for more detail. The instances shown may vary depending on the applications or features running. The number of objects available depends on the Windows NT features that are installed. For example, a special set of TCP/IP counters shows up only if the SNMP service is loaded along with Service Pack 1 or later, and disk performance counters show up only if `DISKPERF -y` is run. (The `DISKPERF` utility must be run from a command line, and after it is run, you must restart your Workstation in order for the counters to begin reporting statistics on your disk drives.)

As an example, the object called PhysicalDisk is broken down into counters such as Avg. Disk Bytes/Read, Disk Writes Per Second, and %Disk Time. These counters can show data regarding all physical disks combined or regarding each physical disk separately (each *instance*). See Figure 6.5. This approach of breaking down the system into objects, counters, and instances is carried throughout all aspects of the Performance Monitor.

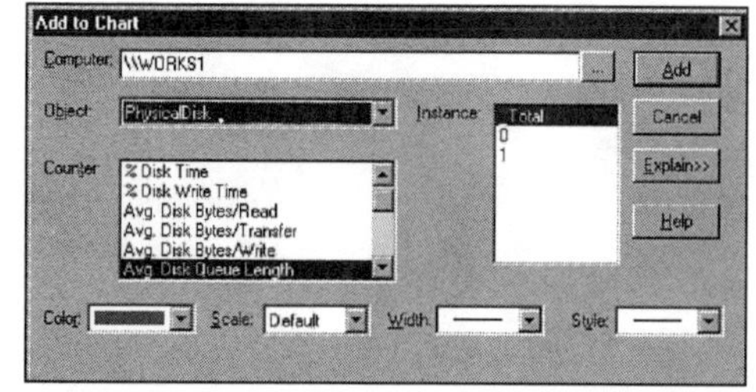


**FIGURE 6.5**
A sample of an object, its counters, and the instances of a specific computer.

Objects recorded in the Performance Monitor may vary depending on the current configuration of NT. Table 6.3 shows common objects that are always available.

TABLE 6.3

**COMMON OBJECTS ALWAYS AVAILABLE IN THE PERFORMANCE MONITOR**

| *Object* | *Description* |
|---|---|
| Cache | An area of physical memory that holds recently used data. |
| LogicalDisk | Disk partitions and other logical views of disk space. |
| Memory | Random access memory used to store code and data. |
| Objects | Certain system software objects. |
| Paging File | File used to support virtual memory allocated by the system. |
| PhysicalDisk | Hardware disk unit. |
| Process | Software object that represents a running program. |
| Processor | Hardware unit that executes program instructions. |
| Redirector | File system that diverts file requests to network servers. |
| System | Counters that apply to all system hardware and software. |
| Thread | The part of a process that uses the processor. |

## Using Charts

The Performance Monitor can show the system's performance in an easy-to-read chart format. The default view is the Chart view.

Chart view is the easiest view to use initially. Data can be viewed in a chart format as live data or from a prerecorded log file. Live data must be monitored constantly and evaluated on the spot. A prerecorded log file could have been gathering data for several hours or more and can be monitored at a more convenient time. This section focuses on the use of current or live data; log files are covered in the upcoming section "Using Logs."

To decide which data is going to be presented on the chart, use the Data From command on the Options menu. Two choices are presented: Current Activity (which allows you to view live data) and Log File (which allows you to open a previously recorded log file). Using the ellipse button (...), you can obtain the log filename by browsing the hard drive.

Using either source of data, you must add objects, counters, and instances to the chart. For the logged data source, only objects captured in the log can be displayed. The current data source, however, can use any and all objects, counters, and instances available.

## STEP BY STEP

### 6.3 Adding an Instance of a Counter Within a Specific Object

1. Start Performance Monitor by choosing Start, Programs, Administrative Tools (Common), Performance Monitor.
2. From the View menu, choose Chart.
3. Click the Add Counter button on the toolbar or select the Add To Chart command from the Edit menu.
4. Select the object you want from the Object drop-down list.
5. Select the counter. You can view an explanation of any counter by clicking the Explain button on the right side of the dialog box. The expanded Explain area (Counter Definition) makes it easier to decide which counter to use. Reading the definitions of several counters should clarify the definition and purpose of any counter definition that seems obscure at first.
6. If an instance is relevant, select it. Or, use Total to include all instances.

To remove an item from the chart, select a counter and press the Delete key.

All selected counters display on the same screen using a 0–100 scale. All counters that refer to percentages are perfect under this 0–100 scale. A value of 50 shows 50 percent usage of the resource. Counters that measure exact figures (such as Memory, Available Bytes) are scaled down or up to fit on the screen between 0 and 100. In such cases, the challenge is to figure out what the value on the chart really means: When the value on the chart shows 50, is that 50 bytes or 50,000 bytes?

NOTE

**Read Counter Definitions to Understand What They Are** A counter definition may be longer than the three lines allocated to it in this dialog box. Always scroll all the way to the end of the explanation. Also, read the definitions of several similar counters to get a more detailed understanding. The definitions do not repeat themselves. If a term is explained in the first counter, it is not explained in following counters for the same object.

You can get more information on key words by searching through Help or the TechNet CD.

Each charted value uses a scale shown at the bottom of the screen just before the counter name. A scale of 1.000 indicates that a counter was not scaled up or down. A scale ratio of 0.100 shows the 50 has been multiplied by 0.1 (divided by 10) to produce the displayed value of 5. A ratio of 10 shows that the value was multiplied by 10 to produce the displayed value of 500. Multiply or divide the value on the chart by the scale to get a true value.

Changing the scale ratio can be a little tricky. Only change the ratio if the chart line is flat at 0 or 100. You can change the default value by double-clicking on the counter name at the bottom of the chart. The current value for the ratio is not shown; only the word `Default` appears. Thus, it is not always obvious what the current ratio is. You can use the drop-down list to select an appropriate scale for this counter only. You might have to test several scale ratios to get a relevant chart.

Another way to improve the readability of the chart is to change the maximum value of the chart's scale. The initial values are always 0 to 100. If you want to change those values, select the Options, Chart command and change the Vertical Maximum setting. If all entries on your chart fall in the range of 110–120, they will appear as a flat line at 100 when the maximum is 100. In that case, change the maximum to 150. Likewise, if your chart shows a flat line around 20, set the maximum at 50, and the fluctuations become more apparent. Figure 6.6 shows all chart options.

Chart options affect all counters currently shown. Items such as Vertical Grid and Horizontal Grid can be adjusted to make reading easier. Do not disable the Vertical Labels or Legend option if you need accurate counts.

You can obtain further statistics on any chart line by clicking on the counter name at the bottom of the screen. Just above the list of counters being displayed are the last, average, minimum, and maximum values for the current item. To highlight a chart item on the screen, click on the item name and press Ctrl+H. The emphasized counter is shown in a thick white line.

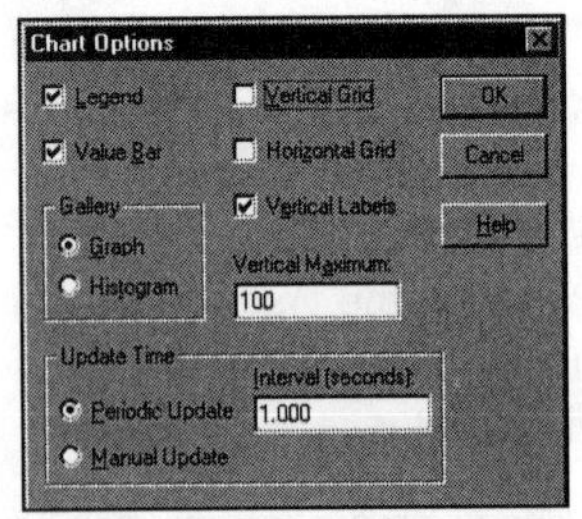


**FIGURE 6.6**
You can view a list of all chart options by choosing the Options, Chart command.

You cannot print charts from Performance Monitor, but you can export them to a tab separated value (.TSV) or comma separated value (.CSV) file. These files contain the data, not the chart lines. (The Export Chart command is found in the File menu.) You can open such files from a spreadsheet or database for analysis and further charting. To print a quick chart, use the PrintScreen button on the keyboard, open a paint program such as MS Paint, and paste. This places a copy of the image in MS Paint that you can then save or print.

## Using Logs

In most cases, just watching current data flowing across the screen is not enough for a thorough analysis. Log files are designed to watch the system for you and record activity in a file that you can review later (see Figure 6.7). You must always start a new log file from the Log view.

> **WARNING**
>
> **You Can't Control Maximum Log Size** You cannot control the maximum size of a Performance Monitor log file, so it might overrun the partition it is on if left unchecked. To prevent this, you may want to create a separate partition just for storing log files. To prevent a log file from crashing the system, always make sure it is stored on a partition other than the system or boot partition.

You can also use log files to compare the system at different times. All object information that can be monitored live can also be logged to a file.

Creating a log and analyzing data from a log are two distinct processes. Creating a log involves selecting the objects to be monitored, specifying the file in which you want to store the logged information, and setting an interval time at which to collect data. You do not select counters or instances for each object. All counters and instances are recorded in the log file. You select individual counters and instances you want to view when you're analyzing the log file.

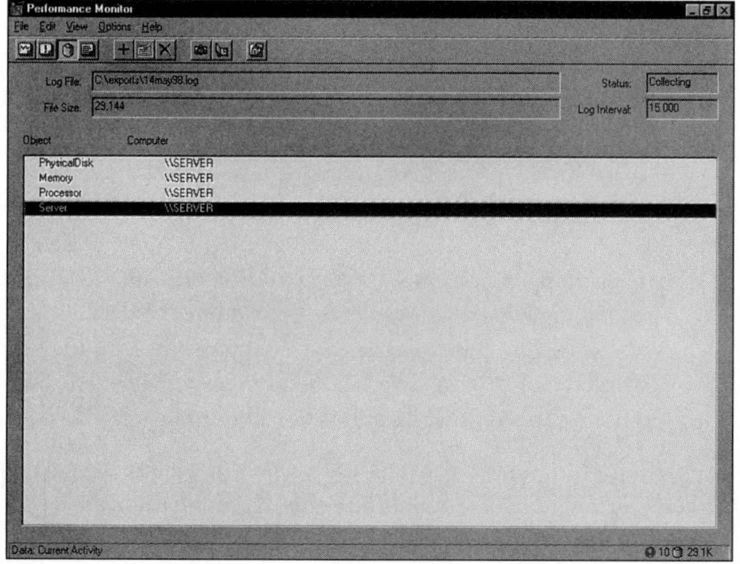


**FIGURE 6.7**
The Log view allows you to capture data to a file for analysis at a later time.

## STEP BY STEP

### 6.4 Start a Log File to Monitor Disk Activity

1. Start Performance Monitor by choosing Start, Programs, Administrative Tools (Common), Performance Monitor.
2. Choose Log from the View menu.
3. Choose the Add to Log command from the Edit menu or use the Add Counter button.
4. To analyze disk activity, add the LogicalDisk and PhysicalDisk counters.
5. From the Options menu, choose the Log command. The Log Options dialog box appears (see Figure 6.8).
6. Enter a filename and location in which to save the logged information.
7. The update interval should be set properly. The default is to take a reading every 15 seconds.
8. Click on the Start Log button to begin.
9. Minimize the Performance Monitor window. You should be able to use the computer normally as long as you're careful not to close the Performance Monitor.
10. While the log is being created, you can insert bookmarks to identify the current activity. To add a bookmark, use the Bookmark command in the Options menu and type a short comment. This comment will appear later in the Time Window feature.

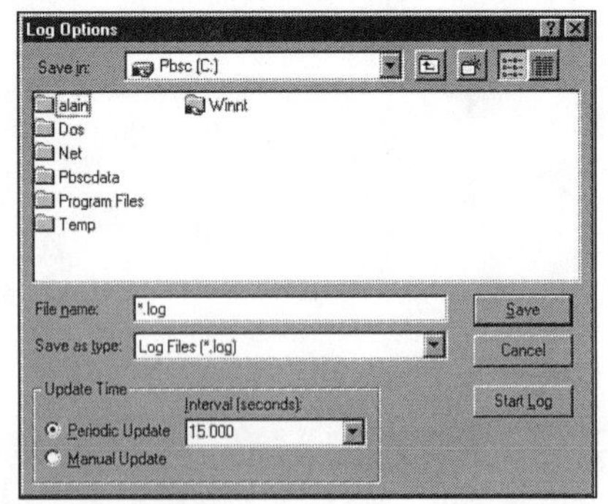


**FIGURE 6.8**
You can view a list of all log options by choosing the Options, Log command.

If a log file is stopped, it cannot be restarted. If a new log file is created using the same name, it overwrites the old one. To stop a log file, use the same Log command in the Options menu. Stop the log only when all data has been collected. You can view the log file after a log has been stopped or while the log is still running.

Performance Monitor also enables you to view or analyze the data captured in a log file. You can display the logged file through the Chart and Report views.

## STEP BY STEP

### 6.5 Viewing a Log File in Chart View

1. Start Performance Monitor by choosing Start, Programs, Administrative Tools (Common), Performance Monitor.
2. Choose Chart from the View menu.
3. In the Options menu, choose Data From.
4. Change from Current Activity to Log File with the name of the log file to be viewed. If necessary, click the ellipsis button (...) to obtain the log filename by browsing the hard drive.
5. Add the counters by using the Add Counter button or the Add to Chart command in the Edit menu.

NOTE **Time Interval and Amount of Detail Are a Trade-Off** The smaller the update time interval, the larger the file will become. It will, however, offer a lot of detail. A larger interval will show a trend, but it may not reflect a specific problem. If a log is to run overnight, do not use a 15-second interval. Try a 15-minute (900-second) or 30-minute (1,800-second) interval instead.

To remove items from the chart, select a counter and press the Delete key.

The process of viewing data is similar to using the Chart view in Current Data mode. Notice that only objects selected to be logged appear in the list. All counters and instances of those objects are available.

Even if the log file records information over several hours or days, the width of the chart screen is not any wider and cannot be scrolled. However, Performance Monitor provides a tool for focusing the view on a particular period of time. To enable that tool, choose the Time Windows command from the Edit menu. The Time Window is a graphical tool that you can drag to indicate the start and end times for a section within the log file that you want to view. You can use a Time Window to view the data one hour at a time by continuously moving the Time Window graph. If bookmarks were recorded during the logging process, you can use them to mark the start or end of the Time Window.

NOTE **Run Another Performance Monitor to Analyze a Log File in Process** To view data from a logged file that has not been stopped, you must open a new copy of Performance Monitor and then follow the same procedure described earlier. This enables you to view the original log file, but it does not affect the capture except to show a slight increase in CPU and memory activity while the second copy of Performance Monitor runs.

All other chart options mentioned earlier in this chapter, such as scales and gridlines, apply to viewing logged data in the Chart view.

## Using Reports

The Report view displays data in a numeric format (see Figure 6.9). With current data, an average of the last three updates is displayed. Data from a log file shows the average value for the Time Windows selected.

To view a report, choose the View, Reports command. To choose the source of the data, choose the Options, Data From command. You must add each counter and instance to the report by using the Add Counter button or the Edit, Add to Report command. To remove an item from the report, select the value and press the Delete key.

The Report view cannot show trends or large fluctuations. You cannot print a report from Performance Monitor, but you can export it as a .CSV or .TSV file and open it in a spreadsheet or word processor.

Report options contain only one item, often the update interval. The interval determines how often the report is updated with new information. This update interval can be set only on a report displaying current data, not one displaying logged data.

## Using Alerts

The Alert view is very different from the three previous views (see Figure 6.10). No data is reported or displayed until a system exceeds a threshold set by the administrator.

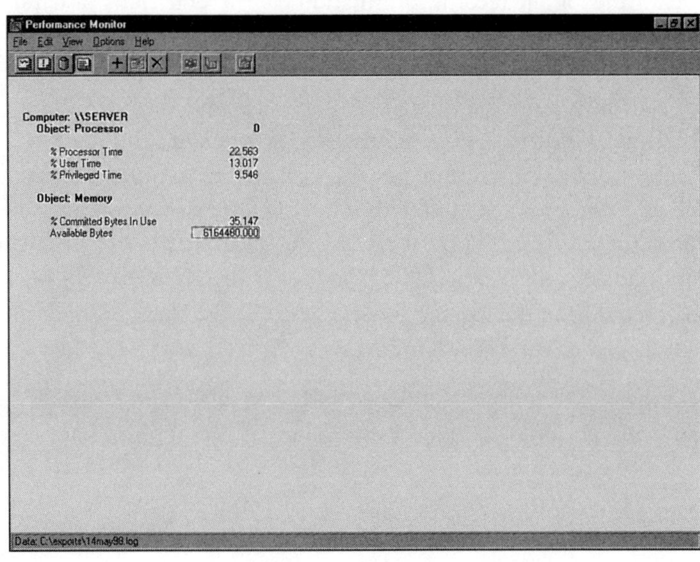


**FIGURE 6.9**
The Report view allows you to see a report of system statistics as of the last reporting interval.

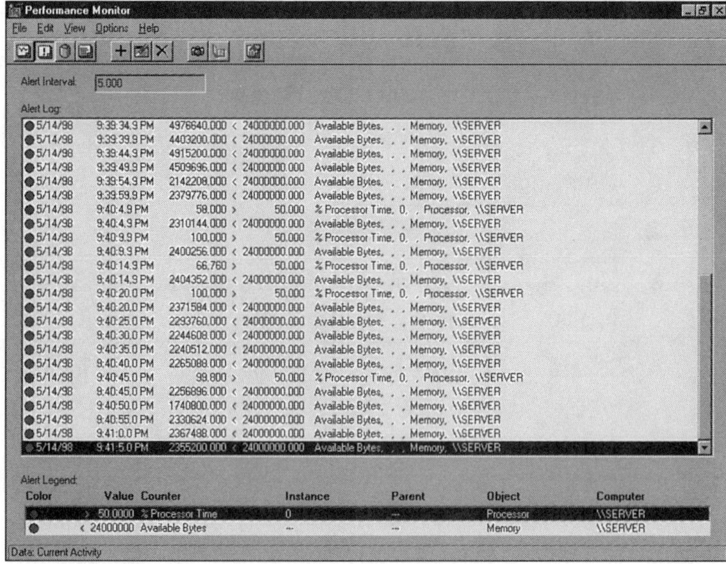


**FIGURE 6.10**

The Alert view allows you to set thresholds for counters and then have Performance Monitor issue alerts when those thresholds are crossed.

You can establish up to 1,000 alerts on a given system. The same objects, counters, and instances are available, and one additional item is added as a condition. When an alert is generated, the system sends an administrative alert message or runs a program. You can set the alerts to react only the first time a threshold is exceeded or each and every time it is exceeded.

You might set one of the following conditions, for example.

> Only alert the administrators if the computer's hard drive space falls below 10-percent free.
>
> or
>
> Alert the administrators when the server's total logons are above 150.

In both these cases, you could set up the system to send a message to the administrator informing him of the situation.

The alert's destination must be configured separately using the Alerts command in the Options menu. All alerts are sent to the same destination. You can enter the destination either as a username or a computer name.

NOTE

**Start the Alerter and Messenger Services** For the alerts to be generated from a computer, both the Alerter service and the Messenger service must be started. For a computer to receive an alert message, the Messenger service must be running. You can start all these services from the Services application in the Control Panel or remotely from a Windows NT Server's Server Manager.

## STEP BY STEP

### 6.6 Setting Up the Alert Destination

1. Change to the Alert view by choosing the View, Alert command.
2. Open the Options menu and choose Alerts.
3. Enter the username or computer name to notify in case of an alert.
4. Select Log Event in Application Log to enable the log feature for all alerts.

For alerts to function, the Performance Monitor must be running at all times. However, because this may slow down a workstation, it should be used for short-term monitoring and troubleshooting only.

## Using Remote Monitoring

You can use the Performance Monitor to monitor other computers on the network. Each time a counter is added to a chart, log, report, or alert, the current computer is used. Any computer that can be remotely administered can be remotely monitored as well.

To select a remote computer to monitor, type the computer name in the Add Counter dialog box or click the ellipsis button (...) and select the specific computer. The full computer name is usually preceded by two backslashes (\\). To add a counter for a computer named salesvr1, for example, you would type **\\salesvr1**. The person doing the remote monitoring must be a member of the Administrators group of the target computer. In a Windows NT domain environment, a user in the group Domain Admins is always a member of each workstation's local Administrators group and can remotely administer and monitor the system.

## Saving Settings

Charts, reports, logs, and alerts are modified each time a counter is added or removed and each time options are set. You can save all these settings in a separate Settings file. This will allow charts, reports, logs, or alerts to be generated one time; they could, however, be used several times on current data or several log files, which provides you with consistency when trying to compare systems or situations.

The Performance Monitor can be shut down and restarted quickly when a Settings file is opened. You can even move the Settings file from one computer to another. The Settings page stores the objects, counters, and instances for the computer on which they were set up. Copying the file to another computer does not monitor the new computer; it just makes remote monitoring a little easier to set up.

# Using the Server Tool

The Server tool can be found in the Control Panel. This tool is used to monitor network activity related to shared folders or printers, to set up the Replication utility, and to set up alert destinations for a Windows NT Workstation.

The monitoring section of interest here is the number of remote users and the types of access they are getting on the system. A few remote users accessing a few shares will not have any ill effect on the system. You should be more concerned with understanding this tool so that you can pinpoint any excessive number of connections. All remote network accesses are performed as background processes; they may not be readily noticeable to the user.

The Server tool (shown in Figure 6.11) offers three methods of viewing remote users and their activity on the system. The three methods offer pretty much the same information with a slightly different focus. These methods are listed and described in Table 6.4.

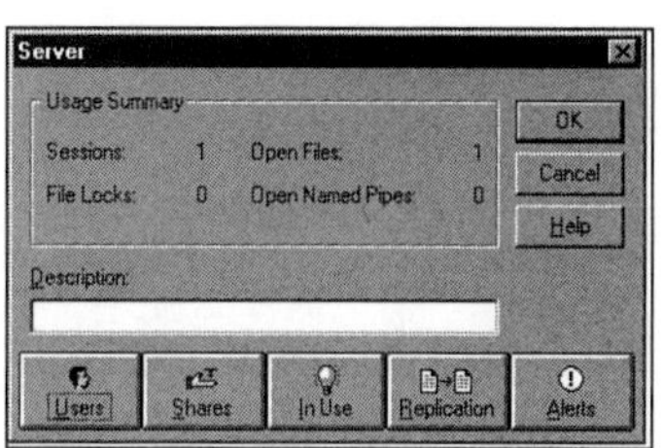


**FIGURE 6.11**
The Server dialog box displays one session connected and one file opened.

TABLE 6.4

**REMOTE USER MONITORING TOOLS IN THE SERVER MANAGER**

| *Button* | *Description* |
|---|---|
| Users | This lists all users remotely connected to the system. Selecting a specific user lists all the shares to which the user is connected. Additionally, information such as how long the user has been connected and whether he is using the Guest account is available. By clicking the Users button, you can disconnect any user from the share. |
| Shares | The Shares button shows the same information as the Users button, except that it lists the shares initially. Selecting a specific share lists all the users connected to it. You can also use the Shares button to disconnect someone from a given share. |
| In Use | The In Use button goes one step further than the two previous items: It lists the resource being connected to and the type of access. A list of files that may be opened with Read Only permission is listed as such. You can close off resources from here, disconnecting the current users. |

The Server dialog box exists on Windows NT Workstations and Servers alike. A Windows NT domain controller also includes a Server Manager icon that enables you to perform the same tasks you can from the Server dialog box on all Windows NT systems in the domain.

Disconnecting a user or a share initially has little effect on remote users because Windows NT and Windows 95 use a persistent connection technique to reconnect lost connections as soon as the resource is needed. You might disconnect a user to close connections from systems after hours or to prepare for a backup for which all files must be closed. To completely remove someone permanently from a share, you must change the share permissions beforehand and then disconnect the user. When the persistent connection is attempted, the permissions are re-evaluated and access is denied.

## Using the WinMSD Utility

WinMSD stands for Windows Microsoft Diagnostic. This utility is part of Windows NT Workstation 4.0 and can be run from the Start menu's Run command. The utility is not used to make changes to a system. Its primary function is to provide a summary report on the current status of the system. This utility displays nine categories of information, from the services' status to the size of the current pagefile, as well as device drivers used on the system (see Figure 6.12).

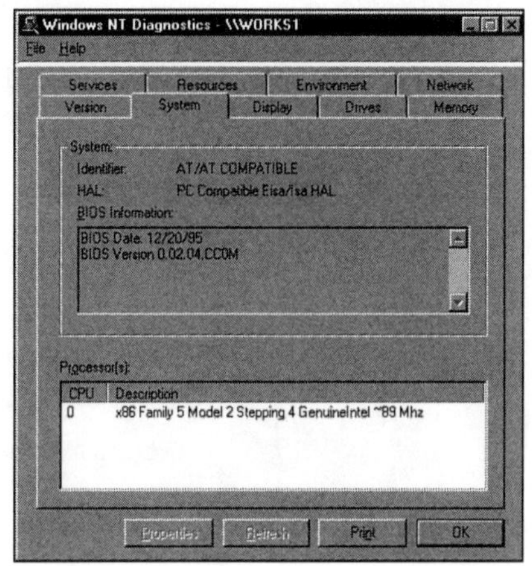


**FIGURE 6.12**
The System tab of Windows NT's Diagnostic utility.

You can produce a printed report showing all details from all the tabs. This information is only accurate at the time WinMSD is started. It does not monitor or update its information automatically while running. However, you can click a Refresh button at the bottom of the dialog box to update information.

Table 6.5 lists the tabs from the WinMSD utility and describes the purpose of each one. WinMSD will prove very useful when comparing two systems. Network administrators can use also WinMSD to view information on remote systems; however, slightly less information is available with remote viewing of WinMSD.

**TABLE 6.5**

**WINMSD SUMMARY INFORMATION**

| *WinMSD Tab* | *Information Displayed* |
|---|---|
| Version | The Licensing screen showing the registered owner and the CD key. The product version and build are also displayed here. This same information is available by right-clicking the My Computer icon and selecting Properties. |
| System | The type of computer and CPU chip used. The system BIOS date and version can also be found here. |
| Display | The display adapter BIOS information and the current adapter settings, including memory on the card and display drivers being used. |
| Drives | All local drives on the system. The properties of each drive reveal the usage in bytes and clusters. |
| Memory | The pagefile size and usage are displayed in kilobytes. (The WinMSD Memory tab is similar to the Task Manager's Memory tab.) |
| Services | All Windows NT services and their current status. The properties of each service show the executable running the service and services that depend on the current service. |
| Resources | The four critical resources for each device: IRQ, I/O port, DMA, and memory. Information can also be listed per device. |
| Environment | The environment variables for the system as well as for the local user. These variables can be set through the System application in the Control Panel. |
| Network | General information about the logon status, transport protocols in use on the system, device settings of the network card, and overall statistics of network use. |

Most of the information available in WinMSD can be configured through the Control Panel and the Registry Editor. You can run this diagnostic tool from DOS as MSD.COM. From the Start menu, choose Run, and then type **MSD**. This DOS version offers slightly different information, such as a list of TSRs and a list of all device drivers.

---

### USING RESOURCE KIT UTILITIES

You can use Resource Kit utilities to augment the built-in tools such as Task Manager and Performance Monitor. These tools are not available on the Windows NT Workstation CD. You can purchase the Windows NT Workstation 4.0 Resource Kit separately either in a book format (which includes a CD) or as part of the Microsoft TechNet CD.

These utilities go beyond everyday analysis. They usually provide a behind-the-scenes look at system activities. Programmers will find this information useful. You can find the three mentioned here in the \i386\perftool\meastool directory of the utility CD for Intel-based computers.

The Resource Kit text explains the purpose and use in far more detail than is expected for the exam (and thus provided in this book). Here's a sample of the utilities available from the Windows NT Resource Kit.

| **Utility** | **Description** |
|---|---|
| Process Explode (Pview) | A full breakdown of each process as to all threads used with each priority, memory address space allocated, and security rights. |
| Process Viewer (Pviewer) | Contains less information per process than Pview, but enables remote monitoring of other Windows NT Workstations (assuming the proper access rights have been granted). |
| Process Monitor (Pmon) | A command line utility showing processes information much like the Processes tab of Task Manager. |

---

These are not all the tools available on the market today. With the exception of the Resource Kit tools, however, this is a complete list of built-in tools always available within Windows NT Workstation 4.0. Several third-party vendors offer utilities you can purchase. In some cases, those might even perform better than the built-in items described in this section. Microsoft does not always support these third-party tools and may not be willing to assist someone whose system may have been damaged by these utilities.

## IDENTIFYING AND RESOLVING PERFORMANCE PROBLEMS

Identify and resolve a given performance problem.

The Task Manager and Performance Monitor are used to determine whether performance is suffering in any way. A major cause of performance degradation is bottlenecks—that is, one or more resources operating at or near 100 percent of capacity.

The four major components that can be monitored and enhanced fall under the following groupings:

- Memory
- Processor
- Disks
- Network

The following sections offer details related to those items.

### Identifying Bottlenecks

By properly identifying one or more bottlenecks, you can help focus attention on the appropriate resources and help determine a course of action. The tricky part is that one resource may seem to be the culprit and thus the bottleneck when, in fact, another resource is really at fault.

Consider, for example, a CPU running at or near 100 percent consistently. At first it would seem that a new and faster CPU is in order. When you look deeper, you may find that the CPU is so busy swapping memory pages from RAM to the pagefile and back that it has no time for anything else (see Figure 6.13). Adding more RAM reduces page swapping and would be the solution in this scenario, not a faster CPU.

Figure 6.13 shows how only one reading of CPU usage may lead you to believe the CPU is inadequate, when in fact the CPU is very busy each time an application is started due to lack of memory. There are three lines on this chart: The two lines that spike are CPU usage and PageFaults, and the third line shows the size of the pagefile. Each time an application is started, in this example, the system cannot find room in physical memory to load it into physical memory and must page information to the pagefile. The CPU is mostly used to perform the paging, not to run the application. Memory bottlenecks are described in full detail later in this chapter.

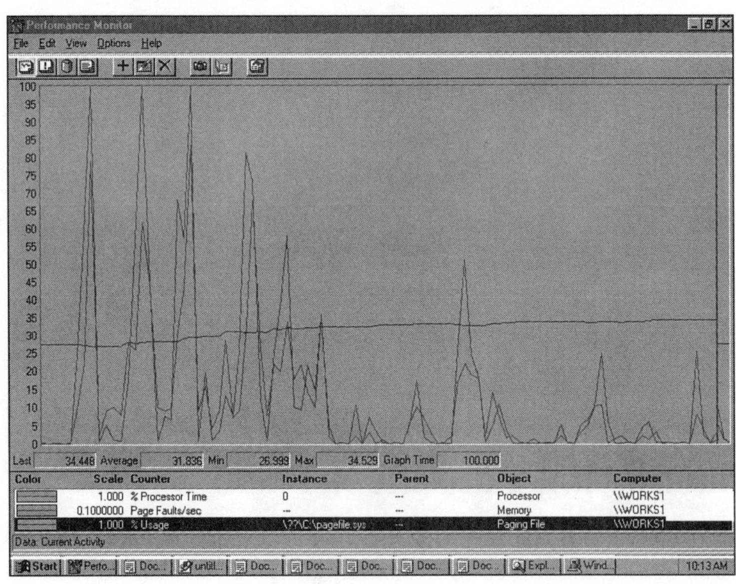


**FIGURE 6.13**
The Performance Monitor showing heavy CPU usage due to memory paging.

To determine what constitutes a bottleneck, you must understand each resource and know its baseline or optimum operating level. Is it a bottleneck if the hard drive is reading 150 bytes per second, or if the CPU is at 75 percent? No exact figure can be given for each resource, but Microsoft has a few guidelines that you can follow. The best way for an individual to analyze a given situation is to maintain a baseline log of appropriate resource counters under normal or basic operating use of the system. You can compare the baseline log in situations of extreme stress or to determine whether a change to the system has any impact on performance.

NOTE

**Look at All Bottlenecked Resources Before Forming a Conclusion** You should always look at all bottlenecked resources, not just the first one you find, because resources are often dependent on one another.

## Creating a Baseline Log

You can create a baseline log by using the Log feature from Performance Monitor as described in the section "Using Logs." A log file does not have to be very large to show pertinent information; the main thing is that the log be created while the system is being used in its normal or basic state. If you can create a log when a system is freshly installed, you can use that log to determine the impact of configuration changes or additional components added at a later date.

You can create a baseline log for each object individually or as a complete set. Creating a complete set is more flexible, but the file will be larger (see Figure 6.14).

**STEP BY STEP**

### 6.7 Creating a Baseline Log

1. Restore the system to its initial state. Make sure that no applications or additional items are running. The system should be at rest.
2. Start a log file on all objects to be tested.
3. Let the log run for at least five minutes, and then stop it.
4. Keep this file on hand. You will use it to compare with current activities or new logs at a later date.

The following four sections show which counters to follow and log to pinpoint possible bottlenecks and system deficiencies.

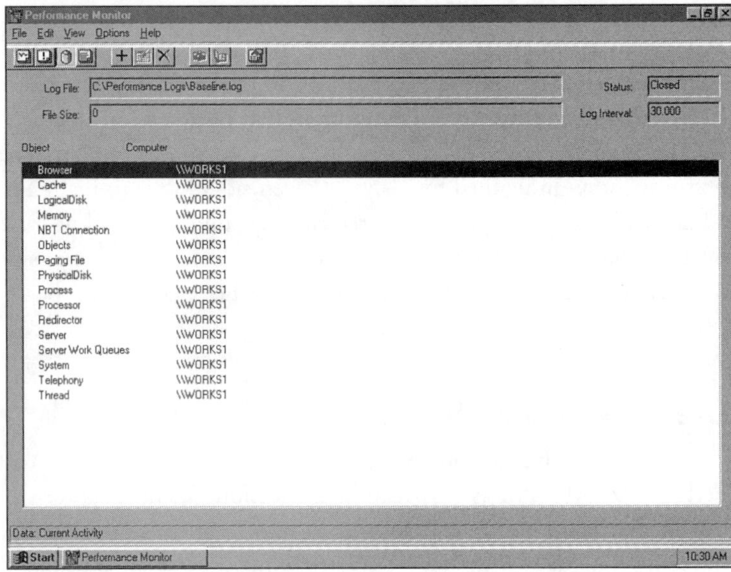


**FIGURE 6.14**
All objects ready to be logged as BASELINE.LOG.

## Pinpointing Memory Bottlenecks

The amount of physical memory (RAM) in a computer is probably the most significant factor when it comes to system performance. More is definitely better in respect to memory. The amount of RAM will depend on the typical use of the workstation (running applications or sharing folders) and the expectations of the user.

Windows NT Workstation 4.0 uses a virtual memory mechanism to store and retrieve information for the processor. Along with real memory capacity (that is, the amount of physical RAM), Windows NT also makes use of a pagefile system. As soon as Windows NT Workstation runs out of RAM to store information, it makes up virtual memory by using space on the hard drive. All information presented to the processor always comes from physical memory. When information is required and is not found in the physical memory, Windows NT has to read the pagefile on the hard drive and transfer the information to physical memory before it can be used.

The action of moving information between the pagefile and physical memory is called *paging*. Windows NT always returns to physical memory and tries to retrieve any information deposited there earlier. If the information cannot be found, the system returns a *page fault*. A soft page fault is returned if the information is found in a different area of physical RAM. A hard page fault is returned if Windows NT has to look in the pagefile on the hard drive to find the information requested. Hard page faults take more time and require greater use of the CPU and system resources than do soft page faults; therefore, hard page faults should be monitored.

Every application that runs under Windows NT 4.0 is allocated a linear 4GB address space in which it can store data (of that 4GB, 2GB are reserved for operating system functions, so really only 2GB are left over for the application). Most systems today will not have 4 or more gigabytes of RAM, so a pagefile is used to handle the supplement. By allocating each application its own set of memory space, the system prevents a poorly written application from trying to use another application's memory. This problem might still be encountered with 16-bit applications, however, because they share the same 4GB space.

The Virtual Memory Manager is responsible for keeping track of each application's address space, the real list of physical memory, and the pagefile memory used to store the information. When physical memory reaches its limit, Windows NT moves some information from the physical space that it occupies to the pagefile. When the information is needed again, it is paged back into physical space.

The memory object is definitely of interest, but you cannot forget that Windows NT Workstation also uses logical disks to create a pagefile (used as virtual memory), as well as processor time to perform the paging. So the following Performance Monitor objects are of interest:

- Memory
- Paging File
- Process
- Logical Disk
- Processor

These items are listed in order of importance and, if monitored as a group, will indicate whether a bottleneck has occurred due to lack of physical memory. As you should remember, selecting an object for a log will include all the counters and instances as well. A Memory baseline log file could be created with these four objects and used in a comparison.

You can use all the memory counters to determine a bottleneck. For the Memory object, three specific counters should be monitored: Page Faults, Pages Input/Sec, and Page Reads/Sec. See Table 6.7 for a list of all objects, counters, and instances and their purposes.

> EXAM TIP
>
> **Always Answer Questions Based on Microsoft's Documentation**
> All Microsoft documentation shows the pagefile calculation to be RAM + 12MB for the minimum and RAM + 12MB + 50MB for the maximum on Windows NT Workstation (despite what testing will show you). In the exam, always quote Microsoft's numbers. There would never be a choice of answers showing 11 and 12; only 12 will be listed.

You should monitor the size of the pagefile to see whether it is always increasing. Excessive paging may just be a short-term phenomenon and could be due to a one-time increase in demand. When the pagefile is constantly pushing the upper limits, there may be cause for concern. Each time the system is started, a pagefile of the minimum parameter is generated. As more pagefile is required, the pagefile is allowed to grow until it reaches the maximum parameter setting. The default size of the pagefile is based on the amount of physical RAM present when Windows NT Workstation was installed. The installation procedure creates a pagefile with a minimum size of RAM + 11MB and a maximum size of RAM + 11MB + 50MB.

For the Paging File object, the %Usage Counter is used to monitor the percentage of the pagefile being used. For the Process object, the Page File Bytes (using the instance total) shows the current amount of the pagefile being used in bytes. These two counters in effect show the same information. However, some people might find it easier to view the actual numbers than to have to calculate the size of the percentage.

The Process object identifies the activity performed by an individual process or total processes on the system. The same counters are found in other areas and may reflect the same results. The Process object helps determine which process (application or operating system) may be causing a problem on the system. The counters to keep under observation are Page File Bytes (as mentioned earlier), Pool Nonpaged Bytes, and Page Faults/Sec.

The Pool Nonpaged Bytes counter represents the amount of physical memory an application is using that cannot be moved to the pagefile. If this number keeps increasing while an application runs, it can indicate that a poorly written application is using up more physical memory and forcing the system to use more pagefile space. In this scenario, the pagefile counters and CPU usage may be showing a memory bottleneck when, in fact, the culprit may be only one application. Microsoft refers to these types of applications as *leaky memory applications.*

The LogicalDisk object will not have the same significance as the previous objects do, but it may help point out inefficiencies from the disks rather than from memory. The pagefile is stored on one or more physical disks, and it is important to identify where the pagefiles are being stored. Each counter shows an instance for total disk as well as each logical disk.

## STEP BY STEP

### 6.8 Identifying the Location of the Pagefile

1. From the Start menu, choose Settings, Control Panel.
2. Double-click on the System icon.
3. Select the Performance tab.
4. Click on the Virtual Memory Change button.

A physical disk may contain several logical disks if the disk has been partitioned. The logical disk counters identify the access to a particular storage area, not the entire disk. For more information on how to improve virtual memory disk usage, see the section "Optimizing System Performance," later in this chapter.

The Average Disk Queue Length counter shows the number of entries waiting to be read or written to the disk. Pagefile items fall into the queue like any other request. If the queue is too slow and cannot process paging requests fast enough, the system seems to be slow due to paging when, in fact, it is the disk that cannot handle the request. In this case, you want to make sure the bottleneck is being caused by insufficient memory and that the disk's performance is adequate. You are looking for a small disk queue or at least one no different than that of normal circumstances. This number should be less than 2 in an optimum scenario.

Finally, the CPU object may show the amount of work being done to satisfy the paging request on the system. If the CPU is very busy before paging starts, it will have an effect on overall performance. As with the LogicalDisk object, you are not interested in the performance of the CPU as such. Instead, you need to make sure the processor is not slowing down the paging process and is not the real cause of the bottleneck.

The counters to follow for the processor are the %Processor Time, %Privilege Time, and DPC Rate. The percent of processor time shows just how busy the processor is performing all tasks. The percent of privilege time excludes all tasks being performed for applications. Most device drivers and paging are performed in privileged processor time; all display and printing tasks are in user processor time. DPC stands for Deferred Procedure Call and refers to tasks waiting to be processed that are placed in a queue. Another indicator of the processor queue is the Processor Queue Length counter for the System object. This counter should not remain above 2 for any significant length of time.

Another indicator of a memory bottleneck is found in the Task Manager's main screen. It indicates the Total Commit Bytes and Total Physical Memory. If the Total Commit is larger than Total Memory, a memory bottleneck may exist.

Table 6.6 enumerates all the counters that may be used to determine a memory bottleneck. The first few items (Memory and Paging File) offer a significant insight into a bottleneck scenario. The last few (Process, LogicalDisk, and Processor) are meant to rule out other possible factors that may be slowing down the system.

## Pinpointing Processor Bottlenecks

The processor (CPU) on any computer is generally busy processing information. However, like a child with a low attention span, even when there is nothing to do, the processor needs to be doing something. To ensure that there is always something going on with the processor, when there is nothing else to do, Windows NT runs an idle process. This idle process generally measures the effective processor inactivity (or availability). Most counters take this idle process into account and display information on all processes except the idle process.

A bottleneck may occur if too many items are waiting in a queue to be processed at one time or if an item takes a long time to make it through the queue. With so much emphasis on NT's capability to run multithreaded applications in a multitasking environment, the CPU must be performing at its peak capacity in order to not slow down the overall system down.

**TABLE 6.6**

**COUNTERS SUMMARY**

| *Object* | *Counter* | *Purpose* |
|---|---|---|
| Memory | Page Faults | Page faults include both soft and hard page faults. Microsoft suggests that a count of more than five page faults per second on an ongoing basis is problematic. |
| | Pages Input/Sec | Represents the number of pages the system had to retrieve from the hard drive to satisfy page faults. Thus it represents the number of hard page faults per second. This number is compared to the total Page Faults/Sec counter to determine the percentage of hard page faults. |
| | Page Reads/sec | This shows the number of times per second that pages are transferred into memory from the pagefile. This indicator can also be used to show a disk bottleneck that might be created by a memory shortage. |
| Paging File | %Usage | This shows the percentage of the pagefile in use. |
| Process | Page File Bytes | Make sure to use the total of all instances to get a full reading. The actual size (in bytes) of the pagefile in use. |
| | Pool Nonpaged Bytes | The amount of physical memory being used that cannot be moved to the pagefile. |
| | Page Faults/Sec | This same counter appears under Memory. In the Process object, it can be further broken down to show the number of faults being generated per process. |
| LogicalDisk | Avg. Disk Queue Length | The number of items waiting in a queue to be read from or written to the disk. This number should be less than 2 under optimum usage. |
| Processor | %Processor Time | The total amount of time the CPU is performing tasks other than the idle process. |
| | %Privilege Time | The time used by the operating system only to perform system tasks such as paging. |
| | DPC Rate | A deferred procedure call queue that indicates how many procedures are placed in the queue waiting for the processor. |

The processor may run fine for most applications and situations, and a log file should be generated during these times. When a problem does manifest itself, there will be a baseline value to use in comparison. For more information on creating a baseline log, see the section "Creating a Baseline Log," earlier in this chapter.

As described in the preceding section, memory bottlenecks may sometimes have the effect of excessive use of the CPU and lead someone to believe the CPU is too slow. Always try to eliminate the suspicion of memory bottlenecks before you spend too much time evaluating the CPU.

Each computer has at least one processor, and much more powerful systems may have two or more. Windows NT Workstation supports up to two processors in its original configuration. Even when a system has multiple processors, a bottleneck can still occur. However, a system with two processors that share the work equally is less likely to be the source of a bottleneck under multithreaded applications.

Microsoft's recommendation is that a single processor system should not be above 75-percent usage for any significant length of time. A multiple processor system should not exceed 50-percent usage for any significant length of time. Another main component of CPU usage is the queue of items waiting to be processed. Microsoft's guideline on the queue is that it be less than two entries most of the time. See Figure 6.15 for a sample chart showing a system with a CPU usage well below the 75 percent in some cases, but then at 100 percent. The chart also shows a large number of entries in the queue (20 to 35 on average).

Applications that are single-threaded—this includes all DOS and 16-bit applications as well as some 32-bit applications—behave the same way on a single- or multiple-processor system. When several processes are executed at the same time from different applications, it can cause the CPU utilization to increase. A quick temporary solution to this is to close down applications not being used at the present time and reopen them as needed. 32-bit applications that are multithreaded, however, will run several processes at once and may tie up a processor even if it is the only application running.

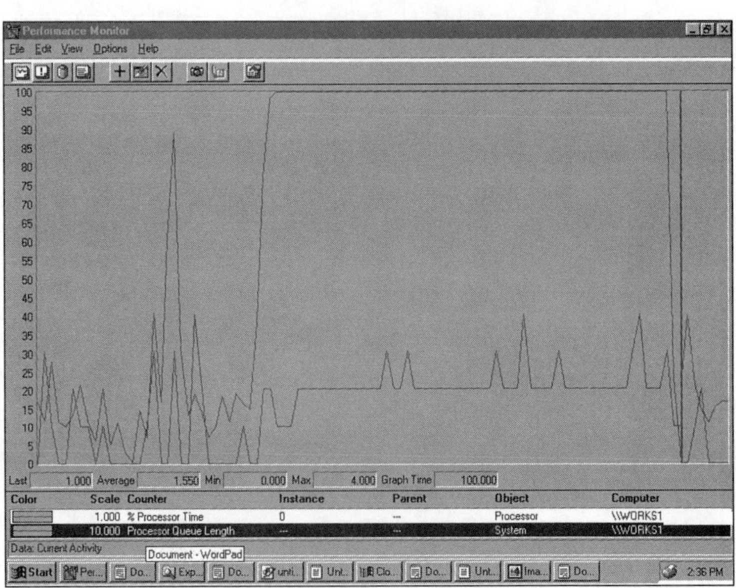


**FIGURE 6.15**
CPU usage of 100 percent and a queue of 30 clearly indicate a processor bottleneck. If this situation persists, a faster processor is in order.

In a multiprocessor system, there can be two types of processing: *synchronous* and *asynchronous.* Windows NT Workstation uses a synchronous environment in which all processors can be used simultaneously. Several single-threaded applications can share both processors, and multithreaded applications can run several threads on one or spread threads across processors. An asynchronous processing system would run only the OS on one processor and all applications on the second. Even when the OS is not using its processor, it is not released for applications to use.

A few counters can be used to determine a processor bottleneck. Most counters use a process of sampling rather than a full count. This sampling may be misleading during a short monitoring period that uses averages. The average CPU usage in a 15-second interval may be very low or very high just because the sampling has taken few readings. A longer sampling period usually deals with this problem. Counters that deal with counts or exact numbers will not be as affected by the sampling errors.

The objects and counters listed in Table 6.7 are monitored to determine a possible processor bottleneck.

**TABLE 6.7**

**OBJECTS AND COUNTERS USED TO MONITOR PROCESSOR BOTTLENECKS**

| *Object* | *Counter* | *Description* |
|---|---|---|
| Processor | %Processor Time | The total amount of time the processor is busy, excluding the idle process. This includes user processing and privileged processing time. This counter should be below 75 percent over time. |
| System | Processor Queue Length | The number of threads waiting to be processed by all processors on the system. This does not include threads being processed. |

The solution to resolving CPU bottlenecks depends on the number of processors as well as their speed and the type of applications (single-threaded or multithreaded) being run on the system. A multithreaded application benefits more from multiple processors just because many tasks are performed simultaneously. The processor is overrun in the short term as the application is executing. With multiple processors, threads can be spread across the processors. For single-threaded applications, multiple processors would only help if several applications are running simultaneously; otherwise, a faster CPU helps process information faster, thus reducing the amount of entries in the queue.

After you determine that a bottleneck is caused by the processor, you need to complete a further investigation on processes, threads, and priorities. This additional investigation will help clarify whether a single application or thread is generating the bottleneck. If a specific application is causing the problem, you might have the option of upgrading the application instead of the CPU. Some 16-bit applications monopolize the CPU, whereas their 32-bit counterparts work quite well.

Although the exam does not get into this level of detail, more information on processor bottlenecks—as well as details on threads and priorities—can be found in the Windows NT Workstation 4.0 Resource Kit (see Chapter 13, "Detecting Processor Bottlenecks").

## Pinpointing Disk Bottlenecks

Disk performance affects many components on Windows NT Workstation 4.0. The pagefile system runs off of a disk, the processor is busy searching or seeking for information on a disk, and file sharing uses the disk along with disk caching to provide information to clients.

These same components may be creating disk bottlenecks due to their limitations. When at all possible, eliminate memory or CPU bottlenecks before trying to monitor disk performance. All components, such as memory, CPU, caches, and disk, must work together to accomplish proper overall system throughput. Calculating the speed of a disk may not be very relevant, and a faster disk may not always enable the overall system to perform any faster if other bottlenecks are present.

A log of disk activity can help compare results on several disks under similar circumstances. The Save Settings feature should be used to start tests on different machines or several hard drives. For more information on how to use saved settings, see the section "Saving Settings," earlier in this chapter.

The most important objects and counters are not available by default in Windows NT Workstation 4.0. You must activate them with the DISKPERF utility by typing `diskperf -y` at a command prompt and then restarting the computer. You must be part of a local machine's Administrators group in order to activate the disk counters on it. Table 6.8 describes the `diskperf` command and its switches.

**TABLE 6.8**

**DISKPERF AND ITS SWITCHES**

| *Command* | *Description* |
|---|---|
| `diskperf` | Shows whether the DiskPerf objects are active |
| `diskperf -y` | Activates the disk counters |
| `diskperf -ye` | Activates the disk counters on mirror, stripe sets, and other noncontiguous partition sets |
| `diskperf -n` | Deactivates disk counters |

Another method of activating the DISKPERF utility is to start it using the Device Manager in the Control Panel. After DISKPERF has run, two main objects are available: PhysicalDisk and LogicalDisk. Without DISKPERF, these counters show up in the Performance Monitor but have readings of 0. The PhysicalDisk object refers to the actual hard drive placed in the system. This hard drive would be identified as disk 0 for the first one, disk 1 for the second, and so on. The logical disks can be subsets of the physical disks. Disk or drive C: may be the full size of disk 0, or it may take up only a portion of a primary or extended partition. All counters shown under both PhysicalDisk and LogicalDisk are identical. Several counters appear only under one or the other.

Two types of possible bottlenecks exist when it comes to disks. The amount of disk space available and the access time of the disk. The counters used and solutions required differ greatly.

When a system's disks become too full, other symptoms might show up, such as the pagefile having no room to grow or an application being unable to save or update files. Hard drives are also used for temporary files created by applications and the operating system. Checking the hard drive via the disk's properties shows only the current free disk space. Using Performance Monitor, you can set up an alert to create an entry in the Event Viewer.

NOTE

**Recommended Hard Drive Size**
A basic rule of thumb for hard drive space is that a hard drive should not be at more than 85 percent of capacity after all necessary applications are installed and configured.

To monitor the amounts of available hard drive space, use the Free Megabytes counter for the LogicalDisk object. You can use this counter to show free space for each drive separately or for the total of all instances.

The second area of concern is the efficiency at which requests are being handled by the hard drive and the overall usage of the hard drive. Microsoft makes the following three recommendations regarding usage of a typical hard drive:

- Disk activity should not be above 85 percent usage as shown by the %Disk Time counter in the PhysicalDisk or LogicalDisk object.
- The number of requests waiting in the queue should not exceed two, as shown in the Current Disk Queue Length counter of the PhysicalDisk or LogicalDisk object.
- Paging should not exceed five page faults per second as shown in Page Reads/Sec, Page Writes/Sec, and Page Faults counters of the Memory object. (Refer to the section on memory bottlenecks for a more thorough discussion.)

WARNING

**Performance Monitor Uses Computer Resources**
Performance Monitor is an application like any other, and as such, it uses system resources. Be aware of the activity you might be creating on a disk as you are monitoring or logging information. Monitoring disk writes of drive C: using a log that is also being stored on drive C: will increase disk activity and alter the results.

Monitoring drives for a comparison is fairly simple as long as the same conditions apply to both disks. Certain factors might affect how one disk performs compared to another, though. Two of the factors are noted here:

- The type of disk partition could be FAT or NTFS.
- The controller card and type of drive might be IDE, SCSI, or SCSI-2.

Keep all this in mind when two test results are compared. Changing just one of these factors might have the desired result of improving overall system performance, but it might also hide other areas of inefficiency.

Table 6.9 shows a list of common counters used to determine a bottleneck situation.

**TABLE 6.9**

**DISK BOTTLENECK COUNTERS**

| *Object* | *Counter* |
|---|---|
| LogicalDisk/PhysicalDisk | %Disk Time |
| LogicalDisk/PhysicalDisk | Avg. Disk Queue Length |
| LogicalDisk/PhysicalDisk | Current Disk Queue Length (known in previous versions as Disk Queue Length) |
| LogicalDisk/PhysicalDisk | Avg. Disk Sec/Transfer |
| LogicalDisk/PhysicalDisk | Disk Bytes/sec |
| LogicalDisk/PhysicalDisk | Avg. Disk Bytes/Transfer |
| LogicalDisk/PhysicalDisk | Disk Transfers/sec |
| LogicalDisk/PhysicalDisk | %Free Space |
| LogicalDisk/PhysicalDisk | Free Megabytes |

You can use several other counters to interpret disk activity. This may not necessarily show a bottleneck, but it can help you understand how the system resources are being used by certain applications. For a complete list of all counters and explanations, go to the counters list in the Performance Monitor and use the Explain button.

One thing you have to be careful of is that although several counters may seem to complement one another, when you add the figures up, the result is more than 100 percent. The over-calculation is due to the Performance Monitor's methods of gathering information. Performance Monitor does not time the actual disk activity; it times the I/O requests, which includes processing and queuing time. When many items are in the queue, the numbers tend to be larger. When the queue is properly serviced, this exaggeration is not as significant.

For example, the %Disk Read Time added to the %Disk Write Time should equal the %Disk Time. But it does not always work out that way. For more information on this discrepancy, see the article titled

"Troubleshooting the Disk Activity Counters" in Chapter 14, "Detecting Disk Bottlenecks," of the Windows NT Workstation 4.0 Resource Kit.

## Pinpointing Network Bottlenecks

Monitoring network activity can only be done on a system connected to the network. Network terminology is used within this chapter, and there is an expectation of networking basics on the part of the reader. Non-networked systems do not require monitoring of network activities, and this section may be skipped.

Network activity on certain systems causes bottlenecks even if all other aspects of the system are performing in an optimum state. The network components pertain to information being shared from the system of information accessed from a remote system. Typically, a Windows NT Workstation's primary function is not that of a file or print server, and the number of requests made of the system does not have any negative effect.

Understanding network traffic, though, can help you eliminate overall network congestion. Network activity uses system resources and could lead to conclusions of inadequate memory, disk, or processor usage when the source of the bottleneck is in fact the network card.

In the earlier sections on pinpointing bottlenecks, it was mentioned several times to focus the attention on very few items simultaneously to get a better understanding of the activity of a particular resource. In the case of network efficiency, the focus is not on the system itself but mostly on the number of remote hosts connected to the system and the amount of information being requested.

You have three main tools to monitor network activity on the system: the Performance Monitor, the Server tool in the Control Panel, and Network Monitor. The Network Monitor can watch the packets going out of and coming into the Workstation, but it is not a very good tool for general analysis because the information is very finely detailed. The Performance Monitor offers counters that can monitor the amount of bytes transmitted as well as errors encountered over several protocols, the Server service, and the Redirector service (client). These counters, however, cannot show the remote computers or users involved in this network activity. The Server icon in the Control Panel can display all the shares on a system as well as which user at which computer is connected to that share. Figure 6.16 shows a sample system's Server icon with a user connected to a shared folder.

The Server icon can be used only to monitor local resources. For more information on all the sharing components of the Server icon, see the section entitled "Using the Server Tool," earlier in this chapter.

The Performance Monitor counters are not all initially present for network monitoring. Some counters that deal specifically with TCP/IP network traffic are not installed and must be added separately. Installing the SNMP (Simple Network Management Protocol) service adds the TCP/IP counters. The network or system administrators are the only users able to add network services.

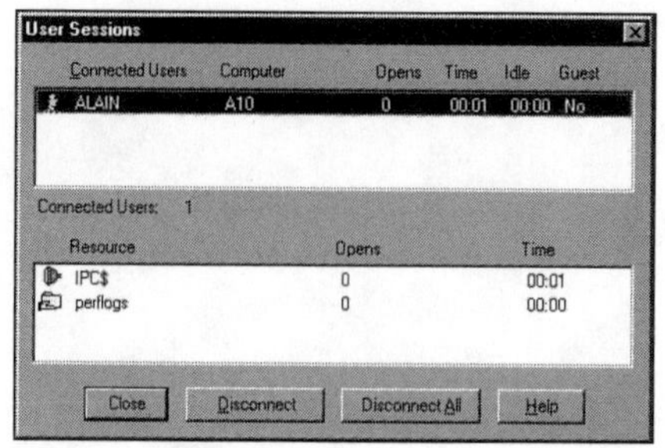


**FIGURE 6.16**
Any Windows NT Workstation can behave as a small server in a domain or workgroup environment to share folders or printers with remote users.

## STEP BY STEP

### 6.9 Adding SNMP Services

1. From the Control Panel, double-click the Network icon.
2. Select the Services tab.
3. Select the Add button and select SNMP services.
4. Accept all dialog boxes and identify the Windows NT Workstation 4.0 source files if needed.
5. Restart the computer.

After the SNMP service is loaded, a TCP/IP system has five additional counters available:

- TCP
- UDP
- IP
- ARP
- ICMP

The full detail of these counters is beyond the scope of this book. The focus here is on counters that show information transmission.

Regardless of the network protocol being used, there are counters to monitor simple read or write request from the network card. These counters are always available under the Redirector and Server objects. Individual protocol counters are under the protocol names themselves. Table 6.10 displays a list of relevant counters from various objects used to monitor network activity on the system.

**TABLE 6.10**

**NETWORK COUNTERS**

| *Object* | *Counter* | *Description* |
|---|---|---|
| Server | Bytes Total/Sec | The total activity of the system as a peer server on the network. |
| Server | Files Opened Total | The total number of files opened by remote systems. This calculates the amount of I/O requests. |
| Server | Errors Access Permission | This counter shows the number of client requests that have failed. A remote user may be attempting to access resources that have been restricted. The system must process these requests, thus taking up system resources for nothing. It may also identify possible hackers trying to gain access to the system. |
| Redirector | Bytes Total/Sec | The Redirector is the client portion of the network initiated by the local system. |
| NetBEUI | Bytes Total/Sec | The Bytes handles the NetBEUI protocol only. This can be useful in determining which protocols are not used much and could be removed. |
| TCP | Segments/Sec | The amount of information being handled by the TCP/IP protocol. |
| NWLink | Bytes Total/Sec | There are three objects for NWLink: IPX, SPX, and NetBIOS. All three have the same counter of bytes transferred per second using the NWLink protocol. |

## Monitoring with the Event Viewer

A part of the operating system is constantly monitoring for possible errors committed by either applications or other parts of the operating system. It should be noted that only 32-bit applications can log errors in the Application log. Event monitors are always active and keep track of these errors in the following three logs, which you can view with the Event Viewer:

- System log
- Security log
- Application log

By default, the System and Application logs can be viewed by any user logged into the Workstation. However, only an Administrator can view the Security log.

The System log reports errors originating from the operating system. This does not mean the Windows NT Workstation has crashed or is misbehaving. This log keeps track of services or devices that may not have started because of equipment failure or configuration errors.

The Security log is unavailable unless the Auditing feature is active in the System Policy of the User Manager. By default, the Windows NT Auditing feature is not active on a new system installation. This log does not provide relevant information as to system performance; it monitors users' and system activities with respect to user rights and permissions. When Auditing is active, it may require the use of several system resources. Auditing should be disabled to reflect a true reading of processor, disk, and memory performance.

The Application log keeps track of 32-bit application errors. A misbehaving application could be tying up system resources consistently with little benefit to the overall system performance. You may need to upgrade these applications or just restart them to correct the situation. Applications under Windows NT have very little interaction directly with devices or device drivers. They can, however, report whether an error has occurred as the device was being requested or used.

## Reading Event Viewer Logs

In both the System and Application logs, Windows NT categorizes the entries as Information, Warning, or Error. Table 6.11 shows the icons available in the System and Application logs. In the Security log, there are Success or Failure entries to perform the activity sections.

**TABLE 6.11**

**EVENT VIEWER ICONS**

| *Icon* | *Description* |
|---|---|
| | Mostly information about successful activities. |
| | The warnings are indirectly the result of critical errors. The system can still function properly, but some features may not be available. These warnings should be used to support or understand critical errors. |
| | The error message indicates a service or device that failed to start up properly. The system may still function, but none of the dependent features are available. You should address these errors quickly. |

Understanding the error codes and types can make it easier to solve the problem. Figure 6.17 shows a typical list of log entries.

Each log entry can be expanded by double-clicking anywhere on the line. The Event Detail page shown in Figure 6.18 then appears. This example shows that the network device driver for the Intel TokenExpress adapter failed to started because a device was not functioning properly. The network card or cable may be defective.

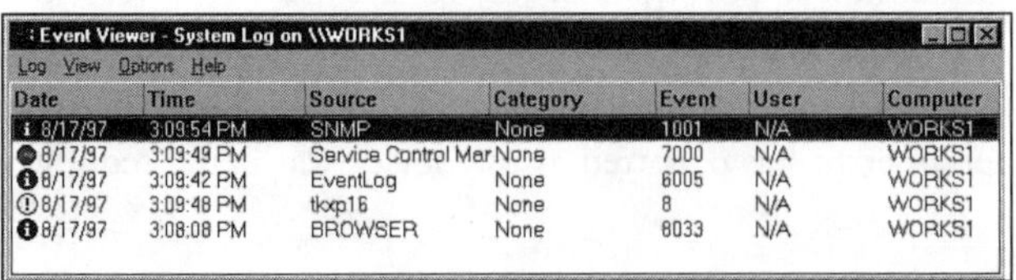


**FIGURE 6.17**
The Service Control Manager reported an error of the event type 7000 by the system.

Additional information appears in the log to help clarify the source and type of message. The Event ID is located in the upper-right corner of the detail screen and can be used during searches in the Help system, when using Microsoft's TechNet CD, or when communicating with a support center.

Table 6.12 offers a complete list of additional information in the Event Detail page.

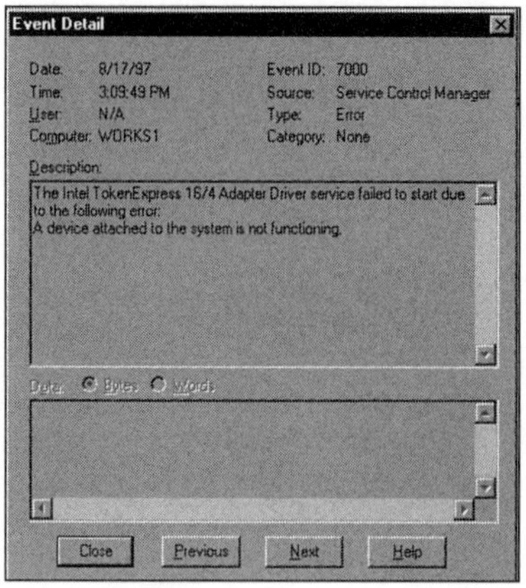

**TABLE 6.12**

**EVENT DETAILS**

| *Item* | *Description* |
|---|---|
| Date | The date the event was logged. |
| Time | The time the event was logged. |
| User | The username responsible for the event being logged. If `N/A` appears, in means the error was not a result of user interaction. Each Windows NT Workstation has a built-in hidden system account responsible for starting up the system and performing system-wide functions. |
| Computer | The name of the computer from which the event was initiated. Most of the time, it is the local computer name. If an alert was set up in Performance Monitor and a computer destination for alert was set up, the name of the computer would be a remote system, not the local one. |
| Event ID | The code that has been assigned to the error. It is used in searches or support calls. A recurring error always displays the same event ID and can be easily recognized. |
| Source | The source indicates which part of Windows NT or which application found the event and reported it to the log. |
| Type | The type is the same as the icon shown in the list: Information, Warning, and Error. |
| Category | Several errors will not have a category. The Audit feature categorizes the events as logon, logoff, policy change, and so on. |

**FIGURE 6.18**
The Intel network card driver failed to initialize due to hardware problems.

NOTE

**About TechNet** The TechNet CD is a compilation of current information about all Microsoft's products. It is an invaluable tool. For more information on using Microsoft's TechNet CD system, see Chapter 7, "Troubleshooting."

## Filtering for Events

The size of a current log or an archive file can make it very difficult to find a specific problem. Using a filter can remove from the view all events that do not match the criteria. You can set criteria based on any of the detail options shown in Table 6.12.

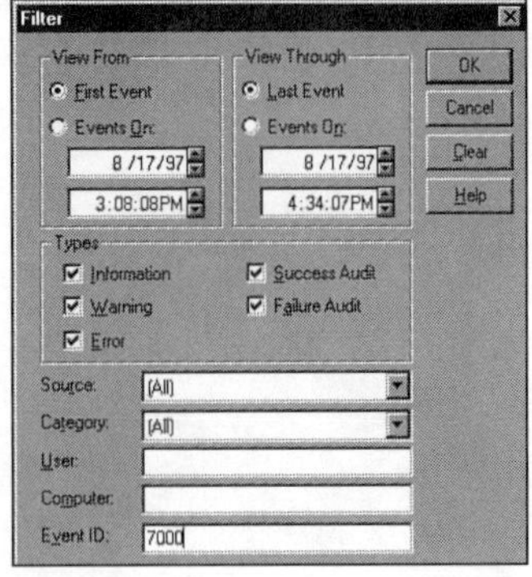


**FIGURE 6.19**
The filter is based on all events with an Event ID of 7000.

The filter performs only on the current information being displayed. The log may need to be refiltered if new information is added while it is being analyzed. The full list of events does not have to be displayed between filtered views; the system always bases the filter criteria on all events currently in the log. See Figure 6.19 for an example of filter criteria.

---

## STEP BY STEP

### 6.10 Filtering a Log or Archive

1. Select the log or open an archive file.
2. Choose Filter Events from the View menu.
3. Complete the dialog box. All selections are cumulative, and an event must meet all conditions for it to be listed.
4. Open Events and evaluate the situation.
5. Return the view to all events by choosing the View, All Events command.

---

## Managing Log Settings

All three logs have settings that you can manage separately. The size of the logs as well as the actions to be taken when a log is full are set for each log via the Log Settings command on the Log menu. The default values for a log are to use up to 512KB of memory to store events and remove entries that have been in the log for seven days. Three options can be set to clean up logs:

- Overwrite Events as Needed
- Overwrite Events Older Than *X* Days
- Do Not Overwrite Events (Clear Log Manually)

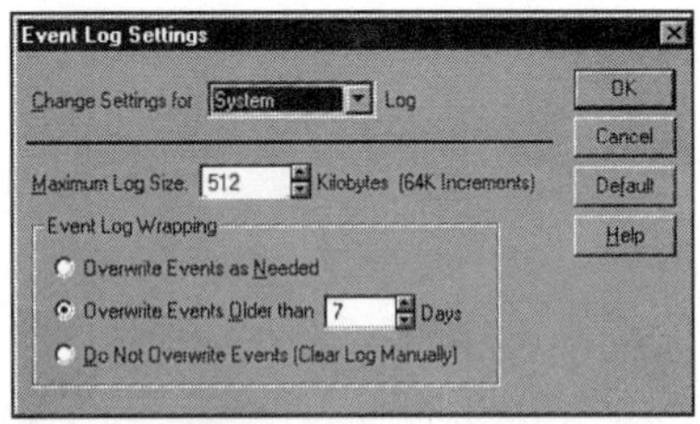


**FIGURE 6.20**
The settings for the System log use a 512KB buffer and keep entries for up to seven days.

The system warns with a message box that the log is full unless the Overwrite Events as Needed option is selected. If the log is full and is not cleared manually, new events cannot be logged (see Figure 6.20).

A larger log keeps track of more information but uses more system resources. Clearing and saving logs is a more efficient method for keeping track of events and possible trends.

## Archiving and Retrieving a Log

The default file format used for archiving a log is an .EVT file format, which can be viewed only from the Event Viewer. You can also save in a .TXT format for viewing in a word processor or a spreadsheet.

Archiving a log refers to saving it to file. You can do this while clearing or by using the Log, Save As command. The Event Viewer is a 32-bit utility. Its Save As routine uses all the standard 32-bit saving features, such as long filenames and Create New Folder. All three logs must be saved separately.

Saving the log file cannot be automated; it is an administrator's task to save the log files at least before they reach their maximum size. All logs can be saved in the same folder and used to determine whether a trend of errors or warnings is occurring.

To open an archived log file, choose the Log, Open command and select the appropriate .EVT file. An archive file contains only one of the three types of logs. When you open an archive file, the system prompts for the type of log being opened. The Categories column is not displayed properly if the log type is not valid. If that happens, just reopen the file using a different file type.

Current logging does not stop when an archive log is being viewed. To return to an active log of the current computer, choose the correct log type from the Log menu.

Although the steps for monitoring performance cannot be laid out exactly, the tools and methods described in these sections will help you identify problem areas. The resources available and the time constraints do not always make it possible to analyze a system and tune it to 100-percent efficiency. There will always be a tradeoff between system performance and providing the time and money to make it happen.

# OPTIMIZING SYSTEM PERFORMANCE

Optimize system performance in various areas.

Now that you understand the available tools and the areas of greatest concern, it is time to look at techniques for improving the overall performance of the Windows NT Workstation 4.0 operating system. Not all the techniques listed here are appropriate in all situations or for all users. Microsoft has shipped Windows NT Workstation 4.0 optimized for the majority of users working in a typical environment. The improvement in performance might be only a slim one or two percent, but it could require a lot of work and money to make it happen.

Messing around with system configuration can be hazardous. In all cases, you should back up all critical system files and settings before making any changes. The effect of the changes should also be monitored and compared with a baseline log that was created before the changes were implemented. (See the section "Creating a Baseline Log," earlier in this chapter.)

## Making a Safe Recovery

You can make a safe recovery if you took the proper steps before any major changes were made to the system. Recovery techniques take time and are often overlooked by impatient users. Unless the machine can be completely torn down and rebuilt, it is much faster to recover a damaged system than to start all over.

The Registry files form the core of the configuration of the Windows NT operating system. Windows NT 4.0 has several Registry files that contain specific information about the hardware, software, and user settings.

These files are stored in the %winroot%\system32\config folder. The %winroot% is a system variable that represents the folder where Windows NT is installed. It is usually named WINNT. The system variable %winroot% is used to refer to this directory in batch files or configuration screens. The Admin$ name is the share name of this WINNT folder on all Windows NT systems and can be accessed only by members of the Administrators group from remote systems.

Several methods enable users to recover from system configuration changes:

- Creating an emergency repair disk
- Using NT's Backup to restore the Registry
- Using the LastKnownGood configuration
- Using hardware profiles

## Creating and Maintaining an Emergency Repair Disk

The best way to make a copy of all necessary Registry files is to create and maintain an emergency repair disk (ERD). The disk includes all hardware and software configuration items, as well as security account database information. You can use this disk to restore a corrupted Registry. The backup copy of these files can be stored in two locations when an ERD is created. The disk has one copy, and the %winroot%\repair folder has a second identical copy. The copy on the hard drive is not very useful if the system has crashed.

Having created an emergency repair disk, you can use it with the three Setup disks required to install Windows NT Workstation to effect a repair. The ERD is not bootable and cannot be used without those three disks. For more information on the repair process, see Chapter 7.

There is no menu command or icon for creating the emergency repair disk. Instead, you run the RDISK utility from a command prompt or from the Start, Run command. This brings up a graphical tool you can use to create the disk or just update the repair folder (see Figure 6.21).

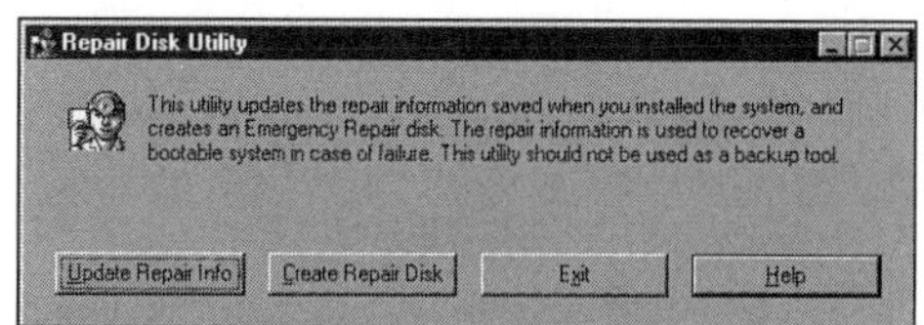


**FIGURE 6.21**
RDISK is used to create an emergency repair disk. All disks are unique to the system they were created on.

The RDISK utility offers two options: Update Repair Info and Create Repair Disk. When run by an administrator, Update Repair Info updates the repair folder and then prompts you to create a disk; when any other user runs this utility, an error message appears, telling that person the update failed. Create Repair Disk creates a disk without updating the repair folder. You should create and maintain an emergency repair disk. You should also have a backup copy of the disk for a system dealing with critical information.

## Creating Hardware Profiles

Creating a hardware profile is one of the safest and fastest methods for making and testing changes to a system without risking the loss of system integrity. Hardware profiles are also used to control when the network settings are loaded on laptops that may be connected to the network or set up to run as a standalone. This setting can be established quickly through the Properties button of the profile.

A hardware profile starts off as an identical copy of the current system's configuration. Part of the Registry is duplicated, and then all device and device-related configuration changes are made to the copy profile and tested. If a particular configuration fails, the system can just be rebooted into the original configuration without any ill effects. Only device and device-related items are stored in a profile. Although most Registry settings are always available to all profiles, the Registry Editor should not be used to modify profiles. Using the Devices and Services icons provides safer methods for changing a profile.

All systems have a hardware profile initially named Original Configuration. The system starts up using this configuration without prompting the user. A hardware profile copy is not modified by the system, only by current configuration changes that are made when the copy is in use.

If a copy exists, prior to logon but after the BOOT.INI displays the list of operating systems, Windows NT brings up a prompt as to which hardware profile is to be used for this session. The system has a timeout setting of 30 seconds, so if no choice is made in that time, it will load the default profile. Figure 6.22 shows the system's Hardware Profiles tab with two hardware profiles defined. You can modify the timeout period as well as the default choice in the system's properties dialog box.

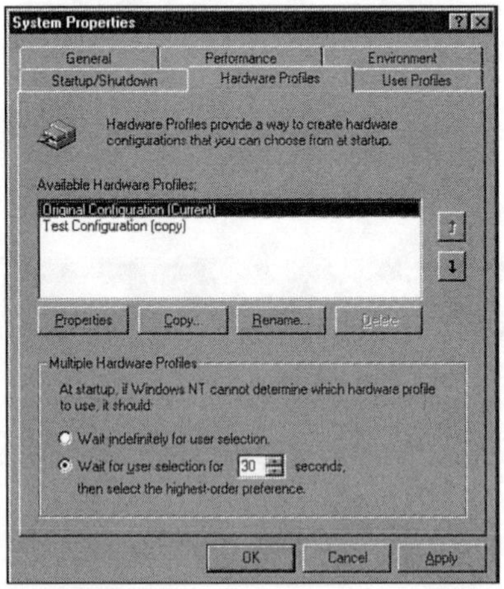

**FIGURE 6.22**

The default Original Configuration loads after 30 seconds if no choice is made at startup.

## STEP BY STEP

### 6.11 Creating a Hardware Profile for Testing System Changes

1. From the Control Panel, double-click the System icon.
2. Select the Hardware Profiles tab.

3. Click on the Copy button.
4. Enter a new name for the new profile.
5. Enter a Wait for Selection time or choose Wait Indefinitely. The default hardware profile is always the first listed. You can use the arrows on the side of the list to change the order.

The profile is now in place and can be selected when the system restarts. Always restart the system using the testing profile before you make any changes to the system. When you have completed all the testing, the copy profile can be deleted. A successful testing profile can be renamed, and the original configuration can then be deleted. Anytime there are two or more configurations, Windows NT prompts the user to choose a profile during startup.

Hardware profiles are easier to use than the ERD. However, the ERD may still be needed if changes are made to the system that corrupt the Registry. The hardware profiles are stored in the Registry.

## Using the LastKnownGood Configuration

A temporary copy of the hardware's original profile is made after every successful logon. This temporary copy is called the LastKnownGood configuration. It is replaced each time the user logs on.

Configuration changes are written to the Registry in the Current control set. Upon successful logon, a copy of this control set is copied to the LastKnownGood set, which can be retrieved if a system is restarted after failed configuration changes. During the startup procedure, Windows NT displays the message `Press the spacebar now to load Last Known Good Configuration`. This message appears for a short time only. If the LastKnownGood configuration is loaded, it replaces the last set that failed. All changes that were made to the system during the last session are lost.

NT's startup procedure can be misleading. Services and devices are started before, during, and after the Ctrl+Alt+Delete logon security box appears. After a user has logged on to the system, it updates the LastKnownGood even if devices or services fail after logon. Always wait for the system to load all devices and services before logging on.

If a device or service fails, Windows NT displays an error message. You can then turn off the power to the system and restarted with the LastKnownGood still intact.

## STEP BY STEP

### 6.12 Invoking the LastKnownGood Configuration

1. Do not log on to the system if an error appears or if the last configuration changes have caused problems.
2. Turn off the computer and wait 10 seconds before turning it on again.
3. Choose Windows NT from the Boot menu.
4. When you see the message `Press the spacebar now to load Last Known Good Configuration`, press the spacebar.
5. Press L to invoke the LastKnownGood configuration.
6. Log on to the system normally. All settings should be restored to their state prior to the last set of failed changes.

Because the LastKnownGood configuration is not always reliable, hardware profiles and emergency recovery disks are recommended as well.

## Configuring the Operating System

You can tune several aspects of Windows NT. Having faster hardware is always an asset, but is not always realistic in the short term. From the operating system's perspective, Windows NT is a set of services that run devices to provide resources to the user. Tuning these items can be done quickly without you having to upgrade or invest a large amount of money.

The following sections cover areas such as Windows NT services, Windows NT device drivers, and Registry components. These components can be modified on the system, and their benefits can be seen instantly. A warning always appears when you tamper with default system values. Be careful and always have backup mechanisms in place so you can recover from any unexpected results.

## Running Windows NT Services

Windows NT Workstation 4.0 is made up of a series of services that run in conjunction with one another to provide the operating system. A default set of services is loaded with a typical installation, and the user or applications can install additional services. Not all services are required to run Windows NT Workstation 4.0. The default set of services is chosen to satisfy most common users and systems. Disabling unused services frees up system resources such as memory and the CPU. You cannot disable all services through hardware profiles, but you can stop them manually.

WARNING

**Services Are Often Interdependent** Several services may depend on one another. Stopping a service may have very significant effects on the overall system's operations. Consult the WinMSD utility for service dependencies before you stop a service. In addition, use hardware profiles when possible to test the effects of stopping a service.

Table 6.13 lists some of the services you can disable using hardware profiles. The information displayed in this table is extracted from Microsoft's TechNet CD and shows memory usage of certain Windows NT services. Stopping these services reduces Windows NT Workstation's functionality but frees up memory.

**TABLE 6.13**

**SAMPLE MEMORY USAGE PER SERVICE**

| *Service Pool* | *Nonpaged Bytes* | *Private Bytes* | *Working Set Bytes* |
|---|---|---|---|
| AtSrv | 10,308 | 253,952 | 765,952 |
| ClipBook Server | 1,908 | 237,568 | 1,114,112 |
| Network DDE | 11,142 | 368,640 | 1,286,144 |
| Nmagent | 2,532 | 1,810,432 | 2,727,936 |
| Alerter (thread in SERVICES.EXE) | 52 | 4,096 | 24,576 |
| Messenger (thread in SERVICES.EXE) | 156 | 16,384 | 49,152 |
| Spooler | 11,452 | 618,496 | 1,105,920 |
| Telephony Services | 12,624 | 499,712 | 1,433,600 |

## Disabling Devices

Devices, like services, can be disabled on a per–hardware profile basis. Most devices set up initially are required to run the hardware attached or included in the system. During normal operation of the system, some devices may not be used; they are using system resources for nothing. You can disable a device as described in Step by Step 6.13, but remember to always use hardware profiles first to test the impact on the system.

**STEP BY STEP**

**6.13 Disabling a Device Safely**

1. Double-click the Devices icon in the Control Panel.
2. Select the device from the list.
3. Click on the HW/Profiles button.
4. Select a test profile if one exists.
5. Click on the Disable button.

The Original Configuration should be left intact. You can use this profile to return the system to proper working order at any time.

## Running Tasks and Applications

Each application runs one or more tasks in the Task Manager. You should close unused tasks to free up system resources. Some tasks are needed to operate Windows NT, but others are applications themselves. Windows NT services are also shown as tasks, but they cannot be closed with the Task Manager. Windows NT services must be closed from the Services application in the Control Panel. (See the preceding section, "Running Windows NT Services.")

When applications are not in use, you should close or at least minimize them. Surprisingly, an application running in an open window takes up significantly more memory than the same application would if minimized. When moving from one application to another, do not use the Alt+Tab feature or the taskbar buttons because they move the selected application to the foreground but do not minimize other applications.

Not all applications run as effectively under Windows NT Workstation 4.0. DOS, 16-bit, 32-bit, OS/2, and UNIX applications are treated very differently on the system. A 32-bit application designed to run on Windows NT performs better and more efficiently than any other type. That is because only 32-bit applications run in the main subsystem without additional effort. 32-bit applications are designed to take advantage of the Pentium processor, and they are most likely multithreaded. For all other types, Windows NT emulates their native operating system environment. This emulation requires more system resources, but it offers better compatibility.

All DOS applications are run in an NTVDM. This is a Windows NT Virtual DOS Machine that represents all the aspects of single computer. It leads the DOS application to believe it is the only application running on the computer. All 16-bit applications run in a WOW (Windows on Windows) session on top of an NTVDM. The WOW is meant to represent Windows 3.1/3.11.

OS/2- and UNIX-based applications run in their respective subsystems, which start along with the applications. The Task Manager shows these NTVDMs and other subsystems in use, along with their memory requirements.

Applications running as tasks will have a higher priority on the workstation and seem to be more responsive to the user. Windows NT Workstation 4.0 offers a foreground/background priority setting. All applications are written with a set of base priorities for each of its threads. The base priority of the thread is used to determine how much CPU time it can have in relation to other threads. A thread running at a priority of 12 runs before a thread with a priority of 8. Windows NT dynamically modifies the priority of threads to ensure that all threads get some time on the CPU.

Priorities range from 1 to 31 and are set by the programmer. A normal thread level is 8 for most user-based application tasks. Most operating system tasks run at a priority above 15. Although the user cannot change the exact value of the thread's priority, it can be boosted.

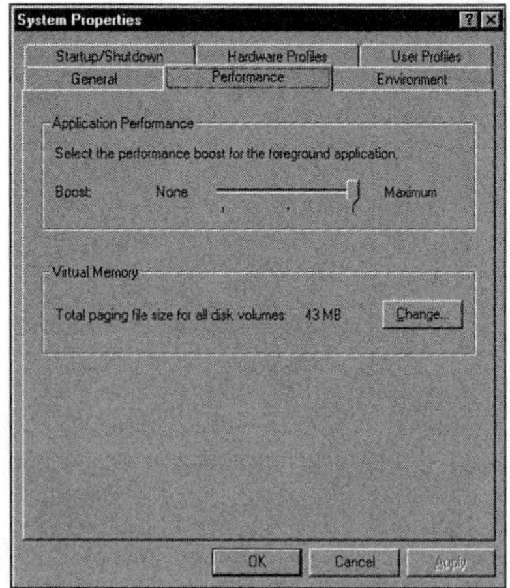


**FIGURE 6.23**
The Boost setting may be set to None to prevent foreground applications from dominating the CPU.

A simple method for changing the background tasks is to set the Application Performance Boost found on the System application's Performance tab. A Maximum boost increases the thread's priority by two levels when running in the foreground. The Minimum boost increases the priority by one, and the None boost does not increase the thread priority at all (see Figure 6.23).

You can boost individual applications from the command line. To access the command line, open the Start menu and choose Programs, Command Prompt. (An alternative is to choose Start, Run and type **CMD**.)

Four switches can be used with the `start` command to change the priority of a given application. They are listed in Table 6.14.

You can check a process's current priority by using utilities such as the Process Monitor and Process Viewer from the Windows NT Resource Kit. (See the sidebar "Using Resource Kit Utilities," earlier in this chapter.) The only situation in which the option of running applications in a higher priority level will manifest itself is on a system where the CPU is very busy. The same example could be repeated using the `/realtime` switch.

**TABLE 6.14**

**START COMMAND SWITCHES FOR CHANGING PRIORITY**

| *Switch* | *Effect on Priority* |
|---|---|
| `start /low` | This actually lowers the base priority of the application to 4. The effect is to increase the overall performance of other applications. Running an application with a priority 4 as a background application takes longer to complete any task. |
| `start /normal` | This switch runs the application using the normal priority of 8. It can be used for applications that normally run at values lower than 8. |
| `start /high` | This sets application priority to a value of 13. Most applications run much faster if they require a lot of CPU time. This improves the performance of an application that reads and writes to the hard disk. |
| `start /realtime` | This switch increases the base priority to 24. The `/realtime` switch is not recommended for applications that use the CPU extensively. You may not be able to interact with the system, and the mouse or keyboard commands may not be able to interrupt the CPU. Only users with Administrator privileges can use the `/realtime` switch. |

## Virtual Versus Physical Memory

You can almost always add physical memory to a computer with positive results. *Memory is the single most significant factor in overall system performance.* However, adding more memory may not be possible in the short term for several reasons: the cost of upgrading can be a barrier, or the system may not have any space to quickly add additional memory chips.

There are alternatives to purchasing more memory. After Windows NT has been tuned to make the best use of its current memory, modifying the location and size of the pagefile may have an effect on the system.

The pagefile is defined using a minimum and maximum size on a given hard drive. On a system with several hard drives, moving the pagefile to a drive that is faster or not used as much improves read and write requests. Placing the pagefile on a drive other than that of the operating system can result in problems during a memory dump. Memory dumps cause the information in physical memory to be stored in the pagefile during a crash. If the pagefile is on a different drive from the operating system, the dump will not be successful.

When the system starts, a pagefile is created at the minimum level. The operating system increases the size of the file to accommodate demand up until the maximum level is attained. You can monitor the current usage of the pagefile in Performance Monitor and the Task Manager. Increasing the size of the pagefile requires system resources and may result in a fragmented pagefile. These factors affect system performance. The minimum size of the pagefile should be large enough to accommodate current uses.

Another technique is to create additional pagefiles stored on different drives. The read and write operations may be handled faster. This depends on the current activity on the drives and the drive's own performance issues. Windows NT supports one pagefile on each logical disk. Placing pagefiles on multiple logical drives on the same physical disk does not affect the system much. Because there is only one physical reader on each physical disk, it takes longer to read.

You can make all changes to the pagefile from the Performance tab of the System properties. To make changes, select the Change button in the Virtual Memory section. See Figure 6.24 for details on virtual memory assignment.

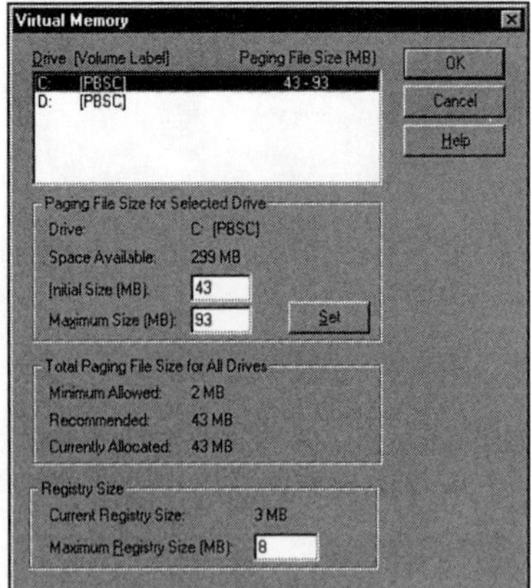


**FIGURE 6.24**
The initial size of the pagefile was 43MB. That is 32MB RAM + 11MB. The new value increases performance.

The maximum size of the pagefile could be left intact. The recommendation is to always keep a 50MB buffer between the minimum and maximum sizes. This buffer ensures that the pagefile can grow to accommodate short-term demands.

## Reviewing Disk Usage

Other than pagefile activity, the disks are used constantly by the operating system to read information and write data. The speed and efficiency of the drive is important, and hardware issues are very important when selecting a hard drive type and speed.

### Making Hardware Choices

Hard drive and controller types can make a big difference on performance. The following are some examples of transfer rates:

- Some IDEs (integrated drive electronic) have a 2.5MB/sec throughput.
- ESDI has a 3MB/sec throughput.
- SCSI-2 has a 5MB/sec throughput.
- Fast SCSI-2 can have a 10MB/sec throughput.

Exact figures can be seen in the manufacturer's documentation. Using a 32-bit controller card instead of a 16- or 8-bit controller will have significant impact on the system.

Although these options improve performance, they may not be realistic in the short term. The cost of these new controller cards may make an upgrade unaffordable.

### Choosing Partition Size and Disk Format

You can partition each hard drive into different sizes and format them using FAT or NTFS. Large partitions may be easier to use because a single drive letter references them. It is not always better to use one logical disk per physical disk. The size and format of the partition determines the size of the cluster being used for storage. A *cluster* is the smallest storage unit on a hard drive.

When formatted as FAT, a larger partition must use a larger cluster; that can result in inefficient use of the hard drive. If 12KB of data is stored to a hard drive that uses a 4KB cluster, the data uses three full clusters and wastes none. If the same 12KB of data is stored in a 32KB cluster, however, it uses only one cluster and wastes 20KB of space in the cluster. NTFS partitions are not bound by the same cluster size limitation that FAT is. NTFS is designed for larger partitions. The maximum size of an NTFS partition is 16 exabytes.

Creating two 500MB partitions will prove more beneficial than using a 1GB partition on the same drive. There are limits to the number of partitions that can be supported by each physical drive. With Windows NT, you can have up to four partitions on each drive. There are two types of partition: primary and extended. There can be only one extended partition per physical drive. Logical drives can be created in the extended partition to allow for even smaller storage areas. It is all based on the size of the cluster that's used.

DOS and NT support FAT partitions. NTFS partitions can be accessed only from within NT. NTFS offers much more security and data-integrity features. In addition, NTFS uses a B-tree method for file access, which is much faster than traditional FAT searches on large partitions. However, disk access on FAT partitions is actually faster for small partitions.

Partitions larger than 512MB should be converted to NTFS to reduce the cluster size. Partitions smaller than 512MB can be converted to NTFS, but because NTFS requires additional space to operate, it may in fact offer less disk space. There are many other factors to consider when choosing between FAT and NTFS. This discussion, however, focuses on disk space only.

## Disk Access Issues

The operating system, the pagefile, programs, and data may be stored on a single hard drive. This may not be very efficient and can slow down overall system performance.

Placing the operating system on a separate partition improves the I/O request. When a pagefile is used constantly, it should be placed on a partition away from the operating system. On a system with multiple disks and multiple controller cards, the improvements can be substantial.

Applications and data files should share the same physical disk—at least all data files being used by an application. When the disk reads information from one file and then must move the disk heads to a completely separate area of the disk, it takes a little longer.

Disk compression has an effect on disk access. Windows NT Workstation 4.0's compression can be implemented on NTFS partitions only. The compression is done on a per-drive, per-folder, or per-file basis. Although compressing information on the drive improves disk storage capacity, it degrades access time. Finding the information on the disk remains the same, but uncompressing it to pass it on to the CPU takes a little more time.

You should never compress heavily used files and programs that access the hard disk frequently. Compression under NTFS was designed for the NT Workstation and does not have a major impact, but it can be noticeable in some cases. The pagefile will not be compressed even if it is selected. Applications and common data files should not be compressed. Data files and applications that are seldom used may be compressed while they sit idle. They can always be uncompressed for use, or Windows NT can uncompress them while they are being used. Considering the low price of hard drives these days, compressed drives should be used at a minimum.

NT Workstation 4.0 creates a backward-compatible short filename (8.3 characters) for each long filename. This takes up little space on the drive but uses processor time. This short name generation can be disabled on a system running only Windows NT and using only 32-bit programs that do not require the traditional 8.3 filenames. Short names can still be used, but NT will not create short names when a long name is given.

To disable short name generation, use REGEDT32.EXE to set a Registry DWORD value of 1 in the following Registry location:

```
SYSTEM\CurrentControlSet\Control\Filesystem\
NtfsDisable8dot3NameCreation
```

Always be careful when making Registry changes. The Registry Editor does not warn you of any syntax errors or missing entries.

## Cleaning Up Disk Space

Fragmentation occurs in all cases when the operating system saves, deletes, and moves information to a hard drive. A file is fragmented if it is stored in several non-consecutive clusters on the hard drive.

Windows NT attempts to store information in the first continuous block of clusters. When a continuous block is not available, the file is stored in several non-consecutive blocks and is said to be *fragmented.* The disk can be fragmented even if files are not fragmented. There may be clusters unused in areas not large enough to store any one complete file.

Fragmentation slows down disk access time because the read heads must move to several locations on the disk to read one file. Currently, Windows NT Workstation 4.0 does not offer a defragmentation tool. However, third-party disk utilities can do the job. From within Windows NT, just moving a large amount of information from one drive to another and back again re-creates a larger continuous block of clusters that will store data more efficiently.

When multiple users share a computer, Windows NT creates a separate user profile, and all users share the same Recycle Bin. These two items may not amount to much for one user. By default, Windows NT uses up to 10 percent of each drive to store deleted files. On a system with a 2GB drive, the space used could be up to 200MB. User profiles maintain a separate list of files for each user in the Recycle Bin if file security has been applied. If a file is marked as No Access to user1 on drive C:, user1 will not be able to see it in the Recycle Bin.

## STEP BY STEP

### 6.14 Reducing Disk Usage for a Multiple-User Workstation

1. Reduce the size of the Recycle Bin that is available to each user.
2. Only use one hard drive for the Recycle Bin.
3. Review the contents of the Recycle Bin regularly and delete older items.
4. Delete unused user profiles.

To modify the properties of the Recycle Bin, right-click on the Recycle icon and select Properties. To delete unused user profiles, open the System application in the Control Panel and select the User Profiles tab. Every new user to log on to a Windows NT Workstation automatically gets his or her own profile. This profile is a copy of the default profile. A roaming profile is stored on the server and is copied down to each NT computer used during logon.

All improvements in performance come at a price. As you learned earlier, there will always be faster and newer hardware available. Changing NT's internal configuration may improve performance slightly, but in some cases it does so at the expense of losing a service or resource. Always consider the impact of the changes before implementation and be prepared to reverse them if problems occur. The basic configuration generated with a standard installation may be more than adequate for most systems.

## Case Study: Closing MS Word Slows System

### ESSENCE OF THE CASE

Here are the essential elements in this case:

- Word exits and system slows.
- Mouse is sluggish, program restoration is slow, and video display is slow.
- Reboot returns system performance to normal.

### SCENARIO

Mary calls to tell you of some trouble she is having with her NT Workstation. Mary primarily uses two applications: Microsoft Word 97 and Lotus Notes. Because Lotus Notes is her email program, she leaves it running all the time and simply minimizes it unless she wants to use email. She runs Word when she needs it and then shuts it down when she does not. She is finding, however, that occasionally something weird will happen when she exits Word. When she exits the word processor and maximizes Lotus Notes, she first notices that the expansion of Notes is slow. She also sees that the movement of her mouse pointer is jerky—like it is being hindered by something. Finally, when composing email, she finds that the screen display of her typing is quite a bit behind what she is doing on the keyboard, sometimes taking a couple of seconds for characters to be displayed.

## CASE STUDY: CLOSING MS WORD SLOWS SYSTEM

Not knowing what to do in those situations, she has been restarting NT (with Start, Shutdown, of course). When NT restarts, everything is fine until the problem arises again. She would like you to at least get her system to a place where she does not have to restart her machine all the time.

### ANALYSIS

In situations like this, it is often helpful to discover what else is running when an application fails. When queried, Mary says that sometimes she is running other applications when the system becomes unresponsive and other times she is not. The commonality seems to be exiting from Word.

You ask her to call you when the problem occurs next and she does. The first thing that you ask her to do is to start the Task Manager to discover what is running in the background that may be causing problems. When she brings up the Task Manager, she sees on the Applications tab that Lotus Notes is in a Running state. At the bottom of the dialog box, she also sees that the CPU usage is running at 100 percent. Clicking on the Processes tab, she scrolls through the list of applications, reading them off as she goes. As she approaches the end she reads, "NLNOTES.EXE, TASKMGR.EXE, and WINWORD.EXE."

At your request, she reads from the CPU column beside WINWORD.EXE that it's fluctuating between 98 and 100. Somehow, Word did not completely close when she exited, and it is taking up all the processor cycles trying desperately (but unsuccessfully) to close. When she clicks on WINWORD.EXE and clicks the End Process button, the entry disappears and her system becomes responsive again immediately.

As you reflect on the situation, you realize that her solution to the problem accomplished the same thing yours did, only in a more radical and time-consuming way. When she restarted her system, she stopped the WINWORD.EXE process, and her performance returned to normal when the restart was complete.

You instruct her to perform the same process termination if this problem should occur again. In the meantime, she is keeping track of what she does in Word just before the system becomes unresponsive in an attempt to isolate the problem to something that Microsoft can help her work out.

## CHAPTER SUMMARY

### KEY TERMS

Before you take the exam, make sure you are comfortable with the definitions and concepts for each of the following key terms:

- Task Manager
- Performance Monitor
- applications
- processes
- objects
- counters
- instances
- Chart view
- Report view
- Log view
- Alert view
- Windows Microsoft Diagnostic (WinMSD)
- bottleneck
- baseline
- DISKPERF
- Event Viewer
- emergency repair disk (ERD)
- hardware profile
- device

This chapter began with a discussion of the tools available to monitor system performance, namely Task Manager, Performance Monitor, the Server Manager, and the WinMSD tool. For all of them, you were introduced to the basic operation and, where applicable, display characteristics that can be changed.

You were then guided through some methods and recommendations for determining where bottlenecks and other problems are occurring. You do that by using Performance Monitor and Event Viewer.

Finally, you looked at system optimization. You learned about recovering from system failure, as well as service and device configuration. In addition, you studied optimization factors involved in running tasks and applications, memory, and disks.

## APPLY YOUR LEARNING

The following section allows you to assess how well you understood the material in the chapter. The exercises provide you with opportunities to engage in the sorts of tasks that comprise the skill sets the objectives reflect. Review and exam questions test your knowledge of the tasks and concepts specified in the objectives. Answers to the review and exam questions follow in the answers sections. For additional review- and exam-type questions, see the Top Score test engine on the CD-ROM that came with this book.

## Exercises

These exercises give you practice at using performance monitoring tools effectively to pinpoint bottlenecks. They also demonstrate safe methods of reconfiguring a system to maximize its potential.

### 6.1 Reducing Available Memory

This exercise demonstrates how to modify the BOOT.INI file to enable Windows NT to access a restricted amount of memory.

Before you can create a situation that results in a memory bottleneck, you may need to reduce the amount of RAM a computer has. On an Intel-based computer, a startup switch called `MAXMEM` can be added to the BOOT.INI file to limit the amount of memory the system can use. The same bottleneck may result even if you don't use the `MAXMEM` switch, but on computers with 16MB of RAM or more, it may take time to manifest itself.

To reduce the amount of physical RAM that Windows NT uses, change the `startup` command in the BOOT.INI file by adding the `/Maxmem` switch. The minimum amount of RAM that Windows NT Workstation will run on is 12MB. Reduce the amount of RAM to 12, and the system will almost immediately show a memory bottleneck. You're using the `/MAXMEM` switch only to test or simulate a shortage of memory; make sure you do not leave it on the system after the test.

**Estimated Time:** 10 minutes

1. Run Windows NT Explorer by choosing Start, Programs, Windows NT Explorer.
2. Open the C: drive and locate the BOOT.INI file in the right pane.
3. You should always make a copy of a file that you intend to modify in case the file needs to be restored later. Right-click on the file and select Copy. Then right-click anywhere on the C: drive and select Paste. The copy of the file is now called "copy of BOOT."
4. Right-click on the original BOOT.INI file and select Properties. Remember that if the extensions are hidden, you will not see "BOOT.INI," but only "BOOT."
5. Click once to remove the check mark from the Read Only check box so that the file may be modified. Close Properties.
6. Double-click on the BOOT.INI file to open and edit it. If the file is not associated with any program, you can select Notepad from the dialog box presented.
7. At the end of the first line in the `[operating system]` section, add the following entry: **/maxmem:12**.
8. Exit and save the file with the new entry. The BOOT.INI file is now ready to start up Windows NT with only 12MB of RAM available.
9. Restart the computer.

## APPLY YOUR LEARNING

### 6.2 Creating a Memory Log

This exercise demonstrates how to create a log to monitor memory usage and determine whether a bottleneck is being created by lack of memory on the system. Exercise 6.2 is guaranteed to show a bottleneck if you have already completed Exercise 6.1. For a true test of the system, either do not complete Exercise 6.1 or reverse the effects before proceeding.

**Estimated Time:** 30 minutes

1. Start Windows NT under basic conditions. No additional software or hardware conflicts are occurring. This may not always be possible, but you should try to reduce as many factors as possible to focus the analysis on the memory component.
2. Open Performance Monitor by choosing Start Programs, Administrative Tools (Common), Performance Monitor.
3. To change to the Log view, choose the View, Log command.
4. Select the Add Counter icon or choose the Edit, Add Counter command.
5. From the list of objects, select the following and add them to the log:
   - Memory
   - Process
   - Page File
   - LogicalDisk
6. Open the Options menu and choose Log.
7. Give the log file a name, such as **MEMTEST.LOG**, and select a folder for storage. The size of this log should not be considerable. (Always make sure the hard drive used to store the log file has sufficient space if the log is going to run overnight.)
8. Change the interval to 30 seconds and click the Start Log button.
9. Let the log record for at least 20 to 30 minutes while the system is performing normal tasks. A longer logging period offers more accurate averages and trends.
10. Minimize the Performance Monitor and start programs that are used frequently on the system. You can insert bookmarks into the log file to help decipher the information later during analysis.
11. Return to Performance Monitor and stop the log.

> WARNING
>
> **Don't Create a Bottleneck Where None Should Exist** Do not overdo this test. A memory bottleneck can always be forced if enough applications are started simultaneously. However, you do not want to show a bottleneck if one does not really exist. Simply run the system under normal circumstances.

**APPLY YOUR LEARNING**

### 6.3 Evaluating the Log File

This exercise helps you understand and interpret the results from the log you recorded in Exercise 6.2.

**Estimated Time:** 15 minutes

1. In the Performance Monitor, open the Options menu and choose Data From.
2. Select to view data from a log, and then type in the filename or browse for the log file called MEMTEST.LOG.
3. Choose the View, Chart command.
4. Add the following counters to the chart:
   - Memory: Page Faults/Sec
   - Memory: Page Inputs/Sec
   - Paging File: %Use
5. If the Page Faults/Sec counter is consistently above 10 and the Page Inputs/Sec is also spiking, the system is low on RAM. Verify the %Use counter of the pagefile to see whether it is increasing over time. This indicates whether the pagefile demands are becoming more extensive as new applications are loaded or whether it is only used when the application starts. Additional paging that occurs when an application starts may not be much of a concern, as long as paging demands return to lower or normal levels after the application is running.

### 6.4 Creating a Hardware Profile

In this exercise, you create a hardware profile that you will use to make and test hardware and software changes without risking permanent damage to the Windows NT Workstation 4.0 operating system. You must create this hardware profile before you can start Exercise 6.5.

**Estimated Time:** 10 minutes

1. Right-click on the My Computer icon and select Properties. (This is the same as opening the System application in the Control Panel.)
2. Select the Hardware Profiles tab.
3. Click on the Copy button.
4. Type **Test Configuration** as the new name for the test profile.
5. Select Wait Indefinitely so the system will give you time to make a choice and will not load any default configuration. The default hardware profile is always the first listed.
6. Restart the system. Choose the Windows NT Workstation 4.0 item from the Boot menu.
7. Two new hardware configurations will appear: the Original Configuration and your Test Configuration. At this first logon, the Test Configuration is identical to the Original Configuration because no changes have been made.

## APPLY YOUR LEARNING

### 6.5 Improving Memory Performance

This exercise shows the impact on memory usage when certain services are stopped. You *must* complete Exercise 6.4 before attempting this exercise. Note, however, that the changes you make can be quickly reversed if the desired results are not achieved.

**Estimated Time:** 15 minutes

1. The MEMTEST.LOG file you created in Exercise 6.2 will be used here as a baseline log before changes are made to the system. If the MEMTEST.LOG file is not available, create one now.
2. Boot the computer and choose the Test Configuration. No changes have been made yet to this profile.
3. From the Control Panel, select the Services icon.
4. Click on the Spooler service.
5. Click on the HW Profile button and disable only the Test Configuration. (Disabling the Spooler disables printing capabilities.)
6. Click on the Server service and disable it for the Test Configuration. (This means that administrators cannot remotely administer your system, and you will not be able to share folders.)
7. Click on any other service you think is not required and disable it as well for the Test Configuration.
8. Restart the computer using the same Test Configuration.
9. Create a new memory log called **MEMTESTAFTER.LOG** and perform the same operations as for MEMTEST.LOG for about the same amount of time.
10. Compare the values in the MEMTEST.LOG (no system improvements) with MEMTESTAFTER.LOG (with the system improvements). If the values are not significantly better, it may not have been worth making the improvements.
11. Reboot the computer using the Original Configuration. If the changes did not improve your system, delete the Test Configuration from the System application in the Control Panel.

## Review Questions

1. You have an application that has stopped responding. How can you shut down this application?
2. When several applications run simultaneously, your system slows down considerably. How can you verify the amount of memory being used by each application?
3. You are planning to upgrade the amount of RAM in your computer. How can you find out how much memory you need to purchase?
4. Your computer runs on a network, and you are sharing folders. You find that your machine tends to slow down every once in a while for no apparent reason. How can you monitor the activity caused by other network users on your system?
5. You are experiencing an intermittent `out of memory` problem and cannot reproduce it for your support department. How can you save the Performance Monitor screens that you have seen to show them to the support department?

**APPLY YOUR LEARNING**

## Exam Questions

1. Which tool can provide information about CPU utilization? (Choose all that apply.)

   A. Performance Monitor

   B. WinMSD

   C. Task Manager

   D. CPU Manager

2. Which counters could be used to identify a physical memory shortage? Pick two.

   A. Thread: %User Time

   B. Memory: Page Faults/Sec

   C. Processor: %Processor Time

   D. LogicalDisk: %Free Space

3. Where can someone find a list of all applications currently running on the system?

   A. From the Start menu

   B. Using the Task Manager

   C. Using the Control Panel's Application icon

   D. On the taskbar

4. You are thinking of stopping an unused service. Before doing so, however, you want to check on service dependencies. Which Windows NT tool could you use?

   A. The Services application in the Control Panel

   B. The Task Manager's Services tab

   C. WinMSD and the properties of a service

   D. The System icon

5. The Processes tab of Task Manager shows some information regarding memory usage that is not listed. How can you view more information in this same window? (Choose all that apply.)

   A. Use the Performance Monitor's memory counters.

   B. Open two Task Manager windows.

   C. From the View menu, choose Select Columns.

   D. Change the size of the window using the mouse.

6. You have decided to optimize your Windows NT Workstation 4. How can you safely make the changes?

   A. Record a log on the system. The log can be used to reconstruct the system at a later time.

   B. Use the hardware profiles feature and make a test configuration. If a failure occurs, the system can be restarted using the Original Configuration.

   C. Document all changes in the WinMSD utility. The system will recover automatically.

   D. Make sure the user profiles are enabled. All changes made to the system will affect only the current user.

7. What is the relationship between counters, instances, and objects in Performance Monitor?

   A. Objects are categories that contain specific counters for all instances.

   B. An object is a unit of each instance. A counter is used only to determine the number of events occurring on a system.

## APPLY YOUR LEARNING

C. Performance Monitor uses counters only.

D. All objects are divided into counters. Each counter can be monitored for a given instance or a total instance.

8. A baseline log was created a few weeks ago and is stored on the local hard drive in a logs folder. Which tool could you use to view this log? (Choose all that apply.)

   A. From the System icon, use Log view and select the log file.

   B. Use the Performance Monitor.

   C. A log file can be viewed only by Microsoft.

   D. Use the Event Viewer.

9. What are the two objects used to monitor disk activity?

   A. DiskPerf

   B. PhysicalDisk

   C. HardDisk

   D. LogicalDisk

10. You have decided to stop unused services using hardware profiles. Which of the following services can be stopped without preventing the user from connecting with other computers? (Choose all that apply.)

    A. Browser

    B. Redirector

    C. Spooler

    D. Server

11. You have been monitoring disk activity in a log for the last eight hours. Yet when you display the counters, they all read 0. What is the meaning of these readings?

    A. The disk has been still for the entire logging period.

    B. The Performance Monitor is not functioning correctly and needs to be reinstalled.

    C. The DISKPERF utility was not enabled.

    D. The PhysicalDisk counter was not enabled.

12. After making several configuration changes to the system, you reboot and log on. Several seconds after you have logged on, the system presents an error dialog box. You reboot again and use the LastKnownGood setting. The same error appears. What could be the problem?

    A. The LastKnownGood works only with hardware profiles.

    B. The LastKnownGood was updated after you logged on, replacing the good configuration with the current one.

    C. The LastKnownGood was not told to update on exit. You must boot up using the letter L and tell the system to update the LastKnownGood.

    D. None of the above.

13. What are some of the factors that affect disk performance? (Choose all that apply.)

    A. The partition size

    B. The amount of information on the disk

    C. The names of the files

    D. The DISKPERF utility

## APPLY YOUR LEARNING

14. How does upgrading to 32-bit applications make a difference on the system? Pick all that apply.

    A. 32-bit applications run faster because they are only written by Microsoft.

    B. 32-bit applications run directly in the system's win32 module, and no emulation is required.

    C. 32-bit applications cannot run under Windows NT.

    D. 32-bit applications run faster because they can be multithreaded.

15. The hard drive on your Windows NT 4.0 computer seems to be full. You investigate the C: drive using Explorer and find that very little software is loaded. What could be using up so much hard drive space? (Choose all that apply.)

    A. The disk is fragmented.

    B. Several Recycle Bins are at full capacity.

    C. The DISKPERF utility is active.

    D. The size of a FAT partition is very large, using large clusters.

16. If you lose your emergency recovery disk, you can create a new one from any other Windows NT Workstation 4.0 computer. True or False?

    A. True

    B. False

17. The system has generated an error code. What tool can you use to review the error code? (Choose all that apply.)

    A. The Performance Monitor

    B. The System application in the Control Panel

    C. The Event Viewer

    D. The Task Manager

18. You need to quickly free up system memory without restarting the system. What can be done? (Choose all that apply.)

    A. Close any applications or files that are not required.

    B. Minimize all background applications.

    C. Run a 16-bit application in its own memory address space.

    D. Increase the size of the pagefile.

19. You have been logging disk objects for the last few days. What are you looking for in the log to indicate whether a disk bottleneck is occurring?

    A. CPU activity above 85 percent consistently

    B. PageFaults/Sec counter above 2

    C. Consistent increases in the size of the pagefile

    D. Disk usage above 85 percent

## Answers to Review Questions

1. Use the Task Manager's Applications tab, select the application, and then click on End Task. For more information, see the section "Using the Task Manager."

2. Use the Task Manager and compare the Memory column of each process. Each application uses

## APPLY YOUR LEARNING

one or more processes. For more information, see the section "Using the Task Manager."

3. Under normal use of your computer, compare the total physical memory with the total committed memory in the Performance tab of the Task Manager. If total committed and peak are always higher than physical memory, you may want to purchase RAM to bring your physical memory up to the total commit or peak values. For more information, see the section "Pinpointing Memory Bottlenecks."

4. Use the Performance Monitor to track the amount of bytes read or bytes written to your disk under the Network object. For more information, see the section "Pinpointing Network Bottlenecks."

5. Use the Performance Monitor and create a log file during normal use of your computer. If an error occurs, you can pass on the log file. Include objects such as Processor, Memory, PhysicalDisk and Paging File. The support department can then analyze this log file. For more information, see the section "Using Logs."

## Answers to Exam Questions

1. **A and C** are correct. The Performance Monitor offers CPU usage counters, and the Task Manager shows the CPU usage in a chart. For more information, see the sections "Pinpointing Processor Bottlenecks" and "Using the Performance Tab."

2. **B and C** are correct. The Page Faults counter shows the number of requests that are not found in physical memory, and processor time may indicate a lot of paging activity being processed. For more information, see the section "Pinpointing Processor Bottlenecks."

3. **B** is correct. Between the Application tab and the Processes tab, all the applications (both foreground and background) are listed. For more information, see the section "Using the Application Tab."

4. **C** is correct. WinMSD offers a list of all services and their properties and shows the dependencies. For more information, see the section "Running Windows NT Services."

5. **C** is correct. The View, Select Column command offers up to 14 columns of information. If all columns are selected, a scroll bar appears because the size of the window cannot be changed. For more information, see the section "Using the Processes Tab."

6. **B** is correct. The hardware profile can be used to make changes to a given profile without affecting the original profile. For more information, see the section "Creating Hardware Profiles."

7. **D** is correct. An *object* is a category of hardware or software that is monitored for statistical information (for example, Processor). A *counter* is a specific statistic for a particular object (for example, %Processor Time). Finally, an instance is a definable unit of the counter (for example, if a computer has two processors, you could monitor counters for either instance, both instances, or the total of both instances). For more information, see the section "Using the Performance Monitor."

8. **B** is correct. Performance Monitor logs can only be viewed using the Performance Monitor. For more information, see the section "Using Logs."

## APPLY YOUR LEARNING

9. **B and D** are correct. DiskPerf is not an object; it only activates objects. HardDisk is not an object either. For more information, see the section "Pinpointing Disk Bottlenecks."

10. **A, C, and D** are correct. The Redirector is the client software that connects the Workstation to a Server service on another system. For more information, see the section "Running Windows NT Services."

11. **C** is correct. The DISKPERF utility enables disk counters. For more information, see the section "Pinpointing Disk Bottlenecks."

12. **B** is correct. The LastKnownGood configuration is written with the configuration at the last successful logon. Because you logged on before the problem was repaired, the faulty configuration was written to LastKnownGood, and now you will not be able to use it to recover your system. For more information, see the section "Using the LastKnownGood Configuration."

13. **A, B, and D** are correct. Large FAT partitions may waste disk space. A full disk tends to be fragmented because there is less room to store data continuously, and running the DISKPERF utility will slow down the disk. For more information, see the sections "Choosing Partition Size and Disk Format" and "Disk Access Issues."

14. **B and D** are correct. Not only do 32-bit applications not need any kind of translation or emulation to run on NT, they also can be multithreaded, which enables them to take advantage of multiple processors if they are available. For more information, see the section "Running Tasks and Applications."

15. **A, B, and D** are correct. Disk fragmentation creates holes on the disk that are not used. NT can use one Recycle Bin per hard drive. The default size is 10 percent of space. Large clusters on a FAT partition may waste disk space. For more information, see the section "Choosing Partition Size and Disk Format."

16. **B** is correct. Parts of the Registry are stored on the ERD and are unique to each system. For more information, see the section "Creating and Maintaining an Emergency Repair Disk."

17. **C** is correct. The Event Viewer stores errors generated by applications and the operating system. For more information, see the section "Monitoring with the Event Viewer."

18. **A and B** are correct. Applications that are opened will be stored in memory, and full-screen applications take up more memory than do minimized applications. For more information, see the section "Running Tasks and Applications."

19. **D** is correct. The Disk Usage counter may spike above 85 percent, but it should not remain that high. Page Faults and the pagefile have to do with memory bottlenecks. CPU Usage reflects CPU or memory bottlenecks. For more information, see the section "Identifying and Resolving Performance Problems."

## Suggested Readings and Resources

The following are some recommended readings in the area of monitoring and optimization for NT Workstation:

1. Microsoft Official Curriculum course 922: *Supporting Microsoft Windows NT 4.0 Core Technologies*
    - Module 18: Troubleshooting Resources
2. Microsoft Official Curriculum course 689: *Supporting Microsoft Windows NT Server 4.0 Enterprise Technologies*
    - Module 2: Microsoft Windows NT Server 4.0 Analysis and Optimization
3. Microsoft TechNet CD-ROM
    - *Concepts and Planning – MS Windows NT Server 4.0*
        - Chapter 8: Monitoring Performance
4. Web sites
    - `www.microsoft.com/train.cert`
    - `www.prometric.com/testingcandidates/assessment/chosetest.html` (take online assessment tests)

## Objectives

Microsoft provides the following objectives for "Troubleshooting":

**Choose the appropriate course of action to take when the boot process fails.**

- This objective is necessary because someone certified in the use of Windows NT Workstation technology must understand the NT boot process and be able to troubleshoot and resolve problems that occur when booting. This includes configuration problems and boot failures resulting from hardware problems.

**Choose the appropriate course of action to take when a print job fails.**

- This objective is necessary because someone certified in the use of Windows NT Workstation technology must understand the NT print process and architecture and be able to troubleshoot and resolve problems relating to printing. This includes configuration of printers as well as resource access problems.

**Choose the appropriate course of action to take when the installation process fails.**

- This objective is necessary because someone certified in the use of Windows NT Workstation technology must understand the process of installing Windows NT Workstation and be able to troubleshoot and resolve problems that occur in the installation process. This includes faulty media, problems with hardware configuration, and failure of automation.

CHAPTER 7

# Troubleshooting

## OBJECTIVES

**Choose the appropriate course of action to take when an application fails.**

- This objective is necessary because someone certified in the use of Windows NT Workstation technology must understand the subsystems involved in running applications and be able to troubleshoot and resolve problems that occur when executing applications. This includes configuring subsystems and execution priority.

**Choose the appropriate course of action to take when a user cannot access a resource.**

- This objective is necessary because someone certified in the use of Windows NT Workstation technology must understand security and connectivity in Windows NT and be able to resolve problems that prevent resource access. This includes password, sharing, and permission problems.

**Modify the Registry using the appropriate tool.**

- This objective is necessary because someone certified in the use of Windows NT Workstation technology must understand the NT Registry and the tools that can be used to modify it. These include the Control Panel, REGEDIT.EXE, and REGEDT32.EXE.

**Implement advanced techniques to resolve various problems.**

- This objective is necessary because someone certified in the use of Windows NT Workstation technology must understand all facets of NT and be able to use all resources at his or her disposal to solve any problems that occur. These include monitors and logs.

## OUTLINE

This chapter will help you prepare for the "Troubleshooting" section of Microsoft's Exam 70-73 by introducing you to a variety of troubleshooting techniques. These techniques cover problems relating to booting, printing, installation, application execution, and resource access.

## Study Strategies

- In a poll that Microsoft conducted among troubleshooters to determine what made for successful troubleshooting, more than half of the troubleshooting successes could be related to experience—either with the computer system or with the specific problem. This indicates that the best knowledge to have is knowledge of how the system works and what problems you might face. Just as bank tellers are trained not on how to spot counterfeit money but on how to spot the real stuff, you should focus most of your attention not on what might go wrong and how to fix it but on how a good working Windows NT Server looks. In this way, you will be able to more easily detect a problem and determine its cause.

- Troubleshooting questions on the Windows NT Server exam are rarely as straightforward as, "You are troubleshooting a problem with RAS...." Instead, a need for troubleshooting is implied in scenario questions, and you will have to put your troubleshooting skills to work to figure out what is the best course of action.

  Scenario questions on the Windows NT Server exam are often worded so as to confuse you into thinking a particular piece of information is important when it is not. Become familiar with working systems, and when you are familiar, you will instantly know if something is wrong (like the bank teller who handles a piece of counterfeit money after thousands of real bills have passed through her hands). Then your experience and instincts will tell you where to go to solve the problem.

- Having said all that, you still must have a good methodology for troubleshooting, and you must know what kinds of problems are likely to crop up both in a production environment and on the exam. Become very familiar with the categories of troubleshooting covered in this chapter and understand the problems that might arise from incorrect configuration or system failure. Also know what solutions make the most sense in a given situation.

## INTRODUCTION

The modern digital computer contains numerous components that interact with one another: both hardware and software. The potential for malfunctions, a poorly performing system, and general system failure always exists. The key to successful troubleshooting is to isolate the component or module responsible for the trouble, fix or modify the problem, and test the results. Often the issue at hand isn't easily isolated and may not arise out of one simple factor. Catastrophic failure is the easiest problem to fix, because the problem is always there to be analyzed. The intermittent problems are the most troublesome—and challenging.

The best weapon any professional can have in his or her arsenal when attempting to troubleshoot a system problem is the knowledge of how the underlying system is supposed to work. With that knowledge, and using the various diagnostic tools that Microsoft includes with Windows NT Workstation 4.0, you can fix many if not all of the common problems you encounter.

This chapter builds on the information you learned in Chapter 6, "Monitoring and Optimization," using many of the same tools and techniques. The basic difference between the information presented in that chapter and in this one is that problems discussed in this chapter are essentially showstoppers that require you to find a solution so your client can proceed to his additional work.

## GENERAL TROUBLESHOOTING TECHNIQUES

Microsoft presents a basic troubleshooting model that it identifies using the acronym DETECT. The letters in DETECT stand for the words Discover, Explore, Track, Execute, Check, and Tie-up. The following list outlines the DETECT troubleshooting model.

- *Discover the problem.* Talk to users and look at the systems in question to determine what the problem is. Find out what software is running and what versions of operating systems and service packs are being used. Gather as much information as you can to figure out what the real problem is. It may take a lot of work to go from point A when the user says, "My computer won't work" to point B when you discover that the user has been receiving a message indicating the primary domain controller could not be located.

- *Explore the boundaries.* Determine the scope of the problem and whether it is reproducible. Does it happen only at specific times of the day? Is other software running when it happens? Is the same problem occurring in other locations on your site? And does TechNet record the problem as common and solvable?
- *Track the possible approaches.* Brainstorm—either alone or with others—to determine the possible approaches to solving the problem. Include solutions that have been tried in the past (especially if they have been successful).
- *Execute an approach.* Implement the approach that you determine is most likely to succeed. Don't forget to consider possible problems that might occur and take steps to avoid making the problem worse. If it is possible that some working system might be rendered inoperable by your changes, back up the data or disconnect it from the network. Be sure to make copies of all the files you propose to change, especially the Registry.
- *Check for success.* Determine if your solution worked, and consider whether the solution is permanent or whether the system is likely to return to the problem state. If it is likely to reoccur, will the same fix work again, and can a user implement it him- or herself?
- *Tie up loose ends.* Document your successes and failures as you work through the problem. Then gather the notes you made during the brainstorming and implementation of your solution so that you will have them for similar solutions. If you feel that the solution you used was not the best (even though it resulted in a successful repair), be sure to document that so you can try another solution next time. Also be sure that the user who placed the call (if it was someone other than you who discovered the problem) is satisfied that the problem is resolved; this will instill confidence in you and in your systems.

What follows are a number of sections in which specific problems are discussed. Be sure to keep in mind that the information presented really only helps you with the exploration and tracking stages of the troubleshooting model. The rest must be up to you to work out in the situations in which you find yourself.

# Assessing Boot Process Failures

Choose the appropriate course of action to take when the boot process fails.

When you know that your workstation's hardware is functioning correctly, Windows NT Workstation's failure to start up properly and load the Windows NT shell may be a boot process problem. The key to solving problems of this type is to understand the logical sequence that your workstation uses when starting up. Windows NT shows you various boot sequence errors, the meaning of which should help you determine the problem with your system. You can also diagnose the BOOT.INI file to determine the nature of any potential problems, and you can use your emergency repair disks to boot your system and repair common boot process failure problems.

A boot failure is an obvious error, and one of the most common problems you will encounter. When you or your client can't start your computer, you know you have a problem. And it's the kind of problem that forces you to stop what you are doing and fix it before you can go on to further work.

## The Boot Sequence

Your computer begins the boot sequence after the Power On Self Test (POST) completes itself. When you turn on the power to your computer, the first series of messages you see are hardware related and are not associated with the boot process. Your memory is tested, for example, and then your bus structure is tested. Your computer runs a series of tests. These tests signal to peripheral devices and sense their replies to check for successful I/O performance. You may see a series of messages stating that your mouse and keyboard are detected, noting the appearance of an IDE drive, indicating whether a SCSI adapter is detected, providing response from any devices on that SCSI chain, and so forth. Failure at this stage isn't a boot sequence problem.

The boot sequence initiates when the hard drive's master boot record (MBR) is read into memory and begins to load the different portions of the Windows NT operating system. Windows NT Workstation runs on different microprocessor architectures. The exact boot sequence depends on the type of microprocessor on which you have installed Windows NT Workstation.

## The Windows NT Boot Process

The boot process begins when your computer accesses the hard drive's master boot record (MBR) to load Windows NT. If your system fails during the Power On Self Test (POST), the problem isn't NT-related; it is a hardware issue. What happens after the MBR program loads depends on the type of computer you are using.

### The Intel Boot Sequence

Windows NT loads on an Intel x86 computer by reading a file called the NTLDR or NT Loader into memory from the boot sector of the startup or active partition on your boot drive. NTLDR is a hidden system file set to be read-only. NTLDR is located in the root folder of your system partition and can be viewed in the Windows NT Explorer when you set the View All File Type option. The NTLDR file initiates the following process:

1. NTLDR initializes the 32-bit flat memory model required by the Windows NT kernel to address RAM.
2. NTLDR initializes the minifile system driver to access the system and boot partitions.
3. NTLDR displays the Boot Loader menu on your monitor to provide you the choice of which operating system to use. These selections are stored in the BOOT.INI file in your systemroot directory.
4. After you select an operating system, a hardware detection routine is initiated. For Windows NT, the NTDETECT.COM program is responsible for this routine, and it creates a hardware list that it passes to the NTLDR program.

5. The operating system kernel is then loaded. The NTOSKRNL.EXE file located in the %systemroot%\System32 folder is called to load the kernel of Windows NT. The menu is replaced by the OS Loader V4.00 screen.
6. A blue screen appears while the Hardware Abstraction Layer (HAL) is being loaded. To execute this, the HAL.DLL is called with a set of routines that isolate operating system functions from I/O.
7. Next, the HKEY_LOCAL_MACHINE\System hive of the Registry is read and the system is loaded. Registry hives are stored as files in the %systemroot%\System32\Config folder.
8. The boot time drivers HKEY_LOCAL_MACHINE\System\CurrentControlSet\Control\ServiceGroupOrder are loaded. For each driver that's loaded, a dot is added to the OS Loader screen.
9. The list of supported hardware devices is handed off from NTDETECT.COM to NTOSKRNL.EXE.
10. After NTOSKRNL.EXE executes, the computer's boot phase finishes, and the software you have installed begins to be loaded.

NOTE

**Non-NT Operating Systems in the Boot Loader Menu** If you install Windows NT Workstation over a previous installation of MS-DOS or Windows 95, the previous operating system will appear in the menu as MS-DOS or WINDOWS. When they are loaded and executed, these systems call the BOOTSECT.DOS file. BOOTSECT.DOS loads and hands off at the end of the boot process to the operating system component responsible for I/O communication. In Windows 95, that file is the IO.SYS file.

NOTE

**Display Driver Names at Startup** If you enter the `/sos` switch in the BOOT.INI file, Windows NT will list the drivers' names in the OS Loader screen as Windows NT Workstation starts up.

## The RISC Boot Sequence

A RISC computer contains the NTLDR software as part of its BIOS. Therefore, the boot phase of a RISC-based computer is both simpler and faster than the boot phase of an Intel x86 computer. A RISC computer keeps its hardware configuration in its BIOS, which obviates the need for the NTDETECT.COM file. Another item kept in firmware is the list of all valid operating systems and how to access them. This means that a RISC computer doesn't use a BOOT.INI file, either.

A RISC computer boots by loading a file called OSLOADER.EXE. After reading the hardware configuration from the BIOS and executing, OSLOADER.EXE hands off the boot process to the NTOSKRNL.EXE. Then the HAL.DLL is loaded, followed by the system file, which ends the RISC Windows NT boot process.

## BOOT.INI

NTLDR may invoke the Boot Loader menu, but BOOT.INI, an editable text file, controls it. (It is read-only, so you must remove that attribute before editing it.) BOOT.INI is the only .INI file that Windows NT uses—if, indeed, you can actually say that NT uses it. After all, Windows NT is not loaded at the time this file is called on.

BOOT.INI has only two sections: `[boot loader]` and `[operating systems]`. The `[boot loader]` section defines the operating system that boots by default, and the `[operating systems]` section defines the other operating systems that can be booted.

The BOOT.INI file contains paths to boot files for the operating systems listed in it. In NT operating systems, this path is defined in ARC format; otherwise, the path is presented as a DOS path. DOS paths, such as "C:\MSDOS," are very straightforward and require no explanation. ARC paths, on the other hand, can be very obscure in their contraction and interpretation. It is, therefore, necessary to discuss them at this point.

### ARC Paths

ARC paths provide a means of defining the location of a file based on physical location—specifically, based on the controller card, physical disk, and partition on which the directory is stored. Because the drive labeled G: could be physically anywhere, the ARC path convention was adopted as the way to tell the NT boot process where the boot files are located.

An ARC path can take one of two forms:

multi(0)disk(0)rdisk(0)partition(1)\WINNT

or

scsi(0)disk(0)rdisk(0)partition(1)\WINNT

The first parameter (either multi or scsi) identifies the physical number of the controller being referenced, starting from 0 and counting up from there. If multi is used, it indicates either a non-SCSI controller or a SCSI controller with its BIOS enabled. If scsi is used, it indicates a SCSI controller with its BIOS disabled.

The second and third parameters (disk and rdisk) are really a set of alternatives: Only one is used in any circumstance. Both the disk and rdisk parameters indicate the physical disk (associated with the controller indicated in the previous parameter). If the first parameter is multi, the disk parameter is ignored and the rdisk parameter is used. If the first parameter is scsi, the disk parameter is used and the rdisk parameter is ignored. Like the controller parameter, the counter associated with the hard disk parameter begins at 0 and increments from there.

The fourth parameter (partition) indicates the partition on the disk specified in either the second or the third parameter. Unlike the first three parameters, the counter for the partition begins at 1 and increments from there.

The final parameter is the path on the partition described in which the NT boot files are located. This path is frequently (but not always) WINNT.

The ARC path of each NT installation on any given computer is automatically placed into the BOOT.INI file in the system partition. If nothing ever changes on your server, you will never have to manipulate that file. However, if new partitions are created on your hard drives or if new hard drives or disk controllers are installed, the ARC paths might need to be updated.

ARC paths are based on physical configuration of your computer. When the configuration changes, the ARC paths in your BOOT.INI file are not automatically modified. As a result, some changes will render your system unbootable. This will not prevent NT from functioning properly after it is booted; however, it may prevent it from starting properly. In order to understand this, you need to understand how ARC numbers are assigned to partitions.

When you create a new partition using the Disk Administrator, the ARC numbers assigned to the partitions are re-evaluated. The numbers are generated according to the following pattern:

1. The first primary partition on each disk gets the number 1.
2. Each additional primary partition is then given a number, incrementing up from 1.
3. Each logical drive is then given a number in the order they appear in the Disk Administrator.

For example, suppose you have a hard drive partitioned like the one shown in Figure 7.1.

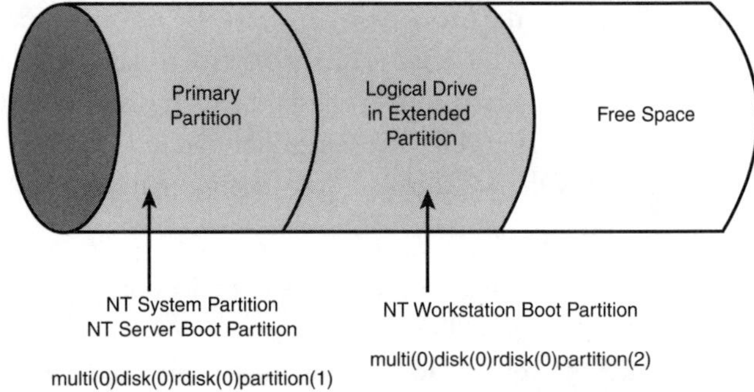


**FIGURE 7.1**
In the original configuration, the Workstation boot files are stored on partition 2.

As you can see, a primary partition contains the system and boot information for NT Server, and the first logical drive contains the boot files for NT Workstation. All is well until you create a new primary partition in the free space on the hard drive (see Figure 7.2).

When you create the new primary partition, that partition gets the number which is one more than the first primary partition; in this case, the new partition is now the number 2. This makes the partition with the Workstation files number 3. Unfortunately, because the BOOT.INI file still thinks it is to go to partition 2, when you choose Workstation from the boot list, the boot fails and you see this message:

```
Windows NT could not start because the following file is
missing or corrupt
<winntroot>\system32\ntoskrnl.exe
Please reinstall a copy of the above file
```

To resolve this problem, you have three options:

- You can boot to an operating system that will still start (in this case, NT Server will still boot) and then change the BOOT.INI file from there.

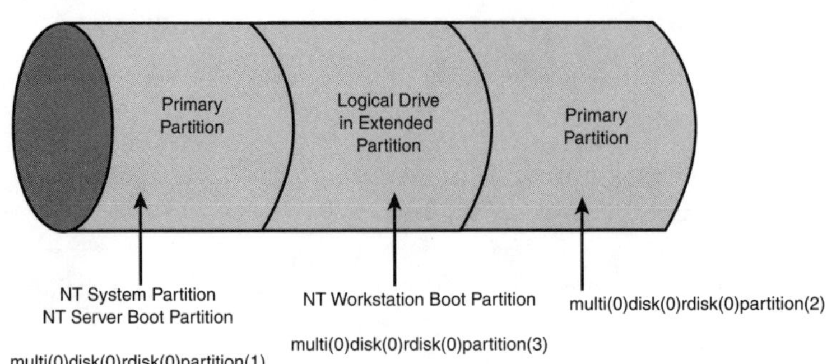


**FIGURE 7.2**
In the new configuration, the Workstation boot files are stored on partition 3 because the new primary partition is now partition 2.

- You can boot from a recovery disk that has the correct BOOT.INI file and then modify the BOOT.INI file from within Workstation. (See "Boot Disk Recovery" for more information on creating a recovery disk.) This method is often used on a system that has only one operating system to boot.
- If your system partition is formatted FAT, you can boot to DOS, use the `attrib` command with the `-h -r -s` switches to make it modifiable, edit BOOT.INI from DOS, and then reboot.

WARNING

**Do Not Ignore Messages in Disk Administrator** The NT Disk Administrator will not change your BOOT.INI file. However, if you create a partition in the NT Disk Administrator that necessitates the modification of the BOOT.INI file, a message will inform you of that. Do not ignore those messages because you may leave your NT Server unbootable. Although the solution to this boot problem is relatively simple, if you do not recognize the problem immediately, you might become frustrated and might reinstall NT unnecessarily.

## The [boot loader] Section

The `[boot loader]` section of BOOT.INI defines the operating system that will be loaded if the user doesn't make a selection within a defined period of time. By default, you see something like this:

```
[boot loader]
timeout=30
default=multi(0)disk(0)rdisk(0)partition(1)\WINNT
```

The timeout parameter is the length of time (in seconds) that NTLDR has to wait for the user to make a decision. If timeout is set to 0, the default operating system loads immediately. If it is set to –1, the menu remains onscreen until the user makes a decision.

The default parameter defines the actual path, in ARC-compliant form, to the directory that contains the files for the default operating system—which usually is the last operating system installed, unless someone has changed this entry. The easiest way to change the default operating system and the timeout setting is by using the Control Panel's System application.

## STEP BY STEP

### 7.1 Changing the Operating System That Boots by Default

1. Open the Control Panel and double-click the System icon.
2. Click the Startup/Shutdown tab to display that page of settings (see Figure 7.3).

*continues*

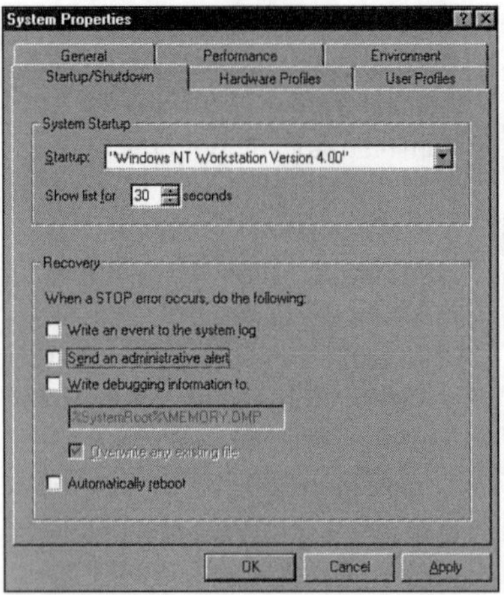


**FIGURE 7.3**
You can change the default operating system on the Startup/Shutdown tab in the System Properties dialog box.

*continued*

3. From the Startup pull-down list, choose the operating system you want to boot by default.
4. If desired, modify the Show List For field to specify how long the system should wait before booting the default operating system automatically.
5. Click the OK button to write the changes to the BOOT.INI file.

Step by Step 7.1 outlines the preferred method of modifying the BOOT.INI file. You can edit BOOT.INI directly, but remember that a mistyped character in NOTEPAD.EXE or EDIT.COM could prevent your system from booting properly.

### The `[operating systems]` Section

The `[operating systems]` section contains a reference for every operating system available to the user from the Boot Loader menu, as well as any special switches necessary to customize the Windows NT environment. One of these entries must match the default= entry in the `[boot loader]` section. Otherwise, you end up with two entries onscreen for the same OS, one of which has "(default)" after it. In all likelihood, only one of these will work. Trial-and-error should quickly discern which one.

Note that the paths are in ARC format with a label in quotation marks, which displays as an onscreen selection. Here's an example of an `[operating systems]` section:

```
multi(0)disk(0)rdisk(0)partition(1)\WINNT="Windows NT
➥Workstation ~Version 4.00"
multi(0)disk(0)rdisk(0)partition(1)\WINNT="Windows NT
➥Workstation ~Version 4.00 [VGA mode]" /basevideo /sos
c:\="Windows 95"
```

This example shows two entries for the same Windows NT Workstation installation, but the second one includes two switches (`/basevideo` and `/sos`) that customize the Windows NT boot and load process. These and other BOOT.INI switches are covered in the next section.

## BOOT.INI Switches

This section describes several useful switches you can include in the `[operating systems]` section of BOOT.INI. The only way to include a switch is to manually edit the BOOT.INI file. If you decide to do so, be sure to remove the read-only attribute from the file before editing it, and be sure that you save the altered file as a text file if you use a word processor that normally saves in another format.

Here are the available switches:

- `/basevideo` The `/basevideo` switch tells Windows NT to load the standard VGA driver instead of the optimized driver written for your video card, which is useful, for example, if your monitor breaks and is replaced by one that doesn't support the same resolution or refresh rate that your last one did. If you can't see, it is awfully hard to get into Control Panel to change the video settings. Selecting the VGA mode entry uses the standard VGA 640×480, 16-color driver that works with almost every monitor.
- `/sos` The `/sos` switch enumerates to the screen each driver as it loads during the kernel load phase. If Windows NT hangs during this phase, you can use the `/sos` switch to determine which driver caused the problem.
- `/noserialmice=[COMx|COMx,y,z_]` When Windows NT boots, NTDETECT.COM looks for, among other things, the presence of serial mice. Sometimes this detection routine misfires and identifies modems or other devices as serial mice. Then, when Windows NT loads and initializes, the serial port is unavailable and the device is unusable because Windows NT is expecting a serial mouse. In other instances, the serial mouse detection signal can shut down a UPS connected to the serial port.

  By itself, the `/noserialmice` switch tells NTDETECT.COM not to bother looking for serial mice. Used with a specific COM port(s), NTDETECT.COM still looks for serial mice, but not on the port(s) specified.
- `/crashdebug` The `/crashdebug` switch turns on the Automatic Recovery and Restart feature, which you can also configure using the Control Panel's System application. In fact, when you configure this feature through Control Panel, what you are

doing is merely adding this switch to the OS path in BOOT.INI.

- `/nodebug` Programmers often use a special version of Windows NT that includes debugging symbols useful for tracking down problems in code. This version of Windows NT runs slowly compared to the retail version, owing to the extra overhead in tracking every piece of executing code. To turn off the monitoring in this version of NT, add the `/nodebug` switch to the OS path in BOOT.INI.
- `/maxmem:`*n* Memory parity errors can be notoriously difficult to isolate. The `/maxmem` switch helps. When followed with a numeric value, this switch limits Windows NT's usable memory to the amount specified in the switch. This switch also is useful for developers using high-level workstations, who want to simulate performance on a lower-level machine.
- `/scsiordinal:`*n* If your system has two identical SCSI controllers, you need a way to distinguish one from the other. The `/scsiordinal` switch is used to assign a value of 0 to the first controller and 1 to the second.

An example of the use of some of these switches appears in the `[VGA]` BOOT.INI choice. This choice allows you to boot with a generic video driver to repair a video configuration failure. In the case of that boot choice, the following example BOOT.INI line could accomplish it:

```
multi(0)disk(0)rdisk(0)partition(1)\WINNT=
"Windows NT Workstation ~Version 4.00 [VGA mode]"
➥/basevideo /sos
```

This line uses the `/basevideo` switch to ensure that generic video drivers are used, and it also uses the `/sos` switch to enumerate the drivers as they load. This line is created by default by the Windows NT installation process whenever NT is installed on a computer.

## The Load Process

After the boot portion of the operating system loads, your device drivers are loaded, and the boot process is handed off to the operating system kernel. In Windows NT, this portion of the startup occurs when the screen turns a blue color and the text shrinks. At that point, the kernel is initializing. The operating system begins to read various hives in the Windows NT Registry. One of the first hives read is the CurrentControlSet, which is copied to the CloneControlSet, and from which a HARDWARE key is written to RAM. The System hive is read to determine whether any other drivers need to be loaded into RAM and initialized. When that is complete, the kernel initialization phase ends.

The Session Manager then reads the System hive in the Registry to determine which programs need to run before Windows NT itself is loaded. Typically, the AUTOCHK.EXE program (a stripped-down version of CHKDSK.EXE) runs and reads the file system.

Other programs defined in the HKEY_LOCAL_MACHINE\SYSTEM\CurrentControlSet\Control\SessionManager\BootExecute key are run, and a page file is then created in the location specified by the HKEY_LOCAL_MACHINE\SYSTEM\CurrentControlSet\Control\Session Manager\Memory Management key. The Software hive is read next, and then the Session Manager loads other required subsystems defined in the HKEY_LOCAL_MACHINE\SYSTEM\CurrentControlSet\Control\SessionManager\Subsystems\Required key. This ends the portion of the boot process in which services are loaded into RAM.

NOTE

**Use the Resource Kit Utilities for More Diagnostic Capabilities** The Windows NT Resource Kit contains a more detailed description of the boot process than that presented here. That kit also contains some additional tools for determining which drivers have loaded and for performing other diagnostic functions.

After services are loaded, the Windows WIN32 Subsystem starts to load. This is where Windows NT Workstation switches into a graphics (GUI) mode. The WinLogon module runs, and the Welcome dialog box appears. The Windows operating system is still loading at this point, but the user can enter his username, domain, and password to initiate the logon process. After the Service Controller (SERVICES.EXE) loads and initializes the Computer Browser, Workstation, Server, Spooler, and other services, the request for logon is passed to the domain controller for service.

The SERVICES.EXE program is a central program in the Windows NT operating system. It initializes various system DLL files. Should this file become damaged, you would have to reinstall Windows NT Workstation.

The following DLLs provide operating system services:

- *Alerter (ALRSVC.DLL).* Provides messaging services and event alerts.
- *Computer Browser (BROWSER.DLL).* Provides a way for locating resources on the network.

- *EventLog (EVENTLOG.DLL).* Notes and enters events into the three log files.
- *Messenger (MSGSVC.DLL).* Provides interapplication communications that enable one application to communicate with another.
- *Net Logon (NETLOGON.DLL).* Contains the code required to request resource validation from domain servers.
- *NT LM Security Support Provider (NTMSSOS.DLL).* Provides security support.
- *Server (SRVSVC.DLL).* Enables Windows NT Workstation to provide limited network services to other computers.
- *TCP/IP NetBIOS Helper (lMHSVC.DLL).* Handles IP address resolution.
- *Workstation (WKSSVC.DLL).* Enables a Windows NT Workstation computer to access resources on the network. Workstation includes services that enable the computer to log on to a domain, to connect to shared resources such as printers and directories, and to participate in client/server applications running over the network.

## LastKnownGood Recovery

NOTE

**LastKnownGood Updated at User Logon** A successful logon is considered the completion of the boot process. To mark the event, Windows NT Workstation updates the LastKnownGood control set key in the Registry with information about what was loaded and the current system configuration at startup.

The LastKnownGood configuration provides a method for recovering your previous system setup. When you create a specific configuration for Windows NT, that information is stored in your Registry in a group called a *control set*. The LastKnownGood control set is updated every time you log in, enabling you to recover from a hardware configuration error—provided that you use this method immediately after discovering the error on the first boot attempt and do not try to log on a second time. If you log in with a hardware configuration problem, that will be recorded as part of the LastKnownGood configuration, and you will not be able to use LastKnownGood to recover in the future.

The information contained in the LastKnownGood configuration is stored in the Registry in the HKEY_LOCAL_MACHINE\SYSTEM\CurrentControlSet key.

## STEP BY STEP

### 7.2 Invoking the LastKnownGood Configuration

1. Reboot your system.
2. When a message appears asking you whether you want to boot the LastKnownGood configuration, press the spacebar.
3. From the Hardware Profile/Configuration Recovery menu, select a hardware profile. Then press the L key for the LastKnownGood configuration.

If a critical system error is encountered, Windows NT Workstation might default to the LastKnownGood configuration of its own accord. This isn't always true, but it is a frequent occurrence. Should basic operating system files be damaged, however, you cannot use the LastKnownGood configuration; instead, you must boot up using a boot floppy and then recover your system as described in the next few sections.

## Boot Sequence Errors

The most common boot sequence errors occur when the operating system components required for the boot process cannot be found or are corrupted. Often a modification to the BOOT.INI file leads to a failure to boot properly. If you or your client has recently made a modification to the startup files, you should suspect that to be the problem first.

Catastrophic hardware failure is not a common problem, but it does happen—particularly in older equipment. If a hard drive stops operating, it is obvious because your computer sounds different. Also, when you open the case of the computer and listen to it, you won't hear the hard drive spin up and achieve its operating speed.

Much less obvious are hardware errors that prevent your system from starting but don't appear to alter the performance of your system noticeably. If your hard drive develops a bad disk sector and that sector contains the operating system components responsible for booting your computer, for example, the computer will appear to function correctly. This particular problem can be solved by reestablishing the boot files on another portion of your hard drive.

Certain error messages appear when there is a problem with the BOOT.INI file. If you get one of these error messages and the Windows shell doesn't load, you should suspect the BOOT.INI file and use a boot disk or an emergency repair disk (ERD) to repair the BOOT.INI file. (You will learn how to create an ERD later in this chapter.)

This message indicates that the Windows NT Loader file is either damaged or corrupted:

```
BOOT: Couldn't find NTLDR
Please insert another disk
```

Typically, the error with the NTLDR file occurs early in the boot process.

If you see a repeated sequence of error messages indicating that Windows NT Workstation is checking hardware, there is a problem with the NTDETECT.COM file. Those messages look like this:

```
NTDETECT V1.0 Checking Hardware...
NTDETECT V1.0 Checking Hardware...
NTDETECT V1.0 Checking Hardware...
```

It is possible for Windows NT to load even if the BOOT.INI file is missing. If that is the case, the NTLDR instructs Windows NT to start loading files it finds in the *<default>*\WINNT folder. If the operating system was installed in another location, an error message will appear, indicating that the NTOSKRNL.EXE file is missing or corrupt. The following error message appears when the BOOT.INI file is damaged or when it points to a location that no longer contains the Windows NT Workstation operating system files:

```
Windows NT could not start because the following file is
➥missing or corrupt:
\<winnt root>\system32\ntoskrnl.exe
Please re-install a copy of the above file.
```

This message indicates that the Windows NT operating system kernel has failed to load. The problem most often occurs when someone has inadvertently renamed the folder containing the operating system files without realizing the consequences of that action. The solution is to use your boot disk to gain access to the system and then to rename the folder back to the location specified in the BOOT.INI file. It is less common to see a change in the BOOT.INI file giving rise to this problem because that requires a knowledgeable user's action.

Another potential reason the kernel might not have loaded is that you used the Disk Administrator to create a partition with free space. If you change the number of the partition that contains your Windows NT operating system files, the pointer in the BOOT.INI file will no longer point to the correct location. To fix this problem, you need to edit the pointer and correct the partition number so that BOOT.INI can locate your Windows NT operating system files.

When there is a problem with the boot sector, the following error message appears during startup:

```
I/O Error accessing boot sector file
Multi(0)disk(0)rdisk(0)partition(1):\bootsect.dos
```

This error message may indicate a problem with your hard drive. You should boot from a boot disk and run the RDISK utility.

Windows NT Workstation also posts a more specific message when it can determine that the error in locating the boot sector is hardware related. The operating system checks hardware (as you learned earlier) by testing it during startup. A lack of response to one of those tests generates the following message:

```
OS Loader V4.00
Windows NT could not start because of a computer disk
➥hardware configuration problem.
Could not read from the selected boot disk. Check boot
➥path and disk hardware.
Please check the Windows NT™ documentation about hardware
➥disk configuration and your hardware reference manuals for
additional information.
```

The preceding message might indicate that the pointer in the BOOT.INI file that should locate the Windows NT operating system actually references a damaged or nonexistent device. Or it might mean that the specified partition doesn't contain a file system that Windows NT can access with the boot loader.

Finally, you may see a STOP error if the Windows NT Loader cannot resolve the appropriate partition that contains your operating system files. This error takes the following form:

```
STOP: 0x000007E: Inaccessible Boot Device
```

This error appears when the hard disk controller has difficulty determining which is the boot device—which might happen if your computer contains an Adaptec SCSI disk controller, for example, and there is an ID number conflict. Another instance in which this error occurs is when the master boot record (MBR) is corrupted by a virus or a disk error.

> NOTE
> **SCSI Preferred over IDE** As a general rule, SCSI drives are faster than IDE drives and are preferred by the operating system. Don't mix and match these two drive types. If you have a SCSI disk controller and SCSI drives, use those to store your boot partition.

If your workstation has an internal IDE drive and a SCSI disk drive with an ID number set to 0, you will also see the "inaccessible boot device" error. The 0 ID number is used to specify which disk is the internal disk, and this drive conflicts with a boot partition on the IDE drive. Any bootable SCSI disks may also be booted in preference to your internal IDE drive, so you may want to make all SCSI drives nonbootable to prevent the SCSI disk controller from booting that SCSI drive. (Some disk adapters dynamically assign SCSI device numbers, but they aren't particularly common.) If the Windows NT DETECT program in the boot loader assigns the SCSI bus adapter the number 0, the reference in the BOOT.INI file to your internal IDE drive becomes inaccurate.

If your system proceeds through the load phase and boots correctly but still seems to be malfunctioning, you should check the system event log to see whether any system messages were written to the log.

The system log may display errors, warnings, or informational events that can explain the conditions leading to the anomaly you observed due to an error in the boot sequence. To view the system log, first choose Start, Programs, Administrative Tools, Event Viewer. Then select the Log menu and choose the System Log command to open the system log. Figure 7.4 shows a system log listing various events.

## Boot Disk Recovery

If your hard disk system partition or the files become corrupted, you can start the system from a floppy disk provided you have a recovery disk available and that the boot partition is still intact. After you start your system using the floppy disk, Windows NT will run as normal, and you will be able to repair boot problems.

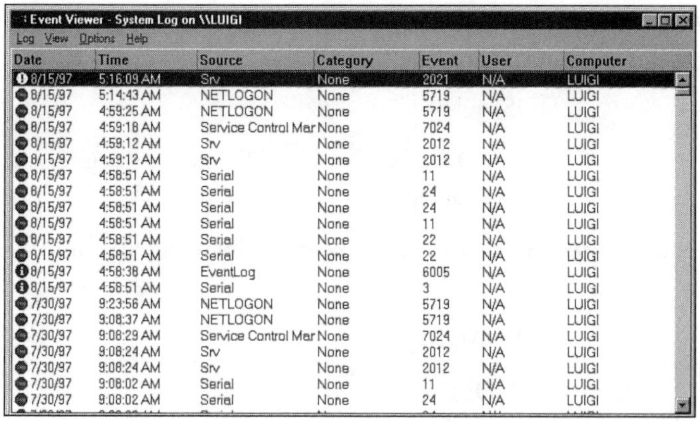

Event Viewer - System Log on \\LUIGI

Log View Options Help

| Date | Time | Source | Category | Event | User | Computer |
|---|---|---|---|---|---|---|
| 8/15/97 | 5:16:09 AM | Srv | None | 2021 | N/A | LUIGI |
| 8/15/97 | 5:14:43 AM | NETLOGON | None | 5719 | N/A | LUIGI |
| 8/15/97 | 4:59:25 AM | NETLOGON | None | 5719 | N/A | LUIGI |
| 8/15/97 | 4:59:18 AM | Service Control Mar | None | 7024 | N/A | LUIGI |
| 8/15/97 | 4:59:12 AM | Srv | None | 2012 | N/A | LUIGI |
| 8/15/97 | 4:59:12 AM | Srv | None | 2012 | N/A | LUIGI |
| 8/15/97 | 4:58:51 AM | Serial | None | 11 | N/A | LUIGI |
| 8/15/97 | 4:58:51 AM | Serial | None | 24 | N/A | LUIGI |
| 8/15/97 | 4:58:51 AM | Serial | None | 24 | N/A | LUIGI |
| 8/15/97 | 4:58:51 AM | Serial | None | 11 | N/A | LUIGI |
| 8/15/97 | 4:58:51 AM | Serial | None | 22 | N/A | LUIGI |
| 8/15/97 | 4:58:51 AM | Serial | None | 22 | N/A | LUIGI |
| 8/15/97 | 4:58:38 AM | EventLog | None | 6005 | N/A | LUIGI |
| 8/15/97 | 4:58:51 AM | Serial | None | 3 | N/A | LUIGI |
| 7/30/97 | 9:23:56 AM | NETLOGON | None | 5719 | N/A | LUIGI |
| 7/30/97 | 9:08:37 AM | NETLOGON | None | 5719 | N/A | LUIGI |
| 7/30/97 | 9:08:29 AM | Service Control Mar | None | 7024 | N/A | LUIGI |
| 7/30/97 | 9:08:24 AM | Srv | None | 2012 | N/A | LUIGI |
| 7/30/97 | 9:08:24 AM | Srv | None | 2012 | N/A | LUIGI |
| 7/30/97 | 9:08:02 AM | Serial | None | 11 | N/A | LUIGI |
| 7/30/97 | 9:08:02 AM | Serial | None | 24 | N/A | LUIGI |

**FIGURE 7.4**
The system log in the Event Viewer application allows you to see successful and unsuccessful system events.

Most computers default to trying the floppy drive as the primary boot device, and then they move to the hard drive should the floppy drive fail. If your computer is configured to start from the hard drive, you must change this in your computer's BIOS setup. Press the keystroke displayed in the startup sequence to open your computer's setup. Then change the boot sequence so it will start from the floppy drive before attempting to boot from a recovery disk. If your Windows NT Workstation computer does not have a floppy drive, you will not be able to use this recovery feature.

A recovery disk contains the same files that are stored on the system partition of your hard disk—the ones that initiate and control the startup process.

## STEP BY STEP

### 7.3 Creating a Recovery Disk

1. Format a floppy disk from within Windows NT. This first step is important because a disk formatted from any other operating system will not boot Windows NT.

2. *For Intel-based servers,* copy the following files onto the disk:

   - NTLDR
   - NTDETECT.COM
   - BOOT.INI

*continues*

NOTE

**Boot Disk Files Are All Generic** The files on the recovery disk are hardware specific, but unlike the Registry, none of them are installation specific. This means that, although you should create a recovery disk before a problem occurs, you could create one later from any Windows NT computer (Workstation or Server) that has the same processor platform. The only tricky part to using a recovery disk created in that way is replacing NTBOOTDD.SYS should your computer need it.

NTBOOTDD.SYS is the driver for a SCSI drive that does not have its BIOS enabled. You can obtain it by copying NTBOOTDD.SYS from another machine with the same SCSI driver or by copying it from the NT Server or Workstation CD. Be aware, however, that this file is not called NTBOOTDD.SYS; it is called by the name of the drive type on the CD. Therefore, you will have to locate the proper driver and copy it to your disk, changing its name to NTBOOTDD.SYS in the process.

*continued*

- BOOTSECT.DOS (if you want to be able to boot to DOS)
- NTBOOTDD.SYS (for SCSI disks without SCSI BIOS enabled)

*For RISC-based servers,* copy the following files onto the disk:

- OSLOADER.EXE
- HAL.DLL
- *.PAL from System partition (for ALPHA-based servers)

3. Modify the BOOT.INI file for the server for which you are creating the boot disk.
4. Test the disk by inserting it into the floppy drive of the machine in which it is to be used and rebooting. If all is well, the disk should initiate boot, and then Windows NT should load normally.

## The Emergency Repair Process

The installation process enables you to create an emergency repair directory and emergency repair disk, both of which are backup copies of Registry information (which come in handy if you can't boot Windows NT because of missing or corrupt files). The emergency repair process can help you fix a troubled Windows NT installation.

### Emergency Repair Directory Versus Emergency Repair Disk

Installation always creates the emergency repair directory. You can find it in <winnt_root>\REPAIR. You can create an emergency repair disk as well. Do you need both? Well, no, not really. The directory serves just as well as the disk unless the directory itself becomes corrupt or the drive itself dies, in which case you're stuck. The disk serves as a backup in case of an extreme emergency.

Both the directory and disk are computer specific, at least in part. Although you can sometimes borrow an emergency repair disk from another computer, you generally should assume otherwise. Keep a separate emergency repair disk for each computer, and tag it with the serial number of the computer because names and locations change over time. Don't leave these disks in the hands of users. Keep them with an administrator in a secure but accessible location.

Table 7.1 lists and describes the files on the emergency repair disk.

**TABLE 7.1**

**FILES ON THE EMERGENCY REPAIR DISK**

| *File* | *Description* |
|---|---|
| SETUP.LOG | A text file that contains the names of all the Windows NT installation files, along with checksum values for each. If any of the files on your hard drive are missing or corrupt, the emergency repair process should detect them with the aid of this hidden, system, and read-only file. |
| SYSTEM._ | A compressed copy of the Registry's System hive. This is the Windows NT control set collection. |
| SAM._ | A compressed copy of the Registry's SAM hive. This is the Windows NT user accounts database. |
| SECURITY.__ | A compressed copy of the Registry's Security hive. This is the Windows NT security information, which includes SAM and the security policies. |
| SOFTWARE._ | A compressed copy of the Registry's Software hive. This hive contains all Win32 software configuration information. |
| DEFAULT._ | A compressed copy of the system default profile. |
| CONFIG.NT | The VDM version of the MS-DOS CONFIG.SYS file. |
| AUTOEXEC.NT | The VDM version of the MS-DOS AUTOEXEC.BAT file. |
| NTUSER.DA_ | A copy of the file NTUSER.DAT (which contains user profile information) from the directory winnt_root\profiles\Defaultuser. |

## RDISK.EXE

Both the emergency repair disk and directory are created during installation, but neither is updated automatically at any time thereafter. To update the emergency repair information, use the hidden utility RDISK.EXE. To start RDISK, choose Start, Run and type **RDISK**. Because RDISK.EXE is in the search path (\<winnt_root>\SYSTEM32), you do not have to specify the full path. Some administrators just add the RDISK program to the Administrative Tools group.

RDISK offers two options for administrators: Update Repair Info and Create Repair Disk (see Figure 7.5). These tasks can be performed only by members of the Administrators group; everyone else will be told that the processes fail.

### Update Repair Info

The Update Repair Info button updates only the emergency repair directory, although it does prompt for the creation/update of an emergency repair disk immediately following successful completion of the directory update. Always update the directory before creating the disk because the disk will be created using the information in the directory.

### Create Repair Disk

If the information in the repair directory is up-to-date, you may choose to create or update an emergency repair disk. You don't have to use a preformatted disk for the repair disk. RDISK formats the disk regardless.

A significant limitation of RDISK that you should definitely know about is that it will not update the DEFAULT._, SECURITY, or SAM files in the repair directory (or disk). In other words, you may update your repair disk week-to-week, but none of your account changes are being backed up. To do a complete emergency repair update, you must run RDISK.EXE using the undocumented `/S` switch. This takes a while, especially if your account database is quite large. It is better, however, than losing all your accounts if and when disaster strikes.

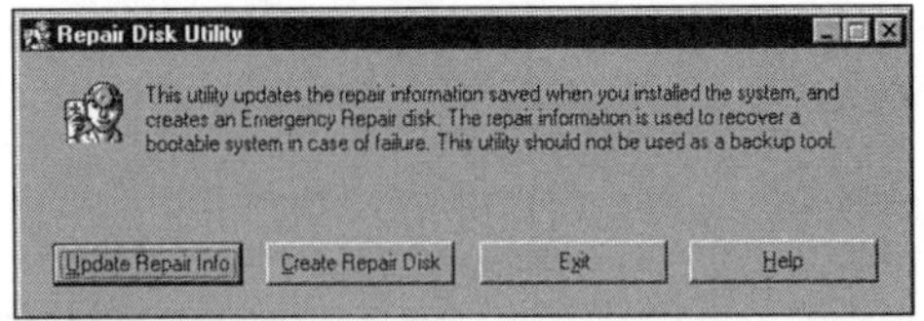


**FIGURE 7.5**
The Emergency Repair Disk utility allows you to update the repair information stored in the \Repair folder and allows you to create a new repair disk based on that information.

## Starting the Emergency Repair Process

Regarding the emergency repair directory and the emergency repair disk, you need to recognize that you can't boot from either or use either from within Windows NT. To actually invoke the emergency repair process, you must access the original three Windows NT Setup disks. If you don't have the original disks handy, you can generate them from the CD by using the `WINNT32` command and the `/OX` switch. Chapter 2, "Installation and Configuration," includes more information on the WINNT32.EXE program. Because these disks are generic, any set will do, regardless of which Windows NT Server machine they were created on. In fact, you can create them from any machine that has a functioning CD-ROM drive (if you don't do it from an NT machine, however, you have to use the `WINNT` command instead of `WINNT32`).

In the installation process, you had the choice to either install Windows NT or repair an existing installation. Pressing R on this screen invokes the emergency repair process. Don't be concerned when the Setup process then continues its pace through the rest of the three setup disks. That is normal.

The emergency repair process gives you several options. You can select any or all of the options in the emergency repair menu. (The default is to undertake all repair options.) After you select your repair options, Setup attempts to locate your hard drive. When it finds your hard drive, Setup asks whether you want to use an emergency repair disk or whether you want Setup to search for your repair directory. You then encounter a series of restoration choices based on the repair options you select and the problems Setup uncovers as it analyzes your system. The next few sections discuss the emergency repair options.

> **WARNING**
>
> **NT Does Not Support an Emergency Repair That Spans More Than One Disk** A large limitation for an NT implementation of any significant size is that the emergency repair information can become larger than a single disk can handle. Unfortunately, if this happens, NT will not prompt you for a second disk when creating the ERD; instead, it will abort with an error message telling you that the emergency repair disk is full. Although failure of this process is beyond the scope of the NT Workstation exam, it would be well worth your while to investigate ways to reduce the size of the total repair package that NT tries to copy to your repair disk. If you search Microsoft TechNet using the term "Emergency Repair," you will find many helpful articles.

### Inspect Registry Files

At this point, the process gets computer-specific. If your Registry becomes corrupt, only your own emergency repair disk can save you—no one else's can. You granularly select to repair any combination of the System, Software, Default, and Security/SAM hives, and these are copied directly from the repair directory or disk. You don't need the original source CD or disks for this procedure.

### Inspect Startup Environment

The files required to boot Windows NT were listed earlier in this chapter. If any of these files is mistakenly deleted or becomes corrupted, choose Inspect Startup Environment to repair them. You can use anyone's emergency repair disk for this option because these files are generic across all Windows NT installations (for the same platform, anyway). You do need to produce the original installation CD, however, before the repair process can replace the files.

> WARNING
>
> **Applied Service Packs May Cause Verification to Fail** If you have applied Service Packs to your Windows NT Server system, validation will fail because Service Packs often modify NT system files. The validation process checks the current system files against the files on the CD-ROM and flags them as being corrupt if they are not the same. However, sometimes files are flagged as being corrupt only because the repair process recognizes the valid changes that the Service Packs have made. You can check this by examining the FILES.LST file on each Service Pack to determine which files have been changed. If you suspect a file is corrupt, replace it, but be sure to reapply the Service Pack after your system has been repaired.

### Verify Windows NT System Files

This option often takes time, but it systematically inspects every file in the Windows NT directory tree and compares each with the checksum values in SETUP.LOG. If it determines that any files are missing or corrupt, the repair process attempts to replace them. Again, you need the original disks or CD when using this option.

### Inspect Boot Sector

If you upgrade to a new version of DOS and suddenly find that you cannot boot to Windows NT anymore, your boot sector probably has been replaced. The MS-DOS or Windows 95 SYS command is notorious for trashing the Windows NT boot sector. The emergency repair disk solves this problem, and you don't even need a computer-specific ERD. You can borrow one from anybody.

## ASSESSING PRINT JOB FAILURES

Choose the appropriate course of action to take when a print job fails.

A single standardized print model under Windows replaces the individual print models of applications under MS-DOS, something more easily understood. The downside is that when problems arise, they affect your entire application suite and maybe an entire workgroup.

Keep in mind that Windows retains the older model for printing for MS-DOS applications that run in Windows NT Workstation from the command prompt. These applications require their own printer drivers to print anything other than ASCII output. If you are using WordPerfect 5.1, for example, you must have both WordPerfect and a printer driver installed. Some MS-DOS applications may require that you turn on the printer port prior to printing by using a command such as this:

```
NET USE LPT1: \\servername\printername
```

One of the benefits of Windows printing is that the operating system handles all print job output in a standardized manner, regardless of the application from which you are printing. Windows NT, being a network operating system, enables you to define network printers that are available as shared resources for other Windows NT Workstations to print to. Any client or server on a network can serve as the print server to a network printer. In addition, you can set up local printers that are not shared to other network computers, but that need to be managed by their owners.

## Understanding the Windows Printing Subsystem

The printing subsystem is modular and works hand-in-hand with other subsystems to provide printing services. When a printer is local, and a print job is specified by an application, data is sent to the Graphics Device Interface (GDI) for rendering into a print job in the printer language of the print device. The GDI is a module between the printing subsystem and the application requesting the printing services. This print job is passed to the spooler, which is a .DLL. The print job is then written to disk as a temporary file so that it can survive a power outage or your computer's reboot. Print jobs can be spooled using either the RAW or the EMF printer language.

The client side of the print spooler is winspool.drv, and that driver makes a Remote Procedure Call (RPC) to the SPOOLSS.EXE server side of the spooler. When the printer is attached to the same computer, both files are located on the same computer. When the printer is attached to a Windows NT Workstation in a peer-to-peer relationship, those files are located on different computers.

SPOOLSS.EXE calls an API that sends the print job to a router (SPOOLSS.DLL), which sends the print job to the computer with the local printer, where the LOCALSPL.DLL library writes the file to disk as a spooled file. At this point, the printer is polled by LOCALSPL.DLL to determine whether the spooled print job is capable of being processed by the printer, and any necessary alterations are made.

The print job is then turned over to a separator page processor and is despooled to the print monitor. The print device receives the print job and raster image processes it to a bitmap file that is then sent to the print engine to be output.

For network printers, the process is very much the same, but client requests and server services are more clearly defined and separate. The routers found in the spooler modules (WINSPOOL.DRV, SPOOLSS.EXE, and SPOOLSS.DLL) are identical to those used for a local printer. A local print provider on the client LOCALSPL.DLL is matched to a remote print provider on the server side (WIN32SP.DLL for Windows print servers or NWPROVAU.DLL for NetWare print servers). In the network printing process, the print processors and print monitors may use several different server DLLs, each one of which is required by a supported operating system.

You generally install a printer using the Add Printer Wizard that you access by choosing Start, Settings, Printers. By stepping through the wizard, you create a virtual printer with a name that you provide. You can create any number of virtual (or logical, if you will) printers that use the same physical printer for a number of purposes. If you want to print differently, to have different security schemes, or to provide different access times, you must create multiple virtual printers. You can then use the following methods of manipulating printers:

- Double-click on the printer to see any spooled jobs, provided you have the privilege to do so.
- Right-click on a printer to view a shortcut menu that provides several actions. You can use this menu to delete a printer that no longer exists, for example. You can use the Default Printer command to set the default printer for a Windows NT Workstation from the shortcut menu.
- Right-click on a printer and select the Properties command from the shortcut menu to access the Printer Properties and modify any number of settings.

## Using a Basic Error Checklist

Any number of things can go wrong when you attempt to print to a printer. In many cases, Windows NT alerts you to an error, and in some cases, Windows NT actually tells you what the error type is.

Here is a standard checklist of the most common solutions to printing problems.

If the print job spools, but it will not print, do the following:

- Make sure that your printer is turned on and that all the connections are secure.
- See if the paper tray is empty and needs to be refilled.
- Make sure a piece of paper is not jammed in the printer.
- Check the printer for an error condition that prevents print processing.

The preceding solutions are so simple that it's easy to waste time and overlook them. It is amazing how many printer problems disappear when you restart your printer. If that fails to work, restart Windows NT Workstation (that is, assuming that your printer worked before you specified the print job).

If none of these solutions seems to work, try the following:

- Verify that the printer you think you printed to is either the default printer or was selected within the application from which the print job was sent.
- Print a simple text file from Notepad. This often verifies whether the print problem is application-specific. Try printing from DOS to test the DOS subsystem if that is the problem environment.
- Print to a different printer, or substitute another printer on the same printer port. This helps determine whether the printer is malfunctioning.
- Check the amount of available hard disk space on your system partition to see whether there was room to create the temporary spooled print file.

- Print to a file, and then copy that file to the printer port in question. If you can print in this manner, you should suspect the spooler or a data-transmission error. Otherwise, you are probably dealing with a hardware, device driver, or application error.

At the very worst, you can try reinstalling the printer and supplying a new or updated printer driver. These are the usual sources of printer drivers:

- The Windows NT operating system distribution disks.
- The setup disks that came with your printer.
- The printer manufacturer's BBS or Web site.
- Microsoft's technical support line. You can contact Microsoft at 206-882-8080. Microsoft's current printer driver library is on the Windows NT Driver Library disk.

If you observe the problem printing to a printer immediately after you install the printer, you should probably suspect a configuration issue. Make sure that you assigned the correct port in the Configure Port dialog box of the Add Printer Wizard. To check port settings after the fact, open a printer's Properties dialog box by right-clicking on the printer in the Printers folder and selecting Properties. In addition, you may suspect that the printer driver is incorrect, especially if you printed a test page after installation and it came out garbled. If the driver is incorrect, you can modify it from the General tab of the printer Properties dialog box.

## STEP BY STEP

### 7.4 Modifying Printer Configuration via the Printer Properties Dialog Box

1. From the Start menu, choose Settings, Printers to open the Printers dialog box.
2. Right-click the printer you are troubleshooting and choose Properties from the shortcut menu.

3. From the General tab, you can change the printer driver and print a test page.
4. From the Port tab, you can configure port settings or change the port to which you are printing.

## Printers As Shared Resources

Network printers are shared resources. You must own the printer (have created or installed it), be an administrator, or be assigned the rights to use a printer in some way to be able to view, modify, and use a printer. Different levels of rights can be assigned by an owner or an administrator. You assign shared rights by selecting the Sharing command on a printer's shortcut menu, which brings up the Sharing tab of the Printer Properties dialog box (see Chapter 3, "Managing Resources," for a review of printer configuration and sharing).

Creating additional printer shares for the same physical printer proves useful for the following reasons:

- Each share can have a different printer setup.
- You can assign different access privileges to groups of users.
- Each group can have different printing priorities.
- You can control access to the printer at different times for each group.
- You can use one share for a network printer and another share name for a local printer.

If a user cannot connect to a printer, he may not have been given the right to access that printer. An administrator will be able to view and modify printers on any Windows NT Workstation.

If you have MS-DOS clients on the network and you want them to see a printer share, you must use a file naming convention that DOS recognizes. Names can be up to eight characters long but cannot contain spaces or any of the following characters:

? * # | \ / = > < %

To hide a printer share, add a dollar sign character to the end of the share name, as in *sharename$*. Any printer with that kind of a name will not show up in the Connect To Printer dialog box that is one of the steps in the Add a Printer Wizard. A user must know that this printer share exists and be able to enter both the correct name and the correct path to the printer share to connect to that printer.

## Solving Print Spooler Problems

Any print job spooled to a printer is written as a temporary file to the %systemroot%\System32\Spool\Printers folder. The file is deleted after the printer indicates that the job has been printed. The most common print spool problem is a lack of available disk space. If you print high-resolution graphics, you might have print jobs as large as 20MB to 80MB per file for a 32-bit image at standard page size. Not surprisingly, it doesn't take many print jobs like that to overwhelm the typical Windows NT Workstation configuration.

WARNING

**Corrupted Spool Files Are Not Deleted** Should your spooled files become corrupted, they will be orphaned and will remain in the spool folder taking up valuable space.

When you print to the spooler, two files are created for each print job: an .SPL file, which is the actual print job spool file, and an .SHD file, which is a shadow file. The shadow file contains additional information about the print job that is not part of the print job itself, such as its owner, priority, and so forth. If your computer crashes, .SPL and .SHD files remain in the default spool file until the service restarts and they are processed and printed. After they are printed, these files are deleted from disk.

You can print directly to a printer from your application by turning off the print spooling feature. Before you print, open the Scheduling tab of the Printer Properties dialog box and select the Print Directly to the Printer radio button. When the printer next becomes available, your document prints. Until that point, you cannot use the application from which you sent the print job. However, you can task switch to another application and continue working until your printing application becomes available again.

### Spooler Performance Problems

You can solve spooler performance problems by increasing the priority that Windows NT Workstation assigns to the Spooler service. By default, Windows NT assigns this service a rating of 7, which is consistent with other background processes. You can increase the rating to 9 to improve the performance of the spooler to the level of a foreground operation. Only consider doing this, however, as a temporary measure to print a large print job or if your workstation is used heavily as a print server. Changing this rating permanently degrades the performance of other services and applications on the workstation.

To change the priority of the Spooler service, open the REGEDT32 application and change the value of the PriorityClass of type REG_DWORD in the following key:

HKEY_LOCAL_MACHINE\System\CurrentControlSet\Control\Print

Set that value to the priority class required. If you enter a value of 0 or no value, NT substitutes with the default value for a background process, which is 7 for Windows NT Workstation.

NOTE

**Defragmentation of Hard Drives Improves Printer Performance**
One very simple and effective way to improve printer performance is to defragment your hard drive on a regular basis.

## Changing the Default Spool Folder

Should you run out of room on your system partition for spooled print jobs, you can specify a different default spool folder. You make such a change in the Advanced tab of the Server Properties dialog box, which you access by double-clicking on the Server icon in Control Panel.

**STEP BY STEP**

### 7.5 Changing the Location of Spooled Documents

1. Create a new spool directory.
2. Choose Start, Settings, Printers.
3. Open the File menu and select the Server Properties command.
4. Click the Advanced tab, and then enter the location of the spool file directory.
5. Click OK.

You may want to create the spool folder on an NTFS volume and set security for this folder. You can edit the Registry to change the value of the DefaultSpoolDirectory of type REG_SZ in the following key of the Registry:

> HKEY_LOCAL_MACHINE\System\CurrentControlSet\Control \Print\Printers

After you enter the new folder and its path, save the change and restart your machine to put the change into effect. Any spooled job in the original location will be lost but will not be deleted. You must delete the TEMP file manually.

If you want to, you can assign an individual spooled folder for each virtual printer. Find your printers in the following key:

> HKEY_LOCAL_MACHINE\System\CurrentControlSet\ Control\Print\~Printers*printername*

Then enter the folder and its path as the data in the SpoolDirectory value for that key. Again, you need to restart the workstation to effect the change.

## Enabling Printer Logging

You can enable event logging for your spooler by adding a check mark to the Enable Spooler Event Logging check box on the Advanced tab. Doing so enables you to track who has used a printer, when the person used it, and what he or she requested.

---

**STEP BY STEP**

### 7.6 Enabling Auditing on a Printer

1. Enable file and object access auditing in the User Manager.
2. To enable printer auditing for a specific printer share, open the Security tab of the Printer Properties dialog box and click the Auditing button.
3. In the Printer Auditing dialog box, click the Add button (see Figure 7.6).

4. In the Add Users and Groups dialog box, select a group or user to be audited.
5. Click OK to return to the Printer Auditing dialog box.
6. Select a user or group, and then click the check boxes in the Events to Audit section to track events you want to log for that particular user and group.
7. Click OK.

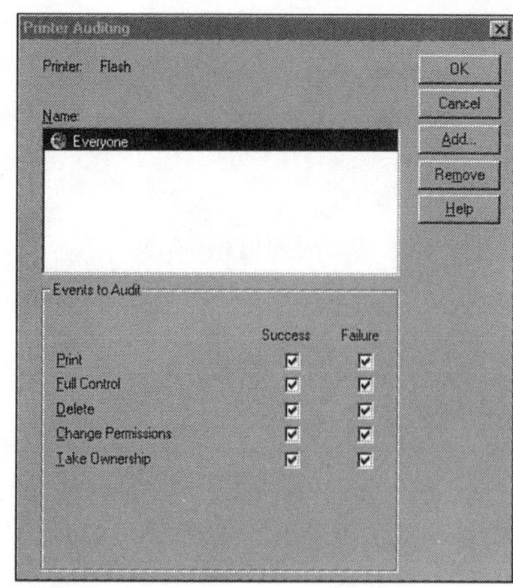


**FIGURE 7.6**
The Printer Auditing dialog box allows you to configure auditing to track printer use and access.

Use the Event Viewer utility in the Administrative Tools folder to view logged events.

## Using the Print Troubleshooter

To help you solve printer problems, Windows NT comes with an interactive printing troubleshooter that's part of the online Help system.

### STEP BY STEP

#### 7.7 Accessing the Print Troubleshooter

1. Choose the Help command from the Start menu.
2. Click on the Index tab, and then enter the keyword **troubleshooting** into the Type the Word(s) You Want to Find text box (see Figure 7.7).
3. Double-click on the problem type and follow the instructions in the Help system.

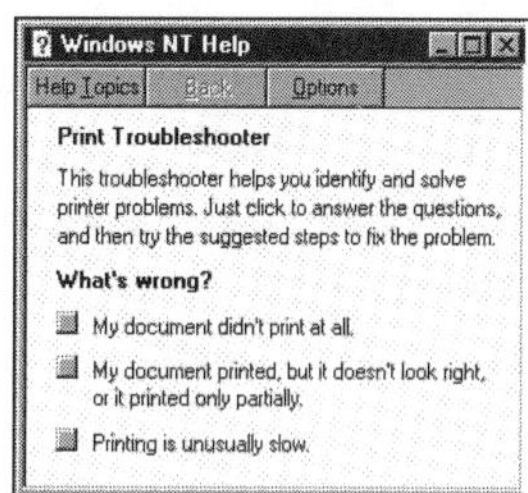


**FIGURE 7.7**
The Print Troubleshooter topic in the Help system guides you through systematic printer troubleshooting.

Printers are among the most important network resources in many organizations. Therefore, you will be called on often to solve problems that crop up with printer shares and printer hardware. This section reviewed some of the most common problems.

# ASSESSING INSTALLATION FAILURES

Choose the appropriate course of action to take when the installation process fails.

The Windows NT Setup program makes installation errors much less common than they used to be. Several categories of errors may still occur after an installation, but they are also easier to track down and eliminate.

## Installation Disk Errors and Upgrades

Infrequently, there will be a problem with the CD that you have obtained to perform the Windows NT Workstation installation. Typically, a Read error is posted; less frequently, the installation may not complete itself and you may not be able to determine why.

To obtain a replacement disk, contact Microsoft at 800-426-9400. Have your registration number handy; the sales and support staff requires it to process your request. New media requests under the warranty are generally sent without cost. If the upgrade is a slipstream upgrade, however, you may be charged postage.

A note about slipstream upgrades and Service Packs is also in order. Many small problems are often repaired as part of a minor version change in the operating system. If you have a problem related to an installation, either get the latest version of the operating system from Microsoft or download any available Service Pack from the Microsoft Web site.

NOTE

**Download and Install the Latest Service Pack** A Service Pack is a self-running program that modifies your operating system. It isn't uncommon within the lifetime of an operating system to have two or three Service Packs. As of the writing of this book, Service Pack 4 was available in Beta form for Windows NT Workstation 4.0. You should try to install the latest Service Pack because it generally solves a lot more problems than it creates.

## Inadequate Disk Space

The Windows NT's Setup program examines the partition that you specify you want Windows NT Workstation installed in for the amount of free space it contains. If you don't have adequate free space, the installation stops and fails. At that point, you need to take corrective action to proceed with the installation.

In some respects, the Setup program is both smart and stupid. It protects your files in the Recycle Bin by not deleting them, which is wise. On the other hand, it leaves any number of .TEMP files that could be safely deleted scattered about your disk.

To free up some room on your disk, consider doing any of the following:

- Empty your Recycle Bin.
- Delete any .TEMP files you find in the various locations they are stored in (for example, the Print Cache folder).
- Delete any files you find in your Internet browser's cache folder or any other cache folder you have.
- Uninstall any programs you no longer need.
- Compress any files you use only on an infrequent basis.
- Go into the Disk Administrator and change the size of the system partition that you want to use for your installation.
- Create a new partition with adequate room for the installation.
- Compress your NTFS partition to make more room.
- Search for and delete all .TMP or .TEMP files

Several other methods enable you to reclaim or recover lost disk space, and it's possible to get really creative in this area. The methods listed here, however, are often sufficient to help you get over the crunch.

## Disk Configuration Errors

If you inherit a configuration with a nonsupported SCSI device adapter, you may not be able to boot your newly installed Windows NT Workstation operating system. If that happens, boot to a different operating system and try starting WINNT on the installation CD. You can also use a network installation to try to rectify the problem. If none of these solutions works, you may be forced to replace the adapter with one recommended on the Hardware Compatibility List.

NOTE **Check All Hardware Against the Latest HCL** The best way to ensure that you are using hardware compatible with Windows NT Workstation is to check the Hardware Compatibility List (HCL) to see whether the device is approved for use and supported.

## Inability to Connect to a Domain Controller

The error message `Cannot Connect to a Domain Controller` is one of the more common error messages you might see when you install Windows NT Workstation, change your hardware configuration, or change network settings. There are a number of potential solutions to this problem.

Carefully verify that you are entering the correct username and password and that the Caps Lock key is not on. The next thing you should check is to make sure that the account name you are using is listed in the User Manager for Domains on the primary domain controller. An incorrect password generates a different error message than does the lack of user account. You should also check to see whether the machine account has been added to the User Manager for the primary domain controller.

Next, open the Network Control Panel and confirm that the network bindings are properly installed on the Bindings tab. Some bindings, such as TCP/IP, require not only computer names, but also IP addresses and subnet masks. If two machines on the network have the same IP address, you get an error condition. Failure to enter the subnet mask also prevents your workstation from finding and connecting to a domain controller to get its network identity properly verified.

The failure to connect to a domain controller is a very common problem. Unfortunately, the error message isn't descriptive of the problem.

## Domain Name Error

If you make a mistake selecting the domain name, you get an error message when you attempt to log on. The solution is obvious when you realize what the problem is. Just go back and select the correct domain name.

## ASSESSING APPLICATION FAILURES

Choose the appropriate course of action to take when an application fails.

Unlike in MS-DOS and earlier versions of Windows, an application failure in NT Workstation won't bring your system to a complete halt. Most application failures are recoverable, and in many cases, you won't even need to reboot your computer to re-establish a working configuration. That is not to say that a system crash is impossible—it just happens very infrequently.

Most often the worst actors are applications written for MS-DOS or 16-bit Windows applications. These programs tend to crash more frequently than do 32-bit Windows applications (which is a good reason to upgrade).

When an application malfunctions, bring up the Task Manager and shut the process down. You can access the Task Manager by using either your keyboard or your mouse (which is useful in case either is hung up by the malfunction).

### STEP BY STEP

#### 7.8 Closing an Application Using Your Keyboard

1. Press Ctrl+Alt+Delete to open the Windows NT Security dialog box.
2. Press the Tab key repeatedly until the Task Manager button is selected, and then press Enter to open the Task Manager.
3. Press the Tab key until one of the tabs at the top of the dialog box is selected, and then use the right or left arrow key to move to the Applications tab (see Figure 7.8).
4. Tab into the applications list and use the up and down arrow keys to select the offending application.
5. Press Tab until the End Task button is selected, and then press Enter to shut down the application.
6. Press Alt+F+X to exit the Task Manager.

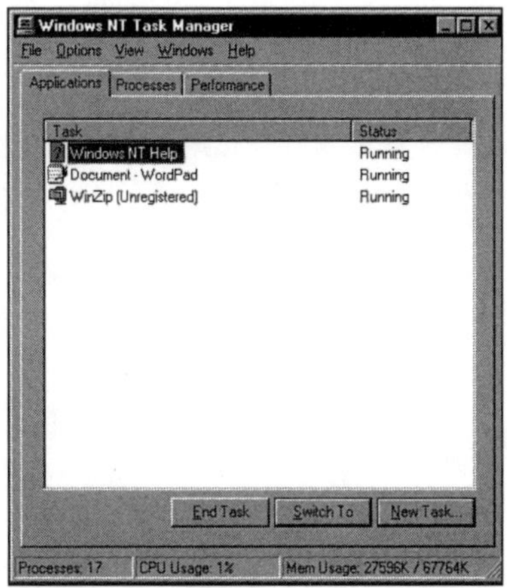


**FIGURE 7.8**
The Applications tab of the Task Manager allows you to terminate unresponsive applications.

If your keyboard is unresponsive or if you just prefer to use your mouse, you can close an unresponsive application using the mouse.

**STEP BY STEP**

**7.9 Closing an Application Using Your Mouse**

1. Right-click the taskbar and choose Task Manager from the menu that appears.
2. Click the Applications tab, and then select the application you want to terminate.
3. Click the End Task button to shut down the task.
4. Choose the File, Exit Task Manager command to close the Task Manager.

## Using the Application Log

Many errors are logged into the Application log for native Windows NT applications. The developer of the application determines the events that are logged, their codes, and meanings. Often an application's manual or online Help system documents what events will appear in the Application log, as well as your ability to control the events that are noted.

## Service Failures

Some applications run as services on Windows NT Workstation. Internet Information Server's three tools (WWW, FTP, and Gopher), for example, are all services. Services are started, stopped, and paused either from within their central administrative tool (for IIS that tool is the Internet Service Manager) or from within the Services Control Panel. If you want to configure a service so that it runs automatically when your workstation boots, more often than not you will set this from the Services application in Control Panel.

Sooner or later, though it's sad to say, you will see the following infamous error message when your Windows NT Workstation starts up after the load phase:

```
One or more services failed to start. Please see the Event
➥Viewer for details.
```

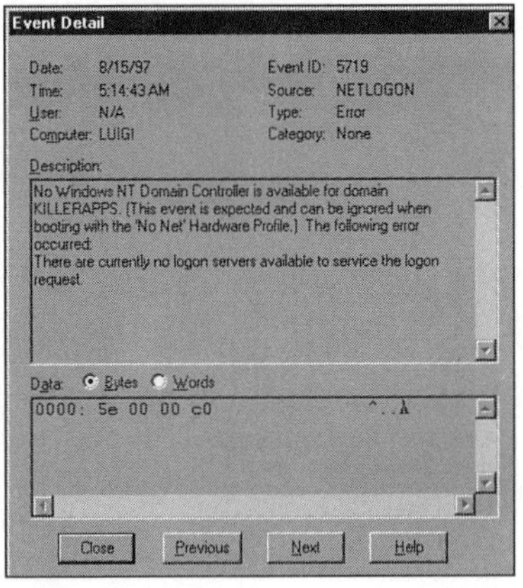


**FIGURE 7.9**
The Event Detail dialog box gives you detailed information about an event in the Event Log.

When you open the Event Viewer, you will be able to analyze the cause of the failure or, at least, the result. Open the System log using the Event heading in the Event Viewer and look for an Event code of 6005. That code marks an informational message that indicates the EventLog service has started. Any event prior to that is a boot event and should be resolved. Double-click on an event message to view an Event Detail dialog box (see Figure 7.9).

One of the problems with the Event Viewer is the cryptic nature of its messages. Another is the fact that the messages logged often show only the result, and not the cause of a failure. For example, in Figure 7.10, you see the System log of an NT Workstation.

As you can see in Figure 7.10, this workstation has recorded three separate logon events (numbered 6005), each of which is marked by the starting of the EventLog service. Two of these were successful; however, the middle one was not. The last event recorded in the unsuccessful login was a failure in the NetLogon service; in fact, the detail indicates that a domain controller could not be located for logon validation. When that error occurred, an actual error message was displayed to the user informing him that an error had occurred. Unfortunately, a number of things could cause such an error. For example, this error could be caused by any of the following:

- No domain controller is present on the network.
- Although there is a domain controller, the workstation does not share a protocol with it.
- The Workstation service for the NT Workstation has not been configured to start at system start.
- The NetLogon service was not configured to start during startup.
- The network adapter has been configured incorrectly.

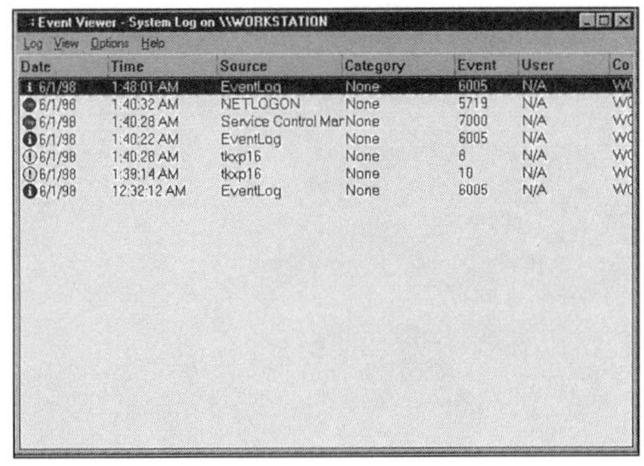


**FIGURE 7.10**
The System log in the Event Viewer can be used to determine the cause of service failure.

- The network adapter is broken.
- The network cable is simply not connected to the computer properly (which happens to be the problem in this case).

Because many services depend on others to start properly, you can't stop at a single error and decide to fix it without first looking at the other errors that occurred in the same time frame. If you look at Figure 7.10 again, you'll see that a Service Control Manager message indicated the adapter driver didn't start because of a faulty device. Then, just before the EventLog message, you'll see two warnings about the tkxp16 device (which is the token ring adapter card on this workstation). One indicates that the adapter could not be opened; the other indicates a "lobe wire fault," which means the cable connections should be checked.

By looking through all of the error messages, you can often detect the source of the problem instead of being hung up looking at the results of the problem. Had you simply stopped at the error that said you couldn't log on, you might have spent a good deal of time trying to figure out where the domain controller in your domain was and why it wasn't responding. Unfortunately, not only are those searches frequently fruitless, but they often cause a troubleshooter to reconfigure components that were never faulty to begin with.

This illustrates the interconnected nature of services and device startup. This chapter will not even attempt to provide a detailed analysis of these interrelationships because such an analysis requires advanced knowledge of Windows NT architecture and the Registry. What can be said is that if services fail on startup, the Event Log will give you an idea where to look for solutions. Begin with the messages around the start of the Event Log because it is close to the start of NT startup. Work your way up the list to determine what failed first, and then look at what failed as a result. By seeking out the initial problem, you will be able to get to the root of the problem sooner than if you try to treat all the resulting symptoms (which may cause you much frustration and may cause you to reconfigure a service that is not in error).

# ASSESSING USER RESOURCE ACCESS FAILURES

Choose the appropriate course of action to take when a user cannot access a resource.

In order to access a resource in Windows NT, you must meet three criteria:

1. You must have a name and password recognized by the NT computer the resource is on.
2. The resource must be available to you from where you are.
3. You must be given permission to use the resource.

If someone is having trouble accessing a resource, any or all of the preceding could be the problem.

## Usernames and Passwords

In an environment in which an NT Workstation is participating in a workgroup, a user will log on to a local NT Workstation and then access local or network resources. In order for the user to access resources on the local or network computers, the account and password combination the user logs in with must also be valid on the machine that holds the resource. This means that if a user logs in to an NT Workstation with the name Fred using a password of *password* and then tries to access a resource on another Workstation, that Workstation must have an account called Fred for which the password is *password.* Failing that, the user attempting to access the resource must be able to provide a valid name and password combination to the NT Workstation that holds the resource if he or she is challenged for such a username and password.

For example, if a user is logging in to a domain from an NT Workstation, the user must have a valid user account in the domain and must be able to provide the password for it. Assuming she supplies that information, the account she specifies must be recognized by all the machines that hold resources the user wants to access—just like in a workgroup). Fortunately, in a domain environment, most of the machines that have available resources also belong to the domain and will, therefore, recognize the user's account.

If a user cannot log on, a number of problems could be preventing it:

- The user may be using an incorrect name or password.
- The user's account may be disabled (by the Administrator) or locked out (because of too many incorrect passwords).
- The password may have expired (which requires a password change).

The problem of an incorrect name is easily remedied: Simply have the user log on using a valid username. If one is not available, create one using User Manager. The password problem is also easily remedied: Make sure the user is using the correct capitalization for the password (remember that passwords in Windows NT are case sensitive). If that fails, you can go into the User Manager (logged in as an Administrator), reset the password to something known, and then have the user log in again.

If the user's account is disabled from the User Manager, the account can be enabled again by an administrator going into User Manager and clearing the Account Disabled check box in the user's properties. If the user's account has been locked out because of too many incorrect password attempts, the account can be unlocked by an administrator going into User Manager and clearing the Account Locked check box in the user's properties. If the account has been locked because the user forgot his or her password, you may also have to change the password to something the user knows to prevent future lockouts.

If the user's password has expired, the user simply has to change his or her password from the Login dialog box. If this is not possible, you will have to enter User Manager and reset the password from the user's account properties.

If you hear that many users are having problems with passwords expiring too frequently or lockout happening too often, you might want to change the account policy in User Manager. The account policy controls how frequently passwords expire, the lockout policy, and other password features.

## STEP BY STEP

### 7.10 Changing Password Options

1. Open the User Manager by choosing Start, Programs, Administrative Tools.
2. Choose the Account command from the Policies menu.
3. In the Account Policy dialog box, select the options you desire, and then click OK (see Figure 7.11).

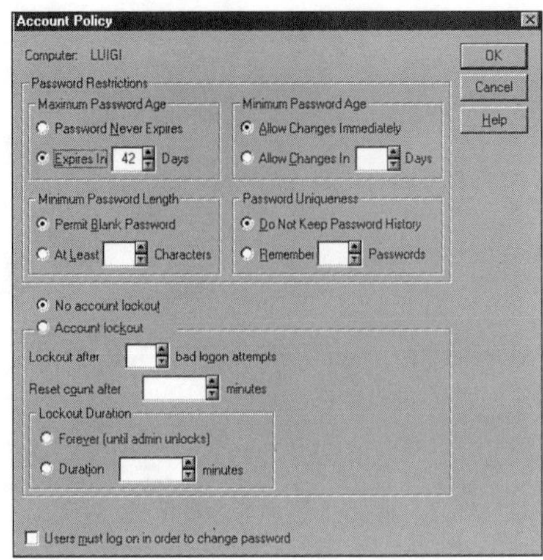


**FIGURE 7.11**
The Account Policy dialog box gives you a forum for modifying password options for all users on your Windows NT Workstation.

The following account policy options pertain to this discussion:

- Minimum and maximum password age before a password expires
- The minimum length of a password
- Whether blank or no character passwords are permitted
- Whether a password list is maintained for an account and allows the user to cycle between passwords
- How many failed attempts to log on to a given account results in an account lockout

If you use the Account Lockout feature, it is important to enter a Lockout Duration. After an account is locked for that duration, it becomes useable again and a user can again attempt to access the account.

To change your own password, you can press Ctrl+Alt+Delete and then click the Change Password button in the Windows NT Security dialog box (see Figure 7.12). The use of the Ctrl+Alt+Delete keystroke to initiate a logon or password change is meant to prevent the posting of a spoofed Password Change dialog box, that is, a program written to simulate a logon dialog box that would thereby allow a hacker to steal your user and password combination.

After the user logs on properly, the next step requirement for accessing resources is that the resource must be available on the network.

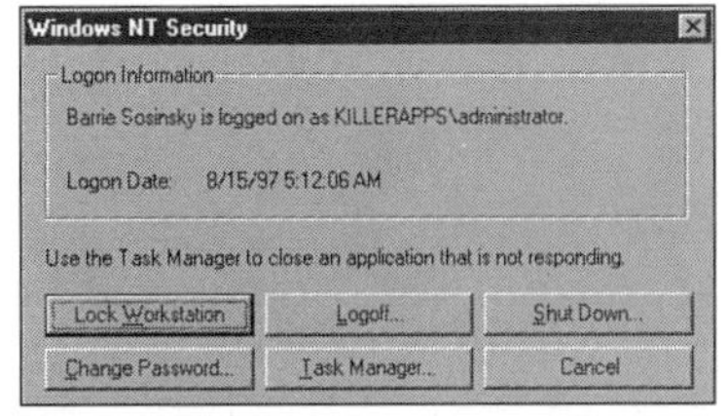


**FIGURE 7.12**
The Windows NT Security dialog box appears when you press the key combination Ctrl+Alt+Delete.

## Resource Availability

A frequent cause of access problems is that resources are simply not available to the user over the network. Even when the user provides a username and password that the machine sharing the resource accepts, the problem of resource availability might still be present. In order for users to access a resource over the network, the following criteria must be met:

- The machine holding the resource must be accessible.
- The machine must be booted with the Server service started.
- The resource must be shared.
- Printer resources must be functioning properly.

It may seem obvious to say that the machine must be accessible, but remember that not all users understand the way networks operate. The machine must be on the same LAN segment (either physical or logical), or there must be some way to access it through a router. If a user calls to tell you that she cannot access a resource on a computer, she may not understand that when she moves a laptop from one location to another, certain resources might not be available. In addition, logical accessibility is required. The computer from which the user is trying to access a resource must be running the same protocol as the machine sharing the resource. In addition, some protocols have configuration settings that must be the same for both machines. For example, the TCP/IP addresses must share the same network address or be passed through a router. If TCP/IP addresses are configured manually, it's possible that the address has been changed by a well-meaning user who was trying to make it easier to remember the IP address of a machine.

It may also seem obvious to say that a machine must be booted. But that can also be a cause of access problems. If a machine is not booted with the operating system that is sharing the resources, the resources will not be available. Similarly, if the machine is down for maintenance or if it has crashed, it will have to be restarted or repaired before resources will be available again. In addition, if the user is attempting to access resources on an NT machine, the capability of sharing resources is dependent on having the Server service running. If it is not running, no resources will be available on the network. This can be checked from the Services dialog box (accessible by double-clicking the Services icon in the Control Panel). If the Server service is not running, you should start it. If it cannot be started, verify that the network adapter is functioning correctly and is configured correctly.

Finally, the resource must be shared. A user may be used to logging in to a specific machine and locally accessing a resource. That user is then surprised when the resource is not available elsewhere. Make sure that the resource has been shared for general use because, unlike NetWare resources, nothing is shared by default on an NT machine.

In the case of shared printers, they must have been configured properly and shared, just like files. Establishing this configuration includes making sure that the physical setup is correct, that the correct drivers have been installed, and that the print device is turned on and has paper in it.

The final stumbling block to resource access is permission to use the resource.

## Resource Permissions

If a user has logged in properly and the resource is available on the network but the user cannot access it, the problem is probably related to permissions. As you learned in Chapter 3, permissions can be applied to shared resources or to local resources (provided that the resources are on volumes formatted with NTFS). If a user can see a resource in Network Neighborhood but is denied access, or if he can read a file but cannot change it, permissions are probably to blame.

Check the share-level permissions, check the NTFS permissions, and check to see if the user is part of a group that has been assigned No Access. Remember that permissions of the same type (share-level or NTFS) are cumulative for the user and all groups the user belongs to, except when one of those is No Access, in which case the user gets no access. Also remember that if share-level and NTFS permissions are both present, the least of the permissions becomes the effective permission.

Printer permissions interact the same as file permissions, and you will need to check what users and groups have what access in order to determine if a user ought to have permission to access a resource and what the access needs to be changed to if it is inappropriate.

# MODIFYING THE REGISTRY

Modify the Registry using the appropriate tool in a given situation.

The Registry is hierarchical, and each branch is referred to as a hive. Individual sub-branches are called keys, each of which is a binary file. The top or first key of a hive is the primary key, and each key is composed of subkeys that take value entries. Most Registry entries are permanent, although some are session dependent, transient, and never written to disk. An example of a transient key is the HKEY_LOCAL_MACHINE\Hardware, which is generated via automatic hardware detection by the Hardware Recognizer (NTDETECT.COM for Intel computers). The Hardware key is an example of a session value. Another transient value is the information written as part of a logon for a session, including security tokens.

When you install software, either a program or a part of the operating system (such as a device driver or service) writes new subkeys and value entries to the Registry. Uninstall these components to remove the information. Subkeys and value entries store information about hardware settings, driver files, and environmental variables that need to be restored—basically anything the application developer requires reference to.

Only members of the Administrators and Power Users groups can access the Registry by default. You can assign other users rights to modify all or part of the Registry by hives, but you should think long and hard before doing so. The potential to compromise security or corrupt an installation is high. By default, all users can see the Registry files, but they cannot edit, delete, or copy Registry files without specific permission to do so.

## Using the Registry Editor

You use the Registry Editor to view and modify the Windows NT Registry. Of the two versions of the Registry Editor, REGEDT32.EXE and REGEDIT.EXE, the former is more generally useful and offers more options.

To discourage their casual use, Microsoft did not include these programs on the Start menu or in the Administrative Tools folder where you might expect to find them. These programs are located in the WINNT folder, but you can add them to your Start menu if you want.

Whenever you change a setting in a Control Panel application or alter your desktop, you are writing changes to the Registry associated with the user account profile with which you logged on. If you want to view and modify Registry information relating to services, resources, drivers, memory, display, or network components, you can use the Windows NT Diagnostic program (WinMSD). This utility is found in the <*System Root*>\System32 folder or in the Administrative Tools folder on the Programs submenu of the Start menu. When you make a change in WinMSD, you are limited in what you can alter and protected from making destructive changes.

> WARNING
>
> **Proceed with Caution** When you alter a value in the Registry using the Registry Editor, the changes you can make are unlimited—and can be hazardous to your computer's health. If you delete or modify a required key, you could cause your computer to malfunction. The only recovery methods you can count on in that instance are reinstalling Windows NT or using the repair disk. Proceed with caution when working in the Registry, and consider wandering around with the files opened as read-only (choose the Read Only command from the Registry Editor menu) to begin with.

The following list outlines the six root keys and their subtrees:

- *HKEY_CLASSES_ROOT.* This subtree stores OLE, file, class, and other associations that enable a program to launch when a data file is opened. Although HKEY_ CLASSES_ROOT is displayed as a root key, it is actually a subkey of HKEY_LOCAL_MACHINE\Software.
- *HKEY_CURRENT_USER.* All user settings, profiles, environment variables, interface settings, program groups, printer connections, application preferences, and network connections for each user are stored in the subkeys of this root key.
- *HKEY_LOCAL_MACHINE.* This subkey contains information that identifies the computer on which the Registry is stored. Information in this key includes settings for hardware such as memory, disk drives, network adapters, and peripheral devices. Any software that supports hardware (such as device drivers, system services, system boot parameters, and other data) is also stored in this subkey.
- *HKEY_USERS.* All data on individual user profiles is stored in this subkey. Windows NT stores local profiles in the Registry, and the values are maintained in this subkey.
- *HKEY_CURRENT_CONFIG.* This key contains the current configuration for software and any machine values. Among the settings stored in this root key are display device setup and control values required to restore the configuration when the program is launched or your computer starts up.

- *HKEY_DYN_DATA.* This last key in the Windows NT Registry holds transient or dynamic data. This root key cannot be modified by the user.

When the system loads the Registry, most of the data is stored in the HKEY_LOCAL_MACHINE and HKEY_USERS keys.

If you make a mistake and delete a key or value in the Registry Editor, you cannot use an Undo command to recover from the error. However, turning on the Confirm On Delete command on the Options menu offers a limited safeguard. But even that isn't foolproof; as everyone knows, it is easy to confirm a deletion and repent the mistake later. The only way to undo an important Registry deletion is to use the LastKnownGood configuration.

## STEP BY STEP

### 7.11 Reversing a Critical Deletion

1. Close the Registry Editor.
2. Immediately restart your computer.
3. Hold down the spacebar as Windows NT loads and select the LastKnownGood option.

When Windows NT boots your system this way, it uses the backup copy of the Windows NT Registry. Any changes you made to your system since your last startup are discarded. The LastKnownGood configuration at least enables you to recover from any critical deletion you might make in the Registry—provided that you recognize the error before you log on to your computer successfully again.

## Backing Up the Registry

The most important thing you can do to protect your system's configuration is to back up the Registry files. When you create an ERD (as described earlier in this chapter), you back up specific hives of the Registry. You should keep a full backup of the Registry on hand.

The Registry files are located in the %system root% \System32\Config folder. For most installations, the %system root% is typically C:\WINNT. Individual users' Registry data is written to the NTUSER.DAT file stored in that user's folder at the location C:\WINNT\Profiles\<*username*>\NTUSER.DAT. When a user logs on to his workstation, a Profile folder is created for him with an NTUSER.DAT file that will hold his user profile. Roaming profiles for a domain are stored in the original copy of the NTUSER.DAT file on the domain controller.

The following CONFIG folder files store direct information on Registry hives:

- DEFAULT
- NTUSER.DAT
- SAM
- SECURITY
- SOFTWARE
- SYSTEM
- USERDIFF
- USERDIFR

Several files are associated with each Registry hive in the CONFIG folder. The first and primary file takes no extension. The CONFIG directory also contains auxiliary files for the Registry, which are the backup, log, and event files. These files have the same names as in the preceding list, but they have .LOG, .EVT, or .SAV extensions. The System file also has a SYSTEM.ALT file associated with it. The .EVT event files are viewable in the Event Viewer and contain audited events. .LOG files store changes that can be rolled back. The .SAV files are part of the LastKnownGood boot configuration that enables you to restore your Registry based on your last booted session. (The LastKnownGood option was described earlier in this chapter.)

The .LOG file is a backup file that enables changes to be rolled back. It serves as a fault-tolerance feature because changes are written to the .LOG file first. When the data is completely written in the .LOG file, the process of updating the matching Registry hive begins. First, the data section to be changed is marked, and then the data is transferred. When the data transfer is completed, the update flag is reset to indicate successful transfer. Should there be a problem or should your computer malfunction during the transfer, the update is started again from scratch.

The SYSTEM file is updated in a somewhat different manner because your computer relies on that key to start up. The duplicate SYSTEM.ALT file operates as the replacement for a .LOG file, and the entire file is mirrored and replicated. Then in the event of a crash, the backup file is used, and the entire file is replaced.

It is unnecessary to back up the entire Registry. Much of the information is transitory and session-dependent. Only specific portions of the Registry need be protected. The files of greatest importance are the SYSTEM and SOFTWARE files. They are generally small and can fit on a single floppy disk. You should also note that the SAM and SECURITY files can't be modified and cannot be copied or backed up.

To back up the Registry, use the RDISK program described earlier in this chapter and set that option. Do not try to copy the files directly to a disk. You can also back up individual hive files from within the Registry Editor by saving a branch using the Save Key command on the Registry menu. You can use the Restore Key command to load those backup files.

The hives of the Registry are locked and cannot be accessed to be copied directly. In a dual-boot system, or if you boot your system using MS-DOS or some other operating system, these files are not locked and may be copied directly. You could copy those files to another drive or volume.

You can view Registry files on a FAT volume from any other operating system. If the file system is an NTFS volume, only a Windows NT or Linux system running a disk access utility can view, read them, and copy the files. On Windows NT, one program that can do this is NTFSDOS.EXE.

For a temporary copy of a key, use the Restore Volatile command instead of the Restore Key command. Restore Volatile loads the key in the Registry Editor, but it does not load that key again in a future session after your computer reboots.

## Changing the Registry Size

Normally, the default size of the Windows NT Workstation Registry is sufficient for most configurations. If you have a large organization and store a lot of user profiles and application data configurations, you may find that the Registry runs out of room. Then you may need to alter the maximum size of the Registry.

### STEP BY STEP

#### 7.12 Changing the Maximum Registry Size

1. Double-click the System icon in the Control Panel folder.
2. Click the Performance tab, and then click the Change button in the Virtual Memory section to view the Virtual Memory dialog box (see Figure 7.13).
3. Enter a size in the Maximum Registry Size (MB) text box, and then click OK.

The Registry size can be somewhat larger than the value entered in the System application of Control Panel. It is related to the size of your paging file, which is related to the amount of installed RAM in your system. When the Registry exceeds the size you set, it brings your system to a halt with a STOP error. This problem very rarely occurs unless you attempt to reduce the size of the Registry artificially. Keep a maximum Registry size about 2MB larger than the current size in the Virtual Memory dialog box.

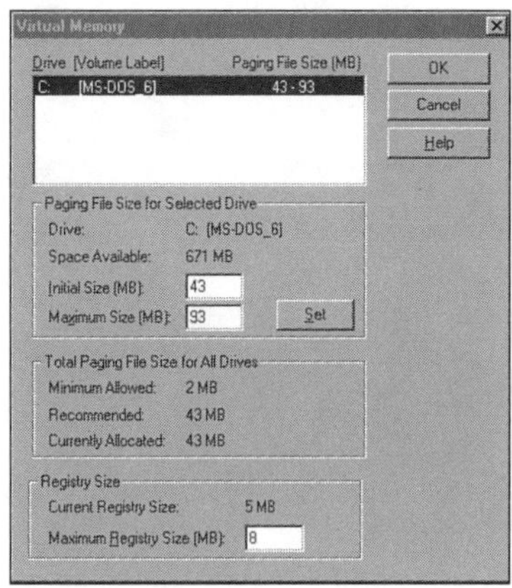


**FIGURE 7.13**
The Virtual Memory dialog box allows you to modify the maximum Registry size.

## Troubleshooting the Registry

Several problems may be directly related to Registry errors. The most common problems are the following:

- Your computer won't boot properly or at all.
- Your computer looks or works differently than it once did.
- Your computer won't shut down correctly.

- The "Blue Screen of Death" (resulting from a STOP error) appears.
- A software or hardware component that operated correctly stops working even though no physical changes have been made to the files or to the device.
- Something stops working after you add new software or hardware, and the two are not known to be incompatible.

Most of these error conditions are at least correctable from backup. The one really frightening error is the STOP error because you can't access your machine. To clear the Blue Screen of Death, try booting from your boot disk and running the CHDSK program to repair the type of errors associated with disk and file problems. The CHDSK.EXE program is located in the <*System Root*>\System32 directory.

# USING ADVANCED TECHNIQUES

Implement advanced techniques to resolve various problems.

Windows NT comes with several diagnostic tools to help you optimize and tune the system and to correct error conditions. In many ways, the operating system is meant to be *self-tuning* and to require that relatively few settings be altered to make the computer run well. To track errors, Windows records a system of events in log files. These events can be tracked and controlled, and they prove very useful in troubleshooting. This section delves into the event logs in some detail.

To aid in solving network problems, Windows NT also offers you the Network Monitor. This utility enables you to examine and analyze network performance and utilization. Common network issues are also discussed in this section.

## Working with the Event Logs and Event Viewer

Events are actions that occur on your system. The system itself generates events and records them in the System and Security log files. Applications record their events in the Application log. You see standard events, and you can audit resources to add additional events. Many application developers use the event system to aid in analysis of their application. The Event Viewer enables you to view the event logs and analyze them.

The event logs are normally viewed by anyone who cares to see the information. You can also remotely view an event log if you have the permission to do so on another machine.

An administrator may want to restrict access to these logs so that the information is secure and can't be erased. To restrict who can open the System or Application logs, you can set the following key:

HKEY_LOCAL_MACHINE\System\CurrentControlSet\Services \EventLog\-*<log_name>*

so that the RestrictGuestAccess value of type REG_DWORD is set to 1. When the RestrictGuestAccess is set to 0 or doesn't exist, the default condition is for anyone to access these two logs.

The log files are a first-in first-out (FIFO) system. When the ultimate limit of a log file is reached, the oldest events are deleted to make room for new events. The default size is 512KB, and the oldest event stored is up to one week old. You can modify these settings from within the Event Viewer.

## STEP BY STEP

### 7.13 Changing the Settings of the Event Logs

1. Open the Event Viewer (see Figure 7.14).
2. Choose the Log Settings command from the Log menu.
3. Select the log type in the Change Settings for Log list box in the Event Log Settings dialog box (see Figure 7.15).

*continues*

*continued*

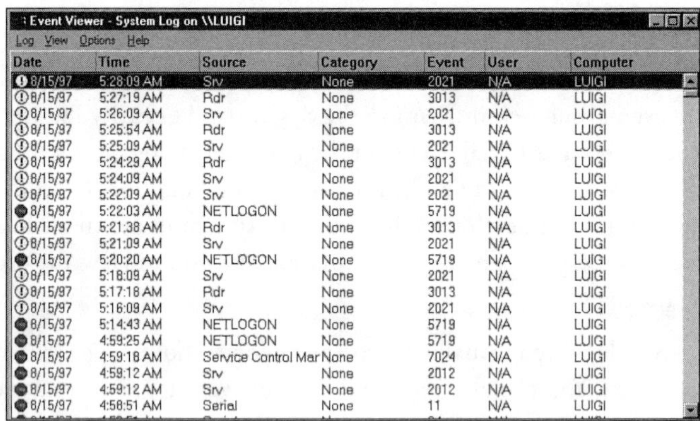

Event Viewer - System Log on \\LUIGI
Log View Options Help
Date Time Source Category Event User Computer
8/15/97 5:28:09 AM Srv None 2021 N/A LUIGI
8/15/97 5:27:19 AM Rdr None 3013 N/A LUIGI
8/15/97 5:26:09 AM Srv None 2021 N/A LUIGI
8/15/97 5:25:54 AM Rdr None 3013 N/A LUIGI
8/15/97 5:25:09 AM Srv None 2021 N/A LUIGI
8/15/97 5:24:29 AM Rdr None 3013 N/A LUIGI
8/15/97 5:24:09 AM Srv None 2021 N/A LUIGI
8/15/97 5:22:09 AM Srv None 2021 N/A LUIGI
8/15/97 5:22:03 AM NETLOGON None 5719 N/A LUIGI
8/15/97 5:21:38 AM Rdr None 3013 N/A LUIGI
8/15/97 5:21:09 AM Srv None 2021 N/A LUIGI
8/15/97 5:20:20 AM NETLOGON None 5719 N/A LUIGI
8/15/97 5:18:09 AM Srv None 2021 N/A LUIGI
8/15/97 5:17:18 AM Rdr None 3013 N/A LUIGI
8/15/97 5:16:09 AM Srv None 2021 N/A LUIGI
8/15/97 5:14:43 AM NETLOGON None 5719 N/A LUIGI
8/15/97 4:59:25 AM NETLOGON None 5719 N/A LUIGI
8/15/97 4:59:18 AM Service Control Mar None 7024 N/A LUIGI
8/15/97 4:59:12 AM Srv None 2012 N/A LUIGI
8/15/97 4:59:12 AM Srv None 2012 N/A LUIGI
8/15/97 4:58:51 AM Serial None 11 N/A LUIGI


**FIGURE 7.14**
The Event Viewer gives you access to the three event logs.

4. Set the size of the log in the Maximum Log Size spinner.
5. Select one of the radio buttons in the Event Log Wrapping section to determine what happens to old events.
6. Close first the Event Log Settings dialog box and then the Event Viewer.

A prudent administrator makes a habit of checking the event logs on a regular basis. Many events occur so frequently that they can overwhelm the event logs and make it difficult to determine what other error conditions or trends exist. By analyzing the event logs, you can determine what event types are worth keeping and how often they should be noted.

Another useful option available through the Event Viewer is the export of event logs to data files. Several different output formats are offered to enable you to more easily analyze the data in the logs. You can export your log data out to text files (.TXT), event log files (.EVT), spreadsheet files (.SYLK), and database data file (.DBF) formats, among others. Numerous third-party tools help you analyze Windows NT Workstation log files.

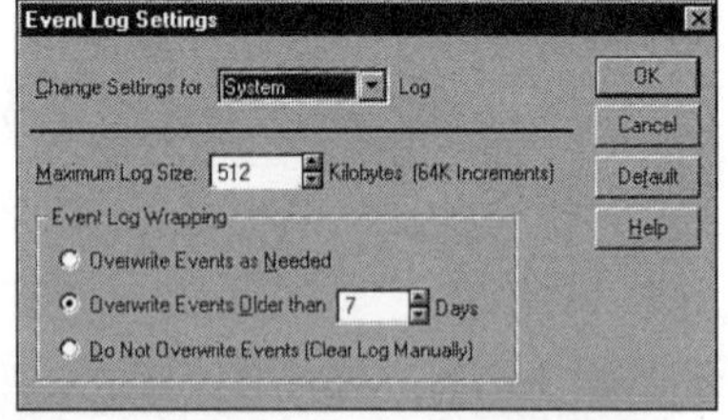


**FIGURE 7.15**
The Event Log Settings dialog box allows you to modify the settings for any or all of the three event logs.

If you want additional information about an event, double-click on the event to view the Event Detail dialog box (refer to Figure 7.9), which offers the following information for the event:

- Date of event
- Time of event

- User account that generated the event (When applicable, this information is recorded in the Security log.)
- Computer on which the event occurred
- Event ID (the actual event code)
- Source or component that recorded the error
- Type of event: Error, Information, or Warning
- Category of event
- Description of event
- Data describing the event in hexadecimal form

NOTE

**Know How to Use the Event Viewer** The Event Viewer (like the Performance Monitor) is one of the Windows NT operating system's central diagnostic tools. Learning how to use this tool well will reward the administrator with a better running workstation, less time spent tracking down errors, and a lower-stress existence.

You can find many of the error messages in the documentation and resource kits for Windows NT Workstation. Microsoft also keeps a technical database that contains many reasons for which error messages are generated. You can search the Knowledge Base on the Microsoft Web site (as a premium service) or on the Microsoft network to obtain information regarding errors stored in the logs.

Another database on CD-ROM is delivered to programmers as part of their subscription to the Microsoft Developer Network program. This database contains information about not only error conditions, but internal error codes of interest to programmers. Programmers with all levels of participation in MSDN receive this database.

The Event Log is very flexible. You can turn event logging on and off for a number of resources by specifying the auditing properties for that resource. Many developers use these logs to record information specific to their applications.

The Event Log is almost an embarrassment of riches. To help you find the particular event you need, the Event Viewer offers a find and search function. You can also filter the Event Log derived from your own computer by using the View menu commands to sort by any of the following items:

- Computer
- Event date and time
- Event ID
- Event type

- User
- Source of the event

## Network Diagnostics

Numerous network problems arise relating to both hardware and software configuration. Some of these problems require that you experiment with cabling and couplings; others can be solved with software that comes with Windows NT Workstation.

If you have a complex network installation, you may require diagnostic equipment to test your hardware. Often you can test individual components by rearranging their positions in the network (swapping cables or boards) and isolating the offending piece of hardware.

Windows NT comes with a utility called the Network Monitor that can prove very useful in diagnosing network activity. This Administrative Tools utility collects and filters network packets and can analyze network activity. However, this utility diagnoses only the computer that it is running on. A copy of Network Monitor that is capable of monitoring all network traffic on your LAN is available with the Microsoft BackOffice product SMS.

The Network Monitor is a supplementary component of the Windows NT Workstation installation. To install this program, open the Network Control Panel's Service tab and click on the Add button. After Windows NT Workstation builds its list of services, you can select the Network Monitor from the list.

Network Monitor is both statistical and graphical. In the four panes of the Network Monitor, the current activity appears in real-time (see Figure 7.16).

The Graph pane in the upper-left corner shows the following bar graphs:

- % Network Utilization
- Broadcasts Per Second
- Bytes Per Second
- Frames Per Second
- Multicast Per Second

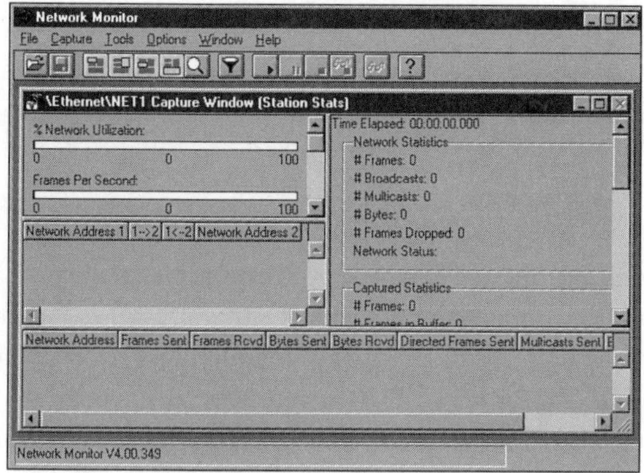


**FIGURE 7.16**
The Network Monitor utility allows you to view frames coming into and going out of your workstation.

These parameters indicate the level of activity your network is experiencing and how saturated your network bandwidth is.

The Session Stats pane shows you which nodes are communicating and the number of frames (of the first 128 measured) sent and received from each.

The Total Stats pane (on the right half of the Network Monitor) provides complete network statistics in the following categories:

- Captured Statistics
- Network Card (Mac) Error Statistics
- Network Card (Mac) Statistics
- Network Statistics
- Per Second Statistics

You must scroll to see each of the panels in the pane for these different categories.

The last pane at the bottom of the window is the Station Stats pane. Information here shows what your workstation is communicating to the network. Click on a column head to sort by that category. The following categories appear:

- Broadcasts Sent
- Bytes Rcvd
- Bytes Sent
- Directed Frames Sent

- Frames Rcvd
- Frames Sent
- Multicasts Sent
- Network Address

An amazing number of network problems are related to TCP/IP protocol addressing. Make sure that your workstation either has a unique address or uses a DHCP (Dynamic Host Configuration Protocol) service for its TCP/IP assignment. Also verify that the subnet address you entered in the TCP/IP Properties dialog box is correct.

## STEP BY STEP

### 7.14 Viewing TCP/IP Settings

1. Double-click the Network icon in Control Panel.
2. Click the Protocols tab of the Network dialog box.
3. Select the TCP/IP protocol, and then click Properties to view the Microsoft TCP/IP Properties dialog box (see Figure 7.17).
4. Examine the settings to see whether they are correct.

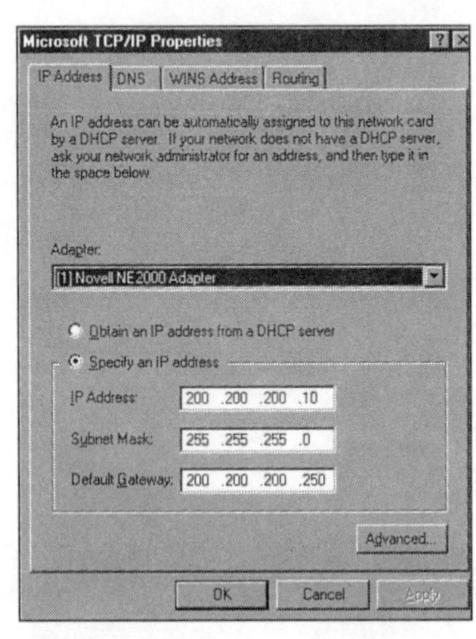


**FIGURE 7.17**
The Microsoft TCP/IP Properties dialog box allows you to view and modify TCP/IP settings.

The PING utility is also included in Windows NT Workstation. You can ping other computers on the network to see whether they are active. Actually, you can ping your own workstation with the specific address, the default gateway, or any computer on the Internet or your intranet. Use the `PING` command in a command prompt session without any other parameters to see an informational screen detailing its use.

## Resource Conflicts

Many configuration errors are resource conflicts. These take the form of duplicate interrupt or I/O assignments or SCSI devices having duplicate or improper assignments. You may see these problems when you first boot your system, or they may show up later when a device doesn't work properly.

Check the Event Log to see what error events are listed. Also run the Windows diagnostic program WinMSD (in the Administrative Tools folder) to examine your resource settings. You can roll back errors in software by using the LastKnownGood configuration.

## Using the Windows NT Diagnostics Program

The Windows NT Diagnostics program is the worthy successor to the MSD program found in Windows 3.1. This dialog box (see Figure 7.18) shows you information on many of the Registry items found in the HKEY_LOCAL_MACHINE subtree. Using WinMSD, you can obtain detailed information and reports on the state and configuration of your workstation. You cannot use this diagnostic tool to change any configuration settings, but you can use it to determine what conditions exist so that you can fix a problem.

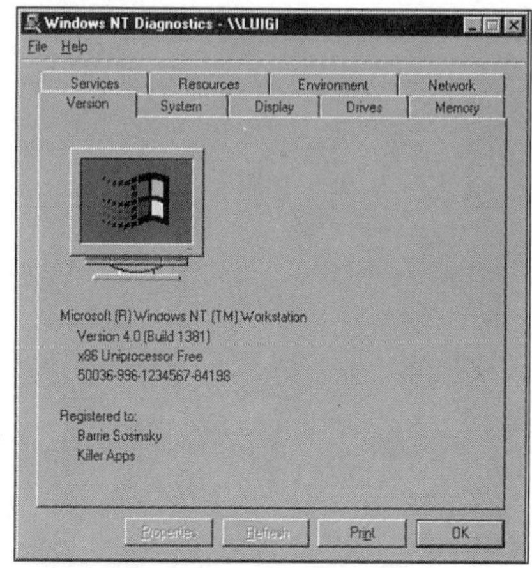


**FIGURE 7.18**
The Windows NT Diagnostics tool.

This dialog box contains the following tabs:

- *Display.* Information on your video adapter, its firmware, and any adapter settings is found on this tab.
- *Drives.* This tab offers a list of drives and volumes in a hierarchical display. Drives include floppy disk drives, hard disk drives, CD-ROM drives, optical drives, and mapped drives through any network connections. If you double-click on a drive letter, the Drive Properties dialog box appears. The Drive Properties dialog box shows you cluster size, bytes per sector, the current status of the use of the disk, and the file system in use.
- *Environment.* All environmental variables in use for a command prompt session appear on this tab.
- *Memory.* This tab shows the installed memory, virtual memory, and usage of both.
- *Network.* The network tab shows installed logons, transports (protocols and bindings), settings, and statistics. Figure 7.19 shows the Transports display of the Network tab.

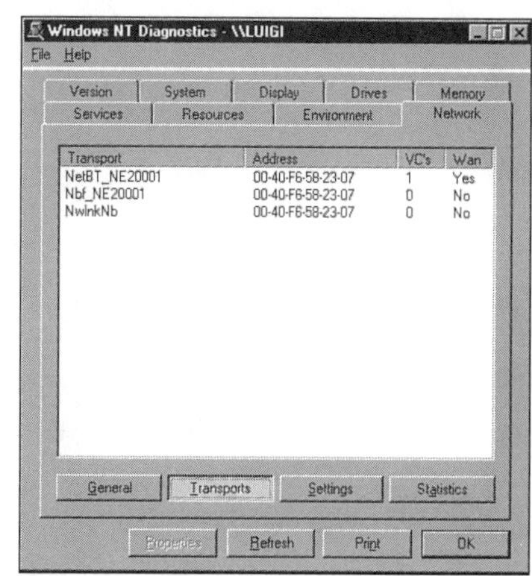


**FIGURE 7.19**
The Transports listing of the Network tab of the WinMSD dialog box.

- *Resources.* When you open this tab, the listing of device assignments appears. Shown here are the IRQ, port numbers, DMA channels, and UMB locations used by each device. If you suspect a device conflict, this is the place to go to attempt to locate the suspect.
- *Services.* The information stored in the HKEY_LOCAL_MACHINE\System\CurrentControlSet\Services key is displayed on this tab. If you select a service and click on the Devices button, the information stored in the HKEY_LOCAL_MACHINE\System\CurrentControlSet\Control key appears, along with the status of that control.
- *System.* This tab shows the information stored in the HKEY_LOCAL_ MACHINE\Hardware key, including the CPU type and information on other installed devices.
- *Version.* The information stored in the HKEY_LOCAL_MACHINE\Software\Microsoft\Windows\NT\CurrentVersion key is shown on this tab. You will find the operating system version, build number, and Service Pack update, and the registered owner of the software.

Windows NT ships with several utilities for evaluating a workstation's configuration and performance. By being proficient in the use of these tools, a savvy administrator can solve many problems and prevent others from occurring.

## Using Additional Resources

In the introduction to this chapter, you learned that successful troubleshooting had a variety of components. Two major components were knowledge of the system and prior experience with the problem. Fortunately, not all knowledge and experience must come firsthand. If you have access to people who have more knowledge and experience than you, they can be valuable troubleshooting resources. In addition, a variety of sources of good information are available in subscription form. These include Microsoft's TechNet, Knowledge Base, and Developer Network. In addition, a variety of periodicals can give you up-to-date articles by experts in the NT field (*Windows*

*NT Magazine* is a prime example). As well, don't forget the Official Microsoft Courses (available in an ATEC near you) and the Microsoft Web site.

All of these resources are invaluable for you as an NT expert to use in those situations when your knowledge is simply not enough to troubleshoot the problem. You should attempt to get your hands on as many of these resources as you can because they will more than pay for themselves the first time they yield an answer that saves you hours or days of work.

## CASE STUDY: FORGOTTEN ADMINISTRATOR PASSWORD

### ESSENCE OF THE CASE

Here are the essential elements in this case:

- The administrator account on an NT Workstation is inaccessible due to loss of password.
- Due to loss of Administrator account, all administrative access has also been lost.

### SCENARIO

You are the administrator charged with maintaining a network of 15 NT Workstations operating in a workgroup. The users have varying knowledge of NT, but all share the understanding that you do all the system maintenance. As a result, you are the only one who knows the Administrator account on each PC, and you maintain the same password on each for administrative ease.

At the behest of a user who's desperate to share a directory for another user to access, you give out the administrative password. Because you are busy at the time, you promptly forget that you have done so.

A couple of weeks later you get a call from the same user. Now it seems that he wants to remove the share he created, but he has a problem. After getting the password to the Administrator account, he "played around a bit." Not only did he create a bunch of shares, but he also changed the Administrator password "just to see if you could do that," and now he has forgotten it. As much as he has tried to remember the password, he is now convinced that he has lost it forever.

*continues*

## CASE STUDY: FORGOTTEN ADMINISTRATOR PASSWORD

*continued*

### ANALYSIS

The problem here is one of access and ends up being a sort of "chicken and egg" scenario. Without a useable Administrator account (or at least an account with administrator access), you cannot perform account maintenance. But if you are unable to perform account maintenance, you cannot get back your Administrator account. So you are forced to exit the loop and turn to restoration methods. Two possible solutions are available, both of which have potentially detrimental consequences. The first is to restore the accounts database from an emergency repair disk, and the second is to restore the Registry from a tape backup. In both cases, the possible danger is that the restoration may not be current enough to solve your problem, or it may be too current and may simply restore the problem.

Fortunately, you have been diligent in updating the emergency repair information on the hard disk of each workstation as you made changes to accounts and disk structures. As a result, the /Repair directory on the user's machine is as up-to-date as the last change you made using the Administrator account. Therefore, no changes that the user made himself will be present in these updates, which will serve to remove the password change when you restore.

You take the following action to restore the accounts database:

1. Run RDISK and choose the Create Repair Disk option.
2. Using the three Setup disks that came with the NT Workstation CD-ROM (or that you created with `WINNT32 /ox`), you restart the system. Then, using the repair disk, you restore the SAM.
3. If any changes were made to the system after the last repair directory update, you will have to redo them manually.

## CHAPTER SUMMARY

This chapter covered a variety of troubleshooting methods. It began with a suggested approach to troubleshooting (the DETECT model) and moved on to present a number of symptoms and solutions. Some of the specific areas covered in this chapter were booting, printing, installation, applications, access and permissions, and the Registry.

The objective of this chapter was to give you a framework for understanding the kinds of issues that may arise when troubleshooting NT Workstation problems, both in a production environment and on the exam.

**KEY TERMS**

Before you take the exam, make sure you are comfortable with the definitions and concepts for each of the following key terms:

- DETECT
- HCL
- MBR
- NTLDR
- NTDETECT.COM
- NTOSKRNL.EXE
- BOOT.INI
- ARC path
- `/sos`
- LastKnownGood
- BOOTSECT.DOS
- NTBOOTDD.SYS
- OSLOADER.EXE
- recovery disk
- emergency repair disk
- RDISK.EXE
- Event Viewer
- Security log
- System log
- Application log
- hive
- Network Monitor
- service
- REGEDIT.EXE
- REGEDT32.EXE

## APPLY YOUR LEARNING

The following section allows you to assess how well you understood the material in the chapter. The exercises provide you with opportunities to engage in the sorts of tasks that comprise the skill sets the objectives reflect. Review and exam questions test your knowledge of the tasks and concepts specified in the objectives. Answers to the review and exam questions follow in the answers sections. For additional review- and exam-type questions, see the Top Score test engine on the CD-ROM that came with this book.

## Exercises

These lab exercises enable you to practice troubleshooting Windows NT Workstation, as well as to create resources that will help you resolve a variety of problems.

### 7.1 Creating a Boot Floppy Disk and Emergency Repair Disks

In this exercise, you create a set of disks that enable you to start your workstation in case of boot failure and to repair a workstation that doesn't boot properly.

**Estimated Time:** 20 minutes

To create the boot floppy, follow these steps:

1. Insert a blank floppy disk in the disk drive and format that disk.
2. Open the Windows NT Explorer and select the BOOT.INI, NTLDR, and NTDETECT.COM files.
3. Copy these files to the floppy disk to create the NT boot floppy disk.
4. Restart your computer without removing the floppy disk from the drive. If the disk is valid, it will boot your computer.
5. Label the disk and store it in a secure location.

To create a set of emergency repair disks, follow these steps:

1. Choose Start, Programs, Command Prompt.
2. Type **RDISK /S** and press the Enter key.
3. Click on the Create Repair Disk button in the Repair Disk Utility dialog box (refer to Figure 7.3).
4. Insert a formatted floppy disk, and then click on the OK button.
5. After Windows NT Workstation creates the ERD, remove the floppy disk, write-protect it, and store it in a safe location.
6. Click the Exit button to close RDISK.
7. Click the Close box.

### 7.2 Displaying Device Drivers at Startup

This exercise explores how to have the BOOT.INI file enumerate your drivers when the kernel is loading.

**Estimated Time:** 15 minutes

1. Choose Start, Programs, Accessories, Notepad.
2. Select the Open command from the File menu.
3. Select All Files from the File of Type list box, and then select the BOOT.INI file in the root directory.

## APPLY YOUR LEARNING

4. Find the line in the BOOT.INI file that reads `Windows NT Server Version 4.00 [VGA]` followed by the `/basevideo` and `/sos` switches. If your system uses a VGA driver, skip to step 6.
5. Choose the File, Save As command and save the BOOT.INI file to a different name, such as BOOT.BAK.
6. In the BOOT.BAK file, delete the `/basevideo` switch but leave the `/sos` switch intact. Modify the bracket text to read **Windows NT Server Version 4.00 [SOS]**.
7. Select the File, Save As command and save the file as the BOOT.INI file in the root directory. (Note that the file BOOT.INI is read-only, system, and hidden. You will probably have to change the attributes to be able to save the file.)
8. Exit Notepad and reboot your system.
9. Select the SOS option from the boot menu when it appears. As your device drivers are loaded, each one is listed onscreen in ARC format.
10. Log on to Windows NT Workstation.
11. Restore the original BOOT.INI file with the VGA configuration and the `/basevideo` switch. Then reboot to test your system.

## Review Questions

1. What phase of the startup process displays the blue screen with a series of dots added to the screen?
2. How can you restore your workstation's previous configuration?
3. How do you create a boot floppy?
4. How do you share a printer so that it is available to others on the network?
5. What is a Service Pack?
6. What are the most common reasons that a user can't log on to a domain?
7. How can you tell which service has failed?
8. What is a user profile and what does it control?
9. Who "owns" a resource?
10. Why is much of the Windows NT Registry not worth backing up?
11. How long do events remain in an Event Log?
12. What utility is most useful for determining resource conflicts?

## Exam Questions

1. When is the LastKnownGood Configuration overwritten?

   A. When you request an update on the Startup/Shutdown tab of the Control Panel's Services application.

   B. When you start up your computer.

   C. When you shut down your computer.

   D. When you log on successfully to your workstation.

2. An error message appears, saying that a service failed to load. Where would you go to determine the nature of the problem?

   A. The Services tab of the Control Panel's Network application

## APPLY YOUR LEARNING

B. The User Manager for Domains

C. The System log in the Event Viewer application

D. The Control Panel's Services application

3. Which file is not required on a boot disk for an x86 Windows NT Workstation?

   A. BOOT.INI

   B. NTLDR

   C. NTDETECT.COM

   D. NTBOOTDD.BAT

4. Which of the following programs creates an ERD?

   A. FORMAT

   B. RDISK

   C. RECOVER

   D. ERD

5. Your print job spools, but it does not print. Which of the following could *not* be the reason?

   A. The printer is turned off.

   B. The paper tray is empty.

   C. The printer's memory is full.

   D. Your hard drive is full.

6. How do you hide a printer share?

   A. Move the file to your system WINNT folder.

   B. Add a dollar sign after the share name.

   C. Set an option in the Printer Properties dialog box.

   D. Create a hidden spool folder.

7. What happens when you don't have adequate space for an installation?

   A. The Setup program detects this, stops, and cancels the operation.

   B. The space available is used to overwrite as many files as possible.

   C. Your installation becomes corrupted.

   D. You are given the choice of installing MS-DOS as a temporary measure.

8. Which one of the following should you *not* do to reclaim space on your disk?

   A. Delete any TEMP files you find in various locations (for example, in the print cache folder).

   B. Empty your Recycle Bin.

   C. Uninstall any programs that you no longer need.

   D. Change your file system.

9. Which methods can you use to open the Task Manager?

   A. Select the Task Manager from the Administrative Tools folder.

   B. Click on the Task Manager button in the Windows NT Security dialog box.

   C. Select the Task Manager command from the Start menu's Status bar shortcut menu.

   D. Press Ctrl+Esc.

10. Which of the following user profiles does not exist?

    A. Default user profile

    B. A user account profile

## APPLY YOUR LEARNING

C. Anonymous user profile

D. Roaming profiles

11. How do you control what action is taken when your workstation encounters a STOP error?

    A. Use the Control Panel's System application to specify the action.

    B. No action is possible; the computer logs an error and reboots.

    C. Use the Control Panel's Network application to specify the action.

    D. Reboot to MS-DOS and enter the RECOVER command.

## Answers to Review Questions

1. The blue screen appears when the Hardware Abstraction Layer (HAL) loads. Each dot represents a device driver being loaded. For more information, see the section "The Intel Boot Sequence."

2. The LastKnownGood configuration is offered as a step in the startup process. Press the spacebar to return to that configuration. Each time you successfully log on to Windows NT Workstation, the LastKnownGood configuration is changed. For more information, see the section "LastKnownGood Recovery."

3. Format a floppy disk and copy the hidden system files: BOOT.INI, NTLDR, NTBOOTDD.SYS, and NTDETECT.COM in your %systemroot% to that floppy disk. For more information, see the section "Boot Disk Recovery."

4. You can specify that a printer is to be shared in the Add Printer Wizard. After the fact, you can select the Sharing command from a printer's shortcut menu and configure the printer share from the Sharing tab of the Printer Properties dialog box. For more information, see the section "Printers As Shared Resources."

5. A Service Pack is a program that Microsoft releases to update Windows NT Workstation (or another application). Service Packs are numbered for each version of the operating system, and greater numbers are given to later versions. It's a good idea to use Service Packs to stay current. For more information, see the section "Installation Disk Errors and Upgrades."

6. Either the username and password have been entered incorrectly, or the user account doesn't exist. For more information, see the section "The Load Process."

7. Open the Event Viewer and examine the System log to see what error events are listed. Then check for details to determine the cause. For more information, see the section "Service Failures."

8. A user profile is a collection of Registry settings that control the look and feel of your workstation, commands on the Start menu, available applications, printers, and other resources. Profiles come in two forms: default, which is related to a specific user, or roaming, which is stored on the network to enable a user to move from workstation to workstation. For more information, see the section "The Emergency Repair Process."

## APPLY YOUR LEARNING

9. The creator of the resource owns that resource and has full rights and privileges to it. An administrator can access a resource and modify it and can take ownership of that resource away from the original owner. Doing so, however, causes the original owner to be locked out of his ownership position. For more information, see the section "Assessing User Resource Access Failures."

10. Much of the Windows NT Registry describes transient settings that are session dependent. Two of the Registry hives describing Security and SAM settings cannot be backed up. For more information, see the section "Backing Up the Registry."

11. Events remain in the Event Log for seven days or until the log fills up and additional space is required. Events are removed in a first-in first-out manner. For more information, see the section "Working with the Event Logs and Event Viewer."

12. The Windows NT Diagnostics program lists the various devices that you have installed on your workstation and the settings they have for IRQs, I/O ports, DMA, and so forth. Through examination of this utility, you can determine what conflicts might exist. For more information, see the section "Using the Windows NT Diagnostics Program."

## Answers to Exam Questions

1. **D** is correct. A successful logon overwrites changes in the Registry for the LastKnownGood configuration. For more information, see the section "LastKnownGood Recovery."

2. **C** is correct. Any system failure is written as an event in the System log. For more information, see the section "Service Failures."

3. **D** is correct. Choice D is fictitious. All the other choices are essential files that are copied to the floppy boot disk. For more information, see the section "The Intel Boot Sequence."

4. **B** is correct. RDISK creates and updates emergency repair disks. For more information, see "The Emergency Repair Process."

5. **D** is correct. A full hard drive has no effect on a previously spooled print file because that file has already been written to disk. For more information, see the section "Solving Print Spooler Problems."

6. **B** is correct. By adding a dollar sign to the end of a sharename, you can hide that share from view. For more information, see the section "Printers As Shared Resources."

7. **A** is correct. Early in the process, Setup examines the file system and the disk size and assesses the amount of free space you have and the amount that's required. If you don't have enough free space, the installation is aborted. This is true even if you are overwriting enough files to free up sufficient disk space for the installation. For more information, see the section "Assessing Installation Failures."

8. **D** is correct. Changing the file system permanently deletes all the data on your disk. In almost all instances, this is neither necessary nor required. For more information, see the section "Inadequate Disk Space."

## APPLY YOUR LEARNING

9. **B and C** are correct. A is incorrect because there is no command for the Task Manager on the Start menu. D is incorrect because the keystroke used to open the Task Manager is Ctrl+Shift+Esc. For more information, see the section "Assessing Application Failures."

10. **C** is correct. A, B, and D all exist and support both local and remote users on a network. Choice C is incorrect because there is no "guest" or anonymous user profile, only the default profile. For more information, see the section "The Emergency Repair Process."

**A** is correct. The System Control Panel contains a setting for the action to be taken when a STOP error occurs. For more information, see the section "Boot Sequence Errors."

**Suggested Readings and Resources**

The following are some recommended readings in the area of Troubleshooting:

1. Microsoft Official Curriculum course 770: *Installing and Configuring Microsoft Windows NT Workstation 4.0*
   - Module 2: Installing Windows NT Workstation 4.0
   - Module 3: Working with Windows NT Workstation 4.0
   - Module 4: Configuring
2. Microsoft Official Curriculum course 803: *Administering Microsoft Windows NT 4.0*
   - Module 8: Administering Network Printers
   - Module 9: Auditing Resources and Events
3. Microsoft Official Curriculum course 922: *Supporting Microsoft Windows NT 4.0 Core Technologies*
   - Module 2: Installing Windows NT
   - Module 3: Configuring the Windows NT Environment
   - Module 17: The Windows NT Boot Process
   - Module 18: Troubleshooting Resources
4. Microsoft Official Curriculum course 689: *Supporting Microsoft Windows NT 4.0 Enterprise Technologies*
   - Unit 3: Microsoft Windows NT Server 4.0 Network Analysis and Optimization
   - Unit 4: Troubleshooting Microsoft Windows NT Server 4.0 in an Enterprise Environment
5. *MS Windows NT Server 4.0 Networking Guide* (Microsoft Press; also available in the Windows NT Server Resource Kit)
   - Chapter 2: Network Security and Domain Planning
   - Chapter 12: Troubleshooting Tools and Strategies
6. *MS Windows NT Server 4.0 Resource Guide* (Microsoft Press; also available in the Windows NT Server Resource Kit)
   - Chapter 2: Printing
   - Chapter 4: Planning a Reliable Configuration
   - Chapter 5: Preparing for and Performing a Recovery
   - Chapter 6: Troubleshooting Startup and Disk Problems
   - Chapter 8: General Troubleshooting
7. Microsoft TechNet CD-ROM
   - *Concepts and Planning: MS Windows NT Server 4.0*
     - Chapter 9: Monitoring Events
     - Chapter 10: Monitoring Your Network
8. Web sites
   - `www.microsoft.com/ntserver` (check out the online seminars)
   - `www.microsoft.com/train_cert`
   - `www.prometric.com/testingcandidates/assessment/chosetest.html` (take online assessment tests)

PART 

# FINAL REVIEW

Fast Facts: Windows NT Workstation 4 Exam

Fast Facts: Windows NT Server 4 Exam

Fast Facts: Windows NT Server 4 Enterprise Exam

Fast Facts: Networking Essentials Exam

Study and Exam Prep Tips

Practice Exam

# Fast Facts: Windows NT Workstation 4 Exam

Now that you have thoroughly read through this book, worked through the exercises, and picked up as much hands-on exposure to NT Workstation as possible, you're ready to take your exam. This chapter is designed to be a last-minute cram for you as you walk out the door on your way to the exam. You can't re-read the whole book in an hour, but you will be able to read this chapter in that time. This chapter is organized by objective category and summarizes the basic facts you need to know regarding each objective. If you know what is in here, chances are the exam will be a snap.

## PLANNING

Remember: Here are the elements that Microsoft says they test on in the "Planning" section of the exam.

- Create unattended installation files.
- Plan strategies for sharing and securing resources.
- Choose the appropriate file system to use in a given situation. File systems and situations include: NTFS, FAT, HPFS, security, and dual-boot systems.

The files used for unattended installation are

- An unattended answer file (UNATTEND.TXT)
- A uniqueness database file (a .UDF file)
- SYSDIFF.EXE
- WINDIFF.EXE

Some switches available for WINNT32.EXE are useful for unattended installations:

- `/u:answerfile` (where *answerfile* might be UNATTEND.TXT, for example)

- `/s:sourcepath` (where *sourcepath* might be e:\i386, for example)
- `/udf:userid,x:\udf.txt`

The content of the $OEM$ directory is copied to the destination machine before NT is installed to allow for additional file or application installation after NT has been installed.

SYSDIFF.EXE can be used to create a snapshot file, a difference file, and/or an .INF file.

.INF files are preferred over difference files because .INF files contain instructions on how to install the software, whereas the difference file contains the whole software package in one large file.

WINDIFF.EXE is used to compare one NT system to another.

The built-in groups in NT Workstation are

- Users
- Power Users
- Administrators
- Guests
- Backup Operators
- Replicator

Table 1 lists the default rights assigned to users or groups on an NT Workstation.

Table 2 lists the built-in capabilities of the built-in groups.

**TABLE 1**
**ASSIGNMENT OF DEFAULT USER RIGHTS**

| *Right* | *Administrators* | *Power Users* | *Users* | *Guests* | *Everyone* | *Backup Operators* |
|---|---|---|---|---|---|---|
| Access This Computer from the Network | X | X | | | | X |
| Back Up Files and Directories | X | | | | | X |
| Change the System Time | X | X | | | | |
| Force Shutdown from a Remote System | X | X | | | | |
| Load and Unload Device Drivers | X | | | | | |
| Log On Locally | X | X | X | X | X | X |
| Manage Auditing and Security Log | X | | | | | |
| Restore Files and Directories | X | | | | | X |
| Shut Down the System | X | X | X | | X | X |
| Take Ownership of Files or Other Objects | X | | | | | |

**TABLE 2**
**BUILT-IN USER CAPABILITIES**

| *Built-In Capability* | *Administrators* | *Power Users* | *Users* | *Guests* | *Everyone* | *Backup Operators* |
|---|---|---|---|---|---|---|
| Create and Manage User Accounts | X | X | | | | |
| Create and Manage Local Groups | X | X | | | | |
| Lock the Workstation | X | X | X | X | X | X |
| Override the Lock of the Workstation | X | | | | | |
| Format the Hard Disk | X | | | | | |
| Create Common Groups | X | X | | | | |
| Share and Stop Sharing Directories | X | X | | | | |
| Share and Stop Sharing Printers | X | X | | | | |

The following special groups are maintained by NT:

- Network
- Interactive
- Everyone
- Creator Owner

Table 3 shows the advantages and disadvantages of storing home directories on a server and on a local computer.

Table 4 shows the advantages and disadvantages of running applications from a server and from a local machine.

**TABLE 3**
**HOME DIRECTORIES ON THE SERVER VERSUS HOME DIRECTORIES ON THE LOCAL COMPUTER**

| *Server-Based Home Directories* | *Local Home Directories* |
|---|---|
| Centrally located so that users can access them from any location on the network. | Available only on the local machine. For roaming users (who log in from more than one computer on the network), the directory is not accessible from other systems. |
| During a regular backup of the server, information in users' home directories is also backed up. | Often users' local workstations are not backed up regularly as part of a scheduled backup process. If a user's machine fails, the user cannot recover the lost data. |
| Windows NT does not provide a way to limit the size of a user's directory. Thus, if a lot of information is being stored in home directories, the directories use up a lot of server disk space. | If a user stores a lot of information in his home directory, the space is taken up on his local hard drive instead of the server. |
| If the server is down, the user won't have access to her files. | The user has access to his files even when the network is down because the files are stored locally. |
| Some network bandwidth is consumed due to the over-the-network access of data or files. | No network traffic is generated by a user accessing his or her files. |

**TABLE 4**
**SHARED NETWORK APPLICATIONS VERSUS LOCALLY INSTALLED APPLICATIONS**

| *Shared Network Applications* | *Locally Installed Applications* |
|---|---|
| Take up less disk space on the local workstation. | Use more local disk space. |
| Easier to upgrade/control. | Upgrades must "touch" every machine locally. |
| Use network bandwidth. | Use no network bandwidth for running applications. |
| Slower response time because applications are accessed from the server. | Faster, more responsive. |
| If the server is down, users can't run applications. | Users can run applications regardless of server status. |

NT Workstation supports the following file formats:

- FAT16 (a universal standard format)
- NTFS (an NT proprietary format)
- CDFS (CD-ROM format)

NT Workstation does not support these file formats:

- FAT32 (supported by Windows 95 OSR2 and Windows 98)
- HPFS (supported by OS/2)

Table 5 provides a comparison between FAT and NTFS.

**TABLE 5**
**COMPARISON OF NTFS AND FAT FILE SYSTEMS USING WINDOWS NT WORKSTATION**

| *Feature* | *FAT* | *NTFS* |
|---|---|---|
| Support for long filenames (up to 255 characters) | Yes | Yes |
| Compression | No | Yes |
| Security | No | Yes |
| Dual-boot capabilities with non–Windows NT systems | Yes | No |
| Maximum file/partition size | 4GB | 16EB |
| Recommended partition size | 0–400MB | 400MB–16EB |
| Capability to format a floppy | Yes | No |
| Recoverability (transaction logging) | No | Yes |

# INSTALLATION AND CONFIGURATION

Remember: Here are the elements that Microsoft says they test on in the "Installation and Configuration" section of the exam.

- Install Windows NT Workstation on an Intel platform in a given situation.
- Set up a dual-boot system in a given situation.
- Remove Windows NT Workstation in a given situation.
- Install, configure, and remove hardware components for a given situation. Hardware components include: network adapter drivers, SCSI device drivers, tape device drivers, UPSs, multimedia devices, display drivers, keyboard drives, and mouse drivers.
- Use Control Panel applications to configure a Windows NT Workstation computer in a given situation.
- Upgrade to Windows NT Workstation 4.0 in a given situation.
- Configure server-based installation for wide-scale deployment in a given situation.

NTHQ.EXE (available on the Workstation CD-ROM) can be used to evaluate a computer for NT installation. It is used to verify hardware and produce a report indicating which components are and are not on the HCL.

Table 6 lists the minimum hardware requirements for NT Workstation installation.

NT Workstation supports four installation types. Table 7 lists the components installed with each of the four installation types.

**TABLE 6**
**WINDOWS NT WORKSTATION 4.0 MINIMUM INSTALLATION REQUIREMENTS**

| *Component* | *Minimum Requirement* |
|---|---|
| CPU | 32-bit Intel x86-based (80486/33 or higher) microprocessor or compatible (the 80386 microprocessor is no longer supported) |
| | Intel Pentium, Pentium Pro, or Pentium II microprocessor |
| | Digital Alpha AXP-based RISC microprocessor |
| | MIPS Rx400-based RISC microprocessor |
| | PowerPC-based RISC microprocessor |
| Memory | Intel x86-based computers: 12MB RAM |
| | RISC-based computers: 16MB RAM |
| Hard disk | Intel x86-based computers: 110MB |
| | RISC-based computers: 148MB |
| Display | VGA or better resolution |
| Other drives | Intel x86-based computers require a high-density 3 1/2" floppy drive and a CD-ROM drive (unless you are planning to install Windows NT over a network) |
| Optional | Network adapter card |
| | Mouse or other pointing device, such as a trackball |

**TABLE 7**
**VARYING COMPONENTS IN FOUR SETUP OPTIONS**

| *Component* | *Typical* | *Portable* | *Compact* | *Custom* |
|---|---|---|---|---|
| Accessibility options | X | X | None | All options |
| Accessories | X | X | None | All options |
| Communications programs | X | X | None | All options |
| Games | | | None | All options |
| Windows Messaging | | | None | All options |
| Multimedia | X | X | None | All options |

Windows NT Workstation can be installed using a variety of procedures given different circumstances:

- Locally, by using the three Setup floppy disks and a CD-ROM
- Locally, by using the CD-ROM and creating and using the three Setup floppy disks
- Locally, using the CD without Setup floppy disks, but by booting instead to an operating system that recognizes the CD-ROM
- Locally, by booting to the CD-ROM from a computer that recognizes the CD-ROM as a boot device
- Over the network, by creating and using the three Setup floppy disks
- Over the network, but without the Setup floppies

When you're installing NT on a computer with an existing operating system present, if the computer recognizes either the CD-ROM or a supported network adapter and connection to a network share on which the installation files are present, you can use one of two programs to install NT:

- **WINNT.EXE.** For installation from existing non-NT operating systems
- **WINNT32.EXE.** For installation or upgrade from existing NT installations

Table 8 describes the switches available for use with WINNT.EXE and WINNT32.EXE.

Dual booting is a method of installing two operating systems on a single machine and letting the user choose which will boot at startup time (only one can be booted at any time).

**TABLE 8**
**SWITCHES FOR MODIFYING THE WINNT.EXE AND WINNT32.EXE INSTALLATION PROCESSES**

| *Switch* | *Effect* |
|---|---|
| `/b` | Prevents creation of the three Setup boot disks. Create a temporary folder named $WIN_NT$.~BT and copy to it the boot files that would normally be copied to the three floppies. The contents of the temporary folder are used instead of the Setup boot disks to boot the machine when the user is prompted to restart. |
| `/c` | Skips the step of checking for available free space. (This switch cannot be used with WINNT32.EXE.) |
| `/I:`*`inf_file`* | Specifies the name of the Setup information file. The default filename is DOSNET.INF. |
| `/f` | Prevents verification of files as they are copied. (This switch cannot be used with WINNT32.EXE.) |
| `/l` | Creates a log file called $WINNT.LOG, which lists all errors that occur as files are being copied to the temporary directory. (This switch cannot be used with WINNT32.EXE.) |
| `/ox` | Creates the three Setup boot disks and then stops. |
| `/s:`*`server_path`* | Specifies the location of the installation source files. |
| `/u` | Allows all or part of an installation to proceed unattended (as detailed in Chapter 1, "Planning"). The `/b` option for floppyless installation is automatically invoked, and the `/s` option for location of the source files must be used. The `/u` option can be followed with the name of an answer file to fully automate installation. |
| `/udf` | During an unattended installation, specifies settings unique to a specific computer, which are contained in a uniqueness database file (see Chapter 1). |
| `/w` | This *undocumented* flag enables the WINNT.EXE program to execute in Windows (normally, it must be executed from an MS-DOS command prompt). |
| `/x` | Prevents creation of the three Setup boot disks. You must already have the three boot disks. |

NT Workstation can dual boot with any of the following operating systems:

- MS-DOS
- Microsoft Windows (3.1, 3.11, 95, 98)
- OS/2
- Microsoft Windows NT (Server or Workstation, any version)

Dual booting with an operating system other than NT (Server or Workstation) requires that at least the primary partition be formatted FAT.

If you remove NT Workstation from a machine, you must SYS (for the OS that remains) on the primary partition to remove the following:

- All paging files (C:\PAGEFILE.SYS)
- C:\BOOT.INI, C:\BOOTSECT.DOS, C:\NTDETECT.COM, C:\NTLDR (these are hidden, system, read only files)
- *.PAL (on Alpha computers)
- NTBOOTDD.SYS (on computers with SCSI drives with the BIOS disabled)
- The *winnt_root* folder
- The C:\Program files\Windows Windows NT folder

Most device drivers not written for NT 4.0 will not work with NT 4.0 (that includes network adapter drivers for NT 3.51 and Windows 95).

All mass storage device installation and settings (including those for tape drives and IDE hard drives) are configured from the SCSI icon in the Control Panel.

During boot, NT's automatic hardware detection process can cause a UPS to shut off because of a pulse that's sent through the COM port to detect a serial mouse. This can be prevented by including the `/noserialmice` switch in the boot line of the BOOT.INI file.

# MANAGING RESOURCES

Remember: Here are the elements that Microsoft says they test on in the "Managing Resources" section of the exam.

- Create and manage local user accounts and local group accounts to meet given requirements.
- Set up and modify user profiles.
- Set up shared folders and permissions.
- Set permissions on NTFS partitions, folders, and files.
- Install and configure printers in a given environment.

Using local groups to assign rights and permissions on an NT Workstation can reduce administrative overhead.

The following account policies can be set from the User Manager:

- **Maximum Password Age.** This option enables you to specify how long a user's password is valid. The default is that passwords expire in 42 days.
- **Minimum Password Age.** This specifies how long a user must keep a particular password before she can change it again. If you force a user to change her password, and you leave this set to Allow Changes Immediately, after the user has changed her password once, she can change it right back to the old one. If you are requiring password changes for security reasons, this breaks down your security. For that reason, you may want to set a minimum password age.
- **Minimum Password Length.** The default on Windows NT is to allow blank passwords. Once again, for security reasons, you may not want to allow this. You can set a minimum password

length of up to 14 characters, which is the maximum password length allowed under Windows NT.

- **Password Uniqueness.** If you want to force users to use a different password each time they change their passwords, you can set a value for password uniqueness. If you set the password uniqueness value to remember two passwords, when a user is prompted to change her password, she cannot use the same password again until she changes her password for the third time. The maximum password uniqueness value is 24.
- **Lockout After Bad Logon Attempts.** Setting a value for this option prevents the account from being used after this number is reached, even if the right password is finally entered. If you set this value to five, which is the default when Account Lockout is enabled, on the sixth attempt, a person cannot log on to Windows NT—even if the user (or hacker) types in the correct username and password.
- **Reset Counter After.** This value specifies when to refresh the counter for bad logon attempts. The default value is 30 minutes. That means if Account Lockout is set to five and a user tries to log on unsuccessfully four times, he can stop, wait 45 minutes, and then try again. The counter will have been reset by then, and he can try to log on five more times before the account will be locked out.
- **Lockout Duration.** This value specifies how long the account should remain locked if the lockout counter is exceeded. It is generally more secure to set Lockout Duration to forever so that the administrator must unlock the account. That way, the administrator is warned of the activity on that account.
- **Users Must Log On to Change Password.** This setting requires a user to log on successfully before changing his password. If a user's password expires, the user cannot log on until the administrator changes the password for the user.

Home directories can be created so that each user who logs on has a specific location on the local machine or the network where he or she can store personal information.

In order to use RAS, a user must be granted dial-in permission in the User Manager.

You create new accounts through User Manager. Two accounts are created automatically when NT is installed: Administrator and Guest.

The following password options can be configured for a user when the account is created:

- **User Must Change Password at Next Logon.** When this is selected (which is the default when creating new users), the user is prompted to change his password when he logs on to Windows NT. This setting is not compatible with the account policy that forces a user to log on to change his password. If both are selected, the user must contact the administrator to change the password.
- **User Cannot Change Password.** Setting this option prevents a user from changing her password. If both this setting and User Must Change Password are selected, you get an error message stating that you cannot check both options for the same user when you attempt to add the account.
- **Password Never Expires.** You can use this option to override the setting for password expiration in the Account Policy. This option tends to be used for accounts that will be assigned to services, but it can be granted to user accounts as well. If you have both this option and User Must Change Password at Next Logon selected, a warning tells you that the user will not be required to change her password.

- **Account Disabled.** Instead of deleting a user's account when he or she leaves the company, it is a good idea to disable the account. If the user will be replaced, it is likely that the new individual who's hired will need the same rights and permissions the previous user had. By disabling the account, you prevent the previous employee from accessing your Windows NT Workstation or domain. When the new individual is hired, however, you can rename the old account to the new name and have the user change the password.
- **Account Locked Out.** This option is visible only if you have Account Lockout enabled in the Account Policy. You, as an administrator, can never check this box; it will be grayed out. The only time this box is available is when a user's account has been locked out because it has exceeded the specified number of bad logon attempts. If the Lockout Duration is set to forever, the administrator must go into that user's account and uncheck the Account Locked Out check box.

Table 9 lists the buttons available from a user's Properties dialog box in User Manager.

### TABLE 9
### USER PROPERTY BUTTONS IN USER MANAGER

| *Button* | *Enables You to Modify...* |
|---|---|
| Groups | The groups the user is a member of |
| Profile | The user's profile path, login script path, and home directory location |
| Account | The user's account expiration date and account type |
| Hours | The hours a user can log in to the computer |
| Dialin | Whether the user can dial in using RAS and what callback features (if any) are enabled |

You can create account templates to reduce the amount of administration that's required to create groups of similar accounts. Accounts created from a template inherit the template's configuration for the following features:

- Account Description option
- User Must Change Password at Next Logon option
- User Cannot Change Password option
- Password Never Expires option
- Group memberships
- All user-environment profile properties
- All dial-in properties

In account configuration, the %UserName% variable can represent individual users' login names whenever they're needed to access or create a folder. (For example, you might use it when creating home folders called by the users' login names.)

When a user leaves the company, it is always better to disable his account than to delete it for the following reasons:

- A disabled account cannot be used to log in (rendering it unuseable).
- Deleting an account also deletes the SID associated with it, thus removing the permissions for that user from all locations on the network.
- A user whose account is deleted will have to have her permissions restored everywhere if she should return.
- Renaming an account grants the permissions of the former user to the new user.

Local groups can be created to grant access to Workstation resources and to assign users' rights on the system. The following local groups are created when NT Workstation is installed:

- **Administrators.** The Administrators group has full control over the Windows NT Workstation. This account has the most control on the computer. However, members of the Administrators group do not automatically have control over all files on the system. By using an NTFS partition, a user can configure a file's permissions to restrict access from the administrator. If the administrator needs to access the file, she can take ownership of the file and then access it. Administrative privilege is one of three levels of privilege you can assign to a user in Windows NT. It is the highest level of privilege that can be assigned.
- **Guests.** The Guests group is used to give someone limited access to the resources on the Windows NT Workstation. The Guest account is automatically added to this group. The Guests group is one of the three levels of privilege you can assign to a Windows NT user account.
- **Users.** The Users group provides a user with the necessary rights to use the computer. By default, all accounts created on Windows NT Workstation are put into the Users group, except for the built-in Administrator and Guest accounts. User privilege is one of the three levels of privilege you can assign in Windows NT.
- **Power Users.** The Power Users group gives members the ability to perform certain system tasks without giving them complete administrative control over the machine. One of the tasks a power user can perform is the sharing of directories. An ordinary user on Windows NT Workstation cannot share directories.
- **Backup Operators.** The Backup Operators group gives its members the ability to bypass the security placed on any file when using the NT Backup utility. This allows them complete resource access, but only for the specialized job of backing up files, not for general access.
- **Replicator.** The Replicator group is used only to enable directory replication. This process allows file transfer to take place between an export computer (which must be an NT Server) and an import computer (which can be NT Workstation or NT Server). You will not see questions regarding this group and its service on the NT Workstation exam; but if you want more information, you can consult the NT Server book in this MCSE series.

Group accounts cannot be renamed.

User profiles fall into two categories: local and roaming. In addition, roaming user profiles fall into two categories: mandatory and personal. A local profile is located on a specific machine and takes effect only when a user logs onto that machine. A roaming profile is available over the network and can be accessed from any machine that has network connectivity to the machine holding the profile. Mandatory profiles (which have the extension .MAN) are read only and, therefore, cannot be changed by a user.

Shared folders allow users to access Workstation resources from the network (by default, no resources are made generally accessible to users over the network).

The following permissions are available on shared folders:

- **No Access.** If a user or group is given the No Access permission to a shared folder, that user or group cannot open the shared folder even though he will see the shared folder on the network. The

No Access permission overrides all other permissions a user or group might have to the folder.

- **Read.** The Read permission allows a user or group to display files and subfolders within the shared folder. It also allows the user or group to execute programs that might be located within the shared folder.
- **Change.** The Change permission allows a user or group to add files or subfolders to the shared folder and to append or delete information from existing files and subfolders. The Change permission also encompasses everything included within the Read permission.
- **Full Control.** If a user or group is given the Full Control permission, that user or group has the ability to change the file permissions and to perform all tasks allowed by the Change permission.

In order to share a folder on an NT Workstation, you must have that right. It is given by default to the built-in Administrators and Power Users groups.

You can share a folder remotely by using the Server Manager. Shares can be created, modified, or removed from a folder through the folder share permissions (accessible by right-clicking the folder and choosing Sharing).

If a user is given individual permission to access a folder and is also a member of one or more groups which are given access, the user's effective permission is the combination of the permissions (the highest level). This is true unless one of the permissions is No Access, in which case the No Access permission prevails over all others.

The permission granted to a share is also the permission granted to the tree structure inside that share. Sharing one folder within another shared folder gives two points of access and, potentially, two levels of access to the same resource.

Shared permissions apply only to network access; NTFS permissions apply both over the network and locally.

Table 10 describes the access permissions available on NTFS.

**TABLE 10**
**STANDARD NTFS PERMISSIONS**

| *Permission* | *Folder* | *File* |
|---|---|---|
| Read (R) | Enables the user to display the folder and subfolders, attributes, and permissions | Enables the user to display the file, its attributes, and its permissions |
| Write (W) | Enables the user to add files or folders, change attributes for the folder, and display permissions | Enables the user to change file attributes and add or append data to the file |
| Execute (X) | Enables the user to make changes to subfolders, display permissions, and display attributes | Enables the user to run a file if it is an executable and display attributes and permissions |
| Delete (D) | Enables the user to remove the folder | Enables the user to remove the file |
| Change Permission (P) | Enables the user to modify folder permissions | Enables the user to modify file permissions |
| Take Ownership (O) | Enables the user to take ownership of the folder | Enables the user to take ownership of a file |

Table 11 lists the standard NTFS file permissions and the granular permissions that comprise them.

**TABLE 11**
**STANDARD NTFS FILE PERMISSIONS**

| *Standard File Permission* | *Individual NTFS Permissions* |
|---|---|
| No Access | (None) |
| Read | (RX) |
| Change | (RWXD) |
| Full Control | (All Permissions) |

Table 12 lists the standard NTFS folder permissions and the default file permissions for files within those folders.

You (or any user) can take ownership of an NTFS resource provided that you meet one or more of the following criteria:

- **You must be the owner of the file or folder.** You must be the user who created it.
- **You must have been granted Full Control.** This includes the ability to Change Permissions (P).
- **You must have been given special access to Change Permissions (P).** A user can be given just this one permission to a file or folder.
- **You must have been given special access to Take Ownership (O).** With the ability to Take Ownership, a user can give himself the right to Change Permissions (P).
- **You must be a member of the Administrators group.**

If a user is granted individual NTFS permissions to a resource and is also a member of one or more groups that have been granted access, the effective permission for the user is the cumulative permission from all the access levels. This is the case unless any level is No Access, in which case the No Access level prevails over all others.

When shared permissions are combined with NTFS permissions for accessing a resource over the network, the lowest permission (share or NTFS) prevails. If the user is accessing locally, however, only NTFS permission applies.

**TABLE 12**
**STANDARD NTFS FOLDER PERMISSIONS**

| *Standard Folder Permissions* | *Individual NTFS Folder Permissions* | *Individual NTFS File Permissions* |
|---|---|---|
| No Access | (None) | (None) |
| Read | (RX) | (RX) |
| Change | (RWXD) | (RWXD) |
| Add | (WX) | (Not Applicable) |
| Add & Read | (RWX) | (RX) |
| List | (RX) | (Not Applicable) |
| Full Control | (All) | (All) |

When you copy a file from one folder to another, the permissions of the destination folder are applied to the new copy of the file. When you move a file from one folder to another and the folders are on different partitions, the permissions on the destination folder apply to the moved file. When you move a file from one folder to another on the same partition, the file retains its original permissions.

It's important that you remember the definitions of the following printing terms:

- **Printer**. The software component for printing. Also referred to as a *logical printer*, it is the software interface between the application and the print device.
- **Print device.** The actual hardware the paper comes out of. This is what you would traditionally think of as a printer. In Windows NT terminology, however, it is called a print device.
- **Print job.** The information that is sent to the print device. It contains both the data and the commands for print processing.
- **Print spooler.** A collection of DLLs (Dynamic Link Libraries) that accept, process, schedule, and distribute print jobs.
- **Creating a printer.** The process of defining a printer from your Windows NT Workstation. When you create a printer, you specify that the machine on which you are creating it will be the print server for that print device. You must create a printer if no other Windows NT system has created it yet, or if the print device is on a non–Windows NT operating system such as Windows 95.
- **Connecting to a printer.** A process that is necessary when the print device has already been defined by another Windows NT system and a printer has been created on that Windows NT system. If that is the case, in order to use the printer, you just need to connect to the printer from your Windows NT Workstation.
- **Print server.** The computer that created the printer and on which the printer is defined. Typically this is a Windows NT Server. However, a Windows NT Workstation or even a Windows 95 system can act as a print server.
- **Print queue.** The list of print jobs on the print server that are waiting to print.
- **Printer driver.** The software that enables applications to communicate properly with the print device.
- **Spooling.** The process of storing documents on the hard disk and then sending them to the printer. After the document has been stored on the hard disk, the user regains control of the application.

You can configure a printer pool by assigning two or more printer ports to the same printer and enabling printer pooling.

To allow other users to access a printer over the network, you must share the printer. Printer permissions can be set to control access to a printer. Table 13 lists those permissions.

**TABLE 13**
**CAPABILITIES GRANTED WITH PRINTER PERMISSIONS**

| *Capability* | *Full Control* | *Manage Documents* | *Print* | *No Access* |
|---|---|---|---|---|
| Print documents | X | X | X | |
| Pause, resume, restart, and cancel the user's own documents | X | X | X | |
| Connect to a printer | X | X | X | |
| Control job settings for all documents | X | X | | |
| Pause, restart, and delete all documents | X | X | | |
| Share a printer | X | | | |
| Change printer properties | X | | | |
| Delete a printer | X | | | |
| Change printer permissions | X | | | |

In a printer's properties dialog box, you can set the availability of the printer to allow it to hold documents until a certain time of the day.

Spool settings include the following options:

- **Spool Print Documents So Program Finishes Printing Faster.** If you choose this option, the documents will spool. This option has two choices within it:
  - *Start Printing After Last Page Is Spooled.* This prevents documents from printing until they are completely spooled. The application that is printing is not available during the spooling. To use this option, you must have enough space on the partition of the spool directory to hold the entire print job.
  - *Start Printing Immediately.* This enables a document to start printing before it has spooled completely, which speeds up printing.
- **Print Directly to the Printer.** This prevents the document from spooling. Although it speeds up printing, this is not an option for a shared printer, which would must support multiple incoming documents simultaneously.
- **Hold Mismatched Documents.** This prevents incorrect documents from printing. Incorrect documents are those that do not match the configuration of the printer.
- **Print Spooled Documents First.** Spooled documents will print ahead of partially spooled documents, even if they have a lower priority. This speeds up printing.
- **Keep Documents After They Have Printed.** Documents remain in the spooler after they have been printed.

If the print queue becomes jammed, you can clear corrupted print items by stopping and restarting the Spooler service from the Services icon in the Control Panel. The spool directory is, by default, located in Systemroot\system32\spool\printers, but that location can be changed via the File menu in the printer properties dialog box.

# CONNECTIVITY

Remember: Here are the elements that Microsoft says they test on in the "Connectivity" section of the exam.

- Add and configure the network components of Windows NT Workstation.
- Use various methods to access network resources.
- Implement Windows NT Workstation as a client in a NetWare environment.
- Use various configurations to install Windows NT Workstation as a TCP/IP client.
- Configure and install Dial-Up Networking in a given situation.
- Configure Microsoft Peer Web Services in a given situation.

NDIS 4.0 enables the following on an NT Workstation computer:

- An unlimited number of network adapter cards.
- An unlimited number of network protocols can be bound to a single network adapter card.
- Independence between protocols and adapter card drivers.
- Communication links between adapter cards and their drivers.

The major characteristics of TCP/IP include the following:

- Routing support
- Connectivity with the Internet
- Interoperability with most possible operating systems and computer types
- Support as a client for Dynamic Host Configuration Protocol (DHCP)
- Support as a client for Windows Internet Name Service (WINS)
- Support as a client for Domain Name System (DNS)
- Support for Simple Network Management Protocol (SNMP)

The following are the major characteristics of NWLink:

- Connectivity with NetWare resources
- Routing support
- Supported by a wide variety of other operating systems
- Large installation base

The main characteristics of NetBEUI include

- No routing support.
- Transmissions are broadcast-based and, therefore, generate a lot of traffic.
- Fast performance on small LANs.
- Small memory overhead.
- No tuning options.

DLC protocol is primarily used for connecting NT Workstations to printers directly attached to the network through network interface cards.

Two network programming interfaces are available to allow programmers to access the network:

- **NetBIOS (Network Basic Input/Output System).** The original network API supported by Microsoft. IBM originally developed NetBIOS.
- **Windows Sockets (also called WinSock).** A newer network API originally developed by the UNIX community. Now Microsoft also supports it.

Table 14 describes the IPC mechanisms available in NT Workstation.

The Network applet in the Control Panel allows you to change names, services, protocols, adapters, and bindings for network configuration.

In order to be part of an NT domain, an NT computer must have an account that was created by someone with the right to add computer accounts in the domain (by default, an administrator).

If NWLink is installed and NT is left to autoconfigure the frame type, NT will expect 802.2 frames unless others are detected, in which case it will configure to the frame type it sees first. To use multiple NWLink frame types, you must make a Registry setting change.

Client Services for NetWare gives an NT Workstation the capability to access files and printers from a NetWare server, provided that NWLink is also installed on the Workstation. When installed on an NT Workstation, NWLink allows the workstation to connect to an application running on a NetWare server.

**TABLE 14**
**TYPES OF INTERPROCESS COMMUNICATIONS**

| *IPC Mechanism* | *Typical Uses* |
|---|---|
| Named pipes | Named pipes establish a guaranteed bidirectional communications channel between two computers. After the pipe is established, either computer can read data from or write data to the pipe. |
| Mailslots | Mailslots establish a unidirectional communications channel between two computers. Receipt of the message is not guaranteed, and no acknowledgment is sent if the data is received. |
| Windows Sockets (WinSock) | WinSock is an API that enables applications to access transport protocols such as TCP/IP and NWLink. |
| RPCs | RPCs enable the various components of distributed applications to communicate with one another via the network. |
| Network Dynamic Data Exchange (NetDDE) | NetDDE is an older version of an RPC that is based on NetBIOS. |
| Distributed ActiveX Component Object Model (DCOM) | DCOM is an RPC based on Microsoft technology; it enables the components of a distributed application to be located on multiple computers across a network simultaneously. |

TCP/IP is the default protocol installed on NT Workstation and requires at least a TCP/IP address and subnet mask to function properly. You can configure an NT Workstation to automatically receive TCP/IP configuration information from a DHCP server by selecting the Obtain Address from DHCP Server option button in the TCP/IP Properties dialog box. Two tools, IPCONFIG and PING, can be used to test the configuration and function of TCP/IP on your NT Workstation.

NT Workstation can act as a RAS client or a RAS server with one concurrent incoming connection. As a client, it can connect to servers using the SLIP, PPP, and PPTP protocols; as a client, it supports incoming connections using PPP or PPTP. Whether acting as a RAS client or a RAS server, an NT Workstation must have the RAS service installed. Table 15 lists the features of the three line protocols mentioned here.

PPTP connections require a PPP or LAN connection to a server with a Virtual Private Network (VPN) configured on it and provide for secure and encrypted communication.

In order for a user to log on to an NT Workstation using RAS, the user account must be configured in User Manager to allow dialin.

Peer Web Services allows for FTP, WWW, and Gopher connections from Internet or intranet clients.

**TABLE 15**
**RAS LINE PROTOCOLS AND FEATURES**

| *Feature* | *SLIP* | *PPP* | *PPTP* |
|---|---|---|---|
| Supports NT as server | No | Yes | Yes |
| Supports NT as client | Yes | Yes | Yes |
| Passes TCP/IP | Yes | Yes | Yes |
| Passes NetBEUI | No | Yes | Yes |
| Passes NWLink | No | Yes | Yes |
| Supports DHCP over RAS | No | Yes | No |
| Requires PPP or LAN connection | No | No | Yes |
| Supports VPNs | No | No | Yes |
| Supports password encryption | No | Yes | Yes |
| Supports transmission encryption | No | No | Yes |

# RUNNING APPLICATIONS

Remember: Here are the elements that Microsoft says they test on in the "Running Applications" section of the exam.

- Start applications on Intel and RISC platforms in various operating system environments.
- Start applications with various priorities.

NT Workstation supports (to a greater or lesser extent) applications written for the following operating systems:

- Windows NT and Windows 95
- MS-DOS
- Windows 3.x
- OS/2
- POSIX

MS-DOS applications invoke an NT Virtual DOS machine, which emulates a DOS environment. Windows 16-bit applications invoke an NT Virtual DOS machine (unless one is already running) and then run a Win16 emulator called WOW.EXE.

By default, Win16 applications all run in the same NTVDM. However, if desired, you can configure them to run in separate NTVDMs. The following list summarizes the advantages and disadvantages of running Win16 applications in separate NTVDMs.

**Advantages:**

- Win16 applications will now use preemptive multitasking. An ill-behaved Win16 application will no longer prevent other Win16 applications from executing normally because each Win16 application will have its own memory space and thread of execution.
- Win16 applications will now be more reliable because they will not be affected by the problems of other Win16 applications.
- Win16 applications can now take advantage of multiprocessor computers. When Win16 applications are run in a common NTVDM, they must share a single thread of execution. The generation of individual NTVDMs also creates individual threads of execution, and each thread can potentially be executed on a different processor. The operating system could now schedule each NTVDM's thread of execution to run on whichever processor is available. In a system with multiple processors, this can lead to multiprocessing. If the Win16 applications were running in a common NTVDM, their single thread of execution would be able to run only on a single processor, no matter how many processors existed on the computer.
- Windows NT will enable Win16 applications running in separate memory spaces to continue to participate in OLE and dynamic data exchange (DDE).

**Disadvantages:**

- There is additional overhead in running separate NTVDMs.
- Some older Win16 applications did not use the standards of OLE and DDE. These applications would not function properly if they were run in separate memory spaces. These applications must be run in a common memory space to function correctly. Lotus for Windows 1.0 is an example of this type of application.

NT offers four methods for running Win16 applications in separate NTVDMs:

- Anytime you start a Win16 application from the Start menu using the Run option, you can select the Run in Separate Memory Space option. This technique must be applied every time an application is run from the Run dialog box.
- At a command prompt, you can start a Win16 application using the command syntax `start /separate` *`application`*. For example, to start Word 6.0 you could type the following:

  ```
  start /separate c:\office16\word\winword.exe
  ```

  This technique must be applied every time the application is run from a command prompt.
- Shortcuts that point to Win16 applications can be configured to always run in a separate memory space. To do that, use the appropriate option on the Shortcut tab of the properties dialog box for the shortcut. Although this causes an application to run in a separate memory space every time the shortcut is used, it applies only to the particular shortcut that's modified, and not to any other shortcuts that have been created to that application.
- You can configure all files with a particular extension to always run in a separate memory space when the data document is double-clicked on in the Windows NT Explorer. To do this, you edit the File Types tab of the View, Options properties.

The OS/2 subsystem allows you to run OS/2 1.x character-based applications on Intel machines. On RISC machines, you must run OS/2 applications in NTVDMs by using the `/FORCEDOS` switch when running the applications from a command prompt or shortcut. You configure OS/2 applications by editing a CONFIG.SYS file using an OS/2 text editor. This creates a temporary file that is then converted to Registry settings (no CONFIG.SYS file is actually stored on the hard drive).

NT provides POSIX.1 support in its POSIX subsystem. This subsystem supports the following features for POSIX applications:

- **Case-sensitive file naming.** NTFS preserves case for both directory and filenames.
- **Hard links.** POSIX applications can store the same data in two differently named files.
- **An additional time stamp on files.** This tracks the last time the file was accessed. The default on FAT volumes is to track only the last time the file was modified.

Application support differs across different hardware platforms. Table 16 lists the kinds of support that applications have. *Binary* means that the same application will run across all hardware platforms; *source* means that a different compile is required for each hardware platform.

### TABLE 16
### APPLICATION COMPATIBILITY ACROSS WINDOWS NT PLATFORMS

| *Platform* | *MS-DOS* | *Win16* | *Win32* | *OS/2* | *POSIX* |
|---|---|---|---|---|---|
| Intel | Binary | Binary | Source | Binary | Source |
| Alpha | Binary | Binary | Source* | Binary** | Source |
| Mips | Binary | Binary | Source | Binary** | Source |
| PowerPC | Binary | Binary | Source | Binary** | Source |

* Third-party utilities such as Digital FX!32 enable Win32-based Intel programs to execute on Digital Alpha AXP microprocessors. Although these utilities are interpreting the code on-the-fly, they end up performing faster on the Alpha as a result of the increased processor speed.
** Only bound applications can be run on the three RISC hardware platforms. They will run in a Windows NTVDM because the OS/2 subsystem is not provided in RISC-based versions of Windows NT.

All applications run at a default priority set by the application itself (between 0 and 31). This priority determines its relative access to the CPU and, as a result, how quickly it responds to user interaction.

You can assign priority levels to applications through the use of command prompt switches. Table 17 lists the priority levels, their base priorities, and the commands you use to assign them.

NT boosts the priority of the application in the foreground by anywhere from 0 to 2 points (this ensures that foreground applications are more responsive than background applications). The "boost from" base is set on the Performance tab of the Control Panel's System application.

### TABLE 17
### BASE PRIORITY LEVELS UNDER WINDOWS NT

| *Priority Level* | *Base Priority* | *Command Line* |
|---|---|---|
| *Low* | *4* | `start /low` *`executable.exe`* |
| *Normal* | *8* | `start /normal` *`executable.exe`* |
| *High* | *13* | `start /high` *`executable.exe`* |
| *Realtime* | *24* | `start /realtime` *`executable.exe`* |

# MONITORING AND OPTIMIZATION

Remember: Here are the elements that Microsoft says they test on in the "Monitoring and Optimization" section of the exam.

- Monitor system performance by using various tools.
- Identify and resolve a given performance problem.
- Optimize system performance in various areas.

Task Manager (accessible by right-clicking the taskbar and choosing Task Manager) allows you to see and end applications and processes on your system.

Performance Monitor allows you to monitor counters for specific computer and application objects and to tune the performance of your computer based on what you find.

In order to monitor disk counters, you must first enable them through the use of the command `DISKPERF -y` (or `DISKPERF -YE` for volume sets and RAID disks).

Table 18 describes the objects you will find in the Performance Monitor (others may be present depending on the services or applications you have installed).

Four views are available in the Performance Monitor:

- **Chart view.** Real-time line graphs of counters.
- **Log view.** Stored statistics useable by other views at a later time.
- **Alert view.** Monitored thresholds that generate events if the thresholds are crossed.
- **Report view.** Real-time text-displayed statistics on counters.

Performance Monitor can be used to monitor a local machine or an NT Server or Workstation to which the user has Administrative rights.

**TABLE 18**

**COMMON OBJECTS ALWAYS AVAILABLE IN THE PERFORMANCE MONITOR**

| *Object* | *Description* |
|---|---|
| Cache | The file system cache is an area of physical memory that holds recently used data. |
| Logical Disk | Disk partitions and other logical views of disk space. |
| Memory | Random access memory used to store code and data. |
| Objects | Certain system software objects. |
| Paging File | File used to support virtual memory allocated by the system. |
| Physical Disk | Hardware disk unit. |
| Process | Software object that represents a running program. |
| Processor | Hardware unit that executes program instructions. |
| Redirector | File system that diverts file requests to network servers. |
| System | Counters that apply to all system hardware and software. |
| Thread | The part of a process that uses the processor. |

The Server Manager allows you to see who is currently logged on to a computer and what resources they are using, to see available shares on your Workstation, to start or stop sharing resources, and to see what type of access is being made to all in-use resources.

WINMSD allows you to view configuration information about your computer.

You may want to monitor and tune the following components:

- Memory
- Processor
- Disks
- Network

The Event Viewer allows you to view information logged to any of three logs:

- **System log.** A log of events detected by NT that have to do with system functioning (the starting and stopping of services or their failure).
- **Security log.** A log of audited events that have to do with resource access (success or failure).
- **Application log.** A log of events recorded by applications running on NT that are configured to create such events.

You can archive any of these logs for viewing at a later time or for event archive.

An emergency repair disk enables you to recover Registry and system settings should they become corrupt. By performing the following two steps, you can be sure your ERD remains up-to-date:

1. Using the RDISK.EXE utility, update the Repair directory to save the repair information on your hard drive.
2. Using the RDISK.EXE utility, write the Repair information to a floppy disk.

You can perform a repair by booting to and using the three installation disks required to install NT from a CD-ROM and by specifying that you want to repair your system when asked.

The LastKnownGood configuration is a set of Registry settings that record the state of the NT configuration at the time of the last successful login. If you encounter problems with your system resulting from a change you've made in the current session, reboot and choose to restore LastKnownGood. Every time you log in, the LastKnownGood configuration is overwritten with the current configuration of your hardware (whether it functions properly or not).

## TROUBLESHOOTING

Remember: Here are the elements that Microsoft says they test on in the "Troubleshooting" section of the exam.

- Choose the appropriate course of action to take when the boot process fails.
- Choose the appropriate course of action to take when a print job fails.
- Choose the appropriate course of action to take when the installation process fails.
- Choose the appropriate course of action to take when an application fails.
- Choose the appropriate course of action to take when a user cannot access a resource.
- Modify the Registry using the appropriate tool in a given situation.
- Implement advanced techniques to resolve various problems.

The acronym DETECT can be used to define the troubleshooting process:

| | |
|---|---|
| D | Discover the problem |
| E | Explore the boundaries |
| T | Track the possible approaches |
| E | Execute an approach |
| C | Check for success |
| T | Tie up loose ends |

Table 19 identifies the files involved in the boot process for both Intel and RISC machines.

**TABLE 19**
**BOOT PROCESS FILES**

| *Intel* | *RISC* |
|---|---|
| NTLDR | OSLOADER.EXE |
| BOOT.INI | NTOSKRNL.EXE |
| NTDETECT.COM | |
| NTOSKRNL.EXE | |
| NTBOOTDD.SYS (for SCSI drives with BIOS disabled) | |

In the NT boot process (in BOOT.INI), ARC paths define the physical position of the NT operating system files. ARC paths follow one of two formats:

scsi(0)disk(0)rdisk(0)partition(1)*folder*
multi(0)disk(0)rdisk(0)partition(1)*folder*

The first type, scsi ARC paths, define hard drives that are SCSI but have the BIOS disabled. The relevant parameters are

- **scsi.** The SCSI controller, starting from 0.
- **disk.** The physical disk, starting from 0.
- **partition.** The partition on the disk, starting from 1.
- ***\folder.*** The folder in which the NT files are located.

The second type, multi ARC paths, define hard drives that are non-SCSI or are SCSI with the BIOS enabled. The relevant parameters are

- **multi.** The controller, starting from 0.
- **rdisk.** The physical disk, starting from 0.
- **partition.** The partition on the disk, starting from 1.
- ***\folder.*** The folder in which the NT files are located.

Partitions are numbered according to the following pattern:

1. The first primary partition on each disk gets the number 1.
2. Each additional primary partition is then given a number, incrementing up from 1.
3. Each logical drive is then given a number in the order they appear in the Disk Administrator.

Switches on boot lines in the BOOT.INI file define additional boot parameters. Table 20 lists the switches you need to know and their functions.

**TABLE 20**
**BOOT.INI SWITCHES**

| *Switch* | *Function* |
|---|---|
| /basevideo | Loads standard VGA video driver (640×480, 16-color) |
| /sos | Displays each driver as it is loaded |
| /noserialmice | Prevents autodetection of serial mice on COM ports, which can disable a UPS connected to the port |

A recovery disk can be used to bypass problems with a system partition. This disk must be formatted in NT and will contain the files listed in Table 21 (broken down by hardware platform).

**TABLE 21**
**FILES ON THE RECOVERY DISK**

| *Intel* | *RISC* |
|---|---|
| NTLDR | OSLOADER.EXE |
| NTDETECT.COM | HAL.DLL |
| BOOT.INI | *.PAL (for Alpha machines) |
| BOOTSECT.DOS (allows you to boot to DOS) | |
| NTBOOTDD.SYS (the SCSI driver for a hard drive with SCSI BIOS not enabled) | |

An emergency repair disk can be used to repair an NT system if the Registry becomes corrupted. The repair disk must be used in conjunction with the three setup disks used to install NT.

The RDISK program allows you to update the \REPAIR folder, which in turn is used to update your repair disk.

The following list identifies possible sources of installation problems:

- Media errors
- Insufficient disk space
- Non-supported SCSI adapters
- Failure of dependency service to start
- Inability to connect to the domain controller
- Error in assigning domain names

Application failures generally result from incorrect application configuration, not from incorrect NT configuration.

If applications do not run, check the following:

- An MS-DOS application may be trying to access hardware directly.
- Two Win16 applications running in the same NTVDM may be conflicting.
- Win32 applications may be compiled for a different processor.

Services are interrelated: If one service fails, it may affect others as well. Therefore, you need to make sure that you get to the root of a service failure, and you're not just treating the symptoms.

Two programs are available for viewing and modifying the Registry:

- REGEDIT.EXE
- REGEDT32.EXE

The Network Monitor tool can be used to analyze network traffic in and out of the adapter on an NT Workstation computer.

# Fast Facts

## Windows NT Server 4 Exam

Now that you have thoroughly read through this book, worked through the exercises and got as much hands on exposure to NT Server as you could, you've now booked your exam. This chapter is designed as a last minute cram for you as you walk out the door on your way to the exam. You can't re-read the whole book in an hour, but you will be able to read this chapter in that time.

This chapter is organized by objective category, giving you not just a summary, but a rehash of the most important point form facts that you need to know. Remember that this is meant to be a review of concepts and a trigger for you to remember wider definitions. In addition to what is in this chapter, make sure you know what is in the glossary because this chapter does not define terms. If you know what is in here and the concepts that stand behind it, chances are the exam will be a snap.

## Planning

Remember: Here are the elements that Microsoft says they test on for the "Planning" section of the exam.

- Plan the disk drive configuration for various requirements. Requirements include: choosing a file system and fault tolerance method
- Choose a protocol for various situations. Protocols include: TCP/IP, NWLink IPX/SPX Compatible Transport, and NetBEUI

Minimum requirement for installing NT Server on an Intel machine is 468DX/33, 16MB of RAM, and 130MB of free disk space.

The login process on an NT Domain is as follows:

1. WinLogon sends the user name and password to the Local Security Authority (LSA).

2. The LSA passes the request to the local NetLogon service.
3. The local NetLogon service sends the logon information to the NetLogon service on the domain controller.
4. The NetLogon service on the domain controller passes the information to the domain controller's Security Accounts Manager (SAM).
5. The SAM asks the domain directory database for approval of the user name and password.
6. The SAM passes the result of the approval request to the domain controller's NetLogon service.
7. The domain controller's NetLogon service passes the result of the approval request to the client's NetLogon service.
8. The client's NetLogon service passes the result of the approval request to the LSA.
9. If the logon is approved, the LSA creates an access token and passes it to the WinLogon process.
10. WinLogon completes the logon, thus creating a new process for the user and attaching the access token to the new process.

The system partition is where your computer boots and it must be on an active partition.

The boot partition is where the WINNT folder is found and it contains the NT program files. It can be on any partition (not on a volume set, though).

NT supports two forms of software-based fault tolerance: Disk Mirroring (RAID 1) and Stripe Sets with Paritiy (RAID 5).

Disk Mirroring uses 2 hard drives and provides 50% disk space utilization.

Stripe sets with Parity use between 3 and 32 hard drives and provides a (n-1)/n*100% utilization (n = number of disks in the set).

Disk duplexing provides better tolerance than mirroring because it does mirroring with separate controllers on each disk.

NT Supports 3 file systems: NTFS, FAT, and CDFS (it no longer supports HPFS, the OS/2 file system nor does it support FAT32, a file system used by Windows 95).

The following table is a comparison of NTFS and FAT features:

Table 1.1 shows a quick summary of the differences between file systems:

### SUMMARY TABLE 1
### FAT VERSUS NTFS COMPARISON

| *Feature* | *FAT* | *NTFS* |
|---|---|---|
| File name length | 255 | 255 |
| 8.3 file name compatibility | Yes | Yes |
| File size | 4 GB | 16 EB |
| Partition size | 4 GB | 16 EB |
| Directory structure | Linked list | B-tree |
| Local security | No | Yes |
| Transaction tracking | No | Yes |
| Hot fixing | No | Yes |
| Overhead | 1 MB | >4 MB |
| Required on system partition for RISC-based computers | Yes | No |
| Accessible from MS-DOS/ Windows 95 | Yes | No |
| Accessible from OS/2 | Yes | No |
| Case-sensitive | No | POSIX only |
| Case preserving | Yes | Yes |

| *Feature* | *FAT* | *NTFS* |
|---|---|---|
| Compression | No | Yes |
| Efficiency | 200 MB | 400 MB |
| Windows NT formattable | Yes | Yes |
| Fragmentation level | High | Low |
| Floppy disk formattable | Yes | No |

The following is a table to summarize the protocols commonly used by NT for network communication:

**SUMMARY TABLE 2**
**PRIMARY PROTOCOL USES**

| *Protocol* | *Primary Use* |
|---|---|
| TCP/IP | Internet and WAN connectivity |
| NWLink | Interoperability with NetWare |
| NetBEUI | Interoperability with old Lan Man networks |

The main points regarding TCP/IP are as follows:

- Requires IP Address, and Subnet Mask to function (default Gateway if being routed)
- Can be configured manually or automatically using DHCP server running on NT
- Common address resolution methods are WINS and DNS

## INSTALLATION AND CONFIGURATION

Remember: Here are the elements that Microsoft says they test on for the "Installation and Configuration" section of the exam.

- Install Windows NT Server on Intel-based platforms.
- Install Windows NT Server to perform various server roles. Server roles include: Primary domain controller, Backup domain controller, and Member server.
- Install Windows NT Server by using various methods. Installation methods include: CD-ROM, Over-the-network, Network Client Administrator, and Express versus custom.
- Configure protocols and protocol bindings. Protocols include: TCP/IP, NWLink IPX/SPX Compatible Transport, and NetBEUI.
- Configure network adapters. Considerations include: changing IRQ, IObase, and memory addresses and configuring multiple adapters.
- Configure Windows NT server core services. Services include: Directory Replicator, License Manager, and Other services.
- Configure peripherals and devices. Peripherals and devices include: communication devices, SCSI devices, tape devices drivers, UPS devices and UPS service, mouse drivers, display drivers, and keyboard drivers.
- Configure hard disks to meet various requirements. Requirements include: allocating disk space capacity, providing redundancy, improving security, and formatting.
- Configure printers. Tasks include: adding and configuring a printer, implementing a printer pool, and setting print priorities.
- Configure a Windows NT Server computer for various types of client computers. Client computer types include: Windows NT Workstation, Microsoft Windows 95, and Microsoft MS-DOS-based.

The Hardware Compatibility list is used to ensure that NT supports all computer components.

NT can be installed in 3 different configurations in a domain: Primary Domain Controller, Backup Domain Controller, and Member Server.

Two sources can be used for installation files: CD-ROM or network share (which is the hardware specific files from the CD copied onto a server and shared).

Three Setup diskettes are required for all installations when a CD-ROM is not supported by the operating system present on the computer at installation time (or if no operating system exists and the computer will not boot from the CD-ROM.)

WINNT and WINNT32 are used for network installation; WINNT32 for installations when NT is currently present on the machine you are installing to and WINNT when it is not.

The following table is a summary of the WINNT and WINNT32 switches:

### SUMMARY TABLE 3
### WINNT AND WINNT32 SWITCH FUNCTIONS

| *Switch* | *Function* |
|---|---|
| /B | Prevents creation of the three setup disks during the installation process |
| /S | Indicates the location of the source files for NT installation (e.g., /S:D:\NTFiles) |
| /U | Indicates the script file to use for an unattended installation (e.g., /U:C:\Answer.txt) |
| /UDF | Indicates the location of the uniqueness database file which defines unique configuration for each NT machine being installed (e.g., /UDF:D:\Answer.UDF) |
| /T | Indicates the place to put the temporary installation files |
| /OX | Initiates only the creation of the three setup disks |
| /F | Indicates not to verify the files copied to the setup diskettes |
| /C | Indicates not to check for free space on the setup diskettes before creating them |

To remove NT from a computer you must do the following:

1. Remove all the NTFS partitions from within Windows NT and reformat them with FAT (this ensures that these disk areas will be accessible by non-NT operating systems).
2. Boot to another operating system, such as Windows 95 or MS-DOS.
3. Delete the Windows NT installation directory tree (usually WINNT).
4. Delete pagefile.sys.
5. Turn off the hidden, system, and read-only attributes for NTBOOTDD.SYS, BOOT.INI, NTLDR, and NTDETECT.COM and then delete them. You might not have all of these on your computer, but if so, you can find them all in the root directory of your drive C.
6. Make the hard drive bootable by placing another operating system on it (or SYS it with DOS or Windows 95 to allow the operating system with does exist to boot).

The Client Administrator allows you to do the following:

- Make Network Installation Startup disk: shares files and creates bootable diskette for initiating client installation.
- Make Installation Disk Set: copies installation files to diskette for installing simple clients like MS-DOS network client 3.0.

- Copy Client-Based Network Administration Tools: creates a folder which can be attached to from Windows NT Workstation and Windows 95 clients to install tools for administering an NT Server from a workstation.

# MANAGING RESOURCES

Remember: Here are the elements that Microsoft says they test on for the "Managing Resources" section of the exam.

- Manage user and group accounts. Considerations include: managing Windows NT groups, managing Windows NT user rights, administering account policies, and auditing changes to the user account database.
- Create and manage policies and profiles for various situations. Policies and profiles include: local user profiles, roaming user profiles, and system policies.
- Administer remote servers from various types of client computers. Client computer types include: Windows 95 and Windows NT Workstation.
- Manage disk resources. Tasks include: copying and moving files between file systems, creating and sharing resources, implementing permissions and security, and establishing file auditing.

Network properties dialog box lets you install and configure the following:

- Computer and Domain names
- Services
- Protocols
- Adapters
- Bindings

When configuring NWLink ensure that if more than one frame type exists on your network that you don't use AutoDetect or only the first frame type encountered will be detected from then on.

The following table shows you three TCP/IP command-line diagnostic tools and what they do:

**SUMMARY TABLE 4**
**TCP/IP COMMAND LINE DIAGNOSTIC TOOLS**

| *Tool* | *Function* |
|---|---|
| IPConfig | Displays the basic TCP/IP configuration of each adapter card on a computer (with/all displays detailed configuration information) |
| Ping | Determines connectivity with another TCP/IP host by sending a message that is echoed by the recipient if received |
| Tracert | Traces each hop on the way to a TCP/IP host and indicates points of failure if they exist |

Network adapter card configuration of IRQ and I/O port address may or may not be configurable from the Network Properties dialog box; it depends on the card.

To allow NT computers to participate in a domain, a computer account must be created for each one.

Windows 95 clients need special profiles and policies created on a Windows 95 machine and then copied onto an NT Server to participate in domain profile and policy configuration.

Windows 95 clients need printer drivers installed on an NT Server acting as a print controller to print to an NT controller printer.

Typical services tested for NT Server are listed and described in the following table:

### SUMMARY TABLE 5
### NT SERVER SERVICES AND THEIR FUNCTIONS

| *Service* | *Function* |
|---|---|
| DNS | Provides TCP/IP address resolution using a static table and can be use for non-Microsoft hosts |
| WINS | Provides TP/IP address resolution using a dynamic table and can be used for Microsoft hosts |
| DHCP | Provides automatic configuration of TCP/IP clients for Microsoft clients |
| Browser | Provides a list of domain resources to Network Neighborhood and Server Manager |
| Replicator | Provides import and export services for automated file distribution between NT computers (Servers can be export and import, Workstations can only be import) |

REGEDT32.EXE and REGEDIT are used to view and modify registry settings in NT.

The five registry subtrees are:

- **HKEY_LOCAL_MACHINE.** Stores all the computer-specific configuration data.
- **HKEY_USERS.** Stores all the user-specific configuration data.
- **HKEY_CURRENT_USER.** Stores all configuration data for the currently logged on user.
- **HKEY_CLASSES_ROOT.** Stores all OLE and file association information.
- **HKEY_CURRENT_CONFIG.** Stores information about the hardware profile specified at startup.

REGEDT32.EXE allows you to see and set security on the registry and allows you to open the registry in read-only mode, but does not allow you to search by key value.

NT checking for serial mice at boot may disable a UPS. To disable that check, place the /noserialmice in the boot line in the BOOT.INI file.

The SCSI adapters icon in the Control Panel lets you add and configure SCSI devices as well as CD-ROM drives.

Many changes made in the disk administrator require that you choose the menu Partition, Commit Changes for them to take effect.

Although you can set drive letters manually, the following is how NT assigns letters to partitions and volumes:

1. Beginning from the letter C:, assign consecutive letters to the first primary partition on each physical disk.
2. Assign consecutive letters to each logical drive, completing all on one physical disk before moving on to the next.
3. Assign consecutive letters to the additional primary partitions, completing all on one physical disk before moving on to the next.

Disk Administrator allows for the creation of two kinds of partitions (primary and extended) and four kinds of volumes (volume set, stripe set, mirror set, and stripe set with parity). The following table is a summary of their characteristics:

## SUMMARY TABLE 6
## PARTITION CHARACTERISTICS

| *Object* | *Characteristics* |
|---|---|
| Primary partition | Non-divisible disk unit which can be marked active and can be made bootable. |
| | Can have up to four on a physical drive. |
| | NT system partition must be on a primary. |
| Extended partition | Divisible disk unit which must be divided into logical disks (or have free space used in a volume) in order to function as space storage tool. |
| | Can have only one on a physical drive. |
| | Logical drive within can be the NT boot partition. |
| Volume Set | Made up of 2-32 portions of free space which do not have to be the same size and which can be spread out over between 1 and 32 disks of many types (IDE, SCSI, etc.). |
| | Can be added to if formatted NTFS. |
| | Cannot contain NT boot or system partition. |
| | Removing one portion of the set destroys the volume and the data is lost. |
| | Is not fault tolerant. |
| Stripe Set | Made up of 2-32 portions of free space which have to be the same size and which can be spread out over between 2 and 32 disks of many types (IDE, SCSI, etc.). |
| | Cannot be added to and removing one portion of the set destroys the volume and the data is lost. |
| | Is not fault tolerant. |
| Mirror Set | Made up of 2 portions of free space which have to be the same size and which must be on 2 physical disks. |
| | Identical data is written to both mirror partitions and they are treated as one disk. |
| | If one disk stops functioning the other will continue to operate. |
| | The NT Boot and System partitions can be held on a mirror set. |
| | Has a 50% disk utilization rate. |
| | Is fault tolerant. |
| Stripe Set with Parity | Made up of 3-32 portions of free space which have to be the same size and must be spread out over the same number of physical disks. |
| | Maintains fault tolerance by creating parity information across a stripe. |
| | If one disk fails, the stripe set will continue to function, albeit with a loss of performance. |
| | The NT Boot and System partitions cannot be held on a Stripe Set with Parity. |
| | Is fault tolerant. |

Disk Administrator can be used to format partitions and volumes either FAT or NTFS.

If you have any clients who access a shared printer that are not using NT or are not using the same hardware platform as your printer server then you must install those drivers when you share the printer.

By assigning different priorities for printers associated with the same print device you can create a hierarchy among users' print jobs, thus ensuring that the print jobs of some users print sooner than others.

By adjusting the printer schedule you can ensure that jobs sent to particular printers are only printed at certain hours of the day.

A printer has permissions assigned to it. The following is a list of the permissions for printers.

- **No Access.** Completely restricts access to the printer.
- **Print.** Allows a user or group to submit a print job, and to control the settings and print status for that job.
- **Manage Documents.** Allows a user or group to submit a print job, and to control the settings and print status for all print jobs.
- **Full Control.** Allows a user to submit a print job, and to control the settings and print status for all documents as well as for the printer itself. In addition, the user or group may share, stop sharing, change permissions for, and even delete the printer.

Printer pools consist of one or more print devices that can use the same print driver controlled by a single printer.

MS-DOS users must have print drivers installed locally on their computers.

The assignment of permissions to resources should use the following procedure:

1. Create user accounts.
2. Create global groups for the domain and populate the groups with user accounts.
3. Create local groups and assign them rights and permissions to resources and programs in the domain.
4. Place global groups into the local groups you have created, thereby giving the users who are members of the global groups access to the system and its resources.

The built-in local groups in a Windows NT Domain are as follows:

- Administrators
- Users
- Guests
- Backup Operators
- Replicator
- Print Operators
- Server Operators
- Account Operators

The built-in global groups in an NT Domain are as follows:

- Domain Admins
- Domain Users
- Domain Guests

The system groups on an NT server are as follows:

- Everyone
- Creator Owner

- Network
- Interactive

The built-in users on an NT server are as follows:

- Administrator
- Guest

The following table describes the buttons on the User Properties dialog box and their functions:

### SUMMARY TABLE 7
### Buttons on the User Properties Dialog Box

| *Button* | *Function* |
|---|---|
| Groups | Enables you to add and remove group memberships for the account. The easiest way to grant rights to a user account is to add it to a group that possesses those rights. |
| Profile | Enables you to add a user profile path, a logon script name, and a home directory path to the user's environment profile. You learn more about the Profile button in the following section. |
| Hours | Enables you to define specific times when the users can access the account. (The default is always.) |
| Logon To | Enables you to specify up to 8 workstations from which the user can log on. (The default is all workstations.) |
| Account | Enables you to provide an expiration date for the account. (The default is never.) You also can specify the account as global (for regular users in this domain) or domain local. |

The following table is a summary of the account policy fields:

### SUMMARY TABLE 8
### Account Policy Fields

| *Button* | *Function* |
|---|---|
| Maximum Password Age | The maximum number of days a password can be in effect until it must be changed. |
| Minimum Password Age | The minimum number of days a password must stay in effect before it can be changed. |
| Minimum Password Length | The minimum number of characters a password must include. |
| Password Uniqueness | The number of passwords that NT remembers for a user; these passwords cannot be reused until they are no longer remembered. |
| Account Lockout | The number of incorrect passwords that can be input by a user before the account becomes locked. Reset will automatically set the count back to 0 after a specified length of time. In addition the duration of lock-out is either a number of minutes or forever (until an administrator unlocks it). |
| Forcibly disconnect remote users from server when logon hours expire | In conjunction with logon hours, this checkbox enables forcible disconnection of a user when authorized hours come to a close. |
| Users must log on in order to change password | Ensures that a user whose password has expired cannot change his or her password but has to have it reset by an administrator. |

Account SIDs are unique; therefore, if an account is deleted, the permissions cannot be restored by recreating an account with the same name.

Local profiles are only available from the machine on which they were created, whereas roaming profiles can be accessed from any machine on the network.

A mandatory profile is a roaming profile that users cannot change. They have the extension .MAN.

Hardware profiles can be used with machines that have more than one hardware configuration (such as laptops).

The System Policy editor (POLEDIT) has two modes, Policy File mode and Registry Mode.

The application of system policies is as follows:

1. When you log in, the NT Config.pol is checked. If there is an entry for the specific user, then any registry settings indicated will be merged with, and overwrite if necessary, the users registry.
2. If there is no specific user entry, any settings for groups that the user is a member of will be applied to the user.
3. If the user is not present in any groups and not listed explicitly then the Default settings will be applied.
4. If the computer that the user is logging in on has an entry, then the computer settings are applied.
5. If there is not a computer entry for the user then the default computer policy is applied.

Windows 95 policies are not compatible with NT and therefore Windows 95 users must access a Windows 95 policy created on an Windows 95 machine and copied to an NT machine and named Config.Pol.

The Net Use command line can be used to map a drive letter to a network share; using the /persistent switch ensures that it is reconnected at next logon.

FAT long file names under NT have 8.3 aliases created to ensure backward compatibility. The following is an example of how aliases are generated from 5 files that all have the same initial characters:

| | |
|---|---|
| Team meeting Report #3.doc | TEAMME~1.DOC |
| Team meeting Report #4.doc | TEAMME~2.DOC |
| Team meeting Report #5.doc | TEAMME~3.DOC |
| Team meeting Report #6.doc | TEAMME~4.DOC |
| Team meeting Report #7.doc | TE12B4~1.DOC |

A long file name on a FAT partition uses one file name for the 8.3 alias and then one more FAT entry for every 13 characters in the name.

A FAT partition can be converted to NTFS without loss of data through the command line

CONVERT <drive>: /FS:NTFS

NTFS supports compression as a file attribute that can be set in the file properties.

Compression can be applied to a folder or a drive and the effect is that the files within are compressed and any file copied into it will also become compressed.

Compression can be applied through the use of the COMPACT.EXE program through the syntax

COMPACT <file or directory path> [/switch]

The available switches for COMPACT are as follows:

### SUMMARY TABLE 9
### COMPACT SWITCHES

| *Switch* | *Function* |
|---|---|
| /C | Compress |
| /U | Uncompress |
| /S | Compress an entire directory tree |
| /A | Compress hidden and system files |
| /I | Ignore errors and continue compressing |
| /F | Force compression even if the objects are already compressed |
| /Q | Display only summary information |

Share-level permissions apply only when users access a resource over the network, not locally. The share-level permissions are:

- **No Access**. Users with No Access to a share can still connect to the share, but nothing appears in File Manager except the message You do not have permission to access this directory.
- **Read.** Allows you to display folder and file names, display file content and attributes, run programs, open folders inside the shared folder.
- **Change.** Allows you to create folders and files, change file content, change file attributes, delete files and folders, do everything READ permission allows.
- **Full Control.** Allows you to change file permissions and do everything change allows for.

Share-level permissions apply to the folder that is shared and apply equally to all the contents of that share.

Share-level permissions apply to any shared folder, whether on FAT or NTFS.

NTFS permissions can only be applied to any file or folder on an NTFS partition.

The actions that can be performed against an NTFS object are as follows:

- Read (R)
- Write (W)
- Execute (X)
- Delete (D)
- Change Permissions (P)
- Take Ownership (O)

The NTFS permissions available for folders are summarized in the following table:

### SUMMARY TABLE 10
### NTFS FOLDER PERMISSIONS

| *Permission* | *Action permitted* |
|---|---|
| No Access | none |
| List | RX |
| Read | RX |
| Add | WX |
| Add & Read | RXWD |
| Change | RXWD |
| Full Control | RXWDPO |

The NTFS permissions available for files are summarized in the following table:

**SUMMARY TABLE 11**
**NTFS FILE PERMISSIONS**

| *Permission* | *Action permitted* |
|---|---|
| No Access | none |
| Read | RX |
| Add & Read | RX |
| Change | RXWD |
| Full Control | RXWDPO |

If a user is given permission to a resource and a group or groups that the user is a member is also given access then the effective permission the user has is the cumulation of all of the user permissions. This applies unless any of the permissions are set to No Access in which case the user has no access to the resource.

If a user is given permission to a shared resource and is also given permission to that resource through NTFS permissions then the effective permission is the most restrictive permission.

The File Child Delete scenario manifests itself when someone has full control to a folder but is granted a permission which does not enable deletion (Read or No Access, for example). The effect is that a user will be able to delete files inside the folder even though sufficient access does not appear to be present.

To close the File Child Delete loophole, do not grant a user Full Control access to a folder but instead, use special Directory permissions to assign RXWDPO access, this eliminates the File Child Delete permission.

Access Tokens do not refresh and a user needs to log off and log back on if changed permissions are to take effect.

## MONITORING AND OPTIMIZATION

Remember: Here are the elements that Microsoft says they test on for the "Monitoring and Optimization" section of the exam.

- Monitor performance of various functions by using Performance Monitor. Functions include: processor, memory, disk, and network.
- Identify performance bottlenecks.

Performance monitor has 4 views: chart, alert, log, and report.

The subsystems that are routinely monitored are: Memory, Disk, Network, and Processor.

Disk counters can be enabled through the command line:

Diskperf –y

Or

Diskperf –ye (for RAID disks and volumes)

## TROUBLESHOOTING

Remember: Here are the elements that Microsoft says they test on for the "Troubleshooting" section of the exam.

- Choose the appropriate course of action to take to resolve installation failures.
- Choose the appropriate course of action to take to resolve boot failures.

- Choose the appropriate course of action to take to resolve configuration errors.
- Choose the appropriate course of action to take to resolve printer problems.
- Choose the appropriate course of action to take to resolve RAS problems.
- Choose the appropriate course of action to take to resolve connectivity problems.
- Choose the appropriate course of action to take to resolve fault tolerance problems. Fault-tolerance methods include: tape backup, mirroring, stripe set with parity, and disk duplexing.

The acronym DETECT can be used to define the troubleshooting process and stands for:

- Discover the problem.
- Explore the boundaries.
- Track the possible approaches.
- Execute an Approach.
- Check for success.
- Tie up loose ends.

An NTHQ diskette can test a computer to ensure that NT will successfully install on it.

The following list identifies possible sources of installation problems:

- Media errors
- Insufficient disk space
- Non-supported SCSI adapter
- Failure of dependancy service to start
- Inability to connect to the domain controller
- Error in assigning domain name

The files involved in the boot process are identified in the following table for both Intel and RISC machines:

**SUMMARY TABLE 12**
**FILES INVOLVED IN THE BOOT PROCESS**

| *Intel* | *RISC* |
|---|---|
| NTLDR | OSLOADER.EXE |
| BOOT.INI | NTOSKRNL.EXE |
| NTDETECT.COM | |
| NTOSKRNL.EXE | |

In the NT boot process (in BOOT.INI) ARC paths define the physical position of the NT operating system files and come in two forms:

Scsi(0)disk(0)rdisk(0)partition(1)\WINNT
Multi(0)disk(0)rdisk(0)partition(1)\WINNT

SCSI arc paths define hard drives which are SCSI and which have their bios disabled. The relevant parameters are:

- SCSI: the SCSI controller starting from 0
- DISK: the physical disk starting from 0
- PARTITION: the partition on the disk stating from 1
- \folder: the folder in which the NT files are located

MULTI arc paths define hard drives which are non-SCSI or SCSI with their bios enabled. The relevant parameters are:

- MULTI: the controller starting from 0
- RDISK: the physical disk starting from 0

- PARTITION: the partition on the disk stating from 1
- \folder: the folder in which the NT files are located

Partitions are numbered as follows:

1. The first primary partition on each disk gets the number 0.
2. Each additional primary partition then is given a number, incrementing up from 0.
3. Each logical drive is then given a number in the order they appear in the Disk Administrator.

Switches on boot lines in the boot.ini file define additional boot parameters. The following table lists the switches you need to know about and their function:

### SUMMARY TABLE 13
### BOOT.INI FILE SWITCHES

| *Switch* | *Function* |
|---|---|
| /basevideo | Loads standard VGA video driver (640x480, 16 color) |
| /sos | Displays each driver as it is loaded |
| /noserialmice | Prevents autodetection of serial mice on COM ports which may disable a UPS connected to the port |

A recovery disk can be used to bypass problems with system partition. Such a disk contains the following files (broken down by hardware platform):

### SUMMARY TABLE 14
### FILES ON A FAULT-TOLERANT BOOT DISKETTE

| *Intel* | *RISC* |
|---|---|
| NTLDR | OSLOADER.EXE |
| NTDETECT.COM | HAL.DLL |
| BOOT.INI | *.PAL (for Alpha machines) |
| BOOTSECT.DOS (allows you to boot to DOS) | |
| NTBOOTDD.SYS (the SCSI driver for a hard drive with SCSI bios not enabled) | |

An Emergency repair disk can be used to recover an NT system if the registry becomes corrupted and must be used in conjunction with the three setup diskettes used to install NT.

The RDISK programs allows you to update the \REPAIR folder which in turn is used to update your repair diskette.

The Event Viewer allows you to see three log files: System Log, Security Log, and Application Log.

The Windows NT Diagnostics program allows you to see (but not modify) configuration settings for much of your hardware and environment.

The course of action to take when a stop error occurs (blue screen) can be configured from the System Properties dialog box (in the Control Panel) on the Startup/Shutdown tab.

To move the spool file from one partition to another, use the Advanced Tab on the Server Properties dialog box; this can be located from the File, Server Properties menu in the printers dialog box.

Common RAS problems include the following:

- User Permission: user not enabled to use RAS in User Manager for Domains.
- Authentication: often caused by incompatible encryption methods (client using different encryption than server is configured to receive).
- Callback with Multilink: Client configured for callback but is using multilink; server will only

call back to a single number, thereby removing multilink functionality.

- Autodial at Logon: Shortcuts on desktop referencing server-based applications or files causes autodial to kick in when logon is complete.

User can't login may be caused by a number of factors including:

- Incorrect user name or password
- Incorrect domain name
- Incorrect user rights (inability to log on locally to an NT machine, for example)
- Netlogon service on server is stopped or paused
- Domain controllers are down
- User is restricted in system policies from logging on at a specific computer

The right to create backups and restore from backups using NT Backup is granted to the groups Administrators, Backup Operators, and Server Operators by default.

NT Backup will only backup files to tape, no other media is supported.

The following table summarizes the backup types available in NT backup:

**SUMMARY TABLE 15**
**BACKUP TYPES AVAILABLE IN NTBACKUP**

| *Type* | *Backs Up* | *Marks?* |
|---|---|---|
| Normal | All selected files and folders | Yes |
| Copy | All selected files and folders | No |
| Incremental | Selected files and folders not marked as backed up | Yes |
| Differential | Selected files and folders not marked as backed up | No |
| Daily Copy | Selected files and folders changed that day | No |

The local registry of a computer can be backed up by selecting the Backup Local Registry checkbox in the Backup Information dialog box.

Data from tape can be restored to the original location or to an alternate location and NTFS permissions can be restored or not, however, you cannot change the names of the objects being restored until the restore is complete.

Backup can be run from a command line using the NTBACKUP command in the syntax:

Ntbackup backup path [switches]

Some command line backup switches are shown in the following table:

**SUMMARY TABLE 16**
**NTBACKUP COMMAND LINE SWITCHES**

| *Switch* | *Function* |
|---|---|
| /a | Append the current backup to the backup already on the tape |
| /v | verify the backed up files when complete |
| /d "text" | Add an identifying description to the backup tape |
| /t option | specify the backup type. Valid options are: normal, copy, incremental, differential, and daily |

To recover from a failed mirror set you must do the following:

1. Shut down your NT server and physically replace the failed drive.
2. If required, boot NT using a recovery disk.

3. Start the Disk Administrator using the menu Start, Programs, Administrative Tools (Common), Disk Administrator.

4. Select the mirror set by clicking on it.

5. From the Fault Tolerance menu choose Break Mirror. This action exposes the remaining partition as a volume separate from the failed one.

6. Reestablish the mirror set if desired by selecting the partition you desire to mirror and a portion of free space equal in size and choosing the menu Fault Tolerance, Establish Mirror.

To regenerate a stripe set with parity do the following:

1. Shut down your NT server and physically replace the failed drive.

2. Start the Disk Administrator using the menu Start, Programs, Administrative Tools (Common), Disk Administrator.

3. Select the stripe set with parity by clicking on it.

4. Select an area of free space as large or larger than the portion of the stripe set that was lost when the disk failed.

5. Choose Fault Tolerance, Regenerate.

Hopefully, this has been a helpful tool in your final review before the exam. You might find after reading this that there are some places in the book you need to revisit. Just remember to stay focused and answer all the questions. You can always go back and check the answers for the questions you are unsure of. Good luck!

# Fast Facts

## Windows NT Server 4 Enterprise Exam

The fast facts listed in this section are designed as a refresher of key points and topics that are required to succeed on the Windows NT server 4.0 in the Enterprise exam. By using these summaries of key points, you can spend an hour prior to your exam to refresh key topics, and ensure that you have a solid understanding of the objectives and information required for you to succeed in each major area of the exam.

The following are the main categories Microsoft uses to arrange the objectives:

- Planning
- Installation and configuration
- Managing resources
- Connectivity
- Monitoring and optimization
- Troubleshooting

For each of these main sections, or categories, the assigned objectives are reviewed, and following each objective, review material is offered.

## Planning

Plan the implementation of a directory services architecture. Considerations include the following:

- Selecting the appropriate domain model
- Supporting a single logon account
- Enabling users to access resources in different domains

The main goals of directory services are the following:

- One user, one account
- Universal resource access
- Centralized administration
- Directory synchronization

To ensure that you are selecting the best plan for your network, always address each of the goals of directory services.

The requirements for setting up a trust are as follows:

- The trust relationship can be established only between Windows NT Server domains.
- The domains must be able to make an RPC connection. To establish an RPC connection, you must ensure that a network connection exists between the domain controllers of all participating domains.
- The trust relationship must be set up by a user with administrator access.
- You should determine the number and type of trusts prior to the implementation.
- You must decide where to place the user accounts, as that is the trusted domain.

Trust relationships enable communication between domains. The trusts must be organized, however, to achieve the original goal of directory services. Windows NT domains can be organized into one of four different domain models:

- The single-domain model
- The single-master domain model
- The multiple-master domain model
- The complete-trust model

Table 1 summarizes the advantages and disadvantages of the domain models.

**TABLE 1**
**PROFILING THE DOMAIN MODELS**

| *Domain Model* | *Advantages* | *Disadvantages* |
|---|---|---|
| Single-domain model | Centralized administration. | Limited to 40,000 user accounts.<br>No trust relationships.<br>No distribution of resources. |
| Single-master domain model | Centralized administration.<br>Distributed resources. | Limited to 40,000 user accounts. |
| Multiple-master domain model | Unlimited number of user accounts; each master domain can host 40,000 user accounts.<br>Distributed resources.<br>Complex trust relationships. | No centralized administration of user accounts. |
| Complete-trust model | Unlimited number of user accounts; each domain can host 40,000 user accounts.<br>Complex trust relationships. | No centralized administration of user accounts. |

Plan the disk drive configuration for various requirements. Requirements include choosing a fault-tolerance method.

Windows NT Server 4 supports the following fault-tolerant solutions:

- RAID Level 0 (disk striping)
- RAID Level 1 (disk mirroring)
- RAID Level 5 (disk striping with parity)

A comparison of the three fault-tolerance options might help to summarize the information and to ensure that you have a strong understanding of the options available in Windows NT Server 4 (see Table 2).

Choose a protocol for various situations. The protocols include the following:

- TCP/IP
- TCP/IP with DHCP and WINS
- NWLink IPX/SPX Compatible Transport Protocol
- Data Link Control (DLC)
- AppleTalk

Windows NT Server 4 comes bundled with several protocols that can be used for interconnectivity with other systems and for use within a Windows NT environment. You examine the various protocols, then try to define when each protocol best fits your network needs. The protocols discussed to prepare you for the enterprise exam are the following:

- **NetBEUI.** The NetBEUI protocol is the easiest to implement and has wide support across platforms. The protocol uses NetBIOS broadcasts to locate other computers on the network. This process of locating other computers requires additional network traffic and can slow down your entire network. Because NetBEUI uses broadcasts to locate computers, it is not routable; in other words, you cannot access computers that are not on your physical network. Most Microsoft and IBM OS/2 clients support this protocol. NetBEUI is best suited to small networks with no

**TABLE 2**
**SUMMARY OF FAULT-TOLERANCE OPTIONS IN WINDOWS NT SERVER 4**

| *Disk Striping* | *Disk Mirroring/ Disk Duplexing* | *Disk Striping with Parity* |
|---|---|---|
| No fault tolerance. | Complete disk duplication. | Data regeneration from stored parity information. |
| Minimum of two physical disks, maximum of 32 disks. | Two physical disks | Minimum of three physical disks, maximum of 32 disks. |
| 100 percent available disk utilization. | 50 percent available disk utilization. | Dedicates the equivalent of one disk's space in the set for parity information. The more disks, the higher the utilization. |
| Cannot include a system/boot partition. | Includes all partition types. | Cannot include a system/boot partition. |
| Excellent read/write performance. | Moderate read/write performance. | Excellent read and moderate write performance. |

requirements for routing the information to remote networks or to the Internet.

- **TCP/IP.** Transmission Control Protocol/Internet Protocol, or TCP/IP, is the most common protocol—more specifically, it is the most common suite of protocols. TCP/IP is an industry-standard protocol that is supported by most network operating systems. Because of this acceptance throughout the industry, TCP/IP enables your Windows NT system to connect to other systems with a common communication protocol.

  The following are advantages of using TCP/IP in a Windows NT environment:

  - The capability to connect dissimilar systems
  - The capability to use numerous standard connectivity utilities, including File Transfer Protocol (FTP), Telnet, and PING
  - Access to the Internet

  If your Windows NT system is using TCP/IP as a connection protocol, it can communicate with many non-Microsoft systems. Some of the systems it can communicate with are the following:

  - Any Internet-connected system
  - UNIX systems
  - IBM mainframe systems
  - DEC Pathworks
  - TCP/IP-supported printers directly connected to the network

- **NWLink IPX/SPX Compatible.** The IPX protocol has been used within the NetWare environment for years. By developing an IPX-compatible protocol, Microsoft enables Windows NT systems to communicate with NetWare systems.

  NWLink is best suited to networks requiring communication with existing NetWare servers and for existing NetWare clients.

  Other utilities must be installed, however, to enable the Windows NT Server system to gain access into the NetWare security. Gateway Services for NetWare/Client Services for NetWare (GSNW/CSNW) must be installed on the Windows NT server to enable the computer to be logged on to a NetWare system. GSNW functions as a NetWare client, but it also can share the connection to the Novell box with users from the Windows NT system. This capability enables a controlled NetWare connection for file and print sharing on the NetWare box, without requiring the configuration of each NT client with a duplicate network redirector or client.

- **DataLink Control.** The DLC protocol was originally used for connectivity in an IBM mainframe environment, and maintains support for existing legacy systems and mainframes. The DLC protocol is also used for connections to some network printers.

- **AppleTalk.** Windows NT Server can configure the AppleTalk protocol to enable connectivity with Apple Macintosh systems. This protocol is installed with the Services for the Macintosh included with your Windows NT Server CD-ROM. The AppleTalk protocol enables Macintosh computers on your network to access files and printers set up on the Windows NT server. It also enables your Windows NT clients to print to Apple Macintosh printers.

  The AppleTalk protocol is best suited to connectivity with the Apple Macintosh.

# INSTALLATION AND CONFIGURATION

Install Windows NT Server to perform various server roles. Server roles include the following:

- Primary domain controller
- Backup domain controller
- Member server

The following are different server roles into which Windows NT Server can be installed:

- **Primary Domain Controller.** The Primary Domain Controller (PDC) is the first domain controller installed into a domain. As the first computer in the domain, the PDC creates the domain. This fact is important to understand because it establishes the rationale for needing a PDC in the environment. Each domain can contain only one PDC. All other domain controllers in the domain are installed as Backup Domain Controllers. The PDC handles user requests and logon validation, and it offers all the standard Windows NT Server functionality. The PDC contains the original copy of the Security Accounts Manager (SAM), which contains all user accounts and security permissions for your domain.
- **Backup Domain Controller.** The Backup Domain Controller (BDC) is an additional domain controller used to handle logon requests by users in the network. To handle the logon requests, the BDC must have a complete copy of the domain database, or SAM. The BDC also runs the Netlogon service; however, the Netlogon service in a BDC functions a little differently than in a PDC. In the PDC, the Netlogon service handles synchronization of the SAM database to all the BDCs.
- **Member server.** In both of the domain controllers, PDC or BDC, the computer has an additional function: The domain controllers handle logon requests and ensure that the SAM is synchronized throughout the domain. These functions add overhead to the system. A computer that handles the server functionality you require without the overhead of handling logon validation is called a *member server.* A member server is a part of the domain, but it does not need a copy of the SAM database and does not handle logon requests. The main function of a member server is to share resources.

After you have installed your computer into a specific server role, you might decide to change the role of the server. This can be a relatively easy task if you are changing a PDC to a BDC or vice versa. If you want to change a domain controller to a member server or member server to a domain controller, however, you must reinstall into the required server role. A member server has a local database that does not participate in domain synchronization. In changing roles, a member server must be reinstalled to ensure that the account database and the appropriate services are installed.

Configure protocols and protocol bindings. Protocols include the following:

- TCP/IP
- TCP/IP with DHCP and WINS
- NWLink IPX/SPX Compatible Transport Protocol
- DLC
- AppleTalk

You install a new protocol in Windows NT Server through the Network Properties dialog box.

> NOTE
> **NetBEUI Not Discussed** This list does not include the NetBEUI protocol, as there are no configuration options available for this protocol.

Following are the protocols, and the configuration options available with each:

- **TCP/IP.** The following tabs are available for configuration in the Microsoft TCP/IP Properties dialog box:
  - **IP Address.** The IP Address tab enables you to configure the IP address, the subnet mask, and the default gateway. You also can enable the system to allocate IP address information automatically through the use of the DHCP server.

    An IP address is a 32-bit address that is broken into four octets and used to identify your network adapter card as a TCP/IP host. Each IP address must be a unique address. If you have any IP address conflicts on your computer, you cannot use the TCP/IP protocol.

    Your IP address is then grouped into a subnet. The process you use to subnet your network is to assign a subnet mask. A *subnet mask* is used to identify the computers local to your network. Any address outside your subnet is accessed through the default gateway, also called the *router*. The default gateway is the address of the router that handles all routing of your TCP/IP information to computers, or hosts, outside your subnet.
  - **DNS.** The DNS tab shows you the options available for configuring your TCP/IP protocol to use a DNS server. The Domain Name System (DNS) server translates TCP/IP host names of remote computers into IP addresses. Remember that an IP address is a unique address for each computer. The DNS server contains a database of all the computers you can access by host name. This database is used when you access a Web page on the Internet. Working with the naming scheme is easier than using the IP address of the computer.
  - **WINS Address.** The WINS Address tab enables you to configure your primary and secondary Windows Internet Names Services (WINS) server addresses. WINS is used to reduce the number of NetBIOS broadcast messages sent across the network to locate a computer. By using a WINS server, you keep the names of computers on your network in a WINS database. The WINS database is dynamic.

    In configuring your WINS servers, you can enter your primary WINS server and a secondary WINS server. Your system searches the primary WINS server database first, then the secondary database if no match was found in the primary one.
  - **DHCP Relay.** The DHCP relay agent is used to find your DHCP servers across routers. DHCP addresses are handed out by the DHCP servers. The client request, however, is made with a broadcast message. Broadcast messages do not cross routers; therefore, this protocol might place some restrictions on your systems. The solution is to use a DHCP relay agent to assist the clients in finding the DHCP server across a router.

In configuring your DHCP relay agent, you can specify the seconds threshold and the maximum number of hops to use in searching for the DHCP servers. At the bottom of the tab, you can enter the IP addresses of the DHCP servers you want to use.

- **Routing.** In an environment in which multiple subnets are used, you can configure your Windows NT Server as a multihomed system. In other words, you can install multiple network adapters, each connecting to a different subnet. If you enable the Enable IP Forwarding option, your computer acts as a router, forwarding the packets through the network cards in the multihomed system to the other subnet.

◆ **NWLINK IPX/SPX Compatible.** The configuration of the NWLink protocol is simple in comparison to the TCP/IP protocol. It is this simplicity that makes it a popular protocol to use.

The NWLink IPX/SPX Properties dialog box has two tabs:

- **General.** On the General tab, you have the option to assign an internal network number. This eight-digit hexadecimal number format is used by some programs with services that can be accessed by NetWare clients.

  You also have the option to select a frame type for your NWLink protocol. The frame type you select must match the frame type of the remote computer with which you need to communicate. By default, Windows NT Server uses the Auto Frame Type Detection setting, which scans the network and loads the first frame type it encounters.

- **Routing.** The Routing tab of the NWLink IPX/SPX Properties dialog box is used to enable or disable the Routing Information Protocol (RIP). If you enable RIP routing over IPX, your Windows NT Server can act as an IPX router.

◆ **DLC.** The configuration of DLC is done through Registry parameters. The DLC protocol is configured based on three timers:

- **T1.** The response timer
- **T2.** The acknowledgment delay timer
- **Ti.** The inactivity timer

The Registry contains the entries that can be modified to configure DLC. You can find the entries at

HKEY_LOCAL_MACHINE\SYSTEM\CurrentControlSet\Services\DLC\Parameters\ELNKIII *adapter name*

◆ **AppleTalk.** To install the AppleTalk protocol, you install Services for Macintosh.

Table 3 reviews the protocols that you can configure for your NT enterprise (including the subcomponents—tabs—of each protocol).

**TABLE 3**
**PROTOCOLS TO CONFIGURE**

| *Protocol* | *Subcomponent (Tab)* |
|---|---|
| TCP/IP | IP Address<br>DNS<br>WINS Address<br>DHCP Relay<br>Routing |
| NWLink IPX/SPX Compatible | General<br>Routing |
| AppleTalk | General<br>Routing |

The binding order is the sequence your computer uses to select which protocol to use for network communications. Each protocol is listed for each network-based service, protocol, and adapter available.

The Bindings tab contains an option, Show Bindings for, that can be used to select the service, adapter, or protocol you want to modify in the binding order. By clicking the appropriate button, you can enable or disable each binding, or move up or down in the binding order.

Configure Windows NT Server core services. Services include the following:

- Directory Replicator
- Computer Browser

In this objective, you look at configuring some of the core services in the Windows NT Server. These services are the following:

- **Server service.** The Server service answers network requests. By configuring Server service, you can change the way your server responds and, in a sense, the role it plays in your network environment. To configure Server service, you must open the Network dialog box. To do this, double-click the Network icon in the Control Panel. Select the Services tab. In the Server dialog box, you have four optimization settings. Each of these settings modifies memory management based on the role the server is playing. These options are the following:
    - **Minimize Memory Used.** The Minimize Memory Used setting is used when your Windows NT Server system is accessed by less than 10 users.

      This setting allocates memory so a maximum of 10 network connections can be properly maintained. By restricting the memory for network connections, you make more memory available at the local or desktop level.
    - **Balance.** The Balance setting can be used for a maximum of 64 network connections. This setting is the default when using NetBEUI software. Like the Minimize setting, Balance is best used for a relatively low number of users connecting to a server that also can be used as a desktop computer.
    - **Maximize Throughput for File Sharing.** The Maximize Throughput for File Sharing setting allocates the maximum amount of memory available for network connections. This setting is excellent for large networks in which the server is being accessed for file and print sharing.
    - **Maximize Throughput for Network Applications.** If you are running distributed applications, such as SQL Server or Exchange Server, the network applications do their own memory caching. Therefore, you want your system to enable the applications to manage the memory. You accomplish this by using the Maximize Throughput for Network Applications setting. This setting also is used for very large networks.
- **Computer Browser service.** The Computer Browser service is responsible for maintaining the list of computers on the network. The browse list contains all the computers located on the physical network. As a Windows NT Server, your system plays a big role in the browsing of a network. The Windows NT Server acts as a master browser or backup browser.

The selection of browsers is through an election. The election is called by any client computer or when a preferred master browser computer starts up. The election is based on broadcast messages.

Every computer has the opportunity to nominate itself, and the computer with the highest settings wins the election.

The election criteria are based on three things:

- The operating system (Windows NT Server, Windows NT Workstation, Windows 95, Windows for Workgroups)
- The version of the operating system (NT 4.0, NT 3.51, NT 3.5)
- The current role of the computer (master browser, backup browser, potential browser)

- **Directory Replicator service.** You can configure the Directory Replicator service to synchronize an entire directory structure across multiple servers.

  In configuring the directory service, you must select the export server and all the import servers. The export server is the computer that holds the original copy of the directory structure and files. Each import server receives a complete copy of the export server's directory structure. The Directory Replicator service monitors the directory structure on the export server. If the contents of the directory change, the changes are copied to all the import servers. The file copying and directory monitoring is completed by a special service account you create. You must configure the Directory Replicator service to use this service account. The following access is required for your Directory Replicator service account:

  - The account should be a member of the Backup Operators and Replicators groups.
  - There should be no time or logon restrictions for the account.
  - The Password Never Expires option should be selected.
  - The User Must Change Password At Next Logon option should be turned off.

  When configuring the export server, you have the option to specify the export directory. The default export directory is C:\WINNT\system32\repl\export\.

  In the Import Directories section of the Directory Replication dialog box, you can select the import directory. The default import directory is C:\WINNT\system32\repl\import.

  Remember that the default directory for executing logon scripts in a Windows NT system is C:\WINNT\system32\repl\import\scripts.

Configure hard disks to meet various requirements. Requirements include the following:

- Providing duplication
- Improving performance

All hard disk configuration can be done using the Disk Administrator tool. The different disk configurations you need to understand for the enterprise exam are the following:

- **Stripe set.** A stripe set gives you improved disk read and write performance; however, it supplies no fault tolerance. A minimum of two disks is required, and the configuration can stripe up to 32 physical disks. A stripe set cannot include the system partition.
- **Volume set.** A volume set enables you to extend partitions beyond one physical disk; however, it supplies no fault tolerance. To extend a volume set, you must use the NTFS file system.
- **Disk mirroring.** A mirror set uses two physical disks and provides full data duplication. Often referred to as RAID level 1, disk mirroring is a

useful solution to assigning duplication to the system partition, as well as any other disks that might be in the system.

- **Stripe set with parity.** A stripe set with parity enables fault tolerance in your system. A minimum of three physical disks is required, and a maximum of 32 physical disks can be included in a stripe set with parity. A stripe set with parity cannot include the system partition of your Windows NT system.

The solution that supplies the best duplication and optimization mix is the stripe set with parity.

Configure printers. Tasks include the following:

- Adding and configuring a printer
- Implementing a printer pool
- Setting print priorities

The installation of a printer is a fairly simplistic procedure and is not tested heavily on the exam; however, the printer pool is a key point. The items to remember about printer pools are as follows:

- All printers in a printer pool must be able to function using the same printer driver.
- A printer pool can have a maximum of eight printers in the pool.

Configure a Windows NT Server computer for various types of client computers. Client computer types include the following:

- Windows NT Workstation
- Windows 95
- Macintosh

The Network Client Administrator is found in the Administrative Tools group. You can use the Network Client Administrator program to do the following:

- **Make a Network Installation Startup Disk.** This option creates an MS-DOS boot disk that contains commands required to connect to a network server and that automatically installs Windows NT Workstation, Windows 95, or the DOS network clients.
- **Make an Installation Disk Set.** This option enables the creation of installation disks for the DOS network client, LAN Manager 2.2c for DOS, or LAN Manager 2.2c for OS/2.
- **Copy Client-Based Network Administration Tools.** This option enables you to share the network administration tools with client computers. The client computers that can use the network administration tools are Windows NT Workstation and Windows 95 computers.
- **View Remoteboot Client Information.** This option enables you to view the remoteboot client information. To install remoteboot, go to the Services tab of the Network dialog box.

When installing a client computer, you must ensure that your Windows NT system is prepared for and configured for the client. The Windows clients can connect to the Windows NT server without any configuration required on the server; however, some configuration is required on the client computers. For the Apple Macintosh client, the NT server must install the services for the Macintosh, which includes the AppleTalk protocol. This protocol enables the seamless connection between the Windows NT system and the Apple clients.

# MANAGING RESOURCES

Manage user and group accounts. Considerations include the following:

- Managing Windows NT user accounts
- Managing Windows NT user rights
- Managing Windows NT groups
- Administering account policies
- Auditing changes to the user account database

AGLP stands for Accounts/Global Groups/Local Groups/Permissions. When you want to assign permissions to any resource, you should follow a few simple rules. All user accounts are placed into global groups, and global groups get assigned into local groups. The local groups have the resources and permissions assigned to them.

When you are working with groups across trust relationships, the following guidelines are useful:

- Always gather users into global groups. Remember that global groups can contain only user accounts from the same domain. You might have to create the same named global group in multiple domains.
- If you have multiple account domains, use the same name for a global group that has the same types of members. Remember that when multiple domains are involved, the group name is referred to as DOMAIN\GROUP.
- Before the global groups are created, determine whether an existing local group meets your needs. There is no sense in creating duplicate local groups.
- Remember that the local group must be created where the resource is located. If the resource is on a Domain Controller, create the local group in the Domain Account Database. If the resource is on a Windows NT Workstation or Windows NT Member Server, you must create the group in that system's local account database.
- Be sure to set the permissions for a resource before you make the global groups a member of the local group assigned to the resource. That way, you set the security for the resource.

Create and manage policies and profiles for various situations. Policies and profiles include the following:

- Local user profiles
- Roaming user profiles
- System policies

You can configure system policies to do the following:

- Implement defaults for hardware configuration—for all computers using the profile or for a specific machine.
- Restrict the changing of specific parameters that affect the hardware configuration of the participating system.
- Set defaults for all users in the areas of their personal settings that the users can configure.
- Restrict users from changing specific areas of their configuration to prevent tampering with the system. An example is disabling all Registry editing tools for a specific user.
- Apply all defaults and restrictions on a group level rather than just a user level.

Some common implementations of user profiles are the following:

- Locking down display properties to prevent users from changing the resolution of their monitor. Display properties can be locked down as a whole or on each individual property page of display properties. You adjust this setting by clicking the Control Panel, Display, Restrict Display option of the Default User Properties dialog box.
- Setting a default color scheme or wallpaper. You can do this by clicking the Desktop option of the Default User Properties dialog box.
- If you want to restrict access to portions of the Start menu or desktop, you can do this by clicking the Shell, Restrictions option of the Default User Properties dialog box.
- If you need to limit the applications that the user can run at a workstation, you can do so by clicking the System, Restrictions option of the Default User Properties dialog box. You can also use this option to prevent the user from modifying the Registry.
- You can prevent users from mapping or disconnecting network drives by clicking the Windows NT Shell, Restrictions option of the Default User Properties dialog box.

Profiles and policies can be very powerful tools to assist in the administrative tasks in your environment. The following list reviews each of the main topics covered in this objective:

- **Roaming profiles.** The user portion of the Registry is downloaded from a central location, allowing the user settings to follow the user anywhere within the network environment.
- **Local profiles.** The user settings are stored at each workstation and are not copied to other computers. Each workstation that you use will have different desktop and user settings.
- **System policies.** System policies enable the administrator to restrict user configuration changes on systems. This enables the administrator to maintain the settings of the desktop of systems without the fear that a user can modify them.
- **Computer policies.** Computer policies allow the lockdown of common machine settings that affect all users of that computer.

Administer remote servers from various types of client computers. Client computer types include the following:

- Windows 95
- Windows NT Workstation

This objective focuses on the remote administration tools available for your Windows NT Server. The following list summarizes the key tools:

- **Remote Administration Tools for Windows 95.** Allows User Manager, Server Manager, Event Viewer, and NTFS file permissions to be executed from the Windows 95 computer.
- **Remote Administration for Windows NT.** Allows User Manager, Server Manager, DHCP Manager, System Policy Editor, Remote Access Admin, Remote Boot Manager, WINS Manager, and NTFS file permissions to be executed from a Windows NT machine.
- **Web Based Administration.** Allows for common tasks to be completed through an Internet connection into the Windows NT Server.

Manage disk resources. Tasks include the following:

- Creating and sharing resources
- Implementing permissions and security
- Establishing file auditing

Windows NT has two levels of security for protecting your disk resources:

- Share permissions
- NTFS permissions

NTFS permissions enable you to assign more comprehensive security to your computer system. NTFS permissions can protect you at the file level. Share permissions, on the other hand, can be applied only to the folder level. NTFS permissions can affect users logged on locally or across the network to the system where the NTFS permissions are applied. Share permissions are in effect only when the user connects to the resource through the network.

The combination of Windows NT share permissions and NTFS permissions determines the ultimate access a user has to a resource on the server's disk. When share permissions and NTFS permissions are combined, no preference is given to one or the other. The key factor is which of the two effective permissions is the most restrictive.

For the exam, remember the following tips relating to managing resources:

- Users can be assigned only to global groups in the same domain.
- Only global groups from trusted domains can become members of local groups in trusting domains.
- NTFS permissions are assigned only to local groups in all correct test answers.
- Only NTFS permissions give you file-level security.

## CONNECTIVITY

Configure Windows NT Server for interoperability with NetWare servers by using various tools. The tools include the following:

- Gateway Service for NetWare
- Migration Tool for NetWare

Gateway Service for NetWare (GSNW) performs the following functions:

- GSNW enables Windows NT Servers to access NetWare file and print resources.
- GSNW enables the Windows NT Servers to act as a gateway to the NetWare file and print resources. The Windows NT Server enables users to borrow the connection to the NetWare server by setting it up as a shared connection.

The Migration Tool for NetWare (NWCONV) transfers file and folder information and user and group account information from a NetWare server to a Windows NT domain controller. The Migration Tool can preserve the folder and file permissions if it is being transferred to an NTFS partition.

Connectivity between Windows NT and a NetWare server requires the use of GSNW. If the user and file information from NetWare is to be transferred to a Windows NT Server, the NetWare Conversion utility, NWCONV, is used for this task. The following list summarizes the main points in this section on NetWare connectivity:

- GSNW can be used as a gateway between Windows NT clients and a NetWare server.
- GSNW acts as a NetWare client to the Windows NT Server, allowing the NT server to have a connection to the NetWare server.

- GSNW is a service in Windows NT, and is installed using the Control Panel.
- For GSNW to be used as a gateway into a NetWare server, a gateway user account must be created and placed in a NetWare group called NTGATEWAY.
- In configuring the GSNW as a gateway, you can assign permissions to the gateway share by accessing the GSNW icon in the Control Panel.
- For GSNW to be functional, the NWLINK IPX/SPX protocol must be installed and configured.
- To convert user and file information from a NetWare server to a Windows NT server, you can use the NWCONV.EXE utility.
- NWCONV requires that GSNW be installed prior to any conversion being carried out.
- To maintain the NetWare folder- and file-level permissions in the NWCONV utility, you must convert to an NTFS partition on the Windows NT system.

Install and configure multiprotocol routing to serve various functions. Functions include the following:

- Internet router
- BOOTP/DHCP Relay Agent
- IPX router

Multiprotocol routing gives you flexibility in the connection method used by your clients, and in maintaining security. Check out the following:

- **Internet router.** Setting up Windows NT as an Internet router is as simple as installing two network adapters in the system, then enabling IP routing in the TCP/IP protocol configuration. This option enables Windows NT to act as a static router. Note that Windows NT cannot exchange Routing Information Protocol (RIP) routing packets with other IP RIP routers unless the RIP routing software is installed.
- **IPX router.** You enable the IPX router by installing the IPX RIP router software by choosing Control Panel, Networks, Services.

  After installing the IPX RIP router, Windows NT can route IPX packets over the network adapters installed. Windows NT uses the RIP to exchange its routing table information with other RIP routers.

The inclusion of the industry-standard protocols, and tools to simplify the configuration and extension of your NT network into other environments, makes this operating system a very powerful piece of your heterogenous environment. The following are the main factors to focus on for this objective:

- A strong understanding of the functionality of each of the Windows NT protocols—with a strong slant toward TCP/IP and the configuration options available. Understanding and configuration of the DHCP server are also tested on this exam.
- The services used to resolve the IP addresses and names of hosts in a TCP/IP environment. DNS service, WINS Service, the Hosts file, and the LMHosts files are among the services tested.
- The routing mechanisms available in Windows NT. These mechanisms are powerful, and largely unknown to the vast majority of NT administrators. Ensure that you review the configuration and functionality of Internet or IP routing, as well as the IPX routing tools available.

Install and configure Internet Information Server, and install and configure Internet services. Services include the following:

- The World Wide Web
- DNS
- Intranets

Internet Information Server (IIS) uses Hypertext Transfer Protocol (HTTP), File Transfer Protocol (FTP), and the Gopher service to provide Internet publishing services to your Windows NT Server computer.

IIS provides a graphical administration tool called the Internet Service Manager. With this tool, you can centrally manage, control, and monitor the Internet services in your Windows NT network. The Internet Service Manager uses the built-in Windows NT security model, so it offers a secure method of remotely administering your Web sites and other Internet services.

IIS is an integrated component in Windows NT Server 4.0. The IIS services are installed using the Control Panel, Networks icon or during the installation phase. The following list summarizes the key points in installing and configuring IIS:

- The three Internet services included in IIS are HTTP, FTP, and Gopher.
- HTTP is used to host Web pages from your Windows NT server system.
- FTP is a protocol used for transferring files across the Internet using the TCP/IP protocol.
- Gopher is used to create a set of hierarchical links to other computers or to annotate files or folders.
- The Internet Service Manager is the utility used to manage and configure your Internet services in IIS.
- The Internet Service Manager has three views that you can use to view your services. The three views are Report View, Servers View, and Services View.

Install and configure Remote Access Service (RAS). Configuration options include the following:

- Configuring RAS communications
- Configuring RAS protocols
- Configuring RAS security

RAS supports the Serial Line Internet Protocol (SLIP) and Point-to-Point Protocol (PPP) line protocols, and the NetBEUI, TCP/IP, and IPX network protocols.

RAS can connect to a remote computer using any of the following media:

- **Public Switched Telephone Network (PSTN).** (PSTN is also known simply as the phone company.) RAS can connect using a modem through an ordinary phone line.
- **X.25.** A packet-switched network. Computers access the network through a Packet Assembler Disassembler (PAD) device. X.25 supports dial-up or direct connections.
- **Null modem cable.** A cable that connects two computers directly. The computers then communicate using their modems (rather than network adapter cards).
- **ISDN.** A digital line that provides faster communication and more bandwidth than a normal phone line. (It also costs more, which is why not everybody has it.) A computer must have a special ISDN card to access an ISDN line.

RAS is designed for security. The following are some of RAS's security features:

- **Auditing.** RAS can leave an audit trail, enabling you to see who logged on when and what authentication they provided.

- **Callback security.** You can enable the RAS server to use callback (hang up all incoming calls and call the caller back), and you can limit callback numbers to prearranged sites that you know are safe.
- **Encryption.** RAS can encrypt logon information, or it can encrypt all data crossing the connection.
- **Security hosts.** In case Windows NT is not safe enough, you can add an extra dose of security by using a third-party intermediary security host—a computer that stands between the RAS client and the RAS server and requires an extra round of authentication.
- **PPTP filtering.** You can tell Windows NT to filter out all packets except ultra safe Point-to-Point Tunneling Protocol (PPTP) packets.

RAS can be a very powerful and useful tool in enabling you to extend the reaches of your network to remote and traveling users. The following list summarizes main points for RAS in preparation for the exam:

- RAS supports SLIP and PPP line protocols.
- With PPP, RAS can support NetBEUI, NWLINK, and TCP/IP across the communication line.
- RAS uses the following media to communicate with remote systems: PSTN, X.25, Null Modem cable, and ISDN.
- The RAS security features available are auditing, callback security, encryption, and PPTP filtering.
- To install RAS, click the Network icon in the Control Panel.

## MONITORING AND OPTIMIZATION

Establish a baseline for measuring system performance. Tasks include creating a database of measurement data.

You can use numerous database utilities to analyze the data collected. The following are some of the databases that Microsoft provides:

- Performance Monitor
- Microsoft Excel
- Microsoft Access
- Microsoft FoxPro
- Microsoft SQL Server

The following list summarizes the key items to focus on when you are analyzing your computer and network:

- Establish a baseline measurement of your system when functioning at its normal level. Later, you can use the baseline in comparative analysis.
- Establish a database to maintain the baseline results and any subsequent analysis results on the system, to compare trends and identify potential pitfalls in your system.
- The main resources to monitor are memory, the processor, the disks, and the network.

The following list summarizes the tools used to monitor your NT server that are available and are built into Windows NT Server 4.0:

- Server Manager
- Windows NT Diagnostics
- Response Probe

- Performance Monitor
- Network Monitor

Monitor performance of various functions by using Performance Monitor. Functions include the following:

- Processor
- Memory
- Disk
- Network

To summarize the main views used within Performance Monitor, review the following list:

- **Chart view.** This view is very useful for viewing the objects and counters in a real-time mode. This mode enables you to view the data in a graphical format. You can also use the chart view to view the contents of a log file.
- **Log view.** This view enables you to set all the options required for creating a log of your system resources or objects. After this log is created, you can view it by using the chart view.
- **Alert view.** Use the alert view to configure warnings or alerts of your system resources or objects. In this view, you can configure threshold levels for counters and can then launch an action based on the threshold values being exceeded.
- **Report view.** The report view enables you to view the object and counters as an averaged value. This view is useful for comparing the values of multiple systems that are configured similarly.

When monitoring the disk, remember to activate the disk counters using the command diskperf –y. If you do not enter this command, you can select counter but will not see any activity displayed. In the case of a software RAID system, start diskperf with the -ye option.

When you want to monitor TCP/IP counters, make sure that SNMP is installed. Without the SNMP service installed, the TCP/IP counters are not available.

Performance Monitor is a graphical utility that you can use for monitoring and analyzing your system resources within Windows NT. You can enable objects and counters within Performance Monitor; it is these elements that enable the logging and viewing of system data.

In preparing you for this objective, this section introduces numerous objects and counters that you use with Performance Monitor. To prepare for the exam, you need to understand the following key topics:

- The four views available in Performance Monitor are the report view, the log view, the chart view, and the alert view.
- The main resources to monitor in any system are the disk, the memory, the network, and the processor.
- Each of the main resources is grouped as a separate object, and within each object are counters. A counter is the type of data available from a type of resource or object. Each counter might also have multiple instances. An instance is available if multiple components in a counter are listed.
- To enable the disk counters to be active, you must run the DISKPERF utility.

Monitor network traffic by using Network Monitor. Tasks include the following:

- Collecting data
- Presenting data
- Filtering data

Network Monitor is a network packet analyzer that comes with Windows NT Server 4. Actually, two versions of Network Monitor are available from Microsoft.

The first version comes with Windows NT Server 4 (simple version). This version can monitor the packets (frames) sent or received by a Windows NT Server 4 computer. The second version comes with Microsoft Systems Management Server (full version). This version can monitor all traffic on the network.

By fully understanding the various components found while analyzing traffic, you will be more successful in locating potential network bottlenecks and offering relevant optimization recommendations. The main components that need to be monitored with your network traffic analysis are the following:

- Locate and classify each service. Analyze the amount of traffic generated from each individual service, the frequency of the traffic, and the overall effect the traffic has on the network segment.
- Understand the three different types of frames: broadcast, multicast, and directed.
- Review the contents of a frame and ensure that you can find the destination address, source address, and data located in each frame.

The following points summarize the key items to understand in building a strong level of knowledge in using Network Monitor as a monitoring tool:

- Two versions of Network Monitor are available: the scaled-down version that is built into the Windows NT Server operating system, and the full version that is a component of Microsoft Systems Management Server.
- The Network Monitor windows consist of four sections: Graph, Session Statistics, Station Statistics, and Total Statistics.
- After Network Monitor captures some data, you use the display window of Network Monitor to view the frames. The three sections of the display window are the Summary pane, the Detail pane, and the Hexadecimal pane.

Identify performance bottlenecks and optimize performance for various results. Results include the following:

- Controlling network traffic
- Controlling the server load

To optimize the logon traffic in your Windows NT network, you should consider four main points:

- Determine the hardware required to increase performance.
- Configure the domain controllers to increase the number of logon validations.
- Determine the number of domain controllers needed.
- Determine the best location for each of the domain controllers.

The following are a few good points to follow in optimizing file-session traffic:

- Remove any excess protocols that are loaded.
- Reduce the number of wide area network (WAN) links required for file transfer.

The following are three points to consider when attempting to optimize server browser traffic:

- Reduce the number of protocols.
- Reduce the number of entries in the browse list.
- Increase the amount of time between browser updates.

Trust relationships generate a large amount of network traffic. In optimizing your system, attempt to keep the number of trusts very low.

## TROUBLESHOOTING

Choose the appropriate course of action to take to resolve installation failures.

Troubleshooting a Windows NT system requires that you have a strong understanding of the processes and tools available to you. To be an effective troubleshooter, first and foremost you must have experience. The following is a list of some common installation problems:

- Hard disk problems
- Unsupported CD-ROMs
- Network adapter problems and conflicts
- Naming problems (each computer must be uniquely named, following the NetBIOS naming conventions)

Always use the hardware compatibility list to ensure that your components are supported by Windows NT.

Choose the appropriate course of action to take to resolve boot failures.

For startup errors, try the following:

- Check for missing files that are involved in the boot process, including NTLDR, NTDETECT.COM, BOOT.INI, NTOSKRNL.EXE, and OSLOADER (RISC).
- Modify BOOT.INI for options.
- Create an NT boot disk for bypassing the boot process from the hard disk.
- Use the Last Known Good option to roll back to the last working set of your Registry settings.

Choose the appropriate course of action to take to resolve configuration errors. Tasks include the following:

- Backing up and restoring the Registry
- Editing the Registry

You can resolve many problems that you encounter within Windows NT by configuring the Registry. However, before you make any Registry configurations, you must have a strong understanding of the keys within the Registry and always back up the Registry prior to making any modifications to ensure a smooth rollback if additional problems occur. The following are the main tools used to modify the Registry:

- REGEDT32
- REGEDIT

For configuration problems, remember the following:

- Using the Registry for configuration and troubleshooting can cause additional problems if you do not maintain a full understanding of the Registry.
- Always back up the Registry prior to editing the contents.
- You can back up and restore the local Registry by using REGEDT32.

Choose the appropriate course of action to take to resolve printer problems.

For troubleshooting printers, you should do the following:

- Understand and review the overview of the printing process.
- Understand the files involved in the printing process.
- As a first step in troubleshooting a printer, always verify that the printer is turned on and online.
- Note that the most common errors associated with a printer are an invalid printer driver or incorrect resource permissions set for a user.

Choose the appropriate course of action to take to resolve RAS problems.

The following is a list of some of the problems that you might encounter with RAS:

- You must ensure that the protocol you are requesting from the RAS client is available on the RAS server. There must be at least one common protocol or the connection will fail.
- If you are using NetBEUI, ensure that the name you are using on the RAS client is not in use on the network to which you are attempting to connect.
- If you are attempting to connect using TCP/IP, you must configure the RAS server to provide you with an address.

You can use the Remote Access Admin tool to monitor the ports as well as the active connections of your RAS server.

Numerous RAS settings can cause some problems with your RAS connections. Ensure that you understand the installation process, as well as any configuration settings required to enable your RAS server. You can avoid some of the common problems that can occur by doing the following:

- Ensuring that the modem and communication medium are configured and functional prior to installing RAS. It can be very difficult to modify settings after the installation, so it is recommended to have all hardware tested and working first.
- Verifying that dial-in permissions have been enabled for the required users. This small task is commonly forgotten in your RAS configuration.

Choose the appropriate course of action to take to resolve connectivity problems.

To test and verify your TCP/IP settings, you can use the following utilities:

- IPCONFIG
- PING

The most effective method for troubleshooting connectivity is to understand thoroughly the installation and configuration options of each of the network protocols. If you understand the options available, you can narrow down the possible problem areas very quickly. Also ensure that you use utilities such as IPCONFIG and PING to test your connections.

Choose the appropriate course of action to take to resolve resource access and permission problems.

You should keep in mind two main issues about permissions:

- The default permissions for both share and NTFS give the Windows NT group Everyone full control over the files and folders. Whenever you format a drive as NTFS or first share a folder, you should remove these permissions. The Everyone group contains everyone, including guests and any other user who, for one reason or another, can connect to your system.
- The NTFS folder permission delete takes precedence over any file permissions. In all other cases, the file permissions take precedence over the folder permissions.

Choose the appropriate course of action to take to resolve fault-tolerance failures. Fault-tolerance methods include the following:

- Tape backup
- Mirroring
- Stripe set with parity

In using the NTBACKUP tool, the primary thing that you need to do is to determine the frequency and type of backup that you will do. There are three main types of backups that you might want to perform:

- **Full.** This backs up all the files that you mark, and marks the files as having been backed up. This is the longest of the backups because it transfers the most data.
- **Differential.** This backs up all the files that have changed since the last backup. A differential backup does not mark the files as being backed up. As time passes since the last full backup, the differentials become increasingly larger. However, you need only reload the full backup and the differential to return to the position of the last backup.
- **Incremental.** This backs up any files that have changed since the last backup, and then marks them as having been backed up. If your system crashes, you need to start by loading a full backup and then each incremental backup since that full backup.

If you are mirroring the system partition, the disks and partitions should be absolutely identical. Otherwise, the MBR/DBR (master boot record/disk boot record) that contains the driver information will not be correct.

Although ARC naming looks complicated, it is really rather simple. The name is in four parts, of which you use three. The syntax is as follows:

```
multi/scsi(#)disk(#)rdisk(#)partition(#)
```

The following list outlines the parts of the name:

- **multi/scsi.** You use either multi or scsi, not both. Use multi in all cases except when using a scsi controller that cannot handle int13 (hard disk access) BIOS routines. Such cases are uncommon. The number is the logical number of the controller with the first controller being 0, the second being 1, and so forth.
- **disk.** When you use a scsi disk, you use the disk parameter to indicate which of the drives on the controller is the drive you are talking about. Again, the numbers start at 0 for the first drive and then increase for each subsequent drive.
- **rdisk.** Use this parameter for the other controllers in the same way as you use the disk parameter for scsi.
- **partition.** This is the partition on the disk that you are pointing at. The first partition is 1, the second is 2, and so forth. Remember that you can have up to four primary partitions, or three primary and one extended. The extended partition is always the last one, and the first logical drive in the partition will have the partition's number. Other drives in the extended partition each continue to add one.

**Breaking a mirror set.** The boot floppy will get the operating system up and running. You should immediately back up the mirrored copy of the mirror set. To back up the drive, you must break your mirror set. To do this, perform the tasks outlined in Step by Step FF.1.

## STEP BY STEP

### FF.1 Breaking the Mirror Set

1. Run the Disk Administrator.
2. From the Disk Administrator, click the remaining fragment of the mirrored set.
3. Choose Fault Tolerance, Break Mirror set from the menu.

At the end of these three steps, you should notice that the mirror set has been broken, and you can now back up the drive.

**Regenerating a stripe set with parity.** Fixing a stripe set with parity is simple. Perform the tasks outlined in Step by Step FF.2 to regenerate your stripe set with parity.

## STEP BY STEP

### FF.2 Regenerating the Stripe Set

1. Physically replace the faulty disk drive.
2. Start the Disk Administrator.
3. Select the stripe set with parity that you need to repair and then Ctrl+click the free space of the drive you added to fix the stripe set.
4. Choose Fault Tolerant, Regenerate. Note that this process can take some time, although the process takes less time than restoring from tape.

   The drives regenerate all the required data from the parity bits and the data bits, and upon completion your stripe set with parity is completely functional.

- **Share permissions.** A common problem when troubleshooting share resources is in the share permissions. Ensure that the minimum functional permissions have been assigned. Always remove the Everyone group from having full control of a share.
- **Combining NTFS and share permissions.** When combining these permissions, remember that NT uses the most restrictive of the permissions when combining. As a rule, use the NTFS permissions as the highest level of permissions, and use the share permissions mainly for access to the folder or share.
- **Tape backups.** In any system that you are using, ensure that you have a good backup strategy. Any component in your system can be faulty, and it is your responsibility to have a recovery plan in case of emergencies.
- **Disk mirroring.** If you are implementing disk mirroring in your system, ensure that you have created a fault-tolerant boot disk that you can use in case of drive failure. By having this disk preconfigured and handy, you can break the mirror set and replace the drive with very little downtime for your server.
- **Stripe set with parity.** This system automatically regenerates data if a drive is faulty. Although your system performance will dramatically decline, it is still a functional box and you risk no possibility of losing any data. If you find that a drive in your stripe set is faulty, replace the drive and use the regenerate command from the Disk Administrator.

Perform advanced problem resolution. Tasks include the following:

- Diagnosing and interpreting a blue screen
- Configuring a memory dump
- Using the event log service

Three utilities come with Windows NT that enable you to work with the memory dump files that are created. You can find all of these utilities on the Windows NT Server CD-ROM. Each utility can be a very helpful tool. The following list briefly describes these utilities:

- **DUMPCHK.** This utility checks that the dump file is in order by verifying all the addresses and listing the errors and system information.
- **DUMPEXAM.** This creates a text file that can provide the same information that was on the blue screen at the time the stop error occurred.

You need the symbol files and the kernel debugger extensions as well as IMAGEHLP.DLL to run DUMPEXAM.

- **DUMPFLOP.** This utility backs up the dump file to a series of floppies so that you can send them to Microsoft.

The following list summarizes the key points required for this objective:

- The Event Viewer is a very powerful troubleshooting tool. The three logs that can be viewed through the Event Viewer are the system log, the application log, and the security log.
- Cross-reference the events in the Event Viewer with knowledge base articles found on Microsoft TechNet for troubleshooting help.
- Interpreting blue screens can be very difficult. Use memory dump files and the following utilities to view your memory dumps to help you isolate the problem:
  - DUMPCHK
  - DUMPEXAM
  - DUMPFLOP
- If the problem persists, you might have to use the kernel debugger that is included on the NT Server CD-ROM in the \Support\debug folder.
- You can use the kernel debugger to monitor a remote machine through a null modem, or by using the RAS service into a machine that is connected to the problematic computer through a null modem.

# Fast Facts

## Networking Essentials Exam

Twelve chapters of this book have looked at objectives and components of the Microsoft Networking Essentials exam. After reading all of that, what is it that you must really know? What should you read as you sit and wait in the parking lot of the testing center—right up until the hour before going in to gamble your $100 and pride?

The following material covers the salient points of the 12 previous chapters and the points that make excellent test fodder. Although there is no substitute for real-world, hands-on experience, knowing what to expect on the exam can be equally meaningful. The information that follows is the networking equivalent of *Cliffs Notes*, providing the information you must know in each of the four sections to pass the exam. Don't just memorize the concepts given; attempt to understand the reason why they are so, and you will have no difficulties passing the exam.

## Standards and Terminology

The Standards and Terminology section is designed to test your understanding and knowledge of terms used in networking, as well as some of the more common standards that have been implemented in the industry.

### Define Common Networking Terms for LANs and WANs

The Networking Essentials exam does not really test on definitions of terms. You are asked questions though, and, based on these questions, you need to understand the definitions of the terms used in order to successfully answer the questions.

The best mechanism to study for this area would be to be able to review the key terms found in every chapter and provide the correct definition for each term. Below is a list of some of the more general networking terms you should be aware of.

- **peer-to-peer networking**. A networking model where both the services and the client are performed by the same computer.
- **client/server networking**. A networking model where a specific role of providing services or acting as a client (not both) is performed by a computer.
- **centralized computing**. A form of computing where all the processing is done by one central computer.
- **distributed computing**. A form of computing where all the processing is shared by many different computers.
- **file services**. Services allowing for the storage and access of files.
- **print services**. Services that allow the sharing of a printer.
- **file and print server**. A server that provides file and print services.
- **application server**. A server that provides some high-end application used by many different computers.
- **token-ring network**. A network that follows a logical topology of a ring, but a physical topology of a star. The computers are connected to a concentrator known as an MSAU or MAU. Computers rely on the possession of a token before the transmission of data on the network. This type of network is known as a deterministic network.
- **ethernet network**. This type of a network is run as a logical bus, but can take on the physical topology of a bus or a star. The concentrator used by these computers, when in a star topology, is called a hub. This type of network is known as a contention-based network because each device contends with every other device for network access.
- **LAN**. Also known as a Local Area Network. Often characterized by fast transmission speeds and short distances between devices, and by the fact that the company running the network has control over all devices and transmission media.
- **WAN**. Also known as a Wide Area Network. When compared to a LAN, a WAN is often characterized by lower data transmission rates and the coverage of long distances, and by the fact that a third party is involved with the supply and maintenance of the transmission media.

## Compare a File and Print Server with an Application Server

A file server is a service that is involved with giving access to files and directories on the network. The purpose of the file server is to give large numbers of users access to a centrally stored set of files and directories.

A print server is a computer or device that gives large number of users access to a centrally maintained printing device. A computer that is a file server often acts as print server, too. These types of computers are known as file and print servers.

An application server is responsible for running applications such as Exchange Server or SQL Server on the network. Application servers perform services that often require a more advanced level of processing than a user's personal computer is able to provide.

## Compare User-Level Security with Access Permission Assigned to a Shared Directory on a Server

User-level security is a security model in which access to resources is given on a user-by-user basis, a group-by-group basis, or both. This type of access restriction allows an administrator to grant access to resources and affords users seemless access to those resources. User-level security is offered by Windows NT in both the workgroup and domain models.

The permissions to a shared directory are:

- **Read**. The user is allowed to read files within a share. He can also see all files and subdirectories.
- **Change**. The user can modify existing files and directories and create new files and directories within the share.
- **Full Control.** The user can see, modify, delete, and take ownership of all files and directories within the share.
- **No Access**. The user cannot access any files or directories within the share.

Share-level permissions apply to anyone accessing the share over the network and do not apply to users who are interactive on the computer where the share resides. Share-level permissions can be set on both FAT and NTFS partitions.

## Compare a Client/Server Network with a Peer-to-Peer Network

A client/server network is one in which a computer has a specific role. A server is a computer, often with more RAM, more hard drive space, and a faster CPU than the other machines. A server services requests from clients. These requests could be for the use of files and printers, application services, communication services, and database services.

Clients are the computers on which users work. These computers typically are not as powerful as servers. Client computers are designed to submit requests to the server.

Peer-to-peer networks are made up of several computers that play the roles of both a client and a server; thus there is no dedicated computer running file and printer services, application services, communication services, or database services.

## Compare the Implications of Using Connection-Oriented Communications with Connectionless Communications

In general, connection-oriented communication differs from connectionless communication as follows:

- **Connection-oriented mode**. Error correction and flow control are provided at internal nodes along the message path.
- **Connectionless mode**. Internal nodes along the message path do not participate in error correction and flow control.

In connection-oriented mode, the chain of links between the source and destination nodes forms a kind of logical pathway connection. The nodes forwarding the data packet can track which packet is part of which connection. This enables the internal nodes to provide flow control as the data moves along the path. For example, if an internal node determines that a link is malfunctioning, the node can send a notification message backward through the path to the source computer. Furthermore, because the internal node distinguishes among individual, concurrent connections in which it participates, this node can transmit (or forward) a "stop sending" message for one of its connections without stopping all communications through the node. Another feature of connection-oriented communication is that internal nodes provide error correction at each link in the chain. Therefore, if a node detects an error, it asks the preceding node to retransmit.

SPX and TCP are two major examples of connection-oriented protocols.

Connectionless mode does not provide these elaborate internal control mechanisms; instead, connectionless mode relegates all error-correcting and retransmitting processes to the source and destination nodes. The end nodes acknowledge the receipt of packets and retransmit if necessary, but internal nodes do not participate in flow control and error correction (other than simply forwarding messages between the end nodes).

IPX and UDP are two major examples of connection-oriented protocols.

The advantage of connectionless mode is that connectionless communications can be processed more quickly and more simply because the internal nodes only forward data and thus don't have to track connections or provide retransmission or flow control.

## Distinguish Whether SLIP or PPP Is Used as the Communications Protocol for Various Situations

Two other standards vital to network communication are Serial Line Internet Protocol (SLIP) and Point-to-Point Protocol (PPP). SLIP and PPP were designed to support dial-up access to networks based on the Internet transport protocols. SLIP is a simple protocol that functions at the Physical layer, whereas PPP is a considerably enhanced protocol that provides Physical layer and Data Link layer functionality.

Windows NT supports both SLIP and PPP from the client end using the Dial-Up Networking application. On the server end, Windows NT RAS (Remote Access Service) supports PPP but doesn't support SLIP. In other words, Windows NT can act as a PPP server but not as a SLIP server.

### PPP

PPP was defined by the Internet Engineering Task Force (IETF) to improve on SLIP by providing the following features:

- Security using password logon
- Simultaneous support for multiple protocols on the same link
- Dynamic IP addressing
- Improved error control

Different PPP implementations might offer different levels of service and negotiate service levels when connections are made. Because of its versatility, interoperability, and additional features, PPP has surpassed SLIP as the most popular serial-line protocol.

### SLIP

Developed to provide dial-up TCP/IP connections, SLIP is an extremely rudimentary protocol that suffers from a lack of rigid standardization in the industry, which sometimes hinders different vendor implementations of SLIP from operating with each other.

SLIP is most commonly used on older systems or for dial-up connections to the Internet via SLIP-server Internet hosts.

Certain dial-up configurations cannot use SLIP for the following reasons:

- SLIP supports the TCP/IP transport protocol only. PPP, however, supports TCP/IP, as well as a number of other transport protocols, such as NetBEUI, IPX, AppleTalk, and DECnet. In addition, PPP can support multiple protocols over the same link.
- SLIP requires static IP addresses. Because SLIP requires static, or preconfigured, IP addresses, SLIP servers do not support the Dynamic Host Configuration Protocol (DHCP), which assigns IP addresses dynamically or when requested. (DHCP enables clients to share IP addresses so that a relatively small number of IP addresses can serve a larger user base.) If the dial-up server uses DHCP to assign an IP address to the client, the dial-up connection won't use SLIP.
- SLIP does not support dynamic addressing through DHCP so SLIP connections cannot dynamically assign a WINS or DNS server.

## Define the Communication Devices that Communicate at Each Level of the OSI Model

- **Repeater**. Operates at the Physical layer of the OSI model. The purpose of a repeater is to regenerate a signal, allowing a signal to travel beyond the maximum distance specified by the transmission media.
- **Hub**. Operates at the Physical layer. A hub is a concentrator that connects 10BASE-T cabling together on an Ethernet network. Some hubs also have the capability to act as a repeater.
- **MSAU**. Operates at the Physical layer. An MSAU performs the same purpose of a hub, but is used on token-ring networks.
- **Network Interface Card (NIC)**. Operates at the Data Link layer. A NIC is responsible for converting information in a computer to a signal that will be sent on the transmission media.
- **Bridge**. Operates at the Data Link layer of the OSI mode. A bridge is responsible for isolating network traffic on a cable segment. It performs this task by building address tables that contain the MAC address or hardware addresses of devices on ether side of it.
- **Router**. Operates at the Network layer of the OSI model. It is responsible for connecting different segments that have dissimilar logical network addresses.
- **Gateway**. Can appear at any level of the OSI model but is primarily seen at the Network layer and higher. The purpose of a gateway is to convert one network protocol to another.

## Describe the Characteristics and Purpose of the Media Used in IEEE 802.3 and IEEE 802.5 Standards

The various media types used by the IEEE 802.3 and 802.5 are discussed below.

### IEEE 802.3

This standard defines characteristics related to the MAC sublayer of the Data Link layer and the OSI Physical layer. Except for one minor distinction—frame type—IEEE 802.3 Ethernet functions identically to DIX Ethernet v.2.

The MAC sublayer uses a type of contention access called *Carrier Sense Multiple Access with Collision Detection (CSMA/CD)*. This technique reduces the incidence of collision by having each device listen to the network to determine whether it's quiet ("carrier sensing"); a device attempts to transmit only when the network is quiescent. This reduces but does not eliminate collisions because signals take some time to propagate through the network. As devices transmit, they continue to listen so they can detect a collision should it occur. When a collision occurs, all devices cease transmitting and send a "jamming" signal that notifies all stations of the collision. Each device then waits a random amount of time before attempting to transmit again. This combination of safeguards significantly reduces collisions on all but the busiest networks.

The IEEE 802.3 Physical layer definition describes signaling methods (both baseband and broadband), data rates, media, and topologies. Several Physical layer variants also have been defined. Each variant is named following a convention that states the signaling rate (1 or 10) in Mbps, baseband (BASE) or broadband (BROAD) mode, and a designation of the media characteristics.

The following list details the IEEE 802.3 variants of transmission media:

- **lBASE5**. This 1-Mbps network utilizes UTP cable with a signal range up to 500 meters (250 meters per segment). A star physical topology is used.
- **10BASE5**. Typically called Thick Ethernet, or Thicknet, this variant uses a large diameter (10 mm) "thick" coaxial cable with a 50-ohm impedance. A data rate of 10 Mbps is supported with a signaling range of 500 meters per cable segment on a physical bus topology.
- **10BASE2**. Similar to Thicknet, this variant uses a thinner coaxial cable that can support cable runs of 185 meters. (In this case, the "2" only indicates an approximate cable range.) The transmission rate remains at 10 Mbps, and the physical topology is a bus. This variant typically is called Thin Ethernet, or Thinnet.
- **10BASE-F**. This variant uses fiber-optic cables to support 10-Mbps signaling with a range of four kilometers. Three subcategories include *10BASE-FL* (fiber link), *10BASE-FB* (fiber backbone), and *10BASE-FP* (fiber passive).
- **10BROAD36**. This broadband standard supports channel signal rates of 10 Mbps. A 75-ohm coaxial cable supports cable runs of 1,800 meters (up to 3,600 meters in a dual-cable configuration) using a physical bus topology.
- **10BASE-T**. This variant uses UTP cable in a star physical topology. The signaling rate remains at 10 Mbps, and devices can be up to 100 meters from a wiring hub.
- **100BASE-X**. This proposed standard is similar to 10BASE-T but supports 100 Mbps data rates.

### IEEE 802.5

The IEEE 802.5 standard was derived from IBM's Token Ring network, which employs a ring logical topology and token-based media-access control. Data rates of 1, 4, and 16 Mbps have been defined for this standard.

## Explain the Purpose of NDIS and Novell ODI Network Standards

The *Network Driver Interface Specification (NDIS)*, a standard developed by Microsoft and the 3Com Corporation, describes the interface between the network transport protocol and the Data Link layer network adapter driver. The following list details the goals of NDIS:

- To provide a vendor-neutral boundary between the transport protocol and the network adapter card driver so that an NDIS-compliant protocol stack can operate with an NDIS-compliant adapter driver.

- To define a method for binding multiple protocols to a single driver so that the adapter can simultaneously support communications under multiple protocols. In addition, the method enables you to bind one protocol to more than one adapter.

The *Open Data-Link Interface (ODI)*, developed by Apple and Novell, serves the same function as NDIS. Originally, ODI was written for NetWare and Macintosh environments. Like NDIS, ODI provides rules that establish a vendor-neutral interface between the protocol stack and the adapter driver. This interface also enables one or more network drivers to support one or more protocol stacks.

# PLANNING

The planning section on the exam tests your ability to apply networking components and standards when designing a network.

## Select the Appropriate Media for Various Situations

Media choices include:

- Twisted-pair cable
- Coaxial cable
- Fiber-optic cable
- Wireless

Situational elements include:

- Cost
- Distance limitations
- Number of nodes

Summary Table 1 outlines the characteristics of the cable types discussed in this section.

Summary Table 2 compares the different types of wireless communication media in terms of cost, ease of installation, distance, and other issues.

### SUMMARY TABLE 1
### COMPARISON OF CABLE MEDIA

| *Cable Type* | *Cost* | *Installation* | *Capacity* | *Range* | *EMI* |
|---|---|---|---|---|---|
| Coaxial Thinnet | Less than STP | Inexpensive/easy | 10 Mbps typical | 185 m | Less sensitive than UTP |
| Coaxial Thicknet | Greater than STP Less than Fiber | Easy | 10 Mbps typical | 500 m | Less sensitive than UTP |
| Shielded Twisted-Pair (STP) | Greater than UTP Less than Thicknet | Fairly easy | 16 Mbps typical up to 500 Mbps | 100 m typical | Less sensitive than UTP |
| Unshielded twisted-pair (UTP) | Lowest | Inexpensive/easy | 10 Mbps typical up to 100 Mbps | 100 m typical | Most sensitive |
| Fiber-optic | Highest | Expensive/ Difficult | 100 Mbps typical | Tens of Kilometers | Insensitive |

**SUMMARY TABLE 2**
**COMPARISON OF WIRELESS MEDIA**

| *Cable Type* | *Cost* | *Installation* | *Distance* | *Other Issues* |
|---|---|---|---|---|
| Infrared | Cheapest of all the wireless | Fairly easy; may require line of sight | Under a kilometer | Can attenuate due to fog and rain |
| Laser | Similar to infrared | Requires line of site | Can span several kilometers | Can attenuate due to fog and rain |
| Narrow band radio | More expensive than infrared and laser; may need FCC license | Requires trained technicians and can involve tall radio towers | Can span hundreds of kilometers | Low power devices can attenuate; can be eavesdropped upon; can also attenuate due to fog, rain, and solar flares |
| Spread spectrum radio | More advanced technology than narrow band radio, thus more expensive | Requires trained technicians and can involve tall radio towers | Can span hundreds of kilometers | Low power devices can attenuate; can also attenuate due to fog, rain, and solar flares |
| Microwave | Very expensive as it requires link to satellites often | Requires trained technicians and can involve satellite dishes | Can span thousands of kilometers | Can be eavesdropped upon; can also attenuate due to fog, rain, and solar flares |

## Select the Appropriate Topology for Various Token-Ring and Ethernet Networks

The following four topologies are implemented by Ethernet and token-ring networks:

- **Ring**. Ring topologies are wired in a circle. Each node is connected to its neighbors on either side, and data passes around the ring in one direction only. Each device incorporates a receiver and a transmitter and serves as a repeater that passes the signal to the next device in the ring. Because the signal is regenerated at each device, signal degeneration is low. Most ring topologies are logical, and implemented as physical stars. Token-ring networks follow a ring topology.
- **Bus**. Star topologies require that all devices connect to a central hub. The hub receives signals from other network devices and routes the signals to the proper destinations. Star hubs can be interconnected to form tree or hierarchical network topologies. A star physical topology is often used to physically implement a bus or ring logical topology that is used by both Ethernet and token-ring networks.
- **Star**. Star topologies require that all devices connect to a central hub. The hub receives signals from other network devices and routes the signals to the proper destinations. Star hubs can be interconnected to form tree or hierarchical network topologies. A star physical topology is often used to physically implement a bus or ring logical topology that is used by both Ethernet and token-ring networks.
- **Mesh**. A mesh topology is really a hybrid model representing a physical topology because a mesh topology can incorporate all of the previous topologies. The difference is that in a mesh

topology every device is connected to every other device on the network. When a new device is added, a connection to all existing devices must be made. Mesh topologies can be used by both Ethernet and token-ring networks.

## Select the Appropriate Network and Transport Protocol or Protocols for Various Token-Ring and Ethernet Networks

Protocol choices include:

- DLC
- AppleTalk
- IPX
- TCP/IP
- NFS
- SMB

### Data Link Control (DLC)

The Data Link Control (DLC) protocol does not provide a fully functioning protocol stack. In Windows NT systems, DLC is used primarily to access to Hewlett-Packard JetDirect network-interface printers. DLC also provides some connectivity with IBM mainframes. It is not a protocol that can be used to connect Windows NT or 95 computers together.

### AppleTalk

AppleTalk is the computing architecture developed by Apple Computer for the Macintosh family of personal computers. Although AppleTalk originally supported only Apple's proprietary LocalTalk cabling system, the suite has been expanded to incorporate both Ethernet and token-ring Physical layers. Within Microsoft operating systems, AppleTalk is only supported by Windows NT Server. Windows NT Workstation and Windows 95 do not support AppleTalk. AppleTalk cannot be used for Microsoft to Microsoft operating system communication, only by NT servers supporting Apple clients.

The LocalTalk, EtherTalk, and TokenTalk Link Access Protocols (LLAP, ELAP, and TLAP) integrate AppleTalk upper-layer protocols with the LocalTalk, Ethernet, and token-ring environments.

Apple's *Datagram Deliver Protocol (DDP)* is a Network layer protocol that provides connectionless service between two sockets. The AppleTalk Transaction Protocol (ATP) is a connectionless Transport layer protocol. Reliable service is provided through a system of acknowledgments and retransmissions. The *AppleTalk File Protocol (AFP)* provides file services and is responsible for translating local file service requests into formats required for network file services. AFP directly translates command syntax and enables applications to perform file format translations. AFP is responsible for file system security and verifies and encrypts logon names and passwords during connection setup.

### IPX

The *Internetwork Packet Exchange Protocol (IPX)* is a Network layer protocol that provides connectionless (datagram) service. (IPX was developed from the XNS protocol originated by Xerox.) As a Network layer protocol, IPX is responsible for internetwork routing and maintaining network logical addresses. Routing uses the RIP protocol (described later in this section) to make route selections. IPX provides similar functionality as UDP does in the TCP/IP protocol suite.

IPX relies on hardware physical addresses found at lower layers to provide network device addressing. IPX also uses sockets, or upper-layer service addresses, to deliver packets to their ultimate destinations. On the client, IPX support is provided as a component of the older DOS shell and the current DOS NetWare requester.

# TCP/IP

TCP/IP is a broad protocol that covers many different areas. This summary presents some of the most important protocols within the TCP/IP protocol suite.

## Internet Protocol (IP)

The *Internet Protocol (IP)* is a connectionless protocol that provides datagram service, and IP packets are most commonly referred to as IP datagrams. IP is a packet-switching protocol that performs the addressing and route selection.

IP performs packet disassembly and reassembly as required by packet size limitations defined for the Data Link and Physical layers being implemented. IP also performs error checking on the header data using a checksum, although data from upper layers is not error-checked.

## Transmission Control Protocol (TCP)

The *Transmission Control Protocol (TCP)* is an internetwork connection-oriented protocol that corresponds to the OSI Transport layer. TCP provides full-duplex, end-to-end connections. When the overhead of end-to-end communication acknowledgment isn't required, the User Datagram Protocol (UDP) can be substituted for TCP at the Transport (host-to-host) level. TCP and UDP operate at the same layer.

TCP corresponds to SPX in the NetWare environment (see the NetWare IPX/SPX section). TCP maintains a logical connection between the sending and receiving computer systems. In this way, the integrity of the transmission is maintained. TCP detects any problems in the transmission quickly and takes action to correct them. The tradeoff is that TCP isn't as fast as UDP, due to the number of acknowledgments received by the sending host.

TCP also provides message fragmentation and reassembly and can accept messages of any length from upper-layer protocols. TCP fragments message streams into segments that can be handled by IP. When used with IP, TCP adds connection-oriented service and performs segment synchronization, adding sequence numbers at the byte level.

## Windows Internet Naming Services (WINS)

Windows Internet Naming Service (WINS) provides a function similar to that of DNS, with the exception that it provides a NetBIOS name to IP address resolution. This is important because all of Microsoft's networking requires the capability to reference NetBIOS names. Normally NetBIOS names are obtained with the issuance of broadcasts, but because routers normally do not forward broadcasts, a WINS server is one alternative that can be used to issue IP addresses to NetBIOS name requests. WINS servers replace the need for LMHOSTS files on a computer.

## Domain Name System (DNS)

The Domain Name System (DNS) protocol provides host name and IP address resolution as a service to client applications. DNS servers enable humans to use logical node names, utilizing a fully qualified domain name structure to access network resources. Host names can be up to 260 characters long. DNS servers replace the need for HOSTS files on a computer.

## Network File System (NFS)

*Network File System (NFS)*, developed by Sun Microsystems, is a family of file-access protocols that are a considerable advancement over FTP and Telnet. Since Sun made the NFS specifications available for public use, NFS has achieved a high level of popularity.

## Server Messaging Blocks (SMB)

One protocol that is slightly independent is Microsoft's Server Messaging Blocks (SMB). SMBs are Microsoft's equivalent to NCP packets. Like NCP packets, SMBs operate at the Application layer of the OSI model.

SMBs allow machines on a Microsoft network to communicate with one another. Through the use of SMBs, file and print services can be shared. SMBs can use TCP/IP, NWLink (IPX/SPX), and NetBEUI because SMBs utilize a NetBIOS interface when communicating. For more information on NetBIOS names, see the following section.

# Select the Appropriate Connectivity Devices for Various Token-Ring and Ethernet Networks

Connectivity devices include:

- **Repeaters**. Repeaters regenerate a signal and are used to expand LANs beyond cabling limits.
- **Bridges**. Bridges know the side of the bridge on which a node is located. A bridge passes only packets addressed to computers across the bridge, so a bridge can thus filter traffic, reducing the load on the transmission medium.
- **Routers**. Routers forward packets based on a logical (as opposed to a physical) address. Some routers can determine the best path for a packet based on routing algorithms.
- **Brouters**. A brouter is a device that is a combination of a bridge and a router, providing both types of services.
- **Gateways**. Gateways function under a process similar to routers except that gateways can connect dissimilar network environments. A gateway replaces the necessary protocol layers of a packet so that the packet can circulate in the destination environment.

# List the Characteristics, Requirements, and Appropriate Situations for WAN Connection Services

WAN connection services include:

- X.25
- ISDN
- Frame relay
- ATM

## X.25

X.25 is a packet-switching network standard developed by the International Telegraph and Telephone Consultative Committee (CCITT), which has been renamed the International Telecommunications Union (ITU). The standard, referred to as *Recommendation X.25*, was introduced in 1974 and is now implemented most commonly in WANs.

At the time X.25 was developed, this flow control and error checking was essential because X.25 was developed around relatively unreliable telephone line communications. The drawback is that error checking and flow control slow down X.25. Generally, X.25 networks are implemented with line speeds up to 64 Kbps, although actual throughput seems slower due to the error correction controls in place. These speeds are suitable for the file transfer and terminal activity that comprised the bulk of network traffic when X.25 was defined, most of this traffic being terminal connections to mainframes. Such speeds, however, are inadequate to provide LAN-speed services, which typically require speeds of 1 Mbps or better. X.25 networks, therefore, are poor choices for providing LAN application services in a WAN environment. One advantage of X.25, however, is that it is an established standard that is used internationally. This, as well as lack of other services throughout the world, means that X.25 is more of a connection service to Africa, South America, and Asia, where a lack of other services prevails.

## ISDN

The original idea behind ISDN was to enable existing phone lines to carry digital communications, and it was at one time touted as a replacement to traditional analog lines. Thus, ISDN is more like traditional telephone service than some of the other WAN services. ISDN is intended as a dial-up service and not as a permanent 24-hour connection.

ISDN separates the bandwidth into channels. Based upon how these channels are used, ISDN can be separated into two classes of service:

- **Basic Rate (BRI)**. Basic Rate ISDN uses three channels. Two channels (called B channels) carry the digital data at 64 Kbps. A third channel (called the D channel) provides link and signaling information at 16 Kbps. Basic Rate ISDN thus is referred to as 2B+D. A single PC transmitting through ISDN can use both B channels simultaneously, providing a maximum data rate of 128 Kbps (or higher with compression).
- **Primary Rate (PRI)**. Primary Rate supports 23 64 Kbps B channels and one 64 Kbps D channel. The D channel is used for signaling and management, whereas the B channels provide the data throughput.

In a BRI line, if the line was currently being used for voice, this would only allow one of the B channels to be available for data. This effectively reduces the throughput of the BRI to 64 Kbps.

## Frame Relay

Frame Relay was designed to support the *Broadband Integrated Services Digital Network (B-ISDN)*, which was discussed in the previous section. The specifications for Frame Relay address some of the limitations of X.25. As with X.25, Frame Relay is a packet-switching network service, but Frame Relay was designed around newer, faster fiber-optic networks.

Unlike X.25, Frame Relay assumes a more reliable network. This enables Frame Relay to eliminate much of the X.25 overhead required to provide reliable service on less reliable networks. Frame Relay relies on higher-level protocol layers to provide flow and error control.

Frame Relay typically is implemented as a public data network and, therefore, is regarded as a WAN protocol. The scope of Frame Relay, with respect to the OSI model, is limited to the Physical and Data Link layers.

Frame Relay provides permanent virtual circuits that supply permanent virtual pathways for WAN connections. Frame Relay services typically are implemented at line speeds from 56 Kbps up to 1.544 Mbps (T1).

Customers typically purchase access to a specific amount of bandwidth on a frame-relay service. This bandwidth is called the *committed information rate (CIR)*, a data rate for which the customer is guaranteed access. Customers might be permitted to access higher data rates on a pay-per-use temporary basis. This arrangement enables customers to tailor their network access costs based on their bandwidth requirements.

To use Frame Relay, you must have special Frame Relay-compatible connectivity devices (such as frame-relay-compatible routers and bridges).

### Asynchronous Transfer Mode (ATM)

*Asynchronous Transfer Mode (ATM)* is a high-bandwidth switching technology developed by the ITU Telecommunications Standards Sector (ITU-TSS). An organization called the ATM Forum is responsible for defining ATM implementation characteristics. ATM can be layered on other Physical layer technologies, such as Fiber Distributed Data Interface (FDDI) and SONET.

Several characteristics distinguish ATM from other switching technologies. ATM is based on fixed-length 53-byte cells, whereas other technologies employ frames that vary in length to accommodate different amounts of data. Because ATM cells are uniform in length, switching mechanisms can operate with a high level of efficiency. This high efficiency results in high data transfer rates. Some ATM systems can operate at an incredible rate of 622 Mbps; a typical working speed for an ATM is around 155 Mbps.

The unit of transmission for ATM is called a cell. All cells are 53 bytes long and consist of a 5-byte header and 48 bytes of data. The 48-byte data size was selected by the standards committee as a compromise to suit both audio- and data-transmission needs. Audio information, for instance, must be delivered with little latency (delay) to maintain a smooth flow of sound. Audio engineers therefore preferred a small cell so that cells would be more readily available when needed. For data, however, large cells reduce the overhead required to deliver a byte of information.

*Asynchronous delivery* is another distinguishing feature of ATM. "Asynchronous" refers to the characteristic of ATM in which transmission time slots don't occur periodically but are granted at irregular intervals. ATM uses a technique called *label multiplexing*, which allocates time slots on demand. Traffic that is time-critical, such as voice or video, can be given priority over data traffic that can be delayed slightly with no ill effect. Channels are identified by cell labels, not by specific time slots. A high-priority transmission need not be held until its next time slot allocation. Instead, it might be required to wait only until the current 53-byte cell has been transmitted.

## IMPLEMENTATION

The Implementation section of the exam tests your knowledge of how to implement, test, and manage an installed network.

### Choosing an Administrative Plan to Meet Specified Needs, Including Performance Management, Account Management, and Security

Administrative plans can be broken down into three areas: performance management, account management, and security.

## Performance Management

Performance management is best done through the establishment of a baseline of the network performance and a baseline of a computer's performance. Based upon the information in a baseline, the administrators of the network can establish when network or computer performance is abnormal.

## Account Management

Account management within Windows NT is done through the use of groups. In a workgroup model, there exist local groups, or groups that are local to the computer. These groups are not seen on other machines in the network. Users are placed into these local groups and assigned permissions to resources, such as printers, shares, or files and directories.

Windows 95 computers do not have built-in groups. There also is no account database on a Windows 95 computer to provide user accounts.

Windows NT domain models do make use of user accounts and groups. Like the workgroup model, the domain model has user accounts and local groups. A domain model also has global groups. Global groups reside on a domain controller and can be referenced as a resource user by any Windows NT computer within the domain sharing resources.

## Security

Windows 95 computers have the capability to provide share-level security, which involves password protecting resources.

Windows NT computers can provide user-level security, in which users are granted access to resources on a user or local group basis (workgroups and domains support this) and a global group basis (only domains support this).

# Choosing a Disaster Recovery Plan for Various Situations

Disaster recovery applies to many different components on the network. The following sections describe the most common issues and solutions used in a disaster recovery program.

## Uninterruptible Power Supply (UPS)

An uninterruptible power supply (UPS) is a special battery (or sometimes a generator) that supplies power to an electronic device in the event of a power failure. UPSs commonly are used with network servers to prevent a disorderly shutdown by warning users to log out. After a predetermined waiting period, the UPS software performs an orderly shutdown of the server. Many UPS units also regulate power distribution and serve as protection against power surges. Remember that in most cases, a UPS generally does not provide for continued network functionality for longer than a few minutes. A UPS is not intended to keep the server running through a long power outage, but rather to give the server time to do what it needs before shutting down. This can prevent the data loss and system corruption that sometimes result from sudden shutdown.

## Tape Backup

Tape backups are done to store data offline in the event that the hard drive containing the data fails. There are three types of tape backups:

- **Full backup**. Backs up all specified files.
- **Incremental backup**. Backs up only those files that have changed since the last backup.
- **Differential backup**. Backs up the specified files if the files have changed since the last backup. This type doesn't mark the files as having been backed up, however. (A differential backup is

somewhat like a copy command. Because the file is not marked as having been backed up, a later differential or incremental backup will back up the file again.)

## RAID 1

In level 1, drives are paired or mirrored with each byte of information being written to each identical drive. You can duplex these devices by adding a separate drive controller for each drive. Disk mirroring is defined as two hard drives (one primary, one secondary) that use the same disk channel or controller cards and cable. Disk mirroring is most commonly configured by using disk drives contained in the server. Duplexing is a form of mirroring that involves the use of a second controller and that enables you to configure a more robust hardware environment.

## RAID 5

RAID 5 uses striping with parity information written across multiple drives to enable fault-tolerance with a minimum of wasted disk space. This level also offers the advantage of enabling relatively efficient performance on writes to the drives, as well as excellent read performance.

Striping with parity is based on the principle that all data is written to the hard drive in binary code (ones and zeros). RAID 5 requires at least three drives because this version writes data across two of them and then creates the parity block on the third. If the first byte is 00111000 and the second is 10101001, the system computes the third by adding the digits together using this system:

1+1=0, 0+0=0, 0+1=1, 1+0=1

The sum of 00111000 and 10101001 is 10010001, which would be written to the third disk. If any of the disks fail, the process can be reversed and any disk can be reconstructed from the data on the other two. Recovery includes replacing the bad disk and then regenerating its data through the Disk Administrator. A maximum of 32 disks can be connected in a RAID 5 array under Windows NT.

# Given the Manufacturer's Documentation for the Network Adapter, Install, Configure, and Resolve Hardware Conflicts for Multiple Network Adapters in a Token-Ring or Ethernet Network

The following resources are configurable on network adapter cards:

- IRQ
- Base I/O port address
- Base memory address
- DMA channel
- Boot PROM
- MAC address
- Ring speed (token-ring cards)
- Connector type

Not all network adapter cards have all of these resources available for configuration. These resource settings on the network adapter card must be different than the settings found on other components used within the computer.

Some network adapter cards use jumper settings to configure these settings, others use software, and others can have this done through the operating system software, such as Windows 95 and Windows NT. The method of configuration is dependent upon the manufacturer.

## Implementing a NetBIOS Naming Scheme for All Computers on a Given Network

NetBIOS is an interface that provides NetBIOS-based applications with access to network resources. Every computer on a Windows NT network must have a unique name for it to be accessible through the NetBIOS interface. This unique name is called a computer name or a NetBIOS name.

On a NetBIOS network, every computer must have a unique name. The computer name can be up to 15 characters long. A NetBIOS name can include alphanumeric characters and any of the following special characters:

! @ # $ % ^ & ( ) - _ ' { } . ~

Note that you cannot use a space or an asterisk in a NetBIOS name. Also, NetBIOS names are not case sensitive.

## Selecting the Appropriate Hardware and Software Tools to Monitor Trends in the Network

The hardware and software tools described in the next five sections are used to monitor trends in a network.

### Protocol Analyzer

This can be a hardware or software tool to analyze the traffic in a network. Protocol analyzers capture packets on a network and display their contents. The software version of this tool supplied by Microsoft is Network Monitor. Network Monitor ships with Windows NT as a scaled-down version that can only capture data between the host computer and those to which the host talks.

### Event Viewer

This software tool is found on Windows NT. It reports one of three event types:

- **System Events**. Those generated by the operating system.
- **Application Events**. Those generated by any application that is programmed to make event calls to the Event Viewer.
- **Auditing**. Any auditing being performed on NTFS partitions or by users interacting with the network.

### Performance Monitor

Windows NT's Performance Monitor tool lets you monitor important system parameters for the computers on your network in real time. Performance Monitor can keep an eye on a large number of system parameters, providing a graphical or tabular profile of system and network trends. Performance Monitor also can save performance data in a log for later reference. You can use Performance Monitor to track statistical measurements (called *counters*) for any of several hardware or software components (called *objects*).

## System Monitor

Windows 95 includes a program called System Monitor that also allows information to be collected on the Windows 95 machine in real time. System Monitor collects information on different categories of items on the system. System Monitor is not as detailed as Windows NT's Performance Monitor.

## Simple Network Management Protocol (SNMP)

SNMP is a TCP/IP protocol used to perform management operations on a TCP/IP network. SNMP-enabled devices allow for information to be sent to a management utility (this is called a *trap*). SNMP devices also allow for the setting and extraction of information (this is done by the issuance of a `set` or `get` command) found in their Management Information Base (MIB).

# TROUBLESHOOTING

The Troubleshooting section of the exam covers many of the topics covered in previous sections. Emphasis of this section is to test your understanding of what can cause problems, and how to fix them.

## Identifying Common Errors Associated with Components Required for Communications

The utilities described in the next four sections can be used to diagnose errors associated with components required for communications.

## Protocol Analyzers

Protocol analyzers are either hardware or software products used to monitor network traffic, track network performance, and analyze packets. Protocol analyzers can identify bottlenecks, protocol problems, and malfunctioning network components.

## Digital Volt Meter (DVM)

Digital volt meters are handheld electronic measuring tools that enable you to check the voltage of network cables. They also can be used to check the resistance of terminators. You can use a DVM to help you find a break or a short in a network cable.

DVMs are usually inexpensive battery-operated devices that have either a digital or needle readout and two metal prongs attached to the DVM by some wires a foot or more in length. By sending a small current through the wires and out through the metal prongs, resistance and voltages of terminators and wires can be measured.

## Time-Domain Reflectometers (TDR)

Time-domain reflectometers send sound waves along a cable and look for imperfections that might be caused by a break or a short in the line. A good TDR can detect faults on a cable to within a few feet.

## Oscilloscope

An oscilloscope measures fluctuations in signal voltage and can help find faulty or damaged cabling. Oscilloscopes are often more expensive electronic devices that show the signal fluctuations on a monitor.

Several diagnostic software tools provide information on virtually any type of network hardware, as well. A considerable number of diagnostic software packages are available for a variety of prices.

A common software tool distributed with most network cards is a Send/Receive package. This software tool allows two computers with network cards and cables to connect to each other. This tool does not rely on a networked operating system, nor can it be used to send data. It simply sends packets from one computer to the other, establishing that the network cards and underlying transmission media are connected and configured properly.

## Diagnosing and Resolving Common Connectivity Problems with Cards, Cables, and Related Hardware

Most network problems occur on the transmission media or with the components that attach devices to the transmission media. All of these components operate at the Physical, DataLink, or Network levels of the OSI model. The components that connect PCs and enable them to communicate are susceptible to many kinds of problems.

### Troubleshooting Cables and Connectors

Most network problems occur at the OSI Physical layer, and cabling is one of the most common causes. A cable might have a short or a break, or it might be attached to a faulty connector. Tools such as DVMs and TDRs help search out cabling problems.

Cabling problems can cause three major problems: An individual computer cannot access the network, a group of computers cannot access the network, or none of the computers can access the network.

On networks that are configured in a star topology, an individual cable break between the computer and hub or MSAU causes a failure in communication between that individual computer and the rest of the network. This type of cable break does not cause problems between all of the other computers on the network.

A cable break in cables connecting multiple hubs causes a break in communications between the computers on one side of the cable break and the computers on the other side of the cable break. In most cases, the communications between computers within the broken segment can continue.

In the case of MSAU, the breakage of a cable connecting MSAUs often causes all computers on the ring to fail because the ring is not complete. A break in the cable on a bus topology also causes all computers on the network segment to be unable to communicate with any other computers on the network.

Try the following checks when troubleshooting network cabling problems:

- With 10BASE-T, make sure the cable used has the correct number of twists to meet the data-grade specifications.
- Look for electrical interference, which can be caused by tying the network cable together with monitor and power cords. Fluorescent lights, electric motors, and other electrical devices can cause interference if they are located too close to cables. These problems often can be alleviated by placing the cable away from devices that generate electromagnetic interference or by upgrading the cable to one that has better shielding.
- Make sure that connectors are pinned properly and crimped tightly.
- If excess shielding on coaxial cable is exposed, make sure it doesn't ground out the connector.
- Ensure that coaxial cables are not coiled tightly together. This can generate a magnetic field around the cable, causing electromagnetic interference.

- On coaxial Ethernet LANs, look for missing terminators or terminators with improper resistance ratings.
- Watch out for malfunctioning transceivers, concentrators, or T-connectors. All of these components can be checked by replacing the suspect devices.
- Test the continuity of the cable by using the various physical testing devices discussed in the previous section or by using a software-based cable testing utility.
- Make sure that all the component cables in a segment are connected. A user who moves his client and removes the T-connector incorrectly can cause a broken segment.
- Examine cable connectors for bent or broken pins.
- On token-ring networks, inspect the attachment of patch cables and adapter cables. Remember, patch cables connect MSAUs, and adapter cables connect the network adapter to the MSAU.

One advantage of a token-ring network is its built-in capability to monitor itself. token-ring networks provide electronic troubleshooting and, when possible, actually make repairs. When the token-ring network can't make its own repairs, a process called *beaconing* narrows down the portion of the ring in which the problem is most likely to exist.

## Troubleshooting Network Adapter Cards

Network problems often result from malfunctioning network adapter cards. The process of troubleshooting the network adapter works like any other kind of troubleshooting process: Start with the simple. The following list details some aspects you can check if you think your network adapter card might be malfunctioning:

- Make sure the cable is properly connected to the card.
- Confirm that you have the correct network adapter card driver and that the driver is installed properly. Be sure the card is properly bound to the appropriate transport protocol.
- Make sure the network adapter card and the network adapter card driver are compatible with your operating system. If you use Windows NT, consult the Windows NT hardware compatibility list. If you use Windows 95 or another operating system, rely on the adapter card vendor specifications.
- Test for resource conflicts. Make sure another device isn't attempting to use the same resources. If you think a resource conflict might be the problem, but you can't pinpoint the conflict using Windows NT Diagnostics, Windows 95's Device Manager, or some other diagnostic program, try removing all the cards except the network adapter and then replacing the cards one by one. Check the network with each addition to determine which device is causing the conflict.
- Run the network adapter card's diagnostic software. This will often indicate which resource on the network card is failing.
- Examine the jumper and DIP switch settings on the card. Make sure the resource settings are consistent with the settings configured through the operating system.
- Make sure the card is inserted properly in the slot. Reseat if necessary.
- If necessary, remove the card and clean the connector fingers (don't use an eraser because it leaves grit on the card).
- Replace the card with one that you know works. If the connection works with a different card, you know the card is the problem.

Token-ring network adapters with failure rates that exceed a preset tolerance level might actually remove themselves from the network. Try replacing the card. Some token-ring networks also can experience problems if a token-ring card set at a ring speed of 16 Mbps is inserted into a ring using a 4 Mbps ring speed, and vice versa.

## Troubleshooting Hubs and MSAUs

If you experience problems with a hub-based LAN, such as a 10BASE-T network, you often can isolate the problem by disconnecting the attached workstations one at a time. If removing one of the workstations eliminates the problem, the trouble may be caused by that workstation or its associated cable length. If removing each of the workstations doesn't solve the problem, the fault may lie with the hub. Check the easy components first, such as ports, switches, and connectors, and then use a different hub (if you have it) to see if the problem persists. If your hub doesn't work properly, call the manufacturer.

If you're troubleshooting a token-ring network, make sure the cables are connected properly to the MSAUs, with ring-out ports connecting to the ring-in ports throughout the ring. If you suspect the MSAU, isolate it by changing the ring-in and ring-out cables to bypass the MSAU. If the ring is now functional again, consider replacing the MSAU. In addition, you might find that if your network has MSAUs from more than one manufacturer, they are not wholly compatible. Impedance and other electrical characteristics can show slight differences between manufacturers, causing intermittent network problems. Some MSAUs (other than the 8228) are active and require a power supply. These MSAUs fail if they have a blown fuse or a bad power source. Your problem also might result from a misconfigured MSAU port. MSAU ports using the hermaphrodite connector need to be reinitialized with the setup tool. Removing drop cables and reinitializing each MSAU port is a quick fix that is useful on relatively small token-ring networks.

Isolating problems with patch cables, adapter cables, and MSAUs is easier to do if you have a current log of your network's physical design. After you narrow down the problem, you can isolate potential problem areas from the rest of the network and then use a cable tester to find the actual problem.

## Troubleshooting Modems

A modem presents all the potential problems you find with any other device. You must make sure that the modem is properly installed, that the driver is properly installed, and that the resource settings do not conflict with other devices. Modems also pose some unique problems because they must connect directly to the phone system, they operate using analog communications, and they must make a point-to-point connection with a remote machine.

The online help files for both Windows NT and Windows 95 include a topic called the Modem Troubleshooter. The Modem Troubleshooter leads you to possible solutions for a modem problem by asking questions about the symptoms. As you answer the questions (by clicking the gray box beside your answer), the Modem Troubleshooter zeroes in on more specific questions until (ideally) it leads you to a solution.

Some common modem problems are as follows:

- **Dialing problems**. The dialing feature is improperly configured. For instance, the modem isn't dialing 9 to bypass your office switchboard, or it is dialing 9 when you're away from your office. The computer also could be dialing an area code or an international code when it shouldn't. Check the dialing properties for the connection.
- **Connection problems**. You cannot connect to another modem. Your modem and the other modem might be operating at different speeds.

Verify that the maximum speed setting for your modem is the highest speed that both your modem and the other modem can use. Also make sure the Data Bits, Parity, and Stop Bits settings are consistent with the remote computer.

- **Digital phone systems.** You cannot plug a modem into a telephone line designed for use with digital phone systems. These digital phone systems are commonplace in most office environments.
- **Protocol problems.** The communicating devices are using incompatible line protocols. Verify that the devices are configured for the same or compatible protocols. If one computer initiates a connection using PPP, the other computer must be capable of using PPP.

## Repeaters, Bridges, and Routers

Issues dealing with repeaters, bridges, and routers are often more technically advanced than those covered in a book such as Networking Essentials. Companies such as Cisco, Bay Networks, and 3Com have their own dedicated books and courses on dealing with the installation, configuration, and troubleshooting of repeaters, bridges, and routers. In general, there are some basic troubleshooting steps you can do when working with these three devices.

Repeaters are responsible for regenerating a signal sent down the transmission media. The typical problem with repeaters is that they do not work—that is, the signal is not being regenerated. If this is the case, the signal being sent to devices on the other side of the repeater from the sending device will not receive the signal.

Problems with bridges are almost identical to that of a repeater. The signal being sent to devices on the other side of the bridge from the sending device will be received. Other issues with bridges are that the table of which devices are on which interface of the bridge can get corrupt. This can lead from one to all machines not receiving packets on the network. Diagnostic utilities provided by the bridge's manufacturer can resolve this type of problem.

Problems with routers can be complex, and troubleshooting them often involves a high level of understanding of the different protocols in use on the network, as well as the software and commands used to program a router. There are generally two types of router problems.

The first router problem that is commonly found is that packets are just not being passed through because the router is 'dead' or simply not functioning. The second common problem with routers is that the routing tables within the routers are corrupted or incorrectly programmed. This problem either leads to computers on different networks being unable to communicate with each other or to the fact that certain protocols simply do not work.

# Resolve Broadcast Storms

A *broadcast storm* is a sudden flood of broadcast messages that clogs the transmission medium, approaching 100 percent of the bandwidth. Broadcast storms cause performance to decline and, in the worst case, computers cannot even access the network. The cause of a broadcast storm is often a malfunctioning network adapter, but a broadcast storm also can be caused when a device on the network attempts to contact another device that either doesn't exist or for some reason doesn't respond to the broadcast.

If the broadcast messages are viable, a network-monitoring or protocol-analysis tool often can determine the source of the storm. If the broadcast storm is caused by a malfunctioning adapter throwing illegible packets onto the line, and a protocol analyzer can't find the source, try to isolate the offending PC by removing computers from the network one at a time until the line returns to normal.

## Identify and Resolve Network Performance Problems

If your network runs slower than it used to run (or slower than it ought to run), the problem might be that the present network traffic exceeds the level at which the network can operate efficiently. Some possible causes for increased traffic are new hardware (such as a new workstation) or new software (such as a network computer game or some other network application). A generator or another mechanical device operating near the network could cause a degradation of network performance. In addition, a malfunctioning network device could act as a bottleneck. Ask yourself what has changed since the last time the network operated efficiently, and begin there with your troubleshooting efforts.

A performance monitoring tool, such as Windows NT's Performance Monitor or Network Monitor, can help you look for bottlenecks that are adversely affecting your network. For instance, the increased traffic could be the result of increased usage. If usage exceeds the capacity of the network, you might want to consider expanding or redesigning your network. You also might want to divide the network into smaller segments by using a router or a bridge to reduce network traffic. A protocol analyzer can help you measure and monitor the traffic at various points on your network.

# Study and Exam Prep Tips

This chapter provides you with some general guidelines for preparing for the exam. It is organized into three sections. The first section addresses your pre-exam preparation activities, covering general study tips. This is followed by an extended look at the Microsoft Certification exams, including a number of specific tips that apply to the Microsoft exam formats. Finally, it addresses changes in Microsoft's testing policies and how they might affect you.

To better understand the nature of preparation for the test, it is important to understand learning as a process. You probably are aware of how you best learn new material. Maybe outlining works best for you, or maybe you are a visual learner who needs to "see" things. Whatever your learning style, test preparation takes time. While it is obvious that you can't start studying for these exams the night before you take them, it is very important to understand that learning is a developmental process. Understanding the process helps you focus on what you know and what you have yet to learn.

Thinking about how you learn should help you recognize that learning takes place when we are able to match new information to old. You have some previous experience with computers and networking, and now you are preparing for this certification exam. Using this book, software, and supplementary materials will not just add incrementally to what you know. As you study, you actually change the organization of your knowledge to integrate this new information into your existing knowledge base. This will lead you to a more comprehensive understanding of the tasks and concepts outlined in the objectives and related to computing in general. Again, this happens as an iterative process rather than a singular event. Keep this model of learning in mind as you prepare for the exam, and you will make better decisions on what to study and how much to study.

## Study Tips

There are many ways to approach studying, just as there are many different types of material to study. However, the tips that follow should work well for the type of material covered on the certification exams.

### Study Strategies

Although individuals vary in the ways they learn information, some basic principles of learning apply to everyone. You should adopt some study strategies that take advantage of these principles. One of these principles is that learning can be broken into various depths. *Recognition* (of terms, for example) exemplifies a surface level of learning: You rely on a prompt of some sort to elicit recall. *Comprehension or understanding* (of the concepts behind the terms, for instance) represents a deeper level of learning. The ability to analyze a concept and apply your understanding of it in a new way or to address a unique setting represents further depth of learning.

Your learning strategy should enable you to know the material a level or two deeper than mere recognition. This will help you to do well on the exam(s). You will know the material so thoroughly that you can easily handle the recognition-level types of questions used in multiple-choice testing. You will also be able to apply your knowledge to solve novel problems.

## Macro and Micro Study Strategies

One strategy that can lead to this deeper learning includes preparing an outline that covers all the objectives and subobjectives for the particular exam you are working on. You should then delve a bit further into the material and include a level or two of detail beyond the stated objectives and subobjectives for the exam. Finally, flesh out the outline by coming up with a statement of definition or a summary for each point in the outline.

This outline provides two approaches to studying. First, you can study the outline by focusing on the organization of the material. Work your way through the points and subpoints of your outline with the goal of learning how they relate to one another. For example, be sure you understand how each of the main objective areas is similar to and different from one another. Then do the same thing with the subobjectives. Also, be sure you know which subobjectives pertain to each objective area and how they relate to one another.

Next, you can work through the outline and focus on learning the details. Memorize and understand terms and their definitions, facts, rules and strategies, advantages and disadvantages, and so on. In this pass through the outline, attempt to learn detail as opposed to the big picture (the organizational information that you worked on in the first pass through the outline).

Research shows that attempting to assimilate both types of information at the same time seems to interfere with the overall learning process. Separate your studying into these two approaches, and you will perform better on the exam than if you attempt to study the material in a more conventional manner.

## Active Study Strategies

In addition, the process of writing down and defining the objectives, subobjectives, terms, facts, and definitions promotes a more active learning strategy than merely reading the material does. In human information processing terms, writing forces you to engage in more active encoding of the information. Simply reading over it constitutes passive processing.

Next, determine whether you can apply the information you have learned by attempting to create examples and scenarios of your own. Think about how or where you could apply the concepts you are learning. Again, write down this information to process the facts and concepts in a more active fashion.

The hands-on nature of the Step by Step tutorials and the exercises at the end of the chapters provide further active learning opportunities that will reinforce concepts.

## Common Sense Strategies

Finally, you should also follow common sense practices in studying: Study when you are alert, reduce or eliminate distractions, take breaks when you become fatigued, and so on.

# Pre-Testing Yourself

Pre-testing allows you to assess how well you are learning. One of the most important aspects of learning is what has been called "meta-learning." Meta-learning has to do with realizing when you know something well or when you need to study some more. In other words, you recognize how well or how poorly you have learned the material you are studying. For most people, this can be difficult to assess objectively on their own. Therefore, practice tests are useful because they reveal more objectively what you have and have not learned. You should use this information to guide review and further studying. Developmental learning takes place as you cycle through studying, assessing how well you have learned, reviewing, and assessing again, until you feel you are ready to take the exam.

You may have noticed the practice exam included in this book. Use it as part of this process. In addition to the Practice Exam, the Top Score software on the CD-ROM also provides a variety of ways to test yourself before you take the actual exam. By using the Top Score Practice Exams, you can take an entire practice test. By using the Top Score Study Cards, you can take an entire practice exam or you can focus on a particular objective area, such as Planning, Troubleshooting, or Monitoring and Optimization. By using the Top Score Flash Cards, you can test your knowledge at a level beyond that of recognition; you must come up with the answers in your own words. The Flash Cards also enable you to test your knowledge of particular objective areas.

You should set a goal for your pre-testing. A reasonable goal would be to score consistently in the 90-percent range (or better). See Appendix D, "Using the Top Score Software," for more detailed explanation of the test engine.

# EXAM PREP TIPS

Having mastered the subject matter, the final preparatory step is to understand how the exam will be presented. Make no mistake about it, a Microsoft Certified Professional (MCP) exam will challenge both your knowledge and your test-taking skills! This section starts with the basics of exam design, reviews a new type of exam format, and concludes with hints that are targeted to each of the exam formats.

## The MCP Exam

Every MCP exam is released in one of two basic formats. What's being called *exam format* here is really little more than a combination of the overall exam structure and the presentation method for exam questions.

Each exam format utilizes the same types of questions. These types or styles of questions include multiple-rating (or scenario-based) questions, traditional multiple-choice questions, and simulation-based questions. It's important to understand the types of questions you will be asked and the actions required to properly answer them.

Understanding the exam formats is essential to good preparation because the format determines the number of questions presented, the difficulty of those questions, and the amount of time allowed to complete the exam.

## Exam Format

There are two basic formats for the MCP exams: the traditional fixed-form exam and the adaptive form. As its name implies, the fixed-form exam presents a fixed set of questions during the exam session. The adaptive format, however, uses only a subset of questions drawn from a larger pool during any given exam session.

### Fixed-Form

A fixed-form, computerized exam is based on a fixed set of exam questions. The individual questions are presented in random order during a test session. If you take the same exam more than once, you won't necessarily see the exact same questions. This is because two or three final forms are typically assembled for every fixed-form exam Microsoft releases. These are usually labeled Forms A, B, and C.

The final forms of a fixed-form exam are identical in terms of content coverage, number of questions, and allotted time, but the questions themselves are different. You may have noticed, however, that some of the same questions appear on, or rather are shared across, different final forms. When questions are shared across multiple final forms of an exam, the percentage of sharing is generally small. Many final forms share no questions, but some older exams may have ten to fifteen percent duplication of exam questions on the final exam forms.

Fixed-form exams also have a fixed time limit in which you must complete the exam. The Top Score software on the CD-ROM that accompanies this book provides fixed-form exams.

Finally, the score you achieve on a fixed-form exam (which is always reported for MCP exams on a scale of 0 to 1,000) is based on the number of questions you answer correctly. The exam passing score is the same for all final forms of a given fixed-form exam.

The typical format for the fixed-form exam is this:

- 50–60 questions
- 75–90 minute testing time
- Question review is allowed, including the opportunity to change your answers

## Adaptive Form

An adaptive form exam has the same appearance as a fixed-form exam, but it differs in both how questions are selected for presentation and how many questions actually are presented. Although the statistics of adaptive testing are fairly complex, the process is concerned with determining your level of skill or ability with the exam subject matter. This ability assessment begins with the presentation of questions of varying levels of difficulty and ascertains at what difficulty level you can reliably answer them. Finally, the ability assessment determines if that ability level is above or below the level required to pass that exam.

Examinees at different levels of ability will then see quite different sets of questions. Examinees who demonstrate little expertise with the subject matter will continue to be presented with relatively easy questions. Examinees who demonstrate a high level of expertise will be presented progressively more-difficult questions. Both individuals may answer the same number of questions correctly, but because the higher-expertise examinee can correctly answer more-difficult questions, he or she will receive a higher score and is more likely to pass the exam.

The typical design for the adaptive form exam is this:

- 20–25 questions
- 90 minute testing time (although this is likely to be reduced to 45–60 minutes in the near future)
- Question review is not allowed, providing no opportunity to change your answers

### The Adaptive Exam Process

Your first adaptive exam will be unlike any other testing experience you have had. In fact, many examinees have difficulty accepting the adaptive testing process because they feel they were not provided the opportunity to adequately demonstrate their full expertise.

You can take consolation in the fact that adaptive exams are painstakingly put together after months of data gathering and analysis and are just as valid as a fixed-form exam. The rigor introduced through the adaptive testing methodology means that there is nothing arbitrary about what you'll see! It is also a more efficient means of testing that requires less time to conduct and complete.

As you can see from Figure 1, a number of statistical measures drive the adaptive examination process. The one that's most immediately relevant to you is the ability estimate. Accompanying this test statistic are the standard error of measurement, the item characteristic curve, and the test information curve.

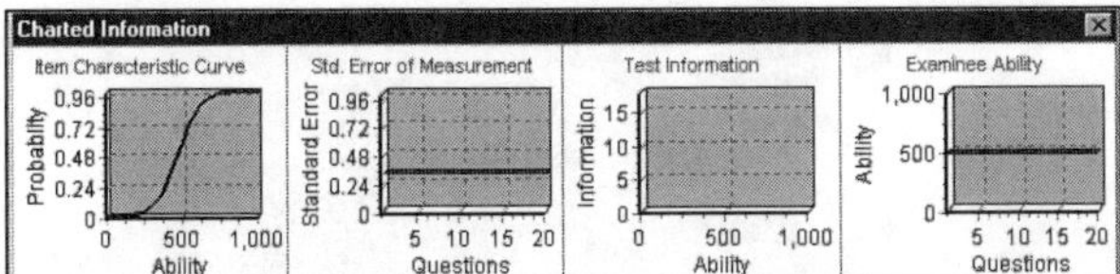


**FIGURE 1**
Microsoft's adaptive testing demonstration program.

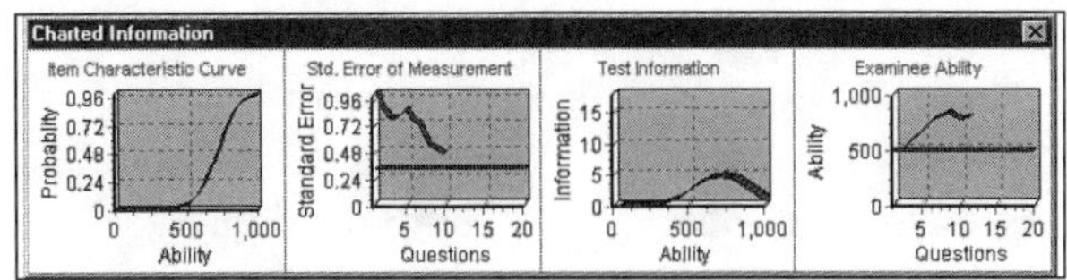


**FIGURE 2**
The changing statistics in an adaptive exam.

The standard error, which is the key factor in determining when an adaptive exam will terminate, reflects the degree of error in the exam ability estimate. The item characteristic curve reflects the probability of a correct response relative to examinee ability. Finally, the test information statistic provides a measure of the information contained in the set of questions the examinee has answered, again relative to the ability level of the individual examinee.

When you begin an adaptive exam, the standard error has already been assigned a target value below which it must drop for the exam to conclude. This target value reflects a particular level of statistical confidence in the process. The examinee ability is initially set to the mean possible exam score, which is 500 for MCP exams.

As the adaptive exam progresses, questions of varying difficulty are presented. Based on your pattern of responses to those questions, the ability estimate is recalculated. Simultaneously, the standard error estimate is refined from its first estimated value of one toward the target value. When the standard error reaches its target value, the exam terminates. Thus, the more consistently you answer questions of the same degree of difficulty, the more quickly the standard error estimate drops and the fewer questions you will end up seeing during the exam session. This situation is depicted in Figure 2.

As you might suspect, one good piece of advice for taking an adaptive exam is to treat every exam question as if it is the most important. The adaptive scoring algorithm is attempting to discover a pattern of responses that reflects some level of proficiency with the subject matter. Incorrect responses almost guarantee that additional questions must be answered (unless, of course, you get every question wrong). This is because the scoring algorithm must adjust to information that is not consistent with the emerging pattern.

## New Question Types

A variety of question types can appear on MCP exams. Examples of multiple-choice questions and scenario-based questions appear throughout this book and the Top Score software. Simulation-based questions are new to the MCP exam series.

### Simulation Questions

Simulation-based questions reproduce the look and feel of key Microsoft product features for the purpose of testing. The simulation software used in MCP exams has been designed to look and act, as much as possible, just like the actual product. Consequently, answering simulation questions in an MCP exam entails completing one or more tasks just as if you were using the product itself.

The format of a typical Microsoft simulation question is straightforward. It presents a brief scenario or problem statement along with one or more tasks that must be completed to solve the problem. The next section provides an example of a simulation question for MCP exams.

## A Typical Simulation Question

It sounds obvious, but the first step when you encounter a simulation is to carefully read the question (see Figure 3). Do not go straight to the simulation application! Assess the problem being presented and identify the conditions that make up the problem scenario. Note the tasks that must be performed or outcomes that must be achieved to answer the question, and then review any instructions on how to proceed.

The next step is to launch the simulator by using the button provided. After clicking the Show Simulation button, you will see a feature of the product, like the dialog box shown in Figure 4. The simulation application will partially cover the question text on many test center machines. Feel free to reposition the simulation or to move between the question text screen and the simulation using hot-keys and point-and-click navigation or even by clicking the simulation launch button again.

It is important to understand that your answer to the simulation question is not recorded until you move on to the next exam question. This gives you the added capability to close and reopen the simulation application (using the launch button) on the same question without losing any partial answer you may have made.

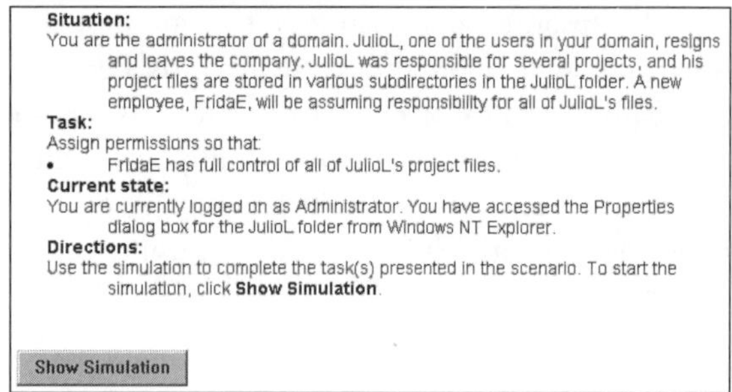

**Situation:**
You are the administrator of a domain. JulioL, one of the users in your domain, resigns and leaves the company. JulioL was responsible for several projects, and his project files are stored in various subdirectories in the JulioL folder. A new employee, FridaE, will be assuming responsibility for all of JulioL's files.
**Task:**
Assign permissions so that:
- FridaE has full control of all of JulioL's project files.

**Current state:**
You are currently logged on as Administrator. You have accessed the Properties dialog box for the JulioL folder from Windows NT Explorer.
**Directions:**
Use the simulation to complete the task(s) presented in the scenario. To start the simulation, click **Show Simulation**.

Show Simulation

**FIGURE 3**
Typical MCP exam simulation question with directions.

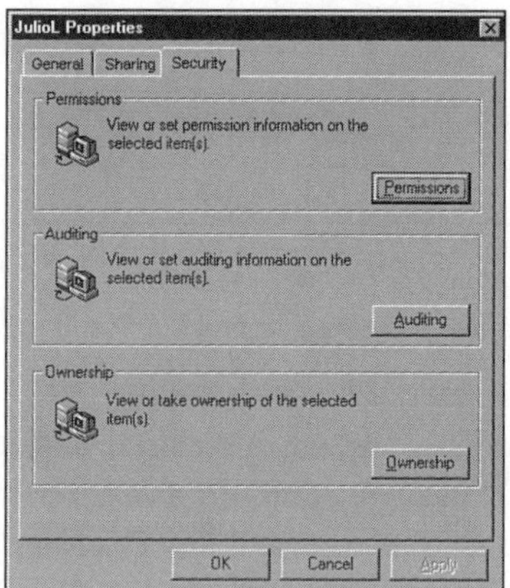


**FIGURE 4**
Launching the simulation application.

The third step is to use the simulator as you would the actual product to solve the problem or perform the defined tasks. Again, the simulation software is designed to function, within reason, just as the product does. But don't expect the simulation to reproduce product behavior perfectly. Most importantly, do not allow yourself to become flustered if the simulation does not look or act exactly like the product. Figure 5 shows the solution to the sample simulation problem.

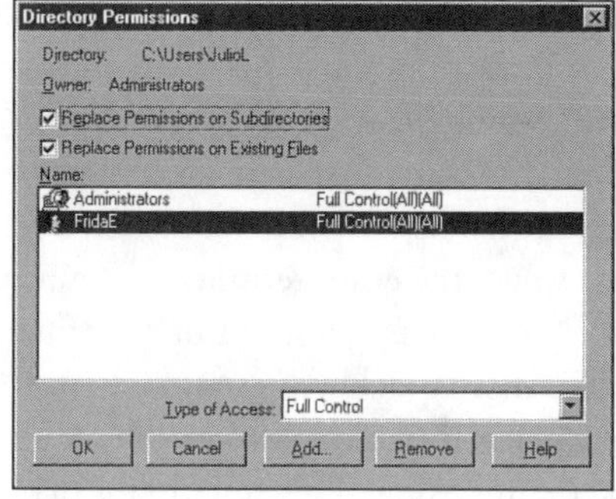


**FIGURE 5**
The solution to the simulation example.

There are two final points that will help you tackle simulation questions. First, respond only to what is being asked in the question. Do not solve problems that you are not asked to solve. Second, accept what is being asked of you. You may not entirely agree with conditions in the problem statement, the quality of the desired solution, or sufficiency of defined tasks to adequately solve the problem. Always remember that you are being tested on your ability to solve the problem as it has been presented.

The solution to the simulation problem shown in Figure 5 perfectly illustrates both of these points. As you'll recall from the question scenario (refer to Figure 3), you were asked to assign appropriate permissions to a new user called FridaE. You were not instructed to make any other changes in permissions. Thus, if you had modified or removed Administrator permissions, this item would have been scored wrong on an MCP exam.

## Putting It All Together

Given all these different pieces of information, the task is now to assemble a set of tips that will help you successfully tackle the different types of MCP exams.

### More Pre-Exam Preparation Tips

Generic exam preparation advice is always useful. Follow these general guidelines:

- Become familiar with the product. Hands-on experience is one of the keys to success on any MCP exam. Review the exercises and the Step by Step tutorials in the book.
- Review the current exam preparation guide on the Microsoft MCP Web site. The documentation Microsoft makes publicly available over the Web identifies the skills every exam is intended to test.
- Memorize foundational technical detail as appropriate. But remember, MCP exams are generally heavy on problem solving and application of knowledge more than they are on questions that require only rote memorization.
- Take any of the available practice tests. We recommend the one included in this book and those you can create using the Top Score software on the CD-ROM. While these are fixed-format exams, they provide preparation that is also valuable for taking an adaptive exam. Because of the nature of adaptive testing, it is not possible for these practice exams to be offered in the adaptive format. However, fixed-format exams provide the same types of questions as adaptive exams and are the most effective way to prepare for either type of exam. As a supplement to the material included with this book, try the free practice tests available on the Microsoft MCP Web site.
- Look on the Microsoft MCP Web site for samples and demonstration items. These tend to be particularly valuable for one significant reason: They allow you to become familiar with any new testing technologies before you encounter them on an MCP exam.

### During the Exam Session

Similarly, the generic exam-taking advice you've heard for years applies when taking an MCP exam:

- Take a deep breath and try to relax when you first sit down for your exam. It is very important to control the pressure you may (naturally) feel when taking exams.
- You will be provided scratch paper. Take a moment to write down any factual information and technical detail that you committed to short-term memory.

- Carefully read all information and instruction screens. These displays have been put together to give you information relevant to the exam you are taking.
- Accept the Non-Disclosure Agreement and preliminary survey as part of the examination process. Complete them accurately and quickly move on.
- Read the exam questions carefully. Reread each question to identify all relevant detail.
- Tackle the questions in the order they are presented. Skipping around won't build your confidence; the clock is always counting down.
- Don't rush, but at the same time, don't linger on difficult questions. The questions vary in degree of difficulty. Don't let yourself be flustered by a particularly difficult or verbose question.

## Fixed-Form Exams

Building from this basic preparation and test-taking advice, you also need to consider the challenges presented by the different exam designs. Because a fixed-form exam is composed of a fixed, finite set of questions, add these tips to your strategy for taking a fixed-form exam:

- Note the time allotted and the number of questions appearing on the exam you are taking. Make a rough calculation of how many minutes you can spend on each question, and use that number to pace yourself through the exam.
- Take advantage of the fact that you can return to and review skipped or previously answered questions. Mark the questions you can't answer confidently, noting the relative difficulty of each question on the scratch paper provided. When you reach the end of the exam, return to the more difficult questions.
- If there is session time remaining when you have completed all questions (and you aren't too fatigued!), review your answers. Pay particular attention to questions that seem to have a lot of detail or that required graphics.
- As for changing your answers, the rule of thumb here is *don't*! If you read the question carefully and completely and you felt like you knew the right answer, you probably did. Don't second-guess yourself. If, as you check your answers, one stands out as clearly incorrect, however, of course you should change it. But if you are at all unsure, go with your first impression.

## Adaptive Exams

If you are planning to take an adaptive exam, keep these additional tips in mind:

- Read and answer every question with great care. When reading a question, identify every relevant detail, requirement, or task that must be performed and double-check your answer to be sure you have addressed every one of them.
- If you cannot answer a question, use the process of elimination to reduce the set of potential answers, and then take your best guess. Stupid mistakes invariably mean additional questions will be presented.
- Forget about reviewing questions and changing your answers. Once you leave a question, whether you've answered it or not, you cannot return to it. Do not skip any questions either. If you do, that question is counted as incorrect!

## Simulation Questions

You may encounter simulation questions on either the fixed-form or adaptive form exam. If you do, keep these tips in mind:

- Avoid changing any simulation settings that don't pertain directly to the problem solution. Solve the problem you are being asked to solve and nothing more.
- Assume default settings when related information has not been provided. If something has not been mentioned or defined, it is a non-critical detail that does not factor in to the correct solution.
- Be sure your entries are syntactically correct, paying particular attention to your spelling. Enter relevant information just as the product would require it.
- Close all simulation application windows after you complete the simulation tasks. The testing system software is designed to trap errors that could result when using the simulation application, but trust yourself over the testing software.
- If simulations are part of a fixed-form exam, you can return to skipped or previously answered questions and change your answer. However, if you choose to change your answer to a simulation question, or if you even attempt to review the settings you've made in the simulation application, your previous response to that simulation question will be deleted. If simulations are part of an adaptive exam, you cannot return to previous questions.

## Final Considerations

Finally, a number of changes in the MCP program will impact how frequently you can repeat an exam and what you will see when you do.

- Microsoft has instituted a new exam retake policy. This new rule is "two and two, then one and two." That is, you can attempt any exam twice with no restrictions on the time between attempts. But after the second attempt, you must wait two weeks before you can attempt that exam again. After that, you will be required to wait two weeks between subsequent attempts. Plan to pass the exam in two attempts; if that's not possible, increase your time horizon for receiving an MCP credential.
- New questions are being seeded into the MCP exams. After performance data has been gathered on new questions, they will replace older questions on all exam forms. This means that the questions appearing on exams will change regularly.
- Many of the current MCP exams will be republished in adaptive format in the coming months. Prepare yourself for this significant change in testing format, as it is entirely likely that this will become the new preferred MCP exam format.

These changes mean that the brute-force strategies for passing MCP exams may soon completely lose their viability. So if you don't pass an exam on the first or second attempt, it is entirely possible that the exam will change significantly in form. It could be updated from fixed-form to adaptive form, or it might have a different set of questions or question types.

The intention of Microsoft is clearly not to make the exams more difficult by introducing unwanted change. Their intent is to create and maintain valid measures of the technical skills and knowledge associated with the different MCP credentials. Preparing for an MCP exam has always involved not only studying the subject matter, but also planning for the testing experience itself. With these changes, this is now more true than ever.

# Practice Exam

This appendix consists of 51 questions representative of what you should expect on the actual exam. There are figures (exhibits) and multiple-choice questions. The answers are at the end of the appendix. It is strongly suggested that when you take this practice exam, you treat it just as you would the actual exam at the test center. Time yourself, read carefully, and answer all the questions to the best of your ability.

Some of the questions are vague and require deduction on your part to come up with the best answer from the possibilities given. Many of them are verbose, requiring you to read a lot before you come to an actual question. These are skills you should acquire before attempting the actual exam. Run through the test, and if you score less than 750 (missing more than 13), try re-reading the chapters containing information where you were weak (use the index to find keywords to point you to the appropriate locations).

## EXAM QUESTIONS

1. You are setting up an NT-based network for a local community college. There are 75 new computers with identical hardware configurations, and all will use Windows NT Workstation 4.0. The IT manager wants you to automate the installation of NT. What's the best way of doing this?

   A. Create a SETUP.INF file that has all the common settings. Copy the I386 directory from the CD to the local hard drive, replace the existing SETUP.INF file, and run SETUP.EXE as usual.

   B. Create an unattended installation file that can be used by all of the new computers.

   C. Run Setup once on one computer, and then do a file copy of the Windows NT installation path to the empty hard drives of all the other computers.

   D. Create an unattended installation with entries for each setting common to all the computers, and create a uniqueness database file (UDF) for the settings that are specific to individual computers (such as IP addresses and computer names).

2. Joan is having problems with users making modifications to the Registry that require her to then rebuild the entire NT Workstation installation. What tool allows her to secure access to individual Registry entries through the use of permissions?

   A. NTFS

   B. REGEDIT.EXE

   C. REGEDT32.EXE

   D. POLEDIT.EXE

3. You are planning the configuration of machines that will be used by internal developers in your company. Because both Windows NT and Windows 95 are used on your network, you have been requested to build machines that dual-boot between Windows 95 and Windows NT Workstation. Which file system should you choose?

   A. FAT

   B. NTFS

   C. HPFS

   D. FAT32

4. A CAD user complains about slow performance when using his CAD application. You are asked to determine whether the performance problems are CPU-related or are the result of low memory. Which of the following tools allow you to monitor both CPU usage and memory usage?

   A. Server Manager

   B. Performance Monitor

   C. Network Monitor

   D. Task Manager

5. Caitlin is preparing a computer for a new hire. She wants to rebuild it completely, so she decides to remove the existing installation of NT Workstation. Besides the installation directory, which of the following root level files need to be removed from the C: drive to ensure a clean removal?

   A. BOOT.INI

   B. NTLDR

   C. NTDETECT.COM

   D. AUTOEXEC.BAT

6. You are asked to configure the NT Workstation for the manager of Operations. Per the IT manager, the manager of Operations is to be granted administrator rights on his machine but not on the domain. How can you do this?

   A. Add him to the Domain Admin group on his machine only.

   B. Add him to the local Administrators group on the domain controller.

   C. Add him to the local Administrators group on his machine only.

   D. None of the above.

7. Which of the following software components are required to allow an NT Workstation to access a NetWare 3.12 file server?

   A. TCP/IP

   B. GSNW

   C. CSNW

   D. NWLink

8. The Marketing department in your company is going to be setting up an intranet server to share interdepartmental information. Your company has a live connection to the Internet with no firewall. How can you ensure that the documents shared on the Marketing department's Peer Web Services server are limited to company use only? Choose only one answer.

   A. Upgrade to NT Server and use Internet Information Server 3.0.

   B. Use NTFS permissions on the directories and HTML files.

   C. By default, deny access to all IP addresses and grant access to only the range of addresses allocated to your company.

   D. Both B and C.

9. You are troubleshooting a bottleneck on a Windows NT computer, and you notice that the Processor Queue Length counter in Performance Monitor is consistently between 4 and 6. What can you do to help this situation?

   A. Add more RAM.

   B. Use a RAID array.

   C. Add additional processors.

   D. Upgrade to a faster processor.

10. You are called in to fix a print problem on a small NT workgroup. In the print queue of the print server, you notice a document that will not print and cannot be deleted. What course of action should you take?

    A. Reinstall the print drivers.

    B. Pause printing, wait about five minutes, and then resume printing.

    C. Use the Emergency Repair Disk to reinstall the Print Processor.

    D. Stop and restart the Spooler from the Control Panel's Services application.

11. Users are complaining that a certain 16-bit application is constantly failing and causing other applications to hang. What can you do to avoid this? Choose only one answer.

    A. Change the shortcuts used to start the application so they use the following command line:

    ```
    Start <application name> /separate
    ```

    B. Change the shortcuts used to start the application so they use the following command line:

    ```
    Start <application name> /high
    ```

    C. Direct users to start the application via the Run command in the Start menu. Tell them to be sure that the Run in Separate Memory Space option is checked.

    D. Both A and C.

    E. None of the above.

12. Which default group will allow a user to share directories on an NT workstation but not to administer the computer?

    A. Local Administrators group

    B. Server Operators

    C. Backup Operators

    D. Power Users

    E. All of the above

13. You are currently using Windows NT Workstation 3.51, but you want to upgrade to version 4.0. What utility allows you to upgrade and, at the same time, continue work on your workstation while the setup files are being copied?

    A. UPGRADE32.EXE

    B. WINNT.EXE

    C. WINNT32.EXE

    D. SETUP.EXE

    E. UPGRADE.BAT

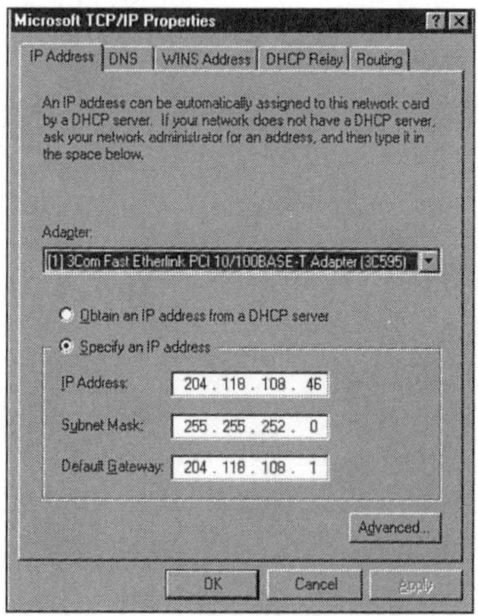


**FIGURE 1**
To answer question 14, refer to this figure.

14. Your company is using TCP/IP for its network protocol (see Figure 1). You do not have a connection to the Internet, and internally, all machines will be residing on a single subnet. Which settings must be configured in the TCP/IP settings to enable communication between computers on the network?

    A. IP address

    B. Subnet mask

    C. Default gateway

    D. All of the above

    E. None of the above

15. Harry is participating in a workgroup. He uses NTFS for his local file system. He wants to share a directory and allow Full Control access to a user whose username is Michele. Which of the following are valid solutions?

    A. Provide Full Control to the Everyone group at the share level and provide Full Control only to Michele at the directory and file level.

    B. Provide Full Control to only Michele at the share level and leave the default NTFS permissions at the file and directory level.

    C. Provide Full Control to Michele at the share level and apply the No Access permission to the Everyone group at the file and directory level.

    D. None of the above.

16. Your network has an NT Server running DHCP services. How can you configure an NT Workstation to be automatically assigned an IP address?

    A. Use the IP Address of the DHCP Server when configuring TCP/IP on the workstation.

    B. From the TCP/IP tab of the Control Panel's Network application, select the Obtain an IP Address from a DHCP Server option, but do nothing else.

    C. Enter the address of the DHCP Server in the Primary WINS Server Address field on the WINS tab in the TCP/IP settings.

    D. None of the above.

17. George is setting up a network for a local hospital. After adding network cards to each machine, he starts NT to try the network. Which of the following items must be known to successfully configure a network card?

    A. The driver name.

    B. IRQ.

    C. I/O address.

    D. None of the above. Plug and Play features will handle all necessary configuration automatically.

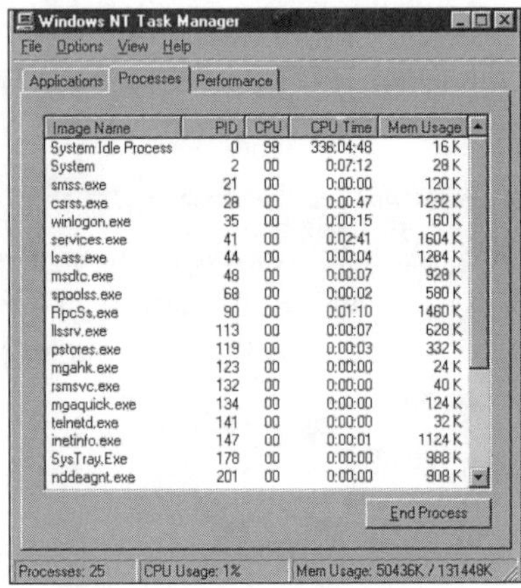


**FIGURE 2**
To answer question 18, refer to this figure.

18. From which tab in Figure 2 can you set thread priority?

    A. Applications.

    B. Processes.

    C. Performance.

    D. None. Thread priority can be set only from the command line.

19. You notice that an application is maxing the CPU out at 100%. You cannot quit out of the application because it is too busy to respond to your request to quit. How can you force the application to quit from the Task Manager?

    A. From the Processes tab, select the process that corresponds to the application and click on the End Process button.

    B. From the Applications tab, select the application and click on the End Task button.

    C. From the Processes tab, select the process that corresponds to the application and set it to a low priority. Then switch to the application and quit by using the appropriate command on the File menu.

    D. All of the above.

20. Chuck is using NT Workstation and is trying to share a file called SUMMARY.TXT to Diane. After successfully mapping a drive letter to the share, Diane attempts to open the file but receives an access denied message. Realizing there is a problem with local NTFS permissions, Chuck adds Diane to the Sales group, which has access to the file. However, Diane still continues to receive the access denied message. What's wrong and how can it be fixed?

    A. Most likely, Diane is being denied access at the share level. To fix it, Chuck needs to give her share access.

    B. Most likely, Diane's password on her local machine is different from the one Chuck assigned to her on his machine. To solve the problem, the passwords must be manually synchronized.

    C. Because Chuck does not have local Administrator privileges, by default, shares that he creates deny access to everyone but himself.

    D. Diane probably has an outdated access token that was created before she was added to the Sales group. To fix the problem, she needs to log off her NT Workstation and log back on.

21. You recently installed 8GB drives for your users. Now you need to allow users to access a single partition and a single drive letter for their files. Security is not an issue. Which file system is most suitable?

    A. FAT

    B. HPFS

    C. NTFS

    D. FAT32

22. You are setting up a scanner for one of your clients. Where would you install the driver for the SCSI controller?

    A. Windows NT Setup

    B. SCSI Adapters application in Control Panel

    C. Devices application in Control Panel

    D. Add/Remove Hardware application in Control Panel

    E. Multimedia application in Control Panel

23. You are installing NT Workstation on an all-Windows NT network. All machines are using version 4.0 and have Pentium II processors. What's the easiest way to install print drivers that will allow your users to print to existing print servers?

    A. Install the driver locally from the CD-ROM as you install Windows NT.

    B. Browse to the printer from Network Neighborhood, right-click on the printer, and select Install.

    C. Use the default Network Printer Installation setup program shared from the print server.

    D. None of the above.

24. Rubin is setting up a Workstation that will be running very memory-intensive applications. He has two physical disks and currently has a default installation of NT. Besides adding memory, what can he do to optimize the performance of his memory-intensive applications?

    A. Use RAID 0, and then install the system files on the stripe set.

    B. Create a single volume set to create one large logical disk.

    C. Put the pagefile on a different physical disk from the system files.

    D. Divide the pagefile between two separate physical disks.

    E. Set the initial size of the pagefile to 2MB for efficiency.

25. Which Registry utility allows you to search for text in Keys, Values, and Data in the Registry? Select all that apply.

    A. REGEDIT.EXE

    B. REGEDT32.EXE

    C. POLEDIT.EXE

    D. CONTROL.EXE

26. You are reconfiguring a system for a new employee who is taking over for a previous employee in the graphics department. You realize that the mouse buttons were configured for a left-handed person. Where can you go to reconfigure the mouse for a right-handed person?

    A. Windows NT Setup

    B. User profiles

    C. Policy Editor

    D. Mouse application in Control Panel

27. Jamie just received a newly purchased tape drive, which is a standard model from a prominent manufacturer. Upon opening the box, he notices there is no driver installation disk. What should he do?

    A. Call Technical Support.

    B. Return the drive for another one.

    C. Plug it in and let Plug and Play handle the rest.

    D. Use the Tape Devices application in Control Panel and attempt to install the driver from the NT Installation CD-ROM.

28. Sophia receives a call from a user complaining that he has modified many of his desktop settings while exploring, and now he can't figure out how to return the desktop to the default settings. What's the best and fastest way to return the desktop to its original settings?

    A. Delete the user account and add a new one with the same username.

    B. Go to the User Profiles tab of the Control Panel's System application, select the user's profile, and click the Delete button.

C. Go to the User Profiles tab of the Control Panel's System application, select the user's profile, and click the Reset button.

D. Reinstall Windows NT.

29. You are setting up a logon script for standard users on your network. Which of the following commands will allow you to map a drive to a server by the name of Vector on the network?

A. `net use \\vector\v`

B. `net use V: \\vector\v`

C. `net use * \\vector\v`

D. `map vector.v * /N`

30. How can you create a user profile?

A. Use the Profile Editor.

B. Log on with an account and configure the desktop as you want it in the profile. Then log off and use that account's profile as a template to copy from.

C. Use the Policy Editor.

D. Create an account to use as a template. Log on and configure the desktop as desired. Open REGEDT32.EXE and save the Registry settings in HKEY_CURRENT_USER. Load this file into the Registry of any users that you want to have this profile.

E. None of the above.

31. Which of the following is a valid access permission (listed in the Type of Access drop-down list shown in Figure 3) for a file on an NTFS partition?

A. Read

B. Write

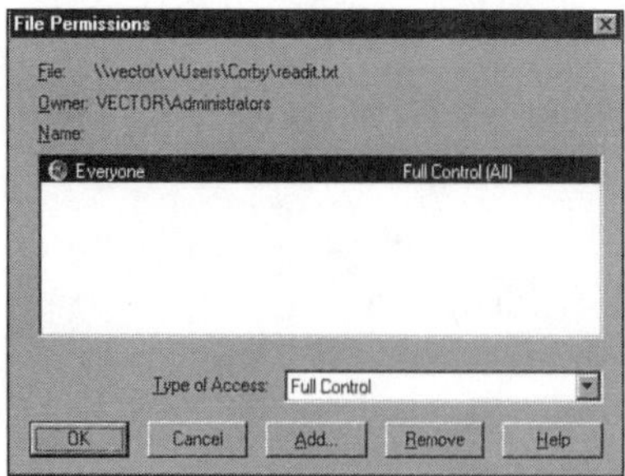


**FIGURE 3**
Questions 31 and 32 refer to this figure.

C. Copy

D. List

32. Figure 3 shows the access permissions for a file on your local system. Why would an "Account Unknown" item appear in the Name list box?

A. This is probably a reference to an account that was previously deleted from the User Manager.

B. The name of the account is unavailable because you do not have Change Permissions permission.

C. It is a non-NT account.

D. The actual name of the account is "Account Unknown."

E. None of the above.

33. Greg is a member of the Sales group. The Operations manager wants to allow Greg to access an Excel file used internally, but he does not want other members of the Sales group to see the file. How can this be achieved with NTFS permissions?

A. Give Greg Read access and give the Sales group Deny access.

B. Give Greg and the Sales group Read access.

C. Give Greg Read access but do not assign any permissions to the Sales group.

D. Give the Sales group Read access.

34. Ron, the owner of a company, wants to ensure that absolutely no one gets access to any local files on his system. He is using NTFS on one single drive (C:). How can this be done using NTFS permissions?

 A. From the root directory, remove all accounts from the permissions list. Add Ron's account and give him Full Control permission. Click OK.

 B. From the root directory, remove all accounts except the Everyone group. Add Ron's account and give him Full Control permission. Change the Everyone group to Deny access. Click OK.

 C. From the root directory, remove all accounts from the permissions list. Add Ron's account and give him Full Control permission. Check the Replace Permissions on Subdirectories option. Click OK.

 D. None of the above.

35. Craig wants to configure his NT Workstation for remote access. Besides his voice line, he has two open lines. What must he do to allow these two lines to be used as remote access lines? Choose only one answer.

 A. Add two modems—one for each line—from the Control Panel's Modems application, and then install Remote Access from the Control Panel's Network application.

 B. Double-click My Computer from the desktop, and then right-click on the Dial-Up Networking icon. Select Sharing and enable both modems for remote access.

 C. Both A and B.

 D. None of the above.

36. You are using Windows NT Workstation as a client on a Novell NetWare network that has a mixture of NetWare 3.11 servers and NetWare 3.12 servers. For some reason, you are able to see and connect to certain NetWare servers but not to all of them. What is wrong?

 A. You need to be configured to connect to both NDS- and bindery-based NetWare servers.

 B. You probably forgot to add a default gateway in your TCP/IP settings.

 C. By default, you are using frame type 802.2. You also need to add 802.3 in order to be backward compatible with the 3.11 servers.

 D. You forgot to add the NWLink Transport Protocol.

37. What is the maximum size for a FAT partition in Windows NT?

 A. 1GB

 B. 2GB

 C. 4GB

 D. 16EB

38. You are currently using Windows 95 and have two partitions. One partition is devoted to the operating system and applications and totals 1GB. The other partition is for files and totals 6GB. You decide to install NT on the operating system partition, with the intent of dual booting. After completing the installation, you notice that the partition devoted to files is unavailable. What is the problem?

 A. The second partition is probably using FAT32, which is not supported in Windows NT 4.0.

B. The second partition was deleted by default during the installation of Windows NT.

C. You forgot to take ownership of the second partition.

D. None of the above.

39. Which of the following is available in Windows NT Workstation and will increase the speed used for general disk I/O?

A. Volume set

B. Stripe set

C. Stripe set with parity

D. Mirror set

40. Joni's organization has several different hardware configurations. However, all desktops will have the same core applications installed, no matter what hardware configurations they are using. Which utility can be used to automate the installation of these applications in a situation where there will be many new installations of NT?

A. UNATTEND.TXT files

B. .UDF files

C. SYSDIFF.EXE

D. SETUPMGR.EXE

41. In a workgroup, what requirements must be met for a user at a Windows NT Workstation to be able to access a file on another Workstation?

A. The user must have a domain user account.

B. A share must be created on the destination directory with the appropriate permissions.

C. Both the source and destination Workstations must have a user account with the same name.

D. The user account on the source Workstation must have an identical password with the account on the destination Workstation.

42. What is the default path used by Peer Web Services for WWW content?

A. C:\InetPub\wwwroot\

B. C:\WebShare\wwwroot\

C. C:\WWWRoot\

D. C:\WebFiles\

43. Which NTFS access permission allows you to see the names of the files in a directory, but does not allow you to open the files themselves?

A. Read

B. Write

C. Browse

D. List

44. When combining share permissions and local NTFS permissions, Windows NT always applies which permissions?

A. Least restrictive

B. Most restrictive

C. Share level

D. File level

45. Mike is configuring the TCP/IP settings for a new NT Workstation installation. The network consists of several TCP/IP subnets. What will he gain by acting as a WINS client?

A. The ability to access Internet domain names

B. The ability to browse non-Windows computers on the network

C. The ability to browse across subnets

D. All of the above

E. None of the above

46. Rex wants to speed up the deployment of NT Workstation. Which of the following provides the fastest method of installation?

A. Install from the CD-ROM.

B. Copy the files in the I386 directory to a share, and then install over the network.

C. Install over the network by connection to a shared CD-ROM.

D. Perform a floppy installation.

47. Which of the following options allows you to upgrade Windows NT 3.51 to 4.0 without creating the three setup floppies?

A. `winnt.exe /b`

B. `winnt.exe /nf`

C. `winnt32.exe /b`

D. `winnt32.exe /o`

48. Device driver configuration settings are stored in the Registry under which of the following keys?

A. HKEY_LOCAL_MACHINE

B. HKEY_USERS

C. HKEY_CLASSES_ROOT

D. HKEY_CURRENT_USER

49. Which of the following components is necessary to connect and use a database server that is running on a NetWare server?

A. CSNW

B. GSNW

C. NWLink

D. All of the above

50. Michele is an administrator of a Windows NT Domain. After a certain accounting employee left the company, she decided to clean up his machine. Upon logging in, she realized that the user had assigned the No Access permission to the Administrators group. What can she do to get around this problem?

A. Try to log on as the previous user, and then make changes to the file and directory permissions.

B. Take ownership of all restricted files, and then use them as normal.

C. Take ownership of all restricted files, and then change the permissions to allow her access.

D. Back up the files to tape, and then reformat the drive.

51. Caitlin is a graphic designer using Windows NT Workstation. Although she has a dual-boot system, she no longer needs Windows 95. She decides that she would like to use NTFS as her file system so she can take advantage of volume sets, especially in light of the very large files she is using. What would be the best method of changing to NTFS?

A. Reformat the hard drive and reinstall Windows NT.

B. Use the Disk Administrator to convert the existing FAT partitions to NTFS.

C. Use the `FORMAT` command to change the existing FAT partitions to NTFS.

D. Use the `CONVERT` command to change the existing FAT partitions to NTFS.

## ANSWERS

1. **D** is correct. Use an UNATTEND.TXT file for common settings and a .UDF file for machine-specific settings.
2. **C** is correct. REGEDT32.EXE allows you to apply permissions to Registry keys.
3. **A** is correct. FAT is the only valid file system for a dual-boot system.
4. **B and D** are correct. Memory and CPU usage can be monitored with both the Task Manager and the Performance Monitor.
5. **A, B, and C** are correct. BOOT.INI, NTLDR, and NTDETECT.COM are all standard NT system files found on the root directory of the active partition.
6. **C** is correct. Adding a user to the local Administrators group gives him administrative access to his own workstation.
7. **C and D** are correct. CSNW and NWLink are necessary for connecting to a NetWare file server.
8. **D** is correct. Both IP blocking and NTFS permissions can be used to secure content provided by Peer Web Services.
9. **C and D** are correct. If the Processor Queue Length is above 2 consistently, the machine needs more processing power.
10. **D** is correct. Stop and restart the Spooler service.
11. **D** is correct. Start the application with the `/separate` command-line argument, or use the Run command that allows you to start it in a separate address space.
12. **D** is correct. To share directories, minimally, you need to be a member of the Power Users group on an NT Workstation.
13. **C** is correct. WINNT32.EXE can be run in the background.
14. **A and B** are correct. If there is only one subnet, the minimum TCP/IP settings necessary are the IP address and subnet mask.
15. **A and B** are correct. Michele must be given explicit permissions at both the share level and the file level, or she must be a member of a group that has Full Control at both levels.
16. **B** is correct. Select Obtain an IP Address from a DHCP Server.
17. **A, B, and C** are correct. The IRQ, I/O address, and driver are needed to set up a network card.
18. **B** is correct. Thread priority is set at the process level.
19. **A and B** are correct. You can force an application to end by ending either the task or the process.
20. **D** is correct. Log off and log back on to update an access token.
21. **C** is correct. NTFS is the only file system available to NT that can handle an 8GB partition.
22. **B** is correct. SCSI controllers are configured from the SCSI Adapters application in Control Panel.
23. **B** is correct. Right-click on the printer from Network Neighborhood and select Install.
24. **C and D** are correct. Separating the disk that contains the system file will increase performance, as will dividing the pagefile across multiple physical disks.
25. **A** is correct. REGEDIT.EXE allows you to search keys, values, and data.
26. **D** is correct. The mouse buttons can be configured from the Mouse application in Control Panel.

27. **D** is correct. Standard Tape Backup Device drivers are included with the Windows NT CD-ROM and can be installed from the Tape Devices application in Control Panel.

28. **B** is correct. To reset a user's desktop to the default, simply delete his user profile.

29. **B and C** are correct. Specify a drive or a wildcard (for the next available drive) when using `net use`.

30. **B** is correct. You create a template user profile by logging in with a user account and configuring the desktop as desired.

31. **A** is correct. Read is the only valid type of access.

32. **A** is correct. The user account was deleted.

33. **C** is correct. Permissions only need to be given to Greg.

34. **C** is correct. Remove all accounts from the list of permissions at the root level, add Ron's account, and choose Replace Permissions on Subdirectories.

35. **D** is correct. Windows NT Workstation allows only one incoming remote access connection.

36. **C** is correct. All frame types used on the network must be used by the NT Workstation.

37. **C** is correct. 4GB is the maximum size of an NT FAT partition.

38. **A** is correct. FAT32 partitions are unreadable under Windows NT 4.0.

39. **B** is correct. Stripe sets increase the speed of I/O operations.

40. **C** is correct. SYSDIFF can be used to install multiple user applications, including files and Registry entries, to an existing Windows NT installation.

41. **B, C, and D** are correct. User accounts need to be created on both workstations with the same password, and a share must be created on the destination.

42. **A** is correct. By default, PWS uses C:\InetPub\wwwroot\ for its path to Web content files.

43. **D** is correct. The List permission allows you to view the filenames in a given directory.

44. **B** is correct. When share and local NTFS permissions are combined, the most restrictive permissions take precedence.

45. **C** is correct. WINS allows you to browse and connect to computers by their name across TCP/IP subnets.

46. **B** is correct. A network installation from a file server is the fastest method of installation.

47. **C** is correct. To upgrade without floppies, use `winnt32.exe /b`.

48. **A** is correct. Driver settings are found in HKEY_LOCAL_MACHINE.

49. **C** is correct. To use a client/server-based application on Novell NetWare, the minimum requirement on NT is that NWLink must be installed.

50. **C** is correct. Take ownership of the files, and then proceed to change the permissions.

51. **D** is correct. CONVERT.EXE allows you to convert a FAT partition to an NTFS permission without data loss.

PART

# Appendixes

APPENDIX A

# Glossary

**/NoSerialMice** A BOOT.INI switch that prevents NT from checking for serial mice on COM ports. This is frequently used to prevent NT from inadvertantly shutting down a UPS connected to the COM port.

**/Separate** A switch used on WIN16 programs run from a command prompt that forces execution of that program in a separate NT Virtual DOS machine.

**/SOS** A BOOT.INI switch indicating that during NT Server or Workstation boot, the list of loading drivers should be displayed. This switch is used for troubleshooting and is normally configured as part of the [VGA] boot option.

## A

**Account Policy** Controls the way passwords must be used by all user accounts of a domain or of an individual computer. Specifics include minimum password length, how often a user must change his or her password, and how often users can reuse old passwords. Account policy can be set for all user accounts in a domain when administering a domain and for all user accounts of a single workstation or member server when administering a computer.

**Alert view** A view in the Performance Monitor in which thresholds for counters are set and then actions are taken when those thresholds are crossed.

**Application log** A server log accessible from the Event Viewer. This log records messages, warnings, and errors generated by applications running on your NT Server or Workstation.

**applications** A computer program used for a particular kind of work, such as word processing. This term is often used interchangeably with "program."

**ARC-path** The Advanced RISC Computing path is an industry standard method of identifying the physical location of a partition on a hard drive. ARC-paths are used in the BOOT.INI file to identify the location of NT boot files.

## B

**base priority** The priority at which a program runs without any user or system intervention.

**baseline** An initial reading of a computer's performance, which is used as a "normal" reading against which other readings can be compared.

**binary compatible** A program having the characteristic of being usable by any hardware platform on which NT runs. DOS and WIN16 programs claim to be binary compatible across all hardware-specific versions of NT.

**binding** A process that establishes the communication channel between a protocol driver (such as TCP/IP) and a network card.

**BOOT.INI** A file located on the system partition of an NT Server or Workstation that's responsible for pointing the boot process to the correct boot files for the operating system chosen in the boot menu.

**BOOTSECT.DOS** A file located on the system partition that contains information required to boot an NT

System to a non-NT operating system (MS-DOS, Windows 95) if a user requests it.

**bottleneck** A system resource that is the limiting factor in speed of processing. All systems have a bottleneck of some sort; the question is whether the bottleneck is significant in the context in which a Server finds itself.

**built-in user accounts** User accounts that are created in the account database automatically and cannot be deleted. Only the Administrator and Guest accounts are built-in.

**built-in Windows NT groups** Groups that are created in the NT accounts database automatically and cannot be deleted. These accounts include the Administrators group and the Guests group.

# C

**Chart view** A view in the Performance Monitor in which a dynamically updated line graph or histogram is displayed for the counters selected in the view configuration.

**Client Services for NetWare (CSNW)** Included with Windows NT Workstation, this enables workstations to make direct connections to file and printer resources at NetWare servers running NetWare 2.x or later.

**counter** A specific component of a Performance Monitor object that has a displayable value. For example, for the object Memory, one counter is Available Bytes.

**CSR subsystem** The Client Server subsystem. Among its many functions is the execution of 32-bit Windows programs.

# D

**default performance boost** The performance boost normally given to programs running in the foreground to allow better performance to the programs that a user is interacting with. This can be set between 0 and 2.

**DETECT** A troubleshooting acronym indicating a recommended method for approaching NT problems. The acronym DETECT stands for Discover, Explore, Track, Execute, Check, Tie-up.

**device** Any piece of equipment that can be attached to a network, such as a computer, a printer, or any other peripheral equipment.

**difference file** Created by the SYSDIFF program, a file that contains a description of the differences between one installation of NT and another. This difference file is used to create an .INF or an executable, both of which are typically used to install applications in conjunction with an automated NT installation.

**DISKPERF** A disk statistic monitor that can be turned on or off. It is required that DISKPERF be turned on to monitor disk performance.

**DLC** A protocol that, in NT, is typically used to communicate with direct interface network printer adapters such as an HP Direct Jet.

**Domain Name System (DNS)** DNS offers a static, hierarchical name service for TCP/IP hosts. The network administrator configures the DNS with a list of hostnames and IP addresses, allowing users of workstations configured to query the DNS to specify remote systems by hostnames instead of by IP addresses. For example, a workstation configured to use DNS name resolution could use the command `PING` *`remotehost`* instead of `PING 1.2.3.4` if the mapping for the system named *remotehost* was contained in the DNS database.

**dual boot** A computer that can boot two different operating systems.

**Dynamic Host Configuration Protocol (DHCP)** A protocol that offers dynamic configuration of IP addresses and related information through the DHCP Server service running on an NT Server. DHCP provides safe, reliable, and simple TCP/IP network configuration, prevents address conflicts, and helps conserve the use of IP addresses through centralized management of address allocation.

## E

**Emergency Repair Disk (ERD)** A floppy disk containing configuration information for a specific NT Server or Workstation. This disk is created and updated using the RDISK utility and can be used in conjunction with the three NT Setup disks to recover from many NT system failures resulting from file and/or Registry corruption.

**Event Viewer** An administrative utility used to look at event logs. Three logs are provided to the Event Viewer: System log, Security log, and Application log.

**extended partition** Created from free space on a hard disk, an extended partition can be subpartitioned into zero or more logical drives. Only one of the four partitions allowed per physical disk can be an extended partition, and no primary partition needs to be present to create an extended partition.

## F

**FAT (File Allocation Table)** A table or list maintained by some operating systems to keep track of the status of various segments of disk space used for file storage. Also referred to as the FAT file system, this method is used to format hard drives in DOS, Windows 95, and OS/2, and can be used in Windows NT.

**File Delete Child** A phenomenon resulting from the presence of the POSIX subsystem that allows someone to delete a file to which he or she has no access (NTFS permission) if he has Full Control to the folder in which the file is located.

`FORCEDOS` A switch used to ensure that OS/2 applications run in an NT Virtual DOS machine instead of in an OS/2 subsystem. This must be used to run OS/2 applications on non-Intel platforms because RISC platforms do not have the OS/2 subsystem.

## G, H

**hard links** A POSIX compatibility feature that allows multiple filenames to point to the same file. Unlike shortcuts, which are files that point to other files, hard links actually are multiple filenames on the same file.

**Hardware Compatibility List (HCL)** The Windows NT Hardware Compatibility List lists all hardware devices supported by Windows NT. The most current version of the HCL can be downloaded from the Microsoft Web page (`microsoft.com`) on the Internet.

**hardware profile** A grouping of hardware devices that make up the current recognized NT hardware. An NT user can use different hardware profiles based on the needs of different situations.

**High Performance File System (HPFS)** Native to the OS/2 operating system, this file system was once supported by NT but is no longer in NT 4.0.

**hive** A section of the Registry that appears as a file on your hard disk. The Registry subtree is divided into hives (named for their resemblance to the cellular structure of a beehive). A hive is a discrete body of keys, subkeys, and values that is rooted at the top of the Registry hierarchy. A hive is backed by a single file and a .LOG file, which are stored in the %SystemRoot%\system32\config folder or the %SystemRoot%\profiles*username* folder. By default, most hive files (Default, SAM, Security, and System) are stored in the %SystemRoot%\system32\config folder. The %SystemRoot%\profiles folder contains the user profile for each user of the computer. Because a hive is a file, it can be moved from one system to another; however, it can be edited only by using Registry Editor.

# I, J, K

**instances** Multiple occurrences of the same object in Performance Monitor. For example, if a computer has two processors, each is recognized as a separate instance of the Processor object and can be monitored separately.

**IPC mechanism** A method, provided by a multitasking operating system, by which one task or process is enabled to exchange data with another. Common IPC mechanisms include pipes, semaphores, shared memory, queues, signals, and mailboxes.

# L

**LastKnownGood configuration** A set of Registry settings that contains the hardware configuration of an NT computer during its last successful login. LastKnownGood can be used to recover from incorrect hardware setup as long as logon does not occur between when the configuration was changed and when LastKnownGood was invoked.

**local group** For Windows NT Workstation, a group that can be granted permissions and rights only for its own workstation. However, it can contain user accounts from its own computer and (if the workstation participates in a domain) user accounts and global groups both from its own domain and from trusted domains.

For Windows NT Server, a group that can be granted permissions and rights only for the domain controllers of its own domain. However, it can contain user accounts and global groups both from its own domain and from trusted domains.

Local groups provide a way to create handy sets of users from both inside and outside the domain, to be used only at domain controllers of the domain.

**Log view** The Performance Monitor view in which the configuration of a log is determined. Logs have no dynamic information; however, the resulting file can be analyzed using any of the other Performance Monitor views.

# M

**Master Boot Record (MBR)** The place on the disk where the initial computer startup is directed to go to initiate operating system boot. The MBR is located on the primary partition.

**multithreaded** A program that has multiple execution strands or threads. On a multiprocessor system, multiple threads can be executed simultaneously and can, therefore, speed execution of the program as a whole.

# N

**NDIS** Acronym for Network Driver Interface Specification, the Microsoft/3Com specification for the interface of network device drivers. All network adapter card drivers and protocol drivers shipped with Windows NT Server conform to NDIS.

**NetBEUI** A network protocol usually used in small, department-size local area networks of 1 to 200 clients. Because it is non-routable, it is not a preferred WAN protocol.

**network monitor** An administrative utility installed on an NT computer when the Network Monitor Tools and Agent service is installed. The network monitor provided with NT allows you to capture and analyze network traffic coming into and going out of the local network card. The SMS version of network monitor runs in a promiscuous mode that allows monitoring of traffic on the local network.

**NT Virtual DOS Machine (NTVDM)** Simulates an MS-DOS environment so that MS-DOS–based and Windows-based applications can run on Windows NT.

**NTBOOTDD.SYS** The driver for a SCSI boot device that does not have its BIOS enabled. NTBOOTDD.SYS is stored on an NT system partition and is required to create a fault-tolerant boot disk.

**NTCONFIG.POL** A file that defines an NT system policy.

**NTDETECT.COM** The program in the NT boot process that's responsible for generating a list of hardware devices. This list is later used to populate part of the HKEY_LOCAL_MACHINE subtree in the Registry.

**NTFS** An advanced file system designed for use specifically within the Windows NT operating system. It supports file system recovery, extremely large storage media, long filenames, and various features for the POSIX subsystem. It also supports object-oriented applications by treating all files as objects with user-defined and system-defined attributes.

**NTFS permissions** Local permissions on NTFS volumes that allow for the restriction of both local and network access to files and folders.

**NTHQ** A program that executes from a floppy disk and that automatically checks the hardware on a computer against the HCL for NT compatibility.

**NTLDR** The program responsible for booting an NT system. It is invoked when an NT computer is started, and it is responsible for displaying the boot menu (from the BOOT.INI file) and starting the NTDETECT.COM program.

**NTOSKRNL.EXE** The program responsible for maintaining the core of the NT operating system. When NTLDR has completed the boot process, control of NT is handed over to the NTOSKRNL.

**NWLink** A standard network protocol that supports routing and can support NetWare client-server applications (when NetWare-aware Sockets-based applications communicate with IPX\SPX Sockets-based applications).

**NWLink frame type** The type of network package generated on a network. In NT configuration, this refers to the type of network packages sent by a NetWare server that an NT client is configured to accept.

# O, P, Q

**object** A specific system category for which counters can be observed in Performance Monitor. Objects whose counters are frequently monitored are Memory, Processor, Network, and PhysicalDisk.

**OS/2** An operating system, originally developed by Microsoft, which is currently owned and maintained by IBM.

**OSLOADER.EXE** On a RISC-based machine, the program that's responsible for the function of the NTLDR on an Intel-based machine.

**Peer Web Server (PWS)** A service that can be installed on NT Workstation, which allows the workstation to publish files over the Internet. Its features include WWW, FTP, and Gopher protocol support.

**Performance Monitor** An administrative application used to monitor object counters on an NT computer to determine bottlenecks in the system and to increase overall efficiency.

**Point-to-Point Protocol (PPP)** A set of industry-standard framing and authentication protocols that is part of Windows NT RAS, which ensures interoperability with third-party remote access software. PPP negotiates configuration parameters for multiple layers of the OSI model.

**Point-to-Point Tunneling Protocol (PPTP)** PPTP is a new networking technology that supports multiprotocol virtual private networks (VPNs), enabling remote users to access corporate networks securely across the Internet by dialing into an Internet service provider (ISP) or by connecting directly to the Internet.

**POSIX** An NT emulation of the UNIX operating system. The POSIX subsystem was implemented in NT to allow UNIX programs to execute and thus fulfill the requirements for some government contracts.

**preemptive multitasking** A multitasking environment in which the operating system decides how long a certain process will have exclusive use of the processor. Windows NT is a preemptive multitasking environment.

**primary partition** A partition is a portion of a physical disk that can be marked for use by an operating system. There can be up to four primary partitions (or up to three if there is an extended partition) per physical disk. A primary partition cannot be subpartitioned.

**print device** The actual hardware device that produces printed output.

**print server** The computer that provides the support for the sharing of one or more printers.

**printer** The software interface between the operating system and the print device. The printer defines where the document will go before it reaches the print device (to a local port, to a file, or to a remote print share), when it will go, and various other aspects of the printing process.

**printer pool** Consists of two or more identical print devices associated with one printer.

**printer priorities** Refers to the relative importance put on certain printers. When one printer that prints to a print device has a higher priority than another printer printing to the same print device, the print jobs of the former will be printed before those of the latter; these print jobs will "jump queue" to take a preeminent place in the print queue while waiting to be printed.

**process** When a program runs, a Windows NT process is created. A process is an object type that consists of an executable program, a set of virtual memory addresses, and one or more threads.

**Program Information File (PIF)** A PIF provides information to Windows NT about how best to run MS-DOS applications. When you start an MS-DOS application, Windows NT looks for a PIF to use with the application. PIFs contain such items as the name of the file, a startup directory, and multitasking options.

# R

**RDISK.EXE** A program used to create and update Emergency Repair Disks and the /REPAIR folder on an NT system.

**recovery disk** A floppy disk that contains the files required by NT to begin the boot process and to point to the boot partition. The files required for an Intel system are: BOOT.INI, NTDETECT.COM, NTLDR, and NTBOOTDD.SYS (if the hard drive is SCSI with BIOS disabled).

**REGEDIT.EXE** One of two Registry editors available in NT. This one has the same interface as the Registry editor available in Windows 95 and provides key value searching.

**REGEDT32.EXE** One of two Registry editors available in NT. This one has a cascaded subtree interface and allows you to set Registry security.

**Remote Access Service (RAS)** A service that provides remote networking for telecommuters, mobile workers, and system administrators who monitor and manage servers at multiple branch offices. Users with RAS on a Windows NT computer can dial in to remotely access their networks for services such as file and printer sharing, electronic mail, scheduling, and SQL database access.

**Report view** A view in the Performance Monitor that displays current counter values in a single-page format.

# S

**scheduling printing** The process by which certain print jobs are sent to printers that are available only at certain times of the day. By doing this, the load on printers can be kept to a minimum during times when many people require access to the same printer for small print jobs.

**Security Identifier (SID)** A unique name that identifies a logged-on user to the security system. Security IDs (SIDs) can identify one user or a group of users.

**Security log** Records security events and can be viewed through the Event Viewer. This helps track changes to the security system and identify any possible breaches of security. For example, depending on the Audit settings in User Manager or User Manager for Domains, any attempts to log on to the local computer may be recorded in the Security log. The Security log contains both valid and invalid logon attempts, as well as events related to resource use (such as creating, opening, and deleting files.)

**service** A process that performs a specific system function and often provides an application programming interface (API) for other processes to call. Windows NT services are RPC-enabled, meaning that their API routines can be called from remote computers.

**shared folder** A folder on a computer to which access has been given to network users through sharing.

**source compatible** A program having the characteristic of only being usable on the hardware platform for which it was compiled. Windows 32-bit programs are source compatible because they need different versions for every hardware platform.

**Spooler service** Software that accepts documents sent by a user to be printed and then stores those documents and sends them, one by one, to available printer(s).

**spooling** A process on a server in which print documents are stored on a disk until a print device is ready to process them. A spooler accepts each document from each client, stores it, and then sends it to a print device when it is ready.

**subnet mask** A 32-bit value that allows the recipient of IP packets to distinguish the network ID portion of the IP address from the host ID portion.

**symmetric multiprocessing** A multiprocessor architecture that allows any process to use any processor, thus ensuring the most effective execution of multithreaded processes. NT uses symmetric multiprocessing. This is an improvement over asymmetric multiprocessing systems in which one processor is used exclusively by the operating system, whether it uses the full capabilities of the processor or not.

**SYSDIFF** A program that is used to create difference files representing the differences between one NT installation and another. *See also* difference file.

**System log** The System log contains events logged by the Windows NT components and can be viewed through Event Viewer. For example, the failure of a driver or other system component to load during startup is recorded in the System log.

# T

**Task Manager** Task Manager enables you to start, end, or run applications; end processes (either an application, application component, or system process); and view CPU and memory use data. Task Manager gives you a simple, quick view of how each process (application or service) is using CPU and memory resources. (Note: In previous versions of Windows NT, Task List handled some of these functions.)

**TCP/IP** An acronym for Transmission Control Protocol/Internet Protocol, TCP/IP is a set of networking protocols that provide communications across interconnected networks made up of computers with diverse hardware architectures and various operating systems. TCP/IP includes standards for how computers communicate and conventions for connecting networks and routing traffic.

# U

**unattended answer file** A file that defines the basic installation characteristics for NT. In essence, it answers the questions that a user would be asked during an interactive installation.

**UNC (Universal Naming Convention) name** A full Windows NT name of a resource on a network. It conforms to the *servername**sharename* syntax, where *servername* is the server's name and *sharename* is the name of the shared resource. UNC names of directories or files can also include the directory path under the share name, with the following syntax:

*servername**sharename**directory**filename*

**uniqueness database file (UDF)** A file that defines the unique characteristics of a number of computers. UDFs are used in unattended NT installations to ensure that the features that must be unique (computer name, for instance) are provided without manual user intervention.

**user profile** Configuration information can be retained on a user-by-user basis and is saved in user profiles. This information includes all the user-specific settings of the Windows NT environment, such as the desktop arrangement, personal program groups and the program items in those groups, screen colors, screen savers, network connections, printer connections, mouse settings, window size and position, and more. When a user logs on, the user's profile is loaded and the user's Windows NT environment is configured according to that profile.

# V, W, X, Y, AND Z

**WINDIFF** A program that enumerates all the differences between two folders or files. This program will show information as specific as line-by-line differences between files or as general as a list of files in two folders that differ.

**Windows Internet Name Service (WINS)** A name resolution service that resolves Windows NT networking computer names to IP addresses in a routed environment. A WINS server handles name registrations, queries, and releases.

**Windows Microsoft Diagnostic (WinMSD)** A program that displays hardware configuration information for the purposes of diagnostics and general system reporting.

**Windows on Windows (WOW)** A WIN16 emulation that runs inside of an NT Virtual DOS machine and allows the execution of WIN16 programs in the 32-bit NT environment.

**WINNT.EXE** The program used to install Windows NT from a non-NT platform.

**WINNT32.EXE** The program used to install or upgrade Windows NT from an NT platform.

APPENDIX B

# Overview of the Certification Process

You must pass rigorous certification exams to become a Microsoft Certified Professional. These certification exams provide a valid and reliable measure of your technical proficiency and expertise. The closed-book exams are developed in consultation with computer industry professionals who have on-the-job experience with Microsoft products in the workplace. These exams are conducted by an independent organization—Sylvan Prometric—at more than 1,200 Authorized Prometric Testing Centers around the world.

Currently Microsoft offers six types of certification, based on specific areas of expertise:

- **Microsoft Certified Professional (MCP).** Persons who attain this certification are qualified to provide installation, configuration, and support for users of at least one Microsoft desktop operating system, such as Windows NT Workstation. In addition, candidates can take elective exams to develop areas of specialization. MCP is the initial or first level of expertise.
- **Microsoft Certified Professional + Internet (MCP+Internet).** Persons who attain this certification are qualified to plan security, install and configure server products, manage server resources, extend service to run CGI scripts or ISAPI scripts, monitor and analyze performance, and troubleshoot problems. The expertise required is similar to that of an MCP with a focus on the Internet.
- **Microsoft Certified Systems Engineer (MCSE).** Persons who attain this certification are qualified to effectively plan, implement, maintain, and support information systems with Microsoft Windows NT and other Microsoft advanced systems and workgroup products, such as Microsoft Office and Microsoft BackOffice. MCSE is a second level of expertise.
- **Microsoft Certified Systems Engineer + Internet (MCSE+Internet).** Persons who attain this certification are qualified in the core MCSE areas and are qualified to enhance, deploy, and manage sophisticated intranet and Internet solutions that include a browser, proxy server, host servers, database, and messaging and commerce components. In addition, an MCSE+Internet–certified professional will be able to manage and analyze Web sites.
- **Microsoft Certified Solution Developer (MCSD).** Persons who attain this certification are qualified to design and develop custom business solutions by using Microsoft development tools, technologies, and platforms, including Microsoft Office and Microsoft BackOffice. MCSD is a second level of expertise with a focus on software development.
- **Microsoft Certified Trainer (MCT).** Persons who attain this certification are instructionally and technically qualified by Microsoft to deliver

Microsoft Education Courses at Microsoft-authorized sites. An MCT must be employed by a Microsoft Solution Provider Authorized Technical Education Center or a Microsoft Authorized Academic Training site.

NOTE

**Stay in Touch** For up-to-date information about each type of certification, visit the Microsoft Training and Certification World Wide Web site at `http://www.microsoft.com/train_cert`. You must have an Internet account and a WWW browser to access this information. You also can call the following sources:

- Microsoft Certified Professional Program: 800-636-7544
- Sylvan Prometric Testing Centers: 800-755-EXAM
- Microsoft Online Institute (MOLI): 800-449-9333

## How to Become a Microsoft Certified Professional (MCP)

To become an MCP, you must pass one operating system exam. The following list contains the names and exam numbers of all the operating system exams that will qualify you for your MCP certification (a * denotes an exam that is scheduled to be retired):

- Implementing and Supporting Microsoft Windows 95, #70-064 (formerly #70-063)
- Implementing and Supporting Microsoft Windows NT Workstation 4.02, #70-073
- Implementing and Supporting Microsoft Windows NT Workstation 3.51, #70-042*
- Implementing and Supporting Microsoft Windows NT Server 4.0, #70-067
- Implementing and Supporting Microsoft Windows NT Server 3.51, #70-043*
- Microsoft Windows for Workgroups 3.11–Desktop, #70-048*
- Microsoft Windows 3.1, #70-030*
- Microsoft Windows Architecture I, #70-160
- Microsoft Windows Architecture II, #70-161

## How to Become a Microsoft Certified Professional + Internet (MCP+Internet)

To become an MCP with a specialty in Internet technology, you must pass the following three exams:

- Internetworking Microsoft TCP/IP on Microsoft Windows NT 4.0, #70-059
- Implementing and Supporting Microsoft Windows NT Server 4.0, #70-067
- Implementing and Supporting Microsoft Internet Information Server 3.0 and Microsoft Index Server 1.1, #70-077

  *OR* Implementing and Supporting Microsoft Internet Information Server 4.0, #70-087

## How to Become a Microsoft Certified Systems Engineer (MCSE)

MCSE candidates must pass four operating system exams and two elective exams. The MCSE certification path is divided into two tracks: the Windows NT 3.51 track and the Windows NT 4.0 track.

The following lists show the core requirements (four operating system exams) for the Windows NT 3.51 track, the core requirements for the Windows NT 4.0 track, and the elective courses (two exams) you can choose from for either track.

The four Windows NT 3.51 track core requirements for MCSE certification are:

- Implementing and Supporting Microsoft Windows NT Server 3.51, #70-043*
- Implementing and Supporting Microsoft Windows NT Workstation 3.51, #70-042*
- Microsoft Windows 3.1, #70-030*

  *OR* Microsoft Windows for Workgroups 3.11, #70-048*

  *OR* Implementing and Supporting Microsoft Windows 95, #70-064

  *OR* Implementing and Supporting Microsoft Windows 98, #70-098
- Networking Essentials, #70-058

The four Windows NT 4.0 track core requirements for MCSE certification are:

- Implementing and Supporting Microsoft Windows NT Server 4.0, #70-067
- Implementing and Supporting Microsoft Windows NT Server 4.0 in the Enterprise, #70-068
- Microsoft Windows 3.1, #70-030*

  *OR* Microsoft Windows for Workgroups 3.11, #70-048*

  *OR* Implementing and Supporting Microsoft Windows 95, #70-064

  *OR* Implementing and Supporting Microsoft Windows NT Workstation 4.0, #70-073

  *OR* Implementing and Supporting Microsoft Windows 98, #70-098
- Networking Essentials, #70-058

For both the Windows NT 3.51 and the Windows NT 4.0 track, you must pass two of the following elective exams for MCSE certification:

- Implementing and Supporting Microsoft SNA Server 3.0, #70-013

  *OR* Implementing and Supporting Microsoft SNA Server 4.0, #70-085
- Implementing and Supporting Microsoft Systems Management Server 1.0, #70-014*

  *OR* Implementing and Supporting Microsoft Systems Management Server 1.2, #70-018

  *OR* Implementing and Supporting Microsoft Systems Management Server 2.0, #70-086
- Microsoft SQL Server 4.2 Database Implementation, #70-021

  *OR* Implementing a Database Design on Microsoft SQL Server 6.5, #70-027

  *OR* Implementing a Database Design on Microsoft SQL Server 7.0, #70-029
- Microsoft SQL Server 4.2 Database Administration for Microsoft Windows NT, #70-022

*OR* System Administration for Microsoft SQL Server 6.5 (or 6.0), #70-026

*OR* System Administration for Microsoft SQL Server 7.0, #70-028

- Microsoft Mail for PC Networks 3.2-Enterprise, #70-037
- Internetworking with Microsoft TCP/IP on Microsoft Windows NT (3.5–3.51), #70-053

  *OR* Internetworking with Microsoft TCP/IP on Microsoft Windows NT 4.0, #70-059
- Implementing and Supporting Microsoft Exchange Server 4.0, #70-075*

  *OR* Implementing and Supporting Microsoft Exchange Server 5.0, #70-076

  *OR* Implementing and Supporting Microsoft Exchange Server 5.5, #70-081
- Implementing and Supporting Microsoft Internet Information Server 3.0 and Microsoft Index Server 1.1, #70-077

  *OR* Implementing and Supporting Microsoft Internet Information Server 4.0, #70-087
- Implementing and Supporting Microsoft Proxy Server 1.0, #70-078

  *OR* Implementing and Supporting Microsoft Proxy Server 2.0, #70-088
- Implementing and Supporting Microsoft Internet Explorer 4.0 by Using the Internet Explorer Resource Kit, #70-079

## How to Become a Microsoft Certified Systems Engineer + Internet (MCSE+Internet)

MCSE+Internet candidates must pass seven operating system exams and two elective exams. The following lists show the core requirements and the elective courses (of which you need to pass two exams).

The seven MCSE+Internet core exams required for certification are:

- Networking Essentials, #70-058
- Internetworking with Microsoft TCP/IP on Microsoft Windows NT 4.0, #70-059
- Implementing and Supporting Microsoft Windows 95, #70-064

  *OR* Implementing and Supporting Microsoft Windows NT Workstation 4.0, #70-073

  *OR* Implementing and Supporting Microsoft Windows 98, #70-098
- Implementing and Supporting Microsoft Windows NT Server 4.0, #70-067
- Implementing and Supporting Microsoft Windows NT Server 4.0 in the Enterprise, #70-068
- Implementing and Supporting Microsoft Internet Information Server 3.0 and Microsoft Index Server 1.1, #70-077

  *OR* Implementing and Supporting Microsoft Internet Information Server 4.0, #70-087
- Implementing and Supporting Microsoft Internet Explorer 4.0 by Using the Internet Explorer Resource Kit, #70-079

You must also pass two of the following elective exams:

- System Administration for Microsoft SQL Server 6.5, #70-026
- Implementing a Database Design on Microsoft SQL Server 6.5, #70-027
- Implementing and Supporting Web Sites Using Microsoft Site Server 3.0, #70-056
- Implementing and Supporting Microsoft Exchange Server 5.0, #70-076

  *OR* Implementing and Supporting Microsoft Exchange Server 5.5, #70-081
- Implementing and Supporting Microsoft Proxy Server 1.0, #70-078

  *OR* Implementing and Supporting Microsoft Proxy Server 2.0, #70-088
- Implementing and Supporting Microsoft SNA Server 4.0, #70-085

## How to Become a Microsoft Certified Solution Developer (MCSD)

MCSD candidates must pass two core technology exams and two elective exams. The following lists show the required technology exams, plus the elective exams that apply toward obtaining the MCSD.

You must pass the following two core technology exams to qualify for MCSD certification:

- Microsoft Windows Architecture I, #70-160
- Microsoft Windows Architecture II, #70-161

You must also pass two of the following elective exams to become an MSCD:

- Microsoft SQL Server 4.2 Database Implementation, #70-021

  *OR* Implementing a Database Design on Microsoft SQL Server 6.5, #70-027

  *OR* Implementing a Database Design on Microsoft SQL Server 7.0, #70-029
- Developing Applications with C++ Using the Microsoft Foundation Class Library, #70-024
- Implementing OLE in Microsoft Foundation Class Applications, #70-025
- Programming with Microsoft Visual Basic 4.0, #70-065

  *OR* Developing Applications with Microsoft Visual Basic 5.0, #70-165
- Microsoft Access 2.0 for Windows-Application Development, #70-051

  *OR* Microsoft Access for Windows 95 and the Microsoft Access Development Toolkit, #70-069
- Developing Applications with Microsoft Excel 5.0 Using Visual Basic for Applications, #70-052
- Programming in Microsoft Visual FoxPro 3.0 for Windows, #70-054

## Becoming a Microsoft Certified Trainer (MCT)

To understand the requirements and process for becoming a Microsoft Certified Trainer (MCT), you need to obtain the Microsoft Certified Trainer Guide document from the following WWW site:

```
http://www.microsoft.com/train_cert/mct/
```

From this page, you can read the document as Web pages, or you can display or download it as a Word file.

The MCT Guide explains the four-step process of becoming an MCT. The general steps for the MCT certification are described here:

1. Complete and mail a Microsoft Certified Trainer application to Microsoft. You must include proof of your skills for presenting instructional material. The options for doing so are described in the MCT Guide.
2. Obtain and study the Microsoft Trainer Kit for the Microsoft Official Curricula (MOC) course(s) for which you want to be certified. You can order Microsoft Trainer Kits by calling 800-688-0496 in North America. Other regions should review the MCT Guide for information on how to order a Trainer Kit.
3. Pass the Microsoft certification exam for the product for which you want to be certified to teach.
4. Attend the Microsoft Official Curriculum (MOC) course for which you want to be certified. You do this so that you can understand how the course is structured, how labs are completed, and how the course flows.

WARNING

**Be Sure to Get the MCT Guide!**
You should consider the preceding steps to be a general overview of the MCT certification process. The precise steps that you need to take are described in detail on the WWW site mentioned earlier. Do not mistakenly believe the preceding steps make up the actual process you need to take.

If you are interested in becoming an MCT, you can receive more information by visiting the Microsoft Certified Training (MCT) WWW site at `http://www.microsoft.com/train_cert/mct/` or call 800-688-0496.

APPENDIX C

# What's on the CD-ROM

This appendix offers a brief rundown of what you'll find on the CD-ROM that comes with this book. For a more detailed description of the newly developed Top Score test engine, exclusive to Macmillan Computer Publishing, see Appendix D, "Using the Top Score Software."

## Top Score

Top Score is a test engine developed exclusively for Macmillan Computer Publishing. It is, we believe, the best test engine available because it closely emulates the format of the standard Microsoft exams. In addition to providing a means of evaluating your knowledge of the exam material, Top Score features several innovations that help you to improve your mastery of the subject matter. For example, the practice tests allow you to check your score by exam area or category, which helps you determine which topics you need to study further. Other modes allow you to obtain immediate feedback on your response to a question, explanation of the correct answer, and even hyperlinks to the chapter in an electronic version of the book where the topic of the question is covered. Again, for a complete description of the benefits of Top Score, see Appendix D.

Before you attempt to run the Top Score software, make sure that autorun is enabled. If you prefer not to use autorun, you can run the application from the CD by double-clicking the START.EXE file from within Explorer.

## Exclusive Electronic Version of Text

As alluded to above, the CD-ROM also contains the electronic version of this book in Portable Document Format (PDF). In addition to the links to the book that are built into the Top Score engine, you can use that version of the book to help you search for terms you need to study or other book elements. The electronic version comes complete with all figures as they appear in the book.

## Copyright Information and Disclaimer

**Macmillan Computer Publishing's Top Score test engine**: Copyright 1998 New Riders Publishing. All rights reserved. Made in U.S.A.

APPENDIX D

# Using the Top Score Software

## Getting Started

The installation procedure is very simple and typical of Windows 95 or Window NT 4 installations.

1. Put the CD into the CD-ROM drive. The autorun function starts, and after a moment, you see a CD-ROM Setup dialog box asking you if you are ready to proceed.
2. Click OK, and you are prompted for the location of the directory in which the program can install a small log file. Choose the default (C:\Program Files\), or type the name of another drive and directory, or select the drive and directory where you want it placed. Then click OK.
3. The next prompt asks you to select a start menu name. If you like the default name, click OK. If not, enter the name you would like to use. The Setup process runs its course.

When setup is complete, icons are displayed in the MCSE Top Score Software Explorer window that is open. For an overview of the CD's contents, double-click the CD-ROM Contents icon.

If you reach this point, you have successfully installed the exam(s). If you have another CD, repeat this process to install additional exams.

## Instructions on Using the Top Score Software

Top Score software consists of the following three applications:

- Practice Exams
- Study Cards
- Flash Cards

The Practice Exams application provides exams that simulate the Microsoft certification exams. The Study Cards serve as a study aid organized around specific exam objectives. Both are in multiple-choice format. Flash Cards are another study aid that require responses to open-ended questions, which test your knowledge of the material at a level deeper than that of recognition memory.

To start the Study Cards, Practice Exams, or Flash Cards applications, follow these steps:

1. Begin from the overview of the CD contents (double-click the CD-ROM Contents icon). The left window provides you with options for obtaining further information on any of the Top Score applications as well as a way to launch them.

2. Click a "book" icon, and a listing of related topics appears below it in Explorer fashion.
3. Click an application name. This displays more detailed information for that application in the right window.
4. To start an application, click its book icon. Then click on the Starting the Program option. Do this for Practice Exams, for example. Information appears in the right window. Click on the button for the exam, and the opening screens of the application appear.

Further details on using each of the applications follow.

## Using Top Score Practice Exams

The Practice Exams interface is simple and straightforward. Its design simulates the look and feel of the Microsoft certification exams. To begin a practice exam, click the button for the exam name. After a moment, you see an opening screen similar to the one shown in Figure D.1.

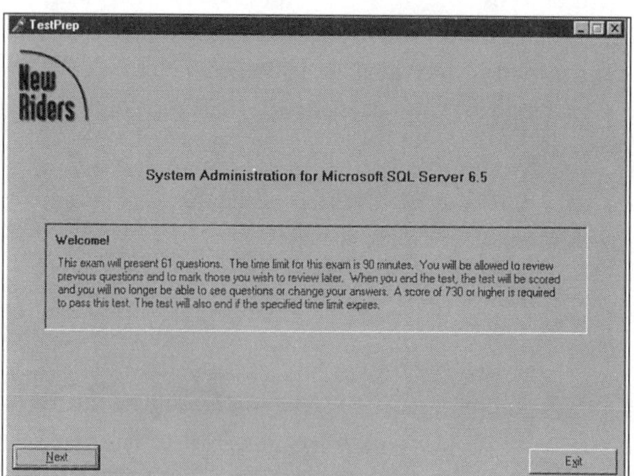


**FIGURE D.1**
Top Score Practice Exams opening screen.

Click on the Next button to see a disclaimer and copyright screen. Read the information, and then click Top Score's Start button. A notice appears, indicating that the program is randomly selecting questions for the practice exam from the exam database (see Figure D.2). Each practice exam contains the same number of items as the official Microsoft exam. The items are selected from a larger set of 150–900 questions. The random selection of questions from the database takes some time to retrieve. Don't reboot; your machine is not hung!

> NOTE
> **Some Exams Follow a New Format**
> The number of questions will be the same for traditional exams. However, this will not be the case for exams that incorporate the new "adaptive testing" format. In that format, there is no set number of questions. See the chapter entitled "Study and Exam Prep Tips" in the Final Review section of the book for more details on this new format.

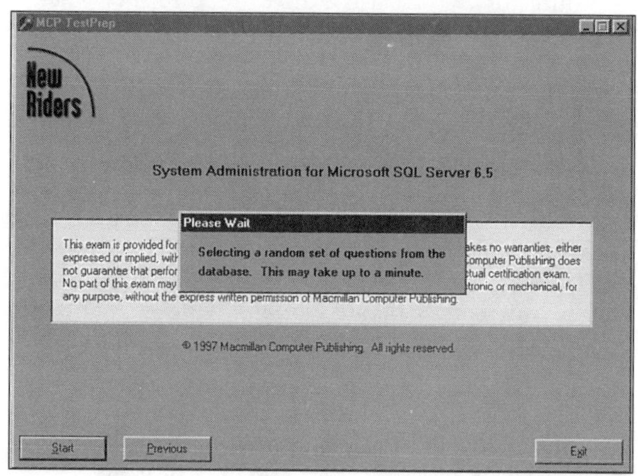


**FIGURE D.2**
Top Score's Please Wait notice.

After the questions have been selected, the first test item appears. See Figure D.3 for an example of a test item screen.

Notice several important features of this window. The question number and the total number of retrieved questions appears in the top-left corner of the window in the control bar. Immediately below that is a check box labeled Mark, which enables you to mark any exam item you would like to return to later. Across the screen from the Mark check box, you see the total time remaining for the exam.

The test question is located in a colored section (it's gray in the figure). Directly below the test question, in the white area, are response choices. Be sure to note that immediately below the responses are instructions about how to respond, including the number of responses required. You will notice that question items requiring a single response, such as that shown in Figure D.3, have radio buttons. Items requiring multiple responses have check boxes (see Figure D.4).

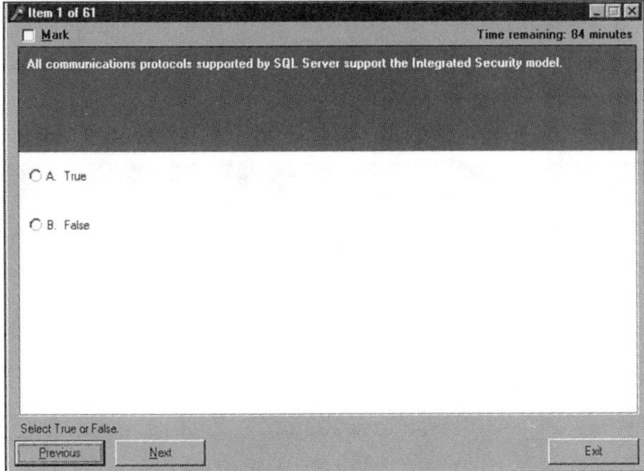


**FIGURE D.3**
A Top Score test item requiring a single response.

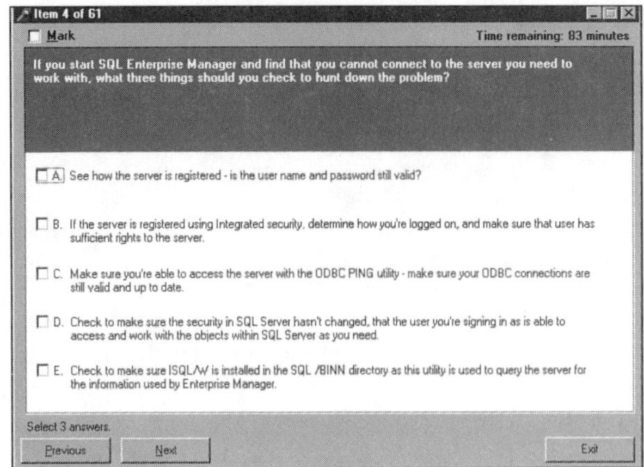


**FIGURE D.4**
A Top Score test item requiring multiple responses.

Some questions and some responses do not appear on the screen in their entirety. You will recognize such items because a scroll bar appears to the right of the question item or response. Use the scroll bar to reveal the rest of the question or response item.

The buttons at the bottom of the window enable you to move back to a previous test item, proceed to the next test item, or exit Top Score Practice Exams.

Some items require you to examine additional information referred to as *exhibits*. These screens typically include graphs, diagrams, or other types of visual information that you will need in order to respond to the test question. You can access Exhibits by clicking the Exhibit button, also located at the bottom of the window.

After you complete the practice test by moving through all of the test questions for your exam, you arrive at a summary screen titled Item Review (see Figure D.5).

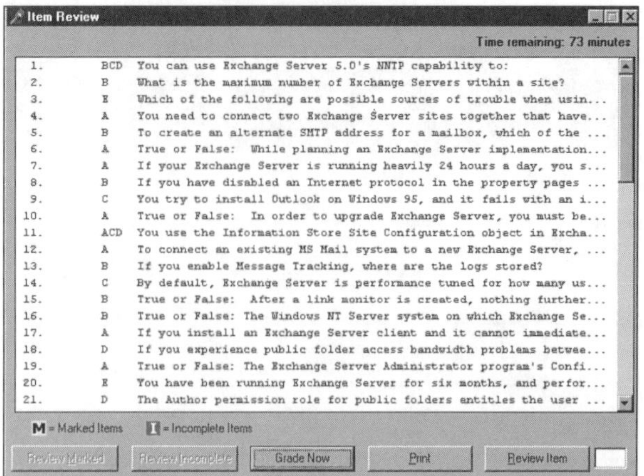


**FIGURE D.5**
The Top Score Item Review window.

This window enables you to see all the question numbers, your response(s) to each item, any questions you have marked, and any you've left incomplete. The buttons at the bottom of the screen enable you to review all the marked items and incomplete items in numeric order.

If you want to review a specific marked or incomplete item, simply type the desired item number in the box in the lower-right corner of the window and click the Review Item button. This takes you to that particular item. After you review the item, you can respond to the question. Notice that this window also offers the Next and Previous options. You can also select the Item Review button to return to the Item Review window.

> **NOTE**
>
> **Your Time Is Limited** If you exceed the time allotted for the test, you do not have the opportunity to review any marked or incomplete items. The program will move on to the next screen.

After you complete your review of the practice test questions, click the Grade Now button to find out how you did. An Examination Score Report is generated for your practice test (see Figure D.6). This report provides you with the required score for this particular certification exam, your score on the practice test, and a grade. The report also breaks down your performance on the practice test by the specific objectives for the exam. Click the Print button to print out the results of your performance.

You also have the option of reviewing those items that you answered incorrectly. Click the Show Me What I Missed button to view a summary of those items. You can print out that information if you need further practice or review; such printouts can be used to guide your use of Study Cards and Flash Cards.

## Using Top Score Study Cards

To start the software, begin from the overview of the CD contents. Click the Study Cards icon to see a listing of topics. Clicking Study Cards brings up more detailed information for this application in the right window.

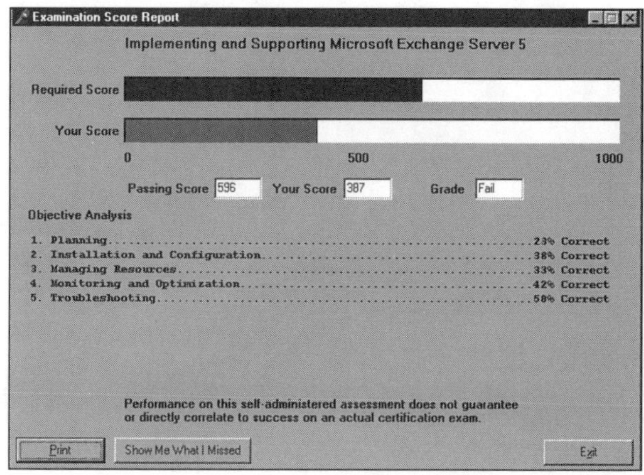


**FIGURE D.6**
The Top Score Examination Score Report window.

To launch Study Cards, click on Starting the Program. In the right window, click on the button for the exam in which you are interested. After a moment, an initial screen similar to that of the Practice Exams appears.

Click on the Next button to see the first Study Cards screen (see Figure D.7).

The interface for Study Cards is very similar to that of Practice Exams. However, several important options enable you to prepare for an exam. The Study Cards material is organized according to the specific objectives for each exam. You can opt to receive questions on all the objectives, or you can use the check boxes to request questions on a limited set of objectives. For example, if you have already completed a Practice Exam and your score report indicates that you need work on Planning, you can choose to cover only the Planning objectives for your Study Cards session.

You can also determine the number of questions presented by typing the number of questions you want into the option box at the right of the screen. You can control the amount of time you will be allowed for a review by typing the number of minutes into the Time Limit option box immediately below the one for the number of questions.

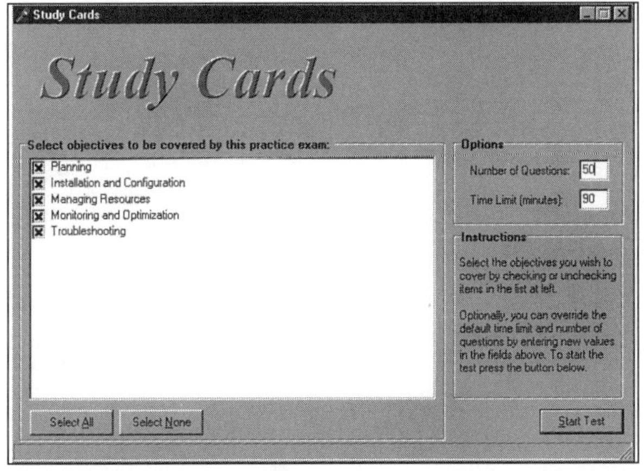


**FIGURE D.7**
The first Study Cards screen.

When you're ready, click the Start Test button, and Study Cards randomly selects the indicated number of questions from the question database. A dialog box appears, informing you that this process could take some time. After the questions are selected, the first item appears, in a format similar to that in Figure D.8.

Respond to the questions in the same manner you did for the Practice Exam questions. Radio buttons signify that a single answer is required, while check boxes indicate that multiple answers are expected.

Notice the menu options at the top of the window. You can pull down the File menu to exit from the program. The Edit menu contains commands for the copy function and even allows you to copy questions to the Windows clipboard.

Should you feel the urge to take some notes on a particular question, you can do so via the Options menu. When you pull it down, choose Open Notes, and Notepad opens. Type any notes you want to save for later reference. The Options menu also allows you to start over with another exam.

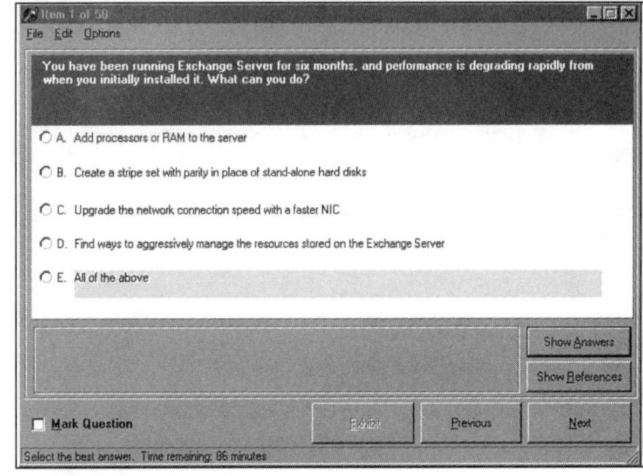


**FIGURE D.8**
A Study Cards item.

The Study Cards application provides you with immediate feedback of whether you answered the question correctly. Click the Show Answers button to see the correct answer, and it appears highlighted on the screen as shown in Figure D.9.

Study Cards also includes Item Review, Score Report, and Show Me What I Missed features that function the same as those in the Practice Exams application.

## Using Top Score Flash Cards

Flash Cards offer a third way to use the exam question database. The Flash Cards items do not offer you multiple-choice answers to choose from; instead, they require you to respond in a short answer/essay format. Flash Cards are intended to help you learn the material well enough to respond with the correct answers in your own words, rather than just by recognizing the correct answer. If you have the depth of knowledge to answer questions without prompting, you will certainly be prepared to pass a multiple-choice exam.

You start the Flash Cards application in the same way you did Practice Exams and Study Cards. Click the Flash Cards icon, and then click Start the Program.

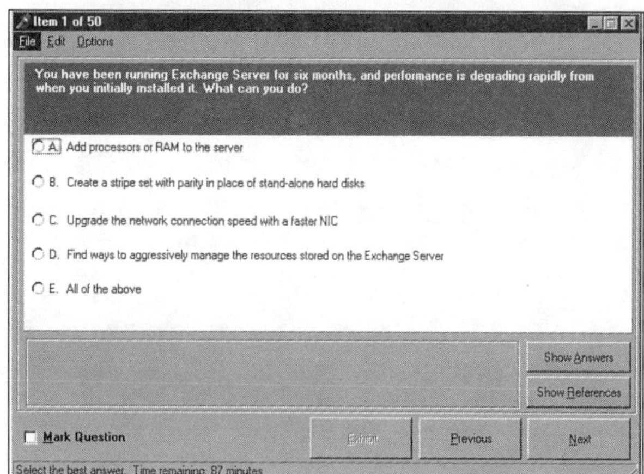


**FIGURE D.9**
The correct answer is highlighted.

Click the button for the exam you are interested in, and the opening screen appears. It looks similar to the example shown in Figure D.10.

You can choose Flash Cards according to the various objectives, as you did Study Cards. Simply select the objectives you want to cover, enter the number of questions you want, and enter the amount of time you want to limit yourself to. Click the Start Test button to start the Flash Cards session, and you see a dialog box notifying you that questions are being selected.

The Flash Cards items appear in an interface similar to that of Practice Exams and Study Cards (see Figure D.11).

Notice, however, that although a question is presented, no possible answers appear. You type your answer in the white space below the question (see Figure D.12).

Compare your answer to the correct answer by clicking the Show Answers button (see Figure D.13).

You can also use the Show Reference button in the same manner as described earlier in the Study Cards sections.

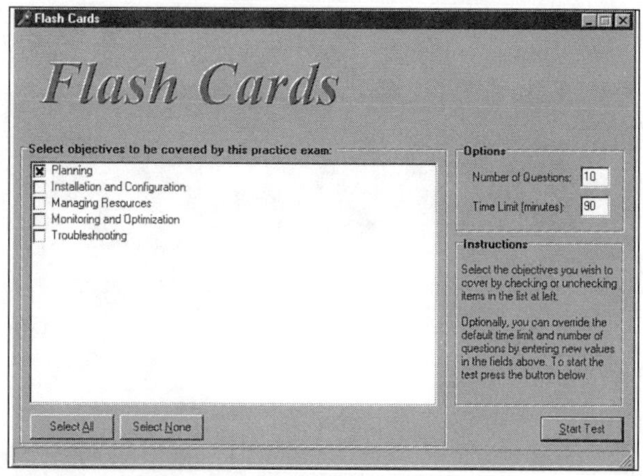


**FIGURE D.10**
The Flash Cards opening screen.

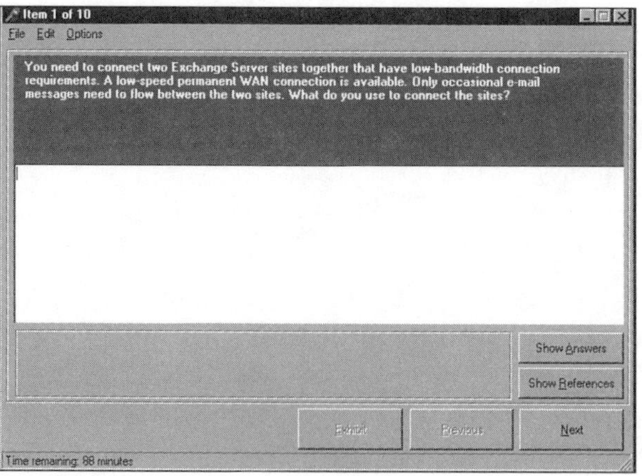


**FIGURE D.11**
A Flash Cards item.

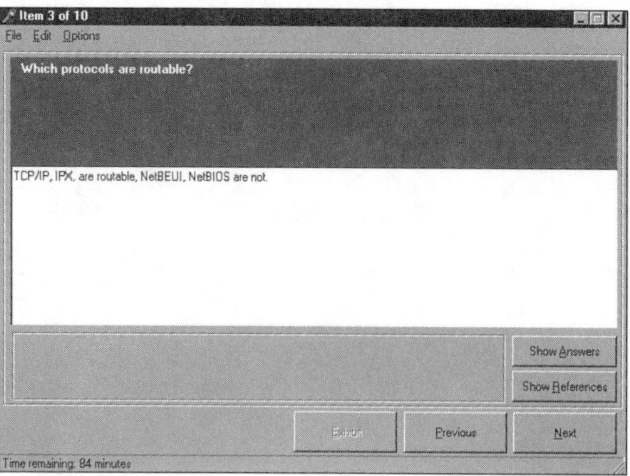


**FIGURE D.12**
A typed answer in Flash Cards.

The pull-down menus provide nearly the same functionality as those in Study Cards, with the exception of a Paste command on the Edit menu instead of the Copy Question command.

Flash Cards provide simple feedback; they do not include an Item Review or Score Report. They are intended to provide you with an alternative way of assessing your level of knowledge that will encourage you to learn the information more thoroughly than other methods do.

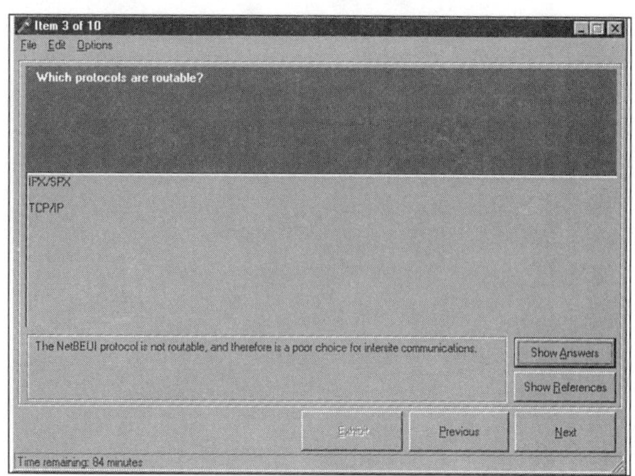


**FIGURE D.13**
The correct answer is shown.

## SUMMARY

The Top Score software's suite of applications provides you with several approaches to exam preparation. Use Practice Exams to do just that—practice taking exams, not only to assess your learning, but also to prepare yourself for the test-taking situation. Use Study Cards and Flash Cards as tools for more focused assessment and review and to reinforce the knowledge you are gaining. You will find that these three applications are the perfect way to finish off your exam preparation.

# Index

## A

# B

## C

# D

# E

# F

# G



# H

# I-J

## K



## L

# M

# N

# O



# P-Q

# R

## S

# U

## V



## W-Z

# NEW RIDERS CERTIFICATION TITLES

## TRAINING GUIDES

### THE NEXT GENERATION

MCSE Training Guide: Networking Essentials, Second Edition

1-56205-919-X, $49.99, 9/98

MCSE Training Guide: Windows NT Server 4, Second Edition

1-56205-916-5, $49.99, 9/98

MCSE Training Guide: Windows NT Server 4 Enterprise, Second Edition

1-56205-917-3, $49.99, 9/98

MCSE Training Guide: Windows NT Workstation 4, Second Edition

1-56205-918-1, $49.99, 9/98

MCSE Training Guide: Windows 98

1-56205-890-8, $49.99, Q4/98

MCSE Training Guide: TCP/IP, Second Edition

1-56205-920-3, $49.99, 10/98

MCSE Training Guide: SQL Server 7 Administration

0-7357-0003-6, $49.99, Q1/99

MCSE Training Guide: SQL Server 7 Design and Implementation

0-7357-0004-4, $49.99, Q1/99

MCSD Training Guide: Solution Architectures

0-7357-0026-5, $49.99, Q1/99

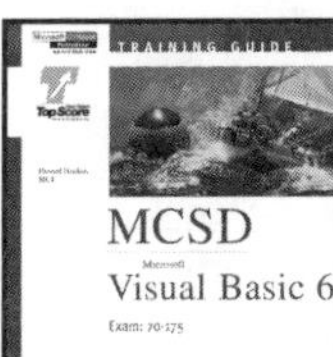


MCSD Training Guide: Visual Basic 6, Exam 70-175

0-7357-0002-8, $49.99, Q1/99

MCSD Training Guide: Microsoft Visual Basic 6, Exam 70-176

0-7357-0031-1, $49.99, Q1/99

## TRAINING GUIDES

### FIRST EDITIONS

*Your Quality Elective Solution*

MCSE Training Guide: Systems Management Server 1.2, 1-56205-748-0

MCSE Training Guide: SQL Server 6.5 Administration, 1-56205-726-X

MCSE Training Guide: SQL Server 6.5 Design and Implementation, 1-56205-830-4

MCSE Training Guide: Windows 95, 70-064 Exam, 1-56205-880-0

MCSE Training Guide: Exchange Server 5, 1-56205-824-X

MCSE Training Guide: Internet Explorer 4, 1-56205-889-4

MCSE Training Guide: Microsoft Exchange Server 5.5, 1-56205-899-1

MCSE Training Guide: IIS 4, 1-56205-823-1

MCSD Training Guide: Visual Basic 5, 1-56205-850-9

MCSD Training Guide: Microsoft Access, 1-56205-771-5

# FAST TRACK SERIES

*The Accelerated Path to Certification Success*

*Fast Tracks* provide an easy way to review the key elements of each certification technology without being bogged down with elementary-level information.

These guides are perfect for when you already have real-world, hands-on experience. They're the ideal enhancement to training courses, test simulators, and comprehensive training guides. *No fluff, simply what you really need to pass the exam!*

## LEARN IT FAST

Part I contains only the essential information you need to pass the test. With over 200 pages of information, it is a concise review for the more experienced MCSE candidate.

## REVIEW IT EVEN FASTER

Part II averages 50–75 pages, and takes you through the test and into the real-world use of the technology, with chapters on:

1) Fast Facts Review Section
2) Hotlists of Exam-Critical Concepts
3) Sample Test Questions
4) The Insider's Spin (on taking the exam)
5) Did You Know? (real-world applications for the technology covered in the exam)

**MCSE Fast Track: Networking Essentials**

1-56205-939-4, $19.99, 9/98

**MCSE Fast Track: TCP/IP**

1-56205-937-8, $19.99, 9/98

**MCSE Fast Track: Windows 98**

0-7357-0016-8, $19.99, Q4/98

**MCSE Fast Track: Internet Information Server 4**

1-56205-936-X, $19.99, 9/98

**MCSE Fast Track: Windows NT Server 4**

1-56205-935-1, $19.99, 9/98

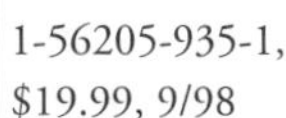

**MCSD Fast Track: Solution Architectures**

0-7357-0029-X, $19.99, Q1/99

**MCSE Fast Track: Windows NT Server 4 Enterprise**

1-56205-940-8, $19.99, 9/98

**MCSD Fast Track: Visual Basic 6, Exam 70-175**

0-7357-0018-4, $19.99, Q4/98

**MCSE Fast Track: Windows NT Workstation 4**

1-56205-938-6, $19.99, 9/98

**MCSD Fast Track: Visual Basic 6, Exam 70-176**

0-7357-0019-2, $19.99, Q4/98

## TESTPREP SERIES

*Practice and cram with the new, revised Second Edition* TestPreps

Questions. Questions. And more questions. That's what you'll find in our New Riders *TestPreps.* They're great practice books when you reach the final stage of studying for the exam. We recommend them as supplements to our *Training Guides.*

What makes these study tools unique is that the questions are the primary focus of each book. All the text in these books support and explain the answers to the questions.

✓ **Scenario-based questions** challenge your experience.

✓ **Multiple-choice questions** prep you for the exam.

✓ **Fact-based questions** test your product knowledge.

✓ **Exam strategies** assist you in test preparation.

✓ **Complete yet concise explanations of answers** make for better retention.

✓ **Two practice exams** prepare you for the real thing.

✓ **Fast Facts** offer you everything you need to review in the testing center parking lot.

*Practice, practice, practice, pass with New Riders* TestPreps*!*

MCSE TestPrep: Networking Essentials, Second Edition

0-7357-0010-9, $19.99, 11/98

MCSE TestPrep: TCP/IP, Second Edition

0-7357-0025-7, $19.99, 12/98

MCSE TestPrep: Windows 95, Second Edition

0-7357-0011-7, $19.99, 11/98

MCSE TestPrep: Windows 98

1-56205-922-X, $19.99, Q4/98

MCSE TestPrep: Windows NT Server 4, Second Edition

0-7357-0012-5, $19.99, 12/98

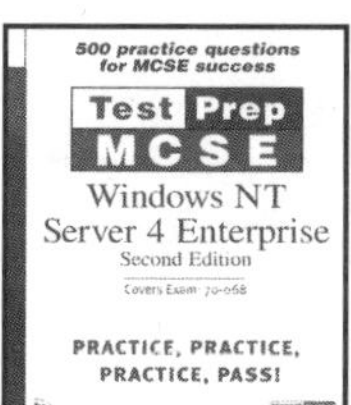


MCSE TestPrep: Windows NT Server 4 Enterprise, Second Edition

0-7357-0009-5, $19.99, 11/98

MCSE TestPrep: Windows NT Workstation 4, Second Edition

0-7357-0008-7, $19.99, 11/98

## FIRST EDITIONS

MCSE TestPrep: SQL Server 6.5 Administration, 0-7897-1597-X

MCSE TestPrep: SQL Server 6.5 Design and Implementation, 1-56205-915-7

MCSE TestPrep: Windows 95 70-64 Exam, 0-7897-1609-7

MCSE TestPrep: Internet Explorer 4, 0-7897-1654-2

MCSE TestPrep: Exchange Server 5.5, 0-7897-1611-9

MCSE TestPrep: IIS 4.0, 0-7897-1610-0

# How to Contact Us

#### IF YOU NEED THE LATEST UPDATES ON A TITLE THAT YOU'VE PURCHASED:

1) Visit our Web site at `www.newriders.com`.

2) Click on the DOWNLOADS link, and enter your book's ISBN number, which is located on the back cover in the bottom right-hand corner.

3) In the DOWNLOADS section, you'll find available updates that are linked to the book page.

#### IF YOU ARE HAVING TECHNICAL PROBLEMS WITH THE BOOK OR THE CD THAT IS INCLUDED:

1) Check the book's information page on our Web site according to the instructions listed above, or

2) Email us at `support@mcp.com`, or

3) Fax us at (317) 817-7488 attn: Tech Support.

#### IF YOU HAVE COMMENTS ABOUT ANY OF OUR CERTIFICATION PRODUCTS THAT ARE NON-SUPPORT RELATED:

1) Email us at `certification@mcp.com`, or

2) Write to us at New Riders, 201 W. 103rd St., Indianapolis, IN 46290-1097, or

3) Fax us at (317) 581-4663.

#### IF YOU ARE OUTSIDE THE UNITED STATES AND NEED TO FIND A DISTRIBUTOR IN YOUR AREA:

Please contact our international department at `international@mcp.com`.

#### IF YOU WISH TO PREVIEW ANY OF OUR CERTIFICATION BOOKS FOR CLASSROOM USE:

Email us at `pr@mcp.com`. Your message should include your name, title, training company or school, department, address, phone number, office days/hours, text in use, and enrollment. Send these details along with your request for desk/examination copies and/or additional information.

## WE WANT TO KNOW WHAT YOU THINK

To better serve you, we would like your opinion on the content and quality of this book. Please complete this card and mail it to us or fax it to 317-581-4663.

Name ____________________

Address ____________________

City ____________ State ________ Zip ____________

Phone ____________ Email Address ____________

Occupation ____________________

Which certification exams have you already passed? ________

Which certification exams do you plan to take? ________

What influenced your purchase of this book?

- ❑ Recommendation
- ❑ Cover Design
- ❑ Table of Contents
- ❑ Index
- ❑ Magazine Review
- ❑ Advertisement
- ❑ Reputation of New Riders
- ❑ Author Name

How would you rate the contents of this book?

- ❑ Excellent
- ❑ Very Good
- ❑ Good
- ❑ Fair
- ❑ Below Average
- ❑ Poor

What other types of certification products will you buy/have you bought to help you prepare for the exam?

- ❑ Quick reference books
- ❑ Testing software
- ❑ Study guides
- ❑ Other

What do you like most about this book? Check all that apply.

- ❑ Content
- ❑ Writing Style
- ❑ Accuracy
- ❑ Examples
- ❑ Listings
- ❑ Design
- ❑ Index
- ❑ Page Count
- ❑ Price
- ❑ Illustrations

What do you like least about this book? Check all that apply.

- ❑ Content
- ❑ Writing Style
- ❑ Accuracy
- ❑ Examples
- ❑ Listings
- ❑ Design
- ❑ Index
- ❑ Page Count
- ❑ Price
- ❑ Illustrations

What would be a useful follow-up book to this one for you? ____________

Where did you purchase this book? ____________

Can you name a similar book that you like better than this one, or one that is as good? Why? ____________

How many New Riders books do you own? ____________

What are your favorite certification or general computer book titles? ____________

What other titles would you like to see us develop? ____________

Any comments for us? ____________

Fold here and Scotch tape to mail

Place
Stamp
Here

New Riders
201 W. 103rd St.
Indianapolis, IN 46290

By opening this package, you are agreeing to be bound by the following agreement:

Some of the software included with this product may be copyrighted, in which case all rights are reserved by the respective copyright holder. You are licensed to use software copyrighted by the publisher and its licensors on a single computer. You may copy and/or modify the software as needed to facilitate your use of it on a single computer. Making copies of the software for any other purpose is a violation of the United States copyright laws.

This software is sold as is without warranty of any kind, either expressed or implied, including but not limited to the implied warranties of merchantability and fitness for a particular purpose. Neither the publisher nor its dealers or distributors assumes any liability for any alleged or actual damages arising from the use of this program. (Some states do not allow for the exclusion of implied warranties, so the exclusion may not apply to you.)

# New Riders Top Score Test Simulation Software Suite

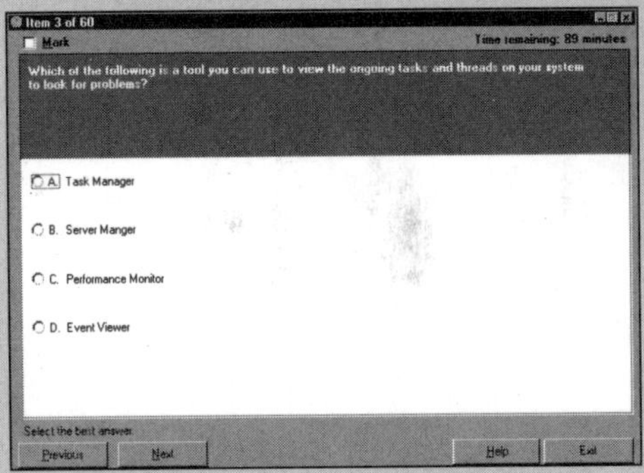


**Practice Exams** simulate the actual Microsoft exams. Option buttons and check boxes indicate whether there is one or more than one correct answer. All test questions are presented randomly to create a unique exam each time you practice—the ideal way to prepare.

**The Item Review** shows you the answers you've already selected and the questions you need to revisit before grading the exam.

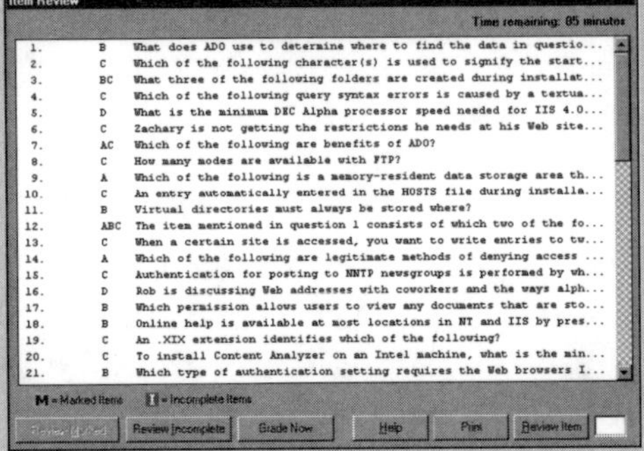


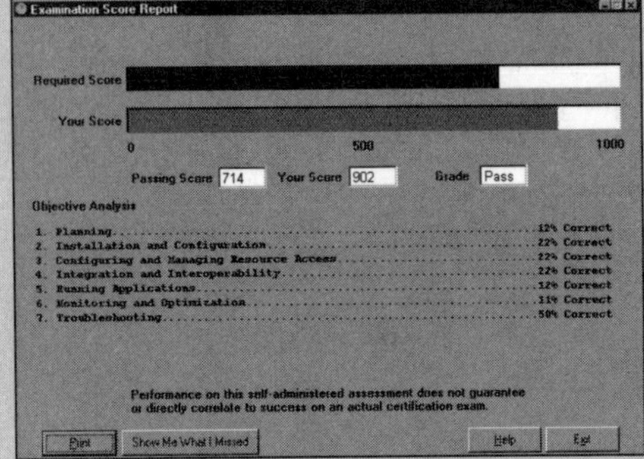


**The Score Report** displays your score for each objective category, helping you to define which objectives you need to study more. It also shows you what score you need to pass and your total score.

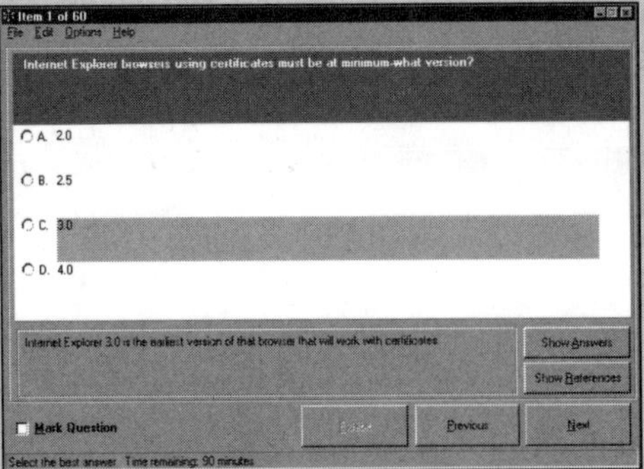


**Study Cards** allow you to test yourself and receive immediate feedback and an answer explanation. Link to the text for more in-depth explanations.